THE CAMBRIDGE WORLD HISTORY

*

VOLUME V

Volume V of *The Cambridge World History* uncovers the cross-cultural exchange and conquest, and the accompanying growth of regional and trans-regional states, religions, and economic systems, during the period 500 to 1500 CE. The volume begins by outlining a series of core issues and processes across the world, including human relations with nature, gender and family, social hierarchies, education, and warfare. Further essays examine maritime and land-based networks of long-distance trade and migration in agricultural and nomadic societies, and the transmission and exchange of cultural forms, scientific knowledge, technologies, and text-based religious systems that accompanied these. The final section surveys the development of centralized regional states and empires in both the eastern and western hemispheres. Together, these essays by an international team of leading authors show how processes furthering cultural, commercial, and political integration within and between various regions of the world made this millennium a "proto-global" era.

BENJAMIN Z. KEDAR is Professor Emeritus of History at the Hebrew University of Jerusalem, founding editor of the journal *Crusades*, and vice-president of the Israel Academy of Sciences and Humanities. The author or editor of thirty books and 140 articles, his interests focus on the crusades and the Latin East, Christian–Muslim relations in the European Middle Ages, the use of aerial photographs as historical sources, and comparative history.

MERRY E. WIESNER-HANKS is Distinguished Professor and Chair of the History Department at the University of Wisconsin-Milwaukee. She is the author or editor of twenty books, including *A Concise History of the World* (Cambridge, 2015), *Early Modern Europe 1450–1789* (Cambridge, 2nd edn 2013), *Women and Gender in Early Modern Europe* (Cambridge, 3rd edn 2008), *Christianity and Sexuality in the Early Modern World: Regulating Desire, Reforming Practice* and *Gender in History: Global Perspectives*.

The Cambridge World History is an authoritative new overview of the dynamic field of world history. It covers the whole of human history, not simply history since the development of written records, in an expanded time frame that represents the latest thinking in world and global history. With over 200 essays, it is the most comprehensive account yet of the human past, and it draws on a broad international pool of leading academics from a wide range of scholarly disciplines. Reflecting the increasing awareness that world history can be examined through many different approaches and at varying geographic and chronological scales, each volume offers regional, topical, and comparative essays alongside case studies that provide depth of coverage to go with the breadth of vision that is the distinguishing characteristic of world history.

Editor-In-Chief

MERRY E. WIESNER-HANKS, *Department of History,*
University of Wisconsin-Milwaukee

Editorial Board

GRAEME BARKER, *Department of Archaeology,*
Cambridge University
CRAIG BENJAMIN, *Department of History,*
Grand Valley State University
JERRY BENTLEY, *Department of History, University of Hawaii*
DAVID CHRISTIAN, *Department of Modern History,*
Macquarie University
ROSS DUNN, *Department of History,*
San Diego State University
CANDICE GOUCHER, *Department of History,*
Washington State University
MARNIE HUGHES-WARRINGTON, *Department of Modern History,*
Monash University
ALAN KARRAS, *International and Area Studies Program,*
University of California, Berkeley
BENJAMIN Z. KEDAR, *Department of History,*
Hebrew University

THE CAMBRIDGE WORLD HISTORY

*

VOLUME V

Expanding Webs of Exchange and Conflict,
500 CE–1500 CE

*

Edited by

BENJAMIN Z. KEDAR

Hebrew University of Jerusalem

and

MERRY E. WIESNER-HANKS

University of Wisconsin-Milwaukee

CAMBRIDGE
UNIVERSITY PRESS

CAMBRIDGE
UNIVERSITY PRESS

University Printing House, Cambridge CB2 8BS, United Kingdom

Cambridge University Press is part of the University of Cambridge.

It furthers the University's mission by disseminating knowledge in the pursuit of
education, learning and research at the highest international levels of excellence.

www.cambridge.org
Information on this title: www.cambridge.org/9780521190749

First published 2015
Paperback edition first published 2017

Printed in the United Kingdom by TJ International Ltd. Padstow Cornwall

A catalogue record for this publication is available from the British Library

ISBN 978-0-521-19074-9 Hardback
ISBN 978-1-108-40772-4 Paperback

In honor and memory of Shmuel N. Eisenstadt (1923–2010) and Sabine MacCormack (1941–2012)

Contents

List of figures   xii
List of maps   xiv
List of table   xv
List of contributors   xvi
Preface   xix

1 · Introduction   1
BENJAMIN Z. KEDAR AND MERRY E. WIESNER-HANKS

PART I:
GLOBAL DEVELOPMENTS

2 · Humans and the environment: tension and co-evolution   43
JOACHIM RADKAU

3 · Women, family, gender, and sexuality   70
SUSAN MOSHER STUARD

4 · Society: hierarchy and solidarity   94
SUSAN REYNOLDS

5 · Educational institutions   116
LINDA WALTON

6 · Warfare   145
CLIFFORD J. ROGERS

Contents

PART II:
EURASIAN COMMONALITIES

7 · Courtly cultures: western Europe, Byzantium, the Islamic world,
India, China, and Japan   179
PATRICK J. GEARY, DAUD ALI, PAUL S. ATKINS, MICHAEL COOPERSON,
RITA COSTA GOMES, PAUL DUTTON, GERT MELVILLE, CLAUDIA RAPP,
KARL-HEINZ SPIEß, STEPHEN WEST AND PAULINE YU

8 · The age of trans-regional reorientations: cultural crystallization
and transformation in the tenth to thirteenth centuries   206
BJÖRN WITTROCK

PART III:
GROWING INTERACTIONS

9 · Trade and commerce across Afro-Eurasia   233
RICHARD SMITH

10 · European and Mediterranean trade networks   257
MICHEL BALARD

11 · Trading partners across the Indian Ocean: the making of
maritime communities   287
HIMANSHU PRABHA RAY

12 · Technology and innovation within expanding webs of exchange   309
DAGMAR SCHÄFER AND MARCUS POPPLOW

13 · The transmission of science and philosophy   339
CHARLES BURNETT

14 · Pastoral nomadic migrations and conquests   359
ANATOLY M. KHAZANOV

PART IV:
EXPANDING RELIGIOUS SYSTEMS

15 · The centrality of Islamic civilization   385
MICHAEL COOK

Contents

16 · Christendom's regional systems   415
MIRI RUBIN

17 · The spread of Buddhism   447
TANSEN SEN

PART V:
STATE FORMATIONS

18 · State formation and empire building   483
JOHANN P. ARNASON

19 · State formation in China from the Sui through the Song dynasties   513
RICHARD VON GLAHN

20 · The Mongol Empire and inter-civilizational exchange   534
MICHAL BIRAN

21 · Byzantium   559
JEAN-CLAUDE CHEYNET

22 · Early polities of the Western Sudan   586
DAVID C. CONRAD

23 · Mesoamerican state formation in the Postclassic period   610
MICHAEL E. SMITH

24 · State and religion in the Inca Empire   638
SABINE MACCORMACK

25 · "Proto-globalization" and "Proto-glocalizations" in the Middle
Millennium   665
DIEGO OLSTEIN

Index   685

Figures

1.1 The Honkōji copy of the 1402 Korean Kangnido map of the world / Pictures From History / Bridgeman Images 3

1.2 Al-Idrīsī's world map, twelfth century (Bodleian Library, Ms. Pococke 375, fols. 3v–4a) 6

1.3 Pietro Vesconte's world map, c. 1321 (Bodleian Library, Ms. Tanner 190, fols. 203v–204r) 8

1.4 Giovanni Leardo's world map, 1448 (DEA Picture Library / Getty Images) 9

3.1 Prince Genji visiting his wife, from Genji Monogatari (The Tale of Genji) (The Art Archive / Alamy) 76

3.2 German family spinning, sixteenth century (Mary Evans Picture Library / Alamy) 78

5.1 Ruins of Buddhist university at Nalanda (photograph by Tansen Sen) 123

5.2 Elite boys enter a calmecac, from the Florentine Codex by Bernardino de Sahagun, c. 1540–85 (Ms palat. 218–220 Book IX. Biblioteca Medicea-Laurenziana, Florence, Italy / Bridgeman Images) 139

6.1 Bulghar warrior on a gold jug (or pitcher) from the Treasure of Nagyszentmiklós (Erich Lessing Culture & Fine Arts Archive) 148

6.2 Mongols and Japanese fight, in a scene from the Mōko Shūrai Ekotoba, a Japanese handscroll made between 1275 and 1293. / Pictures From History / Bridgeman Images 168

6.3 The Battle of Avray in 1364, Master of Mary of Burgundy (fl. 1469–83) (Ms 659 f.271 r. Collection of the Earl of Leicester, Holkham Hall, Norfolk / Bridgeman Images) 173

7.1 Mahmud ibn Sebüktegin receives a robe of honour from the Caliph al-Qādir billāh in 1000, miniature from the 'Jāmi' al-tawārīkh' of Rashīd al-Dīn, c. 1307 (vellum) (Ms Or 20 f.121r. Edinburgh University Library, Scotland. With kind permission of the University of Edinburgh / Bridgeman Images) 187

9.1 Bayon temple in Angkor, market scene (photograph by Benjamin Kedar) 240

12.1 Design for a Chinese water clock, by Su Song, 1088 CE (School of African and Oriental Studies, London, UK / Bridgeman Images) 325

12.2 Geometrical figures for construction, arches and man measuring the height of a tower (facsimile copy, pen & ink on paper), Villard de Honnecourt (fl. 1190–1235) (Ms.Fr.19093 fol.20v. Bibliothèque Nationale, Paris, France / Giraudon / Bridgeman Images) 327

15.1 Islamic coins (photographs by Michael Cook) 397

16.1 Ivory plaque with the Adoration of the Magi, Early Byzantine, early sixth century
(©The Trustees of the British Museum. All rights reserved) 423

16.2 The Holy Family, Joos van Cleve, *c.* 1485–1540/41, Antwerp (Metropolitan Museum
of Art / © SCALA) 425

17.1 Buddhist figures, Longmen Caves, Henan Province (Private Collection
© Leemage / Bridgeman Images) 456

17.2 Pensive Bodhisattva, mid seventh century, Korea (Metropolitan Museum
of Art / © SCALA) 463

20.1 The Birth of the Prophet Muhammad, miniature from the '*Jāmi' al-tawārīkh*' of
Rashīd al-Dīn, *c.* 1307 (vellum) (Ms Or 20 f.42r. Edinburgh University Library,
Scotland. With kind permission of the University of Edinburgh / Bridgeman
Images) 544

22.1 Illustration of Mansa Musa in detail from the Catalan Atlas, 1375 (vellum), Cresques
Abraham (1325–87) (Bibliothèque Nationale, Paris, France / Bridgeman Images) 601

23.1 Chronological outline for Postclassic Mesoamerica 617

23.2 Trends in Postclassic polities 629

24.1 Sacsayhuaman: Inca Ruins (Aivar Mikko / Alamy) 659

Maps

1.1   Eastern hemisphere, 500 CE   36

1.2   Eastern hemisphere, 1000 CE   37

1.3   Eastern hemisphere, 1500 CE   38

5.1   Universities in Europe   127

9.1   Major trade routes of Afro-Eurasia 1300 CE   234

10.1   European/Mediterranean trade in the thirteenth century   278

10.2   European/Mediterranean trade in the fifteenth century   280

11.1   Gujarat   289

14.1   Central Asia, *c.* 1000 CE   364

15.1   The Islamic world   388

16.1   Christianity in 406 CE   417

16.2   Spread of Christianity across Asia   439

17.1   The spread of Buddhism in Asia   449

17.2   Early Buddhist sites in Southeast Asia   459

17.3   The Three Kingdoms in Korea   461

19.1   Tang dynasty China   517

19.2   Xia, Liao and Song Empires   526

19.3   Southern Song, Xia, Jin and Dali   529

20.1   The Mongol conquests and the Four Khanates   536

21.1   Byzantine Empire at the time of Justinian, 555 CE   563

21.2   Byzantine Empire in the eleventh century   573

21.3   Byzantine Empire in 1350 CE   582

22.1   Ghana/Mali/Songhay   591

23.1   Maya sites   615

24.1   Inca expansion   652

Table

1.1   World population (in millions) by major regions, 500–1500 CE   19

Contributors

DAUD ALI, University of Pennsylvania
JOHANN P. ARNASON, La Trobe University, Melbourne
PAUL S. ATKINS, University of Washington
MICHEL BALARD, University of Paris / Panthéon-Sorbonne
MICHAL BIRAN, Hebrew University of Jerusalem
CHARLES BURNETT, Warburg Institute, London
JEAN-CLAUDE CHEYNET, University of Paris-Sorbonne
DAVID C. CONRAD, State University of New York at Oswego
MICHAEL COOK, Princeton University
MICHAEL COOPERSON, University of California, Los Angeles
RITA COSTA GOMES, Towson University, Baltimore
PAUL DUTTON, Simon Fraser University, Burnaby, British Columbia
PATRICK J. GEARY, Institute for Advanced Study, Princeton
BENJAMIN Z. KEDAR, Hebrew University of Jerusalem
ANATOLY M. KHAZANOV, University of Wisconsin-Madison
SABINE MacCORMACK, Notre Dame University
GERT MELVILLE, Technical University of Dresden
DIEGO OLSTEIN, University of Pittsburgh
MARCUS POPPLOW, Technical University of Berlin
JOACHIM RADKAU, University of Bielefeld
CLAUDIA RAPP, University of Vienna
HIMANSHU PRABHA RAY, National Monuments Authority, New Delhi
SUSAN REYNOLDS, University of London
CLIFFORD J. ROGERS, United States Military Academy, West Point
MIRI RUBIN, Queen Mary College, University of London
DAGMAR SCHÄFER, University of Manchester
TANSEN SEN, Baruch College, City University of New York
MICHAEL E. SMITH, Arizona State University
RICHARD SMITH, Ferrum College, Virginia
KARL-HEINZ SPIEß, University of Greifswald
SUSAN MOSHER STUARD, Haverford College, Pennsylvania
RICHARD VON GLAHN, University of California, Los Angeles
LINDA WALTON, Portland State University

STEPHEN WEST, Arizona State University
MERRY E. WIESNER-HANKS, University of Wisconsin-Milwaukee
BJÖRN WITTROCK, Uppsala University
PAULINE YU, American Council of Learned Societies

Preface

The Cambridge Histories have long presented authoritative multi-volume overviews of historical topics, with chapters written by specialists. The first of these, the Cambridge Modern History, planned by Lord Acton and appearing after his death from 1902 to 1912, had fourteen volumes and served as the model for those that followed, which included the seven-volume Cambridge Medieval History (1911–1936), the twelve-volume Cambridge Ancient History (1924–1939), the thirteen-volume Cambridge History of China (1978–2009), and more specialized multi-volume works on countries, religions, regions, events, themes, and genres. These works are designed, as the Cambridge History of China puts it, to be the "largest and most comprehensive" history in the English language of their topic, and, as the Cambridge History of Political Thought asserts, to cover "every major theme."

The Cambridge World History both follows and breaks with the model set by its august predecessors. Presenting the "largest and most comprehensive" history of the world would take at least 300 volumes – and a hundred years – as would covering "every major theme." Instead the series provides an overview of the dynamic field of world history in seven volumes over nine books. It covers all of human history, not simply that since the development of written records, in an expanded time frame that represents the newest thinking in world history. This broad time frame blurs the line between archaeology and history, and presents both as complementary approaches to the human past. The volume editors include archaeologists as well as historians, and have positions at universities in the United States, Britain, France, Australia, and Israel. The essays similarly draw on a broad author pool of historians, art historians, anthropologists, classicists, archaeologists, economists, sociologists, and area studies specialists, who come from universities in Australia, Britain, Canada, China, France, Germany, India, Israel, Italy, Japan, the Netherlands, New Zealand, Singapore, Sweden, Switzerland, and the United States. They include very senior scholars whose works have helped to form the field, and also mid-career and younger scholars whose research will continue to shape it in the future. Some of the authors are closely associated with the rise of world history as a distinct research and teaching field, while others describe what they do primarily as global history, transnational history, international history, or comparative history. (Several of the essays in Volume I trace the development of these overlapping, entangled, and at times competing fields.) Many authors are simply specialists on their topic who the editors thought could best explain this to a broader audience or reach beyond their comfort zones into territory that was new.

Reflecting the increasing awareness that world history can be examined through many different approaches and at varying geographic and chronological scales, each volume offers several types of essays, including regional, topical, and comparative ones, along with case studies that provide depth to go with the breadth of vision that is the distinguishing characteristic of world history. Volume I (Introducing World History [to 10,000 BCE]) introduces key frames of analysis that shape the making of world history across time periods, with essays on overarching approaches, methods, and themes. It then includes a group of essays on the Paleolithic, covering the 95 per cent of human history up to 10,000 BCE. From that point on, each volume covers a shorter time period than its predecessor, with slightly overlapping chronologies volume to volume to reflect the complex periodization of a truly global history. The editors chose the overlapping chronologies, and stayed away from traditional period titles (e.g. "classical" or "early modern") intentionally to challenge standard periodization to some degree. The overlapping chronologies also allow each volume to highlight geographic disjunctures and imbalances, and the ways in which various areas influenced one another. Each of the volumes centers on a key theme or cluster of themes that the editors view as central to the period covered in the volume and also as essential to an understanding of world history as a whole.

Volume II (*A World with Agriculture, 12,000 BCE–500 CE*) begins with the Neolithic, but continues into later periods to explore the origins of agriculture and agricultural communities in various regions of the world, as well as to discuss issues associated with pastoralism and hunter-fisher-gatherer economies. It traces common developments in the more complex social structures and cultural forms that agriculture enabled, and then presents a series of regional overviews accompanied by detailed case studies from many different parts of the world.

Volume III (*Early Cities and Comparative History, 4000 BCE–1200 CE*) focuses on early cities as motors of change in human society. Through case studies of cities and comparative chapters that address common issues, it traces the creation and transmission of administrative and information technologies, the performance of rituals, the distribution of power, and the relationship of cities with their hinterlands. It has a broad and flexible chronology to capture the development of cities in various regions of the world and the transformation of some cities into imperial capitals.

Volume IV (*A World with States, Empires, and Networks, 1200 BCE–900 CE*) continues the analysis of processes associated with the creation of larger-scale political entities and networks of exchange, including those generally featured in accounts of the rise of "classical civilizations," but with an expanded time frame that allows the inclusion of more areas of the world. It analyzes common social, economic, cultural, political, and technological developments, and includes chapters on slavery, religion, science, art, and gender. It then presents a series of regional overviews, each accompanied by a case study or two examining one smaller geographic area or topic within that region in greater depth.

Volume V (*Expanding Webs of Exchange and Conquest, 500 CE–1500 CE*) highlights the growing networks of trade and cross-cultural interaction that were a hallmark of the millennium covered in the volume, including the expansion of text-based religions and the transmission of science, philosophy, and technology. It explores social structures, cultural institutions, and significant themes such as the environment, warfare, education, the family, and courtly cultures on both a global and Eurasian scale, and continues the examination of state formation begun in Volume IV with chapters on polities and empires in Asia, Africa, Europe, and the Americas.

The first five volumes each appear in a single book, but the last two are double volumes covering the periods conventionally known as the early modern and modern, an organization signaling the increasing complexity of an ever more globalized world in the last half-millennium, as well as the expanding base of source materials and existing historical analyses for these more recent eras. Volume VI (*The Construction of a Global World, 1400–1800 CE*) traces the increasing biological, commercial, and cultural exchanges of the period, and explores regional and trans-regional political, cultural, and intellectual developments. The first book within this volume, "Foundations," focuses on global matrices that allowed this increasingly interdependent world to be created, including the environment, technology, and disease; crossroads and macro-regions such as the Caribbean, the Indian Ocean, and Southeast Asia in which connections were especially intense; and large-scale political formations, particularly maritime and land-based empires such as Russia, the Islamic empires, and the Iberian empires that stretched across continents and seas. The second book within this volume, "Patterns of Change," examines global and regional migrations and encounters, and the economic, social, cultural, and institutional structures that both shaped and were shaped by these, including trade networks, law, commodity flows, production processes, and religious systems.

Volume VII (*Production, Destruction, and Connection, 1750–Present*) examines the uneven transition to a world with fossil fuels and an exploding human population that has grown ever more interactive through processes of globalization. The first book within this double volume, "Structures, Spaces, and Boundary Making," discusses the material situations within which our crowded world has developed, including the environment, agriculture, technology, energy, and disease; the political movements that have shaped it, such as nationalism, imperialism, decolonization, and communism; and some of its key regions. The second book, "Shared Transformations?", explores topics that have been considered in earlier volumes, including the family, urbanization, migration, religion, and science, along with some that only emerge as global phenomena in this era, such as sports, music, and the automobile, as well as specific moments of transition, including the Cold War and 1989.

Taken together, the volumes contain about 200 essays, which means the *Cambridge World History* is comprehensive, but certainly not exhaustive. Each volume editor has made difficult choices about what to include and what to leave out, a problem for all world histories since those of Herodotus and Sima Qian more than two millennia ago. Each volume is arranged in the way that the volume editor or editors decided is most appropriate for the period, so that organizational schema differ slightly from volume to volume. Given the overlapping chronologies, certain topics are covered in several different volumes because they are important for understanding the historical processes at the heart of each of these, and because we as editors decided that viewing key developments from multiple perspectives is particularly appropriate for world history.

As with other *Cambridge Histories*, the essays are relatively lightly footnoted, and include a short list of further readings, the first step for readers who want to delve deeper into the field. In contrast to other *Cambridge Histories*, all volumes are being published at the same time, for the leisurely pace of the print world that allowed publication over several decades does not fit with twenty-first-century digital demands.

In other ways as well, the *Cambridge World History* reflects the time in which it has been conceptualized and produced, just as the *Cambridge Modern History* did. Lord Acton envisioned his work, and Cambridge University Press described it, as "a history of the world," although in only a handful of chapters out of several hundred were the principal actors individuals, groups, or polities outside of Europe and North America. This is not surprising, although the identical self-description of the *New Cambridge Modern History* (1957–79), with a similar balance of topics, might be a bit more so. The fact that in 1957 – and even in 1979 – Europe would be understood as "the world" and as the source of all that was modern highlights the power and longevity of the perspective we have since come to call "Eurocentric." (In other languages, there are perspectives on world history that are similarly centered on the regions in which they have been produced.) The continued focus on Europe in the mid-twentieth century also highlights the youth of the fields of world and global history, in which the conferences, professional societies, journals, and other markers of an up-and-coming field have primarily emerged since the 1980s, and some only within the last decade. The *Journal of World History*, for example, was first published in 1990, the *Journal of Global History* in 2005, and *New Global Studies* in 2007.

World and global history have developed in an era of intense self-reflection in all academic disciplines, when no term can be used unselfconsciously and every category must be complicated. Worries about inclusion and exclusion, about diversity and multi-vocality, are standard practice in sub-fields of history and related disciplines that have grown up in this atmosphere. Thus as we editors sought topics that would give us a balance between the traditional focus in world history on large-scale political and economic processes carried out by governments and commercial elites and newer concerns with cultural forms, representation, and meaning, we also sought to include topics that have been important in different national historiographies. We also attempted to find authors who would provide geographic balance along with a balance between older and younger voices. Although the author pool is decidedly broader geographically – and more balanced in terms of gender – than it was in either of the Cambridge Modern Histories, it is not as global as we had hoped. Contemporary world and global history is overwhelmingly Anglophone, and, given the scholarly diaspora, disproportionately insti-tutionally situated in the United States and the United Kingdom. Along with other disparities in our contemporary world, this disproportion is, of course, the result of the developments traced in this series, though the authors might disagree about which volume holds the key to its origins, or whether one should spend much time searching for origins at all.

My hopes for the series are not as sweeping as Lord Acton's were for his, but fit with those of Tapan Raychaudhuri and Irfan Habib, the editors of the two-volume *Cambridge Economic History of India* (1982). In the preface to their work, they comment: "We only dare to hope that our collaborative effort will stimulate discussion and help create new knowledge which may replace before many years the information and analysis offered in this volume." In a field as vibrant as world and global history, I have no doubts that such new transformative knowledge will emerge quickly, but hope this series will provide an entrée to the field, and a useful overview of its state in the early twenty-first-century.

MERRY E. WIESNER-HANKS

Introduction

BENJAMIN Z. KEDAR AND MERRY E.
WIESNER-HANKS

This volume deals with the main processes that furthered cultural, commercial, and political integration within and between various regions of the world from the middle of the first to the middle of the second millennium CE. This span of time – which may be called "the Middle Millennium" – overlaps with the phase in European history commonly known as the Middle Ages, but our decision to consider it as a distinct era, far from displaying a Eurocentric sentiment, is based on the conviction that this millennium amounts to a meaningful period in the history of all main political divisions of the eastern hemisphere.[1] In addition, although the middle of the first millennium is generally not a sharp dividing line in the history of the western hemisphere, the middle of the second millennium certainly is. And in both hemispheres, similar processes occurred during this period: trade networks expanded and matured, interactions among cultures intensified, and, toward the period's end, incipient contacts between the two hemispheres came about.

Contemporary views of the known world:
cartography

True world history is a modern phenomenon: no one who lived before 1500 could have had even an approximate notion of both of the globe's hemispheres, nor did any inhabitant of the western hemisphere have even a vague idea of its shape and extent. In the eastern hemisphere however, some people did attempt to form a view of the known world in its supposed entirety, but restricted in reality to major parts of that hemisphere. Important testimonies to such endeavors are the so-called world

The editors wish to thank the Israel Institute for Advanced Studies, Jerusalem, for its support of an invaluable workshop for the authors in 2011, at which draft chapters were discussed and inter-relationships explored.
1 See Johann Arnason's detailed discussion in Chapter 18 below.

maps. Their geographical distribution and chronological evolution are illustrative of wider developments.[2]

Kwŏn Kŭn, the Neo-Confucian scholar who watched over the making of the Korean world map of 1402, exclaimed that by looking at it "one can indeed know the world without going out of one's door!"[3] His pride was justified, for the map attempts to represent the entire area from Korea and Japan in the east to Africa and the Iberian peninsula in the west: two of the westernmost places marked on it are *Ma-li-xi-li-na* (that is, Marseille) and *Da-la-bu-luo-si* (Tarābulus [Tripoli], Libya). The world map was based on imported maps of China and Japan, as well as on a detailed map of Korea; the depiction of the Arabian peninsula, Africa, the Mediterranean and Europe evidently depended on maps from the Islamic realm that had been brought to Mongol-ruled China and helped there to shape maps whose copies made their way to Korea. The map of 1402 has its flaws: for instance, Korea is larger than Africa, Japan faces southern China, and India and China are amalgamated into a single land mass (see Figure 1.1). Kwŏn Kŭn was right to observe that "it is indeed difficult to achieve precision ... in compressing and mapping [the world] on a folio sheet several feet in size." And yet this map was a unique Korean achievement that not only corroborated Kwŏn Kŭn's conviction that "the world is very wide" but also offered a rough overview of the main components of the world's eastern hemisphere.

Such maps did not exist in East Asia before the advent of the Mongol trans-Eurasian state in the thirteenth century and appear to have remained rare after its demise. Information on the layout of the Islamic realm reached China, but was not integrated into the imperial, Sino-centric cartography. Thus the two famous Chinese maps engraved in 1136 on two sides of a stele – one of them equipped with a grid that allows for the calculation of distances and areas – are almost exclusively focused on China, depicting its coastline and river systems with a remarkable accuracy; the term *Dashi* (realm of Islam), however, figures merely in an annotation beyond the western margin

---

2 For a detailed examination of the maps of all pre-modern civilizations, see J. B. Harley and David Woodward (eds.), *The History of Cartography*, 3 vols. in 6, Chicago and London: University of Chicago Press, 1987–2007; for cartography under Mongol rule see Thomas T. Allsen, *Culture and Conquest in Mongol Eurasia* (Cambridge University Press, 2001), ch. 13; for a longitudinal study of Sino–Muslim relations based on cartography, written texts, and archaeology, see Hyunhee Park, *Mapping the Chinese and Islamic Worlds. Cross-Cultural Exchange in Pre-modern Asia* (Cambridge University Press, 2012).

3 For this and the following quotations of Kwŏn Kŭn (also transliterated as Gwon Geun), see Gari Ledyard, "Cartography in Korea," in Harley and Woodward (eds.), *The History of Cartography*, vol. II, bk 2, 245.

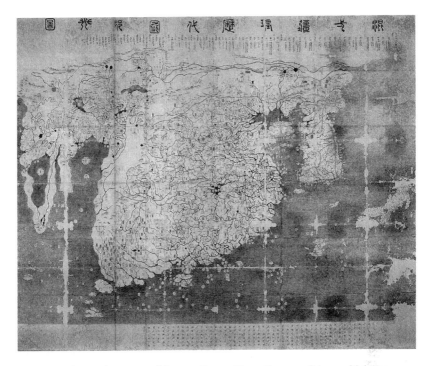

Figure 1.1 The Honkōji copy of the 1402 Korean Kangnido map of the world / Pictures From History / Bridgeman Images

of the second map. Chinese Buddhist cartographers, aware of the foreign origin of their faith, did not place China at the world's center and prominently depicted India and Central Asia, but they, too, provided scant information on countries beyond them, marking *Dashi*, *Lumei* (or Rūm, that is, Byzantium) and *B'wâng-d'ăt* (Baghdad) near the western margins of their maps. Japan possessed general maps of the country as well as Buddhist drawings that focused on a five-partite India, with Turkestan, Japan, China, and Ceylon marked near the margins. The maps of Vietnam prepared in the late fifteenth century were likewise restricted to that country. In pre-Columbian America, maps represented smaller sections of territory: the Aztecs prepared way-finding maps that showed rivers, ranges and localities, and district maps that recorded property ownership, while the Incas carved stone landscapes that appear to have represented actual regions.

The Mongols were different. Keen to form a view of their unprecedentedly far-flung empire and of the lands adjoining it, they not only collected maps of the countries they conquered but also initiated vast cartographical projects in which Muslim scholars played a major role. Thus, the Bukharan astronomer Jamāl al-Dīn (in Chinese transcription, Zha-ma-lu-ding) prepared in 1267 a terrestrial globe for the Grand Khan Qubilai (Kublai, Khubilai) and endeavored in 1286 to prepare, with a Sino–Muslim staff, a massive geographical compendium equipped with maps. As Jamāl al-Dīn put it in his memorandum to the Grand Khan, "Now all of the land from the place of sunrise to sunset has become our territory. And therefore, do we not need a more detailed map? How can we understand distant places? The Islamic maps are at our hands. And therefore, could we combine them [with the Chinese maps] to draw a [world] map?"[4] Jamāl al-Dīn's team completed its work in 1303, relying on Muslim maps deposited at the Imperial Library Directorate in Khanbaliq (Beijing) for the coverage of Islamic and probably also of other foreign countries. At some later date, Shansi (whose Arabic name appears to have been Shams al-Dīn) produced the "Map Book of the Western Countries." While none of these maps has come down to us, the "Map of the Countries of the Northwest" that the Mongol court issued in about 1330, and that focuses on Central Asia but marks also Damascus and Egypt, survives in a post-Mongol collection. The impact of Muslim mapmaking must have been evident also in Li Zemin's contemporaneous "Map of the Vast Diffusion of Resounding Teaching" that contained much information on the "Far West"; this map has not survived, but it surely influenced the depiction of the hemisphere's western part in the Korean map of 1402, because a Chinese map of 1541 that resembles it claims to be based on Li's work. Yet with the collapse of Mongol rule in China in 1368, and the rise of the Chinese Ming dynasty, government-sponsored efforts to utilize Islamic cartographical lore for a better visualization of the known world came to an end. The maritime voyages of Zheng He – the Ming dynasty eunuch admiral of Muslim origin – to Southwest Asia and East Africa in the years 1405–33 made use of knowledge gathered under Mongol rule and gave rise to the unique navigational chart of the route Nanjing – Straits of Singapore – Bay of Bengal – Persian Gulf – Aden – Mogadishu – Malindi (present-day Kenya). A Chinese coin dating from 1403–25, unearthed in 2013 on the island of Manda off the coast of Kenya, may well be a vestige of Zheng He's voyages. These were, however, abruptly discontinued and, to thwart their renewal, most of their documentation was destroyed.

---

4 Quoted by Park, *Mapping the Chinese and Islamic Worlds*, 103.

The Mongol recourse to Islamic maps and geographical lore is not surprising, both because the cartographic achievements in the realm of Islam were remarkable and because the Mongols conquered much of it. Since this realm bordered on all other major civilizations of the eastern hemisphere – those of China, India, Byzantium and Latin Europe, as well as on sub-Saharan Africa – it produced world maps far more accurate than the Korean one that depended on them. Back in the tenth century, members of the Balkhī school of geographers represented the earth in repeatedly copied sets of charts, which consisted of a world map, maps of the Mediterranean and Caspian seas and the Indian Ocean, and maps of seventeen regions of the Muslim world, all displaying geographic forms in a linear, abstract fashion. A much more realistic presentation appears in the circular map that the Muslim cartographer al-Idrīsī prepared in the mid-twelfth century at the court of King Roger II, ruler of the Norman Kingdom of Sicily (see Figure 1.2).

This map purports to show the entire inhabited world, from China (al-Sīn) to Morocco (al-Maghrib al-aqsā), from Poland (Balūniya) to Sofāla (in present-day Mozambique), with an oversize island of Sri Lanka (Sarandīb) marked south of a non-triangular India and with Tibet (al-Tubbat) among the mountains north of it. As on the earlier maps of the Balkhī school, the inhabited world is surrounded by the Encompassing Sea, and a huge Africa extends all the way from its western to its eastern extremity, thus coming close to China; the latter feature reveals the influence of Ptolemy (fl. 150 CE), whose manual for map-makers, the Geography, was translated from Greek into Arabic in the ninth century. Yet these achievements were followed by relative stagnation and thus al-Idrīsī's circular world map resurfaced, with no notable changes, in Ibn Khaldūn's Book of Advice of the late fourteenth century.

In Byzantium, on the other hand, a breakthrough occurred around 1300, when Maximus Planudes used the instructions in Ptolemy's Geography to prepare a world map as well as twenty-six regional ones. His map of the world has a rectangular frame, with the inhabited area placed on a conic graticule whose straight meridians were to merge well beyond the upper, northern frame, and whose parallels were drawn as arcs of circles. The Mediterranean, Europe, the Black Sea, the Persian Gulf and Southeast Asia are depicted far more accurately than on the twelfth-century circular map of al-Idrīsī, yet the two maps share an indistinct China, an oversize Sri Lanka (here called Taprobane) and an eastern extension of Africa that ultimately joins with China, thus rendering the Indian Ocean a closed sea.

Kwŏn Kŭn observed in 1402 that "by looking at maps one can know terrestrial distances and get help in the work of the government." Two

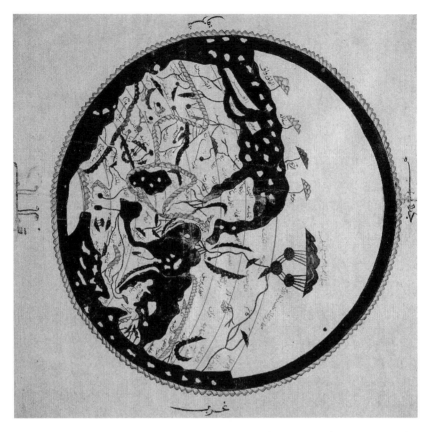

Figure 1.2: Al-Idrīsī's world map, twelfth century, rotated (Bodleian Library, Ms. Pococke 375, fols. 3v–4a)

centuries earlier, the Chinese courtier-turned-teacher Zhang Ruyu observed that "maps of the Empire are of the greatest use to states. At the time when states are first established they are of use in pacification. After the territories are consolidated, they are of use in defence. And during times of restoration, they are of use in the recuperation of lost territories."[5] This utilitarian approach was surely shared by the people who endeavored to prepare

5 Quoted by Hilde De Weerdt, "Maps and Memory: Readings of Cartography in Twelfth- and Thirteenth-Century Song China," *Imago Mundi* 61.2 (2009): 148. The author argues that after the loss of northern China to the Jurchen in 1141, maps of the no-longer-existing unified empire – many of them printed– served in Southern

reliable maps of the Chinese Empire that were based on measurements, by the Mongol rulers who collected and commissioned maps, as well as by Vietnamese and Muslim map-makers. In western Europe, on the other hand, an important aim of world maps was to provide information about major events in sacred history, thus presenting time as well as space, or time superimposed on space, in a manner that recalls local maps produced in other civilizations. As the Franciscan friar Paolino Veneto put it in the early fourteenth century, "I would say that without a world map it is not just difficult but impossible to imagine, or conceive in one's mind, what is said of the sons and grandsons of Noah and of the Four Monarchies and of other kingdoms and provinces, both in theological and secular writings."[6] Consequently, on European world maps one sees Adam, Eve, and the serpent in a Paradise located in the east, or busts of the Apostles at sites where they were said to have been buried, and so on. Physical accuracy was not a major aim, with an oversize Holy Land figuring near the maps' centers. Yet at least one map-maker chose to highlight the area in which he himself lived. This was Stephanus Garsia of the monastery of St Sever in Gascony, who in the mid-eleventh century prepared the most detailed Latin world map of that age that has come down to us: it shows Europe prominently, with a Mediterranean whose northern and southern shores are almost straight, a slim India, and a still more slender China stretching south of the Garden of Eden. On this world map Stephanus not only represented his monastery with a building as big as that symbolizing Constantinople, the largest city in Christendom, but also marked six small places in the monastery's vicinity, while leaving Paris and Marseille unmentioned.

When the First Crusade left for Jerusalem in 1096, many Islamic world maps were significantly more accurate than their European counterparts; Europe had no school of geographers, nor any standardized set of maps. Consequently, a Muslim of that age looking at a world map prepared in the realm of Islam could have obtained a much more realistic idea about the shape of Italy, for example, than a contemporary Latin Christian contemplating the most detailed European map.

Yet this was to change. In the thirteenth century Europeans began to draw portolans – that is, marine charts – that showed very accurately the coastlines

---

Song China as potent reminders of China's dismemberment as well as of the yearning for its reconstitution.

6 Latin text edited in Anna-Dorothee von den Brincken, "Mappa mundi und Chronographia. Studien zur *imago mundi* des abendländischen Mittelalters," *Deutsches Archiv für Erforschung des Mittelalters* 24 (1968): 127.

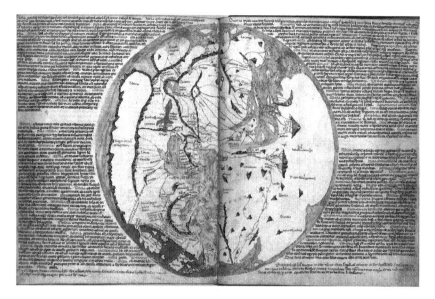

Figure 1.3 Pietro Vesconte's world map, *c.* 1321 (Bodleian Library, Ms. Tanner 190, fols. 203v–204r)

of the Mediterranean and Black Seas, and subsequently these coastlines were incorporated in various world maps. Map-makers gradually improved their craftsmanship, assimilating the best achievements of Islam and Byzantium, and adding information from other sources. The circular world map of the type first attested in al-Idrīsī's treatise must have become known in Italy, because the world map that the Genoese Pietro Vesconte drew up in 1321 is strikingly similar to it, although, thanks to portolan lore, the Mediterranean and Black Seas are far more exactly depicted (see Figure 1.3).

The Catalan Atlas, which the Jewish "Master of Maps and Compasses," Cresques Abraham, prepared in Majorca in 1375, reveals the impact of reports on Inner and East Asia during the Pax Mongolica by such travelers as Marco Polo, while the spotted, brightly colored horses depicted as traversing these areas are inspired by Persian models. Ptolemy's *Geography*, translated into Latin in about 1409, soon began influencing European world maps, as attested by the 1414 map by Pirrus da Noha. And the impact of Portuguese explorations along the western coast of Africa can be observed, for example, on the maps made in about 1450 by the Italian monk, Fra Mauro, and the Venetian cartographer, Giovanni Leardo (see Figure 1.4).

Thus, by 1500 European world maps were far more advanced than those of other contemporaneous civilizations and, after Europeans had reached the

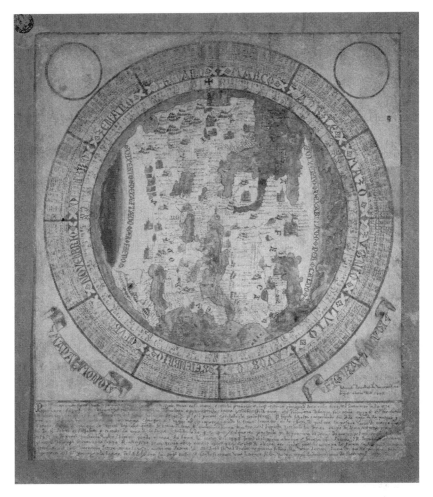

Figure 1.4 Giovanni Leardo's world map, 1448 (DEA Picture Library / Getty Images)

Americas, the New World, too, started to appear on them. In 1507 Martin Waldseemüller was the first to place the name 'America' on a world map: it is marked on the southern part of a slim, elongated continent separated by oceans from Africa and Europe to its east and Asia to its west.

This bird's-eye view of cartography during the Middle Millennium may serve as a simile for the fortunes of the main civilizations during that period: an inward-looking China that opens up under the impact of the Mongol conquest; the realm of Islam, the true Middle Kingdom of the age, whose cultural apogee is followed by a plateau in most Arabic-speaking countries; Byzantium, a storehouse of breakthroughs attained in antiquity; Latin Europe, initially backward but gradually assuming a leading position; and the Mesoamerican and Andean civilizations, each following a distinct path with no habitual contact between them.

Contemporary views of the known world: written histories

Maps are apt to traverse civilizational boundaries with relative ease. Most people who have grasped the principle of using a series of symbols to represent three-dimensional territory on a two-dimensional surface are capable of deciphering a map even though it uses a different set of symbols and is accompanied by legends in an unknown script or language. This is why Korean map-makers were able to incorporate an imported map that showed the unknown lands of the "Far West," and why a Spanish conquistador could comprehend, and put to use, an Aztec cloth map that depicted a coastal region. In short, it is possible to figure out a map's rough meaning without having recourse to its language, or at any rate without mastering it. Hence the cross-civilizational flow of cartographic lore and the capability of situating on one's world map geographical information deriving from distant sources. On the other hand, historical accounts – inasmuch as they are language-bound – cross civilizational borders far less easily. This was one reason why our period witnessed a number of world maps but just one work that may be regarded as a world history of sorts. The other reason was the gap between the relatively widespread desire to form a view of the physical world in its entirety, and the sparse interest in the past of its diverse peoples.

Consequently, the countless records of the past written during the Middle Millennium, though pertaining to a vast variety of genres and revealing widely diverging depths of historical memory, share one fundamental characteristic: their authors focus on their own group or state or civilization, with other groups, states or civilizations mentioned only insofar as they have an impact on that to which the writer belongs. This is true of the Mesoamerican records of dynastic lineages, which may go back for just a few centuries; of China's Standard Dynastic Histories, which form a continuous sequence from pre-imperial times onward; and of Islamic, Byzantine and Western annals and chronicles, which, even when self-styled as universal, start with creation and humanity's legendary beginnings yet very soon converge on their authors' respective civilizations and their immediate predecessors. It is symptomatic of this civilization-centrism that the Standard History of the Mongol dynasty in China, compiled – according to age-old tradition – in the wake of its downfall in 1368, focuses on Mongol rule over China, not on the immense Mongol Empire of which China formed a part. No less telling is the roughly contemporary work of the Florentine Franciscan, Giovanni de' Marignolli (d. 1358), the one Western chronicler with world-historical pretensions who visited China and India: he had nothing to say about the history of these countries and used his Far Eastern experiences primarily to elucidate the early chapters of the biblical book of Genesis.[7]

There were a few exceptions to this lack of curiosity. Theophanes the Confessor (d. 818) stands out among Byzantine historians for dealing not only with events that occurred in the Byzantine Empire but also with those that took place in the realm of its major adversary, the caliphate; each of his annalistic entries starts with the names and regnal years of the ruling emperor and caliph. Indeed, some entries deal exclusively with events within the Islamic realm. Anastasius the Librarian translated Theophanes' work into Latin, in Rome in the early 870s, and consequently some Europeans could read about the rise of *Muamed* (Muhammad), the Arab conquests and the history of the caliphate down to the struggle between the heirs of *Aaron* (Hārūn al-Rashīd). Al-Mas'udi (d. 957), "the Herodotus of the Arabs," may be considered Theophanes' Muslim counterpart, inasmuch as he stands out among Muslim authors for spelling out which Byzantine emperor was the contemporary of which caliph, and for offering much information on Byzantium's internal affairs and its relations with the caliphate as well as with other neighboring countries. The breadth of vision of al-Mas'ūdi – who traveled in West Asia, India and East Africa – was actually much more far-reaching than that of Theophanes. Thus he describes at some length the uprising of *Yānshū* in the year 264 (877–8 CE) and observes that it ushered in a protracted period of lawlessness and political fragmentation in China.[8] This remark refers undoubtedly to the rebellion of Huang Chao (875–84), which critically weakened the Tang dynasty. Similarly, he provides information on India,

---

7 Anna-Dorothee von den Brincken, "Die universalhistorischen Vorstellungen des Johann von Marignola OFM. Der einzige mittelalterliche Weltchronist mit Fernostkenntnis," *Archiv für Kulturgeschichte* 49 (1967): 297–339.

8 Al-Mas'udi, *Les prairies d'or*, §329–35, ed. Charles Barbier de Meynard and Abel Pavet de Courteille, rev. Charles Pellat, vol. I (Beirut, 1966): 163–6; Al-Mas'udi, *Les prairies d'or*, §329–35, trans. Charles Barbier de Meynard and Abel Pavet de Courteille, rev. Charles Pellat, vol. I (Paris, 1962): 124–6.

the Turkic tribes, the Khazars, the Rus', and the Slavs; among the peoples of Africa he mentions the Zanj in the east and the Ghāna in the west. In Egypt he came across a book that a bishop of Girona in Catalonia had presented to the heir of the caliph of Cordova, and culled from it a list of Frankish kings – from the fifth/sixth-century *Q.lūdiyah* (emendable to *Qulūduwīh* = Chlodo-wech, Clovis), down to the tenth-century '*Ludhrīq*, the son of *Qārluh*' (= Louis IV d'Outremer, son of Charles the Simple).[9] The list, garbled and patchy as it is, amounts to the only attempt within the vast Islamic historiography of the age to sketch a chapter of West European history.

In the age of the crusades, just two attempts were made to write the adversary's history. Hamdān al-Athāribī (*c.* 1071–1148), a wine-drinking Muslim poet, physician and administrator, who served first Frankish and then Muslim masters, wrote in Arabic a *History of the Franks who Came Forth to the Land of Islam* – that is, a chronicle of the First Crusade of 1096–9 from a Muslim viewpoint. William of Tyre (*c.* 1130–86), the great chronicler of the Frankish Kingdom of Jerusalem, was commissioned by his patron, King Amaury, to write in Latin, on the basis of books in Arabic, a *History of the Princes of the East* – in other words, a history of the kingdom's Muslim enemies. These extraordinary projects attest to the exceptionality of their originators; that neither of these works survived indicates how much they were out of step with their times. Only in the thirteenth century would there be written in Europe a counterpart to the book King Amaury had commis-sioned – this is the *History of the Arabs* by Rodrigo Jiménez de Rada (*c.* 1170–1247), the archbishop of Toledo, who promoted the crusade against the Almohad Muslims in 1212 and dealt in his book with the history of the Muslims of Spain from its beginnings in the eighth century down to the coming of the Almohads in the twelfth.

The only work written during the Middle Millennium that comes close to an all-hemispheric history is the *Compendium of Chronicles* by Rashīd al-Dīn (*c.* 1247–1318) in Persian and Arabic versions. A Jewish physician who con-verted to Islam in his youth, Rashīd al-Dīn gained the favor of Iran's Mongol rulers and served them for two decades as associate vizier. He relates that two of these rulers, the Ilkhans Ghāzān and Öljeitü, commissioned him to write historical works. Said the latter:

> Until now no one at any time has made a history that contains the stories and histories of all inhabitants of the climes of the world . . . In these days,

9 Al-Mas'udi, *Les prairies d'or*, §914–6: text, vol. ii, 147–8; translation, vol. ii, 344–5.

when, thank God, all corners of the earth are under our control and that of Chinggis Khan's illustrious family, and philosophers, astronomers, scholars, and historians of all religions and nations – Cathay [northern China], Machin [southern China], India, Kashmir, Tibet, Uyghur, and other nations of Turks, Arabs, and Franks – are gathered in droves at our glorious court, each and every one of them possesses copies of the histories, stories, and beliefs of their own people … it is our considered opinion that of those detailed histories and stories a compendium that would be perfect should be made in our royal name.[10]

Öljeitü and his vizier were thus well aware that the envisaged compendium was unprecedented and that it was the vast extension of the Mongol Empire that rendered it feasible.

The resulting work is indeed unmatched in scope, presenting the history of the Mongols, Muhammad and the caliphs, Persia, the Turks, the Chinese, the Jews, the Franks and the Indians. Several components amount to translations into Persian (and Arabic) of imported historical works. Thus, Rashīd al-Dīn's history of China, which lists its dynasties and rulers, is based on a hitherto unidentified Buddhist chronicle; his history of the Franks (western Europeans) is largely derived from some version of Martin of Troppau's *Chronicle of the Popes and the Emperors*; a considerable part of his history of India, and especially the detailed account of the life of the Buddha, relied on the input of Kamalaśrī, a Buddhist informant who hailed from Kashmir; the Mongol intellectual and statesman Bolad provided much information on Mongolian history and on the court of the Grand Khan Qubilai. Rashīd al-Dīn emphasized that, since it was impossible to verify the various histories, he saw it as his duty to faithfully extract them from "reliable standard books" based on continuous tradition, with the responsibility for each text's claims resting solely with the original narrator.[11] Rashīd al-Dīn's repeated disavowal of his own responsibility probably aimed at dissociating himself from assertions in the histories of non-Muslim peoples that conservative Muslim readers might have found offensive. Yet he exhibited also a genuine reluctance to decide between conflicting traditions. Still, his work is more than a mere compendium of extracts, for in the introductions to several histories he

---

10 Rashīd al-Dīn, *Rashiduddin Fazlullah's Jami'u't-tawarikh: Compendium of Chronicles. A History of the Mongols*, trans. Wheeler M. Thackston, vol. I (Cambridge, MA: Harvard University Press, 1998): 6.

11 Rashīd al-Dīn, *Compendium of Chronicles*, 7–9. See also *Die Geschichte der Kinder Israels des Rašīd ad-Dīn*, trans. Karl Jahn (Vienna: Verlag der Österreichischen Akademie der Wissenschaften, 1973): 21; *Die Indiengeschichte des Rašīd ad-Dīn*, trans. Karl Jahn (Vienna: Verlag der Österreichischen Akademie der Wissenschaften, 1980): 19.

makes original statements – for instance, when he provides the earliest description in any language of Chinese woodblock printing and distribution of books, or when he mentions the Franks' ability to depict all countries, islands, mountains and deserts of their part of the world on a *bāb mandū* (a distortion of the Latin *mappa mundi*, "world map").[12] He also rightly underlines the originality of his history of the Jews, which he construed on the basis of the Bible and various later books. Rashīd al-Dīn planned to attach a collection of maps to his compendium but, while there are good reasons to assume that this objective was achieved, the maps did not come down to us.

Rashīd al-Dīn's work, especially his history of the Mongols, was influential in the eastern Islamic realm, that is, in Iran, Central Asia and Mughal India. But his history of the known world found just a single emulator, the Transoxanian Muhammad Banākatī, who in 1317 prepared a rather pedestrian collection of extracts from the *Compendium of Chronicles*. Neither the *Compendium* nor the collection had much impact west of Iran until, in the late seventeenth century, Ottoman and European scholars became aware of Banākatī's book. Rashīd al-Dīn himself succumbed to the machinations of a rival vizier and was charged with having poisoned the Īl-Khān Öljeitü. After a court interrogation during which his Jewish origin was repeatedly mentioned, the seventy-year-old historian was put to death. His severed head was displayed in Tabriz, the capital, as "the head of the Jew who scorned the word of God" and ninety years later his bones were exhumed from his grave in the Muslim cemetery and re-interred in the Jewish one.[13]

While most historians provided few clues as to what had happened beyond the reach of their respective civilizations in the past, knowledge about conditions in distant countries spread through the accounts of pilgrims, returning prisoners of war, merchants and travelers. Thus the Chinese Buddhist monk Xuanzang traveled in 629 to India via Samarkand and Bāmiyān (where he saw the two giant rock statues of standing Buddhas, destroyed by the Taliban in 2001). Upon his return to China in 645 with many hundreds of Sanskrit texts, he left behind a description of the regions of Central and Southern Asia that included information on the Indian caste

---

12 *Die Chinageschichte des Rašīd ad-Dīn*, trans. Karl Jahn (Vienna: Verlag der Österreichischen Akademie der Wissenschaften, 1971): 24; *Die Frankengeschichte des Rašīd ad-Dīn*, trans. Karl Jahn (Vienna: Verlag der Österreichischen Akademie der Wissenschaften, 1977): 54.
13 Walter Fischel, "Über Raschid ad-Daulas jüdischen Ursprung," *Monatsschrift für Geschichte und Wissenschaft des Judentums* 81 (1937): 145–53; Amnon Netzer, "Rashīd al-Dīn and his Jewish Background," *Irano-Judaica* 3 (1994): 118–26.

system. Du Huan, a Chinese captured by the Muslims at the Battle of Talas (751), spent a decade in the 'Abbasid capital of Kūfa (Iraq), and upon his return to China provided an early account about Islam and the Arab conquests; Hārūn b. Yahyā, a Muslim from Ascalon who fell into Byzantine captivity in the late ninth century, brought back much information on Constantinople and Rome. And travel accounts such as those of Benjamin of Tudela and Ibn Jubayr in the twelfth century, of Marco Polo in the thirteenth and of Ibn Battūta and Wang Dayuan in the fourteenth century, throw much light on conditions in far-away countries.

The Middle Millennium for today's historians

Having sketched the growing knowledge about the world's appearance and the largely civilization-centric works of history that were available during the Middle Millennium, let us now turn to the history of that period as it emerges from present-day research. It is a history that differs dramatically from the endeavors of Rashīd al-Dīn, to say nothing of his less ambitious contemporaries, for its scope encompasses much more than the account of political and religious events, spiced with the recording of unusual natural occurrences like comets or bloody rains, which constituted the customary fare of history written in those times. It posits questions about such subjects as ecology and climate, family and gender, social stratification, economy, group mentality, art, and technology, and attempts to ascertain their interrelations.

Present-day research stands out also for the ever-expanding range of sources put to use in its quest for answers. Rashīd al-Dīn's *Compendium* reproduces what he found written "in the well-known books of every nation" and in the reports of "the wise and learned of every group,"[14] but nowadays documents written on parchment or paper – from laws and proclamations to chronicles and poems to merchants' contracts and manuals to private letters and diaries – are increasingly supplemented by other types of documentation, such as inscriptions and coins, or data derived from archaeological finds or pollen analysis.

Occasionally such other types take pride of place. For instance, our knowledge of Cambodian history in the Angkorean period – that is, from the ninth to the fifteenth century – is based primarily on a huge number of

---

14 Rashīd al-Dīn, *Compendium of Chronicles*, 8.

inscriptions incised on stone: Sanskrit inscriptions, in verse, extolling the deeds of kings and the mighty, and Khmer-language inscriptions, in prose, dealing with mundane matters such as the number and names of slaves belonging to a temple. This is not to say that Angkorean Cambodia was devoid of ordinary writing. Zhou Daguan, the Chinese envoy who stayed in Angkor in 1296–7 and left behind a description of the city and of its inhabitants, reported that they used to write on deerskin or similar parchment and employed professional scribes for the composition of petitions[15] – but none of such writings have come down to us.

Similarly, knowledge about Maya history largely depends on a vast number of inscriptions carved on stone; other inscriptions were etched on wooden lintels or incised on pottery. But, unlike the Khmer of Cambodia, the Maya produced also a large number of books consisting of bark paper, and although most of these were burnt by the Spanish conquerors, three or four made their way to Europe and have survived to this day.[16] Knowledge of how to read Maya glyphs, whether carved or written, developed especially in the 1970s and 1980s, and today much understanding of Maya culture depends on written Maya sources. Scholars of the Inca Empire are currently trying to decipher *khipus*, or apparatuses of knotted and colored cords that allowed for the encoding of numbers and possibly also of non-numeric units of information. If they succeed, our understanding of Inca mathematics, accounting, and record-keeping systems may significantly advance.[17]

Archaeology of the Middle Millennium is a rapidly developing subdiscipline that uncovers time and again totally new evidence. For instance, the birch-bark documents that have been emerging from 1951 onwards from the mud of Novgorod and elsewhere in northeastern Europe and that turned out to have been written between the eleventh and fifteenth centuries in a rough local idiom, mainly by urban laymen and also some laywomen, allow for unique glimpses of family life, commerce, litigation, devoutness, and much more.[18] Another example is the unlooted royal tomb discovered in 2013 in Peru, which sheds new light on the Wari polity that predated, and in several respects prefigured, the Inca Empire. Yet archaeology is important not only

15 Chou Ta-kuan, *The Customs of Cambodia*, trans. J. Gilman d'Arcy Paul, 3rd edn (Bangkok: The Siam Society, 1993): 27.
16 See for instance Robert J. Sharer, *The Ancient Maya*, 5th edn (Stanford University Press, 1994): 597–629.
17 These issues are dealt with in detail in chapters 9 and 10 in vol. III of this work.
18 For a brief overview see Simon Franklin, *Writing, Society and Culture in Early Rus, c. 950–1300* (Cambridge University Press, 2002): 35–45, 123–4.

for the history of poorly documented societies but also for those that produced many written sources; for the latter, it holds the promise of studying issues on which the written sources are silent and of generating ever more new data even as the number of written documents that remain unpublished is constantly dwindling. In addition, written sources known for a long time may yield fresh insights or data when examined from new points of view or subjected to quantitative analysis.

The potential of these approaches may be exemplified by some recent studies of the Frankish Kingdom of Jerusalem, founded in the wake of the First Crusade of 1096–9 and brought to its end by the Mamluk conquest of Acre in 1291. Archaeological finds, supplemented by an examination of structures surviving above ground, show that while Frankish domestic architecture in the towns absorbed local influences (especially the courtyard-house design), the planned street-villages and the farms the Franks established in the countryside followed European models, although the scarcity of wood in the kingdom dictated their construction in stone. The excavation of the frontier castle of Vadum Iacob showed that this hotly contested Templar fortress was still being constructed when Saladin conquered and destroyed it in August 1179; the heaps of building materials and the many work implements, as well as the state of the unfinished fortifications, throw light on the construction techniques the Franks employed. The examination of thirteenth-century latrines of Frankish Acre has revealed that many of their users carried in their intestines eggs of fish tapeworm, a species limited to northern Europe at that time: evidently the users must have been crusaders or pilgrims from Europe. An investigation of skeletons excavated in Frankish Caesarea suggests the availability of medical treatment in that town, seeing that numerous fractured tibias healed straight. And a quantitative study of the personal names of some 6,200 persons figuring in the kingdom's surviving charters highlights – as does the study of domestic architecture – an interplay of European and local influences.[19]

In sum, the ever-expanding variety of sources utilizable in the study of the Middle Millennium depends on historians' inventiveness. It also depends on their ability to surmount the absence of direct evidence about a phenomenon by identifying observable facts that can be convincingly presented as its indirect indicators or proxies.

---

19 For details see the works of Boas, Ellenblum, Mitchell et al., and Shagrir listed in the further reading.

Population and history

Robert Lopez – an early practitioner of world history – used to say that since history is the study of humans in time, the first question one should ask about a period under scrutiny is: How many humans were then living? When we pose this question with regard to the Middle Millennium, all we can expect are educated guesses. And there are not many of them. Back in 1979, the French historical demographer Jean-Noël Biraben published a "provisional table" in which he offered estimates of the world's population from 400 BCE to 1970 CE. His estimates for our time frame can be seen in Table 1.1.

Biraben assumes that the world's population more than doubled between 500 and 1500, from 207 to 461 million. In the table's earlier sections, Biraben estimates that by 200 CE the world's population had reached the unprecedented zenith of 257 million, so that during the first 500 years of our period, the world presumably had fewer inhabitants than it had at the earlier peak. The impact of a major pandemic that recurred several times from 541 to 750 is observable, in Biraben's table, in the sharp drop in population after 500 in Southwest Asia, Europe, and North Africa. From the eleventh century onward, however, there were, at any given moment, more people on the planet than during any previous epoch in history, with the most dramatic upsurge – from 299 to 400 million – in our era taking place in the twelfth century. To his list of round dates Biraben added the years 1250 and 1340, which allow him to present conjectures on the demographic impact of the Mongol invasions that had taken place before the first of these dates, and of the Black Death that had erupted after the second. Biraben's estimates have been adopted by subsequent students of the subject,[20] and they are presented here, too, as reasonable approximations, largely based though they are on conjecture.

In any case, there can be no doubt that in the period 500–1500 the planet was much less evenly populated than in more recent times. Hunter-gatherers, sparsely spread out over vast tracts of land, inhabited all of Australia, much of the Americas and considerable parts of southern Africa,

20 See for instance Massimo Livi-Bacci, *A Concise History of World Population*, 4th edn (Oxford: Blackwell, 2007): 26; David Christian, *Maps of Time: An Introduction to Big History* (Berkeley: University of California Press, 2011): 344–5. Alternative estimates of the world's population in the years 1000 and 1500 do not differ dramatically from those by Biraben appearing above: see Angus Maddison, *The World Economy. A Millennial Perspective* (Paris: OECD Publications, 2001): Table B-1, 231.

Table 1.1 *World population (in millions) by major regions, 500–1500*

	500	600	700	800	900	1000	1100	1200	1250	1300	1340	1400	1500
China	32	49	44	56	48	56	83	124	112	83	70	70	84[a]
Indian subcontinent	33	37	50	43	38	40	48	69	83	100	107	74	95
Southwest Asia	41	32	25	29	33	33	28	27	22	21	22	19	23
Japan	5	5	4	4	4	4	5	7	9	10	10	9	10
Rest of Asia	8	11	12	14	16	19	24	31	31	29	29	29	33
Europe	30	22	22	25	28	30	35	49	57	70	74	52	67
USSR	11	11	10	10	11	13	15	17	14	16	16	13	17
North Africa	11	7	6	9	8	9	8	8	9	8	9	8	9
Rest of Africa	20	17	15	16	20	30	30	40	49	60	71	60	78
North America	2	2	2	2	2	2	2	3	3	3	3	3	3
C. and S. America	13	14	15	15	13	16	19	23	26	29	29	36	39
Oceania	1	1	1	1	1	1	2	2	2	2	2	2	3
World	207	208	206	224	222	253	299	400	417	431	442	375	461

Source: Jean-Noël Biraben, "Essai sur l'évolution du nombre des hommes," *Population* 34 (1979): 16.
[a]The current estimates for China, based on adjustments to recorded census figures, are: 609 – 46, 754 – 75, 1003 – 60, 1110 – 125, 1225 – 140, 1290 – 68, 1393 – 73, 1630 – 192. Source: Ge Jianxiong, general ed., *Zhongguo renkou shi* (*A History of Chinese Population*) (Shanghai: Fudan University Press, 2000), vols. II, III, IV. Our thanks to Prof. Richard von Glahn for supplying these data.

while pastoral nomads roamed over northern and Central Asia, the Arabian peninsula and the Sahara. Although agriculture expanded and intensified in this period, so that agricultural villages could be found in far more places in 1500 than in 500, the densely settled civilizations of the age were limited, in the western hemisphere, largely to the Mesoamerican and Andean regions and the ancestral Pueblo homeland, while in the eastern hemisphere they formed a wide belt that extended from the Atlantic coasts of North Africa and Europe all the way to China and Japan. Of the planet's three oceans, only the smallest – the Indian – witnessed cross-littoral navigation and trade.

We know much more about the large settled civilizations of the age than about its outlying, mostly isolated, and sometimes tiny groups of people. Yet modern methods allow us to reconstruct some of their history quite accurately as well. For instance, a recent study based on 1,434 radiocarbon dates suggests radical modifications in the existing view of East Polynesia's early history: the settlement of Samoa in about 800 BCE was followed by a 1,800-years-long pause in colonization activities; then, around 1025–1120 CE, long-distance voyaging resumed and the Society Islands east of Samoa were settled; finally, in the course of a single century – between 1190 and 1293 – seafarers spread out to the most remote islands of East Polynesia, reaching Hawaii in the north, Rapa Nui (Easter Island) in the east, and Auckland Island in the south.[21]

Sporadic trans-civilizational contacts

While the Mesoamerican and Andean civilizations presumably lacked direct, regular relations and were even unaware of each other's existence, the civilizations of the eastern hemisphere either directly bordered on one another or were at least conscious of their distant neighbors. Consequently, regular trans-civilizational relations were limited to the Old World, where they were of paramount importance in furthering large-area integration during our period. Yet it would be wrong to assume that sporadic contacts, presumably far more widespread, were of necessity historically meaningless.

Take for example the Parisian goldsmith Guillaume Boucher, whom the Mongols took prisoner in Hungary in 1241 and who, at the behest of the

---

21 Janet M. Wilmshurst, Terry L. Hunt, Carl P. Lipo and Atholl J. Anderson, "High-Precision Radiocarbon Dating Shows Recent and Rapid Initial Human Colonization of East Polynesia," *Proceedings of the National Academy of Sciences of the United States of America* 108/5 (2011): 1815–20.

Grand Khan Möngke, constructed a semi-mechanical fountain that spurted out four different beverages to the khan's courtiers and guests in the Mongol capital of Qara-Qorum.[22] Boucher's very presence in Qara-Qorum would have remained unknown had not the Franciscan friar William of Rubruck arrived there in 1254 and met him. William engaged Boucher's adoptive son as translator from Mongol into French, and vice versa, and took part in a Buddhist–Muslim–Nestorian–Latin religious disputation at the Grand Khan's court. He later recorded all of this in the account of his voyage to the Mongols.[23] The dragoman skills of Boucher's adoptive son crucially determined the course of the unprecedented quadrilateral disputation, which pitted a Latin Christian against a Buddhist for the first time. Friar William did not see fit to relate whether Boucher enlightened his Qara-Qorum acquaintances about Western customs and techniques, but this does not mean that he did not do so: here, as elsewhere, documentation should not be equated with reality. The same is true of the German prisoners whom the Mongols abducted to work in their gold mines, among whom Friar William originally intended to settle. The countless men and women who, in both hemispheres and in innumerable instances, were carried off into slavery, at times over great distances, provide another example of sporadic cultural transmission. At least occasionally they may have transmitted some cultural items to their captors without this leaving any record in written sources. In short, we may assume that underneath the layer of documented cross-cultural connections there is a substratum of shadowy traffic that only occasionally left behind traces. These remain baffling when they are discovered only as long as this level is not taken into consideration.

In the realm of ideas, sporadic transmission could preserve an item's content with astonishing accuracy. The spread of a tale that originated somewhere in the eastern Mediterranean in the wake of the Arab conquests of the 630s provides an arresting example. As the story has it, the Byzantine emperor Heraclius saw in the stars that a circumcised people would lay waste to his realm and therefore ordered that all Jews be killed or baptized, only to realize later on that the calamity was brought on him by another

---

22 An imaginary reconstruction of this fountain, which illustrates Pierre Bergeron's *Voyages faits principalement en Asie* (The Hague, 1735), appears on present-day Mongolian banknotes.

23 See William of Rubruck, *The Mission of Friar William of Rubruck: His Journey to the Court of the Great Khan Möngke*, trans. Peter Jackson (London: The Hakluyt Society, 1990); Benjamin Z. Kedar, "The Multilateral Disputation at the Court of the Grand Qan Möngke, 1254," in Hava Lazarus-Yafeh et al. (eds.), *The Majlis. Interreligious Encounters in Medieval Islam* (Wiesbaden: Harrassowitz, 1999): 162–83.

circumcised people, the Arabs. In the lands of the East this legend was transmitted orally for several generations and first appeared in writing in Arabic works composed 150 years later. But already in about 658 the tale appears in Gaul in a Latin chronicle – striking proof of the story's rapid transmission to the far west of those times. Moreover, this story was copied for centuries, with little or no changes, from one Latin chronicle to another until, early in the fourteenth century, Rashīd al-Dīn incorporated it into his history of the Franks.[24]

An item could also undergo radical metamorphoses in the course of a sporadic transmission, however. The story of the Bodhisattva – the future Buddha – which in Central Asia assumed a Manichaean guise in which the hero is called the Bodisav prince, was adapted into Arabic in eighth-century Baghdad. It was only slightly Islamicized, rendering the hero's name as Būdāsaf, or – due to some careless copyist – Yūdasaf. In the ninth century the Arabic version gave rise to a Georgian-written, intensely Christianized adaptation that gave the hero's name as Iodasaph. Euthymius the Georgian (c. 955–1028) translated the story into Greek, calling the hero Ioasaph; from the Greek it was translated into Old Slavonic, Armenian and Christian Arabic, the latter giving rise to an Ethiopian version as well as to a de-Christianized Hebrew one. From the mid-eleventh century onward, the Greek version was repeatedly translated into Latin, with the hero rebaptized as Iosaphat, and the Latin versions served in their turn as the basis for adaptations in most of Europe's vernacular languages, from Italy to Iceland and from Portugal to Russia, with episodes from the story utilized time and again. For example, the four caskets figuring in the story – some adorned with gold and jewels, others smeared with tar – gave rise to the two chests, one containing the king's crown, scepter and orb, the other full of earth, in Boccaccio's *Decameron* (x, 1), and to the three caskets of gold, silver and lead in Shakespeare's *Merchant of Venice* (ii.vii.ix). In its turn, the parable of the man who avoids falling into a well by clutching on to a tree at whose root two mice are relentlessly gnawing played a crucial role in Lev Tolstoy's spiritual conversion. Moreover, Josaphat – and his mentor Barlaam – eventually entered the Roman Catholic *Martyrology* under 27 November, while the Georgians commemorated 'Iodasaph, King of the Indians' on 19 May and the Greeks honored the Blessed Ioasaph on 26 August. Although the Portuguese historian Diogo do Couto remarked in about 1612 on the similarity

24 See Benjamin Z. Kedar, *Crusade and Mission: European Approaches toward the Muslims* (Princeton University Press, 1984): 27–8.

between Josaphat and the Buddha, it was only around 1860 that Western scholars established definitely that the saintly Christian prince-turned-hermit was a distant yet unmistakably identifiable reincarnation of India's great spiritual teacher.[25]

When what appears to have been sporadic transmission is attested solely by archaeology, one might wonder whether the transmission was simply accidental. Mesoamerican metallurgy is a case in point. Comparative laboratory studies of Mesoamerican and Andean copper artifacts have revealed that the same fabrication techniques were employed in their production; but while Andean metallurgical traditions evolved over more than a millennium, in Mesoamerica – to be more precise, in present-day west Mexico – well-crafted metal assemblages of the same kind appeared all of a sudden around 800 CE. Hence it stands to reason that Andean metallurgy influenced that of Mexico. Bronze production, too, appears to have reached Mesoamerica from the Andean region, and T-shaped axes that served as money, which spread after c. 1200 over most of Mesoamerica, also followed South American designs.[26] In the Andes, however, bronze served for the manufacture of everyday tools, while Mesoamerican smiths used it primarily for ritual items and for items reserved for the elite. Moreover, recent lead isotope studies of Mexican and Andean copper ores and artifacts point to an adoption of techniques, rather than an import of artifacts. This suggests that some relatively extended interaction must have taken place, and it is plausible to assume that it was not limited just to metallurgy but rather touched also upon subjects that leave no archaeological traces.

Regular trans-civilizational relations

While sporadic contacts ought not to be neglected, pride of place in the study of the movement toward more intense integration of large-area units, and of communication among them, should go to regular interactions. Of these, the

25 The legend has been rightly defined as "one of the most remarkable episodes in the history of literature": Joseph Jacobs, *Barlaam and Josaphat* (London: David Nutt, 1896): viii; on its metamorphoses see David M. Lang, *The Wisdom of Balahvar: A Christian Legend of the Buddha* (London: Allen and Unwin, 1957): 9–65; David M. Lang, "Introduction," in St John Damascene, *Barlaam and Ioasaph*, ed. and trans. G. R. Woodward and H. Mattingly (Cambridge, MA: Harvard University Press, 1967): ix–xxxv; Wilfred C. Smith, *Towards a World Theology: Faith and the Comparative History of Religion* (London: Macmillan, 1981): 7–11, 19–20.

26 For the stages of this fascinating study see the publications by Dorothy Hosler listed in the further reading.

most important were three types: war and conquest that led to the formation of states; the development of trade networks; and the emergence of religious ecumenes. These interactions, whether voluntary or coercive, are at the heart of the present volume.

The first type of regular interaction was political. During our time frame, a number of centralized empires aspired to intense, large-area integration: Byzantium (from its beginnings in the fourth century), China (from the reunification under the Sui dynasty in 589), the 'Abbasid Caliphate in its heyday, the Aztec and Inca Empires (from 1428 and 1438, respectively). Of these, only China succeeded, some hiatuses notwithstanding, in preserving its empire throughout our period and much beyond. The Byzantine Empire, though nominally existing down to the Ottoman conquest of Constantinople in 1453, had already lost some of its most important provinces by the seventh century, and after the Fourth Crusade of 1203–4 was reduced to a dwindling territory. Far more short-lived were the conquest empires of Charlemagne, Chinggis Khan and Timur (Tamurlane), all three of which lacked a durable centralized administration. Smaller political units – for instance, Japan, Angkorean Cambodia, Ethiopia, England – attained a significantly more robust durability. Still, even ephemeral empires could boost long-term connectivity or bequeath a cultural legacy, as the cases of Charlemagne and Chinggis Khan demonstrate.[27] The latter may have affected genetics as well: a famous DNA study suggests that about 8 per cent of the men now living between Uzbekistan and Northeast China carry a chromosome that arguably goes back to Chinggis Khan and his close male relatives.[28]

Regional trade networks, the second type of regular interaction, were more common than empires. In the eastern hemisphere, they were increasingly interlinked and, in about 1250, developed into a loose system that extended in the wake of the Mongol conquests from England to China and persisted for about a century. According to one reconstruction, it was made up of eight circuits: China to the Strait of Malacca, India to the Strait of Malacca, China to the Black Sea, Arabia to East Africa and West India, the eastern Mediterranean to the Persian Gulf, Egypt to the Indian Ocean, and the trans-Mediterranean and West European subsystems;[29] to these one may

---

27 For the Mongol Empire, see chapter 20.
28 See Tatiana Zerjal et al., "The Genetic Legacy of the Mongols," *American Journal of Human Genetics* 72.3 (March 2003): 717–21.
29 See Janet L. Abu-Lughod, *Before European Hegemony: The World System A.D. 1250–1350* (New York: Oxford University Press, 1989). On the Mongol conquests enabling a flow of silver along the upper stratum of monies across much of Eurasia, see Akinobu

add the network that linked sub-Saharan Africa with the Maghreb. The extent to which some contemporaries were aware of these interlinkages is highlighted by the proposal of the Dominican friar William of Adam, in about 1317, to prevent the flow of goods from India via Egypt to Europe by blockading the Gulf of Aden with four crusader war galleys.[30]

There were also trade networks in the western hemisphere. For Late Postclassic Mesoamerica, four exchange circuits have been identified: west Mexico, the Aztec Empire, the Maya zone, and the southern Pacific coastal zone.[31] In addition, archaeological investigations indicate that cacao and scarlet macaws, alongside their ritual roles, were imported from Mesoamerica to the North American southwest; the macaws, in at least one case, were then bred locally, over 500 kilometers north of their natural habitat.[32] In the Inca Empire trade apparently took place only in two regions: in the northernmost periphery of the realm traders procured sumptuary goods for local lords, and traders based in the central Peruvian Chincha Valley used rafts to reach the Guayaquil Gulf (modern Ecuador) and took the land route to the Inca capital at Cuzco.[33] Despite all of these connections, however, it would appear that during the period 500–1500 economic exchange circuits played second fiddle to war and conquest in connecting different populations in both hemispheres.

Religion was a third important ligament of connection. The Buddhist, Christian and Islamic ecumenes, expanding during much of the Middle Millennium, served as the arenas for intense and durable cultural integration. Of these, the largest by far was the Islamic realm, which originated in the Arab conquests of the seventh century and eventually extended from West Africa and Spain to Southeast Asia. The only civilization to border on all

Kuroda, "The Eurasian Silver Century, 1276–1359: Commensurability and Multiplicity," *Journal of Global History* 4 (2009): 245–69.

30 See William of Adam, *How to Defeat the Saracens*, ed. and trans. Giles Constable (Washington, DC: Dumbarton Oaks Research Library and Collection, 2012): 96–116; see also 9, n. 37.

31 Michael E. Smith and Frances F. Berdan, "Spatial Structure of the Mesoamerican World System," in Michael E. Smith and Frances F. Berdan (eds.), *The Postclassic Mesoamerican World* (Salt Lake City: University of Utah Press, 2003): 29–30.

32 Patricia L. Crown and W. Jeffrey Hurst, "Evidence of Cacao Use in the Prehispanic American Southwest," *Proceedings of the National Academy of the United States of America* 106/7 (2009): 2110–13; Andrew D. Somerville, Ben A. Nelson and Kelly J. Knudson, "Isotopic Investigation of Pre-Hispanic Macaw Breeding in Northwest Mexico," *Journal of Anthropological Archaeology* 29 (2010): 125–35.

33 Frank Salomon, "A North Andean Status Trader Complex under Inka Rule," *Ethnohistory* 34 (1987): 63–77; María Rostworowski de Díez Canseco, *History of the Inca Realm*, trans. Harry B. Iceland (Cambridge University Press, 1999): 159–62, 209–14.

other major ones of the eastern hemisphere, it played a crucial role in the communication among them. The borders between the religious ecumenes were not stable: for instance, Buddhism lost present-day Afghanistan to Islam, and Islam lost Spain to Latin Christendom. Nevertheless, the ecumenes enjoyed far more durability than the empires, with the exception of China.

Communication and transmission of knowledge among large-area units assumed various forms. Some are closely documented, such as the translation of philosophical and scientific treatises in eighth/ninth century Baghdad or in twelfth/thirteenth century Spain. The migration of literary motifs, on the other hand, can often be established only through a painstaking scrutiny of apparently unconnected texts.[34] Similarly, the study of the diffusion of crops or techniques can rely but rarely on an explicit mention of a transcultural borrowing; usually historians have to rely on indirect evidence, such as the geographical diffusion of a crop or a technique whose chronological progress can be unquestionably attested. The spread of paper is a case in point. Widely used in China by the third century, paper reached the Islamic realm soon after its creation, and came to be manufactured in Samarkand after 751, in Baghdad in about 794, in Egypt in the tenth century and in Játiva (Muslim Spain) in the eleventh century; by the end of the twelfth century there were 472 paper mills in Fez (Morocco). Some Egyptian paper was exported to India. In Europe paper was first used some time before 1000 but came to be manufactured only from the thirteenth century onward. The Byzantines apparently never took to paper-making; but from the eleventh century they used imported paper. (In Mesoamerica paper was invented independently.)

The spread of paper exemplifies the ways in which knowledge and technology spread, but also demonstrates the way in which an item could be detached from its original major use as it spread. In China woodblock printing on paper, attested since the eighth century, became very common and set off an information revolution. In the realm of Islam, on the other hand, although paper was extensively adopted for writing, block-printing of books was not emulated. In western Europe, too, paper was used for centuries before Johann Gutenberg, in about 1440, invented printing with movable type.[35]

---

34 See for instance Sharon Kinoshita, "Translatio/n, Empire, and the Worlding of Medieval Literature: The Travels of Kalila wa Dimna," *Postcolonial Studies* 11 (2011): 371–85.

35 See Tsuen-Hsuin Tsien, *Paper and Printing*, vol. v, part 1 of J. Needham (ed.), *Science and Civilisation in China* (Cambridge University Press, 1985); Jonathan M. Bloom, *Paper*

Diasporas fulfilled a major role in the spread of goods and ideas. In the ninth century the Jewish merchants called al-Rādhāniyya (or Radhanites) carried their goods all the way from the land of the Franks to China and back; from the twelfth century onward, Jewish scholars took part in the translation of Arabic treatises into Latin. They could fulfill these functions because in the realm of Islam Jews (and Christians) were accorded protected status, and because in Christendom, despite recurrent bouts of persecution, the theological doctrine that regarded Jews as witnesses to Christianity's truth sanctioned their presence. The Muslim commercial diasporas in West Africa and in Southeast Asia were instrumental in the Islamization of these regions. (The absence of such a Muslim diaspora in western Europe may have resulted, in the early centuries, from the West's commercial insignificance, and in the later ones from the absence of a Christian doctrine sanctioning Muslim presence.) And Chinese diasporic communities spread popular strains of Buddhism in South and Southeast Asia.

While conquest, commerce, and religion furthered the expansion of various webs, and pilgrims, merchants and envoys, as well as some thinkers and tinkers, traveled the roads and seas, and such exceptional men like Rashīd al-Dīn dramatically promoted cross-civilizational awareness, we can only guess to what extent an ordinary person who lived in those times was conscious of these developments or of their actual extent. With most people's horizons limited to the nearby vicinity and bounded by custom, it is probable that few perceived these thickening webs, even as their lives were increasingly affected by them.

Overview of this volume

This volume is divided into five sections, with a final concluding chapter. The first section, "Global developments," provides a series of chapters that are global in scope and focus on structures, institutions and processes that developed long before the Middle Millennium and continue to shape world history today. In Chapter 2, Joachim Radkau examines the interaction between humans and the environment, noting the ways humans shaped nature and nature simultaneously shaped humans in a process of co-evolution. He explores the dynamics of the relationship between humans and nature among agriculturalists and nomads, and evaluates scenarios that

before Print: The History and Impact of Paper in the Islamic World (New Haven, CT: Yale University Press, 2001).

have been proposed for that dynamic, which have ranged from witless exploitation that led to environmental degradation and societal collapse to rugged resilience and sustainability. The Middle Millennium, he concludes, saw gradual acceleration in human alteration of the environment, but this was limited and local; in contrast to today, those who caused environmental damage belonged to the same social group as those affected by it, and lived with its effects. In Chapter 3, Susan Mosher Stuard surveys women, family, gender, and sexuality, noting regional differences in marital patterns and the ways families organized societies. She pays particular attention to the role of religion in structuring patriarchal and paternalistic gender assumptions, and also uses domestic slavery and inheritance systems as examples of the way in which the webs of exchange that grew denser in this era had differential impacts on men and women. Sexual responses and reproduction were apprehended through gender distinctions, and notions of sexuality were communicated in erotic art, law codes, medical treatises, and scientific works. Gender systems remained varied, Stuard concludes, but in general moved from being somewhat diverse and flexible to becoming more rigid in this era, particularly as they applied to women. In Chapter 4, Susan Reynolds examines social hierarchy and solidarity, opening with the central assumption that all societies of which there is any record in this era were more or less unequal, but also all had expectations of proper and just behavior for those at the top, including the ruler. Government came in layers, and growing wealth and economic complexity led to new types of elites and more complex systems of governance, law, and bureaucracy. Societies from the local to the large-scale were also envisaged as solidarities linked by bonds of assumed (though often fictitious) genealogical connection, myths of origin, shared customs, and common interests, but only rarely, Reynolds asserts, did such bonds lead to calls for greater social egalitarianism rather than justice within a hierarchical system. In Chapter 5, Linda Walton surveys educational institutions beyond the household, focusing especially on those that arose with the expansion of Confucianism, Buddhism, Christianity, and Islam, but also describing organized education in Eurasian Judaism and in the Aztec and Inca Empires. Learning was both a path to religious knowledge and a means of fulfilling the secular administrative and legal needs of rulers, dual functions that sometimes stood in tension to one another. Everywhere, Walton concludes, the organization and transmission of knowledge reflected not only diverse cultural values and traditions, but also differing relationships between states, which both utilized and controlled knowledge, and also relationships among elites, whose status depended on their access to knowledge and role in its transmission. In Chapter 6, Clifford J. Rogers provides an analysis of warfare, examining the reasons why wars were fought, who fought them, and how they were fought, including questions of recruitment, equipment, and organization of armed forces as well as strategy, tactics, and logistics. He examines the role of tribute-taking and slave-raiding in warfare, and pays particular attention to patterns of conflict between Eurasian nomadic societies and agro-urban civilizations, exploring why the former were so often able to defeat and overrun the latter despite disadvantages in manpower and resources. At the end of the Middle Millennium, Rogers comments, mastery of gunpowder weapons gave both the Ottomans and Europeans key advantages that allowed them to conquer and hold large areas.

The second section, "Eurasian commonalities," narrows the geographic focus slightly, but includes analyses of developments with broad cultural, political, economic, and social impacts that occurred in parallel across much of Eurasia in this era. In Chapter 7, an author team headed by Patrick J. Geary examines courtly cultures in western Europe, Byzantium, the Islamic world, India, China, and Japan. In all of these regions, courts became centers of power where specialized communities of individuals carried out functions related to the exercise of power, and simultaneously created cultural forms and ceremonial rituals that represented the court to itself and to outsiders. Courts varied widely in their size, organizational complexity, spatial arrangements, physical stability, structure, and gradations of rank, but across Eurasia there was intense competition for power and access to royal favor, which gave rise to particular codes of behavior that sought to teach courtiers how to survive and advance and that distinguished men and women participating in court life from those outside the court. Courts exchanged novel and precious cultural products of display and consumption and directly or indirectly borrowed practices and values from other courtly cultures, thus creating, the authors conclude, a Eurasian system of exercising and representing power. In Chapter 8, Björn Wittrock examines a series of transmutations, renovations, and reorientations from the eleventh to the thirteenth centuries within various Eurasian cultural ecumenes through which core traditions and cultural legacies were reinterpreted and rearticulated in the face of challenges posed by economic, political, and social change. He notes that these occurred across Eurasia, but pays particular attention in this chapter to China, Japan, and Western Christendom. Wittrock argues that these reorientations involved a process of "cultural crystallization" by which these ecumenes were distinctly formed and became clearly demarcated from each other, both in their self-image and the view of other societies, in terms of their cultural order, cosmological focus, historical consciousness, and other aspects of life.

The third section, "Growing interactions," highlights networks of long-distance trade and migration in agricultural and nomadic societies, and the transmission and exchange of knowledge and technologies that accompanied these. In Chapter 9, Richard Smith provides a broad overview of trade and commerce across Afro-Eurasia during the Middle Millennium, noting that by the fifteenth century "a more professional merchant class moved larger cargoes of more varied commodities longer distances to more destinations serving a wider consumer base than could have been imagined at the close of the fifth century." He divides this huge area into three categories of zones: engines such as China and the Islamic heartland that were centers of production, consumption, and exchange; passageways such as Central Asia or the sea routes of Southeast Asia; and cul-de-sacs such as western Europe and West Africa. Smith traces the ways in which cataclysms such as the Mongol conquest and pandemic disease, as well as technological innovations and political decisions, shaped the ability of any zone to gain or maintain its status as a commercial engine. In Chapter 10, Michel Balard examines the northwestern portion of the Afro-Eurasian zone, Europe from the north Baltic Sea to the eastern Mediterranean. He discusses merchants and their associations, the commercial techniques invented for raising and handling capital, new forms of paper and metal currency, changes in ships and navigational routes, expanded fairs and markets, methods of obtaining governmental protection, and the wide variety of luxury goods, subsistence products, raw materials, and human cargo that merchants handled. Balard concludes that despite ups and downs, by the fifteenth century the Mediterranean and the north of Europe were tied together by numerous land and sea routes and were experiencing strong economic growth in what might be termed a first globalization of trade. In Chapter 11, Himanshu Prabha Ray examines another segment of the Afro-Eurasian trading zone, the dynamic maritime communities of the Indian Ocean. She finds that local demand and local fishing and sailing communities played an important and steady role, but Hindu, Muslim, Buddhist, and Jewish institutions and merchants coming from elsewhere also shaped trade. Partnerships were established across religious affiliations and ethnic boundaries that connected coastal cities to each other and to distant trading centers, while in southern India merchant associations dominated commerce, founded temples, and employed private armies. Ray notes that evidence for seafaring communities comes from historical and archaeological sources, but also cautions that a holistic understanding of cultural interaction across the maritime world must take into account diverse channels of communication, including oral transmission by priests and pilgrims, traders and sailors, wandering storytellers and entertainers.

This third section moves from trade to other types of interactions. In Chapter 12, Dagmar Schäfer and Marcus Popplow explore technology and innovation within expanding webs of exchange. They note that while earlier historiography tended to emphasize sudden technological breakthroughs, change actually occurred continuously, as people invented and adapted tools, machines, designs, methods, and processes deliberately to address new environmental or other circumstances, and also playfully or because of changing tastes and patterns of consumption. State or elite interests often acted as the catalysts, but artisanal experts and everyday practitioners held the basis of technical knowledge and stabilized its circulation. The motivations for innovation and methods of transmission were manifold, Schäfer and Popplow argue, and no culture was hostile toward technology or ignorant of it, but used innovations for both reform and the continuation of traditions. Turning from the practical to the theoretical, in Chapter 13 Charles Burnett discusses the transmission of science and philosophy, commenting that writers during the Middle Millennium and modern scholars have both regarded questions about the cultural origins of scientific knowledge as essential. Contemporary legends about the transmission of science reflect some degree of reality, for certain courts or cities stand out as hubs of learning and intellectual exchange, where books and mobile practitioners brought new ideas, although these were also to be guarded lest they fall into the wrong hands. Burnett concludes that ideas became transformed and appropriated to new situations and cultures as they moved, and that in at least some cases their transmission transcended religious and other types of boundaries. In Chapter 14, Anatoly M. Khazanov examines one type of boundary crossing that was particularly evident during the Middle Millennium, large-scale pastoral nomadic migrations and conquests. He analyzes the economic and political causes for pastoral nomadic migrations in this period, and discusses similarities and differences in three parts of Afro-Eurasia: the Eurasian steppes, semi-deserts and deserts; the Near and Middle East and North Africa; and India. Khazanov asserts that nomadic conquests brought significant cultural and economic changes, including the spread of Turkic languages and the flow of ideas and goods through long-distance trading, but did not ultimately alter sociopolitical structures drastically or permanently, because nomadic rulers had to adopt or adjust to the pre-existing institutional infrastructure, administrative models, and religious situation of conquered states.

The fourth section, "Expanding religious systems," focuses on three religions that proved to be so portable that by the end of the Middle Millennium they could legitimately be termed "world religions." In Chapter 15, Michael Cook explores the centrality of Islamic civilization, which by the fifteenth century stretched east/west from Southeast Asia to West Africa, and north/south from the bend in the Volga River to Madagascar. He begins with a bird's-eye view of differences among regions within this vast area as Islam interacted with and superseded earlier civilizations and cultural formations, and then highlights the components that helped to bind Islamic civilization together, including institutions, traditions of scholarship, and language. Cook argues that Islam is the only world religion that was also a world civilization, and suggests that this may have resulted from the complementary fusing early in its spread of the strong ethnic, religious, and political identity of the Arabs with the elaborate literary traditions of the Fertile Crescent. In Chapter 16, Miri Rubin examines Christendom's regional systems, first discussing central features of Christian life, including rituals, the veneration of saints and the Virgin Mary, bishops and other clergy, and collective worship, and the implications of these for polities, communities, and individuals. She surveys areas of the world governed by Christian rulers, those in which Christians lived as large, tolerated indigenous communities (largely under Muslim rulers), and those further east where Christian groups were small. Rubin highlights certain movements, including trade, crusading, and missionary activities, which encouraged links between the Christian regions, concluding that Christian institutions and teaching possessed the potential for inclusion and exclusion, for accommodating diversity as well as encouraging polities to become persecuting societies. In Chapter 17, Tansen Sen surveys the spread of Buddhism, noting that this was a complex multi-directional process that involved the transmission of art forms, literary genres, ritual items, geographical knowledge, and technologies along with religious doctrines. He sees two key turning points, one in the fifth century, after which places such as Sumatra, Japan, and Korea were incorporated into the Buddhist realm and diverse forms of Buddhist teachings adapted to local needs and values emerged, and one in the tenth century, after which there were multiple centers of Buddhism with their own spheres of influence and connections. Sen concludes that the spread of Buddhism triggered vibrant commercial interactions and cross-cultural exchanges that integrated various regions of Asia from Iran to Japan, and transformed the worldviews, political/cultural identities, sacred landscapes, and social lives of numerous people living across most of Asia.

The fifth section of this volume, "State formations," surveys the development of centralized regional states and empires. In Chapter 18, Johann P. Arnason provides an overview of state formation and empire building, linking these processes with the previous section on religion by emphasizing that in this period state formation was everywhere intertwined with religious cultures and institutions. He notes that political developments across Afro-Eurasia and to some extent in parts of the Americas lend support to the idea that the Middle Millennium was a distinct period. Of these, interaction between inner and outer parts of Eurasia was of particular importance for political history, but this did not lead to a unified pattern of state-building among either nomadic pastoralists or sedentary societies. Instead, Arnason asserts, imperial patterns – as distinct from more basic or common forms of statehood – were present in all Eurasian civilizations, though on different levels and with different levels of durability. Chapters 19–24 comprise a series of chapters that explore state-building in various parts of the world. In Chapter 19, Richard von Glahn notes that with the reunification of China under the Sui dynasty in the sixth century, a unified empire became the political ideal and – with fairly brief interruptions – the historical reality from this time onward, and inspired China's neighbors to emulate the Chinese model and form their own more centralized "national states," engendering a multi-state political order that has persisted in East Asia down to modern times. Despite its political and cultural supremacy, however, China faced challenges from within and without that ultimately led to dramatic changes, including a revitalized Confucian model of imperial sovereignty and civil bureaucracy and a rapid monetization of taxes, rents, and other aspects of the economy in part through government interventions. In Chapter 20, Michal Biran examines the Mongols, who embarked on an unprecedented mobilization of peoples, goods, and ideas to forge the largest contiguous empire the world has known, and created an imperial administration and culture that merged their indigenous norms with various elements of their subjects' cultures. She acknowledges the destruction that was part of this empire building, but primarily emphasizes the role of Chinggis Khan and his descendants as active promoters of inter-civilizational exchange that bolstered Eurasian integration and broadened the horizons of the Mongols' subjects and neighbors. Their legacy is complex, Biran asserts, as they triggered a long-lasting cultural effervescence, a thriving artistic and scientific exchange, booming international trade, and a host of religious, ethnic and political changes. In Chapter 21, Jean-Claude Cheynet discusses Byzantium, the only European or Mediterranean state formed in antiquity that survived almost the entire Middle Millennium, despite its geographic position in the path of every people on the move, instability in the succession to the emperorship, and challenges by local elites. This longevity was in part the result of certain advantages – Roman traditions, an influential religious hierarchy, a well-defended capital, and a relatively stable financial system – but also the Byzantines' capacity for adaptation. Cheynet argues that contrary to the image of stability emanating from official discourse and often accepted by later historians, the structures of the Byzantine Empire were regularly transformed to meet new situations. In Chapter 22, David C. Conrad surveys polities that emerged in the Western Sudan from the late eighth century to 1500, including the Soninke kingdom of Wagadu/Ghana, the Mali Empire, the kingdom of Gao that expanded into the Songhay Empire, and other smaller states. All of these drew significant resources from long-distance and trans-Saharan trade in gold, copper, iron tools and weapons, slaves, salt, and other goods. Conrad makes innovative use of oral traditions along with archaeological, epigraphic, linguistic, and written evidence to examine the ways in which these states developed more efficient methods of food production, gained control of sources of artisanal, agricultural, and mineral goods, imposed control over trading centers, and established political dominance.

The final two chapters in the fifth section move across the Atlantic to investigate the Americas, where there are parallels in several places to many of the economic, political, and social processes that characterized Afro-Eurasia in the Middle Millennium. In Chapter 23, Michael E. Smith examines Mesoamerican state formation in the Postclassic period (from the eighth century through the fifteenth), when societies grew and expanded after an interval of collapse, ruralization, and stagnation. Peoples migrated, commercial networks increased in size and scope to encompass a greater diversity of goods, empires and city-states rose and fell, and ideas and styles traveled widely, forming a distinctive art style and a set of common symbols that were used all over Mesoamerica. Smith emphasizes that Postclassic Mesoamerica was very dynamic politically with multiple historical trajectories, but in general polities were smaller, shorter-lived, and less despotic than those of the Classic period, although the large Aztec and Tarascan Empires developed in contradistinction to this trend. In Chapter 24, Sabine MacCormack analyzes the ways in which state and religion were intertwined in the creation of the Inca Empire, the largest imperial state of pre-Columbian America, which at its height stretched over 4,000 kilometers along South America's Pacific coast. Inca rulers expanded their power and their territory in a variety of ways, forging marriage alliances with neighboring lords, waging wars to gather plunder and incorporate new territory, extending a system of roads with way stations, and engaging in diplomacy and negotiation. These practical measures were enhanced, MacCormack asserts, by creation myths and other narrative traditions (later recorded by the Spanish) in which the Inca rulers deliberately portrayed themselves as the founders and originators of civilization in the Andes, giving order to human society just as the Creator had given order to the cosmos, and by the Inca rulers' participation in the religion of their subjects.

The volume ends with a final synoptic chapter, in which Diego Olstein surveys the social, economic, cultural, intellectual, and political developments discussed in the preceding chapters with an eye to forces of regional integration and movements of interaction that led to what Shmuel N. Eisenstadt has termed "proto-globalization." This globalization was "proto" because it was intermittent and fell short of encompassing the globe, and also because local trends often prevailed upon global ones in a process Olstein labels "proto-glocalization," modifying the term invented by economists to describe the adaptation of a global product to local conditions and standards. Glocalization stresses the tensions between the local and global origins of – and inputs into – structures and processes in any given society, as well as tensions in the outcomes of such processes. Olstein thus begins with the local, then looks at the irruption of outside forces that transformed local worlds especially in Afro-Eurasia, including the often intertwined transregional processes of empire building, the expansion of trade networks, and religious conversion. He surveys the various ways these were localized, as ideas, technologies, gender patterns, court traditions, laws, rituals, and educational institutions were adapted and modified in the process of making an impact upon local arrangements. The combination of limiting conditions for a globalized world and the presence of powerful external forces that permeated so many local lives, he concludes, suggests that expanding webs of exchange and conquest did indeed make the Middle Millennium a "proto-global" era.

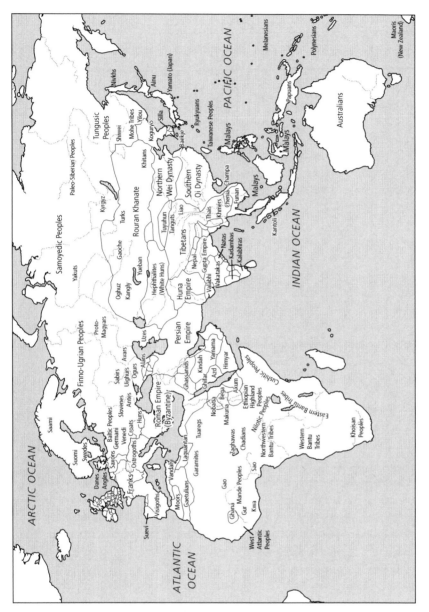

Map 1.1. Eastern hemisphere, 500 CE

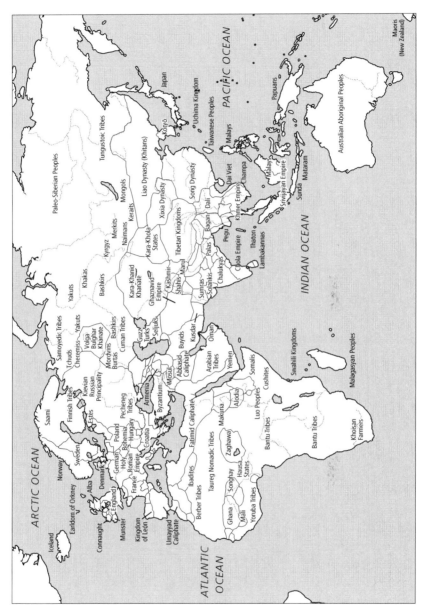

Map 1.2. Eastern hemisphere, 1000 CE

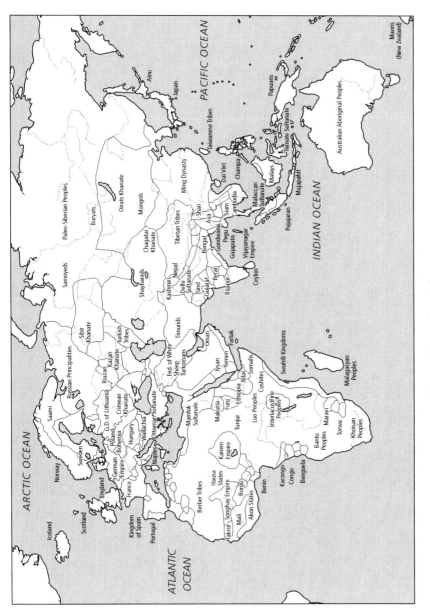

Map 1.3. Eastern hemisphere, 1500 CE

FURTHER READING

Abu-Lughod, Janet L. *Before European Hegemony. The World System* A.D. *1250–1350*. New York: Oxford University Press, 1989.

Allsen, Thomas T. *Culture and Conquest in Mongol Eurasia*. Cambridge University Press, 2001.

Beasley, W. G. and E. G. Pulleyblank (eds.), *Historians of China and Japan*. London: Oxford University Press, 1961.

Bentley, Jerry H. "Hemispheric Integration, 500–1500 CE." *Journal of World History* 9 (1998): 237–54.

Biraben, Jean-Noël. "Essai sur l'évolution du nombre des hommes." *Population* 34 (1979): 13–25.

Bloom, Jonathan M. *Paper before Print: The History and Impact of Paper in the Islamic World*. New Haven, CT: Yale University Press, 2001.

Boas, Adrian J. *Domestic Settings. Sources on Domestic Architecture and Day-to-Day Activities in the Crusader States*. Leiden: Brill, 2010.

Brentjes, Sonja. "Revisiting Catalan Portolan Charts: Do They Contain Elements of Asian Provenance?" In Philippe Forêt and Andreas Kaplony (eds.), *The Journey of Maps and Images on the Silk Road*. Leiden: Brill, 2008: 181–201.

Chandler, David P. *A History of Cambodia*. Boulder, CO: Westview Press, 1983.

Christian, David. *Maps of Time: An Introduction to Big History*. Berkeley, CA: University of California Press, 2011.

Cook, Michael. *A Brief History of the Human Race*. New York, NY: W. W. Norton, 2003.

Edson, Evelyn. *The World Map, 1300–1492: The Persistence of Tradition and Transformation*. Baltimore, MD: The Johns Hopkins University Press, 2007.

Edson, Evelyn and Emilie Savage-Smith. *Medieval Views of the Cosmos: Picturing the Universe in the Christian and Islamic Middle Ages*. Oxford: Bodleian Library, 2004.

Ellenblum, Ronnie. *Crusader Castles and Modern Histories*. Cambridge University Press, 2007.

Harley, J. B., and David Woodward (eds.) *The History of Cartography*, 3 vols. University of Chicago Press, 1987–2007.

Hosler, Dorothy. "Ancient West Mexican Metallurgy: South and Central American Origins and West Mexican Transformations." *American Anthropologist* 90 (1988): 832–55.

    The Sounds and Colors of Power. The Sacred Metallurgical Technology of Ancient West Mexico. Cambridge, MA: MIT Press, 1994.

    "Metal Production." in Michael E. Smith and Frances F. Berdan, eds., *The Postclassic Mesoamerican World*. Salt Lake City, UT: University of Utah Press, 2003: 159–71.

Hosler, Dorothy, and Andrew Macfarlane. "Copper Sources, Metal Production, and Metals Trade in Late Postclassic Mesoamerica." *Science* 273, 5283 (1996): 1819–24.

Kedar, Benjamin Z. "Reflections on Maps, Crusading and Logistics." In John H. Pryor (ed.), *Logistics of Warfare in the Age of the Crusades*. Aldershot: Ashgate, 2006: 159–83.

Krawulsky, Dorothea. *The Mongol Īlkhāns and their Vizier Rashīd al-Dīn*. Frankfurt: Peter Lang, 2011.

Lang, David M. *The Wisdom of Balahvar: A Christian Legend of the Buddha*. London: Allen and Unwin, 1957.

Livi-Bacci, Massimo. *A Concise History of World Population*, 4th edn. Oxford: Blackwell, 2007.

Lopez, Robert S. *Civilizations, Western and World: From Prehistory to the End of the Old Regime*. Boston, MA: Little, Brown and Co., 1975: 1–319.

Marcus, Joyce. *Mesoamerican Writing Systems. Propaganda, Myth, and History in Four Ancient Civilizations*. Princeton University Press, 1992.

Mitchell, Piers D., Evilena Anastasiou, and Danny Syon. "Human Intestinal Parasites in Crusader Acre: Evidence for Migration with Disease in the Medieval Period." *International Journal of Paleopathology* 1 (2011): 132–7.

Olschki, Leonardo. *Guillaume Boucher: A French Artist at the Court of the Khans*. Baltimore, MD: The Johns Hopkins Press, 1946.

Park, Hyunhee. *Mapping the Chinese and Islamic Worlds. Cross-Cultural Exchange in Pre-modern Asia*. Cambridge University Press, 2012.

Ptak, Roderich. "Images of Maritime Asia in Two Yuan Texts: *Daoyi zhilue* and *Yiyu zhi*." *Journal of Sung-Yuan Studies* 25 (1995): 47–75 [The *Daoyi zhilue* is the account by Wang Dayuan, based on his voyages in the 1330s].

Rostworowski de Díez Canseco, María. *History of the Inca Realm*. Trans. Harry B. Iceland, Cambridge University Press, 1999.

Shagrir, Iris. *Naming Patterns in the Latin Kingdom of Jerusalem*. Oxford: Linacre College, Unit for Prosopographical Research, 2004.

Sharer, Robert J. *The Ancient Maya*, 5th edn. Stanford University Press, 1994.

Shboul, Ahmad M. H. *Al-Mas'ūdī and His World. A Muslim Humanist and his Interest in Non-Muslims*. London: Ithaca Press, 1979.

Tedlock, Dennis. *2000 Years of Mayan Literature*. Berkeley, CA: University of California Press, 2010.

Tsien, Tsuen-Hsuin. *Paper and Printing*. Vol. v, part 1 of Joseph Needham (ed.), *Science and Civilisation in China*. Cambridge University Press, 1985.

Xuanzang. *The Great Tang Dynasty Record of the Western Regions*. Trans. Li Rongxi, Berkeley, CA: Numata Center for Buddhist Translation and Research, 1996.

PART I

★

GLOBAL DEVELOPMENTS

2

Humans and the environment: tension and co-evolution

JOACHIM RADKAU

'When the world was half a thousand years younger', wrote Johan Huizinga in the opening of his *The Autumn of the Middle Ages*, 'all events had much sharper outlines than now. The distance between sadness and joy, between good and bad fortune, seemed to be much greater than for us; every experience had that degree of directness and absoluteness that joy and sadness still have in the mind of a child . . . Sickness contrasted more strongly with health. The cutting cold and the dreaded darkness of winter were more concrete evils.'[1] This immediacy also shaped the connection between humans and their environment: in essence this relationship was still very direct, mediated neither by technical media nor administrative apparatuses, and also much less so by money than in later periods. When Ibn Battuta (1304–1368/9 or 1377) described the abundance of China, the splendid plums and chicken eggs as large as goose eggs in the West were among the first things he praised:[2] as Karl Marx would have said, he paid attention not to the exchange value of products but to their utility value; more precisely, to their enjoyment value along with the natural conditions that gave rise to such products.

The nature that surrounded humans, from which they lived and which at times threatened them, was still very concrete in all its diversity; it would not have occurred to anyone to invent for it the abstract label 'environment'. And it was full of energy and life. In northern climes – whether in western Europe or East Asia – people were happy about spring; in regions of the south, which had periods of drought, they were happy about the rainy period. The more human settlements in the wake of population growth

1 Johan Huizinga, *The Autumn of the Middle Ages*, trans. Rodney J. Payton and Ulrich Mammitzsch (University of Chicago Press, 1996): 1, 22.
2 Ibn Battuta, *Travels in Asia and Africa 1325–1354*, trans. H. A. R. Gibb (Varanasi: Pilgrims Publishing, 2007): 282–3.

moved away from springs, the more people discovered the vital value of pure water: this discovery, which pervades all cultures, is to this day a leitmotif of environmental policy. Needless to say, the refreshing power of clear water was experienced most intensely in arid regions. Whereas hundreds of cisterns had been dug in Constantinople during the Byzantine period,[3] the Ottoman rulers built aqueducts in an effort to return to running water, which alone was regarded as pure in Islam.

Among the countless testimonies to the culture- and epoch-spanning bond of humans with animals, plants, and bubbling springs, the appreciation for the *bee* seems especially important. The bee – to the cultivation of which Virgil had already devoted the entire fourth book of his *Georgica*, and which for Bernard of Clairvaux represented the Holy Spirit – this winged creature exemplary for its diligence and cooperation that seeks out fragrant blossoms and extracts and providently collects their sweet essence, honey; and for all that contemporaries did not yet understand the importance of the bee to the pollination of the blossoms![4] With palpable delight, Max Weber quoted the eighth-century Kansuan Verse Inscription of the Brahman prince Śivagana about the season when he built his hermitage, where the buzzing of the bees mixes with an erotic shiver – for Weber a key to understanding happiness and the hope for salvation in the Indian 'Middle Ages': 'Swarms of bumble bees are everywhere and more than ever the gleam in the eyes of lovely women tells of their love ... Laughingly they hastily avert their half-closed eyes and only the quiver of their brows betrays the joy in their hearts. The wives of the pilgrims, however, see the land lighted with the flowers of mango trees and hear the humming sound of drunken bees.'[5]

The Egyptian Dhu'n-Nun (died 859), one of the earliest Islamic mystics, discovered nature as God's witness, like pantheists of other religions across the ages. As one of his prayers intoned: 'O God, I never hearken to the voices of the beasts or the rustle of the trees, the splashing of the waters or the song of the birds, the whistling of the wind or the rumble of the thunder but I sense in them a testimony to Thy Unity.'[6] Theorists distinguish a half-dozen

3 Elif Ada Deniz, *A Tale of Water* (Istanbul: Unicon Consulting Group 2009): 81.
4 Gerd Heinz-Mohr, *Lexikon der Symbole. Bilder und Zeichen der christlichen Kunst* (Düsseldorf: Eugen Diederichs, 1971): 51; May R. Berenbaum, *Blutsauger, Staatsgründer, Seidenfabrikanten. Die zwiespältige Beziehung von Mensch und Insekt* (Heidelberg: Spektrum Akademischer Verlag, 1997): 128–30.
5 Max Weber, *The Religion of India: The Sociology of Hinduism and Buddhism*, trans. Hans H. Gerth and Don Martindale (Glencoe, IL: The Free Press, 1958): 190.
6 Annemarie Schimmel, *Islam: An Introduction* (Albany, NY: State University of New York Press, 1992): 106.

or more different definitions of 'nature' and thereby often decide that the concept is random. Despite this ambiguity, however, the concept 'nature' could not and cannot be done away with.[7] Norbert Elias recommends that we regard 'nature' not so much as an idea, but as 'a symbol that represents a synthesis on a very high level'[8] – a synthesis of long, vital collective experiences. And there is much to Edward O. Wilson's *biophilia hypothesis*, according to which all humans are endowed with an innate love of the nature that surrounds them even if this love, much like Eros, has multiple variations[9].

The most famous nature contemplations in medieval Europe – Albertus Magnus' tractates *De animalibus*, *De vegetabilibus*, and *De creaturis* – are characterized by a vivid perception, even if formally they are commentaries on Aristotle. According to tradition, Albertus spent many years as a mendicant wandering from monastery to monastery, from the North Sea to Italy, and from Austria to Brabant; his writings on nature attest not only to a knowledge of classical literature, but also to a good deal of personal observation.[10] Today, when even the World Bank's report on agriculture (2008) warns against the worldwide degradation of soils, Albertus' observations in *De vegetabilibus* about the newly cleared and the fallow land are of particular interest. He praises the fallow land as a way of rejuvenating the aging soil, understands the soil as a living thing – the very thing that even Justus Liebig, the nineteenth-century pope of chemistry, refused to believe. Of course, the teachings of Albertus were not learned speculations, but a mirror of peasant experience of the three-field system that had been spreading in the West since the Carolingian period. The same applies to his warnings against soil erosion on mountain slopes and his recommendation to plough at the same level, not from the top down: this was nothing other than the 'contour plowing' that the Soil Conservation Service of President Roosevelt's New Deal, alarmed by the Dust Bowl, rediscovered from ancient agrarian cultures.

This basic problem of farming sloping terrain is the same everywhere. A global environmental history can be reconstructed, at least in rough

7 On the 'mysterious regenerative power of the nature idea', see Joachim Radkau, *Nature and Power: A Global History of the Environment*, trans. Thomas Dunlap (New York: Cambridge University Press, 2009): 17–19.

8 Norbert Elias, 'Über die Natur', *Merkur* 40 (1986): 471.

9 Stephen R. Kellert and Edward O. Wilson (eds.), *The Biophilia Hypothesis* (Washington, DC: Island Press, 1993).

10 Clarence J. Glacken, *Traces on the Rhodian Shore. Nature and Culture in Western Thought from Ancient Times to the End of the 18th Century* (Berkeley: University of California Press, 1967): 227–8.

outline, even where a broad basis of field research is lacking, because natural laws come into play – along with basic traits of human nature, which are deeply shaped, though not entirely determined, by evolution and corporeal reality. Moreover, one can identify in humans a 'second nature' that is formed by ways of life and therefore varies from culture to culture, but which possesses a remarkable resilience against short-term fluctuations.[11] The environmental historian therefore has good reason to borrow from the work of anthropologists and to pay special attention to how certain ways in which nature is used simultaneously shape humans. It is by virtue of this, above all, that some basic features of the Middle Millennium emerge, even if a broad foundation of details is missing.

A three-realms model

Reconstructing the human relationship to nature depends not on general but on specific driving forces: not on the natural instincts of human beings, but on the 'second nature' of a way of life shaped by culture and generation-spanning experience. Strategies of planning ahead can be expected to be more likely in regions of the world with periods of cold or drought, where humans will starve if they fail to make provisions. According to Fernand Braudel, the entire civilized world, looked at from its vital basis, divides into three realms: one governed by wheat, one by rice, and one by corn (maize). Their origins are lost in the darkness of prehistory. It is only in the Middle Millennium that they take on sharper contours for the historian, contours that shed greater light on the dynamic of the relationship between humans and nature. I propose a somewhat modified three-fold classification: first, the great irrigation systems; second, the nomadic realms; and third, the combination of rainfed agriculture and animal husbandry that became characteristic for broad regions of Europe.

The great irrigation systems

For the period 200–1000 CE, John R. and William H. McNeill have emphasized that 'the spread of rice paddies in southern Asia affected more persons than any other single transformation of the age'.[12] In all of world history, the

---

11 Joachim Radkau, 'Wendezeiten der Umweltgeschichte. Die Spuren der menschlichen Natur', in Ernst Peter Fischer and Klaus Wiegandt (eds.), *Die Zukunft der Erde. Was verträgt unser Planet noch?* (Frankfurt: Fischer Verlag 2005): 60–97.

12 John R. McNeill and William H. McNeill, *The Human Web: A Bird's-Eye View of World History* (New York: W. W. Norton & Co., 2006): 96.

great irrigation systems are virtually the archetypal example of how a form of agriculture shapes all of society, political administration, ways of thought, and not least the relationship to the environment. In his *Steps to an Ecology of the Mind*, a cult book of environmentalism, Gregory Bateson offered a fascinating account, based on years of first-hand experience on Bali, of how the social constraints of terrace farming, along with all of its religious rituals, 'become so much a second nature of the Balinese that the individual Balinese . . . has continual anxiety lest he make an error.'[13]

Karl August Wittfogel became famous and infamous for his theory of the 'hydraulic society' – also known as the 'Asiatic mode of production'. In his Communist phase, he theorized that large irrigation systems had early on compelled a collective mode of production, while in his later anti-Communist phase, he propounded the view that these irrigation systems represented the historical roots of totalitarianism. Wittfogel's tendency toward ecological determinism has been rightly criticized: history has shown that it is by no means true that irrigation systems compel a centralized bureaucracy. History is replete with examples of local management of irrigation systems, even in China; in fact, it raises doubts as to whether even in Egypt, the classic land of irrigation, a successful overseeing of hydraulic systems from a distant centre using pre-modern means of communication was at all possible.

Elinor Ostrom also looked at hydraulic societies and found in them examples of a successful communal management of the environment.[14] For Huizinga, water management was the very foundation of the cooperative structures in the Netherlands: 'A country divided by watercourses such as ours must needs have a considerable measure of regional autonomy'; only the combined energy on the ground was able to maintain the dykes and canals.[15] But if irrigation systems do not *compel* bureaucratic centralism, they do offer an *incentive* for ambitious rulers along rivers surrounded by arid regions to enlarge their sphere of power and tax revenues by expanding these networks into the desert.

And for that very reason, such systems become ecologically fragile: the high rate of evaporation in hot areas leads to an increasing salinization of the soil unless the salt is immediately washed away again by adequate drainage.

13 Gregory Bateson, *Steps to an Ecology of Mind* (Northvale, NJ: Jason Aronson, 1972): 128.
14 Elinor Ostrom, *Governing the Commons. The Evolution of Institutions for Collective Action* (Cambridge University Press, 1990).
15 Johan Huizinga, *Dutch Civilization in the Seventeenth Century*, trans. Arnold J. Pomerans (New York: Harper and Row, 1969): 16.

From the time of the Sumerians until today, the universal rule around the world has been that human efforts are focused initially on irrigation only, while drainage is neglected. While every farmer in regions around the world where rainfed agriculture was combined with pasture farming knew that he had to regenerate the fertility of his land with fertilizers, and was able to distinguish well-fertilized from poorly fertilized fields, soil salinization tended to be an insidious process that was not clearly comprehended, and where the countermeasures were often not understood or not available because of a lack of water.[16] Hence we encounter early on an environmental degeneration of the modern kind: an ecological instability inherent in a method of production.

This seems to be contradicted by the oldest and – in the West – the most famous example of a large-scale irrigation society: Egypt. In all of world history it offers the most impressive case of a sustainable agrarian economy across five millennia, until the construction of the Aswan Dam (completed in 1971) that robbed the Nile Valley of nutrients. But at its core this was natural, not artificial, irrigation, even if the water of the Nile was distributed into thousands of canals; the tides of the Nile also took care of drainage and prevented soil salinization without the need for special human efforts. The situation was different in Mesopotamia, and there we find indications that soil salinization already troubled the Sumerians and prompted them to switch their cultivation from wheat to the more salt-resistant barley.[17] Yet high cultures continued in Mesopotamia for millennia afterwards: it would appear that the irrigation systems there became overextended and increasingly ecologically fragile only under the 'Abbasids.[18]

Even Andrew M. Watson – who identified a major innovative boost in the early Islamic world after the Arab conquests when the water wheel (*noria*) was widely adopted and became the foundation of multifarious garden cultures – believes it is evident that

> at its peak the new agriculture was exceedingly fragile ... The fertility and moisture of the soil had to be protected by techniques that were often very labour-consuming and which might not be effective in the face of climate changes; water tables, on which some irrigation works depended, had to be maintained by preventing excessive runoff of rainwater and by husbanding groundwater.

16 Peter Christensen, *The Decline of Iranshahr. Irrigation and Environments in the History of the Middle East 500 B. C. to A. D. 1500* (Copenhagen: Museum Tusculanum Press, 1993): 51, 73.

17 Radkau, *Nature and Power*, 95–6.   18 Christensen, *Decline*, 104, 252–3.

The overall impression of Near East agriculture in later centuries, Watson argued, pointed at ecological decline.[19] For the rising Ottoman Empire, the fact that large-scale irrigation projects did not take off in core regions until the most recent times may have been unexpectedly fortunate, although champions of agrarian progress long lamented this.

Be that as it may: we should be careful with sweeping stories of decline. It would seem that in India, as far as we can tell at the moment, larger irrigation systems emerged only in the Gupta period (320–550 CE) and thereafter. But at all times, village irrigation systems prevailed in India, and all in all there are no signs of an ecological crisis.[20] In warm and humid Southern China as well, Mark Elvin has spoken of an 'agrarian revolution' in the eleventh and twelfth centuries in the form of a rapid expansion of wet-rice farming on terraces.[21] On occasion he has characterized all of Chinese agricultural history as '3000 years of unsustainable growth';[22] however, clear signs of an ecological decline in China are evident only over the last three centuries, at the earliest,[23] not over three millennia. And today, under the banner of a return of 'permanent agriculture', the careful return of 'night soil' – human waste – is being rediscovered as a centuries-old basic principle of Chinese agriculture, and described as 'turning waste into treasure'.

Zhong Gongfu has described the 'mulberry dike-fish pond ecosystem' of Chinese wet-rice farming in the Pearl River delta as the model of an inherently sustainable agricultural economy.[24] The small fish that swam in the irrigated rice paddies not only provided food for the peasants and fertilizer for the fields, they also ate the insects that carried the malaria pathogen. But they did not eat all of the insects: swamp fever was also part of Chinese history, though not with the intensity that one would have

---

19 Andrew M. Watson, *Agricultural Innovation in the Early Islamic World: The Diffusion of Crops and Farming Techniques, 700–1100* (Cambridge University Press, 1983): 108, 139–41.

20 Ranabir Chakravarti, 'The Creation and Expansion of Settlements and Management of Hydraulic Resources in Ancient India', in Richard H. Grove et al. (eds.), *Nature and the Orient. The Environmental History of South and Southeast Asia* (New Delhi: Oxford University Press, 1998): 97–102.

21 Mark Elvin, *The Pattern of the Chinese Past: A Social and Economic Interpretation* (Stanford University Press, 1973): 113–30.

22 Mark Elvin, '3000 Years of Unsustainable Growth: China's Environment from Archaic Times to the Present', *East Asian History* 6 (1993): 7–46

23 Peter C. Perdue, *Exhausting the Earth. State and Peasant in Hunan 1500–1850* (Cambridge, MA: Harvard University Press, 1987): 87–9, 131–3; John F. Richards, *The Unending Frontier: An Environmental History of the Early Modern World* (Berkeley: University of California Press, 2003): 130–1, 144.

24 Zhong Gongfu, 'The Mulberry Dike-Fish Pond Complex: A Chinese Ecosystem of Land-Water Interaction on the Pearl River Delta', *Human Ecology* 10 (1982): 191–202.

expected from a country of irrigation cultures in a warm climate. Ibn Battuta, who made it all the way to China on his travels, was told that life in the warm south was much more dangerous than in the north because of virulent fevers. One can infer from this that Chinese expansion southward was long impeded by malaria. Wet-rice farming could develop fully only after the inhabitants had evolved a kind of immunity against malaria – or had become accustomed to life with malaria and to premature death.

Among the ancient American cultures, the famous – and to this day exemplary – cultivated terraces of the Inca[25] stand in contrast to the extensive slash-and-burn economy of the Maya, which was not consistent with their urban concentrations. Studies of soil archaeology at Lake Pátzcuaro in the highlands of Mexico point to soil degradation already during the Aztec period. Much like Marvin Harris, for whom Aztec cannibalism had a very practical cause in a lack of protein, Elizabeth Dore has given this blanket verdict: 'In spite of the prevalence of scholarship and myth about a pristine pre-Conquest America, there is increasing evidence that pre-Columbian people were systematically incapable of sustaining the ecosystems upon which their societies depended.'[26] To this day, the history of irrigation systems, especially of terrace farming, is exceedingly ambivalent from an ecological perspective: stabilization and destabilization lie close together here. Next to planting trees, terraces are the best countermeasure to soil erosion; but if the peasant communities that are necessary for their upkeep – which is very labour-intensive – decay, a veritable chain reaction of eroding topsoil can be set off.

The nomadic realms

Nomadism is a way of life all its own, which produced a distinctive type of person and reached its historical climax in the Middle Millennium, before the storms of nomads were crushed by the artillery fire of sedentary powers – or the leaders of the nomadic hordes themselves became rulers of sedentary cultures, like the Mughals in Northern India. In contrast to what used to be believed, nomadism is not a mere continuation of prehistoric hunting and

---

25 J. Donald Hughes, *An Environmental History of the World: Humankind's Changing Role in the Community of Life* (London: Routledge, 2001): 99–104.
26 Marvin Harris, *Cannibals and Kings* (New York: Random House, 1977); Elizabeth Dore, 'How Sustainable Were pre-Columbian Civilizations?' in Helen Collinson (ed.), *Green Guerillas. Environmental Conflicts and Initiatives in Latin America and the Caribbean* (Nottingham: Russell Press, 1996): 47.

gathering: rather, it presupposes the breeding of riding animals as well as sedentary cultures to trade with or plunder.

But what did the nomads mean for their environment? To this day, the question to what extent deserts and steppes are natural in origin or owe their spread in part to their nomadic inhabitants is one of the greatest mysteries of environmental history. Precisely because our knowledge is so fragmentary and many findings are equivocal, the issue is vulnerable to politics and ideologies. Like few other landscapes, the desert tempts observers into ecological determinism; but there are also multiple possible stories about the impact of nomads on their environment.

To the French colonizers of North Africa as well as to Walter Clay Lowdermilk, who came out of the Soil Conservation Service of the New Deal and whose doctrines became the gospel of the Zionist settlers in Palestine, the matter was clear: nomads, children of the desert, transform all regions they invade into a desert by destroying irrigation systems or letting them decay. Similar verdicts are found to this day, particularly focusing on overgrazing.[27]

The ideological content of such verdicts has been criticized, however, and others point to the fragility of many irrigation systems and the ecological merits of nomads, who by their very mobility avoided the overgrazing of arid regions. The geographer Horst G. Mensching, who gathered clues to the history of desertification and nomadism in North Africa, has been left with the impression, in part on the basis of aerial photographs, that the wandering pasture farming of the Arab nomads, who conquered large areas of North Africa after the collapse of Roman rule, 'caused far less damage' compared to classical irrigation farming 'and rather helped to regenerate the ecosystem of the steppe, since excessive overgrazing did not take place'.[28]

But if the traditional notion that the nomads were the misfortune of the lands they overran is open to challenge, for it reflects all too obviously the partisan perception of sedentary cultures, this does not mean that the exact opposite is true. Modern ethnologists who study nomadic populations are often fascinated by the care with which these people treat their animals and pay attention also to the pasture plants. The benefits of mobility were

27 Bernard Campbell, *Human Ecology: The Story of Our Place in Nature from Prehistory to the Present*, 2nd edn (New York: A. de Gruyter, 1995): 157–8; David R. Montgomery, *Dirt – The Erosion of Civilization* (Berkeley: University of California Press, 2007).
28 Horst G. Mensching, 'Die Verwüstung der Natur durch den Menschen in historischer Zeit: Das Problem der Desertifikation', in Hubert Markl (ed.), *Natur und Geschichte* (Munich: Oldenbourg, 1983): 164–5.

lessened during the time of the great nomadic conquests, for the ecological conditions of the steppe go along with a thin settlement, not a concentration of power. Power concentrations stood in tension with the ecology of their living space. Since the sparse steppe vegetation was quickly overgrazed by the mass of riding animals, nomads were forced into a heightened mobility: there was a convergence between aggressiveness and ecological constraints.

A stable balance between humans and nature does not fit into this overall picture. That applies not only to the warriors of a Chinggis Khan and Timur. Even for the Mediterranean region, John McNeill, on the basis of field research from the Atlas to the Taurus range, concluded: 'Instability is an inherent condition of pastoralism.'[29] And one should not forget in all of this that the nomads who made global history were, strictly speaking, often only semi-nomads. Babur (1483–1530), the first of the Mughal rulers, who in India longed to return to the gardens of Samarkand and cried with homesickness when he cut a melon, professed himself in his memoirs a passionate lover of nature – both wild and garden nature.[30]

European combining of rainfed agriculture with animal husbandry

After the intensive, garden-like economy of irrigated terraces and the nomad-ism of the mounted peoples, the combination of farming and animal hus-bandry that became characteristic for central and western Europe reminds one of the Hegelian resolution of thesis and antithesis in the synthesis; but we should beware of constructing an ecological harmony in Europe. Georges Bertrand highlights the 'triologie agraire' of French agriculture: '*ager, saltus, silva* (field, pasture, forest)'; in his view, a true ecological balance between the three was achieved only with the introduction of legumes – which regenerate the soil's nutrients – by the agrarian reformers of the eighteenth and nineteenth centuries.[31] However, the three-field system, the precursor to the later crop rotation, had spread in western and central Europe already in the Middle Ages.

---

29 John R. McNeill, *The Mountains of the Mediterranean World. An Environmental History* (Cambridge University Press, 1992): 279.

30 Stanley Lane-Poole, *Babar* (Delhi: Low Price Publications, 1997, original publication 1898): 12, 149.

31 Georges Bertrand, 'Pour une histoire écologique de la France rurale', in George Duby and Armand Vallon (eds.), *Histoire de la France rurale* (Paris: Editions du Seuil, 1975), vol. 1: 83–5.

If the origins of the Western *Sonderweg* that proved very successful in the course of the modern period go back to the Middle Ages, it would undoubtedly be mistaken to date a superiority of the Western economic system already back to that period. In fact, the British agrarian historian Michael M. Postan believed he could detect evidence that agriculture over the course of the High Middle Ages in England as well as in other European regions had slid into an 'ecological trap': not only through its expansion into unsuitable marginal zones, but also through the exhaustion of the soil. Animals were needed to provide fertilizer, but their pasture was the forest – the watered pasture was only an invention of the early modern period – and it was being pushed back by reclamation.[32]

But this condemnation of traditional agriculture reflects the view of modern agrarian reformers, and is not based on broad field research. Joan Thirsk has argued vigorously against the 'Postan orthodoxy', which saw crises everywhere: she asserts that in equal measure one can discover in the peasant world of the Middle Ages a broad spectrum of flexibility. The diversity of this economic system – from extensive animal husbandry to intensive horticulture – supposedly stabilized it against crises, whether they were caused by weather or population growth. Decline in one sector could have gone hand in hand with growth in another.[33] No doubt, here, too, there is not only a single master story!

For Max Weber, the transition from antiquity to the Middle Ages amounted to a restorative return to a barter economy, a regeneration through a recovered contact to the soil; for Marc Bloch, on the other hand, the collapse of the urban culture of antiquity in the early Middle Ages was accompanied by a technological innovation that led directly to modernity: the introduction of the heavy plough pulled by oxen and suited to the heavy soils of northern Europe.[34] Bloch believed that this technological innovation triggered an entire chain reaction: it was now possible to conquer areas for agriculture into which the light Mediterranean plough had not been able to penetrate; the peasants had to keep animals, and they had to come together,

---

32 Michael M. Postan, *The Medieval Economy and Society* (London: Penguin, 1972): 26–7, 63–5.

33 Joan Thirsk, *Alternative Agriculture: A History from the Black Death to the Present Day* (Oxford University Press, 1997): 254–5; similarly, William Chester Jordan, *The Great Famine: Northern Europe in the Early Fourteenth Century* (Princeton University Press, 1996): 26–7.

34 Joachim Radkau, *Max Weber: A Biography*, trans. Patrick Camiller (Cambridge: Polity Press, 2009): 70–2; Marc Bloch, *Les Caractères originaux de l'histoire rurale française* (Paris: Armand Colin, 1952), vol. 1.

since they needed broad fields for these ploughs and were often able to keep the needed oxen only collectively. For Lynn White, Jr, who followed in Bloch's tracks, the crucial point was the *mental* effect: the heavy plough 'had helped to change the northern peasants' attitude towards nature, and thus our own ... once man had been part of nature; now he became her exploiter'.[35] With this insight, White became the founding father of a pessimistic environmental history.

His bold leap from the heavy plough to the 'great transformation' in the relationship between humans and nature contains a speculative element, however, and requires broad empirical verification. In the background one recognizes specific American experiences. Under the impact of the Dust Bowl, Edward H. Faulkner, the prophet of conservation tillage, published a general attack on the plough in 1943 with the provocative title *Plowman's Folly*, a polemic whose stridency was never equalled in less erosion-threatened Europe. It was simultaneously a major assault on conventional peasant mentality and habits in dealing with the soil.

Medieval farming was not inherently ecologically stable, but required ecological reserves: not only forests, but on barren soils, also heathlands for heather-sod composting, or marl, the subject of a later saying that it made 'rich fathers and poor sons', since it tempted farmers into overusing the land.[36] In sandy regions of northern Germany, heather-sod cutting, which can be demonstrated for the period after around 1000 CE, amounted to a veritable 'agricultural revolution' that made permanent agriculture possible in the first place.[37] This situation can be interpreted in two contrary directions: as the early establishment of an economic form with a broad ecological footprint that lacked an inherent sustainability and possessed a tendency toward a colonization of its environment; but also as an economic form which, unlike Asian wet-rice cultures, was prevented from pushing population growth to the utmost limits of the food supply precisely by the fact that it required ecological reserves.

For historians of the forest, the fact that medieval peasants used the forests as pasture was definitive proof that they had systematically ravaged the forests as well as the soil. If the forest pasture reduces the commercial yield

35 Lynn White, Jr, *Medieval Technology and Social Change* (Oxford University Press, 1962): 56.
36 Radkau, *Nature and Power*, 76; Marie Collins and Virginia Davis, *A Medieval Book of Seasons* (London: Sidgwick and Jackson, 1991).
37 Heinz Ellenberg, *Bauernhaus und Landschaft in ökologischer und historischer Sicht* (Stuttgart: Ulmer, 1990): 127.

of timber from a forest, however, this in no way means that it ruins the forest ecologically. In this regard, modern conservation experiences have led to a thorough revisionism: forest pasture has been ecologically rehabilitated.

Ester Boserup has further rehabilitated the smallholders of the world and established an entire theory on the argument that intensive, garden-like smallholder agriculture could cushion a growth in population, indeed, that it could be strengthened by it. However, that applies only up to a certain limit.[38] A balance between humans and nature is more or less stable only when it possesses ecological reserves. And a precise balance can be easily upset, whether by crop failures, invasions, or natural events. The combination of farming and animal husbandry possessed its own kind of ecological resilience, especially on heavy soils; however, this took full effect only during the course of the modern period.

Three master stories

To date, there have been three chief approaches to a master story of human–nature interaction that stretches across the millennia: first, the anthropological approach; second, the religious–philosophical approach; and, third, the climatological approach. All three have been applied to the Middle Millennium, and in all three, one must pay heed to the highly hypothetical and speculative element they contain.

The anthropological approach can be seen in impressive large surveys that turned into best sellers, those by Jared Diamond, Tim Flannery, and Marvin Harris[39] All have three characteristics in common: first, a provocative, revisionist tendency vis-à-vis the old idealized image of the noble savage, which is being revived in the new environmentalist ideal of ecological natives; second, a delight in bold flights through world history without agonizing much about the problems of source criticism; third, a penchant for direct leaps from prehistoric culture to modern civilizations, with a tendency to skip the Middle Millennium or give it merely a cursory glance. The whole point is to illustrate through these daring leaps that a tendency

---

38 Ester Boserup, 'Environment, Population and Technology in Primitive Societies', in Donald Worster (ed.), *The End of the Earth: Perspectives on Modern Environmental History* (Cambridge University Press, 1988).

39 Jared Diamond, *Guns, Germs and Steel: A Short History of Everybody for the Last 13,000 Years* (London: Jonathan Cape, 1997); Jared Diamond, *Collapse: How Societies Choose to Fail or Succeed* (New York: Viking, 2005); Timothy F. Flannery, *The Future Eaters: An Ecological History of the Australasian Lands and People* (Sydney: Reed Books, 1994); Harris, *Cannibals and Kings*.

towards the destructive overuse of natural resources has been inherent in human nature since time immemorial: through the dominance of moment-ary cupidity over forethought for a distant future, and through the drive – grounded in the sexual urge – to constantly increase one's own population.

It would be unrealistic not to recognize that such a disposition does in fact exist within humans. This human nature broke through even in a future pope: when the then 28-year-old Enea Silvio Piccolomini confessed to his father in 1443 that he had fathered an illegitimate son, his excuse was nature: 'In all lovers it arouses this appetite so that the human race will be con-tinued.'[40] In the Middle Ages, 'nature' also meant humanity's sexual nature, and it drove humans to multiply without any forward-looking planning with a view towards the limits on resources.

The religious–philosophical approach was made famous above all by Lynn White's Christmas Lecture in 1966, entitled 'The Historical Roots of Our Ecological Crisis', which became a kind of sacred text of early environmental history. Although White came to his subject from the history of technology and considered various historical causes behind the modern environmental crisis, in the end he sought the fundamental reason in the Judaeo-Christian tradition with the Old Testament God's commandment to humans to exer-cise *dominium terrae*, though more so in its Western than its Greek-Orthodox incarnation: 'Especially in its Western form, Christianity is the most anthro-pocentric religion the world has seen.'[41] This Christianity supposedly estab-lished an exploitative relationship to nature that was unique in the history of the world. Since Christianity – like Islam, which stood within the same tradition – rose to become a world power in the Middle Millennium, the logical conclusion would be that the foundations for the modern environ-mental crisis were laid in that period.

But very shortly after White delivered his famous lecture, Clarence J. Glacken published the fruit of a lifetime of study, unsurpassed to this day: *Traces on the Rhodian Shore*. It was filled with a wealth of quotes that pointed to old elements of a close bond to nature: for example, the notion of a 'book of nature', which – alongside sacred scripture – was a source of divine revelation, part of the theological tradition of the Middle Ages.[42]

40 *Reject Aeneas, Accept Pius: Selected Letters of Aeneas Sylvius Piccolomini (Pope Pius II)*, trans. Thomas M. Izbicki, Gerald Christianson, and Philip Krey (Washington, DC: The Catholic University of America Press, 2006): 160.
41 Lynn White Jr, 'The Historical Roots of Our Ecological Crisis', in David and Eileen Spring (eds.), *Ecology and Religion in History* (New York: Harper & Row, 1974): 24.
42 Glacken, *Traces on the Rhodian Shore*, 203–5.

'Is there any more marvellous sight, any occasion when human reason is nearer to some sort of converse with the nature of things, than the sowing of seeds, the planting of cuttings, the transplanting of shrubs, the grafting of slips?' St Augustine had already asked.[43] Niklas Luhmann scoffed at the debate for and against Lynn White: 'When the question is put in such a simple and naive way', one could continue the back-and-forth of citations ad infinitum without ever arriving at a conclusion.[44] Indeed, the only way to make headway is to examine the role of religion in the everyday life of human beings, in the peasant calendar and peasant customs, in the regulation of economic life. However, one can peruse entire piles of books and chapters on the topic of religion and ecology without so much as encountering an awareness of this necessity.

Xavier de Planhol, the author of – to this day, singular – work about the 'cultural–geographic foundations of the history of Islam' detected 'a negative role of Islam everywhere': Islam, itself a religion of the desert, had supposedly advanced 'bedouinization' in an 'unparalleled way', thereby promoting the advance of the steppe and the desert against the forest and the field.[45] Here he followed the one-sidedly negative view of nomadism, but much within the richly varied material that he presents does not fit this image of monotonous destruction. The Islamic realm, too, contains an abundance of flourishing agrarian and horticultural cultures, yet it gives pause that the realm of Islam to this day constitutes the largest, contiguous blank spot on the global landscape of environmentalism.

The third master story is climatological. In recent decades, influenced by the warnings about current climate change, a 'how-climate-made-history' notion has come into fashion. It has not been helpful, however, that historians of climate, though profiting from the growth of interest in the issue, found themselves amidst the worldwide controversy between those who claim that we are currently experiencing a historically exceptional global warming and those who deny it. Some historical facts can be exploited by both parties. Still, the history of climate holds the promise of bestowing on the Middle Millennium an internal unity as well as a dramatic cycle, both based on the hypothesis that the warm period in the High Middle Ages was

43 Peter Brown, *Augustine of Hippo* (Berkeley, CA: University of California Press, 1967): 143.
44 Niklas Luhmann, *Ecological Communication*, trans. John Bednarz, Jr (Cambridge: Polity, 1989): 5.
45 Xavier de Planhol, *The World of Islam: Le monde islamique: essai de géographie religieuse* (Ithaca, NY: Cornell University Press, 1959): 23.

followed by the 'Little Ice Age'. That medieval warm period lessens the drama of the 'hockey stick' climate curve, according to which average temperature was relatively uniform over the centuries and rose alarmingly only during the last decades. Still, most historians of climate have been reluctant to combat the alarmist party, because – all things considered – the lasting impression remains: 'Earth is already almost certainly warmer now than it was during the Middle Ages.'[46]

The basic problem of this genre is that short-term fluctuations of the weather are perceived much more clearly than long-term climate change, with the result that the sources of the older period, when the environment was grasped only with the senses and not through statistics, deal almost exclusively with weather, not with climate. Especially impressive is the research on 'catastrophic' soil erosion in northern German loess regions following an extreme wet period in 1342.[47] At the same time, however, the rice farmers in eastern and southern Asia became more independent from the weather thanks to the expansion of irrigation systems. Another problem is that the effects of climate change are very different in different regions. Given the current state of research, it can be grasped only indistinctly what the 'Medieval Climate Optimum' in western Europe meant for many other regions of the world. The discussion of present-day climate aims, as a rule, at formulating theses about global development, and neglects regional variation. Likewise, the study of earlier times has tended to generalize on the basis of regional findings instead of paying attention to regional differences.[48] A noteworthy exception is Ronnie Ellenblum's thesis that, during the Middle Millennium, varying developments of climate took place in different parts of the world. On the basis of a massive corpus of sources in many languages, he has shown that the warm period in medieval Europe coincided with a period of coldness, drought and hunger in large parts of the eastern Mediterranean, which entailed a region-wide decline in the tenth and eleventh centuries.[49]

---

46 Robert Kunzig and Wallace Broecker, *Fixing Climate: The Story of Climate Science – and How to Stop Global Warming* (London: Profile Books, 2008): 211.

47 Hans-Rudolf Bork, *Bodenerosion und Umwelt. Verlauf, Ursachen und Folgen der mittelalterlichen und neuzeitlichen Bodenerosion* (Braunschweig: Technische Universität, 1988): 34–6, 43–4, 47–8, 198.

48 On this see Joachim Radkau, 'Exceptionalism in European Environmental History', and comment by John McNeill, *Bulletin of the German Historical Institute* 33 (2003): 23–52.

49 Ronnie Ellenblum, *The Collapse of the Eastern Mediterranean: Climate Change and the Decline of the East, 950–1072* (Cambridge University Press, 2012): 251–3. He warns however (258) against 'collapse' schemes derived from climate change.

Scenarios for the Middle Millennium: collapse, crisis, resilience, sustainability

Until now, research into environmental history based on written sources has encompassed the Middle Millennium only sporadically. Although the community of environmental historians has expanded enormously, especially since the 1990s, so far it has focused entirely on the last two – or at best three – centuries. One outlier in the existing literature is the magnum opus of John F. Richards on global environmental history from about 1500 to 1800, *The Unending Frontier*. Its very title suggests, however, that it defines the previous millennium primarily in negative terms: as the period *before* the great colonial expansion of the Western seafaring powers, *before* the emerging global economy, when, in spite of the Mongol onslaught, the silk roads, and sea trade in the Indian Ocean, humanity overwhelmingly still lived in narrow boundaries, in small worlds. Global histories written from a modern retrospective generally prefer the world's growing interconnectedness as their leitmotif; by contrast, to grasp the peculiarity of the preceding age, it would be more suitable to make the autarky of the many small worlds the guiding theme, from environmental to cultural history. Does this apply only to the pre-Columbian era? In their 760-page opus on the premodern history of the Mediterranean, Peregrine Horden and Nicholas Purcell argued vigorously against generalizations even about the Mediterranean region so densely connected through seafaring since antiquity, especially against widespread blanket statements about ecological decline as a result of deforestation. Against this 'Mediterraneism', which had been taken to an extreme by the idea of ecological determinism, they posited the thesis that the true history even in the Mediterranean had unfolded in small worlds. Xenophon's terse comment, 'not every piece of land suffers disease at the same time', could be inscribed as a motto over this major work.[50]

Now, historians whose point is that history unfolds differently elsewhere are always right; but anyone who focuses entirely on differences lapses into a mere accumulation of facts. A global survey of the environmental history of the Middle Millennium must navigate – like Odysseus around Scylla and Charybdis – between this approach and the speculative constructs of ecological determinism.

---

50 Peregrine Horden and Nicholas Purcell, *The Corrupting Sea: A Study of Mediterranean History* (Oxford: Blackwell, 2000): 329, 337.

One scenario that has frequently been applied to the Middle Millennium is that of collapse. Various archaeological findings can be interpreted to suggest that the Maya culture of Tikal, the East African culture of Great Zimbabwe, and the Khmer culture of Angkor were at least in part destroyed by an excessive strain on the environment or by its inadequate management. Around Great Zimbabwe there are indications of soil erosion as a result of deforestation, which may have been caused by the wood needed for smelting works. Most widely discussed and the best researched has been the 'Maya Collapse', which seems to have happened fairly abruptly in the eighth and ninth centuries and without any destructive conquerors, though it did not mean that the Maya people disappeared. In this case researchers arrived at an ecological explanation long before ecology became fashionable, with the conjecture of a vicious cycle of overpopulation, deforestation, soil erosion, and the overuse of the fragile tropical soils. For all the back and forth in the debate, the ecological explanation has remained quite persuasive to this day, even in the eyes of the geographer Herbert Wilhelmy, who in his major work on the rise and fall of Maya culture searched for clues to the contrary.[51]

But the fates of Tikal, Zimbabwe, and Angkor are not, on the whole, as typical of their time as presented in the ecologically pessimistic visions of history. Moreover, the findings are ambivalent: the mere sight of buildings crushed by mighty trees suggests that these cities might have been undone, not by a destroyed nature, but by an overpowering one. The sight of the Maya ruins on the Yucatan peninsula overgrown by the jungle led Arnold Toynbee to believe that the 'forest, like some sylvan boa-constrictor, has literally swallowed them up'.[52] Gazing upon Angkor, which was presumably abandoned as the capital around 1440, the writer Han Suyin, in her introduction to a book about the ancient city, was seized by the same conviction: 'The trees came and overgrew stones and heads and suffocated Angkor.'[53] It would appear that the irrigation system on which the culture of Angkor was based was so unstable under the prevailing geomorphological conditions – the clay-rich soil, the low gradient, the tropical climate – that a weakening of the political organization overseeing its maintenance

51 Herbert Wilhelmy, *Welt und Umwelt der Maya. Aufstieg und Untergang einer Hochkultur* (Munich: Piper, 1981); on this see Radkau, *Nature and Power*, 29–30; a 'classic' discussion in T. Patrick Culbert (ed.), *The Classic Maya Collapse* (Albuquerque: University of New Mexico Press, 1977).
52 Arnold Toynbee, *A Study in History*, abridged by D. C. Somervell (Oxford University Press, 1987), vol. 1: 80.
53 Han Suyin, introduction to Donatello Mazzeo and Chiara Silvi Antonini, *Angkor* (Wiesbaden: Ebeling Verlag, 1974).

triggered a chain reaction that caused rivers to silt up and change their courses, thus destroying the entire system. It is not the eventual collapse of Angkor that is phenomenal, however, but the preceding resilience of this culture. What is more, this collapse was not tantamount to a decline of nature – with a loss of forest, water, and biodiversity. Nor did it mean the loss of all the basic resources of life of the population that lived there. In fact, a majority of the people might have led a more pleasant life following the collapse of Angkor's centralized apparatus of power. James C. Scott titled his *Anarchist History of Upland Southeast Asia* – a pioneering study of the early environmental history of this part of the world – *The Art of Not Being Governed*.[54]

Those authors especially who know of no other historical factors find it easy to turn climate change into the primary actor. For some time now evidence has been accumulating that the 'Medieval Climate Optimum' was followed soon after 1300 by a century of continuous cooling; however, at the current state of research, the 'Little Ice Age' takes on clearer contours only from the sixteenth century and, for now, only in central and northern Europe.[55] Its effects on the Mediterranean are 'still little understood',[56] not to mention those on more southern regions of the world, where the label 'ice age' makes no sense in any case. Visible effects should be expected most readily at the edge of glaciers; and so to this day the end of the Viking settlements is the clearest demarcation of the onset of the Little Ice Age in the Late Middle Ages. But according to the latest findings, even that decline was far less dramatic than Diamond's account in *Collapse*, and to some extent it seems to have consisted quite simply of a switch to food extraction from the sea after the model of the Inuit.[57] In recent years the theme of resilience has moved increasingly to the fore: while searching for the impact of climate change, researchers instead made discoveries about the adaptability of nature and culture.

54 James C. Scott, *The Art of Not Being Governed: An Anarchist History of Upland Southeast Asia* (New Haven, CT: Yale University Press, 2009). He shows how this 'art' is favoured by mountainous nature. For a counter-model focused on lowlands see Victor Lieberman, *Strange Parallels. Southeast Asia in Global Context, c. 800–1830* (Cambridge University Press, 2003), vol. 1.

55 See Wolfgang Behringer, Hartmut Lehmann, and Christian Pfister (eds.), *Kulturelle Konsequenzen der "Kleinen Eiszeit" – Cultural Consequences of the 'Little Ice Age'* (Göttingen: Vandenhoeck, 2005).

56 Brian Fagan, *The Little Ice Age: How Climate Made History 1300–1850* (New York: Basic Books, 2000): xv.

57 Joel Berglund, 'Did the Medieval Norse Society in Greenland Really Fail?' in Patricia McAnany and Norman Yoffee (eds.), *Questioning Collapse. Human Resilience, Ecological Vulnerability, and the Aftermath of Empire* (Cambridge University Press, 2010): 45–70.

Modern environmental awareness emerged as an awareness of crisis; no surprise, then, that environmental historians also initially directed their zeal at uncovering crises in earlier eras. For example, Robert S. Gottfried, in his *The Black Death*, described the plague as 'the most severe environmental crisis in history'.[58] And yet, there is one thing one must not overlook when identifying environmental crises: compared to today, the forms of life during the Middle Millennium, as varied as they were, on the whole possessed three essential elements of an inherent ecological stability. First, those who caused environmental damage, which was usually contained within a local framework, generally belonged to the same social group as those affected by it: this was a major and fundamental difference from today. Second, environmental damage was usually not irreversible, though this point requires closer examination on a case-by-case basis. Third, in typical cases the causal link between cause and effect – so it would appear, at least – was transparent, and one knew what kinds of precautions and countermeasures had to be taken.

Many surveys on forest history that draw on the sources of forest administrations and reflect the self-awareness of modern forestry divide all of history into two major epochs: first the many centuries of predatory exploitation of the forest, the evil time of a haphazard and narrow-minded plundering of the forest by the peasants, followed, beginning in the eighteenth century, by the glorious 'New Age' of sustainable forestry introduced under the guidance of scientifically trained forestry officials. But is the sustainable handling of natural resources, one that is concerned with future generations, in fact an invention of the modern age that presupposes modern science and a state bureaucracy? One must not confuse the history of concepts with real history; quite the contrary: sustainability becomes a major state programme only when it is clearly threatened. It is no accident that the concept of sustainable forestry was first formulated by a Saxon mining administrator: Hanns Carl von Carlowitz in his 1713 book *Sylvicultura oeconomica*.[59] Mining and smelting were the largest wood consumers in the country. Carlowitz, today often acclaimed as the inventor of sustainability, knew very well that his concept was nothing but a transfer of the rules of good housekeeping to forestry.[60]

---

58 Robert S. Gottfried, *The Black Death. Natural and Human Disaster in Medieval Europe* (New York: The Free Press, 1983): 161.
59 Joachim Radkau, *Wood – A History*, trans. Patrick Camiller (Cambridge: Polity Press, 2012): 173.
60 Hanns Carl von Carlowitz, *Sylvicultura Oeconomica* (Leipzig, 1713): 69, 'Der Hauswirt als Vorbild'. On the same page he uses, for the only time, the term 'nachhaltend' [sustaining], on account of which his book has become famous in modern times!

The situation was similar in Japan, the only non-Western country that in pre-modern times sought to institutionalize sustainable forestry; and yet its historian, Conrad Totman, has remarked: 'Rhetoric alone did even less to preserve timber stands than it did to stop erosion because the rhetoricians were the chief lumber consumers ... The protective measures were being taken by the principal forest predators as means of assuring their own access to forest yield, not as ways of preserving forest per se.'[61] State-prescribed sustainability is not an innocent concept; it could function as a battle cry with which major wood consumers, supported by the territorial ruler, pushed the peasants out of the forest. That danger is also contained in the 'sustainable development' proclaimed at the environmental summit in Rio in 1992.

A sustainability that is more or less inherent in a way of life is much more lasting than the kind of sustainability that is recommended to the world at summit meetings and requires forward-looking planning from above. The latter is something that one will search for in vain during the Middle Millennium; the former is something that one can more likely presume to have existed. Let us recall the opening quote from Huizinga: precisely because most people in the old days had their natural resources immediately before their eyes and peasants lived in symbiosis with forest and field, those times had inherent in them a tendency towards a certain sustainability in their dealings with the environment. That sustainability emerges more clearly, the more autonomous villages there were. It is striking that forms of sustainable forestry can be demonstrated earliest in central Europe and in Japan, that is, in world regions in which peasant forest cooperatives are especially well documented.[62]

The thesis about the 'tragedy of the commons' by the American human ecologist Garrett Hardin has become famous and infamous: the notion that shared goods, which are open to common use without coercion from above, are invariably ruined by human selfishness.[63] But this thesis is grounded in the logic of the 'prisoner's dilemma', for it imagines participants as completely isolated individuals. Yet that assumption is entirely absurd with respect to the old villages, where everybody knew everybody else and all were watching one another. A. T. Grove and Oliver Rackham, combative British authors of an ecological history of the Mediterranean region, scoffed

---

61 Conrad Totman, *The Green Archipelago. Forestry in Preindustrial Japan* (Berkeley: University of California Press, 1989): 97, 80.
62 Radkau, *Wood – A History*, 65–7, 295–7.
63 Hardin's essay and accompanying discussion in John A. Baden and Douglas S. Noonan (eds.), *Managing the Commons*, 2nd edn (Bloomington: Indiana University Press, 1998).

at Hardin's thesis: 'This pernicious notion was invented by an American with no experience how commons actually work.'[64]

Elinor Ostrom spent decades constructing a position contrary to that of Hardin, and in 2009 she was the first woman to receive the Nobel Prize in Economics for her work. Combining empirical knowledge grounded in local history and the theoretical logic of models, she demonstrated that a sustainable management of natural resources on the basis of village cooperation is most definitely possible.[65] Her insights are important also for interpreting the findings from medieval environmental history. But what follows from this is not a perfect harmony between humans and nature in those days. In Ostrom's account as well, the sustainable interaction with nature is secured only under certain conditions: the size of the population remains fairly stable, outsiders are kept out of the commons, and some authority guarantees that certain rules are observed. She, too, does not in any way believe that humans possess a natural instinct toward sustainability.

All in all, the impression that emerges is this: while elements of ecological crisis characteristic of the industrial age existed at best in rudimentary form in the Middle Millennium, the relationship between humans and the environment displayed fragile elements already back then – which is why there is reason to pay attention to ecological coefficients in transformation processes of the period. To be sure, given the existing, highly fragmentary state of knowledge, the ambition to write a master story for the entire world, or even merely for individual regions of the world, would be misplaced; most definitely we have not only indications of a degradation of the environment, but also signs of a symbiosis of humans and nature and of a co-evolution of culture and nature. That is precisely why environmental history is a fertile field for discoveries and surprises. But for anyone who elevates pristine nature into the yardstick, the entire history of human civilization is simply one of decline.[66]

Cyclical elements in the history of the relationship between humans and the environment

Instead of a single, large, linear movement in the Middle Millennium, what tends to emerge in environmental history are several *cyclical* movements.

64 A. T. Grove and Oliver Rackham, *The Nature of Mediterranean Europe: An Ecological History* (New Haven, CT: Yale University Press, 2001): 88.
65 Ostrom, *Governing the Commons*.
66 This is the tendency of Vito Fumagalli, *Mensch und Umwelt im Mittelalter* (Berlin: Wagenbach, 1992).

A first, and especially prominent, large cycle, in which world history merges with environmental history, lies in the ebb and flow of the large nomadic expansions: a process that begins in late antiquity and ends in the early modern period. Throughout this entire millennium, the onslaughts of the mounted nomads were a constant threat to the sedentary irrigation cultures of South and East Asia, which, unlike the peasants in the West, did not breed horses, and by interfering with the artful irrigation systems, they also had an ecological dimension. For example, in 1128 a desperate governor of the Northern Song dynasty, in an attempt to ward off the mounted warriors of the Jurchen – who would be followed in short order by the Mongols – opened the dykes of the Yellow River, with the effect that it shifted its estuary watercourses several hundred kilometres southward until the nineteenth century. For the peasants this meant an 'ecological catastrophe', but military considerations took precedence over the maintenance of the irrigation networks.[67]

Another cycle was especially evident in central and western Europe. Initially, the expansion of territorial lordship manifested itself around the world in the clearing of forests, and the growing shortage of wood was one of the weakest points of Islamic civilization of that age. But then a profound change took place, and lordship manifested itself increasingly through the *protection* of the forest. The logging decree in Charlemagne's *Capitulare de villis* already contains the restriction that forests, 'where they are needed', must not be excessively logged. At first this was in service to the royal hunt – as were similar restrictions in England after the Norman invasion of 1066 – but later, especially in central Europe, in the interest of the mining and salt works of the territorial rulers, and in western Europe in service to shipbuilding.[68] Beginning in the fourteenth century, Alpine forests were protected against logging to prevent avalanches and flooding.

Hunting and forest pasture did not play the same role in Asian cultures; and in warm countries, vast quantities of wood were not needed as fuel for the winter. Instead, Indian and Chinese rulers for a long time still looked upon forests with suspicion, as the home of wild peoples who escaped subjugation. It has often been maintained that the inhabitants of the West also looked upon the forest as an enemy; but in view of the multifarious uses

---

67 Christian Lamouroux, 'From the Yellow River to the Huai: New Representations of a River Network and the Hydraulic Crisis of 1128', in Mark Elvin and Liu Ts'ui-jung (eds.), *Sediments of Time. Environment and Society in Chinese History* (Cambridge University Press, 1998): 545–6.
68 Radkau, *Wood – A History*, 57–112.

of the forest for the peasants, this thesis, the product of forest wardens in service to the territorial lords, is not credible. For that reason it is also questionable to what extent the stream of official forest regulations that commenced at the end of the Middle Ages did in fact constitute ecological progress at the time. Forest protection compelled from the top down can bring about the exact opposite. It was therefore crucial that, notwithstanding the many conflicts over the forest, in the end the interests of the lords and the peasants in the preservation of the forest found some common ground and that all those involved were committed to legal regulation in the long run, which meant that the struggle over the forest became a struggle over the law.

A particularly prominent cycle of the Middle Millennium is epidemiological and demographic in nature: it arises out of the first documented appearance of a large plague epidemic at the end of antiquity, of smallpox spread both by the Huns and the Arab warriors, the spread of the plague, which reached its catastrophic climax around 1350, and the subsequent gradual development of immunities among the population. This had the result that population growth settled on a permanent long-term trend with the beginning of the modern period, even though waves of epidemics followed for centuries to come. The situation was inverted only in the New World: there it was the conquistadors who introduced infectious diseases that turned into catastrophic epidemics in lands that had once – if Las Casas is to be believed – been crowded with people, 'like in a beehive'. One can get the impression that the 'Plague of Justinian', which reached the Mediterranean in 541 via Egypt, meant the definitive end of antiquity[69] and inflicted a lasting weakness on the Byzantine Empire, which prepared the ground for the Arab conquests. Although population pressure is periodically evident in the Middle Millennium as a dominant factor in the relationship between humans and the environment, on the whole it is much less so than in the modern period.

Whether this applies also to China is a contested issue among scholars. A Chinese 'Farmer's Lament' from the twelfth century declared: 'If there's a mountain, we'll cover it with wheat. If there's water to be found, we'll use it all to plant rice ... With such labor we exhaust all our strength.'[70] For Qu

---

69 Lester K. Little (ed.), *Plague and the End of Antiquity: The Pandemic of 541–750* (Cambridge University Press, 2007).

70 Vaclav Smil, *The Bad Earth: Environmental Degradation in China* (Armonk, NY: M. E. Sharpe, 1984): 3–4.

Geping, in the 1980s deputy chairman of the environmental protection agency of the People's Republic of China, overpopulation had been China's hereditary evil for millennia, very much in the spirit of Malthus,[71] while Robert B. Marks countered in a similarly sweeping vein that 'the Chinese were in fact very much in control of their reproductive capabilities'.[72]

John R. McNeill has come away with the impression that 'Chinese society was probably the most epidemiologically experienced'.[73] This points to a relatively high degree of immunity, but also to the fact that epidemics were a constant companion in Chinese history; in the historiography they do not appear as epochal events. By contrast, the Black Death constituted a profound turning point in the consciousness of the Western world. In the policy of public hygiene, which – beginning in Ragusa, modern Dubrovnik – emerged out of the traumatic experience of the great epidemics, we have the earliest roots of state environmental protection. Hygienic and environmental problems were concentrated above all in the cities; and the autonomous city, which existed chiefly in the West, was the primary actor in whatever kind of environmental policy existed from the Late Middle Ages to the nineteenth century.

Conclusion

In the chapter on the Middle Ages in his *Environmental History of the World*, J. Donald Hughes noted that in those days the world was still full of unspoiled landscape with a biodiversity which today has long since been forgotten. And yet: 'Elsewhere, the rate at which the humans were altering the face of the Earth was slow but accelerating. It was not proceeding at a steady pace, but it was faster than it had ever been.'[74] Indeed, broadly speaking, one can detect in the course of the Middle Millennium a gradual acceleration in world history, and not least also in the alteration of the environment by humans, especially in retrospect. Here one realizes that the triumph of the water mill in the West, which was impeded in the East by the water regime of the irrigation cultures, already contained the germ

71 Qu Geping and Li Jinchang, *Population and the Environment in China*, trans. Jiang Bazhong and Gu Ran (Boulder, CO: L. Rienner Publishers, 1994).
72 Robert B. Marks, *The Origins of the Modern World. A Global and Ecological Narrative from the Fifteenth to the Twenty-First Century* (Lanham, MD: Rowman & Littlefield, 2007): 104.
73 John R. McNeill, 'China's Environmental History in World Perspective', in Elvin and Ts'ui-jung, *Sediments of Time*, 35.
74 Hughes, *An Environmental History of the World*, 83.

seed of the industrial revolution.[75] Moreover, beyond individual innovations one can detect in the European Middle Ages the 'invention of invention': the emergence of an optimistic attitude toward technological innovations, at least among influential elites, in contrast to the tragic outcome of the ancient myths of Daedalus and Prometheus.

Still, all of this becomes meaningful only from modern hindsight. As late as the second half of the fifteenth century, stagnation was observed in wide areas of Europe in mining. Today, as humanity returns to an awareness of the limits to growth, there is reason to appreciate also the medieval limits to growth as a regulating mechanism in the relationship between humans and nature instead of seeing them merely as barriers to be overcome. If one ran up against the limits of wood resources, it by no means meant an 'energy crisis' at that time, for back then, when most goods were limited, an economy compulsively programmed on growth could not exist yet. It was simply a time in which, as Huizinga reminded us, the world was still very concrete – and which knew growth only as organic, limited growth.

Translated by
Thomas Dunlap

FURTHER READING

Bateson, Gregory. *Steps to an Ecology of Mind.* Northvale, NJ: Jason Aronson, 1972.
Behringer, Wolfgang, Hartmut Lehmann, and Christian Pfister (eds.), *Kulturgeschichte des Klimas. Von der Eiszeit bis zur globalen Erwärmung.* Munich: Beck, 2007.
Bork, Hans-Rudolf. *Bodenerosion und Umwelt: Verlauf, Ursachen und Folgen der mittelalterlichen und neuzeitlichen Bodenerosion.* Braunschweig: Technische Universität, 1988.
Campbell, Bernard. *Human Ecology: The Story of Our Place in Nature from Prehistory to the Present,* 2nd edn. New York, NY: A. de Gruyter, 1995.
Christensen, Peter. *The Decline of Iranshahr: Irrigation and Environments in the History of the Middle East 500 B. C. to A. D. 1500.* Copenhagen: Museum Tusculanum Press, 1993.
Diamond, Jared. *Collapse: How Societies Choose to Fail or Succeed.* New York, NY: Viking, 2005.
Ellenblum, Ronnie. *The Collapse of the Eastern Mediterranean: Climate Change and the Decline of the East, 950–1072.* Cambridge University Press, 2012.
Elvin, Mark. '3000 Years of Unsustainable Growth: China's Environment from Archaic Times to the Present', *East Asian History* 6 (1993): 7–46.
Flannery, Timothy F. *The Future Eaters: An Ecological History of the Australasian Lands and People.* Sydney: Reed Books, 1994.

75 Jochim Varchmin and Joachim Radkau, *Kraft, Energie und Arbeit. Energie und Gesellschaft* (Reinbek: Rowohlt, 1981): 42–4.

Geping, Qu and Li Jinchang. *Population and the Environment in China*. Trans. Jiang Bazhong and Gu Ran, Boulder, CO: L. Rienner Publishers, 1994.

Glacken, Clarence J. *Traces on the Rhodian Shore. Nature and Culture in Western Thought from Ancient Times to the End of the 18th Century*. Berkeley, CA: University of California Press, 1967.

Grove, A. T. and Oliver Rackham. *The Nature of Mediterranean Europe: An Ecological History*. New Haven, CT: Yale University Press, 2001.

Horden, Peregrine and Nicholas Purcell. *The Corrupting Sea: A Study of Mediterranean History*. Oxford: Blackwell, 2000.

Hughes, J. Donald. *An Environmental History of the World: Humankind's Changing Role in the Community of Life*. London: Routledge, 2001.

Humphrey, Caroline and David Sneath (eds.), *Culture and Environment in Inner Asia*. Cambridge University Press, 1996.

Little, Lester K., ed. *Plague and the End of Antiquity: The Pandemic of 541–750*. Cambridge University Press, 2007.

Luhmann, Niklas. *Ecological Communication*. Trans. John Bednarz, Jr, Cambridge: Polity Press, 1989.

McAnany, Patricia and Norman Yoffee (eds.), *Questioning Collapse: Human Resilience, Ecological Vulnerability, and the Aftermath of Empire*. Cambridge University Press, 2010.

McNeill, John R. *The Mountains of the Mediterranean World: An Environmental History*. Cambridge University Press, 1992.

Montgomery, David R. *Dirt – The Erosion of Civilization*. Berkeley, CA: University of California Press, 2007.

Radkau, Joachim. *Nature and Power: A Global History of the Environment*. Trans. Thomas Dunlap, New York: Cambridge University Press, 2009.

Wood – A History. Trans. Patrick Camiller. Cambridge: Polity Press, 2012.

Richards, John F. *The Unending Frontier: An Environmental History of the Early Modern World*. Berkeley: University of California Press, 2003.

Scott, James C. *The Art of Not Being Governed: An Anarchist History of Upland Southeast Asia*. New Haven, CT: Yale University Press, 2009.

White, Lynn Jr. 'The Historical Roots of Our Ecological Crisis', in David and Eileen Spring (eds.), *Ecology and Religion in History*. New York, NY: Harper & Row, 1974.

Medieval Technology and Social Change. Oxford University Press, 1962.

Wilhelmy, Herbert. *Welt und Umwelt der Maya. Aufstieg und Untergang einer Hochkultur*. Munich: Piper, 1981.

3

Women, family, gender, and sexuality

SUSAN MOSHER STUARD

During the Middle Millennium, polities the world over mirrored constituent families, almost all of a paternal and hierarchical character, although this was hardly new. Whether empires, ruled by a caliph or emperor, or city-states where officials were inclined to dictate private behaviors, polities reflected and sometimes shaped family norms. Families staffed households, the basic units of production and reproduction, and authorities taxed households rather than persons, for the most part. For these reasons families remained bulwarks of the regional states, empires, and economic systems that flourished from the Pacific Ocean, to sub-Saharan Africa, Europe, and on beyond the Atlantic Ocean. With rare exception, families were gendered in the sense of separate and distinct expectations for women and men, boys and girls. Almost everywhere women were responsible for child-raising until about age seven, and a negative ratio of women to men existed wherever records have yielded estimable numbers. Once this level of generalization is left behind, the differences in the ways families organized societies argue for significant diversity. Deeply embedded patterns of marriage, child-raising, living arrangements (patrilocality, matrilocality, or neolocality), kinship, and kinship-like ties figured in distinguishing societies from one another, and these patterns reveal dynamic changes holding unique potential for a given region's development.

Whenever historians examine the lives of women, they investigate family and kinship ties focusing on societal assumptions about gender. Histories of men are far less likely to do so since authors assume that gender expectations and family roles fell more lightly on men's shoulders, particularly where men wielded the power and authority that warrants biographical treatment. As an analytical tool of history, however, the study of gender, which is largely acquired and not innate, encompasses the study of men and women.

Gender assumptions were more varied than a high level of generalization casually applied would have us believe. Gender was not a constant, nor was it systematized thinking, but rather remained largely notional in character, thus unexamined. That proved its greatest asset, but also a failing. Women in authority wielding power in their own right gave tacit acknowledgement to women's latent capacities even where gender assumptions denigrated women. In fact the more incapacitating gender dictums were trotted out when expedient, and seldom where women exercised power. In general, gender systems moved from somewhat diverse and flexible to more rigid in this era, while in western Europe schematically polar notions of gender became embedded in prevailing Scholastic dogma. Throughout Asia, North Africa, and Europe, war, conflict, and invasions constituted threats that led to subordinating women through a more pronounced emphasis on gender difference; crowding in this age of population increase may have been a factor as well. The Americas and parts of sub-Saharan Africa appear to have been exceptions to these generalizations.

Women and family in the Islamic world and South Asia

Family patterns over this millennium were subject to change due to the spread of religions, trade, the movement of peoples, and conquest as well as internal developments. The most dramatic early conquests were launched in the name of Allah and his Prophet Muhammad. These Islamic conquests introduced the Quran and shari'a law, and conversion favored the subordination of women, although Islam aimed consciously at protecting women by specifying a marriage gift (*mahr*) to a wife. By the end of the era in East African societies, where conversion was often achieved through trade rather than conquest, shari'a introduced a dower paid to a wife by contract. In al-Andalus (Muslim Iberia) a marriage contract included a similar dower and further stipulated the number of wives a husband might have (polygyny). Similar practices persisted throughout Islam and women were understood to embody the honor of the family. Veiling and the seclusion of women may be more an indication of class status and wealth than gender because minding flocks, migrating across great distances, and field labor did not lend themselves to sequestering women. Labor-intensive households used women's and girls' labor as a matter of course and *'urf*, or exigent custom, structured family life along with religious law throughout Islam. According to all four Islamic law traditions, wives had a right to divorce on the grounds of physical or financial mistreatment, and relatives and neighbors testified in such cases. Divorce for men was a matter of will by repeating the phrase 'I divorce thee' three times. Throughout Islam daughters possessed rights of inheritance, although these were most often exercised at marriage (occurring at or near menarche to an older spouse) rather than upon the death of a father, and portions were smaller than those for sons, who divided property equally when a father died. Nonetheless women were property owners in Islam, and seclusion in women's quarters did not stop women from suing in court at least in some urban centers.

At the highest level of Muslim society a few women achieved powerful roles and elite women were not excluded from the vital spiritual life of Islam. Wealthy women throughout Islam completed the *hajj* (pilgrimage) to Mecca, which was regarded as praiseworthy, provided the rules of propriety were observed. Rabi'a of Basra (713–801) found a position as a venerated Sufi mystic. Convents for women existed in Aleppo by the twelfth and thirteenth centuries, and also in Baghdad and Cairo in the same era. Literacy figured among wealthy women's accomplishments, through tutoring carried out in well-to-do households that valued literate daughters. In the thirteenth century Dayfa Khatun, wife, mother, and grandmother of successive Ayyubid sultans of Aleppo (and niece to the great Saladin) ruled as regent and in her own right, strongly influencing the policies of her dynasty. Like other Ayyubid court women, she was a patron of religious foundations and architecture. The Khanqah al-Farafra for male scholars and the Firdaws Madrasa built for women Sufis benefited from her generosity. Nonetheless Dayfa Khatun expressed her political will through her male secretary Iqbal and was known as "[Her of] the elevated curtain and impregnable veil." She was a pious princess in a political marriage; meanwhile other brides throughout Islam awaited the birth of an heir to confirm their rights as married women within their husband's family.

Islamic invasions brought migrations of families from throughout Asia and even from East Africa to northern India, yet an older pattern of wealthy households that were large, co-residential and contained many generations of dependents persisted. It would be difficult to distinguish dependents whose presence marked a display of family piety from those who were non-free servitors. Furthermore, the status of dependents within such households changed over lifetimes. Girls often married by ten years of age to be raised in their husbands' households, and divorce was rare. Royal married women followed in the tradition of social duty and gave charity of their own personal property (*stridhana*) that lay within their power. Giving food at the door was an extension of Islamic hospitality after the Muslim invasions as well. In the same era Buddhist inscriptions noted women giving charity, and in Jain inscriptions women figured among donors. Islamic India followed familial practices known to other co-resident religious groups, which likely eased tensions among diverse religious communities in India's densely populated cities in the age of invasions.

In northern India women saw a momentous change in their condition with the introduction of kulinism, probably by Raja Vallala Sena of Bengal (r. 1158–69). According to this marital system, a woman was forbidden to wed below her rank, but she could marry up to three ranks superior to her own. The results were likely unforeseen, but included infanticide of Brahminic daughters, and hypergamy, or 'good' marriages, for some brides of lower status. Brahmin men, who married and lived with a carefully chosen first wife, might collect dowries from lower-status women, even if they never met them, a form of polygamy that concentrated wealth in their hands. Of northern India J. Duncan M. Derrett observed, "Everyone believed in caste."[1] Jains became a caste and even Lingayats, who advocated intermarriage, became an endogamous group.[2] Meanwhile in eastern India, cross-cousin marriage preserved women's standing after marriage through the exchange of bridal wealth among closely connected lineages; this pattern exhibited features of both matrilinearity and patrilinearity. Buddhist nuns lived together as single women, while in the south single women dedicated to temples gained authority as donors, according to Tamil inscriptions. In Kashmir women appeared as rulers, advisers, donors, and builders, and in Delhi Princess Radiyya bint Iltutmish ruled in the years 1235–40. Diversity marked women's experience across India.

Women and family in Central and East Asia

The Franciscan William of Rubruck (1220–93), on a mission to Central Asia in 1253–5 said of Mongols before their conversion to Islam that "[i]t is the women's task to drive the wagons, to load the dwellings on them and to unload again, to milk the cows, to make their butter and *grut* (curds) and to dress the skins and stitch them together."[3] Turkic women sometimes ruled in collaboration with husbands, bringing the prestige of their own lineages to

---

1 J. Duncan M. Derrett, "Law and the Social Order in India before the Muhammadan Conquests," *Journal of the Economic and Social History of the Orient* 7:1 (1964): 79–80.
2 Lingayats or Siasaivas were followers of Sankara and Ramanuja and flourished from the twelfth century onward in southern India.
3 *The Mission of Friar William of Rubruck: His Journey to the Court of the Great Khan Möngke 1253–1255.* Trans. Peter Jackson (London: Hakluyt Society, 1990): 90.

sustain their husbands' wars of expansion. Such a powerful wife, or a sister, or a daughter, was expected to manage the encampment and the collected wealth of the dynasty and even defend her people and flocks if called upon to do so. Custom sustained women in such roles and provided them with the control of property that enforced their authority even when it involved ordering out fighting men. Only rarely did a concubine or slave, the favorite of the ruler, achieve such status, since a woman's own lineage sanctioned her in her authority. An epic of the Turks, the late medieval *Oghuz-nama*, first tells a tale of a warrior bride, the Princess Saljan of Trebizond, and later moralizes:

> First comes she who is the pillar that upholds the house. If a respected guest comes to the house when her husband is absent, she gives him food and drink, she entertains him and honors him and sends him on his way. She is of the breed of Ayesha and Fatima, O my Khan! May her babies grow up, may such a wife come to your hearth.[4]

With the conversion to Islam of the Mongol Ilkhan Ghazan in 1295, the authority of some highly placed women continued; the Muslim traveler Ibn Battuta (1304–1368/9 or 1377) was astonished to see the power exercised by the wives of Ozbek, khan of the Golden Horde, in the 1330s.[5]

In China there was a long tradition of property passing to daughters as dowry, and late Song laws designed to keep property within the patriline justified dowering daughters (marriage for daughters was set at age fourteen, sons at sixteen) before division to sons of equitable shares. As women became more identified with their husbands' lineages under the Song (960–1279), few divorced. An unmarried daughter without brothers might inherit three-quarters of an estate with only a quarter going to the agnatic kin. Less interested in the rights of daughters, the Mongol Yuan dynasty (1271–1368) under Qubilai Khan (r. 1260–1295) allowed levirate marriage (with a brother's widow) but with reservations. In addition, because of the close connections between rights to land and military service, a man marrying a single female heir who took on his father-in-law's military service might inherit through his marriage. This influenced practice throughout China, and such households would not become extinct because property passed through women, but a daughter only inherited if she married a man who would perform the required military service. While the Ming Code that followed in

---

4 *Book of Dede Korkut*, ed. Geoffrey Lewis (Harmondsworth: Penguin, 1974): 4.
5 *The Travels of Ibn Battuta*, trans. H. A. R. Gibb, vol. II (Cambridge: The Hakluyt Society, 1958): 480–9.

1397 self-consciously echoed the earlier Tang laws (624, revised 653) on family, it also incorporated Yuan property practices and a daughter only inherited if there was no one of the same surname who could be found.

Successful Chinese households were often units of production for textiles and other export goods like embroidered shoes; thus women with their servants played substantial roles in home production. In the words of the statesman-poet Liu Ji (1311–75), "One who builds a big house will hire many artisans, but there will be one master-artisan, and no one will dare decide on anything that thwarts his plans ... When people of the four quarters obey one ruler, they are settled. When an army of a million men obeys one commander, it triumphs."[6] Widows might perform the role of master of production within a household and, surviving their husbands, they might also fulfill the obligation of preserving a deceased husband's lineage, demonstrating that Confucianism afforded some women important responsibilities. In China, immigrant Muslim textile workers, both women and men, provided a home industry in vertically organized production of cloth of gold. Skilled families were brought to China by Yuan rulers; they produced gold-shot silk equivalent in value to gold itself.[7]

Prosperity emerging in the Song era and continuing through the Yuan years into the Ming era enriched some households, resulting in some leisure for elite women for whom it became fashionable to pursue literacy. With the eleventh-century advent of printing in China, the imperial court lost its dominant role in the production of women's writing, leading to an upsurge in women's poetic compositions throughout China.[8] Women exchanged poetry among households and, increasingly under the Ming, literate women helped educate their sons, who would face formidable examinations in which success promoted the fortunes of any family. Meanwhile in Japan, women wrote poetry and also prose works. Murasaki Shikibu's (973–1014/31) venerated *Tale of Genji* has been called the first psychological novel in world literature (see Figure 3.1).

In China the teachings of Confucius emphasized the cultivation of virtue, with men, at least, understood to be morally perfectible. In the social

6 Liu Ji, *Chengyi bo wenji*, cited in John W. Dardess, "Did Mongols Matter," in *The Song–Yuan–Ming Transition in Chinese History*, ed. Paul Jakov Smith and Richard von Glahn (Cambridge, MA: Harvard University Press, 2003): 132.

7 James C. Y. Watt and Anne E. Wardwell, *When Silk Was Gold: Central Asian and Chinese Textiles* (New York: Metropolitan Museum of Art, 1997).

8 Wilt Idema and Beata Grant, *The Red Brush: Writing Women of Imperial China* (Cambridge, MA: Harvard University Press, 2004): 6.

Figure 3.1 Prince Genji visiting his wife, from Genji Monogatari (The Tale of Genji) (The Art Archive / Alamy)

hierarchy, family and state flourished when all persons knew and performed their assigned duties; this governed the lives of both women and men, which within the family meant nurturing and protecting the old and the young. Beneath the level of high generality, Confucianism tolerated diverse practices, even divorce, proving that China did not possess a uniform culture. Only the most wealthy and prestigious households practiced polygyny and the spread of Buddhism freed a few women from the constraints of family and marriage to become nuns. Foot-binding began among women at court during the Song dynasty, but spread widely only in the Ming era (1368–1644). Diversity in gender assumptions about women and their assigned roles failed to disturb underlying Confucian morality to any measurable extent.

Women and family in Europe

In the fragmented lands of medieval Europe, prone to invasions in the early part of our era and less successful in acculturating new populations than Asia, two distinct family patterns emerged. A Mediterranean large-family unit sanctioned by late Roman and canon (church) law existed in the Byzantine Empire, Italy, and Spain, while a small-family pattern, based on the neolocality of a newly married couple, thrived farther north. Marriage for both men and women occurred relatively late, that is, near twenty years of age. (In the south, men in their twenties married women fourteen to eighteen years of age.) Canon law prohibited divorce, but the powerful could obtain annulments from the church. Consent was grounds for valid marriage but seldom enforced. Marriage practices sustained new families in assarting (opening land to cultivation), or the pursuit of crafts and trade that underlay Europe's economic rise through the medieval centuries. Bride price (*morgencap* or its variants) predominated in both the north and south: by contract a bride received wealth from her husband that she owned and managed. After 1140 in Italy, and thereafter in Spain and southern France, dowry paid by the bride's father to the groom replaced the husband's major marital gift. Henceforth a woman owned her dowry as a natal inheritance, but her husband managed it. He was obligated by law to increase but never squander it, an unrealistic demand for a commercial economy with attendant risks.

Meanwhile under common law in England, a single woman could own property as a *feme sole*, but lost ownership rights over it when she married, only to have them returned to her if she became a widow. Women's property rights had substantial impact on women's familial and economic roles. Where they owned the proceeds of their labor, or anticipated that ownership, women participated in production and trade (see Figure 3.2). The revived Roman dotal regime introduced in the twelfth century in the south curbed women's management of wealth, and their roles in the workplace diminished. This affected families, because women's authority in marriage generally stems from wealth they bring into the marriage over a lifetime.

Although most women married, some single women formed their own households in medieval Europe and others joined together in Christian monasteries. Women numbered among the most venerated saints of their day. The church worked to enclose nuns but under some circumstances it tolerated sisterhoods such as the Beguines, who lived in towns and provided social services to the community. Literacy was an expectation for at least some women in religious houses and orders, and literary works have come down to us from nuns, including the abbess, poet, composer, and scientist Hildegard of Bingen (1098–1179). A few laywomen also wrote wide-ranging works: Anna Komnene (1093–1153) composed *The Alexiad*, a major source of Byzantine political history for the late eleventh and twelfth centuries, that is,

Figure 3.2 German family spinning, sixteenth century (Mary Evans Picture Library / Alamy)

the era of the crusades, and Trotula of Salerno composed a famous treatise on women's diseases.[9]

Medieval Jewish families often lived in uneasy proximity to their Muslim or Christian neighbors, and women's decorous behavior ideally deflected notice that could lead to persecution. By the Late Middle Ages, Jews in Europe were required to wear defining garb, like shoes of mismatched color, but this did not prevent persecution or expulsions. Jewish women married young with a dowry, and both they and Jewish men had the right to initiate divorce. In Cairo Jewish women were not as strictly enclosed as their Muslim neighbors, although contact outside the Jewish community was regarded as more dangerous for women than for men. Jewish women enjoyed more opportunities to pursue literacy and careers than women in the Christian West or Islam. In twelfth-century Cairo, divorced Karima worked as a broker in embroidered textiles, and Licoricia of Winchester became a successful banker and mainstay of her family until her murder in 1277. Jewish women became physicians patronized by their Islamic and Christian neighbors. While ritually disadvantaged, in economic life there was no substitute for

9 *The Trotula: An English Translation of the Medieval Compendium of Women's Medicine*, ed. and trans. Monica H. Green (Philadelphia: University of Pennsylvania Press, 2001).

Jewish widows who perpetuated businesses and collected from debtors, especially non-Jews.

Religion and women

The leading religions of the day did not necessarily seek to discredit women, although they were hierarchical and paternalistic without exception. Each advocated some safeguards for women's rights, but local law or custom easily eroded these.

If the Buddha opened the path of enlightenment to women and men, soon monks subordinated nuns to their rule. Christianity ordained men as priests because they, not women, were made "in the image of Christ," and medieval Talmudic scholars argued for the superiority of man over woman, defined as the "other." Among the proselytizing religions, Islam favored sequestering women, although the Quran only demanded modesty befitting family honor; harems were much older institutions, yet they persisted. When Jews, Christians, Buddhists, or Muslims enclosed women, they intended to shield *men* from temptation. The universal religions of the medieval world all spoke of man as the generic norm, which made women perhaps not less worthy, but in a sense, less human. Still, women mystics in the Christian West like Catherine of Siena, who sent her visionary epistolary admonitions to the pope and European rulers, wrote numerous texts illuminating an alternative experiential Christianity that was distinct from the dominant theology of the age. Cults of female nuns, saints, and mystics compensated somewhat for marginalization, but such spiritual empowerment was limited to a few.

In western Europe, Aristotelian ideas about gender were reintroduced by the universities and schools, and most fully articulated in the thirteenth century by the Scholastic philosopher Thomas Aquinas (1225–74). Scholastics argued about 'woman' as a universal category and employed defining polarities. For Aquinas woman was passive, whereas man was an active agent in the image of God. These new essentialist Scholastic polarities were buttressed with other aligned traits: man was formative, tending toward perfect, odd, one, right, square, at rest, straight, light and good; woman was material, deprived of the tendency toward perfection, even, plural, left, oblong, moving, curved, dark and evil.[10] The very simplicity of the scheme recommended it.

---

10 Ian MacLean, *The Renaissance Notion of Woman: A Study in the Fortunes of Scholasticism and Medical Science in European Intellectual Life* (Cambridge University Press, 1980): 1–7.

Within the particular (non-proselytizing) religions of Asia there were no specific articles of faith or dogma to dictate gender terms. The duality Yin–Yang, in which each partakes of the other, as well as a sexual dyad of Outer and Inner, had emerged early in China and remained remarkably resilient identifiers for female and male, perhaps because they were not justified by religious dogma like polar notions found further west. In South Asia the assumption that only goddesses with consorts were beneficent, while unmarried goddesses were dangerous, influenced gender, but not always in negative ways: male asceticism was revered but feared, and women were assumed to have the power of life (*sakti*) in India, an antidote to asceticism's extremes.[11] In Tamil South Asia, misogynous pronouncements about women were balanced by paeans of praise to women's desirability and beneficence.

Among various peoples of Mesoamerica parallels were drawn between childbirth and warfare, and noted in the daily cycle of the sun god. Comparable praise fell to those who died in battle and those who died in labor: of one who died in childbirth, "her husband and parents rejoiced ... for it was said she went not to the land of the dead but to the heavens, to the house of the Sun."[12]

Although it is difficult to gain specific information about women and religion in North America in this era, it appears that the Iroquois–Algonquin tribes (Haudenosaunee) broke with the male-dominant pattern. Five, sometimes six, united Iroquois tribes expanded their territory through conquest much like Eurasian peoples, but not at the same cost of subordinating women. The *gantowisas* (women's council) came into existence during this era and balanced the male council. Matriliny sanctioned by religious practices characterized longhouse clan culture and the *gantowisas* had the right to determine the agenda for men's council meetings. No less warlike in regard to external enemies, the *gantowisas* successfully advocated peaceful government among the Iroquois tribes, played major roles in forming alliances, and may have participated significantly in creating a constitutional form of government.

Slavery and gender

One topic that may help elucidate Middle Millennium gender assumptions, family life, and sexuality is domestic slavery and the web of exchange that

---

11 Frédérique Apffel Marglin, "Female Sexuality in the Hindu World," in Clarissa W. Atkinson, Constance H. Buchanan and Margaret R. Miles (eds.) *Immaculate and Powerful: The Female in Sacred Image and Social Reality* (Boston: Beacon Press, 1985): 47.

12 Rosemary A. Joyce, *Gender and Power in Prehispanic Mesoamerica* (Austin: University of Texas Press, 2000): 172.

provided slaves to families. Wealthy families worldwide raised comfort levels by recourse to slaves. Contrary to Marc Bloch's sanguine view that slavery was no longer relevant to Western society after the ninth century, European slavery had revived by the thirteenth century and was preponderantly female in composition. In this era slavery was mainly domestic in nature, although wars in the Mediterranean and the Muslim invasions into India introduced a supply of male slaves into trade on a sporadic basis. In Europe female domestic slaves came from foreign lands, and might be labeled schismatics, heretics, or pagans, prompting the Fourth Lateran Council (1215) to sanction unfree condition for them.

In households of this era with their high ratios of hard labor to family welfare and production, slavery answered needs, but so also did contract labor, wage-earners, those receiving bed and board, and non-resident menial workers. Slaves produced goods for trade alongside family members and other servants and dependents. Experience in cloth production raised the prices of some skilled female slaves. In Venice, slaves were hired out to artisans like shoemakers and learned skills, but slaves performed the more onerous tasks associated with production, while free persons assumed skilled and highly recompensed work.

Young female slaves were traded at times to be concubines. In China, skills in music, dance, and recitation were valued, so a slave concubine might be trained in the arts and educated to write to please her master. Accomplished slaves were traded among men, or given as gifts. In Baghdad Ibn Butlan's eleventh-century guide went to lengths to explain how to judge slave girls.[13] The birth of a master's child to a slave in an Islamic household led to the mother's manumission upon the death of the master. This was one of the limitations on slavery prescribed by Muhammad and meant that a few legal means were at hand for women to escape slavery, although this did not imply escape from the family or harem; nevertheless the child of a former woman slave was legitimized and might even become a sultan. In Christian households the birth of a child did not free a slave: the expressed will of the master was necessary. This led to confusion about rights in communities where both religious groups lived, such as Valencia in the Iberian peninsula. In 1261, Christian townspeople here changed their laws to conform to Muslim practice.

13 Murray Gordon, *Slavery in the Arab World* (New York: New Amsterdam, 1989): 66.

Large households in China employed written contracts for enslavement, as did port cities in Northwest India, while in the West, towns recorded slaves by cartularies. China, Northwest India, and Europe demarcated free and slave populations with legal precision because of a general reliance on written contracts to police property rights. In China contracts were based upon the seventh-century Tang Code, and in India on laws in port cities; in Europe, Roman law precedents from the sixth-century Code of Justinian dictated terms. Notable similarities occurred in China and Europe. A contracted sale of an eleven-year-old girl dated 731 in China demanded forty bolts of silk, a high price; the contract specifies the names of all parties, including the slave and guarantors, noting the slave came from inferior classes. In 1281 in Ragusa/Dubrovnik a buyer contracted to buy young Moysa of Hlum or Herzegovina at the steep price of seven and one half *grossi*. Slavs such as Moysa were so common as slaves in Europe that "Slav" is the root of the word "slave" in many European languages.

In South Asian households, slaves were preferred for certain tasks forbidden to those regarded as "untouchable," such as preparing food. From the eleventh century onward, the Muslim invasions of Islam produced slaves at numbers never before seen in this region. In the era of Mahmud of Ghazni's expeditions into northwestern India, 1000–25, newly defeated and enslaved Indians attracted a brisk trade to local markets; this led to a diaspora of Indian slaves into Central Asia. Under the Delhi sultanate (1206–1556) observers wrote of a glut of low-priced Indian slaves in markets. In contrast to Christian slave systems and those elsewhere in the Muslim world, in northern India slaves possessed some rights, including marriage and a father's paternal rights over offspring.

Most religions tolerated slavery and justified the trade in slaves, as did Pope Innocent III at the Fourth Lateran Council. The Prophet Muhammad, in "lightening the fetter [of slavery] riveted it ever more firmly in place" in Islam by demanding some restraints on the absolute authority of slave-owners.[14] In India keeping domestic slaves conferred prestige upon a family, and as an indigenous system reliant on slave-brokers, the trade was not dependent on conquest. China maintained distinct and separate markets for slaves, servants, and male heirs; only female slaves purchased young were likely to change their status over a lifetime if they found favor as concubines. Masters determined legitimacy of all offspring of the household in any case.

14 Ibid., 19

The Tang Code regulated sale of slaves strictly: "Male and female slaves, like money and goods, are for their owner to dispose of," and law codes saw society rigidly divided into privileged, commoners, and inferiors like slaves.[15]

While it would be difficult to locate any state or empire of the Middle Millennium that was economically dependent on slavery, domestic slavery flourished among those wealthy enough to afford slaves. The legal scope of the family included its power over slaves. Women owned slaves, and particularly in the Middle East and Europe a slave sometimes accompanied a bride to her new home. It was a pious act to free slaves in wills in Europe and the Islamic world, and manumission is widely regarded as a softening influence on medieval slavery. However, to put a cynical face on it, manu-mitting an old slave served to lessen the owner's burden for slaves' welfare. The Roman law principle "the child of my slave is my slave" remained a feature of European law and was handed down to plantation enterprises when Europeans began colonization: Crete by the thirteenth century, then the Atlantic islands, finally the Americas.

By the end of the Middle Millennium, slave systems were poised for a take-off. Not only were the first plantation-slave systems developing, but galley-slaves reappeared in the Mediterranean. The fourteenth-century Otto-mans built the first standing army in Europe out of enslaved Christian boys known in the mamluk army as Janissaries; they were forbidden to marry. In China slaves continued to be luxuries, and in Europe the price of slaves rose over the centuries, which meant that domestic slavery was an indication of increasing prosperity and the unequal distribution of wealth among families. Enslavement was often the result of a local war, but many children were sold into slavery by their destitute parents, so that slavery reflected disparity in wealth across regions linked by trade as well as within societies. Slavery was largely condoned, its contractual dimensions and coercive means tolerated.

Domestic slavery, reliant largely on women, characterized the Middle Millennium in much of the eastern hemisphere, and societies maintained the legal systems policing slavery that they had inherited from earlier times although slavery seldom still served as a delivery system for essential agricul-tural labor. Perpetuation of domestic slave systems rested on a master's assumption of paternal rights and ownership of a female slave's offspring. Because they were chattels, women slaves' reproduction rights were bought

---

15 James L. Watson, "The Chinese Market in Slaves, Servants and Heirs," in *Asian and African Systems of Slavery*, ed. James L Watson (Berkeley: University of California Press, 1980): 240–1.

and owned, reinforcing notions of female dependence and passivity. No longer just the property of rulers and a small elite, domestic slaves familiarized a broad spectrum of urban persons with chattel-slavery's coercive capacities.

Sexuality

Gender remains the salient category of analysis when considering sexuality in this era, because sexual responses and reproduction were apprehended through gender distinctions. Travelers' observations reveal how diverse understandings were and how severely societies judged the sexual practices of others. Observations reflected a male gaze that assumed that women were compliant with men's desires. Having remarked on polygyny among the Mongols, Marco Polo (1254–1324) noted that Qubilai Khan provided magnificent and separate palaces for his four wives. The khan's harem included four or five hundred young women selected from the province of Ungut, known for the beauty of its women; this superfluity inspired Polo to wonder. He commented that these young women were later distributed among the khan's nobles as an honor.[16] The Syrian Arab emir Usama ibn Munqidh (1095–1188) asked a Frankish father of a motherless girl leaving the baths of Tyre why he had taken her inside. He answered, "Her mother died, and so she has no one who will wash her hair. I brought her into the bath with me so that I might wash her hair." Usama overcame his misgivings and responded, "[t]hat's a kind thing you're doing." He was more shocked by a Frankish husband in the baths of Maʿarrat al-Nuʿman who had his pubic hair shaved, following local custom, and liked it so well he led in his wife to have the same performed on her and watched as it was done by the Muslim attendant. Easy-going attitudes toward privacy and sexual propriety suggested to Usama that Franks had no shame, and neither did they have the sense to feel jealous when other men approached their wives.[17] Despite their often-touted permissiveness, Indians regarded castration for eunuchs who served as government officials or guarded harems as an abhorrent practice. Western Christians shared this attitude, although they made an exception for

---

16 *The Travels of Marco Polo the Venetian*, trans. Willliam Marsden (Garden City, NY: Doubleday, 1948): 117–99.

17 Usama ibn Munqidh, *The Book of Contemplation: Islam and the Crusades*, trans. Paul M. Cobb (London: Penguin, 2008): 148–50. However, the accuracy of the last observation has been disputed.

the *castrati* who sang for them. Shocking sexual practices were those practised by other cultures.

The female body generally bore the burden of erotic messages in this age. In Japanese painting, provocative nude figures incited desire. In Persian painting the partially and alluringly dressed women of the harem were favored. In the Christian West a clothed woman personifying *luxuria* represented sexual allure through rich fabrics and jewels. With the classical revival of the Renaissance, nudity again entered the repertoire of erotic imagery. High-ranking women and men of the Maya of Mesoamerica wore a long straight tunic, while semi-nude male warrior figures appeared in loincloths that eroticized their genitals.

Scientific thinking tended to approach the issue of sexuality through the lens of gender. The Chinese concept of Outer and Inner explained coitus in terms of dominance and male vitality; Yin–Yang characterized male and female sexual production that gave birth to all things in subsequent generations. In the Christian West active and passive were gendered divisions that explained reproduction following Aristotle or one-seed theory. The West, along with Islam, also respected humoral arguments publicized by Galen (*c.* 130–200/217CE) that explained the generation of sexual organs, their functions, and coitus. This system associated women with moist and cold, and men with dry and hot, stressing the latter as sole generators of seed. In the Islamic world, another inherited ancient discourse on women's production of sperm created a physiological link between a woman's emission of semen and procreation (two-seed theory), and advocated female sexual pleasure that induced women to produce "seed."

Indian society paid little attention to sexuality in public discourse perhaps because there were fewer associations of sexuality with a condition of sin. Early marriage policed sexuality for most families in India with virginity required of brides, although "public" women to whom men had easy access were tolerated here as in the rest of Eurasia. *Kama*, or pleasure, included sexual pleasure and stood as one of the three aims in life along with *dharma* (duty and destiny) and *artha* (wealth). In its instruction manual component, the *Kama Sutra* stressed that women's sexual pleasure held primacy over men's, at least theoretically. Sexuality was tied to creativity, the power of life. Thus sexuality might be viewed as essentially divine activity, and families celebrated it ritually in homes, and in temples within the Hindu, Buddhist, and Jain traditions. In South Asia medical authority promoted ideas about body, mind, and soul that stressed balance (*ayurveda*). Excessive loss of semen created imbalance for men, and biological cycles were advocated to determine when coitus should occur. In Tantric practice male sexual arousal was encouraged but then turned inward in a quest for higher bliss. While such traditions suggest that women were to be prized, rather than demeaned, for their potent sexuality, there is little evidence to attest to this happening. The medical, religious, and philosophical ideas surrounding sexuality appear to have been a male discourse with little direct application to the social and sexual lives of women. Still, the shape-shifting from female to male and back again as well as the transvestism found in the *Rig Vedas* and *Upanishads* held imaginative possibilities for women as well as for men.

Commensurate attitudes toward what was deviant stemmed from similarities in medical and scientific understandings of sexuality and reproduction. Turning to early Sanskrit typologies of sexual orientation, the *Caraka* identified eight sexual abnormalities, and the somewhat later *Susruta* identified six (first two centuries CE). Each list identified a masculine lesbian female as deviant, but all other types were dysfunctions (bent penis, impotence) or sexual behaviors (voyeurs) and practices (same-sex fellators) associated with men. No distinctions were made among sexual practices, anatomical abnormalities and impotence. Homosexual practices, such as taking the bottom or "passive" position in sexual encounters, were viewed as a congenital condition and blame, if any, was assigned to the parents' sexual practices. In India partners of passive men were regarded as normal. More troubling was anal intercourse, due to fear of pollution attached to defecation.

Islam demanded virginity for brides and was less tolerant of homosexuality at least in religious law. The *hadith* (reports of the Prophet's exemplary statements and actions) decreed that both active and passive homosexual partners should be stoned. By Byzantine law, from the eighth-century *Ecloga* onward, active and passive partners were to be punished with the sword. The Frankish canons of Nablus of 1120, evidently influenced by Byzantine legislation, demanded the burning of partners. Yet ardent homoerotic love poetry existed side-by-side with harsh punishments throughout the Middle East. In Islam sultans numbered young boys among the women in their harems. The literature of Sufi mysticism included rapturous love poems addressed to male lovers, which became a way of symbolizing union with the divine. While love poems appear to be about unrequited yearning, they represented a popular literary genre appreciated by a wide swath of society.

For the medieval Christian church, sodomy was abhorrent and secular authorities punished it as a crime, but this was true for all fornication, which was punished by anything from simple fines to capital punishment. Whether male–male or male–female, the crime of sodomy was described as an

86

abomination and drew heavier prosecution as the medieval era progressed. This led to widely varying rulings about which specific acts were encompassed; these ranged from anal intercourse to the crime of heresy.

Christians and Jews attached the sin of adultery to both husband's and wife's out-of-wedlock sexual acts, whereas ancient Rome had understood adultery as a sin of wives only. Unlike Jews, Christians considered celibacy a highly prized condition, even more so virginity. For continence, the twelfth-century *Speculum virginum* (Mirror of Virgins) awarded married women thirtyfold, widows sixtyfold, and virgins one hundredfold in heaven. Accolades were lavished on virginity, an invention of sorts of medieval Christianity.[18] Penitential manuals, church councils, and the Gregorian reform initiatives of the eleventh century enforced chaste behavior on regular and secular clergy but with less-than-perfect outcomes.

China appears to have confronted fewer difficulties with same-sex relations among men. Confucian ethics did not encourage lifelong celibacy although Buddhism did; both expected women to be virgins at marriage. While homosexual men were recognized as deviant, this did not shame a family or lineage. Male prostitutes worked in towns and some were transvestites who garnered considerable public notice. A wealthy man might pursue a homoerotic relationship within his home by bringing in a man or boy in place of a concubine for his pleasure. While obscure language often veiled homoerotic sentiments in poetry, the envoy Tao Gu, in his *Records of the Extraordinary*, stated flatly, "Nowadays in the capital those who sell themselves number more than ten thousand. As to the men who offer their own bodies for sale, they enter and leave places shamelessly."[19] Same-sex marriages were sometimes celebrated in China.

In some places sexual and gender categories became interwoven, but in others they were not. In China male homosexuality and lesbianism were not seen as related, nor was there a scientific classification for "homosexual"; active and passive roles defined deviance. In India males with cross-gender behavior or characteristics were compared to disorderly and lewd young girls or prostitutes; as such, they might be seen as a third gender. Muslims neither celebrated homosexuality nor regarded it as particularly heinous, despite religious condemnation; avoidance ruled, and homosexuals never constituted

---

18 *Listen, Daughter: The "Speculum Virginum" and the Formation of Religious Women in the Middle Ages*, ed. Constant J. Mews (New York: Palgrave, 2001): 171.

19 Bret Hinsch, *Passions of the Cut Sleeve: The Male Homosexual Tradition in China* (Berkeley: University of California Press, 1990): 92.

a third gender. In North America, men who dressed and acted as women (called *berdache* later by Europeans but today more generally known as "two-spirit people") were considered a third gender and some apparently took husbands. In western Europe the category of a third gender was sometimes attached to the celibate, which included all priests and monks who were reliably celibate, and women consecrated as holy virgins. A wide range of behaviors characterized groups that fell outside heterosexual typologies.

The old assumption that women who engaged in sex with women escaped condemnation has lost credence in the face of research. Women attracted to women were not regarded as dangerous to the social order to the same degree as men attracted to men, but in the West such women were punished as sinners, albeit "silent sinners."[20] In Islam, which acknowledged same-sex desire in women, the terms *sahiqu*, *sahhaqa*, and *musahiqa* denoted action or behavior rather than emotional attachment. In Arabic erotic literature, lesbians were noted as women who met together and taught each other how to achieve pleasure, and in religious law lesbian acts were punished less severely than male homosexual acts. In Indian medical literature, the masculine woman or lesbian was not blamed; instead, like her male counterpart, responsibility was assigned to her parents. In China, Ming literature viewed lesbians as a male fantasy of utopian polygamy: where there is love between two women, no jealousy exists and they unite with the same man. Rivalry is eliminated so a man enjoys his pleasure without jeopardizing peace and harmony in the home.[21] Throughout Eurasia, men expressed doubt that women derived pleasure from same-sex relations.

Despite the endemic shortage of women in this era that left many men without partners, nuclear families were presumed to contain and police intimate relations and were expected to form the chief bulwark against sexual excess and deviance for both men and women. Not surprisingly, sex trades flourished where unmarried men congregated. Islam advocated polygamy and concubinage in families as one solution to women's sexual excess and deviance, sacrificing the benefits from the solidarity of a monogamous pair invested in their offspring. With sex ratios unfavorable to women here as elsewhere, lifelong Muslim bachelors were deprived of licit sexual lives, which jeopardized their full manhood as understood by Islam. The more

20 Louis Crompton, "The Myth of Lesbian Impunity: Capital Laws from 1270–1791," *Journal of Homosexuality* 6 (1980/81): 13–25.
21 See Tze-lan Deborah Sang, *The Emerging Lesbian: Female Same-Sex Desire in Modern China* (Chicago: University of Chicago, 2003): 49.

monogamous West never contained and policed male sexuality successfully, although religious and civic authorities increasingly regulated family sexual practices. Jewish rabbis exhorted husbands to restrain lust and Christian priests tried to forbid coitus in Lent and on Holy Days, that is, much of the calendar year.

Conclusion

Gender assumptions and women's experience provide litmus tests of family flexibility, resilience, and the capacity to use the talents of all. Women in the Middle Millennium had dynamic histories, but this is not to say that gendered expectations for women were perforce benign by any stretch of the imagination. Indeed, in regulating families, religious and civil authorities superintended family members strictly and frequently imposed restrictions on women. Gender expectations changed little for men; patriarchal institutions dominated throughout, and except for lands with little or no contact with Eurasia, became more hierarchical *among* men – favoring wealth and advanced age at the expense of youth – by the end of the Middle Millennium than when it began.

Gender was a cultural artifact that imposed on men's and women's lives harshly and restrictively at times, at others more leniently, as circumstances and mores dictated. Under threat of war or conquest or loss, sequestering women often intensified, but traditions of women warriors, from samurai maidens in Japan to shieldmaidens in Scandinavia, suggest that under threat women sometimes escaped from gender imperatives, and societies imagined that women and men shared capabilities. The weight of gendered scientific reasoning fell heavily on thinking about sexual acts and behaviors; this represented an enduring legacy from the era to modern times.

Chinese law codes' expectations created sufficient commensurability through rulings on marriage, paternal rights over children, and inheritance so the contour of "family" itself was manifest, and the same appears true for the customs of time-tested kin groupings in India. Islamic conquest imposed shari'a law that defined family in India, Southeast Asia, and across the Middle East and North Africa, although Islam failed to eliminate regional differences in its wide reach. Among Jews, legal writings, ethical preaching, and local rabbis defined family, demanding submissive roles for Jewish women, although this could lead to rebellion as well as compliance. Christian Europe was exceptional because "family" as an entity attaining definition first occurred in medieval times, as David Herlihy has argued.[22] Thereafter monogamous families evolved, becoming more hierarchical, while civil and ecclesiastical laws increasingly oversaw family life.

Around the world marriage had become more monogamous by 1500, with Christian Europe and European Jewry rejecting polygyny, and Chinese marriages among commoners remaining monogamous; India reflected a comparable pattern. Monogamous marriage meant care for elderly parents and more investment in offspring's welfare, such as reliable marriage gifts for daughters and inheritance for sons at the death of a father.

In the West both law and gender constructs permitted women's participation in economic growth in the early phases of the Commercial Revolution, but then disadvantaged women during later phases, when wealth was increasingly concentrated in the hands of a few; often women were reduced to unacknowledged and menial roles in the economy. In the Mediterranean region, among Jews and Christians dowry in coin awarded to daughters allowed land and other wealth to be held intact for sons until their father's death. Thereafter legal partnerships – contracts like *fraterna* (pact of brothers) and *societas* (association) – prolonged joint family ownership, encouraging continuation of business "houses" like banks that promoted economic growth. In addition, the inheritance system of primogeniture, which governed royal holdings and peerages in England and France by the thirteenth century, spread socially and in time would result in an infinite right to entail landed property in some European countries, resulting in a further concentration of wealth.

According to Timur Kuran, both joint family ownership and primogeniture benefited the West when compared to Islam, where partible inheritance under shari'a law called for the immediate partition of assets to offspring at the death of a father.[23] Earlier Muslims had taught Westerners about contractual business instruments; ironically, Muslim business enterprises remained short-lived while the West would benefit from more enduring contractual arrangements because Westerners applied contract law to kin liaisons.

In this age, public institutions promoted family welfare but also monitored family behaviors. Islam embarked on private provision of public welfare,

---

22 David Herlihy, *Opera Muliebria: Women and Work in the Middle Ages* (New York: McGraw Hill, 1990).

23 Timur Kuran, "Why the Middle East Is Economically Underdeveloped," in *The Development Economics Reader*, ed. Giorgio Secondi (New York: Routledge, 2008): 107–25.

including schools, through the *waqf* system of pious foundations directed by donors. Gains in literacy increased families' access to political information in China through government schools, including charity schools. In the West religious and civic foundations like orphanages emerged and schools opened up a world of information to youth. Meanwhile, care of elders remained a largely unmediated family obligation.

Late marriage for both women and men, as practiced in the northwest of Europe, still benefited the economy in 1500 since late-marrying women, like their husbands, brought wealth to marriage, along with marketable skills, while women's child-bearing years were truncated, resulting in smaller families. Plague and war also served as positive checks on population growth, but these factors were not unique to Europe. Since most lands linked by trade grew in wealth in this period, families prospered in many locales, but in the West Jews and Christians experienced prosperity as higher per capita income, while more easterly lying societies with earlier marriage and higher birth rates were set for future population increase. In the long run this placed Western families on an enhanced footing as they entered modern times.

FURTHER READING

Primary sources

Le Lettere di Margherita Datini a Francesco di Marco, 1384–1410. Ed. Valeria Rosati. Prato: Cassa di risparmio e depositi, 1977.

Letters of Catherine of he Sienna. Trans. Suzanne Noffke, 4 vols. Tempe, AZ: Arizona Center for Medieval and Renaissance Studies, 2000-7.

The Mission of Friar William of Rubruck: His Journey to the Court of the Great Khan Möngke 1253–1255. Trans. Peter Jackson. London: Hakluyt Society, 1990.

Murasaki Shikibu. *The Tale of Genji.* Trans. Edward G. Seidensticker. New York, NY: Alfred A. Knopf, 1976.

The Travels of Ibn Battuta, A. D. 1325–1354. Trans. H. A. R. Gibb, 5 vols. Cambridge: Hakluyt Society, 1958–2000.

Secondary sources

Amer, Sahar. "Medieval Arab Lesbians and Lesbian-Like Women," *Journal of the History of Sexuality* 18, 2 (2009): 215–36.

Ardren, Traci, ed. *Ancient Maya Women.* Walnut Creek, CA: AltaMira Press, 2002.

Birge, Bettine. "Women and Confucianism from Song to Ming: The Institutionalization of Patrilineality," in Paul Jakov Smith and Richard von Glahn (eds.), *The Song–Yuan–Ming Transition in Chinese History.* Cambridge, MA: Harvard University Press, 2003: 212–40.

Bloch, Marc. *Slavery and Serfdom in the Middle Ages*. Trans. William R. Beer. Berkeley, CA: University of California Press, 1975.

Blumenthal, Debra. *Enemies and Familiars: Slavery and Mastery in Fifteenth-Century Valencia*. Ithaca, NY: Cornell University Press, 2009.

Boswell, John. *Same-Sex Unions in Premodern Europe*. New York, NY: Villard, 1994.

Brown, Carolyn Henning. "The Gift of a Girl," *Ethnology* 22, 1 (1983): 43–62.

Brundage, James. *Law, Sex, and Christian Society in Medieval Europe*. University of Chicago Press, 1987.

Bynum, Caroline Walker. *Holy Feast and Holy Fast*. Berkeley, CA: University of California Press, 1987.

Goitein, S. D. *A Mediterranean Society: The Jewish Communities of the Arab World as Portrayed in the Documents of the Cairo Geniza*, vol. III: *The Family*. Berkeley, CA: University of California Press, 1978.

Goldman, Robert P. "Transsexualism, Gender and Anxiety in Traditional India," *Journal of the American Oriental Society* 113, 3 (1993): 374–491.

Grossman, Avraham. *Pious and Rebellious: Jewish Women in Medieval Europe*. Trans. Jonathan Chipman. Waltham, MA: Brandeis University Press, 2004.

Gulik, Robert Hans van. *Sexual Life in Ancient China*. Leiden: Brill, 1961.

Hambly, Gavin R. G., ed. *Women in the Medieval Islamic World*. New York, NY: St Martin's Press, 1998.

Hansen, Valerie. *Negotiating Daily Life in Traditional China*. New Haven, CT: Yale University Press, 1995.

Hay, David. *The Military Leadership of Matilda of Canossa, 1046–1115*. University of Manchester Press, 2008.

Haynal, John J. "European Marriage Patterns in Perspective," in D. V. Glass and D. E. C. Eversley (eds.), *Population in History. Essays in Historical Demography*. Chicago University Press, 1961: 101–43.

Herlihy, David. *Opera Muliebria: Women and Work in Medieval Europe*. New York, NY: McGraw Hill, 1990.

Joyce, Rosemary A. *Gender and Power in Prehispanic Mesoamerica*. Austin, TX: University of Texas, 2001.

Karras, Ruth Mazo. *Sexuality in Medieval Europe: Doing unto Others*, 2nd edn, New York, NY: Routledge, 2012.

Ko, Dorothy, JaHyun Kim Haboush and Joan R. Piggott (eds.), *Women and Confucian Cultures in Premodern China, Korea, and Japan*. Berkeley, CA: University of California Press, 2003.

Maclean, Ian. *The Renaissance Notion of Woman: A Study in the Fortunes of Scholasticism and Medical Science in European Intellectual Life*. Cambridge University Press, 1980.

Mann, Barbara Alice. *Iroquoian Women: The Gantowisas*. New York, NY: Peter Lang, 2000.

Marglin, Frédérique Apffel. "Female Sexuality in the Hindu World," in Clarissa W. Atkinson, Constance H. Buchanan and Margaret R. Miles (eds.). *Immaculate and Powerful: The Female in Sacred Image and Social Reality*. Boston, MA: Beacon, 1985: 39–80.

Mews. Constant J. ed. *"Listen, Daughter". The Speculum Virginum and the Formation of Religious Women in the Middle Ages*. New York, NY: Palgrave, 2001.

Murray, Stephen O. and Will Roscoe. *Islamic Homosexualities*. New York University Press, 1997.

Neel, Carol, ed. *Medieval Families: Perspectives on Marriage, Household, and Children*. University of Toronto Press in Association with the Medieval Academy of America, 2004.

Orr, Leslie C. *Donors, Devotees, and Daughters of God: Temple Women in Medieval Tamilnadu*, New York, NY: Oxford University Press, 2000.

Ramaswamy, Vijaya. *Walking Naked: Women, Society, Spirituality in South India*, 2nd edn, Shimla: Indian Institute of Advanced Study, 2007.

Rangachari, Devika. *Invisible Women, Visible Histories. Gender, Society and Polity in North India (Seventh to Twelfth Century CE)*. New Delhi: Manohar, 2009.

Rowson, Everett K. "The Categorization of Gender and Sexual Irregularity in Medieval Arabic Vice Lists," in Julia Epstein and Kristina Straub (eds.), *Body Guards: The Cultural Politics of Gender Ambiguity*. New York, NY: Routledge, 1991: 50–99.

Smith, Richard M. "Geographical Diversity in the Resort to Marriage in Late Medieval Europe," in P. J. P. Goldberg (ed.), *Woman is a Worthy Wight: Women in English Society c. 1200–1500*. Wolfeboro Falls, NH: Alan Sutton, 1992: 16–59.

Sweet, Michael J. and Leonard Zwilling. "The First Medicalization: The Taxonomy and Etiology of Queerness in Classical Indian Medicine," *Journal of the History of Sexuality* 5, 4 (1993): 590–607.

Trautman, Thomas R. *Dravidian Kinship*. Cambridge University Press, 1981.

Wiesner-Hanks, Merry E. *Gender in History: Global Perspectives*. 2nd edn. Oxford: Blackwell, 2001.

4

Society: hierarchy and solidarity

SUSAN REYNOLDS

This chapter argues that during the Middle Millennium people in all the societies about which enough information can be gleaned were reckoned to be more or less unequal. So far as the information goes, most people seem to have taken their inequality for granted and regarded it as just, so long as those above them treated them according to their society's ideas of justice. The different ranks and statuses in any society were generally regarded as forming a hierarchy, that is, 'the principle by which the elements of a whole are ranked in relation to the whole'.[1] A society here will be taken to be 'a network of social interaction at the boundaries of which is a certain level of interaction cleavage between it and its environment . . . a unit with boundaries [which] contains interaction that is relatively dense and stable; that is, it is internally patterned when compared to interaction that crosses its borders'.[2] Many such societies were more or less coterminous with polities, that is, units of government, whether these were independent or formed a subordinate layer of government within a larger polity. Envisaging one's own society and polity as a natural, given whole promoted a measure of solidarity. Hierarchy and solidarity went together. Solidarity did not exclude internal conflict any more than hierarchy meant that equality was never valued. Equality between such people within each rank as ought to be equal was prized and there were very occasional demands for wider equality, though even the most radical do not seem to have extended to women, servants, or slaves.

   The chief problem for a historian of medieval Europe in tackling any aspect of these thousand years of the history of the whole world is, of course,

---

1 Louis Dumont, *Homo Hierarchicus: The Caste System and its Implications*, trans. Mark Sainsbury (London: Weidenfeld and Nicolson, 1970): 66.
2 Michael Mann, *Sources of Social Power, 1: A History of Power from the Beginning to A.D. 1760* (Cambridge University Press, 1986): 13.

lack of knowledge of so much of it. Paradoxically, however, almost as great is the problem caused by the domination of the historiography of the period by that of Europe. The very period is the one conventionally assigned to the Middle Ages in Europe. The medieval label has been transferred to periods of Asian history previously thought to have had characteristics once attributed to the European Middle Ages, but the characteristics and the centuries described as medieval vary. A range of words and patterns applied to the European Middle Ages has been used for other areas in what are called their middle ages, sometimes without further definition. An obvious example is feudalism, a construct of eighteenth- and nineteenth-century historiography that came to embrace two quite different concepts, one about relations of vassalage and fiefholding in the ruling class and the other, formulated by Marx and Engels, about relations between the landowning class and the peasantry.[3] Difficult, if not impossible, as it is to fit the evidence about the European Middle Ages into the bulging feudal framework, it is even more difficult to make sense of other societies when they are squashed into it by the use of words like fief, enfeoffment, feudatory, or vassal in ways that assume they each have a general, though generally undefined, meaning irrespective of date or context.

Other words can also be misleading. 'Villages' can be nucleated rural settlements, units of exploitation, or units of government. The word 'guild' is confusing for comparisons. In our period it was sometimes used in northern Europe for associations of craftsmen but more often for various other kinds of associations that generally combined conviviality and mutual help. Many historians, however, apply it chiefly, if not exclusively, to craft associations, even in Italy, where the word was never used. 'Serf' is also unhelpful as it is used to cover different disabilities and obligations in different bits of European history. People at the bottom of other agricultural societies, however oppressed, may not have been either oppressed in the ways supposedly characteristic of European 'serfdom' or specifically categorized as 'unfree'. Some Anglophone historians of China use words familiar in their own societies, like sheriff, but some use words like prefect, prefecture, or commandery, which are not. Some historians of India in this period use the word 'cess' to denote rents, though it seems to have been used in Europe only in Ireland, and 'demesne', which, though it may look suitably medieval, was a coinage of post-medieval English lawyers that is harder to interpret

---

3 Susan Reynolds, 'The Use of Feudalism in Comparative History', in Benjamin Z. Kedar (ed.), *Explorations in Comparative History* (Jerusalem: Magnes Press, 2009): 191–217.

(and pronounce) than 'domain'. 'Manor' is a word which in European (and especially English) history denotes an institution that changed much in our period and therefore lacks perspicuity even there. 'Gentry' is one peculiar to England, where it normally denotes a status-group that might elsewhere be considered minor nobility but had local peculiarities. Applying it to France poses problems. Applying it to China poses more.[4] Difficult as the problems of translation are, all these solutions may pose more for the reader.

This borrowing of ideas and words from European history is entirely understandable even if the results are not: the modern kind of critical and professional historiography started in Europe and offered a stimulus to critical and professional history elsewhere. But it inevitably also offers superficial analogies that would hinder attempts at comparison even if some of them had not been based on ideas about medieval Europe that no longer seem to fit the European evidence. This chapter will therefore use words that are as generic, untechnical, and unrelated to particular interpretations of European history, new or old, as possible, in the hope that this may avoid misunderstanding.

Interesting as is the question of the origins of the 'rise of Europe', this chapter will also try to avoid the teleology of searching for them before 1500. They may be discernible but the search lends itself to contrasting stereotypes, whether of dynamic Europe and the timeless East, or of Western liberties and Oriental Despotism, that do not promote the understanding of this period either in Europe or elsewhere.[5] The history of different parts of Europe, moreover, varied too much to fit any stereotype, while variations in the national traditions of historiography developed in the last two centuries have compounded the difficulty of generalizing about it.

Eurasia, with the addition of North Africa, is by far the best recorded part of the world in the Middle Millennium. This chapter will thus focus primarily on this very large part of the world, and then look more briefly at other areas.

Economic foundations of societies in Eurasia

Mongol conquests loomed large to writers both in China and Europe in the thirteenth century, but that was a time of relatively prolific writing and

---

4 Ping-Ti Ho, *The Ladder of Success in Imperial China: Aspects of Social Mobility, 1368–1911* (New York: John Wiley, 1964): 34–40.
5 Jack Goody, *The Eurasian Miracle* (Cambridge: Polity Press, 2010).

recording: the Mongols did not open hitherto untravelled roads any more than did Marco Polo's journeys to the east. As well as maritime traffic around coasts and across the Indian Ocean, people, goods, and ideas travelled from centuries before our period almost to its end along what has become known as the Silk Road.

Despite all the contacts and despite more similarities between the societies of Eurasia than traditional stereotypes suggest, there were many differences in economic and social structures and relations. All societies of which there is any record seem, however, to have been more or less unequal. The least unequal, with fewest layers of government, were the smallest and poorest. Some, like the earlier Mongol–Turkic peoples, were pastoral or hunter-gathering, with little or no agriculture. Some, like those attacked by the young Chinggis Khan, were ostensibly egalitarian, making 'no distinction between great and small, bad and good, high and mean',[6] so that they were held together simply by ties of kinship. Unwritten genealogies and rules of kinship are, however, always manipulable, while the equality was probably enjoyed only by the senior male householders (or tent-holders). It was they who, with authority legitimized by real or fictive kinship, judged disputes, enforced custom, and made decisions for the community. Since that left out sons living under their fathers' authority, as well, of course, as women, servants, and slaves, their societies were not equal in a modern sense. Some of these small, more or less independent societies lasted throughout our period but many became absorbed in larger economies and polities, especially as agriculture developed within them or in neighbouring areas. Until then, those in which authority was both coercive and accepted as legitimate may rather rank as mini-states than as stateless.

Agriculture brought greater populations, greater wealth, greater inequality and power, greater complexity of government, and therefore more cause for conflict. Though already dominant in some areas long before 500 CE, it was extended thereafter and developed through new crops and techniques, in many areas including irrigation. Sometimes this was organized by rulers or those, including monasteries or temples, to whom they gave land, but their responsibility may have been exaggerated: sometimes, especially while there was still land to spare and forests to be cleared, it was done independently by the people who did the actual farming. Everywhere, as populations grew, land as the source of wealth came to be a commodity, and one controlled

---

6 *Secret History of the Mongols*, ed. and trans. Igor de Rachewiltz, 2 vols. (Leiden: Brill, 2006): 1.7 (I § 35).

more strictly by people at the top of local hierarchies than it was in pastoral societies or in those that practised agriculture but were remote from centres of power. In general this meant the imposition of layers of rights above the cultivators of the land and the increase of rules and records about them.

Increased production promoted markets, towns, and trade, both local and long-distance, and with them came more development of more crafts, more movement and mixing of people, both in space and status, and of goods, both everyday and luxury. Local lords and rulers profited from tolls, rents, and taxes. Some towns, like Rome or Qubilai Khan's summer capital at Shangdu (Coleridge's Xanadu) were primarily centres of government and consumption rather than wholesale trade or production. But everywhere they were both a result and a cause of economic, social, and political change. They were centres of literacy, learning and numeracy: tally sticks very like those used in the English exchequer in the twelfth century served similar purposes in the Tibetan Empire four centuries earlier. The population of Eurasia, both urban and rural, was larger in 1500 than in 500, but it did not grow continuously or in all areas: plagues that spread, like famines and wars, along trade routes checked it periodically, notably in the sixth and fourteenth centuries. By the end of the period towns along the Silk Road were dying, though the maritime traffic that replaced it brought increased trade to ports along the coasts of South Asia.

Hierarchy and government in Eurasia

It is impossible to discuss societies in this period without saying something about their government: information about society often comes from records of government while political and social hierarchies and solidarities appear to have been closely related. The growth and growing complexity of economies spread to other areas the complexities of government and society that had long existed in the empires of China, India, the Middle East, and Rome. Monarchy, which Walter Bagehot called 'an intelligible constitution',[7] became the most common form of government. However intelligible, it could cause its subjects anxiety at successions, whether because rules were uncertain or favoured partible inheritance or, in highly organized polities, where central power was worth fighting for. Nevertheless, despite the existence of small states centred on towns, which were sometimes ruled by

7 Walter Bagehot, *The English Constitution* (London: Chapman and Hall, 1867), ch. 2.

councils, contemporaries who wrote fiction or treatises seem often to have assumed that some kind of monarchy was the norm. Whether Anglophone historians call rulers emperors, kings, princes, chiefs, lords, leaders, or anything else is a matter of translation and ethnographical and historiographical tradition which reveals little about the different ways independent polities were governed. The use of different words for different societies makes comparisons difficult. I shall refer simply to rulers and to what they ruled as polities or kingdoms, generally avoiding the controversial word 'state'.

Government in all but the smallest polities came in layers, with authority either delegated through a formal hierarchy of offices over different regions and smaller areas or exercised by people of high status who ruled their own patches within the polity, sometimes, in India and early medieval Europe, with titles translated as 'king.' It is often difficult to distinguish the two kinds of layers of authority, as when rulers gave land, or authority over land, to monasteries in China and Europe, to temples and high-caste groups in India, or to individual great men in any polity.

From the leading householders of the smallest societies to the monarchs of great polities, all rulers seem to have been supposed to protect their people, do justice to them, and consult with those whose status made them worthy of consultation. The prescriptions of the *Arthaśāstra*, written in India some centuries before 500 CE, that 'all action [by rulers] should be preceded by consultation' and that 'in the happiness of the subjects lies the happiness of the king', would have seemed appropriate in any kingdom.[8] Taking counsel did not mean having to follow it, but references to assemblies or councils of great men suggest a certain constraint: counsellors might, for instance, be responsible for communicating and enforcing decisions, which could involve securing a measure of agreement from them. References to a ruler's obligation to do justice, sometimes explicitly to the poor, and to follow custom or law, suggest something different from Oriental Despotism or even absolutism as some historians have envisaged them. Both characterizations seem to derive rather from treatises written to flatter rulers than from evidence about the way government worked in practice. Even some of the treatises that presented their rulers as rulers of the whole world, responsible to gods alone, also suggested that wise rulers ought to take counsel.

---

8 *The Kauṭilya Arthaśāstra*, 2, trans. R. P. Kangle, 2nd edn (Bombay: University of Bombay, 1972): 32 (1.15.1); 47 (1.19.34); cf. e.g. Ann K. S. Lambton, *Landlord and Peasant in Persia* (Oxford University Press, 1953): xix–xxx.

Not all rulers conformed to these ideals. Nor did subordinate officials, though they were probably easier to discipline than were their masters at the top of the political hierarchy, who had no superior to control them. The difficulty of controlling rulers was increased by the acceptance of hierarchy and coercive government, as well as by the need evidently felt by writers of the time to flatter the ruler and emphasize the obligation to obey him. Some rulers nevertheless clearly felt an obligation to do what was considered just. Protecting the poor could help a ruler control subjects of higher status, but it seems to have been often, and certainly not only in Christian kingdoms, thought of as the duty of a ruler. As land became more valuable rulers sometimes tried, without much success, to stop powerful subjects from buying land from peasants. Tang rulers in China (618–907) tried giving peasants equal plots in land for life, primarily to promote agriculture and get taxes, but could not stop larger landowners from acquiring the holdings.

As war-leaders and their followers acquired resources they turned from mere tribute-taking to more systematic collection of taxes, rents, and tolls, and spent more on their courts, rituals, and patronage. In 500 CE literate, record-keeping administration was only vestigially alive in western Europe but it was well established in Byzantium, Iran, Tibet and, of course, China. At least some kingdoms in India probably belong in that list, but they pose problems for an outsider dependent on secondary works, since historians of India have tended to describe kingdoms as bureaucratic without discussing the evidence of anything like bureaucracy in, for instance, Max Weber's sense. Nevertheless, surviving lists of villages and tolls, together with the evidence of literacy in copper-plate and temple inscriptions, suggest that some Indian kings had professional, record-keeping servants. Islamic government under the Umayyads (661–750) and even more afterwards, under the 'Abbasids, adapted and developed the systems they had inherited from their Byzantine and Iranian predecessors, while various forms of bureaucracy began to transform government from the eighth century in Japan and the twelfth in Europe. Bureaucracy made effective control of larger areas possible, but it was no substitute for courts, rituals, patronage, and force in maintaining a ruler's authority. Nor could it always preserve a polity against external attacks and internal conflicts: Byzantine rulers lost control of much of their empire long before its final collapse. The Carolingian Empire in Europe broke up in 889; the Islamic Empire began to fragment politically long before the ending of the Baghdad Caliphate in 1258; central government in Japan lost authority from the ninth century; China, the most obvious bureaucracy of all, which is traditionally depicted as forming one great empire through history, was divided in various ways through much of our period. Meanwhile effective bureaucracy flourished in city-states and other small polities.

Professional administration affected social and political structures by producing new elites of officials alongside landowners so as to open a new road to social mobility. Even in China, however, where examinations were famously used from the seventh century on, with variations and intermissions, to recruit officials, the extent to which this promoted social mobility is disputed: entry to examinations might need a recommendation from an official whose own son did not need to take the examination. Members of the lower grades of village society would be unlikely to have the basic qualifications to start with. Neither in China nor, for instance, in thirteenth-century France did many officials work their way from the bottom to the top of the system. Land remained the chief source of wealth, status, and power, so that the largest landowners remained the top elite. Although armies, like civil services, became more professional so that men of high status (often called 'nobles' by historians) served in them less often, those elites might still retain a military ethos. The traditional view of military and civilian elites in China as separate, and of the non-military ethos of the civilians, has recently been questioned. Islamic armies were more separate from the rest of society, at first because Arab garrisons formed their own settlements in conquered towns, and later because 'slave armies' were recruited largely from outside the empire.

Solidarities within the polities of Eurasia

Beyond the more obvious solidarities of close kin and, in settled societies, of neighbours, the way that units of government were so often referred to as if they were naturally existing collectivities or peoples suggests that they evoked some kind of solidarity. This probably functioned best in relatively small polities. Some, like the nomad polities (generally called empires) of Central Asia, in which the rulers merely took tribute without imposing much government, soon fell apart. Solidarity after the great Islamic conquests belonged at first to the Arab conquerors and apparently never turned into a permanent political, as distinct from religious, unity, which perhaps partly explains the later political fragmentation. Polities that survived in spite of the difficulties of supervision and the strength of local solidarities within them did so less because of despotic power at the centre than because of what looks like acceptance of political unity, hierarchy, and layers of solidarity.

In many polities, both large and small, the legitimation of authority seems to have included an assumed, though fictitious, genealogical connection. Many of these focused on supposed dynasties of rulers but others, most famously that of the Franks, explicitly involved the peoples they ruled, as if they were natural, given communities of descent with distinctive characteristics and customs. Others implicitly subsumed the peoples in the stories of their kings. As more ambitious rulers extended their territories they seem to have often preserved their acquisitions as subordinate units of government so that old solidarities and hierarchies were preserved under the new. The survival of collective (now often called ethnic) names of old units of society and government, whether territorial like the duchies of Germany which had once been kingdoms, or sections of the population like the formerly nomadic groups settled in China under the Mongols, suggests the way that they were taken for granted as having a real and naturally given existence. Language seems to have been less important as a uniting or dividing factor than has often been assumed since the eighteenth century. Assimilation of immigrants or conquered populations, however, became harder when groups had very different economies and cultures (including religions) and when governments ruled them as separate units and kept written records to preserve the memory of difference. This happened, for instance, when the population of China was classified in four ethnic groups with different rights and obligations and the immigrant Mongols had the most privileges. Various kinds of systematic and recorded separation were applied to Jews and Muslims in Europe, non-Muslim groups in the Islamic Empire, and the non-agricultural forest dwellers now known as 'tribals' in India.

The solidarity of whole polities was likely to be felt most strongly by their leading members. For them, even if on occasion broken by jealousy and ambition, it could be fortified by interpersonal relations with the ruler and each other, joint service in armies and councils, patronage, and shared common interests, at least in keeping control of the rest of the population. In Europe members of councils, assemblies, and armies, who formed a very small part of the population of the polity, were often referred to as if they included everyone. Lower down any hierarchy most people probably felt most solidarity with their local communities. The acceptance of inequality and belief in custom and in the necessity of imposed order, together with the hope of protection, seem nevertheless to have generally led to an acceptance, however unconsidered or reluctant, of whatever government was more or less firmly established.

Towns too, despite their internal conflicts, and especially when they had some degree of independence, developed strong senses of solidarity along with myths of origin that belied the sometimes large number of immigrants in their populations. Economic and social hierarchies, except in the largest and richest cities, were lower than those of kingdoms, but urban society, with its servants, day labourers, and (in some cases) slaves, both men and women, was not egalitarian. As in kingdoms, hierarchy and solidarity went together.

Religions in Eurasia

Most societies probably started out with their own gods and religious customs, which might then become liable to influence from those of other societies with which they came into contact. Outside influences are most obvious with the spread of Buddhism, Christianity, and Islam. How far that spread affected the shape of societies is hard to say: although it obviously affected the cultures of societies as well as individuals within them, religions seem to have adapted themselves in practice to economic and social hierarchies. While Christianity, Islam, Buddhism, and some Hindu sects all had egalitarian strands, the societies they inhabited were in practice unequal, with inequality fortified by acceptance of political, social, and religious hierarchy. Churches, monasteries, temples, and mosques, whether in Europe, the Middle East, India, Central Asia, or China, became great landlords and behaved accordingly. People living on lands given to churches, temples or monasteries, sometimes indeed, though perhaps not always, suffered from the change. The most splendid religious buildings and rituals were produced in the more complex and unequal societies. Religious rituals and royal patronage of religious institutions legitimized royal rule, while religious teaching reinforced the obligations to govern justly that seem to have obtained in most societies. Religious sanctions fortified wider political and social norms, notably in the oaths widely used to strengthen obligations.

On the other hand, apart from the economic, fiscal, and political impact of monasteries, the various teachings, cults, and demands of different religions, their festivals, the character of their monks, priests, or hermits, and the degree of their separateness from the rest of society obviously affected the societies in which they were practised. A conflict between church and state has sometimes been seen as peculiar to Europe. The hierarchy of both Roman and Orthodox churches made conflicts between emperors and popes or patriarchs particularly sensational but, though causes of dispute varied, other rulers tangled with local religions too. Chinese rulers and officials worried about the taxes and services they lost to Buddhist monasteries (and fake monasteries) and periodically dissolved some of them and confiscated their lands. Christianity seems to have been unusual in the persistence and fierceness of its internal conflicts and persecution of heretics, its occasional forcible conversion of neighbouring pagans or expulsions of non-Christians, and its wars against Islam, but this impression may be partly the result of fuller records and more research into them. Although a good many large polities outside Europe and some within, like some city-states and Iberian kingdoms, had populations of mixed religions which rubbed along together much of the time and influenced each other, there were occasional conflicts and persecutions, not only those of Jews by Christians. There were, for instance, conflicts and rivalries between sects in India, where untouchability has been cited as 'a form of religious persecution'. Some stories of religious hostilities, however, reflect modern ideas rather than those of the time, as do much later elaborations of the story of the plundering of a temple at Somnath (Gujarat, India) by the Muslim sultan Mahmud of Ghazni in 1026, which culminated in nineteenth-century claims that it reflected permanent antagonism between Hindus and Muslims.[9]

Law in Eurasia

The treatises on law, politics, and theology written by scholars in the literate societies of Eurasia often contain much information about law and the grades of their societies, but they also tend to make rules look both more fixed and more complicated than they may have been in reality. Treatises need to be combined with other evidence and, notably, such records as survive of law in practice. So far as these reflect what the treatises say, that may be as much or more because the authors of treatises started from the assumptions of their societies as because those who judged crimes or disputes knew what the treatises said.

Most societies started from some kind of unwritten customary law. Because it was unwritten it tended to vary, even within one polity, from place to place and from time to time. Rules about such matters as inheritance and the use of land varied between societies and between classes of people

---

9 Romila Thapar, 'Imagined Religious Communities? Ancient History and the Modern Search for a Hindu Identity', *Modern Asian Studies* 23 (1989): 220, and Romila Thapar, *Somanatha: The Many Voices of a History* (New Delhi: Penguin, 2004).

within them, and were variably enforced, cutting across some of the simple contrasts traditionally drawn between east and west or different countries within either. Some societies allowed individuals to avenge wrongs against themselves or their kin without recourse to outside authorities, but disputes seem often to have been settled in assemblies or courts that also legislated and dealt with wider matters of government. Legal decisions might be announced by the ruler, but if he (or occasionally she) was wise, he would make them after taking advice about what was customary and right. In larger polities many crimes and disputes were probably dealt with locally. In that case judgments might be given by a local lord or royal official but again, if he was wise, after consultation dominated by men of higher status – probably the richer, older, and most established in the area – who were supposed to know the community's custom and judge on its behalf.

Many of the surviving records of law concern rights in land, which landowners in agricultural societies particularly wanted to record. Historians have sometimes thought that all the land under either Oriental Despotism or feudalism belonged to the ruler, so that no one else had anything that can now be called rights of property. But although any kingdom in one sense belonged to its king, the evidence of disputes between subjects in Europe, India, and China, for instance, suggests that individuals had rights enforceable against each other in their houses, gardens, and the land they cultivated. Custom might even allow that some of those who owed rents and services had some rights against the ruler or landlord, hard as they might be to enforce. While rents and services might be owed to rulers and landlords, and all the land in a village might come to be considered as in some sense the landlord's land, during much of this period it was only in some sense his. Rights over land are often divided and come in layers, even in modern societies, but modern legal systems generally distinguish rights of government from rights of property as was seldom done in the past. Appeals to rulers by the humble seldom succeeded, but they were supposed to be allowed and were indeed made.

On the other hand, while some historians have thought that all the land belonged to the king, others have thought that at the level of villages or other agricultural communities, property was originally – and even as late as the beginning of this period – communal. Local communities certainly often had common rights over wastes and pastures and even, under rules, over the land of individuals, but these would now count as rights of government or control. People do not seem to have been constrained by the modern distinction between corporate and unincorporated groups: collective action, even by peasants, was allowed unless it was subversive.

How far either advocates or judges were legal experts is a question that has not been much considered by historians more interested in the content of treatises than in the practice of law. The social impact of law, however, changes when it ceases to be the custom of a community and becomes the preserve of a group with some kind of professional and expert knowledge. The growth of more systematic and bureaucratic government brought more royal judges into local communities, sometimes armed with instructions about the rules they were to enforce and even with knowledge of learned treatises on law, so that they tended to override the customary consensus of local elites. The *qadis* who judged Muslims under Islamic law were professionals of a kind, with expert knowledge, though their jurisdiction did not extend to crime. In Europe a big change to law, and particularly property law, came with the emergence of professional advocates around the twelfth century. Law at the level they practised thus became the custom of lawyers and tended to favour those who employed lawyers. Whether law elsewhere became professionalized in ways similar to these, or differently from either, deserves further study.

Local society in Eurasia

The combination of solidarity and hierarchy is clear at the local level of society at which most people lived most of the time. Solidarity there was institutional as well as affective, though of course there was plenty of room for likes and dislikes, affections and discords. Local government, with varying degrees of autonomy or supervision from above, was nearly always conducted through regional and local assemblies of varying degrees of formality. Some Indian land grants and, notably, the tenth-century constitution drawn up for the South Indian village of Uttaramerur[10] show that rulers in India, as in Europe, sometimes formally authorized a degree of local autonomy. That did not mean local democracy. In Europe, the richer and more established men of a village, province, or lord's estate, whether or not it had any formal autonomy, seem to have been the effective decision-makers, though their humbler (male) neighbours might be present. The same probably applied to local headmen and landlords' officials in Iran. In the parts of China under the Song (960–1279), local society was officially graded in nine, or later five, grades. Though things probably worked less neatly in practice, official duties

---

10 K. A. Nilakanta Sastri (ed. and trans.), *Studies in Cōla History and Administration* (Madras University Historical Series 7, 1932): 169–75.

like policing, tax-collection, and settling minor disputes fell even more probably to those in the higher grades. Most Indian village assemblies were restricted to higher castes. Despite the supposed immutability of caste, however, categories and rankings were sometimes adjusted, while genealogies from the end of our period show that Indian individuals occasionally changed caste. In Europe, where in the earlier Middle Ages, and for longer in some areas, the humbler peasants, now often called serfs, were held down in various ways by being classified as unfree at law, some of them crossed the barrier by a recognized procedure of emancipation. Movements up and down local hierarchies no doubt occurred in most other societies. So long as there were towns in which to try one's fortune, or uncleared land not brought under governmental control, geographical mobility could be a means to social mobility. Though society in pastoral or hunter-gatherer areas was less unequal, it was not necessarily more free or comfortable for everyone than in areas where agriculture was dominant and government close. Leaving aside women and the problematical category often called serfs, there were people in many societies who had virtually no rights. The conditions of slavery varied, but people sold away from their homes, for instance, however well-fed they might be, certainly look like what are generally considered slaves. Many societies made legal provision for freeing slaves, especially women in concubinage, but more seems to be written on religious teaching on the merits of manumitting slaves than on actual cases from this period.[11]

The traditional belief that European towns were nurseries of democracy, uniquely distinguished by their collective liberties, and that liberties fostered their growth, is only partly true: some large cities, including Paris, had no significant autonomy, while London's liberties were always subject to royal revision. The city-states of Italy and late medieval Germany were exceptional in Europe. Some towns along the Silk Road were intermittently nearly as independent, while many in other parts of Eurasia were in practice left to run much of their own affairs and pay their dues collectively. Some lived under single rulers while others were ruled by councils of leading citizens, merchants, craftsmen, neighbourhoods or quarters. Adherents of different religions, and even the employed (or unemployed) in many parts of Eurasia acted collectively in ways to which governments had to pay attention, and of which they sometimes made use.

---

11 Though S. D. Goitein and M. A. Friedman (eds.), *India Traders of the Middle Ages: Documents from the Cairo Geniza* (Leiden: Brill, 2008): 632–4, have an example.

Class conflict in Eurasia

However strong the impression that social and political hierarchies and solidarities were generally accepted, that can obviously not be the whole story, even in a very short survey. Leaving aside conflicts within the upper classes, which are well attested in written sources, there was plenty of scope in all but the smallest and poorest societies for conflicts of interest between landlords and peasants, employers and employed. Peasants recognized this, as appears from many records of their complaints and grievances and some of outright revolts. Common provocations were new demands for rents and services from landlords or for taxes and labour services from governments, and suffering caused by civil wars. It is difficult to be sure what protesters – or outright rebels – wanted, since virtually all the records are hostile: peasants may well have limited their demands to what they thought they might get. Nevertheless, however hard it is to know what people at the bottom of society thought, the evidence, such as it is, suggests that many of them wanted what was considered justice within the existing system, and appealed to lords and rulers for it according to its rules. The Zanj (East African slaves) who were used to cultivate salinized marshland in south Iraq rebelled twice in the seventh century, and then more successfully in the ninth. The independent government of the area that they maintained from 869 to 894 does not, however, seem to have been significantly different in structure from others of the time. There is apparently no evidence that its leader wanted to do more than improve conditions for the Zanj themselves. In fourteenth-century China the leader of a popular rebellion who made himself emperor then ruled in the normal way. In southern India in 1426–9, new taxes provoked resistance from groups relatively low down the caste hierarchy but not apparently challenging the hierarchy. In Europe the crucial demand was generally for the legal freedom that secured other rights.

Some millenarian movements suggest more revolutionary aspirations. The demands of some of the rebels in the English Peasants' Revolt of 1381 included the abolition of all lordship except that of the king, the distribution of church property, and the appointment of only one bishop. The rebels from Kent nevertheless said that they held 'with kynge Richarde and with the trewe communes'.[12] As for urban conflicts, most of those that are recorded seem to have been among employers rather than against them

12 *Anonimalle Chronicle, 1333 to 1381*, ed. V. H. Galbraith (Manchester University Press, 1970): 139.

as a class. The so-called 'craft revolution' of later medieval Europe did not empower the poor, though the Florentine revolt of 1378, known as the Tumulto dei Ciompi, came near to doing that and has therefore, like other urban revolts, often been seen as proto-democratic. The government it set up represented workers in the woollen industry and introduced important political and social reforms during the few years it lasted, but even so these did not really amount to a total overthrow of the traditional social hierarchy, which was, after all, supposed to provide justice and protection for the poor. Defective as the evidence is, it seems to show that many, if not most, of the most oppressed accepted the prevailing hierarchies – if only they were justly managed according to the officially accepted rules.

Africa and the Americas

Written sources are so scanty for the rest of the world that it must be discussed more briefly. Archaeology, historical linguistics, and conjectural history deduced from anthropologists' reports about traditions and genealogies all provide clues but these are chronologically uncertain and, while they may suggest the nature of past economies or social or political inequalities, they can say little about structures of authority or social and political ideas.

For sub-Saharan Africa, there are some written sources about Ethiopia and areas visited, settled, or mentioned by Muslims. These, combined with what modern scholars have deduced from other sorts of evidence, suggest varying patterns of hierarchy in different areas and periods. In most of the continent, agriculture, despite regional variations but all apparently without ploughs, was not productive enough to produce social and economic complexity as it did in Eurasia. Cattle may in some areas have done more, but trade was the greatest stimulus. Even before the arrival of Muslim traders, East African ports sustained traffic across the Red Sea and Indian Ocean. Jenne-jeno in Mali, though settled earlier, had probably become an exchange point for trans-Saharan trade by the ninth century. Evidence of iron- and other metalworking and of other crafts at lesser sites suggests more widespread links. Gold and salt may have been the first long-distance commodities, with ivory and slaves later. The masterpieces of sculpture known as the 'bronze' heads of Ife (Nigeria), presumably portraying rulers and other elite people, suggest a population big and rich enough to develop specialized skills. Fewer important urban sites have been found in the centre or south, apart from Great Zimbabwe, which is thought to have profited from trade along the

Limpopo. Elaborate terracing in Nyanga (Zimbabwe), with some stone buildings, suggests a well-organized society, though with little evidence of either towns or hierarchy.

Discussion of social and political structures in Africa is hindered by the customary vocabulary of tribes and chiefs. Europeans got their idea of tribes as groups united by both descent and culture from Roman history and the Bible, but did not use forms of the word to denote 'primitive' independent polities until the late eighteenth century. It was first applied then to indigenous North Americans and later to Africans.[13] People in the many small and economically relatively undifferentiated African societies and polities of our period may have identified themselves by their society or polity, perhaps using kinship terms. Given the malleability of polities, genealogies, and descent myths, these may well have functioned as metaphors, as they did elsewhere, but they do not seem to have generally coincided with modern tribal names. As for the word 'chief', which is often used to mean something less grand than king, prince, or emperor, it joins the other words for rulers already rejected in this chapter in favour of the undifferentiated 'ruler': some African 'chiefs' look like some early medieval European 'kings'.

Many small African societies, even without single rulers ('chiefs'), may have had enough inequality and enough coercive controls not to be unambiguously 'stateless'. Real equality (including women and servants, with no slaves) was probably rare, though on the rash premise that some African hunter-gatherers between 500 and 1500 CE lived like some in the twentieth century, they could have been pretty equal, living in small groups between which individuals (including women) could move at will.[14] Some societies before 1500, however, notably those with recorded or excavated towns or fortresses surrounded by humbler dwellings, had governments that are dignified by historians with the title of kingdoms (as grander than 'chiefdoms'). In some the rulers may have done little but take tribute, but in Ethiopia local government and tax collection were delegated to individuals or monasteries. Ibn Khaldun (d. 1406) says that tales of the wealth, generosity, and just rule of Mansa Musa of Mali, who made the pilgrimage to Mecca

---

13 John Iliffe, *A Modern History of Tanganyika* (Cambridge University Press, 1979): 8–10, 20, 323–4; Terence Ranger, 'The Invention of Tradition in Colonial Africa', in Eric Hobsbawm and T. Ranger (eds.), *The Invention of Tradition* (Cambridge University Press, 1983): 211–62; *Oxford English Dictionary*, 18. 503; Alain Rey (ed.), *Dictionnaire historique de la langue française*, 2 vols. (Paris: Robert, 1993): 2. 2166; Jacob and Wilhelm Grimm (eds.), *Deutsches Wörterbuch*, 16 vols. (Leipzig: Hirzel, 1854–1962): 10, col. 642–4.
14 James Woodburn, 'Egalitarian Societies', *Man*, New Series 17 (1982): 431–51.

in 1324–5, were still being told, along with stories of the tyranny of a later ruler of Mali, who had been deposed by another just one.[15] Mali, like the other polities which dominated West Africa before and after it, was rich enough to support a fairly complex hierarchy and perhaps a corresponding solidarity. Political solidarity was probably stronger in smaller societies, whether with or without 'chiefs', but saying more about them would involve conjectural extrapolation from Eurasia or from the findings of twentieth-century historical linguists and anthropologists.

In North America, Australasia, and the Pacific islands, most societies and polities were smallish and poorish, presumably with relatively low hierarchies. That does not mean that they were egalitarian in the sense that they believed in equality any more than did similar societies in Eurasia. While there were many such societies in Central and South America too, both areas in this period also developed some that were large, complex, and definitely hierarchical. In parts of both areas farmers, despite the absence of iron, ploughs, wheels, or draft animals, developed suitable crops and used terracing, irrigation, and drainage to produce enough food to support specialized crafts as well as large governmental hierarchies. Neither area had coinage but there were apparently markets in Central America where cacao beans and other commodities served as currency. How exchanges between regions and localities worked in South America is obscure, but it apparently went on, presumably by barter, and not only in the Inca state with its system of labour services and storage of food. Central America had writing, though little has survived except in the many (though only partially deciphered) inscriptions. Even though the Inca kingdom, like other South American societies, had no writing, it kept statistical records of tribute, population, and herds on knotted cords. Late in the period both the Aztec and Inca polities kept records that suggest elements of Weberian bureaucracy.

Solidarity is harder to deduce from the available evidence cited in secondary works, but the ceremonial visits of Inca rulers to different regions, dressed in appropriate local fashions, were obviously intended to promote it. So were the ceremonies depicted in temples and other monuments, as well as described by Spanish invaders, reluctant as one may be to envisage human sacrifice as promoting togetherness. War no doubt also strengthened the solidarity of polities here as in the Old World. Though myths of origin may reflect the expectations of Spanish writers, those that told about whole

---

15 J. F. P. Hopkins and N. Levtzion (ed. and trans.), *Corpus of Early Arabic Sources for West African History* (Cambridge University Press, 1981): 334–6.

peoples as they were at the time of telling, as well as about rulers or nobles, may reflect political solidarities as did those of Europe. There seems to be little information about councils and consultation, but there is no obvious reason to think that rulers were any more 'absolute' and free of obligation to take counsel than were rulers elsewhere. Anthropologists and archaeologists indeed stress reciprocal relations between rulers and subjects as forming an apparently distinctive system of ordering relationships. But though reciprocity is particularly obvious in the labour services and provision of food in the Inca polity, the principle of reciprocal, mutual duties of rulers and subjects seems to have underlain the government of Old World societies too. Rulers and others at the top of hierarchies everywhere were supposed to be just as well as generous.

Conclusion

This chapter has not been intended to suggest that everywhere was the same. There were many differences both between continents and between and inside the societies and polities within them. Many derived from geography and the different economies it imposed and were compounded by the ways that custom developed in different societies and parts of societies. Historians of individual societies have studied many of these customs, ranging from rules of kinship, marriage and gender relations, inheritance, and rights of property to rituals, games, and pastimes. What is suggested here is that some of the apparent differences, as well as some apparent similarities, derive from lack of comparison with other societies in the same period or from comparison only with stereotypes such as that contrasting Europe with the Rest. European history of the period needs comparisons as much, or more, than does non-European history: the search for the origins of the modern world distorts the history of Europe between 500 and 1500 as much as it distorts that of other areas. At the end of the period some – untypical – Europeans gained an increasing mastery of the sea so as to 'discover' areas they had not known, or had known only slightly or at second hand, although these 'discoveries' were, of course, already known to those who lived there. But these were not the most important of the changes that had taken place or were still taking place. Populations had risen and fallen, and people had been moving, whether in large or small groups, for short or long distances, though most often, for individuals, relatively short. People in many societies had been learning new technologies and new ideas from others or had developed them for themselves. New religions had spread, whether to whole populations or parts of them, and influenced the societies to which they went, though they perhaps influenced them less than their adherents thought and think. Looking at what changed and what did not may illuminate societies of the time more if one resists the temptation to look at what was to come and award marks to any country, region, or period.

This chapter suggests that assumptions about hierarchy and solidarity were apparently similar everywhere. Hierarchies came in different shapes and layers, but they all assumed political and social inequalities. The smaller and poorer societies were less unequal but not, apparently, because they embodied egalitarian ideas embracing women, children, servants or slaves, and foreigners. Religions that asserted the value of each individual do not seem to have applied the idea to the here and now. Political and social ideas and assumptions seem to have started, not with equal individuals in a state of nature but with given, existing communities. From this followed some kind of solidarity within polities, which was made easier by the acceptance of inequality and hierarchy. All human societies appear to have conflicts, between individuals and between groups. The richer and more complex societies of this period were liable to have more conflicts of interest between economic (and political) classes. Some of these were recognized, if implicitly, by requirements that rulers should protect the poor and weak against the rich and strong. Rulers were sometimes explicitly told to rule according to custom and after consultation with their great men. The necessity of advice and consent from people who represent the community has since 1789 often been taken to be a new progressive idea connected with equality and democracy in contrast to the absolutism of the Old Regime. But that does not make sense for the period studied here. Hierarchy seems to have imposed duties, however often unfulfilled, on the people at the top. Consultation was not at all incompatible with inequality and hierarchy.

Many people at the bottom of hierarchies must, at least intermittently, have felt the injustice of their lot, but it is improbable that they felt about their grievances in the way that they would have if, like white men in the last two centuries (and women and non-whites more recently) they had been told that they were equal citizens with equal rights to participate in politics. The tentative conclusion of this chapter is that societies between 500 and 1500 can be understood better if they are seen against a background of the political assumptions of their time, however little we may share them, not of ours.

FURTHER READING

Bailey, F. G. 'Decisions by Consensus in Councils and Committees; with Special Reference to Village and Local Government in India', in Michael Banton (ed.), *Political Systems and the Distribution of Power*. London: Tavistock Publications, 1965: 1–20.

Bush, M. L. (ed.) *Serfdom and Slavery: Studies in Legal Bondage*. London: Longman, 1996.

Cammarosano, Sandro. 'Social Mobility and the Middle Ages', *Continuity and Change*, 26 (2011): 367–404.

Chatterjee, Indrani and Richard M. Eaton (eds.), *Slavery and South Asian History*. Bloomington, IN: Indiana University Press, 2006.

Cohn, Samuel K., Jr. *Lust for Liberty: the Politics of Social Revolt in Medieval Europe, 1200–1425: Italy, France, and Flanders*. Cambridge, MA: Harvard University Press, 2006.

Di Cosmo, Nicola, ed. *Military Culture in Imperial China*. Cambridge, MA: Harvard University Press, 2009.

Fröhlich, Judith. *Rulers, Peasants and the Use of the Written Word in Medieval Japan*. Bern: Peter Lang, 2007.

Goody, Jack. *The Eurasian Miracle*. Cambridge: Polity Press, 2010.

Haldon, John, ed. *A Social History of Byzantium*. Oxford: Wiley-Blackwell, 2009.

Heitzman, James. *Gifts of Power: Lordship in an Early Indian State*. Oxford University Press, 1997.

Hodgson, Marshall G. S. *Rethinking World History*. Cambridge University Press, 1993.

Jeffcott, Colin. 'The Idea of Feudalism in China, and its Applicability to Song Society', in E. Leach and others (eds.), *Feudalism: Comparative Studies*. Sydney Association for Studies in Society and Culture, 1985: 155–74.

Kedar, Benjamin Z. 'Expulsion as an Issue of World History', *Journal of World History* 7 (1996): 165–80.

Kosambi, Damodar Dharmanand. *Introduction to the Study of Indian History*, revised 2nd edn. Bombay: Popular Prakashan, 1975.

Lapierre, Jean-William. *Vivre sans État? Essai sur le pouvoir politique et l'innovation sociale*. Paris: Éditions du Seuil, 1977.

Marlow, Louise. *Hierarchy and Egalitarianism in Islamic Thought*. Cambridge University Press, 1997.

Mundy, Martha. 'Ownership or Office? A Debate on Islamic Hanafite Jurisprudence Over the Nature of the Military "Fief," from the Mamluks to the Ottomans', in Alain Pottage and Martha Mundy (eds.), *Law, Anthropology, and the Constitution of the Social*. Cambridge University Press, 2004: 142–65.

O'Leary, Brendan. *The Asiatic Mode of Production*. Oxford University Press, 1989.

Pomeranz, Kenneth. *The Great Divergence: China, Europe, and the Making of the Modern World Economy*. Princeton University Press, 2000.

Popovic, Alexandre. *The Revolt of the African Slaves in Iraq in the Third/Ninth Century*, trans. Léon King. Princeton, NJ: Markus Wiener Publishers, 1998.

Reynolds, Susan. *Fiefs and Vassals: The Medieval Evidence Reinterpreted*. Oxford: Clarendon Press, 1994.

'The History of the Idea of Incorporation or Legal Personality: A Case of Fallacious Teleology', in Susan Reynolds, *Ideas and Solidarities of the Medieval Laity: England and Western Europe*. Aldershot: Variorum, 1995, Study vi.

Kingdoms and Communities in Western Europe, 900–1300, 2nd edn. Oxford: Clarendon Press, 1997.

The Middle Ages without Feudalism. Aldershot: Variorum, 2012, Studies V, XV, VI.

Richards, John F., ed. *Kingship and Authority in South Asia*. New Delhi: Oxford University Press, 1998.

Schoenbrun, David Lee. *A Green Place, a Good Place: Agrarian Change, Gender, and Social Identity in the Great Lakes Region to the Fifteenth Century*. Portsmouth, NH: Heinemann, 1998.

Sing, Hira. 'Classifying Non-European, Pre-Colonial Social Formations: More Than a Quarrel Over a Name', *Journal of Peasant Studies* 20 (1993): 317–47.

Twitchett, Denis. 'The Composition of the T'ang Ruling Class: New Evidence from Tunhuang', in Arthur F. Wright and Denis Twitchett (eds.), *Perspectives on the T'ang*. New Haven and London: Yale University Press, 1973: 47–85.

Veluthat, Kesavan. 'Land Rights and Social Stratification', in Upinder Singh (ed.), *Rethinking Early Medieval India: A Reader*. New Delhi: Oxford University Press, 2011: 83–99.

Watts, John. *The Making of Polities*. Cambridge University Press, 2009.

Wickham, Chris. *Framing the Middle Ages: Europe and the Mediterranean 400–800*. Oxford University Press, 2005.

Wood, Ian N. *The Priest, the Temple and the Moon in the Eighth Century*. Brixworth: Friends of All Saints' Church, 2008.

Zuidema, R. Tom. *Inca Civilization in Cuzco*. Trans. Jean-Jacques Decoster. Austin, TX: University of Texas Press, 1986.

5

Educational institutions

LINDA WALTON

Simply defined, "education" means the transmission of learning both within and across generations. As David Christian has argued, collective learning and the ability to reproduce it over generations distinguish humans from other species.[1] Collective learning encompasses a wide range of experience transmitted in both oral and written forms, as well as through practice. In the broadest sense, an "institution" is a practice that becomes regularized as a means to accomplish a task. From this perspective, educational institutions are "customary practices designed to transmit collective learning." Educational institutions thus include not only schools where formal instruction takes place but also informal patterns of learning. As sites where children learned domestic skills, crafts, or trade, the family and household were primary educational institutions throughout the world. Beyond the family and household, organized educational activities created special groups whose particular skills – including, but not limited to, literacy – distinguished them from the rest of society. For example, like universities that provided specialized training and professional credentials, trade and craft apprenticeships exchanged labor for instruction and professional licensure. Recognizing the broad range of activities and purposes subsumed under the topic of "educational institutions," this chapter will focus primarily on institutions of higher education from the perspective of the following questions: What kind of knowledge is valued, and how is it organized and transmitted? What is the relationship of organized knowledge to the state, and how does it control and regulate education? Finally, to what degree does access to knowledge through educational institutions determine social status or political power?

Achieving a fully global perspective on educational institutions between 500 and 1500 is problematic because of the profound imbalance among

---

1 David Christian, "World History in Context," *Journal of World History* 14.4 (Dec., 2003): 445–6.

sources, both primary and secondary. There are abundant materials on the rise of the European university, and a relatively lengthy tradition of scholarship built on them. There are also plentiful sources on schools and the examination system in China, and by extension for parts of East Asia heavily influenced by China, especially Korea and Vietnam. Records of Buddhist monastic schools document their spread throughout South, East, and Southeast Asia, and the role they played in secular, as well as religious, education. Similarly, there are copious resources for regions of the world where Islam took root, because the transmission of religious knowledge was of vital importance in Islamic societies. Beyond Islamic Africa, however, there is little evidence of formal educational institutions in pre-colonial times on that continent. Apart from Spanish accounts of Aztec schools, evidence of formal educational institutions in the Americas before 1500 is also sparse.

Despite varying historical experiences and uneven sources, however, it is nonetheless possible to establish a globally inclusive analytical framework. This chapter demonstrates that the organization and transmission of knowledge reflect not only diverse cultural values and traditions but also differing relationships between states, which both utilized and controlled knowledge, and also relationships among elites, whose status depended on their access to knowledge and role in its transmission.

During this period, the most potent and ubiquitous form of knowledge was religious. Buddhism, Christianity, and Islam all spawned institutions to spread their teachings. As the religions expanded across Afro-Eurasia, these institutions were increasingly harnessed to the goals of states and empires as well as to the aspirations of elites. In regions of the globe not yet penetrated by any of the world religions, such as sub-Saharan Africa and the Americas, formal educational institutions sanctioned by religion under the control of priestly elites also served the needs of states. In China, interdependence between state and elite was grounded in the indigenous political philosophy of Confucianism, which contributed to the creation of one of the world's most distinctive and lasting educational institutions: the civil service examination system.

Confucianism and educational institutions in East Asia

Confucian thinkers regarded education as essential to the cultivation of human nature, and envisioned the ideal society as one governed by scholars. Education as a marker of both status and power was institutionalized in the civil service examination system, which was controlled by the state. Thus access to knowledge determined social status and political power, defining the scholar–official elite of imperial China. Both Confucian ideas and the examination system were also adopted by emerging states on the Korean peninsula, in the Japanese archipelago, and in Vietnam.

China

Systematic efforts to recruit and select officials by means of examinations date from the Tang dynasty (618–907). Tang rulers adopted the examination system to control powerful aristocratic clans, using the Confucian ideal of government by scholars to justify selection for office through examinations. The examination system subverted hereditary privilege by creating a state-controlled process to determine eligibility for court ranks and offices. Tang examinations awarded degrees based on mastery of the Confucian classical tradition, plus poetry and policy debates. The Tang Imperial University provided a scholarly resource for the government and a place for prospective bureaucrats to be trained. Beyond the capital, education took place largely through private tutoring, or in Buddhist monastic institutions (see below).

Throughout the Tang period only members of the aristocracy had the wealth and leisure to acquire the education necessary to pass the examinations. In the subsequent Song dynasty (960–1279), however, the examinations did foster significant social change. In addition to the Imperial University, the government supported schools throughout the empire with land endowments and bequests of woodblock-printed editions of the Confucian classics. Social mobility increased as more people had access to education through government schools, clan or lineage schools, and as commercial printers provided cheap copies of texts. The Song instituted a three-tiered examination system: prefectural, departmental (in the capital), and palace. Students began by registering in their native places, where their family pedigrees were scrutinized. If they then succeeded in passing the prefectural examination, they went on to the departmental examination, and finally, the palace examination, conducted personally by the emperor to determine the ranking of candidates for appointment to high offices. Examination content changed periodically with differing emphases on classics, history, poetry, and policy.

By the latter part of the Song, changes in Confucianism began to affect the examination system. In the eleventh century, Neo-Confucian thinkers turned their attention to the relationship between humans and the cosmos, expanding classical Confucian concern with good government to a new metaphysical realm. Zhu Xi (1130–1200) sought to create a synthesis of these interpretations of the classics and promoted his ideas of moral self-cultivation through teaching in private academies, which flourished during the Southern Song (1127–1279). Academy founders criticized the examinations as a perversion of the true purpose of education because students studied only for success in the examinations rather than for self-cultivation. In the end, however, academies succumbed to the same impulse of examination preparation, although they did promote the notion that the literati elite – whether or not they succeeded in passing the examinations – occupied a cultural niche that set them apart from commoners.

Despite the imposition of foreign rule in the Mongol Yuan dynasty (1271–1368), there was a high degree of continuity in educational institutions. Yuan rulers eventually restored the examination system in 1315, adopting ethnic quotas to retain political control. Neo-Confucian interpretations were adopted as orthodoxy by the Yuan government, and Zhu Xi's teachings became the foundation of both school curriculum and examination content. With the restoration of native Chinese rule in the Ming dynasty (1368–1644), both examinations and schools were promoted by the state. Community schools increasingly provided access to education for a wider social range of students. Eventually, achieving success at even the first level of the examinations awarded a degree that could be used to advance a career – in teaching or the lower levels of officialdom – without passing the higher levels of the examinations. By 1500, mid-way through the Ming, the examination system was thoroughly enmeshed in Chinese society, politics, and culture, and virtually all educational institutions were absorbed with teaching for examination success, remote though an individual's chances to achieve a degree might have been.

Korea

Confucian ideas spread to the Korean peninsula well before the mid-seventh century unification by Silla. Silla's state structure was modeled on that of Tang China, and although Buddhism was dominant, a Confucian academy for the education of officials was established in the capital. A state examination system was introduced briefly in the late eighth century, but soon abandoned. Although Buddhism continued to be influential during the succeeding Koryŏ dynasty (918–1392), Confucianism was promoted by the state. A Chinese-style examination system established to recruit government officials included poetry along with Confucian texts.[2] By the second half of the eleventh century, private schools flourished along with state-sponsored schools for the preparation of candidates.[3]

Koryŏ had close relations with contemporary Song China, and after the disruption of the Mongol conquest, integration into the Mongol Empire brought Korean Confucians into closer contact with intellectual developments in Yuan China, especially Neo-Confucianism. The Chosŏn dynasty (1392–1897) restored native control of the peninsula and heavily promoted Neo-Confucianism as state ideology in both schools and the examinations. Reflecting deeply rooted tribal traditions, access to the examination system was restricted by social status: only members of the *yangban* (hereditary civil and military official families) elite were formally eligible.

Japan

As in Korea, the tribal foundations of aristocratic society shaped the reception of Chinese ideas and educational institutions in Japan. Chinese influence on the Japanese archipelago became substantial in the seventh century and peaked during the Nara period (712–784) with the emergence of a centralized state. Japan's rulers set forth a comprehensive plan for an educational system, including a central university, and civil service examinations. Examination content drew on the Confucian classics, with emphasis on philosophy and history. The model of Confucian education and the examination system borrowed from Tang China were modified to suit the needs of state and society in eighth-century Japan. Admission to the university was determined primarily by the father's rank.[4] Examinations were ancillary to hereditary privilege, which assigned court rank according to ancestry, as in Tang China. Scions of the aristocracy therefore did not flock to the university, but lower-ranking courtiers and sons of provincial officials did, since they could elevate their status by performing well in the examinations. Unlike China, however, the examination system did not survive long enough to produce social change.

The Heian period (794–1185) saw the rise of an aristocratic court culture relatively isolated from Chinese influence, and by the latter part of the Heian period, the university and examination system existed in name only. As

2 Peter H. Lee, *A History of Korean Literature* (Cambridge University Press, 2003): 1.
3 Martina Deuchler, *The Confucian Transformation of Korea: A Study of Society and Ideology* (Cambridge, MA: Council on East Asian Studies, Harvard University Press, 1992): 15.
4 Robert Borgen, *Sugawara no Michizane and the Early Heian Court* (Cambridge, MA: Council on East Asian Studies, Harvard University Press, 1986): 72–3.

warriors expanded their role in society, Confucian-based education fell even more out of favor in the Kamakura (1185–1333) and Ashikaga periods (1336–1573), when Buddhist monastic institutions were the main repositories of learning.

Vietnam

Unlike both Korea and Japan, which selectively adopted and adapted Chinese institutions, Vietnam's incorporation into the Chinese Empire between the second century BCE and the tenth century CE brought a millennium of direct and sustained transmission of Chinese culture into the area, along with a degree of political unification. The Sino–Vietnamese state centered on the Red River Delta, where northern officials absorbed local leaders into the imperial hierarchy and, aided by Chinese immigrants, introduced Chinese-style schools. Once independent of Chinese control in the tenth century, Dai Viet ("Great Viet") nonetheless implemented a Chinese-style civil service examination, although students were tested on their knowledge of Buddhism and Daoism as well as Confucianism. Buddhism remained influential, and Buddhist temples provided monastic education. But Confucian models became more prominent as economic growth favored private landowners with modest wealth who sought opportunities for government office through education for the civil service examinations. Educated men in Dai Viet became familiar with Neo-Confucianism, transmitted through both Chinese immigration and the circulation of texts.[5]

Invasion by Ming China (1407–27) intensified Chinese influence, and Confucian schools were founded for the first time in the countryside. Neo-Confucian ideas were also transmitted and promoted in contrast to the classical Confucianism previously favored by Dai Viet literati.[6] After the expulsion of the Ming, key features of Ming administration were retained, including schools. Dai Viet's first orthodox Chinese-style examinations began in the 1440s, and Neo-Confucianism prevailed as officially sanctioned state ideology. Examinations became the chief means of recruitment for government offices, and by 1500 as many as 30,000 men took the triennial regional examinations. Literacy became a necessary qualification for holding local offices and for economic benefits such as exemption from obligatory unpaid labor.

---

5 Victor Lieberman, *Strange Parallels: Southeast Asia in Global Context, c. 800–1830* (New York: Cambridge University Press, 2003): 357–62.

6 John K. Whitmore, "Literati Culture and Integration in Dai Viet, c. 1430–1840," *Modern Asian Studies* 31.3 (1997): 666.

Buddhism and educational institutions in Asia

Across East Asia Confucianism placed supreme value on humanistic learning, cultivated through study of the Confucian classics as training for government officials. Between 500 and 1500, however, China, Korea, Japan, and Vietnam also belonged to a Buddhist world. Although Buddhism never challenged state power in East Asia, Buddhist values did compete with Confucian ones, and Buddhist monastic institutions complemented Confucian schools. Training monks and nuns to read *sutras* (scriptures) and transmit teachings to lay believers required substantial investment in education. Beginning with its place of origin in the Himalayas, everywhere Buddhism took root, monastic schools were established that provided both religious instruction and community educational resources.

South Asia

Organized education in South Asia came with the Buddhist and Jain reform movements that arose in the sixth century BCE on the northern fringes of the Gangetic plain and in the foothills of the Himalayas. In contrast to the dominant Vedic religion, whose teachings of the Vedas and other texts were orally transmitted from teacher to student, these new monastic religions relied on both oral and written transmission of their teachings in the institutional environment of monastic communities.[7]

Building on a monastic foundation, the most famous Buddhist university was founded at Nalanda in the mid-fifth to mid-sixth century and flourished until the Muslim conquest in the early thirteenth century (see Figure 5.1). Patrons of Buddhism such as the emperor Harsha (r. 606–47) supported Nalanda with endowments, and tax revenues were allocated to the support of the university and its several thousand students and teachers, who lived in residential colleges. Nalanda offered instruction not only in Mahayana Buddhism, but in other Buddhist sects as well, along with the Vedas, philosophy, and secular sciences such as logic, Sanskrit grammar, and medicine. Large libraries endowed by rulers and other wealthy patrons at this and other Buddhist universities housed comprehensive collections of both religious and secular materials. These institutions attracted many students from abroad, including Tibet, China, Korea, and Japan.

---

7 Hartmut Scharfe, *Education in Ancient India* (Leiden: Brill, 2002). Information on Jain education is relatively sparse and will not be addressed here.

Figure 5.1 Ruins of Buddhist university at Nalanda (photograph by Tansen Sen)

The institutionalization of Vedic education was likely influenced by the Buddhist model of monastic schools attached to temples. Vedic colleges attached to many temples were supported by rulers who allocated tax income from farming villages and also by wealthy donors. Emphasis on oral instruction and the primacy of the teacher–student relationship, however, meant that upper-caste Brahmins continued to control Vedic education. But with the thirteenth-century spread of the *bhakti* movement of personal devotion that rejected caste distinctions, support for Brahmin-led Vedic institutions of learning decreased and *bhakti* temples assumed many of the same educational functions for students from a broader social background.

Both Buddhist and Vedic educational institutions served the needs of rulers by training students in secular skills useful to the administration of states and empires in South Asia. Rulers may have patronized these institutions as devotional acts, but there were practical motives behind their support as well. Imperial patronage of Buddhist monastic institutions likewise characterized the relationship between state, religion, and education in East Asia.

East Asia

By 500, Buddhism was well established in China, and institutions of Buddhist education began to flourish. As elsewhere, Buddhist education focused on the *sangha*, the community of monks and nuns. In separate men's and women's houses, novices were trained in Buddhist texts, in liturgy, and in the regulations of monastic life. Buddhist temples and monasteries also provided lay educational resources by teaching basic literacy as well as preaching Buddhism; Confucian texts were part of monastic education along with Buddhist *sutras*.[8] Buddhist priests joined Confucian literati as part of the educated elite. Clerical examinations in scriptural exegesis, modeled on the civil service examinations, were introduced in the Tang both to control the size of the *sangha* and to legitimize the clergy as a body of religious specialists.

Buddhism also had an important influence on education because of its role in the development of printing. Monasteries maintained manuscript libraries used by clerics, but woodblock printing made it possible to expand the number of scripture copies available and thus made Buddhist teachings accessible to a wider literate audience. The desire of Buddhists to spread their beliefs inspired the technology that enabled the teachings of the Buddha to be transmitted more widely. Buddhism's relationship to printing was similar to that of Protestant Christianity, as printing allowed the ideas of Martin Luther and other reformers to spread faster and farther than would have been possible through oral and manuscript transmission alone.

By the eleventh century, the Chan sect began to influence Buddhist education in China. The primary purpose of Chan education was to enable the practitioner to achieve an awakening through individual effort, using techniques such as meditation.[9] Chan followers paid less attention to doctrinal study of the *sutras* and more to the practices and texts that would help them become enlightened. This led to the development of particular genres of texts: "recorded sayings," "lamp records," and "pure rules" (monastic codes). Both "recorded sayings" and "lamp records" were textual means to convey the teachings and enlightenment experiences of Chan masters to their disciples over generations. Monastic codes were designed to provide clear

---

8 Erik Zürcher, "Buddhism and Education in T'ang Times," in Wm. T. de Bary and John W. Chaffee (eds.), *Neo-Confucian Education: The Formative Stage* (Berkeley: University of California Press, 1989): 19–56.

9 Yü Chün-fang, "Ch'an Education in the Sung: Ideals and Procedures," in de Bary and Chaffee, *Neo-Confucian Education*, 60.

guidelines for community life that would also support monks in their quest for enlightenment.

The ideals of Chan education in Song China were transmitted to Korea and Japan, where they became the foundation of Son and Zen monastic education. In Kamakura Japan, Zen monasteries became both repositories of learning akin to the monasteries of medieval Europe and arms of the government. During the Ashikaga period, Buddhist monasteries continued as the primary site of scholarly endeavors and transmission of both Buddhist and Confucian ideas.

Southeast Asia

Southeast Asia between 500 and 1500 presents a dizzying array of different cultures, peoples, and states, but all were influenced by Buddhism, and educational institutions were primarily Buddhist. The transmission of Theravada Buddhism to the kingdom of Pagan (*c.* 950–1300) marked the beginning of monastic education there. Monastic libraries preserved manuscript collections, and the copying of manuscripts was a monastic responsibility. In addition to the education of monks and nuns, lay believers received instruction during obligatory short-term stays in monasteries.[10] Burmese was the language of instruction, but both Sanskrit and Pali were taught for reading Buddhist texts. Indian monks from Nalanda introduced both Mahayana Buddhism and Sanskrit manuscripts on medicine, astrology, and alchemy.

As in Pagan, in the Khmer Empire (*c.* 800–*c.* 1440) Buddhist monasteries monopolized education, despite the prominence of Hinduism along with Buddhism. Monks frequently traveled in their studies. In the thirteenth century, and then in greater numbers from the mid-fourteenth to the sixteenth centuries, Tai, Burmese, Mon, and Khmer monks studied at monasteries across Southeast Asia and in Sri Lanka, spreading Buddhist teachings to new audiences throughout the region.[11] Chiang Mai, the ancient capital of the northern Tai kingdom of Lan Na, was the center of Buddhist education in the region by the fifteenth century.[12] Chiang Mai's temple Wat Suan Dok was home to a major secondary school and monastic university built in 1371.

10 U Sein Maung Oo, "The Development of Burmese Writing and Monastic Education in the Pagan Period," in Yoshiaki Ishizawa and Yasushi Kono (eds.), *Study on Pagan: Research Report* (Rangoon and Tokyo: Institute of Asian Cultures, Sophia University, 1989): 138–44.

11 Lieberman, *Strange Parallels*, 260.

12 Justin McDaniel, *Gathering Leaves and Lifting Words: Histories of Buddhist Monastic Education in Laos and Thailand* (Seattle: University of Washington Press, 2008): 69–75.

Founded in 1454, Wat Phra Singh housed a Buddha image that drew pilgrims from throughout Southeast Asia, and after the building of its monastic library in 1488, it was a center for manuscript preservation and copying.

In both South and Southeast Asia, Buddhism was a powerful stimulus to the development of educational institutions. Initially dedicated to religious training, Buddhist monastic schools also instructed students in basic literacy and secular learning that served the educational needs of rulers of states and empires. In East Asia, Buddhist monastic institutions supplemented Confucian education, which imperial rulers encouraged and supported as training for government officials.

Christianity and the rise of the European university

Like Buddhist monastic institutions in Asia, Christian monasteries nurtured the earliest stages of institutional education in Europe in the era after the collapse of the Roman Empire in the West. The monastic movement in the Latin West flowered with the founding of Monte Cassino by St Benedict of Nursia (c. 480–544) in 529 and his writing of the *Rule of St Benedict*, which led to the institutionalization of reading and education in monasteries. Christian monasteries spread throughout the former Roman provinces, and rulers such as Charlemagne (r. 768–814) sought ways to utilize the educational resources of monasteries in the service of the state. In addition to his court school at Aachen, Charlemagne ordered all monasteries and cathedrals to have schools that would provide free basic education for any boy who could demonstrate his academic abilities. Although not all did, this was the origin of cathedral schools. Charlemagne's support of education was part of a general revival of Latin learning that later scholars termed the "Carolingian Renaissance."

In contrast to the revival of Latin learning in the Carolingian era, the later "Twelfth-Century Renaissance" (c. 1060s–1160s) was precipitated by an influx of new knowledge, partly through Italy and Sicily, but chiefly through the Iberian peninsula. Translations from Arabic and Greek into Latin allowed European scholars to read hitherto unknown works of Plato, Aristotle, Euclid, Galen and Ptolemy, while the rediscovery of Emperor Justinian's *Digest* paved the way for the renewal of Roman jurisprudence. These new bodies of knowledge profoundly altered the educational landscape of medieval Europe and set the stage for the rise of universities.[13]

13 Hunt Janin, *The University in Medieval Life, 1179–1499* (Jefferson, NC and London: McFarland and Company, 2008).

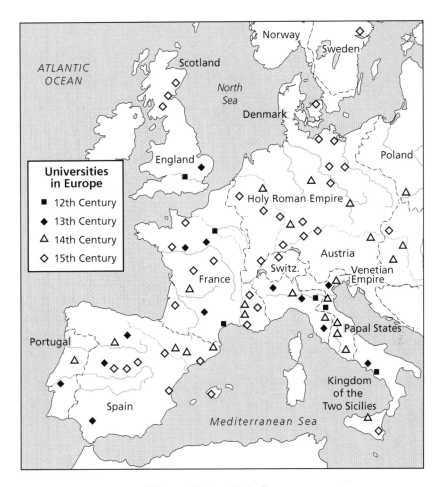

Map 5.1. Universities in Europe

Changes in the European economy and society were equally important to the development of universities (see Map 5.1). A more commercialized economy and larger urban concentrations of population provided greater numbers of students. The medieval university originated in associations of students, or of students and teachers, which were first granted special rights and privileges by both civil and ecclesiastical authorities in the thirteenth century. Only in 1215 was the term *universitas* used for the first time to describe an assembly of teachers and scholars gathered to hear or to read new work. Universities increased educational opportunities for those seeking professional employment in the ecclesiastical or government realms, or as lawyers or physicians.

By the early thirteenth century, there were three major universities in Europe: Bologna, known for the study of both civil and canon (church) law; Paris, where logic, philosophy, and speculative theology reigned; and Oxford, which became a leader in mathematics and the natural sciences. Other universities were gradually established elsewhere in Europe, while in the Byzantine world, a tradition of higher secular and religious education under the aegis of the Eastern Orthodox Church and state in Constantinople fell prey to political turmoil and fragmentation in the thirteenth and four-teenth centuries.[14]

The student bodies at Bologna and Paris were international, organized into "nations" based on their differing origins (for example, English in Paris, German in Bologna).[15] In Italy, most students were laymen, while in north-western Europe almost all were nominally clerics, although not ordained priests. Prospective university students would have to demonstrate a substantial command of Latin. If they had not learned Latin through a cathedral school and their families were prosperous enough, young men could be educated at home with a tutor. Students matriculated through interviews with prospective masters. For the best students, an advanced degree in theology or canon law was the gateway to the upper levels of the church in northern Europe. A degree in civil law or medicine was also a means of advancement. Because women could not become clerics under Church law, it was consequently impossible for them to become university students, but some women did become highly educated as nuns or as daughters of wealthy families with access to tutors.

Clerical status placed university students under the legal authority of the church, but there were economic advantages to clerical status: as clerics, students qualified for benefices (clerical positions that received revenues from endowments). Clashes sometimes erupted between students, who were legally protected by their status as clerics, and civil authorities.

The relationship between the church and universities was also problematic at times. In 1231, for example, a papal bull supported the right of universities to form their own corporate statutes and to strike, which weakened church

14 C. N. Constantinides, *Higher Education in Byzantium in the Thirteenth and Early Four-teenth Centuries, 1204–Ca.1310* (Nicosia: Cyprus Research Centre, 1982).

15 Olaf Pedersen, *The First Universities: Studium Generale and the Origins of University Education in Europe* (Cambridge University Press, 1997).

authorities such as bishops and chancellors. Chancellors were the *ex-officio* directors of teaching in cathedral schools, and they originally had the privilege of conferring the *licentia docendi* (license to teach), which was the first form of university degree. The backing of the pope strengthened the position of the university faculty over the chancellor with regard to the conferral of degrees, which they did after putting candidates through a grueling examination.[16]

Universities provided a structure for faculties to govern their own affairs through elected academic officials. There were initially no university buildings, so classes were held in rented rooms, and larger gatherings could be held in church buildings. Students who were members of religious orders sometimes lived in special houses established by their order; the earliest of these were set up in the 1220s for the use of students in the Franciscan or Dominican orders. Students not in monastic orders initially lodged in rented rooms or hostels. Residential colleges where lay students lived together and studied under a master began to be established, supported by pious foundations through endowments of land, properties, or rents. The first university college was the Sorbonne, founded in 1257, and others followed shortly at Oxford and later elsewhere.[17]

The university curriculum consisted of the seven *artes liberales*: the *trivium* (grammar, rhetoric, dialectical reasoning) and *quadrivium* (music, astronomy, geometry, and arithmetic), followed by one of three advanced subjects (medicine, law, theology). The final examination was given in a student's fourth year, on the threshold of being promoted to *baccalaureus* ("garlanded with laurels"). Masters taught either by lecturing or by means of oral disputation, in which students played an active role in debate. Peter Abelard's *Sic et Non* was the basis for the dialectic method of teaching and the *Summa Theologiae* of Thomas Aquinas provided a template for the question–response pedagogy. These became the foundation of Scholasticism, a rigorous method of learning based on dialectical reasoning as developed by Aristotle (thesis – antithesis – synthesis). Reason was the means by which human beings expressed their faith in the rational order of God's creation and their confidence that it was accessible to human understanding. Scholasticism expanded beyond theology into many other fields, inspiring the application of its method to all knowledge, not just to proving the Christian faith.

16 Walter Rüegg, "Themes," in Hilde de Ridder-Symoens (ed.), *A History of the University in Europe* (Cambridge University Press, 1997 [1992]).
17 Janin, *The University in Medieval Life*, 33.

The *Yeshiva* and education in Judaism

In Judaism study was an act of devotion, and the primary purpose of education was the religious and ethical training of the individual as part of the Jewish community. In theory all Jews were supposed to study the Torah – that is, the Pentateuch or the Five Books of Moses – and at higher levels of education, men were trained in the Talmud, the record of rabbinic discussions of law, ethics, customs, and history. Those who mastered this training became rabbis, or teachers, who held high status in their communities both as repositories of knowledge and as transmitters of learning to others.

Between the Arab conquests in the seventh century, when most Jewish communities lived within the framework of the Islamic realm, and the mid-eleventh century, Jews experienced a religious and cultural renaissance often referred to as the "Gaonic period" (589–1038). The Gaon was the spiritual and academic head of the *yeshiva*, or academy, where scholars gathered to expound and discuss the Torah and the Talmud and to issue authoritative rulings (*responsa*) concerning Jewish law.[18] The Babylonian (in Sura and Pumbeditha along the Euphrates River, later in Baghdad) and the Palestinian (in Jerusalem, then Tyre) *yeshivas* were the centers of Jewish intellectual and religious life in this period. The geographical division corresponded to the production of two pre-Islamic collections of rabbinic discussions on Jewish religion and law, the Babylonian Talmud and the Palestinian Talmud, which then became the main object of study in Jewish schools. The Gaon had the power to levy taxes to support the *yeshiva*, to appoint communal officers, and to respond to both theological and secular questions submitted to the academy from throughout the Jewish diaspora.[19] The exchange of questions and responses with the Gaon were a kind of "correspondence education" in which the Gaon served as an authoritative source of knowledge about Jewish tradition and learning for Jews scattered across Afro-Eurasia.

After the Gaonic period, higher learning continued in local *yeshivas* of various countries. The Jews of northern France, Germany, and England were increasingly subject to persecution by Christian rulers, beginning at the time of the First Crusade (1096). Despite this, Franco–German Jewry produced a corpus of Talmudic and *halakhic* (pertaining to the entire body of religious

18 S. D. Goitein, *A Mediterranean Society, II: The Community* (Berkeley: University of California Press, 1971): 171–211. This is the entire section in which Goitein discusses education, which is highly valuable for those who wish to learn more on the subject.

19 A. Blinderman, "Medieval Correspondence Education: The Responsa of the Gaonate," *History of Education Quarterly* 9.4 (1969): 472.

law) commentaries, represented by the genre known as *tosafot*, which revolutionized the study of rabbinic literature. The shift to Talmud commentators (Tosafists) in northern *yeshivas* roughly corresponded to the transition from monastic schools to cathedral schools in the Christian world, from rote learning of religious texts to a logical analytical approach.[20]

Despite the injunction to all Jews to study the Torah, women were not required to learn Hebrew since they were prohibited from actively participating in public worship. Study of the Torah by women was even proscribed by some medieval rabbis because of the fear that literacy would lead to immorality.[21] As in other societies, however, there is evidence that at least some Jewish women were either teachers or regarded as highly learned. A woman teacher in twelfth-century Cairo was unwilling to abandon her successful career at her husband's behest,[22] while the daughter of the Babylonian Gaon in twelfth-century Baghdad taught in her father's famous *yeshiva*.[23] A sixteenth-century rabbi commented that "many Jewesses in South Germany were, in the beginning of the fifteenth century, noted for their learning ... These women entered into learned discussions with famous rabbis, and the opinions of 'Lady Rabbinists' were cited often with approval."[24]

Mosques and madrasas in the medieval Muslim world

Like their Jewish brethren, Muslims were "People of the Book" for whom the pursuit of learning required of all believers meant the study of sacred texts, coupled with adherence to codes of ethical conduct. Education was essential to religious identity, which transcended ethnic and cultural identities. Oral transmission of religious teachings was as important as the written texts themselves, and both required knowledge of Arabic. As Islam spread with the expansion of the caliphate in the seventh and eighth centuries,

20 Ephraim Kanarfogel, *Jewish Education and Society in the High Middle Ages* (Detroit, MI: Wayne State University Press, 1992): 70–1.
21 Avraham Grossman, trans. Jonathan Chipman, *Pious and Rebellious: Jewish Women in Medieval Europe* (Waltham, MA: Brandeis University Press, 2004): 154–7; 160–2.
22 Renee Levine Melammed, "He Said, She Said: A Woman Teacher in Twelfth-Century Cairo," *AJS Review* 22.1 (1997): 19–35; cf. Goitein, *A Mediterranean Society* II. 185. (Goitein does not deal here with this case, but with women teachers in general.)
23 Grossman, *Pious and Rebellious,* 162.
24 William Chomsky, "Jewish Education in the Medieval Period," *Gratz College Annual of Jewish Studies* 4 (1975): 37.

training in basic Arabic literacy was needed for many people to adopt the new religion. Instruction was offered in "places of writing" adjacent to mosques, in tents, or even out in the open. The curriculum included memorization and recitation of the Quran, reading, writing, and arithmetic, along with instruction in prayer and other religious duties. Boys were given a basic education by lower-level teachers, and for more advanced learning, the task of the *ulama* (Muslim clerics) was to instill knowledge of the sacred text and to interpret it as a guide to moral and ethical behavior. Based on their interpretation of collected opinions, specialists in jurisprudence issued decisions rendering judgments on legal questions, much as the Jewish Gaons.

The mosque was the primary site of higher education in early Islam, a place of teaching as well as worship. Students gathered in study circles around scholars with specialized knowledge of the Quran and other disciplines, including *hadith* (reports of the Prophet's exemplary statements and actions), law, theology, Arabic language and literature, and even non-Islamic sciences (logic, medicine). Students who aspired to become teachers themselves sought learning from a variety of the leading scholars of the time. Recognition as a teacher was eventually formalized in the written *ijaza*, which made official a student's authority to transmit books from his teacher. Hostels for students were sometimes attached to mosques and by the tenth century, the fusion of mosque and hostel produced the madrasa (place of study), a new type of formal educational institution. Although the earliest madrasas were probably in Khurasan (Iran), the model madrasa was the Nizamiyya, built in 1065 by the Seljuk vizier Nizam al-Mulk in Baghdad. Subsequently, madrasas were constructed throughout the Muslim world.

As in the mosque, the curriculum of the madrasa was based on the Quran and associated disciplines, with a special emphasis on law and its subdisciplines. Students were required to attend daily classes and Quran recitation sessions, and to devote themselves fully to study. Memorization and recitation were essential to train students for disputations, in which they were expected to cite texts verbatim. A madrasa typically specialized in one or more of the four schools of Islamic law, and in addition to legal texts, the curriculum might include Quran exegesis, Arabic language and grammar, philosophy, theology, mathematics, astronomy, medicine, and even Sufism (Islamic mysticism).[25] Teaching positions at madrasas were coveted appointments that awarded both salaries and prestige.

---

25 Wadad Kadi, "Education in Islam: Myths and Truths," *Comparative Education Review* 50, 3 (2006): 311–24.

Madrasas were usually not supported by governments, even though high-ranking officials often established them. A madrasa was funded by an endowment (*waqf*) provided by a patron who would then exercise control over it.[26] Madrasa patrons were influential people in power, such as viziers or caliphs, and wealthy philanthropists. Endowments might include shops, mills, houses, land, or even entire villages. The proceeds from these endowments covered the expenses of the madrasas, including faculty salaries and student stipends. Madrasas often became part of an educational–charitable complex that could include a mosque, a hospital, and even a mausoleum. The Ashrafiyya, constructed and endowed by Sultan al-Ashraf Barsbay around 1425, was a major educational complex in late medieval Cairo. It incorporated halls for each of the four schools of Sunni law, rooms for students, a public fountain, and a primary school, as well as a tomb chamber for the founder's family, and a minaret marking it as a place of public worship. Instructional staff received salaries and students were awarded stipends.[27] By funding such complexes, urban elites in cities like Baghdad, Cairo, and Damascus publicly displayed their support of education and community charity, thus transforming their wealth into status.

Madrasas served religious and secular needs throughout the Islamic world, from North Africa and the Mediterranean to Central and South Asia. They promoted Sunni Islam in Shi'a-dominated areas or Islamization in newly conquered regions, such as the Delhi sultanate in India. Saladin founded the first madrasa in Cairo in 1170 to restore Sunni teachings, and under his successors and the Mamluks, madrasas flourished in Egypt and other parts of the eastern Mediterranean. Madrasas arrived in Anatolia beginning in the late eleventh century as part of "an Islamic package" that included mosques, *khanqahs*, hospitals, inns, lodges, and soup kitchens.[28] The *khanqah* – similar institutions were also called *ribat* or *zawiyah* – was originally a center for Sufis, and it often functioned as both a monastery and a school where Sufi masters instructed followers.

26 Said Amir Arjomand, "The Law, Agency, and Policy in Medieval Islamic Society: Development of the Institutions of Learning from the Tenth to the Fifteenth Century," *Comparative Studies in Society and History* 41.2 (1999): 263–93.

27 Jonathan Berkey, *The Transmission of Knowledge in Medieval Cairo: A Social History of Islamic Education* (Princeton University Press, 1992): 47.

28 Gary Leiser, "The Madrasa and the Islamization of Anatolia before the Ottomans," in Joseph E. Lowry, Devin J. Stewart, and Shawkat Toorawa (eds.), *Law and Education in Medieval Islam: Studies in Memory of Professor George Makdisi* (Chippenham: E. J. W. Gibb Memorial Trust, 2004): 175.

A spectrum of institutions across the Islamic world contributed to the transmission of religious knowledge, from mosque to madrasa to *khanqah*. The transmission of knowledge could take place in many different institutional settings because learning was an act of piety dependent on the personal authority of a teacher, not an institution. The multitude of institutions facilitated the exposure of ever-larger numbers of people to religious knowledge. Religious knowledge was also transmitted outside the network of endowed schools, by scholars teaching at home, in study circles, and in other settings, both formal and informal. Such venues expanded the possibilities for women, in particular, to gain access to instruction.

Although elite women endowed madrasas and other institutions, and even played roles in their administration, they could neither attend them as students nor teach in them. But some women could and did become learned teachers of *hadith* by studying with scholars, especially family members, in their homes or studying alongside men in private teaching circles in mosques.[29] Because *hadith* transmission required only certification of study with an authentic transmitter and the ability to memorize revealed texts, women as well as men were able to do this. In the fourteenth century, a woman from Damascus known as 'Aisha studied *hadith* with many teachers and received *ijazas* from scholars in Aleppo, Hama, Nablus, and Hebron. As her fame spread, many flocked to study with her.

The permeability of institutional boundaries, as well as the importance of the *rihla* (a knowledge-seeking journey) for Muslim scholars,[30] is illustrated by the career of the historian and philosopher Ibn Khaldun (1332–1406). A Maghribi by birth, Ibn Khaldun studied in Fez and Granada before his appointment in 1387 to teach at Cairo's newly built al-Zahiriyya madrasa. Upon his return from pilgrimage to Mecca, he was appointed teacher of *hadith* at another madrasa, and at the same time he was placed at the head of the *khanqah* of Baybars, the most important Sufi convent in Egypt. The blurring of distinctions among different kinds of institutions that provided education – mosque, madrasa, *khanqah* – is testimony to the primacy of the teacher–student relationship in Islam over any particular institutional setting and to the relative absence of state control of education. Muslims of all backgrounds had access to learning in a wide range of different settings, from informal study circles to mosques and madrasas. Status was associated with

---

29 Berkey, *Transmission*, Chapter VI.
30 William Granara, "Islamic Education and the Transmission of Knowledge in Muslim Sicily," in Lowry, Stewart, and Toorawa (eds.), *Law and Education in Medieval Islam*, 151.

the reputation and authority of individual teachers to transmit learning, embodied in the granting of *ijaza* to their students, not on access to knowledge through educational institutions. Consequently, Islamic education before 1500 was characterized by an informal system of instruction based on personal relationships between teachers and students, unlike the formal institutionalization of instruction and examination that evolved in the European universities.

Islam and educational institutions in Africa

Pre-Islamic African traditions were transmitted orally. In many places professional narrators recounted traditions and history that they had learned, thus preserving the collective memory of the society. In some places they used this knowledge to remonstrate with the ruler on behalf of the entire population. In West Africa such individuals were called *griots*, and they are mentioned in the accounts of Muslim observers such as al-Bakri, who noted the presence of one at the court of the king of Ghana in 1068. The Berber traveler Ibn Battuta provided the first eyewitness description of *griots* at the court of Mali in the mid-fourteenth century.[31]

By the twelfth century, Islam had spread from North to West Africa, and from the Arabian peninsula to East Africa. Overland trading routes across the Sahara carried Islam to Ghana and Mali, while maritime routes brought Muslim merchants to East African coastal towns such as Kilwa, Malindi, and Mombasa. In the twelfth and thirteenth centuries, Arab clans from Yemen migrated to Mogadishu and contributed to that city's fame as an important center of Islamic learning.[32] Part of northeastern Africa remained impervious to the advent of Islam on the African continent until the fourteenth century, and Ethiopia until today. Christian rulers of the kingdoms of Nubia supported Christian monastic institutions as the primary centers of scholarship and the transmission of learning until Nubia was conquered by the Mamluks. After 1400, Nubians converted to Islam and so became part of the African Islamic world and its traditions of learning.

Quranic learning became a fixture at the courts of Kanem-Bornu, a succession of states stretching from the Niger River through modern Chad

---

31 Thomas A. Hale, *Griots and Griottes: Masters of Words and Music* (Bloomington: Indiana University Press, 1998): 73–4; 79. See also the chapter by David Conrad in this volume.
32 Randall L. Pouwels, *Horn and Crescent: Cultural Change and Traditional Islam on the East African Coast, 800–1900* (Cambridge University Press, 1987): 22–6.

to the deserts of Libya from the eighth through the nineteenth centuries. In the oasis towns and nomadic encampments of the southwestern Sahara, by the eleventh century higher education was provided by an institution known as the *mahadra*, and Sufi lodges were also centers of Muslim learning.[33] By 1500 rural Quranic school settlements dotted the Kanem-Bornu landscape, where families of teachers and scholars congregated with large numbers of students of different ages who served them and helped in the household and fields. These camps of scholars and students shared the itinerant ways of life of nomadic and semi-nomadic groups, and they became common in the western Sahara among the Tuareg (Berber nomadic pastoralists).[34]

In the region of Ghana (*c.* 600–1250) and Mali (1200–1450) in West Africa, one of the earliest centers of Islamic learning was the oasis city of Walata.[35] After 1200, following a shift in trade routes from west to east and the consequent decline of Walata, the gold and salt emporium of Jenne at the southern end of the Niger Inland Delta became an important center of learning.[36] Trade made cities flourish, and learned men with expertise in writing and law were drawn to these cities where their skills were needed. They were also active as religious teachers and medical practitioners, educating the people in Islam, but also in medicine, history, and astronomy. Muslim rulers promoted the teaching of Islam by patronizing mosques, schools, and libraries. The famed Mali ruler Mansa Musa (r. 1312–37) erected mosques and madrasas in Timbuktu and Gao after his pilgrimage to Mecca in 1324.

Strategically located at the meeting point between the fertile Niger Delta and the Sahara, Timbuktu prospered in the fifteenth century, eclipsing Jenne as the center of Islamic learning in the middle Niger region.[37] With numerous schools and private libraries, Timbuktu was known throughout the Muslim world as a center of scholarship in all aspects of Islamic learning. Timbuktu's Sankore mosque provided both a forum for interaction among

---

33 Ghislaine Lydon, "A Thirst for Knowledge: Arabic Literacy, Writing Paper, and Saharan Bibliophiles in the Southwestern Sahara," in G. Krätli and Ghislaine Lydon (eds.), *The Trans-Saharan Book Trade: Manuscript Culture, Arabic Literacy, and Intellectual History in Muslim Africa* (Leiden: Brill, 2011): 40.

34 Stefan Reichmuth, "Islamic Education and Scholarship in sub-Saharan Africa," in Nehemiah Levtzion and R. L. Pouwels (eds.), *The History of Islam in Africa* (Athens: Ohio University Press, 2000): 422–3.

35 Ghislaine Lydon, "Inkwells of the Sahara," in Scott Steven Reese, *The Transmission of Learning in Islamic Africa* (Leiden: Brill, 2004): 45.

36 Albrecht Hofheinz, "Goths in the Lands of the Blacks," in Reese, *The Transmission of Learning in Islamic Africa*, 161.

37 Hofheinz, "Goths," 161; Elias N. Saad, *Social History of Timbuktu: The Role of Muslim Scholars and Notables, 1400–1900* (Cambridge University Press, 1983): 58–60.

scholars and courses of study open to all who could qualify.[38] But the absence in Timbuktu of the institution of *waqf* that could support public libraries meant that the Timbuktu *'ulama*, who came from the city's wealthy families, maintained private libraries as a mark of their scholarly standing rather than endowing public libraries.[39] Unlike the rest of the Muslim world, where aspiring scholars had access to books and instruction irrespective of their social standing, the *'ulama* of Timbuktu were a hereditary elite with control over education.

The Americas

Like written accounts of pre-Islamic Africa by Islamic traders and travelers, the pre-Columbian Americas are chronicled primarily through the writings of outsiders, Spanish priests whose observations of the Maya, Aztecs, and Incas were recorded in the sixteenth century. The Spanish chroniclers testify to the importance of oral tradition and skill in oratory among Mesoamerican peoples. But both the Maya and the Aztecs also left written records in their own script, which can be used along with archaeological evidence to reconstruct Aztec and Maya societies. Although the Maya city-states were constantly warring with each other, training as a warrior was not regarded as highly as education for the priesthood or for administrative duties that fell to the nobility. Maya nobles (males) were instructed in reading and writing hieroglyphs, which provided them with esoteric knowledge that separated them from commoners.

Educational institutions are better documented in Aztec society than elsewhere in Mesoamerica. Between the ages of 12 and 15, Aztec children attended the *cuicacalli* ("House of Song"), the school of the territorial kinship group (*calpulli*) to which they belonged. Some sources suggest that all children attended, and some that only elite boys did. Here they were instructed in the songs and orations that prepared them to take part in major religious ceremonies of the Aztec calendar. Learning these sacred songs and stories also taught them about Aztec cosmology and the place of the Aztec people in it.[40]

---

38 Saad, *Social History of Timbuktu*, 62.
39 B. D. Singleton, "African Bibliophiles: Books and Libraries in Medieval Timbuktu," *Libraries and Culture* 39.1 (2004): 9.
40 David Cárrasco, *Daily Life of the Aztecs* (Westport, CT: Greenwood, 1998), especially Chapter 4.

Education between the ages of 15 and 20 was stratified according to social status. Sons of commoners and lower-ranking nobles went on for further study of history, religion, and music in the *telpochcalli* ("House of Youth"), located in each of Tenochtitlan's city wards.[41] Because warfare was a primary focus of Aztec society, students in the *telpochcalli* received intensive military training, which included accompanying the army on campaigns as burden-bearers in order to gain experience of battle. Boys slept at the *telpochcalli* at night, but ate meals with their families and continued to spend part of the day acquiring the skills to pursue a vocation from their fathers. Sons of the higher-ranking nobility attended one of six or more *calmecacs* ("row of houses"), which were attached to the temples of Tenochtitlan and therefore under the direct control of priests (see Figure 5.2).[42] They lived at the school, which was more like a monastery because of its temple affiliation and supervision by religious authorities. The *calmecac* provided military training, along with more diversified and advanced instruction than that of the *telpochcalli* in religion, astrology, the calendar, writing and oral speech, history, art, song and dance, law, mathematics, government, and architecture. These students were being trained to become priests, scribes, government officials, military leaders, or judges. Students at the *calmecac* spent much of their time memorizing historical and religious material, for they had the responsibility as members of the elite to preserve and transmit Aztec cultural heritage. The patron god of the *calmecac* was Quetzalcoatl, the creator deity who was also "the god of learning and culture, of ancient lore, the god of civilization itself."[43] The patron god of the *telpochcalli* was Tezcatlipoca, the war god. Although schooling ended for girls with the *cuicacalli*, daughters of the nobility had the opportunity to receive further education in temple schools.[44]

In Incan society most children did not receive schooling. There was an institution of higher learning at the Inca capital, Cuzco, for the sons of the nobility. During the reign of the Inca Pachacutec (*c.* 1400–48), the heirs of provincial chiefs were required to reside in Cuzco for education. In the first year, they were instructed in Quechua; in the second, they studied theology

41 E. Calnek, "The Calmecac and Telpochcalli in Pre-Conquest Tenochtitlan," in H. B. Nicholson, N. J. Jorge Klor de Alva, and Eloise Quinones Keber (eds.), *The Work of Bernardino de Sahagun: Pioneer Ethnographer of Sixteenth-Century Aztec Mexico* (Albany, NY, Institute for Mesoamerican Studies: The University at Albany, 1988): 171.

42 J. Marcus, *Mesoamerican Writing Systems: Propaganda, Myth, and History in Four Ancient Civilizations* (Princeton University Press, 1992): 50–1.

43 Brian Fagan, *The Aztecs* (New York: W.H. Freeman, 1984): 244.

44 Inga Clendinnen, *Aztecs: An Interpretation* (Cambridge University Press, 1991): 155–6.

con oraciones, y lagrimas; pa
raque nos declare, su volun
tad.

ꟼ Capitulo quinto, de la
manera de biuir, y exer
cicios, que tenjan los que

Figure 5.2 Elite boys enter a *calmecac* for instruction, from the Florentine Codex by
Bernardino de Sahagún, *c*. 1540–85 (Biblioteca Medicea-Laurenziana, Florence, Italy /
Bridgeman Images)

and ritual; in the third, they learned the interpretation of *khipu*, the knotted strings that were used as a means of record-keeping; and in the fourth year, they learned more about *khipu* and history. The goal of this education was to produce citizens who could serve the state. Attractive young women were chosen to be educated in vast, convent-like places near the Temple of the Sun, and in provincial centers scattered throughout the empire. Here they were taught domestic skills of weaving, spinning, and cooking. They were required to remain virgins, and at marriageable age, four or five of those from the school in the capital were selected as permanent brides of the Sun; others were wed to the Inca or to provincial chiefs.[45]

Among Mayas, Aztecs, and Incas formal educational institutions were directly tied to state needs, especially the training of warriors and priests. Because the state itself was sanctioned by religion, priests played a crucial role in maintaining the state, as warriors did in expanding and defending it. As in other parts of the world, schooling was sharply divided by gender and status, in both practical skills and religious instruction.

Conclusions and comparisons

For the vast majority of the world's population during most of this period, knowledge that transcended the practical concerns of daily life was religious in nature. Religion also provided the setting for education: Buddhist monasteries in Asia, Christian monasteries in Europe, and mosques in the Islamic world. Learning was not an end in itself, but a path to religious knowledge. However, as Buddhism, Christianity, and Islam were fused to expanding states and empires, monasteries and mosques also provided basic education that served the administrative and legal needs of rulers.

Before 1000, in contrast to educational institutions grounded in the spread of these world religions, Confucianism inspired an educational institution that directly served the Chinese state: the civil service examination system. Humanistic ideals of learning derived from Confucian texts were woven together with the practical needs of the state to administer a vast bureaucracy. The influence of Confucianism and the examination system extended throughout East Asia, and Confucian schools coexisted with Buddhist monastic institutions in this region of the world.

45 Terence N. D'Altroy, *The Incas* (London: Blackwell, 2002): 187–91.

In both Judaism and Islam, formal institutions of religious education evolved alongside synagogues and mosques: the *yeshiva* in Judaism and the madrasa in Islam. Islam was the defining religion of states and empires, followed by rulers and subjects alike, but the diasporic conditions of Jewish life meant that individual Jews and their communities resided within states and empires governed by followers of other religions. And yet, Islam was not subject to centralized religious leadership, while through the end of the Gaonic period in the early eleventh century, Judaism was. Both Judaism and Islam relied on the authority of rabbis and ʿulama to determine correct interpretations of sacred texts. Consequently, for both Jews and Muslims, the relationship between teacher and student was paramount. Religious texts were the core of the curriculum, but oral teachings – incorporating the interpretations of a teacher – were also of great importance in the transmission of learning. For Muslims especially, personal authority over a text was the means by which instructors bestowed licenses to teach. Thus, although madrasas and *yeshivas* thrived as places of instruction, education was less tied to specific institutional settings than to particular teachers. Education for both Jews and Muslims was also mobile, as the trope of the "wandering scholar" in Judaism has its counterpart in the custom of the *rihla* for Muslims.

There was tension between the dual functions of education in Buddhist and Christian institutions that provided training to serve the secular needs of rulers as well as instruction for religious purposes. Tension was likewise inherent in Confucian education for the examination system, which juxtaposed instruction in humanistic ideals with the needs of the state to recruit administrators. Tension of this nature was largely absent in Islamic educational institutions because the state was closely aligned with Islam and thus knowledge for state service was not clearly distinct from religious knowledge. Similarly, formal educational institutions in pre- and post-Islamic sub-Saharan Africa and in the Americas were directly tied to state religion and therefore did not generate the kinds of tensions between religious and secular education observed elsewhere. Such tension lay at the very heart of the European university, in which the search for knowledge was embedded in struggles between ruler and pope and in the changing needs of an increasingly urban and commercial economy. It is, however, precisely in the European university that knowledge burst out of its religious confines as a pursuit independent of Christianity. The university in medieval Europe traced its origins to monasteries and cathedral schools, but its antecedents also lay in Greek and Roman thought, enriched by Arab and Byzantine scholarship. Ultimately, this combination of influences created the conditions under which knowledge was no longer defined as religion, although the use of reason as a method of analysis began as a path to faith.

What might be called the "fetish of institutionalization" – the tendency to neglect informal arrangements in favor of more formal structures, or to view them as somehow less "institutional" – can distort the portrayal of diverse historical conditions. The term "institution" can be used in a way that either imposes a fixed quality on fluid and shifting practices or ignores such practices as not "institutions." This problem is most acute in viewing regions beyond Afro-Eurasia not dominated by the world religions, where the historical record of formal educational institutions is sparse. However, in sub-Saharan Africa and the Americas, the transmission of learning was more often woven into the fabric of daily life rather than segregated as a set of formally recognized institutions. Where such institutions did exist – the West African *griot* or the Aztec *calmecac* – their functions were closely aligned with a social and political order produced by the fusion of state and religion.

In contrast, the relationship between state and religion varied greatly across Afro-Eurasia, ranging from Confucian China, where religion was subordinate to and controlled by the state, to the struggle between Church and state in Europe, and finally the Islamic world, where the state represented but did not control religion. Consequently, the functions of educational institutions in Afro-Eurasia correlated with the degree to which state and religion were integrated. Scholar official elites in China and other parts of East Asia influenced by Confucianism achieved social and political status through the state civil service examination system by demonstrating their access to knowledge. Muslim clerics and Jewish rabbis commanded status through their knowledge of religious texts and law, unmediated by the state. European scholars successfully negotiated their independence from Church and state to establish universities that served both and yet began to define knowledge as distinct from either.

FURTHER READING

Arjomand, Said Amir. "The Law, Agency, and Policy in Medieval Islamic Society: Development of the Institutions of Learning from the Tenth to the Fifteenth Century," *Comparative Studies in Society and History* 41, no. 2 (1999): 263–93.

Baskin, Judith. "Some Parallels in the Education of Medieval Jewish and Christian Women," *Jewish History* 5, no. 1 (1991): 41–51.

Bednarski, Steven, and Andrée Courtemanche. "Learning to Be a Man: Public Schooling and Apprenticeship in Late Medieval Manosque," *Journal of Medieval History* 35, no. 2 (2009): 113–35.

Begley, Ronald B., and Joseph W. Koterski. *Medieval Education*. New York, NY: Fordham University Press, 2005.

Berkey, Jonathan P. *The Transmission of Knowledge in Medieval Cairo: A Social History of Islamic Education*. Princeton University Press, 1992.

Callan, Maeve B. "St Darerca and Her Sister Scholars: Women and Education in Medieval Ireland," *Gender & History* 15, no. 1 (2003): 32–49.

Calnek, Edward. "The Calmecac and Telpochcalli in Pre-Conquest Tenochtitlan," in H. B. Nicholson, J. Jorge Klor de Alva, and Eloise Quinones Keber (eds.), *The Work of Bernardino de Sahagún: Pioneer Ethnographer of Sixteenth-Century Mexico*. Albany, NY: Institute for Mesoamerican Studies, The University at Albany, 1988: 169–77.

Chamberlain, Michael. *Knowledge and Social Practice in Medieval Damascus, 1190–1350*, Cambridge Studies in Islamic Civilization. Cambridge University Press, 1994.

Cobban, Alan B. *The Medieval English Universities: Oxford and Cambridge to c. 1500*. Berkeley, CA: University of California Press, 1988.

Constantinides, C. N. *Higher Education in Byzantium in the Thirteenth and Early Fourteenth Centuries, 1204–Ca.1310*. Nicosia: Cyprus Research Centre, 1982.

de Bary, Wm Theodore, and John W. Chaffee (eds.). *Neo-Confucian Education: The Formative Stage*. Berkeley, Los Angeles, London: University of California Press, 1989.

Drijvers, Jan Willem, and A. A. MacDonald. *Centres of Learning: Learning and Location in Pre-Modern Europe and the Near East*. Leiden: Brill, 1995.

Getz, F. "Medical Education in Later Medieval England," *Clio Medica (Amsterdam)* 30 (1995): 76–93.

Goitein, S. D. *A Mediterranean Society, ii: The Community*. Berkeley: University of California Press, 1971.

Gunther, Sebastian. "Be Masters in That You Teach and Continue to Learn: Medieval Muslim Thinkers on Educational Theory," *Comparative Education Review* 50, no. 3 (2006): 367–88.

Jaeger, C. Stephen. *The Envy of Angels: Cathedral Schools and Social Ideals in Medieval Europe, 950–1200*. Philadelphia, PA: University of Pennsylvania Press, 1994.

Janin, Hunt. *The University in Medieval Life, 1179–1499*. Jefferson, NC and London: McFarland and Company, Inc., 2008.

Kadi, Wadad. "Education in Islam: Myths and Truths," *Comparative Education Review* 50, no. 3 (2006): 311–24.

Kanarfogel, Ephraim. *Jewish Education and Society in the High Middle Ages*. Detroit, MI: Wayne State University Press, 1992.

Krätli, G. and Ghislaine Lydon. *The Trans-Saharan Book Trade: Manuscript Culture, Arabic Literacy and Intellectual History in Muslim Africa*. Leiden: Brill, 2011.

Lee, Thomas H. C. *Education in Traditional China: A History*. Leiden: Brill, 2000.

Leiser, Gary. "Medical Education in Islamic Lands from the Seventh to the Fourteenth Century," *Journal of the History of Medicine and Allied Sciences* 38, no. 1 (1983): 48–75.

Lowry, Joseph E., Devin J. Stewart, and Shawkat M. Toorawa (eds.). *Law and Education in Medieval Islam: Studies in Memory of Professor George Makdisi*. Cambridge: E. J. W. Gibb Memorial Trust, 2004.

Mahamid, Hatim. "Waqf, Education and Politics in Mamluk Jerusalem," *The Islamic Quarterly* 50, no. 1 (2006): 33–56.

Makdisi, George. *The Rise of Colleges: Institutions of Learning in Islam and the West.* Edinburgh University Press, 1981.

McDaniel, Justin. *Gathering Leaves and Lifting Words: Histories of Buddhist Monastic Education in Laos and Thailand.* Seattle, WA: University of Washington Press, 2008.

Pedersen, Olaf. *The First Universities: Studium Generale and the Origins of University Education in Europe.* Cambridge University Press, 1998.

Reese, Scott Steven. *The Transmission of Learning in Islamic Africa.* Leiden: Brill, 2004.

Reichmuth, Stefan. "Islamic Education and Scholarship in Sub-Saharan Africa," in Nehemia Levtzion and Randall Lee Pouwels (eds.), *The History of Islam in Africa.* Athens, Oxford, Cape Town: Ohio University Press, 2000: 419–40.

Ridder-Symoens, Hilde de. *Universities in the Middle Ages, A History of the University in Europe*, Vol. 1. Cambridge University Press, 1992.

Saad, Elias N. *Social History of Timbuktu: The Role of Muslim Scholars and Notables, 1400–1900.* Cambridge University Press, 1983.

Scharfe, Hartmut. *Education in Ancient India.* Leiden: Brill, 2002.

Vaughn, Sally N., and Jay Rubenstein. *Teaching and Learning in Northern Europe, 1000–1200: Studies in the Early Middle Ages*, vol. VIII. Turnhout: Brepols, 2006.

6

Warfare

CLIFFORD J. ROGERS

This chapter will be an exploration of warfare itself, not principally of how war affected either the societies of the global community or their inter-action.[1] It will examine why wars were fought, by whom, and how – including questions of recruitment, equipment, and organization of armed forces as well as strategy, tactics, and logistics. There are wide variations in the state of current scholarship and in available source material (which ranges, for broad swathes of time and geography, from very thin to virtually nonexistent). This will of necessity place the emphasis firmly on Eurasia and North Africa.

A principal *Leitmotif* will be the patterns of conflict between nomadic societies and agro-urban civilizations, exploring the question of how the former were so often able to defeat and overrun the latter, despite disadvan-tages in manpower and resources. We will begin with an early example of steppe empire building, followed by examination of three civilizations that had to address the problem of attacks from the steppe: China, Persia, and Byzantium. From there we will move through the geographic and chrono-logical scope of the chapter by a chain of interactions. As we encounter each new society, we will stress what is most distinctive about its military, and what more general topics it best illustrates.

The steppes and the agro-urban empires

Nomadic peoples do not maintain archives, leave relatively scarce archaeo-logical evidence, and rarely produce much by way of historical records. Because the tribes of the great Eurasian steppes often made war on the

---

[1] I owe thanks for comments on this chapter to Stephen Morillo, John France, Tom Nimick, and David Graff, in addition to my fellow contributors to this volume, especially Jean-Claude Cheynet, Anatoly Khazanov, and Benjamin Kedar.

agro-urban civilizations that surrounded them, however, we have numerous descriptions of steppe nomads and their style of fighting dating from across the ancient and medieval periods. Insofar as the evidence allows us to judge, there seems to have been relatively little change in the steppe ways of life and of warfare from the start of our period to the rise of the Mongols in the thirteenth century.

Living by hunting and on the meat and milk of vast herds of horses and other livestock, the nomads had to stay constantly on the move to find good grazing for their animals. Their boys and men spent most of every day on horseback, with bows in hand to shoot small game. These bows, used also for war, were of composite recurved design, allowing for long, powerful draws from short bows suitable for use from the saddle. Steppe warriors could rapidly shoot many arrows for great distances, even while galloping, at targets in any direction, including behind them.[2] The arrows did not have great armor-penetrating ability, but they were most often used against fellow nomads, who (except for the leaders) normally had little or no metal armor, and their unprotected mounts.[3] Battles began with arrows, but were finished mainly with spears. Usually victorious leaders gained the subjection of the defeated, their "strength and labor."[4] Sometimes the defeated fled and lost their grazing lands; sometimes the men were scattered or exterminated and the women and children became the property of the conquerors. A long sequence of victories created a large hegemony; a single defeat might break it up. It took forty-seven campaigns and twenty battles for Ilterish (r. 682–94) to build the Second Eastern Turkic Khaqanate (Qaghanate):

> He made those with dominion lose their dominion
> He made those with a Khaghan lose their Khaghan
> He made the enemy a vassal
> He made those with knees to kneel.[5]

---

2 See Al-Jahiz, "The Virtues of the Turk," in *Nine Essays of al-Jahiz*, trans. William M. Hutchins (New York: Peter Lang, 1989).

3 Metal armor was more common towards the end of our period than at the beginning, and even in the earlier periods leaders did have good armor. In one battle, the Turkic leader Kul Tegin (d. 731), had three horses killed and (according to the inscription describing his deeds) had a hundred arrows strike his armor, but because none touched his face and head, he survived. *Kul Tegin Inscription*, trans. Stefan Kamola, at http://depts.washington.edu/ccalt/database/Bilghe-Qaghan/Kul-Tegin-Inscription.

4 The phrase is used repeatedly in the *Kul Tegin Inscription*.

5 Ibid. The spelling in English of Mongolian and Turkic words is a matter of convention, and to some degree preference. This volume will use 'khan' to mean a ruler, and 'khanate' to mean the state that he ruled. Khagan (Turkic, sometimes spelled qaghan or qagan) or Qa'an (Mongolian) are used to denote the supreme ruler or Great Khan.

Rule tended to pass relatively easily from brother to brother, but not from generation to generation. When the naturally fissiparous character of nomadic polities created opportunities to do so, more settled states outside the steppe often intervened to encourage civil wars and prevent consolidation of power. They did so because they dreaded the military potential of the united steppe. The nomad population was small, but most men were skilled warriors, superb horsemen, inured to hunger, thirst, and bad weather, fierce, seemingly fearless, honed by frequently raiding enemies for "women with beautiful cheeks and geldings with fine rumps."[6] (Raiding for women was so common among the Mongols in the thirteenth century that even arranged marriages were preceded by a ritual abduction "with a semblance of violence."[7]) "They care only about raiding, hunting, horsemanship, skirmishing with rival chieftains, taking booty, and invading other countries," wrote al-Jahiz in the mid-ninth century, "which for them take the place of craftsmanship and commerce and constitute their only pleasure, their glory, and the subject of all their conversation." (See Figure 6.1.)[8]

With each rider using a string of four or more remounts, including mares which could sustain him as well as carry him, nomad armies could go almost anywhere and get there incredibly fast, covering as much as a hundred miles per day. As a ninth-century Chinese policy document explains, military force could not effectively defend a long frontier against such raiders: "for us to mobilise our forces would take at least ten days or a few weeks, while for them to take our men and animals prisoner would take at most a morning or an evening. By the time an imperial army could get there, the barbarians would already have returned home."[9] Retaliatory expeditions were possible, but were expensive to mount, had poor prospects of finding and overtaking a mobile population in a sea of grass, and risked disastrous defeat on the enemy's home turf. The best course of action was normally to pay the "barbarians" protection money (often in the form of silks, grain, or other commodities rather than gold and silver) and make flattering marriage alliances with them, rather than fight them.

---

6 *The History and the Life of Chinggis Khan (The Secret History of the Mongols)*, trans. Urgunge Onon (Leiden: Brill, 1990), chapters 179, 197.
7 William of Rubruck, *The Mission of Friar William of Rubruck*, trans. Peter Jackson (London: Hakluyt Society, 1990): 92.
8 *Life and Works of Jahiz*, ed. Charles Pellat, trans. D. M. Hawke (Berkeley: University of California Press, 1969): 97.
9 *Hsin T'ang-shu*, in *The Uighur Empire, According to the T'ang Dyanstic Histories*, ed. and trans. Colin Mackerras (Columbia, SC: University of South Carolina Press, 1973): 111.

Figure 6.1 Bulghar warrior on a gold jug (or pitcher) from the Treasure of Nagyszentmiklós (Erich Lessing Culture & Fine Arts Archive)

Policies of bribery could work well because settled agro-urban states had vastly greater economic resources than the nomads: agriculture allowed for the support of much larger populations and more division of labor. Skilled urban craftsmen produced fine goods that the steppe leaders valued, and the amount needed to buy safety was limited by the low numbers and material expectations of the nomads. It was not only safer to pay them off, it was also cheaper. The settled empires had to maintain large armies in any case, to defend against other peer states, to sustain the ruling political and military classes in power, and also to insure the nomads could not simply take what they wanted with impunity. Despite the nomads' advantages already noted, a Chinese, Byzantine, or even Ottonian army could, under the right circumstances, inflict a severe defeat on an invading force of horse-archers, or could be used offensively to help one group of nomads defeat another. This was possible because civilized areas had such large populations and economies that they could usually field larger armies than their nomadic enemies even when they armed only 1 or 2 per cent of their populations. They could also provide their soldiers with great capital resources, in the form of armor, weapons, supply wagons and boats, time for military training, and (in relatively small numbers) heavy grain-fed horses. But the warlike capabilities that nomads gained as a by-product of their lifestyle could only be matched by sedentary peoples with focused expense and effort. If "gifts" could keep the steppe leaders on the border happy, then smaller, less expensive imperial forces would suffice. Besides, a friendly khaghan (or would-be khaghan) across the border could not only restrain his people from raiding and act as a shield against more distant peoples, he could also provide horsemen to balance the infantry-heavy armies that agro-urban civilizations tended to produce.

Horsemen, footmen, and empires

The most effective armies comprise balanced forces of cavalry and infantry. The great mobility of horsemen allowed rapid shifting of troops from one region to another in response to developing threats, or to make lightning surprise attacks. The side with superior cavalry would have superior information about enemy movements, could usually choose when to fight and when to avoid combat, and could severely disrupt the enemy's supply arrangements while protecting its own. By pillaging and devastating the enemy countryside and seizing captives for ransom or enslavement, it could fund its own war effort while weakening the enemy leaders and pressuring them either to buy peace or to give battle. Battles were typically won when one side's cavalry defeated the other side's horse, then hit the enemy footmen from the flank or rear. After that, it usually required a vigorous cavalry pursuit to make a victory truly decisive; infantry losses were often far higher after formations were broken up than during the battle itself. Thus, across most of Eurasia and North Africa in most of our period, cavalry was (despite the skepticism of some scholars) the most important military arm. "Riders are the pivot of an army," wrote an Arab in the ninth century: "theirs are the glory days, the famous battles, the vast conquests."[10] Nonetheless, infantry was important too. Footmen were much cheaper to equip, to train, and to maintain, so really large armies had to be made up mostly of infantry. Huge numbers were needed to garrison long frontiers, and sometimes to occupy and retain new conquests. Siege operations – the capture of fortified places, especially walled towns and cities – were a very large part of warfare in this period. Controlling an agricultural area required capturing and retaining the walled towns within it. The ancient techniques of siegecraft used to take an army over, under, or through urban walls remained in use: ladders, siege towers, mines, battering rams, and stone-throwing engines. But fortifications nonetheless gave defenders a huge tactical advantage. A siege-ladder might make it possible for attackers to reach a wall-top, but one man on the ramparts with a rock still had the upper hand over six men on the ladder. Mining was effective but slow. Battering engines were effective against some fortifications, but not against strongly built masonry. Strongholds were much more often taken by starvation and negotiation than by assault. That required encircling and cutting off a town, usually digging ditches and manning them strongly enough to resist sallies by the defenders, which could be concentrated against any point of the perimeter. This took large numbers of soldiers, most of whom could be infantry, though horsemen were needed to secure the besiegers' lines of supply and to defeat a relief army in battle.

Thus, one of the basic problems societies faced in constructing their military forces was how to provide adequate forces both of cavalry and infantry. For agro-urban civilizations, it was often easier and cheaper to acquire the services of skilled but poor steppe horse-archers than to equip, train, and pay native cavalrymen, especially since the former could be hired "off the shelf" when needed and then dismissed back to their herds and yurts in times of peace. But that ran into the second basic problem of military systems: soldiers were needed not just to defeat foreign enemies, but also to maintain domestic power structures, both social and governmental. One reason emperors liked to employ "barbarian" soldiers was that foreigners

---

10 *Life and Works of Jahiz*, 95.

lacked the political and familial connections and cultural credibility that made native generals potential usurpers. But over time, empires tended to become increasingly dependent on the barbarians for fighters. The norm in pre-modern human societies is for a single group to dominate all three basic wellsprings of power and authority: armed force, wealth, and cultural legitimacy (including religion). Sometimes, however, those with wealth and authority drift away from the dangerous burdens of making war. As the sociologist Stanislav Andreski has suggested, this tends to create an unstable situation, because those with arms can rarely be satisfied for long with less than the lion's share of riches and power.[11] Military elites who are subordinated to separate economic and political elites are likely to attempt to seize rule for themselves. Whether they succeed, or force the "civilian" elites to remilitarize in order to defeat them, or fail but so weaken the state that a more martial external power enters as a conqueror, the separation of military and social power is likely to erode or disappear.

Empires only become empires through war, and cannot maintain themselves without using armed force to crush rebellions and defeat invasions. However, one of the main reasons empires "work" – why they appear so frequently in human society – is that their surface area generally expands more rapidly than their perimeter, so that their economic resources expand more rapidly than their defense needs. The larger the polity, the more of its population can be secure from external violence and hence more economically productive. Also, the more stable its political institutions, the less its people will suffer from internal warfare. Thus, the most successful empires are those that have effective systems for collecting wealth in the center, through the exercise of unquestioned authority more than the application of force, and directing adequate resources to the armed forces on the frontiers, while also retaining a strong central reserve to deter or defeat rebellions and to aid the border forces in responding to exceptionally strong threats from outside. When warrior-elites seize power, they create a destabilizing precedent, and also tend to over-use force rather than cheaper and less disruptive authority, both at home and abroad. In the long run, civilizations with elites that are adequately militarized but not principally military tend to be the most prosperous, most stable, and most successful. Both as a result of and as an element of their success, they develop strong intellectual and cultural emphases on the importance of *legitimacy* in rule, and value-sets that grant

---

11 Stanislav Andreski, *Military Organization and Society* (London: Routledge & Kegan Paul, 1968).

prestige and deference to administrative skill, intelligence, and education, not just bravery, aggressiveness, and prowess.

China

Around the start of our period, civil wars and nomad migrations led to the fall of the Western Roman Empire. Similarly, in northern China nomadic warriors had been widely employed during the War of the Eight Princes (291–306), and between 304 and 316 the Wu Hu "barbarian" peoples effectively seized control over the region, beginning the Sixteen Kingdoms period. By 439 the Northern Wei dynasty, descended from Xianbi nomads, had unified North China using a military structure that seems to have set the pattern for the system used by the Sui (589–618) and early Tang emperors to conquer the south. Under the early Tang, Chinese "military families" were given land to farm on the frontier, spared from most taxes, and required to provide infantry soldiers equipped with armor and crossbows or pole-arms, organized into regiments. At little cost to the treasury, this *fubing* (territorial forces) system produced several hundred thousand soldiers who guarded the borders, contributed to major field armies, and, in rotation, annually served one- to two-month stints in the capital. There the *fubing* soldiers gave the emperors a check on the potential power of the other main component of the regular military, the standing Palace Army. Aristocrats of mixed steppe and Han blood served as cavalry in the Imperial Guard, which also provided officers to the *fubing* and the Palace Army. Extra manpower for large campaign armies was provided by short-term conscript infantry. The final main component of Sui and Tang armies was allied or subject cavalry from the steppes. Tang Taizong (599–649), a product of both cultures, took the steppe–Han fusion in a new direction when he managed to become khaghan of the eastern nomads as well as emperor of China. But in 679–82 the Turks threw off the dominance the Chinese had established more through "soft fabrics and deceiving words" – bribes and diplomacy – than through warfare. Their leader, Ilterish Khaghan, launched devastating raids into China to collect booty and slaves to reward his followers and ultimately to force the Tang to pay for peace; unlike plunder, the tribute went directly to the khaghan, who could control its distribution to ensure his own internal power. This enabled the Second Turkish Federation to last through a second generation, but it collapsed after the death of Ilterish's last son in 741.

Meanwhile the *fubing* system had gone into a steep decline, as the lands allocated for its support fell under the control of aristocrats and Buddhist monasteries, and military service became seen increasingly as a burden rather than a privilege. It was a recurring problem in China that Confucian disdain for soldiers – which *was* a factor in Chinese civilization, though its strength and prevalence have doubtless been exaggerated by some modern writers – weakened one of the principal social bonds that rulers used to exert authority over armed men, the conferring of honor. When soldiers were denied honor, they tended to lose material support also, and then they became open to transferring allegiance to new rulers who would reward them better. Empress Wu (690–705) tried to build up the Palace Army to offset the weakness of the *fubing*, but it turned against her and participated in her deposition. Subsequent Tang rulers built up a new, smaller army of well-compensated professional soldiers (*jian'er*) and tribal cavalry.[12] From large new fortresses on the frontier they took the offensive against the nomads. As we will see below, this shift from quantity to quality was part of a remarkable pattern of similar developments in various regions at around the same time. For China, the change succeeded in restoring security and even hegemony in the northwest, at least for a brief time. The new-model forces were so successful that the *fubing* system was formally abolished in 749, and in 751 the Tang were confident enough to launch major campaigns in three directions simultaneously, against the Khitan nomads in the northeast, against the Tibetans in the southwest, and towards Tashkent in the far west. This proved to be mere hubris: all three armies suffered severe battlefield defeats.

Persia and Byzantium

The battle of Talas River, a high-water mark for Chinese expansion to the west and for Arab expansion to the northeast, took place geographically in the very center of sub-taiga Eurasia, at the chronological midpoint of the early medieval period (751). To understand its background we must examine the history of the two great agro-urban empires of the West and the Middle East, Rome and Persia. In the West as in China, the fourth and fifth centuries were a period of invasions and civil wars. As the Chinese Empire lost its northern half to barbarian conquest dynasties, so the Roman Empire lost its western provinces to Goths, Vandals, Lombards, Franks, and other migrating warrior-tribes. In the early sixth century, as Emperor Wu of Liang struggled first to repel and then to reverse Northern Wei advances into South China,

12 David Graff, *Medieval Chinese Warfare, 300–900* (London: Routledge, 2001): 209.

the Roman or "Byzantine" emperors of Constantinople likewise aimed to block new aggressions and to recover lost territories. From 503–638, Byzantium fought a series of wars in Armenia and Mesopotamia against the Sasanian Persians, while simultaneously combating Slavic light infantry in the Balkans, Avar steppe cavalry in the Danube basin, and tough Goths, Vandals, and Lombards in the south and west. In the fourth and early fifth centuries Roman armies, like southern Chinese ones, had retained advantages in infantry and engineers, who were especially important for defending border forts and cities, but also put great emphasis on strengthening their cavalry. Ready forces of armored horsemen, armed with composite bows and lances and supported by drilled, hard-marching foot soldiers with strong tactical defensive capabilities, had the mobility needed to defend long frontiers and the hitting power needed to defeat invaders or rebels in battle. They could also spearhead wars of expansion. The skilled generals of Justinian I (r. 527–65) recovered Italy, North Africa, and the southeastern coast of Spain. But the vast effort and expense of these westward reconquests left the empire weak in the east, and in 540 Antioch, the capital of Syria and one of the greatest Byzantine cities, fell temporarily to Khosro I of Persia (531–79).

The Persians employed skilled engineers, foot archers who shot very rapidly though not very strongly from behind mobile walls of wicker shields, and various other less-skilled infantry, along with war-elephants, but by far the most important element of their army was their cavalry. Allies and subject peoples provided light cavalry, but the cutting edge of the Sasanian armies was the cataphract cavalry, completely encased in iron, well-drilled, and riding large, scale-armored horses. Such troops were very expensive; Khosro increasingly provided life-estates and government funds to horsemen to allow non-nobles to serve.[13]

When these two empires clashed, it was common for the aggressor's concentrated forces to gain an initial advantage, but the numerous urban fortifications in the disputed zone and the practical difficulties of supporting deep offensives (especially against an enemy well-provided with cavalry and practicing a counter-logistical "Vegetian" strategy, which aimed to defeat invaders with famine rather than the sword) meant those advantages were short-lived.[14] Khosro I took Antioch but could not hold it; he defeated a

---

13 Moshen Zakeri, *Sasanid Soldiers in Early Muslim Society* (Wiesbaden: Otto Harrassowitz Verlag, 1995).

14 On Vegetian strategy – a very important concept for understanding warfare in this whole period– see John Gillingham, "Richard I and the Science of War in the Middle Ages," in John Gillingham and J. C. Holt (eds.), *War and Government in the Middle Ages*

Byzantine army in 544, but failed to capture Edessa. In 573 the Romans nearly captured Nisibis, but then lost their own frontier stronghold of Dara. In his last campaign, Khosro drove into Anatolia, failed to take Caesarea in Cappadocia, then retreated in great disorder after a severe battlefield defeat. The frontier flowed back and forth; each side poured out blood and money without making lasting gains to repay the effort.

A more decisive phase of the wars began in the seventh century. Weakened by Lombard attacks in Italy, by Avar-Slav offensives in the Balkans, and by a civil war following the deposition of Emperor Maurice, the Byzantines nearly succumbed to Persian assaults. The Euphrates frontier collapsed in 609; Edessa fell in 610; Antioch, Damascus, Jerusalem, Alexandria, and even Chalcedon (across the Bosphorus from Constantinople) by 617. The Byzantine Empire seemed on the verge of extinction, but the desperate situation called forth an extraordinary effort, funded by the centuries of accumulated treasure in Constantinople and fired by religious enthusiasm for the salvation of Christendom. Between 622 and 625, Heraclius won several battles and pushed the fighting back to the Euphrates. A combined Persian and Avar counter-thrust failed to capture Constantinople in 626, and the next year, in alliance with the Khazar Turks, Heraclius turned the tide, winning another great battle at Nineveh and threatening the Persian capital. The Byzantine emperor urged the Sasanians to make peace before the war "burns up everything."[15] Peace was agreed, and Heraclius returned to Constantinople in triumph, but it was really too late. The charred remains of both empires looked weak enough to tip over easily, and assaults by a new threat soon destroyed one entirely, and cut the other in half.

The Arab explosion

Heraclius had portrayed his campaign as vengeance against the enemies of God, and promised his men the reward of heaven.[16] Roman and Byzantine emperors had long enjoyed near-control of the Orthodox Church,

---

(Woodbridge: Boydell Press, 1984); Clifford J. Rogers, "The Vegetian 'Science of Warfare' in the Middle Ages," *Journal of Medieval Military History* 1 (2003): 1–20; Stephen Morillo, "Battle Seeking: The Contexts and Limits of Vegetian Strategy," ibid., 21–42; and John Gillingham, "'Up with Orthodoxy!': In Defense of Vegetian Warfare," *Journal of Medieval Military History* 2 (2004): 149–58.

15 Walter E. Kaegi, *Heraclius, Emperor of Byzantium* (Cambridge University Press, 2003): 172.
16 Theophanes (the Confessor), *Chronicle of Theophanes*, ed. and trans. Harry Turtledove (Philadelphia: University of Pennsylvania Press, 1982): 16.

supported it against "heretical" forms of Christianity like the Monophysit-
ism prevalent in Egypt and Syria, and expected in return religious leaders'
support for the state. This required some accommodation, for (like
Confucianism) Christianity was the product of a relatively peaceful and
stable imperial environment and (like Confucianism, Daoism, and Buddhism) was at best ambivalent towards both the warrior ethos and the
concentrated wealth elite warriors expected to enjoy. Christian soldiers
did heavy penance for killing even in battle and were supposed to view
war as "the worst of all evils," necessary only because "our enemies
clearly look upon the shedding of our blood as one of their basic duties
and the height of virtue."[17]

The new monotheist religion arising at this same time – Muhammad's
flight from Mecca to Medina was the same year as Heraclius' first victory –
was born in war. War is about making resistance more painful than submission, and effective conquerors work both sides of that equation in just the
ways that Islam encouraged. Fighting infidels until they exhibit "willing
submission, and feel themselves subdued" was not only a virtue, but a
religious duty. Once battle with unbelievers was joined, hellfire awaited
any Muslims who fled, heaven any who died fighting.[18] On the other hand,
Islam enjoined tolerance towards Christians and Jews willing to live peacefully under Muslim dominion, and encouraged the strong to treat the weak
with justice and charity. This was a belief system well designed for empire
building, founded by a conqueror with unified political and religious
authority.

Within a year of Muhammad's death in 632, Abu Bakr, the first caliph, had
forged a united Arab state. Its armies benefitted from the toughness and
mobility of camel-herding nomads; its leaders, from Medina and Mecca,
included skilled generals firmly resolved to extend the boundaries of Islamic
rule. Like steppe forces, Arab armies were huge in relation to the population,
but not large by agro-urban standards. Cavalry was valued, but initially
scarce. Iron helmets and leather shields were normal and mail armor
common.[19] Enemies were defeated by hard fighting and simple infantry
tactics – trench defenses and attacks first with arrows, then spears, then

---

17 John Haldon, *Warfare, State and Society in the Byzantine World, 565–1204* (London:
   Routledge, 1999): 22.
18 Quran 9:29, 4:76; 8:15–16, 4:74, 4:95.
19 Widespread use of mail is indicated by Ibn Ishaq, *The Life of Muhammad*, trans. A.
   Guillaume (New York: Oxford University Press, 2002): 546 (p. 145), 619 (p. 411), 250
   (p. 174), etc.

swords: "that's all there is to it."[20] Like Heraclius, the early caliphs pursued battle-focused strategies. After four Muslim victories in 634–5, Palestine and Syria submitted. Crushing Byzantine and Sasanian defeats at Yarmuk in 636 and Qadisiya in 637 crippled the empires' resistance. By 642, Persia and Egypt were under Arab rule. Soldiers were paid in cash with shares of the tax revenues of conquered provinces. Tax exemptions and what seemed an obvious case of divine favor won many converts to Islam, providing manpower and energy for further expansion despite two civil wars between 657 and 684. By the 730s, the Umayyads ruled an empire stretching from southern France, through Spain, across North Africa and the Middle East, into Transoxania.

Imperial expansion can proceed by a snowball effect, where each newly conquered region gets in on the profits of war by aiding in the conquest of the next, using the prestige and a fraction of the strength of the empire to overturn old balances of power. It is relatively easy to keep control of outlying areas when they are willing springboards for further expansion. But when external conquest stalls, armies concentrated on the periphery have the means and often find motive to turn against the core (sometimes in conjunction with the external enemies whom they had until then been fighting). Tang replaced Sui after failed offensives into Korea; the Carolingian Europe later fragmented after Charlemagne's conquests reached the limits of profitable campaigning; the rebellion of An Lushan's frontier armies fractured China from 755–63. By 732 the overstretched Umayyads in the northwest faced difficult Anatolian terrain skillfully defended by a reformed, though much-reduced, Byzantine army and government.

Constantinople's massive fortifications and still-efficient navy had thrown back a great Islamic offensive in 717–18. Under the pressures of war, the Byzantine preference for civilian pre-eminence had given way to a more efficient system where each province was governed as well as defended by a general officer. The cavalry-heavy "thematic" force structure, which rather like the Tang system relied on local, part-time soldiers who received land grants and provided their own mounts, equipment, and supplies, had been reinvigorated by Leo III, who won Byzantium's first major battlefield victory over the Arabs at Akroinon in 739. Shortly thereafter, in response to a revolt by provincial troops, Constantine V further strengthened the army by the creation of professional heavy cavalry regiments (*tagma*) that received their

20 Hugh Kennedy, *The Army of the Caliphs: Military and Society in the Early Islamic State* (London: Taylor and Francis, 2001): 23.

equipment (as well as lands and wages) from the state. These soldiers formed a central reserve, around which local thematic troops coalesced for major operations. In the north, the Second Turk Confederacy and Tang China prevented further Islamic conquests. In the far west, Umayyad forces were checked by the rising power of the Franks. To the east, deserts and high mountains blocked access to the Rajput kingdoms of northern India. Predictably, stymied frontier troops turned back against the failing central government. The Persian-based 'Abbasids took power in 749/50 (except in Spain, where an Umayyad fugitive established a competing caliphate) and immediately launched the campaign that threw back the Tang in 751, without however allowing a resumption of expansion.

The "Empire of the Franks"

Umayyad forces had also been defeated in Gaul in 721 and 726, then on a larger scale by the Frankish ruler Charles Martel between Poitiers and Tours in 732. In 736, with the aid of the Lombards, Charles nearly eliminated the Islamic toehold north of the Pyrenees.

The Germanic tribes that had moved into Roman Gaul, Spain, and Italy in the fifth century had created numerous small conquest dynasties. As was also common in other areas, their freemen formed a military class supported by native farmers, typically with warriors allocated the revenues of specific estates. The Germans had a long history of interaction with Rome, including service in Roman armies. They co-opted the infrastructure and literate personnel of the Catholic Church to maintain at least rudimentary bureaucracies, with Roman law for Romans and Germanic law for Germans. Common Germans fought mainly in shield-walls with spears, but the elites (who intermarried with surviving Roman aristocrats) were skilled heavy horsemen, wielding swords and lances rather than bows. Although this is a subject of fierce scholarly debate, it seems that by the mid-eighth century, in Gaul as in Anatolia and in China, cavalry had become the principal military arm.[21]

---

21 Bernard S. Bachrach has written extensively in opposition to this claim, most elaborately in "Charles Martel, Mounted Shock Combat, the Stirrup, and Feudalism," *Studies in Medieval and Renaissance History* 7 (1970); compare Clifford J. Rogers, "Carolingian Cavalry in Battle: The Evidence Reconsidered," in *Crusading and Warfare in the Middle Ages: Realities and Representations*, ed. Simon John and Nicolas Morton (Farnham: Ashgate, 2014): 1–11. For "the pre-eminence of cavalry" in Byzantium beginning in the mid-seventh century, see Haldon, *Warfare, State and Society*, 208.

Free Germans owed military service, with their own kit and supplies. In the eighth century, the Carolingian Franks built a large empire by the usual method: near-annual campaigns to secure the submission of neighbors or to crush rebels by inflicting devastation, conducting sieges, and, if the enemy obliged, by fighting battles. Warriors were rewarded with plunder, estates, and women (notably heiresses); subdued peoples contributed to the next round of conquest and gradually integrated into the polity. As the territory under Frankish rule grew, it became impractical for footmen to march from one frontier to another before the start of a campaign. Both this and tactical factors (including the use of the stirrup) led the Franks increasingly to concentrate resources on mounted soldiers. Kings and magnates granted estates to their men for that purpose, as free gifts or as fiefs. At the same time the Tang were diverting resources to the professional frontier armies and Leo III was building up his "cavalry armies,"[22] Charles Martel was redistributing extensive Church lands to his warriors, to support them as heavy cavalry. His grandson Charlemagne required poor freemen to pool resources, so that four men might contribute to sending a fifth, fully equipped, on campaign.[23]

Frankish expansion reached a natural apogee in the mid-ninth century, encompassing lands from the Pyrenees to the Saale, northern Italy, and loose dominion over the Slavic region to the east. External warfare became less profitable; war-leaders struggled to reward their men adequately. Civil wars ensued. The accumulated wealth and weakened condition of the Franks attracted predatory raiders from all directions – Magyars from the eastern steppes, seaborne Vikings and Muslims from the north and south. In the tenth century, local warlords became the focus of military strength and public authority. The spread of castles (strongly fortified, strategically sited lordly residences, which became far more common in Europe than elsewhere) greatly reinforced this trend.

Meanwhile, however, Europe was experiencing a period of remarkable demographic and economic growth, spurred by improved agricultural and mining techniques, which led to growing urbanization, division of labor, and long-distance trade. The European warrior-aristocracy turned the new wealth into stone castles, powerful war stallions, and increasingly heavy mail protection that seems to have been significantly stronger than Byzantine or

22 Ibid.
23 John France, "The Composition and Raising of the Armies of Charlemagne," *Journal of Medieval Military History* 1 (2002): 61–82, offers a balanced discussion.

Islamic armor. The crossbow (long used in China but previously rare in the West) was widely adopted by urban infantry and ships' crews. In a variation on the capitalist mentality of the urban elites developing at this time, the aristocrats expected and got large returns on their military investments by using them for war.

Grand conquests usually begin with internal consolidation, but the rise of the "Empire of the Franks" – the term used by the great thirteenth-century Mosul historian Ibn al-Athir for the spread of western European power from the eleventh century to his own day[24] – was not preceded by the reconstruction of Charlemagne's empire, or even the re-establishment of genuinely strong royal authority in any principal fragment of it. With little slackening of intra-European warfare, armies led by dukes and counts, rather than kings, carried Frenchmen – especially Normans – to power in the British Isles, southern Italy, Sicily, and even Antioch, Jerusalem and Constantinople. Small Iberian kingdoms grew rich and powerful first by using devastating slave-raids to extort tribute from neighboring Muslim states, then by occupying them outright. Despite endemic civil wars, German rulers made Bohemia into an imperial fief, and German military–religious orders conquered and Christianized the Baltic area. Even maritime city-states like Pisa and Genoa participated, seizing Corsica and Sardinia, and sacking Fatimid Mahdiya in 1087. The growth of Christian naval power led by Italian fleets was of great importance to the success of Latin expansion. From the late eighth through the tenth century, the Byzantines and the caliphate – both heirs, to some extent, of the late Roman tradition of an organized, professional navy employing specially designed warships and ship-killing tactics – had been fairly evenly matched in the eastern Mediterranean, while North Africans had held the advantage in the seas further west. Over the course of the eleventh century, however, western European sailors came to dominate the Mediterranean, both in commercial shipping and in naval warfare. The prevailing northerly winds and the relative lack of good harbors on the African coast helped the Europeans maintain this advantage until the rise of Ottoman naval power at the end of our period.

As the "Franks" conquered new territories, they typically left much of the native population on the land, as workers – effectively appropriating the income of the old elites. But some of the conquered lost their possessions – treasures, stores of food, livestock, buildings, lands, even ownership of their

---

24 John Gillingham, "An Age of Expansion, *c.* 1020–*c.* 1204," in Maurice Keen, ed., *Medieval Warfare: A History* (Oxford University Press 2000): 59.

own bodies – both to intimidate the rest and to fuel the conquest. This helps explain how Western warriors (and also steppe nomads) could conquer regions richer and more populous than their own homelands. As Duke William of Normandy observed when his advisors warned him that King Harold of England, whom he planned to attack, disposed of far greater resources than his own: "there is no doubt that whoever is bold enough to dispose of his enemy's possessions as though they were his own will overcome his enemy."[25] But before this dynamic could kick in, the enemy had to suffer military defeats severe enough to allow expropriations to take place, as Harold did at Hastings in 1066. Or at least, the soldiers had to expect that this would occur.

Western Europeans were competent in siege warfare, and by the eleventh century had the upper hand in naval combat, and those facts were necessary for their success, but it was on the battlefield that they proved generally superior to their neighbors. This was clearly seen in the First Crusade (1096–9), when the Westerners consistently defeated Turkish, Arab–Syrian, and Fatimid Egyptian armies alike, often against heavy numerical odds. A principal reason for this was their excellent armor, which Byzantine and Muslim sources describe as making Christian knights (though not their horses) almost invulnerable to arrows.[26] By the thirteenth century, Western knights with double mail over padded gambesons and heavy shields were probably the best-protected soldiers humanity had ever seen. Also, Western knights were the greatest masters of the couched lance technique. Used with high saddles and stirrups, this enabled them to strike with the massive momentum and kinetic energy of a charging stallion concentrated behind a sharp steel lance-head, rather than limiting the power of the blow to the strength of their arms. Generally speaking, no other cavalry could withstand a charge by these horsemen.

When fighting horse-archers, Western tactics were similar to Chinese methods. Footmen armed with powerful crossbows, and sometimes troops of light cavalry, kept the enemy at a distance, protecting the heavy horse behind them. The heavy cavalry stood ready to charge if the mounted bowmen came close enough to really threaten the infantry. Each arm protected the other. With these tactics, winning a decisive battlefield victory

---

25 William of Poitiers, *Gesta Guillelmi*, in Stephen Morillo, ed., *The Battle of Hastings: Sources and Interpretations* (Woodbridge: Boydell, 1996): 8.

26 Clifford J. Rogers, *Soldiers' Lives Through History: The Middle Ages* (New York: Greenwood, 2007): 171–3, 205–6, 214–5, 228–30.

was very difficult unless the enemy made a grave error. Another way to defeat a Western army was to avoid general engagements, pull all food supplies into fortified positions, harass foraging detachments, and force it to retreat from frustration and hunger. This "Vegetian" style of defense (named after the late Roman author who advocated it) was frequently used by western and eastern Europeans and by the Crusader States and was a mainstay of Byzantine strategy. A variation in which swamps, forests and mountains took the place of castles and walled cities was common in less urbanized regions.

At the end of the twelfth century, the frontiers of Latin Christendom had reached a certain equilibrium. Almost all of the Kingdom of Jerusalem was recovered by Saladin after the battle of Hattin in 1187, and in 1195 the fearsome Almohad caliph, Abu Yusuf Ya'qub, led his North Africans to hammer the Castilians at Alarcos. On the other hand, in 1204 a Latin army captured Constantinople, and in 1212 the Spanish smashed the Almohads at Las Navas de Tolosa, then went on to overrun all the remaining Muslim areas of Iberia except Granada, which became a tributary state of Castile. At this point the "Frankish" surge had run its course, not to resume for two centuries.

Indeed, in the mid-thirteenth century Europeans met two strong new adversaries who proved fully a match for them: the Mongols, who won crushing victories in Hungary and Poland, and the Mamluks, who defeated Louis IX's great effort to seize Egypt, beat even the Mongols at 'Ayn Jalut in 1260 (and again in 1281 and 1303), and finally eliminated the last remnants of the Frankish States in the Levant.

Mamluks and Mongols

The Mamluk sultanate was the culmination of a major development in Islamic warfare that began soon after the 'Abbasid revolution of 747–50. By the end of the Umayyad period, the armies of the caliphate had become less Arab-dominated, and less infantry-focused. In the late seventh century the Arabs adopted stirrups, and improved them by making them of iron rather than wood. They were considered "among the best trappings of war both for the lancer who wields his spear and the swordsman," since without them a striking cavalryman "had no support."[27] At Zab in 750, the Syrian army

---

27 Hugh Kennedy, "The Military Revolution and the Early Islamic State," in Niall Christie and Maya Yazigi (eds.), *Noble Ideals and Bloody Realities* (Leiden: Brill, 2006): 199, quoting two ninth-century Muslim authors.

charged on horseback "like a mountain of iron," and the 'Abbasid decision to dismount and fight on foot was a calculated tactical decision, not a default action.[28] Starting in the 820s the future Caliph al-Mu'tasim, having observed the extraordinary loyalty and prowess of Turkic freedmen in a recent civil war, created an elite cavalry force of some 3–4,000 steppe Turks, recruited by a method that was then revolutionary, though it soon became perfectly normal: he bought them. Turkish boys old enough to have developed steppe toughness, horsemanship, and archery skills could be ensconced in an artificial military community and taught Islam, discipline, combat techniques, and absolute devotion to the patron who had rescued them from the slave-markets – a loyalty in theory undivided by familial, factional, or sectarian allegiances. The experiment was so successful that later in the ninth century it could be said that Turkish slaves (mamluks) gave the caliph "an invulnerable armour," and in the tenth century that they not only spearheaded but "constituted" his army.[29]

The mamluk system was designed to solve a problem common to many states in this period. When rulers are expanding their power-bases, they can reward their followers with rich gifts expropriated from the defeated. When a state is growing slowly or not at all, however, resources for the warriors have to come from the limited surpluses generated by agricultural economies. To sustain a service–reward exchange, a ruler must collect taxes from farmers and merchants and redistribute them to fighters. This is feasible but costly (especially when many soldiers are horsemen), as it requires supporting two elites, civil and military. When economic downturns or military pressures require economizing measures, a natural response is to combine the elites, so that soldiers administer lands and collect their revenues, and landholders owe cavalry service. A system which disperses soldiers to estates outside the main fighting season does slow down mobilization and limit opportunities for unit drill, but it also provides on-the-spot capability to respond to local uprisings, brigandage or raids. Moreover, it uses resources more efficiently, since it is much cheaper to move a horseman to 3,000 kg of grain and hay than to do the reverse. Variations on this system were the norm in the West, under the Sasanians, under some conquest dynasties in

---

28 Ibid., 202.
29 Reuven Amitai, "The Mamluk Institution: 1000 Years of Military Slavery in the Islamic World," in Philip D. Morgan and Christopher L. Brown (eds.), *Arming Slaves: From Classical Times to the Modern Age* (New Haven: Yale University Press, 2006): 46, quoting al-Jahiz and al-Istakhri.

China, in Heian Japan, in Silla and Koryŏ Korea, Ayyubid and Mamluk Egypt, and in Byzantium under the theme system, for example.

Hereditary landholding aristocrats, however, view wealth as their birthright, not as a gift from the ruler, and unless campaigning is profitable, military service may become a resented burden. This tendency can be counteracted to a degree by cultural norms defining masculinity and worthiness in terms of prowess and loyalty. But prowess can be demonstrated in civil wars, and in military–aristocratic hierarchies loyalties may focus more on regional magnates than on central courts. The system is more stable when the ruler can freshly endow each new generation of soldiers with his own gifts. The European fief accomplished this at least in theory, as it remained the property of the granting lord, to be recovered and re-granted at each cycle of inheritance. Various empires, including Byzantium, China, and the Delhi Sultanate, have used slave-eunuch generals and administrators to ensure that high offices would regularly revert to the emperor for re-granting. Similarly, mamluks could not pass estates or even mamluk status to their children. Each new ruler could "raise from the dust" a new set of his own warriors – youths dependent on and grateful for his favor, yet possessing martial skills and values that among agro-urban populations normally could be found only among children of aristocrats. (Prestigious standing forces with well-paid commissioned officers, like the Byzantine *tagmata*, some variations of Chinese Palace Armies or Imperial Guards, or the French *compagnies d'ordonnance* at the end of our period, worked on related principles, but did not give the ruler equal opportunities to shape the upbringing of the soldiers or to isolate them from other loyalties.)

The mamluk system consistently created excellent soldiers, and was about as good as any in keeping military power under central control. But even mamluks insulated from external loyalties still had self-interest that could conflict with the desires of their masters – or, more often, with those of their masters' heirs. And the very lack of roots in the broader community that contributed to the mamluks' reliability also ensured a generally high level of tension between the army (and its head, the caliph) and regional elites. The collapse of the 'Abbasid Caliphate's authority began in 861 with a palace coup led by Turkish ex-mamluks. Nonetheless, from the ninth century on, practically every Islamic ruler employed mamluk soldiers, even when the rulers were themselves Turks, whether the leaders of conquest dynasties like the Seljuks, or descended from mamluks who seized power for themselves. A good example of the latter is the Ghaznavids, who from 963–1187 employed Turkic slave-soldiers to extend their control over much of Persia,

Transoxania, and Afghanistan, and for the first time pushed Muslim rule into northern India.

In Egypt, elite mamluks played a key role in defeating the invasion of King Louis IX of France in 1249, but then staged a coup and executed the new sultan, who was promoting his own slaves over the old guard. Rather than installing a puppet sultan, the mamluk leader Qutuz took direct rule, establishing the Mamluk Sultanate which would retain control of Egypt and Syria until 1517. The core of the army continued to be mamluks purchased from the steppes, converted to Islam, and rigorously trained by eunuch drill-sergeants until manhood. They were then manumitted and allowed to rise in rank by merit. Officers were granted *iqta'* (rights to the government revenues from designated lands, which were returned to the government at promotion, disgrace, or death; equivalent to Byzantine *pronoia* or Ottoman *timar*) to support themselves and their men.[30] Mamluks' sons were normal freemen, not mamluks themselves.

Mamluk cavalry were as skilled and disciplined as any soldiers in the world. The outcome in medieval battles, especially cavalry battles, was often determined by the clash not of mass against mass, but of the best troops on each side, who were normally around the army commander. If they were defeated he could be killed. When his banner fell, the army was likely to collapse. This helps explain why elite military households, guards, and mamluk units received so much attention and wealth. The tenth-century Byzantine emperor Nicephoros Phocas, for example, created a special force of a few hundred heavy-armored cataphracts with quadruple the land-allocation of normal horsemen, and wrote that the first principle of tactics was to slam the wedge of cataphracts straight at the enemy commander.[31] At 'Ayn Jalut, after ferocious hand-to-hand fighting, the Mongol general Kitbuqa was killed, and his army defeated.

This was possible partly because the great bulk of the Mongol forces that had overrun Persia and Syria and destroyed Baghdad had already withdrawn from the region, partly because the terrain did not support huge numbers of ponies well, and partly because of internal Mongol politics following the death of the Great Khan. The same considerations had spared western

30 On the iqta' system, see Sato Tsugitaka, *State and Rural Society in Medieval Islam* (Leiden: Brill, 1997).
31 Warren Treadgold, *Byzantium and its Army, 284–1081* (Stanford University Press, 1998): 174; Stephen Morillo, Jeremy Black, and Paul Lococo, *War in World History: Society, Technology and War from Ancient Times to the Present*, vol. 1 (New York: McGraw-Hill, 2008): 155.

Europe from a full-scale assault in 1242. It should not, however, be blithely assumed that a Mongol invasion of the West would have succeeded. The Hungarians fought hard in 1241; after the battle of Mohi the Mongols could not launch the pursuit "to the furthest limits," "to the end," that Chinggis Khan made a distinctive characteristic of their warfare,[32] and Hungary, though devastated, did not submit. Further west the Mongols would have faced even tougher enemies, less open terrain, and stronger and more numerous castles. On the other hand, although they did not there face the combination of castles and urban fortifications that made conquest so difficult in the West, the Mongols did take many great walled cities in West Asia and China using co-opted local manpower and expertise. Perhaps they could have done the same in Europe.

Mongols in China

Like the Umayyads, after reaching an apogee of strength around 750, the Tang had faced a great rebellion led by a frontier commander.[33] Unlike Abu al-'Abbas, who became the first caliph of the 'Abbasid dynasty, the Turkish-Sogdian general An Lushan ultimately failed. In both cases, the following century saw a rise in the power of provincial warlords. In the ninth century, as the Carolingian Empire in Europe fragmented (843) and the mamluk coup of 861 gravely weakened the caliphate, the Huang Chao rebellion (875–84) led to the disintegration of the Tang state by 907. Although the Song dynasty reunited almost all of China by 960, it could make no progress against the nomadic Khitan Liao dynasty ruling the north. Indeed, from 1005 the Song paid an annual tribute to the Liao, and in 1127 lost their capital at Kaifeng and all of northern China to the Jurchen, the successors of the Khitans. Nonetheless, Song advantages in logistics and in siege and riverine warfare (deriving in some small part from use of gunpowder weapons as early as 1132) kept most of China under Chinese rule.[34]

Prior to their invasions of Persia and eastern Europe, the Mongols, temporarily allied with the Song, defeated and absorbed their neighbors the Jurchen (1211–34), using a combination of devastating raids, cooption of Jurchen subjects, and eventually siege warfare. The Mongols, the Song, and

---

32 *Secret History*, 185.

33 In fact, An-Lushan's rebellion in 755 was the third rebellion by a frontier commander since 734. Jonathan Karam Skaff, "'Barbarians at the Gates?' The Tang Frontier Military and the An Lushan Rebellion," *War and Society* 18 (2000): 33.

34 Peter A. Lorge, *The Asian Military Revolution* (Cambridge University Press, 2008), ch. 1.

the Jurchen had been in a three-way military balance, but South China was at a decisive disadvantage against Mongols controlling North China's resources. When the assault on the Song began in 1256, the lands formerly under Jurchen control contributed food, weapons, logistical administrators, riverine forces, and huge numbers of troops (especially infantry). The Mongols also brought in Arab–Persian siege specialists, unequalled in undermining walls and construction of giant stone-throwing trebuchets, when Chinese engineers proved unable to subdue the strongest Song fortifications.

By the time the Mongols completed the conquest of China in 1279, their great empire had split into four independent states, and though he claimed superiority over them all, Qubilai Khan focused his attention on China, which he was the first non-Han emperor to rule completely. The Song, originators of the proverb that good iron is not used to make nails, nor good men to make soldiers, had studiously avoided fostering a martial culture and structured their military to ensure civilian control, even at the cost of efficacy.[35] The new Yuan dynasty retained the services of the traditional Chinese bureaucracy, but imposed a superstructure of Mongol military–political organization, with the warriors firmly in charge. Universal service by Mongol men continued, supported by slave labor and heavy taxation. Mongol princes received giant appanages; soldiers (and favored subjects such as cavalrymen from other steppe peoples) got small estates. North Chinese soldiers were given farms; South Chinese troops were paid from tax revenues. Vast resources went into projects like the extension of the Grand Canal to Beijing, which though extraordinarily beneficial economically, were principally intended to support military logistical requirements.

Warfare on the borders and against rebels in China, Mongolia, and Central Asia was frequent. A series of invasions of Vietnam from 1257–88 met serious military setbacks in the face of guerilla warfare and Vegetian defense, but did end with both the Viet and Champa states as Yuan tributaries. Major seaborne invasions were launched (unsuccessfully) against Java in 1293 and Japan in 1274 and 1281 (see Figure 6.2). In Java the Mongols tried the usual technique of allying with one local power against another, but in this case the beneficiary of their aid, after formally submitting to Yuan overlordship, attacked the Mongol encampment by surprise and forced the fleet to return to China. Japan's successful defense owed a great deal to luck, in the form of "divine wind" storms that wrecked the Mongol fleets both times. It also

35 Yuan-Kang Wang, *Harmony and War: Confucian Culture and Chinese Power Politics* (New York: Columbia University Press, 2010): 16–17.

Figure 6.2 Mongols and Japanese fight, in a scene from the Mōko Shūrai Ekotoba, a Japanese handscroll made between 1275 and 1293. Pictures From History / Bridgeman Images

reflected the effectiveness of *bushi* (aristocratic warriors), who had become the dominant force in Japanese warfare in the late eighth century, with the rise of tax-exempt noble domains, privatization of government, and the consequent decline of a more centralized *fubing*-style military. Their heavy armor, mounted archery skills, and trained swordsmanship put them on a par with Mongol troops. After the Mongol defeat, with neither an external threat to impose unity nor the possibility of external conquests to fund consolidation, territorial magnates with their wooden castles and little private armies became increasingly independent, creating a military environment similar to that of High Medieval Europe.

The Ming and the Indian Ocean

Remarkable achievement though it was, the military structure of Yuan China was as artificial as the new steppe lands created in North China to support Mongol ponies and the man-made river of the Great Canal that sustained the newly built capital at Beijing. Without the profits of continued conquest, the costs of the huge military infrastructure (with over a million men under arms) had to be borne by the native population. Civil wars made the Yuan government weaker, with power shifting to regional warlords as in contemporary Japan or in the late 'Abbasid Caliphate, and despite resisting sinicization Mongol troops lost their hard edge over time. Zhu Yuanzhang, the Han warlord who founded the Ming dynasty (1368–1644), had to reconquer China step by step, fighting both Yuan forces and competing rebels, and his victories put great resources of land under his control. He used them to reward his generals, to create a new native martial nobility, and to distribute military lands to self-supporting farmer-soldiers along *fubing* lines, but not concentrated in frontier areas. To prevent the generals from becoming threats to his authority, the new emperor ensured that field armies were drawn from the regional garrisons, but led by officers from different areas. The political advantages of this system outweighed costs in cohesion and military efficacy. Although Zhu Yuanzhang's early attitudes reflected his later regnal title ("Immensely Martial"), under later Ming emperors civilian precedence over the military was restored nearly to Song levels.

Rather than using military force for real conquests, the late Ming made heavy use of an old Chinese idea: encouraging neighbors to make largely nominal submissions and to pay "tribute" by returning gifts of much greater value than the tribute received. This practice reached its high point with the great "Treasure Fleets" of the eunuch admiral Zheng He, which between 1405 and 1433 sailed as far as East Africa. "When we arrived at the foreign countries," Zheng He's record states, "barbarian kings who resisted [submission] and were not respectful we captured alive, and [pirates] . . . we eliminated." In most places in Southeast Asia force was not needed, as local rulers, awed by the strength of the fleets' size (around 300 ships, some of them gigantic, and 27,000 sailors and marines) and pleased by Chinese gifts, allowed the erection of tablets representing Ming suzerainty.[36] Wars in this region were typically fought to control and tax seaborne trade, which might be combined with the "delight in looting . . . by the light of destructive fires" proclaimed by Chola rulers.[37] Diplomatic treatment of the Ming fleet avoided risk of the latter and cost nothing in terms of the former.

The more powerful states the fleet encountered further west – notably the Vijayangaran empire in southern India and the Mamluk Sultanate – were presumably not asked for submission. The Vijayangaran Empire, which controlled southern India, formed in the mid-fourteenth century when the Delhi sultanate, which had briefly ruled most of the area, began to break apart. The Delhi sultanate had been founded in 1206, after a decisive victory at Tarain (1192) led to the conquest of northern India by Muslim Ghurids. The Hindu Rajput kingdoms employed elephants, large numbers of low-

---

36 Wang, *Harmony and War*, 160, 164 (quotation).
37 G. W. Spencer, "The Politics of Plunder: The Cholas in Eleventh-Century Ceylon," *Journal of Asian Studies* 35 (1976): 405.

quality infantry, and relatively small forces of warrior-caste cavalry, limited by the unsuitability of the area for large-scale horse-breeding. Although their forces won some battles, ultimately they proved unable to cope with armies composed mainly of mamluk cavalry, provided with plenty of horses and weapons of superior quality, and supported by siege engineers employing traction trebuchets. In southern India, however, the heat and the terrain made campaigning difficult for large mounted forces, and the Vijayanagar remained strong until 1565.

Africa, the Atlantic, and the slave trade

Zheng He received tribute even from Mogadishu in East Africa. Muslim Arab–Berber conquerors and settlers had in the ninth and tenth centuries come to dominate the Sahel and the Horn of Africa, relying mainly on cavalry, against which local rulers, lacking either horsemen of their own or disciplined, armored infantry, had no effective response. Further south, climate and forests made horses almost useless, but in the border zone cavalry aristocracies engaged in frequent dry-season slave-raids, the profits of which funded their acquisition of horses and armor imported across the Sahara.[38]

The significance of slave acquisition in fueling the warfare of this period all across the world was very great, and has not been adequately appreciated. Although prices fluctuated greatly, falling dramatically when successful military campaigns flooded the markets with captives, soldiers could often get two months' wages for a typical slave, and much more for a beautiful girl. The sale of the 1,254 inhabitants of the Tunisian island Kerkennah in 1286 provided enough gold to fund a large fleet's operation for two months.[39] Contemporary sources emphasize the "joy" of the Portuguese at the discovery (in 1441) that the coast of west central Africa provided abundant opportunities for brutal and highly profitable slave-raids against near-defenseless villagers.[40] Subsequently the level of slave-raiding warfare in the area rose dramatically, as coastal rulers seized their neighbors to trade to the

---

38 Roland Oliver and Anthony Atmose, *Medieval Africa* (Cambridge University Press, 2008): 7–8.

39 Clifford J. Rogers, "Medieval Strategy and the Economics of Conquest," in Manuel Rojas Gabriel, ed., *Estrategia en la édad media* (Cáceres: Imprenta de la Universidad de Extremadura, forthcoming).

40 E.g. Gomes Eanes de Zurara, *The Chronicle of the Discovery and Conquest of Guinea*, trans. Charles Raymond Beazley and Edgar Prestage, vol. 1 (London: Hakluyt Society, 1896): 50–1.

Portuguese. The Ottomans, similarly, began their rise with constant slave-raiding in Anatolia, and nearly collapsed when Sultan Bayezid was beaten in 1402 by the Mongol–Turkic conqueror Timur, whose own empire building was partly funded by the profits of mass enslavements of tens of thousands of victims.

Europe's military revolutions

The Ottomans were Turks, but at the turn of the fifteenth century their capital (Adrianople/Edirne) and a large portion of their dominion was European, and their territorial heartland was formerly Byzantine Anatolia. Like most Muslim states after 900, the Ottomans employed elite slave-soldiers, but the main strength of their cavalry – the principal arm of their forces – came from free holders of *timar* (similar to *pronoia* and *iqta'*). These armored troopers were equipped and fought much like mamluks, using exceptionally strong composite bows with over 100-pound draw-weights.[41] The *timariots* were complemented by smaller standing forces of highly trained slave-soldiers (*kapikulu*) – including the famous standing regiments of the "Janissary" infantry, who in battle anchored the center while the cavalry enveloped the enemy flanks. Ottoman forces also included strong artillery trains and numerous irregular frontier-raiders and low-quality con-script footmen.

By the end of our period, the Ottomans possessed one of the most effective military organizations the world had ever seen. In the second half of the fifteenth century, the Ottomans conquered Constantinople and most of the Balkans. Between 1514 and 1529, they inflicted crushing defeats on Safavid, Mamluk, and Bohemian-Hungarian armies, conquered the Mamluk sultanate and much of Hungary, and advanced to besiege Vienna. In both West and East, the tactical flexibility, impressive logistical organization, and outstanding discipline of the Turkish forces (especially the *kapikulu*) contrib-uted to success. In the East, the Ottomans' superior infantry and mastery of gunpowder weapons – both muskets and cannon – gave them a key advan-tage. Chinese armies had made significant military use of gunpowder, in rockets, flame-throwers, and guns, from the twelfth century onward, and the technology was widely used throughout Asia in the fourteenth century. But by the mid-fifteenth century, Europeans (including the Ottomans) had

---

41 Adam Karpowicz, "Ottoman Bows – An Assessment of Draw Weight, Performance and Tactical Use," *Antiquity* 81 (2007): 681–2.

handguns and large siege guns that were strong enough to take full advantage of more powerful "corned" (granulated) gunpowder. These weapons harnessed chemical energy to revolutionize both siege warfare and battlefield tactics.

European bombards were the first weapons capable of rapidly breaching strong fortifications, greatly reducing the advantage of the defense in siege warfare which had shaped so much of the warfare of our period. When "great towns, which once could have held out for a year ... now fell in a single month," the art of war was "turned upside-down."[42] In the fourteenth century, partly because Europe was the most heavily fortified region on earth, battle-avoiding Vegetian strategy had been the norm for states on the defensive. Since nearly all troops were by this time paid daily wages, offensive warfare had become very expensive. Sieges required large forces for long periods, and in wars between Christians it was not permitted to recoup the costs by enslaving defeated populations. In the face of a determined and well-conducted defense, invasions often collapsed for lack of money and lack of progress. Small states could resist more powerful neighbors; central governments found it difficult to bring recalcitrant provincial nobles to heel. With the new artillery, the strategic inertia favoring the defense was greatly reduced; to defeat an invader now practically required beating him in open battle. Both conquest and internal consolidation became markedly easier for states with strong artillery trains and armies spearheaded by elite standing forces, like Charles VII's France, the Ottoman Empire, or Ferdinand and Isabella's Spain.

On the battlefield, however, the advantage had already in the fourteenth century shifted from cavalry (which fights only by attacking) to tightly arrayed infantry, and hence from offense to defense. Western plate armor of the late fourteenth century was already the most completely protective ever developed, and to compete with it European infantry deployed the most powerful infantry missile weapons yet developed, steel-bowed crossbows and English longbows. In the early fifteenth century Milanese smiths developed high-carbon quenched steel armor with double the hardness of earlier models, so tough that it was extremely difficult to penetrate with muscle-powered weapons.

---

42 Bernáldez and Guicciardini, quoted in Clifford J. Rogers, "The Artillery and Artillery Fortress Revolutions Revisited," in Nicolas Prouteau, Emmanuel de Crouy-Chanel and Nicolas Faucherre (eds.), *Artillerie et fortification, 1200–1600* (Rennes: Presses universitaires de Rennes, 2011): 75.

Figure 6.3 The Battle of Avray in 1364, Master of Mary of Burgundy (*fl.* 1469–83). This painting, made in 1477, shows weapons of its time, not the time of the battle. Collection of the Earl of Leicester, Holkham Hall, Norfolk / Bridgeman Images)

This was a principal reason for the spread of handguns, which were slow-firing and inaccurate, but by 1400 could launch a ball with ten times the kinetic energy of the strongest longbows' arrows. When protected from charging cavalry by pikemen, entrenchments, or lines of chained war-wagons, handgunners proved increasingly valuable on the battlefield, as well as in sieges (see Figure 6.3). In the fifteenth century, Czech Hussites and Ottoman Janissaries were among the first to show how effective hand-held firearms could be.[43] (Handguns had long been used in China, but they were weaker and more closely equivalent to crossbows.)

At the end of our period European states had developed fortresses, armor, and artillery that were qualitatively superior to any the world had seen before, and infantry missile weapons more powerful than any others. Their ships were also the best ever built (despite being very much smaller than the

43 Clifford J. Rogers, "Tactics and the Face of Battle," in Frank Tallett and D. J. B. Trim (eds.), *European Warfare, 1350–1750* (Cambridge University Press, 2010): 203–35.

Chinese "treasure ships"), and had carried them not only to sub-Saharan Africa, but also to the New World, previously entirely isolated from the military developments of Afro-Eurasia. Spanish explorers encountered peoples whose armaments were on the opposite end of the spectrum from their own: practically the first thing Columbus recorded about the natives of the Caribbean is that they had no armor or metal weapons. The Aztecs, Inca, and Maya did make limited use of bronze, but most Native American military technology was made of stone, bone, leather, and wood. There were of course still wars, which as in Afro-Eurasia were fought largely for political–territorial dominion, acquisition of slaves, and revenge. American weapons were well-suited to disabling and capturing enemy warriors who could be enslaved, adopted, or subjected to elaborate rituals of revenge-torture. Until the fourteenth century, Europeans fighting Europeans had likewise often sought to beat down and capture enemy men-at-arms (to gain the profits of ransom rather than slaves or torture-victims) but crossbows, longbows, pikes, and especially guns were ill-suited for that purpose. By the time they reached the Americas, Europeans generally had little interest in taking captives until the fighting was finished and the enemy routed. Their more "bloody and devouring" style of war,[44] their horses and guns, and (most importantly) steel armor and weapons, gave Europeans huge military advantages over Native Americans, a fact Columbus immediately recognized. He promptly concluded that the crews of his three little ships would have sufficed to conquer an area with double the population of Portugal.[45] In the sixteenth century the Spanish would exploit their one-sided military advantages to extract massive quantities of wealth from the Americas, then pour much of that wealth into the extremely capital-intensive mode of warfare characteristic of late medieval Europe. These resources, in combination with the highly effective military technology and techniques they had already developed by 1500 and a few new innovations, such as *trace italienne* fortresses, would in subsequent centuries solidify and expand the qualitative military edge Europeans had gained even over other advanced Eurasian civilizations.

---

44 Roger Williams, *Key to the Language of the Indians of New England* (London, 1643): 235.
45 Christopher Columbus, *The Journal of Christopher Columbus (During His First Voyage, 1492–1493), etc.*, trans. Clements R. Markham (London: Hakluyt Society, 1893): 137–8.

FURTHER READING

Al-Jahiz, "The Virtues of the Turk," in *Nine Essays of al-Jahiz*, trans. William M. Hutchins. New York, NY: Peter Lang, 1989.

Amitai, Reuven. "The Mamluk Institution: 1000 Years of Military Slavery in the Islamic World," in Philip D. Morgan and Christopher L. Brown (eds.), *Arming Slaves: From Classical Times to the Modern Age*. New Haven, CT: Yale University Press, 2006: 40–78.

Bachrach, Bernard. *Early Carolingian Warfare*. Philadelphia, PA: University of Pennsylvania Press, 2000.

Barfield, Thomas J. *The Perilous Frontier. Nomadic Empire and China 221 B.C. to A.D. 1757*. Cambridge, MA: Blackwell, 1992.

Barua, Pradeep. *The State at War in South Asia*. Lincoln, NE: University of Kansas Press, 2005.

Bennett, Matthew, ed. *The Medieval World at War*. London: Thames and Hudson, 2009.

Crone, Patricia. *Slaves on Horses. The Evolution of the Islamic Polity*. Cambridge University Press, 1980.

France, John. *Western Warfare in the Age of the Crusades, 1000–1300*. Ithaca, NY: Cornell University Press, 1999.

Friday, Kar. *Samurai, Warfare and the State in Early Medieval Japan*. London: Routledge, 2004.

Graff, David. *Medieval Chinese Warfare, 300–900*. London: Routledge, 2001.

Haldon, John. *Warfare, State and Society in the Byzantine World, 565–1204*. London: Routledge, 1999.

Halsall, Guy. *Warfare and Society in the Barbarian West, 450–900*. London: Routledge, 2003.
The History and the Life of Chinggis Khan (The Secret History of the Mongols), trans. Urgunge Onon, Leiden: Brill, 1990.

Kaegi, Walter E. *Heraclius, Emperor of Byzantium*. Cambridge University Press, 2003.

Keen, Maurice, ed. *Medieval Warfare: A History*. Oxford University Press, 2000.

Kennedy, Hugh. *The Army of the Caliphs: Military and Society in the Early Islamic State*. London: Taylor and Francis, 2001.
"The Military Revolution and the Early Islamic State," in Niall Christie and Maya Yazigi (eds.), *Noble Ideals and Bloody Realities*. Leiden: Brill, 2006.

Lorge, Peter A. *The Asian Military Revolution*. Cambridge University Press, 2008.

May, Timothy. *The Mongol Art of War*. Barnsley, England: Pen & Sword, 2007.

Morillo, Stephen, Jeremy Black, and Paul Lococo. *War in World History: Society, Technology and War from Ancient Times to the Present*, vol. 1. New York, NY: McGraw-Hill, 2008.

Rogers, Clifford J. "The Military Revolutions of the Hundred Years' War," *Journal of Military History*, 57 (1993): 241–78..
Soldiers' Lives through History: The Middle Ages. New York, NY: Greenwood, 2007.

Sandhu, Gurcharn Singh. *A Military History of Medieval India*. New Delhi: Vision Books, 2003.

Treadgold, Warren. *Byzantium and its Army, 284–1081*. Stanford University Press, 1998.

Zakeri, Moshen. *Sasanid Soldiers in Early Muslim Society*. Wiesbaden: Otto Harrassowitz Verlag, 1995.

PART II

★

EURASIAN COMMONALITIES

Courtly cultures: western Europe, Byzantium, the Islamic world, India, China, and Japan

PATRICK J. GEARY, DAUD ALI, PAUL S. ATKINS,
MICHAEL COOPERSON, RITA COSTA GOMES,
PAUL DUTTON, GERT MELVILLE, CLAUDIA RAPP,
KARL-HEINZ SPIEß, STEPHEN WEST AND PAULINE YU

Courts are centers of power, whether religious or political, which create specialized communities of individuals who both carry out functions related to the exercise of this power and simultaneously create cultural forms that represent these centers to themselves and to those outside them. Courts were necessary to rulers because these human configurations reproduced on a daily basis their special position within society, setting them apart and making visible to all how the rulers were related to a specific social and cosmic order. In Asia, paradigmatic court traditions took shape in China during the Han dynasty (206 BCE–220 CE) and influenced those in Japan. In western Eurasia, Roman imperial and regional courts set the model for the Byzantine court, the papal court, and the courts of Western barbarian successor kingdoms as well as, to some extent, Islamic courts, although the latter particularly appropriated traditions from the Sasanian courts as did Indian courts. Across Eurasia, in addition to courts created around central authorities, local courts – themselves to a greater or lesser extent modeled on central courts – developed around local power centers, whether religious, administrative, or private.

Power and place

Between 500 and 1500 Constantinople (modern Istanbul) was the site of the most stable court in the world: for almost a millennium, from the late fifth century until 1453 – except for a brief hiatus between 1204 and 1261 when the city was under Crusader rule – it was the permanent residence for the

Byzantine emperors. The papal court, which developed out of late Roman traditions of administration, was also remarkably stable through most of this period, although between 1309 and 1376 it moved to Avignon and then between 1378 and 1417 rival popes, one in Rome and one in Avignon, competed for universal recognition. The caliphate, too, knew considerable continuity in the location of its court. Baghdad, founded in 762 as the successor to the Umayyad capital of Damascus, housed the 'Abbasid court almost continuously until the Mongol invasion of 1258.

Elsewhere, changes in dynasties meant changes in the centers of royal or imperial power. China knew various, at times competing, imperial court cities after the collapse of the Han dynasty in 220, when new regional courts claiming imperial legitimacy arose. These included the Shu court of Chengdu and the Wu court at Jiankang as well as northern centers of power dominated by barbarian rather than Han traditions. The Tang (618–907) re-established unity and attempted to revive Han court traditions at Chang'an (present-day Xi'an). Subsequently Kaifeng remained a major capital city under various names until the Mongols created a new capital at what would become Beijing. The Japanese court followed the Chinese model and early on was located at various sites in the Asuka region until it was finally fixed at Nara in 710. In 784, the capital was moved to Nagaoka, west of what is now Kyoto. Only in 794 was the Heian capital established at present-day Kyoto, where it remained, with a few exceptions (Fukuhara in the twelfth century and Yoshino rivalling Kyoto in the fourteenth) for more than a millennium.

The continuity of these great courts contrasted with the peripatetic courts of India and western Europe. Power in India and post-Roman western Europe was distributed, with numerous smaller court-centered polities, modular in their proliferation but often ranged in unstable relation to one another. In both regions monarchs and their courts were often traveling, both on ritual tours of the kingdom and on military campaigns. In India and to some extent in parts of Europe, these processions were highly ritualized events and presented the court "on the move" – with many of the same functionaries that attended the royal assembly within the palace. Many royal decrees, particularly land grants, were issued from military encampments set up while Indian and European kings were waging war. Royal palaces and administrative centers were often changed from generation to generation by rulers, mostly because of intra- or inter-generational factionalism and strife. Early attempts at establishing fixed locations, such as Ravenna for the Ostrogothic ruler Theodoric or Aachen for the Frankish king and emperor

Charlemagne, remained exceptional and short-lived, only gradually resulting in the creation of fixed administrative centers such as Paris or Westminster.

These radical differences in place corresponded to an equally radical difference in physical organization. Chinese courts were by many orders of magnitude the largest courts in the world, and thanks to their rigid grid-square layouts they were the most organized and complex. Chang'an, the location of the Tang court, by 750 had a population of close to one million. The city's layout was an almost perfect square of 8.6 kilometers by 9.7 kilometers, divided into a grid with the Imperial City and Imperial Palace centered in the north. The Song capitals of Kaifeng and Hangzhou were also vibrant, wealthy, and well-populated cities that undertook impressive construction projects.

While the Chinese court was separated from the rest of the city by imposing walls, the Byzantine court blended into the urban fabric of Constantinople. The palace area occupied the southeastern part of the triangular peninsula on which Constantinople was located, and was thus largely bounded by water. To the north lay the patriarchate and the Church of Holy Wisdom (Hagia Sophia) and to the west the hippodrome where the emperor presided over the horse races and other entertainments in full view of the other spectators. A bronze gate (*Chalke*) decorated with religious and imperial imagery marked the ceremonial entry point into the palace area. The palace itself was an agglomeration of buildings that underwent many alterations in the course of time – residences for the imperial household and the imperial bodyguard, chapels, reception and banqueting halls, but also a private harbor, gardens and a polo ground. Apart from the imperial bodyguards, most courtiers resided in the city and reported for duty when their presence was required. The court itself functioned as the residence for the men, women and children of the imperial family and their immediate servants, who lived in separate male and female quarters. As the center of imperial power, it boasted several reception halls where imperial ceremonials were staged in the presence of courtiers, arranged in strict hierarchical order. Although the Byzantine emperor was believed to be God's viceregent on earth and the palace featured a number of chapels and small churches, the center of religious power was not the court but the nearby Church of Holy Wisdom under the authority of the Patriarch, to which the emperor had privileged access.

Japanese capitals were established on the Chinese model, laid out on a grid according to geomantic principles, with major Buddhist temples and Shinto shrines sited nearby. Indian courts were less formally structured, with the residential interior of the king's palace including women's quarters (*antahpuram*), houses for princes, and often a garden or pleasure park for use by the king and his intimates. The least formal spatial organizations of all were western European courts, which, in keeping with the constant mobility of the court, often consisted of no more than great estates or rural palaces with a residence and throne hall, a palace chapel, and various undifferentiated buildings for the support of the royal family and its retainers. When centers of royal or princely power began to become more established, they were deeply influenced by the architecture of fortifications. This typically included a heavily guarded walled area that enclosed the royal residence, throne hall, living quarters for intimate members of the household, and a palace chapel. Even by the end of the fifteenth century Western monarchies had hardly begun to create fixed royal courts comparable to those of Asia.

Membership and function

Not every royal or imperial court was a center of real political power, and the makeup and roles of courtiers differed enormously across Eurasia. Since the centers of the Chinese and Byzantine empires were the imperial courts themselves, they were the nexus of the imperial households, large civil bureaucracies, and the emperor's personal servants and bureaucrats. Here, however, the similarities end. The Chinese imperial court was highly structured, consisting of four main constituencies: the civil, military, and imperial bureaucracies, and the women's quarters. In the civil bureaucracy the emperor stood at the head of a complex system that radiated from the court to every county in the empire. At the court itself were Grand Councilors, who were heads of the Three Cabinets (the Chancellery, the Secretariat, and the Department of State Affairs); the Censorate and Remonstration Bureau, in charge of monitoring the conduct of officials and the emperor; the State Finance Commission; and the Bureau of Military Affairs. Their offices were located in the capital, across the street from the southern entrances to the Forbidden City. In addition, the Department of State Affairs oversaw the Six Ministries of Personnel (in charge of civil service appointments and transfers), of Revenue, of Rites, of War, of Punishments, and of Public Works; nine courts in charge of ritual and entertainment music, the royal clan, granaries, etc.; and the five bureaus of State Education, Manufacturing, Military Equipment, Construction, and Hydrology. Under the Song the emperor was also in charge of the Hanlin Academy, a personal secretarial service for the emperor as well as personal physicians and other professionals, and of the Department of Private Documents, which included the Court of Historians, Court of Veritable Records for each reign, the Office of Calendar and Astronomy, the Office of Administrative Documents, and the Astronomy Bureau. In addition, a military presence at court consisted of nearly 500,000 men kept near the capital as well as Imperial Guards stationed both in the Forbidden City and in the city, but always within the Inner Wall.

The Chinese court also included numerous eunuchs who were personal attendants on the emperor and the royal clan, particularly women. They performed numerous daily tasks but could on occasion rise to prominence as privy councilor to the emperor, and because of their close personal ties to the imperial family they were given many important ad hoc assignments, such as heading construction and hydrology projects. Finally, there was a graded hierarchy for the many women who populated the eastern part of the rear palaces: the dowager empress, the empress, royal consorts, concubines, and women in waiting. There was, as well, a large network of royal princes and princesses who were housed within the capital (for princes) or sent out in marriage (princesses).

Beginning with the Tang, entry to the imperial Chinese court bureaucracy occurred increasingly through imperial examinations based on the Confucian classics and composition skills, which gave successful candidates access to positions in the government civil service, including service in the imperial court itself. Under the Tang, holders of the highest degree rose from 7 per cent of chief councilors in the early seventh century to over 40 per cent a century later, although the overwhelming majority of Tang officials obtained their positions not through the examination system but through patronage and recommendations. By the Song, the examination system had become so significant that hundreds of thousands of aspirants sat for examinations at all levels, although fewer than 1 per cent of candidates might aspire to the highest degree, *jinshi* (presented scholar), and have access to the imperial palace. Still, aristocratic patronage and nepotism insured that roughly half of the palace bureaucracy rose more through connections than through the examinations.

No other court approached the size or organizational complexity of the Chinese. The Japanese court attempted to introduce an examination system based on the Chinese in the eighth century, but this was soon abandoned in favor of one in which kinship ties and personal connections played a dominant role. Eventually court posts and ranks became more or less hereditary, and the designated heir could expect to attain his father's terminal rank by the end of his career. Women could enter court service as ladies-in-waiting or as consorts to an emperor or prince. Official permission was required to serve as a palace courtier (*tenjōbito*), and men who held one of the highest three ranks were regarded as senior nobles (*kugyō*). Members of the court have occupied the social apex of Japan into the modern age, even during times in which they lacked political and economic power. The imperial family was thus served by elite lineages whose male members served as regents, ministers, and advisers; and whose women might also serve as consorts, ladies-in-waiting, and attendants. Lesser lineages and cadet branches of the elite lines provided personnel to staff the court bureaucracy and govern the provinces.

Japan also followed Chinese models in organizing court personnel, albeit on a lesser scale. Two sets of penal and administrative codes (*ritsuryō*), based on models from Sui- and Tang-dynasty China, were promulgated in the early eighth century. They prescribed a system of ranks for male courtiers from Senior First down to Junior Eighth, lower grade; boys from mid- and high-ranking lineages entered the system at Junior Fifth, lower grade. Rank theoretically entitled the holder to an appropriate office in a branch of the imperial bureaucracy. The most prestigious posts fell under the aegis of the Council of State (*Dajōkan*) and included such offices as Grand Minister of State (*Dajō-daijin*), Minister of the Left, Minister of the Right, Senior Coun-selor, Counselor, Junior Counselor, and Adviser. The court maintained its own military apparatus and a promising courtier might also have a post as an officer in the Imperial Bodyguard. Other ministries were dedicated to func-tions such as Treasury, Punishments, Ceremonial, and Provincial Adminis-tration. Over time various extra-code offices were created to supplement the *ritsuryō* posts, such as the Office of the Chamberlain (*Kurododokoro*), whose head acted as the emperor's private secretary and chief of staff. Members of the imperial family had their own official titles, such as Empress Dowager, Imperial Lady, or ranked Princes and Princesses of the Blood. Ladies-in-waiting were also assigned ranks and offices, mainly associated with their service on the emperor. The central court appointed governors and other provincial officials to administer the country beyond the Kyoto area.

The Byzantine court, like the Chinese and in contrast to the Japanese, was appointed rather than hereditary, although no formal system of accession existed as it did in China. Appointments to the court were considered direct favors of the emperor, who often acted under the influence of powerful advisers. Term limits allowed the emperor to extend his favor to a larger group of people. In the ninth and tenth centuries, a particular court office was especially designated for women. The courtiers received their rewards in an annual ceremony directly from the emperor, in the form of money as well as outfits and insignia appropriate to their office. No entrance exams and no formal restrictions according to ethnicity or status barred access to the court, but a well-developed social network could be instrumental for securing an appointment. In the ninth century, several women of modest origins became imperial consorts as the result of empire-wide "bride shows." In later centuries, political alliances were often cemented by the marriage of a (future) emperor to the daughter of a foreign ruler.

For all of the official titles held by members of the Byzantine court, their actual functions were much less obvious. The most important and influential office at the Byzantine court was that of the Grand Chamberlain, who also had access to the women's quarters. This position was traditionally reserved for eunuchs, who played an important part in public life. The Master of Ceremonies was in charge of staging the imperial ceremonies that took place in various palace buildings, the ceremonies involving the public in the hippodrome and other open spaces of the city, and the religious ceremonies in the Church of Holy Wisdom. His duties included overseeing the elaborate seating arrangements at imperial banquets. Beginning with the late eleventh century, kinship designations were increasingly awarded as court titles. However it is difficult to know whether any official designation refers to a title (and hence an honor) or to an office (and hence a function). Many designations at court do not seem to have carried a clearly defined portfolio of tasks.

The earliest Indian manuals on polity datable to the second to fourth century mention the "examination" of men appointed as dependents, testing their virtues, loyalty, etc. with elaborate ruses and temptations. The implicit hierarchy of court attendance and even royal service was distinct from that of "caste." Though the Brahmin, as intellectual and expert in literate sciences, tended to monopolize strategic and religious roles at court, and his status was therefore traditionally regarded as above that of the king, for all intents and purposes he served the king as a loyal subordinate. Non-religious functions were socially porous at court and a vast range of aspiring groups and local notables sought gainful employment, reputation, fortune, and even lordly or warrior status through court service. Even Brahmins were known to enter military service. In all, the court remained a fluid space as far as caste was concerned.

Surrounding the king or lord were his most intimate counselors (*mantrin*), usually headed by a chief advisor, as well as a royal priest (*purohit*) or spiritual advisor (*rājaguru*) and a court astrologer. He often also had a court jester (*viḍūṣaka*) in attendance, though this figure is more prominent in literary depictions of the court than in court manuals as such. Chief functions among the king's advisors included his "minister of peace and war" (*mahāsandhivigrahaka*) and chamberlain (*mahāpratīhāra*), who controlled access to the king and movement throughout the palace compound. Among the most important tasks performed by the chamberlain and his associates was the monitoring of the entrance to, and seating structure and protocol within, the king's assembly hall. A very large number of lesser functionaries, often with the most generic of titles, resided within the palace complex. The women's quarters were overseen by a special officer and the king met the women there on a daily basis in a manner very similar to his treatment of courtiers and vassals. Elaborate protocols and gift exchange determined which particular women would be selected for nocturnal visitations by the king. Princes were often appointed as "viceroys" to provincial capitals. Revenue officials and structure, particularly the precise interface between imperial administrators and local notables, are not entirely clear from the evidence, though we know that the upper echelons of local institutions were often susceptible to royal influence. The royal court, however, was not primarily a legislative or judicial forum. The king decided legal cases only in situations where intervention was necessary in the mostly local adjudication of justice.

The gradation of rank and title among vassals, courtiers, and other dependents differed regionally and is not always very well understood. There is an emphasis on the wearing of jewelry to indicate rank and status – with higher ranks having more ornamented crowns, armbands, rings, and other jewelry. Bands (*paṭṭa*) probably made of silk supplemented these ornaments as emblems of status. The emissary, or *dūtaka*, was an office of special importance and his qualifications and treatment were generally outlined in the manuals on polity. The messenger had to be able to converse according to florid verbal and gestural protocols when visiting the court of another king – because even when he was entrusted with a written message (usually with the king's seal to attest the authenticity of the message) the most important parts of the letter were only conveyed verbally.

As originally planned, the 'Abbasid Baghdad took the form of a round city containing the caliph's palace, his mosque, and the tax bureaus, the chancellery, and other offices. In practice, however, the center of power was mobile. The early caliphs built new residential complexes outside the round city, or left the capital for extended stays near the Byzantine front. During the later 'Abbasid period, conversely, the caliphs were often confined to their palaces, as military and administrative leadership was diffused to provincial courts.

Figure 7.1 Mahmud ibn Sebüktegin receives a robe of honour from the Caliph al-Qādir billāh in 1000, miniature from the *'Jāmi' al-tawārīkh'* of Rashīd al-Dīn, *c.* 1307 (vellum) (Edinburgh University Library, Scotland. With kind permission of the University of Edinburgh / Bridgeman Images)

At the head of the early 'Abbasid civil hierarchy stood the vizier or chief administrator. Also directly answerable to the caliph, at least in theory, were the military commanders, provincial governors, and judges (see Figure 7.1). In the early period, at least, the so-called "common people" appear to have been given regular access to high officials in order to seek redress of grievances.

Wherever the center of power was located, Arabic literary sources suggest the existence of strict boundaries between the indoors and the outdoors, and between ceremonial and intimate space. Access to the ruler was controlled by a chamberlain, and women's spaces overseen by a female officer called the *qahramanah*. Those empowered to cross the boundaries between gendered spaces included the ruler, eunuchs, and children.

Germanic and Carolingian courts were hierarchically organized with a series of offices and officers of descending importance: the queen and chamberlain, the seneschal (palace arrangements), wine steward, constable (who oversaw travel arrangements), master of lodgings, hunters, and falconers. The queen, with the assistance of the chamberlain, oversaw the domestic activities of the palace and its servants; the count of the palace dealt with judicial matters and petitions; an archchaplain supervised the religious activities of the palace; and, under him, an archchancellor supervised the notaries and scribes who produced the acts and charters of the king. The system was male dominated, though the wives and female offspring of the king had a prominent place at court and some lateral power. Most courts moved with the king from palace to palace, both for reasons of effective regional governance and to spread the expense of maintaining the court over several sites.

The structure of Western courts in post-Carolingian Europe can be described as a combination of three different functions: mechanisms of periodic gatherings of followers and allies (for ritual commensality, for judicial functions, for counsel and political assembly); mechanisms of separation and control of the ruler's physical presence; and mechanisms of sacralization associated with the religious autonomy of the monarchs. Those would correspond, respectively, to the *aula* or hall, to the *cubiculum*/chamber, and to the chapel. The treasury was both associated with the king's physical body (therefore with his chamber), and with the chapel, which most probably originated from the treasury itself. The functional differentiation of those three domains, all of them organized around the figure of the ruler, and its translation into a similar set of offices is recognizable in most post-Carolingian Western courts. The official role of the queen declined from what it had been in Carolingian times in Western royal courts, and other women did not hold formal offices, except in the chamber of the queen, which was almost entirely composed of females. Since Western royal courts remained peripatetic practically until the seventeenth century, the regime of court offices evolved in tandem with this system of life. The court would tend to incorporate more people when it was settled in one place for a longer period, and to reduce its membership whenever it was moving to another residence or seat of power. Functional clusters such as central tribunals, chancelleries, and treasuries tended to be fixed in specific locations after the 1200s, even though the kings continued to move with their regular entourage.

Noble courts in Europe were generally organized by four primary officers: the steward, the chamberlain, the marshal, and the butler. These offices indicate their origins within the household, although in great aristocratic courts they acquired major responsibilities for provisioning, finances, military, and control of the hundreds of persons who might make up the court. Later a master of the Household might oversee all of the court staff. Women at court, under the direction of a mistress of the court, resided primarily in the women's quarters that were only occasionally open to male courtiers – only the lord had unrestricted access.

Competition and courtliness

Neither elaborate systems that recruited courtiers by examination nor hereditary right prevented intense competition at courts, both at the top, as rival claimants sought either to replace rulers or secure their succession, and at the level of the courtiers who jockeyed for influence over rulers. Since the Chinese emperor was the Son of Heaven and ruled only with the Mandate of Heaven, dynastic change normally took the form of conquest by warlords whose victories were evidence that the mandate had been passed on to them because of the failures of their predecessor. Within the dynasty, succession passed from father to son, although disputes involving brothers and mothers advancing favored sons were common. Common, too, was competition among the principal power groups within the court itself: the eunuchs, the Confucian scholar bureaucrats, representatives of the aristocracy and the military. In Japan, even though emperors were blocked from implementing direct rule, multiple consorts competed to ensure that their offspring might succeed to the throne. Likewise the tradition of the *insei* (rule by retired emperor) system, instituted in the eleventh century, by which an elder relative – usually the father – of a young emperor wielded power, spurred rivalries between members of the older generation. By the late thirteenth century rivalries between two hereditary lines of succession to the throne gave rise to rival courts (from 1337 until 1392), the southern at Yoshino and the northern at Kyoto.

Western European courts were likewise competitive places for all: for royal family members, nobles, churchmen, and the women in attendance. While succession in the German kingdom and among ecclesiastical princes, including bishops and the pope, was determined through election, transfer of monarchical power normally followed hereditary rules, and primogeniture came to prevail in most European courts and kingdoms after 1000 CE. Succession through the female line in the absence of a direct male heir and transmission of power to women were also practiced, and competition among sons or in opposition to their fathers occurred frequently, generating factions among courtiers. Inside the court, a combination of personal factors (proximity in childhood or adolescence, individual charisma or skills) and control of specific offices or positions (often transmitted hereditarily) allowed for access to the ruler. The king's personal choice was an active principle in the regime of courtly offices and in the distribution of power and influence, inside the court as well as in the kingdom. This factor determined a specific "moral economy" in Western courts centered on obtaining royal preference and attaching oneself to the person of the ruler. However, competition did not always revolve around specific and formally defined status or positions. A constellation of concepts related to the "love" or "wrath" of the ruler seems to express this shifting terrain, in which the transfer and acquisition of power were seen as the results of personal interaction. As in earlier periods, royal favorites, particularly when they were chosen from outside traditional court circles, became targets of intrigue and blame for unpopular royal policies.

As in Western monarchies, access to the Byzantine emperor and the ability to speak freely in the emperor's presence (*parrhesia*) were highly prized. Competition for access to power or for succession to the throne was not uncommon. Gossip, the spreading of false rumors, and violence, even murder, were the most effective methods to undermine the usual and expected pattern of dynastic succession. A ruling emperor (*augustus*) usually took precautions to secure a smooth transition of power through the appointment of a junior emperor (*caesar*) as his designated successor. In the absence of male offspring, the designated successor was usually either a bureaucrat or a general. A large number of emperors came to power by usurpation, with the backing of the army or the aristocracy.

In the Baghdad court, competition was exacerbated by the loose tradition of succession: caliphs were customarily succeeded by male relatives, usually brothers or sons, but there were few rules beyond that. In theory, the caliph was God's – and later the Prophet's – representative on earth, a distinction available only to members of certain families. Thus, even after the caliph became a figurehead, chosen by whatever military faction happened to be in the ascendant, he was never dispensed with altogether.

Competition was likewise endemic to Indian court life at a number of levels. Though primogeniture was recognized, in practice collateral succession was common, a feature exacerbated by the widespread practice of polygamy as a method of establishing political alliances. Royal houses were thus often filled with generations of princes. The earliest texts on polity consider queens and their sons to be the most serious internal threat to political authority. Queens, whose residential quarters in the palace were separate from the king's, were to be visited only after being cleared of all suspicion by older women. Theoretically arranged in a hierarchy of junior to senior status, queens often had strong rivalries among themselves for the position of the royal favorite, and were often joined by concubines or other independent women who might capture the king's attentions. Competition among princes was potentially even more dangerous. One text on polity notes that they were like "crabs" – devouring their fathers. Competition was not limited to men of royal status, but obtained among vassals, courtiers, and servants as well. The court was imagined as a great circle where success was often measured by one's proximity to its center of power in the form of the lord or king. Such a vision of the court was not far from that of a twelfth-century English courtier who compared the royal court to hell.

Intense rivalry and constant insecurity gave rise in courts across Eurasia to particular codes of behavior that sought to teach courtiers successful skills to survive and advance within these perilous environments. Confucianism, which placed great priority on conservative adherence to tradition, duty to principle rather than to factions, and reforms that would revitalize Confucian ideals (although just what these might be was hotly disputed) dominated Chinese codes of courtly behavior. Japanese courtiers were also expected to uphold Confucian ideals of propriety, benevolence, justice, and rectitude. Yet most conceptions of how a courtier should behave cluster around aesthetics, not ethics, and crystallize in the contested term *miyabi*, sometimes translated as "courtliness," but more literally "to behave in the manner of the capital [as opposed to the rusticated provinces]," connoting restraint, sophistication, and savoir-faire. An alternate interpretation, however, based on the range of meanings associated with the various Chinese characters used to write it, suggests the opposite, linking *miyabi* with unconventionality, freedom, and a turning away from the world of the capital.[1]

In India, a very different and distinct didactic literature, exemplified by works like the *Pañcatantra* and *Hitopadeśa*, provided courtiers with a kind of ethics and strategy of survival in the fiercely competitive world of the court which involved studying the outer countenances and inner dispositions of one's rivals and superiors to detect strengths, weaknesses, and opportunities for political gain. Through translation into Middle Persian and then into Arabic, the Indian ideal proved formative of the Islamic code of refined behavior, called *adab*. The ideal practitioner, usually imagined as a young man, was pleasant though not ostentatious in dress and manners; well-versed in Arabic poetry, the Quran, history, medicine, and other branches of

---

[1] For details, see Joshua Mostow (ed. and trans.), *At the House of Gathered Leaves: Shorter Biographical and Autobiographical Narratives from Japanese Court Literature* (Honolulu, HI: University of Hawai'i Press, 2004): 16–18.

knowledge; and restrained and dignified in bearing, though capable of witty rejoinders as required by a turn in the conversation. *Adab* allowed for a ceremonial loss of restraint in its idealization of love, whether for beardless boys or for women. In practice, advancement probably depended more immediately on the cultivation of reciprocity relations with patrons and dependents alike. *Adab* culture favored both ruinous displays of generosity and graceful acceptance of favors, customs through which the hierarchical order, headed by a God imagined as the Most Bountiful, was maintained.

Western courtly advice on comportment spanned both the ideal and the practical. Young kings received advice manuals called Mirrors for Princes that spelled out courtly virtues and vices, and advised the young ruler how to live a life pleasing to God, manage a family, select a wife, deal with rivals, and conduct wars. From the twelfth century, possibly under the influence of Islamic courtly tradition learned in Spain and the Near East, Western court literature produced an idealization of court behavior, "courtliness." This code of conduct theoretically guided the behavior of both a lord and his followers with an emphasis on self-control and refinement of emotions, eloquence of speech, and service to the lord and his consort. Actual courtly behavior was learned essentially through practice, hence the tradition of sending youths to court from an early age (approximately 14) to serve and to experience the ways of courtly life.

In Byzantium, by contrast, since the tastes and preferences of each individual emperor guided his selection of courtiers and dominated all interactions at court, there was no formal instruction in "courtly behavior." After the eighth century, the expected code of conduct and mode of comportment was similar to that of the great aristocratic families. Ethical and political advice to the emperor was offered in Mirrors for Princes literature (by the deacon Agapetus in the sixth century, Emperor Constantine Porphyrogenitus in the tenth century, Theophylaktos of Ohrid in the eleventh century). An eleventh-century handbook, the *Strategikon* by Kekaumenos, dispenses advice on how to navigate the dangers of a career in the administration or in the military. Foreign-born imperial brides were prepared for their future role by priests and older female members of the court.

Cultural production in the court

In virtually every court, cultural production, both by and for members of the court, developed forms that sought to separate court culture from the rest of society. Paradoxically, these forms tended to be highly imitated by lesser courts and non-court milieux.

As would be expected in a court whose members were largely recruited by examinations on the literary canon, Chinese courtiers, members of the imperial family, and even emperors produced literary works, especially poetry. The rhapsody (*fu*), which combined verse and prose, developed in the second century before the Common Era and continued to be a means of demonstrating knowledge of the classical canon and technical skills. During the Tang dynasty new poetic forms, often with more restrictive forms governing structure and based on balance of the four tones in Middle Chinese, were developed, with Du Fu (712–70), the greatest Chinese poet, the acknowledged master. Court culture included not only poetry but also music, calligraphy, and silk painting. The court and its members patronized artists and artisans in the vast cities surrounding the court as well as performers who, from the Song dynasty on, included urban performing troupes that bridged urban and court cultural modes.

The principal literary genre of the Japanese court was the *waka* poem, a thirty-one syllable verse comprising a sequence of five "lines" of 5,7,5,7 and 7 syllables. Courtiers were expected to be able to compose a passable verse on the themes of love, the seasons, religion, felicitations, laments, or other decorous topics. In early times, poems were usually written for specific social occasions, such as a banquet or a romantic rendezvous; during the twelfth century, the practice of composing sequences on a set of prescribed topics became popular, and such sequences could be matched in poetry contests that were judged and critiqued. From 905 until 1439 compilers produced twenty-one poetic anthologies by imperial command, each work including from about 500 to 3,000 poems, largely by court poets.

In addition, courtiers and, especially, ladies-in-waiting composed prose works based to varying degrees upon their lives at court. Most prominent is the early eleventh-century *Tale of Genji*, generally acknowledged as the central work of Japanese literature. Written by a lady-in-waiting during the period of Fujiwara ascendancy, it is set about a century earlier, during a "golden age" of direct imperial rule. Its hero, the Shining Genji, is the son of an emperor but has been reduced to peer status; the story follows him and his numerous paramours through their romantic and political intrigues. Music was also of great importance, and proficiency in an instrument was another desirable skill that a courtier should possess. Generally, court ladies played the *koto*, a stringed instrument, while gentlemen played the flute. *Gagaku*, the music of the Japanese court, originated in Chinese and Korean forms and in the Shinto ritual music called *kagura*. Its slow, stately melodies and rhythms are achieved with flutes, drums, and various wind instruments, most prominently the oboe-like *hichiriki*. Painting was practiced by amateur and professional artists. Portraiture was not unknown, but the favored subject was the landscape. Illustrated handscrolls were popular, and calligraphy prized as a high art, superior in status to painting. Statuary and sculpture mainly portrayed Buddhist figures and themes.

In India, courts were but one of the three great centers of cultural production in the period between *c.* 300–1300 CE, the others being brahmanical hermitages and temples. Most classical literature in Sanskrit (known as *kāvya*) during this period, including some scientific and religious works, was composed expressly for courtly audiences. Moreover, much literary, hermeneutic and legal intellectualism, not to mention religious writings, though not affiliated with particular courts, nevertheless often evolved in close dialogue with the concerns of the courtly classes. Specialized areas of knowledge and practice, like astrology, prognostication, erotics, gemology and perfumery, were particularly influenced by courtly concerns. Poetic production took several important forms, most ubiquitously the eulogistic poems composed by court poets for ruling kings. These prefaced all the public royal edicts, now preserved in thousands of stone and copper plate inscriptions. These eulogies recorded ancestors of the ruling king and celebrated his heroic and generous deeds. Over time, we see a continued poetic elaboration of these encomia and a steady convergence with the more elaborate literary genres (narrative poems, prose and drama) patronized at court. Kings often called competitions of poetic virtuosity and learning, and the most pre-eminent poets were laurelled with titles like the "Emperor among Poets" (*kavichakravartin*).

At many Islamic courts, high officials competed to reward poets, scholars, and scientists. Some scholars were given rooms in the court complex, though most worked at home. Soon after the accession of the 'Abbasids, paper, imported from China, became widely available. Learned traditions such as poetry, genealogy, biography, Arabic grammar, Quranic exegesis, and *hadith* (reports of the Prophet's exemplary statements and actions) were either committed to writing for the first time, or grew enormously in scope and ambition. A tenth-century list of books available for sale in Baghdad includes works on everything from poetry, law, theology, and history to jokes, obscenities, and fictions. At the behest of the caliphs, their physicians, and other patrons, Nestorian Christian and Sabean scholars produced remarkably accurate translations of ancient Greek philosophical, medical, and other texts.

The most famous patron of the sciences was Caliph al-Ma'mun (813–33), who sponsored the discovery of algebra, the mapping of the known world, and the construction of mechanical devices. The 'Abbasid court was also a center of musical performance, though the most famous musicians – men and women alike – were trained by outside entrepreneurs and seem to have practiced at home in preparation for their gala appearances at the court.

Byzantine imperial patronage resulted in the creation of architecture, monumental painting, mosaics, and the production of works of ivory, gold and silver or enamel as well as manuscripts. Some emperors also supported the creation of literature and poetry. Ample rewards awaited those who performed laudatory speeches (panegyrics) in the presence of the emperor and his court. Many historiographers either enjoyed access to court circles or were themselves members of the court and thus wrote from a privileged position, although rarely at the direct instigation of the emperor.

Western courts, like those of Japan, were but one center of cultural production, the other being major monastic foundations. Early medieval courts sought to continue Roman traditions of Latin poetry and literary production, but with a distinctly Christian cast, attracting scholars and poets both lay and ecclesiastical. With the exception of the Visigothic King Sisebut (c. 565–620 or 621), few early medieval rulers themselves composed literary works. In the late eighth century the Frankish ruler Charlemagne brought together a group of international scholars who wrote Latin poems for the king, produced theological, grammatical, and administrative treatises, and corresponded in letters with each other and the king. His grandson Charles the Bald likewise established a palace school and encouraged the production of painting, poetry, and theological works.

With some exceptions such as the court of Roger II of Sicily and Henry II of England, post-Carolingian royal courts were not primarily centers of cultural production prior to the thirteenth and fourteenth centuries. The exception was the German court of the tenth and early eleventh centuries, where traditional Carolingian and Byzantine traditions of religious writing and manuscript illumination continued to be patronized (if not actually practiced) as part of royal representation. Royal courts were rather centers of consumption of culture, whether Latin clerical culture produced in episcopal and especially monastic environments, or visual and plastic arts (book illumination, gold and silver work) produced by artisans located near courtly centers who relied on court and aristocratic patronage. Courts themselves were centers of the display of these productions as part of the representation of monarchs and courtiers through distinctive dress, manners, and comportment.

While royal courts remained consumers rather than producers of culture, episcopal courts, particularly in the Rhineland and the German speaking regions, played a particularly important role in the development of new modes of comportment and sensitivity derived from classical and Christian precedent. In the twelfth century this clerical tradition, probably influenced by Islamic courtly tradition, developed into a distinctive courtly culture in great aristocratic courts. The ideal of courtliness, discussed above, was demonstrated in speech, in gestures, in speaking, in dancing, and in eating. The highpoint of courtly stylization was the model of "courtly love," an idealization of romantic attachment that contrasted with the crass reality of marriages arranged for family interests. This form of vernacular courtly literature began in the twelfth century, along with a specific courtly literature that celebrated and elevated the dynasties of individual nobles. Music served the same purpose of representing the lord, as did wall painting and manuscript illumination. By the fifteenth century a new form of representation, that of the ruler's portrait, emerged, first in conjunction with religious iconography but increasingly as independent depictions of specific rulers and great lords. Nevertheless, the level of artistic production and display depended enormously on the interests of specific rulers and varied greatly from court to court.

Court ceremonial

Essential to the identity and role of courts as central places of power were the rituals performed by the ruler and his entourage. However, the complexity and choreography of such rituals varied enormously, from the strictly regulated ceremonies performed by the Chinese emperor to maintain the Mandate of Heaven to the chaotic and casual behavior of twelfth-century English courts which, apart from a few "crown wearing" celebrations, seem to have lacked virtually all formality.

Chinese and Japanese courts followed carefully prescribed cycles of annual events through various rites, festivals, banquets, and ceremonies. Court life was highly ritualized, and rites were conducted for births, marriages, deaths, accessions, abdications, and many other events. Reform movements in China often took the form of investigating whether the performance of ancient rituals properly venerated ancestor rulers as well as the appropriate acts required at the change of seasons and through the life cycle. The emperor was visible to the million inhabitants of the capital on a regular basis, moving through the city in impressive parades populated by a panoply of civil and military officials, musicians, and eunuchs that numbered in the thousands. These parades were usually linked to seasonal festivals such as New Year's and were part of a huge government enterprise not only to display imperial power and majesty, but to create a close bond between the court and the citizens of the capital by embedding imperial display within the context of entertainment. In Japan, an elaborate set of protocols governed the ceremonies surrounding the accession and investiture of an emperor. From ancient times a harvest ritual (*Niinamesai*) was performed annually in the eleventh month in which the regnant emperor would make offerings of the year's first rice crop to the deities of heaven and earth, taste the grain himself, and thank them for a bountiful harvest. During the first year of each emperor's reign, this rite was replaced by an elaborate ritual of food offering (*Daijōsai*), in which divination was used to select two paddy fields, which were then consecrated before being specially prepared for harvest. The harvested rice was brought to the new emperor, ritually purified, and prepared for his consumption with the gods.

An annual cycle of rituals in accordance with the liturgical calendar of the year likewise dominated the life of the Byzantine emperor, his family, and his closest associates, as well as that of the Patriarch and his staff. Not only during the Christmas and Easter season, but also on the occasion of feasts of saints, the court participated in rituals in the palace or in the cathedral church of Hagia Sophia, or in processions through the city. Important events in the imperial family – births, marriages, deaths, and of course accessions to the throne – were also marked by rituals. The most common elements in these rituals were prayers, the chanting of Psalms, changes of clothing, and the partaking of symbolic foods. As in China and Japan, banqueting played an important role in court ritual, both to reward dignitaries and to impress foreign visitors. The seating order on these grand occasions was a carefully calibrated affair, and several handbooks of instruction in these matters survive.

In Indian courts, the life cycle rites of the king and courtiers usually conformed to those of the upper castes. The accession of a new king was effected by a "shower-bath into kingship" (*rājyābhiṣeka*). Marriage was an important ritual that was often used to forge dynastic alliances. Hindu kings were polygamous and queens were ranked, with the chief queen (*paṭṭamahādevī*) having pride of place in matters of inheritance – though primogeniture was not always practiced. Princes were often crowned "heir apparent" well before the king died or stepped down. In contrast with most other Eurasian courts, eating was not imbued with a strong communal sociality, and literary texts contain no descriptions of feasts but only briefly mention that the king and intimates ate together. This lack of descriptions of banquets is partly due to the rules of who might dine together current among the upper castes in Hindu society. Sensual descriptions at court rely on the imagery of sound, smell and light rather than gustatory sensation.

Numerous religious ceremonies were practiced by those at court in India. The king had an important place in the consecration and inauguration of large temples, and the procession of deities. The king and his family also had a designated *kuladevatā* or "family deity" that allowed for private royal worship. The court astrologer was consulted before any major social or political undertaking, and propitiatory, prophylactic, and injurious rites were often performed to assist the career of the king. An important festival mentioned in literary texts was the "Spring Festival" or *vasantotsava*, where the god of Love, Kāmadeva, was worshipped and merriment was made in the gardens of the palace.

Early European courts throbbed to the rhythm of rituals. The court participated in weekly church services, which were scripted public performances, accompanied by chanting, and overseen by the king. The king as suzerain entered publicly into oral contracts with his magnates that made them his vassals. The vassalage ceremony was highly ritualized; the vassal with his hands lifted knelt before the lord, swore out loud and in the presence of relics of the saints to be his loyal man and to serve his lord. The lord cupped the man's hands, accepted his pledge with reciprocal words, and often gave him a token of the land he would receive as a benefice. The event was public and called on four of the senses: sight, sound, hearing, and touch. There were formal ceremonies to elevate and crown kings and queens, emperors and empresses, and minor ceremonies for the elevation of officials. There were ceremonies to mark the *adventus* or arrival of dignitaries at court and to mark the king's own leave-taking and arrival at the palace. Gift giving was a formal and expected ritual, as inferiors paid homage to the king. Banquets were structured but less ritualized occasions, but both Charlemagne and Louis the Pious tried to domesticate their courts and disapproved of public excess and inebriation.

In European courts of the thirteenth and fourteenth centuries, courtly ceremonial controlled the distance and proximity to the ruler on a daily basis. Formal ceremonials particularly characterized marriages and funerals, to which thousands of guests might be invited, with elaborate gifts, pageantry, and consumption of rare and extraordinary foods. Increasingly, royal visitations to cities became occasions of elaborate performances, drawing on mythological and heroic literary traditions to portray the ruler, his family, and the devotion of his subjects. By the fifteenth century royal and imperial ceremonial had become a highly regulated affair: in the Golden Bull of 1356 the precise order of imperial prince electors' order in processions and seating was painstakingly spelled out.

Compared with other great courts, Islamic ceremonial was subdued. The accession of a new caliph was effected by an oath of allegiance, sworn to him by senior members of his family and other dignitaries. Such events were marked by largesse to the troops, though there is no record of public celebration. The birth of sons and the designation of an heir were occasions for congratulatory assemblies where poetry was recited. Emissaries of foreign powers, especially the Byzantine Empire, were regaled with displays of troop strength and conspicuous consumption. Even so, the 'Abbasid court did not have anything like the Sasanian or Roman practice of parading representatives of its subject peoples. Public displays of its pretensions to universal authority seem to have been limited to the sending of armies to the provinces and the parading of defeated rebels back to the capital. The later 'Abbasid caliphs are described as emerging from their palaces only to dangle their long sleeves from a balcony for the people to kiss, or to lead prayer once a year at the end of Ramadan.

The court and its critics

Every courtly system generated not only forms of self-representation but also criticism of the prince and those around him. No other courts took this as far as the Chinese, which had Confucian officials in the Censorate and Remonstration Bureau specifically charged with correcting and criticizing imperial decisions and governance, a role that they took seriously even if at times such criticism, often expressed in poetry or formalized reports, led to demotion, exile, and even execution. By contrast, in Japan for much of its history, the court and especially the emperor were considered above criticism; critiques of them became even less relevant as their powers were assumed by the military class. When offered, criticism was expressed indirectly, for example through historical writings, especially by analogies to early Chinese history. By contrast, in India criticism of the court seems to have been as old as courts themselves. The most common form of criticism was directed at kings, who were seen to be as fickle and unreliable as "prostitutes" and "wanton women." This extended to more lengthy criticisms of "royal service." This critical literature seems to have been written by and for Brahmins supported by princes, and numerous authors known to have been patronized by royal courts came to write extended critiques of courtly life.

In Constantinople as in Indian kingdoms, implicit criticism of individual emperors and their politics or of high-ranking officials and their excesses was common and generally penned by those who had themselves been close to the emperor. An unusual document is the sixth-century *Secret History* of Procopius of Caesarea, which depicts the emperor Justinian and his court with exaggerated criticism bordering on caricature. In the fourteenth century, political satire developed into a genre of its own and targeted both the court and the church.

The early 'Abbasid dynasty was viewed by many proto-Sunni Muslims as illegitimate, both because it had been founded as the result of a revolution against the Umayyads, and because at least one of the early caliphs claimed authority to interpret the law without help from the scholars. Literary sources are full of holy men who shout protests at the palace walls and of preachers who reduce caliphs to tears. Certain ascetics declared the court and all its works as ritually impure. The *hadith*-scholar Ibn Hanbal (d. 855), for example, refused to accept gifts from the caliph, or to enter his son's house after the latter did.

The criticism of early Western courts generally came from Romanized churchmen who found the barbarian rulers insufficiently Christian in practice and their palaces sites of violence, sexual immorality, and the arbitrary exercise of power. One persistent tension in the Carolingian world was over the place of churchmen, particularly monks, at secular courts, where they might be corrupted by worldly ways and lose their souls. By the 820s a species of dream literature (written by monks) imagined rulers suffering in afterlife for their licentious habits. More open criticism of the court appeared in the 830s and 840s, one monk likening the court to a brothel and deformed theater of illusions where the worst vices were indulged, the king was deluded, and soothsayers held sway. Noble critics of the king and court generally voted with their feet, by securing the protection of another sovereign, if they could, or abandoning the court and world for a religious life. In later Western courts, criticism came primarily from clerics and was directed at such un-Christian activities as tournaments and courtly immorality. Rather than commenting directly on monarchs, critics often concentrated on royal favorites and advisors, castigating them for providing rulers with "evil counsel." By the fourteenth century, an even more fundamental form of criticism emerged, not from within courtly or ecclesiastical milieux but from those entirely excluded from it, a criticism aimed not only at princes and their courts but at the very idea of nobility: "When Adam delved and Eve span, who was then the gentleman?"

Thus across Eurasia during the fifth through the fifteenth centuries, centers of political power, although varying greatly in size, physical stability, organization, complexity, and structure, nevertheless showed certain commonalities. All were centers of intense competition for power and access to royal favor. They developed specific forms of comportment that regulated this competition and that simultaneously distinguished men and women participating in court life from those outside the court. All were sites of cultural production, consumption and ritual. Moreover, many courts directly or indirectly borrowed practices and values from other court cultures: Regional courts mimicked central court practice, while central courts at times adopted regional forms of culture and comportment. The Chinese court formed the model for Eastern courts such as the Japanese, while the Byzantine, which had absorbed aspects of Persian courts before the Islamic conquest as had those of India, provided a model for Western Christian and Islamic courts, which in turn influenced each other. Through reception of ambassadors as well as the search for new and precious cultural products of display and consumption, Eurasian courts participated, however indirectly, in a Eurasian system of exercising and representing of power.

FURTHER READING

Comparative studies:

Beihammer, Alexander, Stavroula Constantinou and Maria Parani (eds.). *Court Ceremonies and Rituals of Power in Byzantium and the Medieval Mediterranean: Comparative Perspectives.* Leiden: Brill, 2013.

Duindam, Jeroen Frans Jozef. *Royal Courts in Dynastic States and Empires: A Global Perspective.* Leiden: Brill, 2011.

Knechtges, David and Eugene Vance (eds.). *Rhetoric and the Discourses of Power in Court Culture: China, Europe, and Japan.* Seattle: University of Washington Press, 2005.

Lin, Yaofu, ed. *Selected Essays on Court Culture in Comparative Perspective.* Taipei: National Taiwan University Press, 1999.

China

The Cambridge History of China, 13 vols. Cambridge University Press, 1979–2009, vol. I, eds Denis Twitchett and Michael Loewe; vol. III, ed. Denis Twitchett; vol. V, eds. Denis Twitchett and Paul Jacov Smith.

Chaffee, John W. *Branches of Heaven: A History of the Imperial Clan of Sung China.* Cambridge, MA: Harvard East Asia Center, 1999.

Cutter, Robert Joe, and William Gordon Crowell. *Empresses and Consorts: Selections from Chen Shou's Records of the Three States with Pei Songzhi's Commentary*. Honolulu, HI: University of Hawai'i Press, 1999.

Ebrey, Patricia and Maggie Bickford (eds.). *Emperor Huizong and Late Northern Song China: The Politics of Culture and the Culture of Politics*. Cambridge, MA: Harvard University Press, 2008.

Fisher, Carney. *The Chosen One: Succession and Adoption in the Court of Ming Shizong*. London: Allen and Unwin, 1990.

Knechtges, David. *Court Culture and Literature in Early China*. Aldershot: Ashgate, 2002.

(trans.), *Wen xuan, or Selections of Refined Literature*. Princeton University Press, 1982–96.

Kuhn, Dieter. *The Age of Confucian Rule: The Song Transformation of China*. Cambridge, MA: Belknap Press of Harvard Press, 2009.

Li, Huishu. *Empresses, Art, and Agency in Song Dynasty China*. Seattle, WA: University of Washington Press, 2010.

McDermott, Joseph, ed. *State and Court Ritual in China*. Cambridge University Press, 1999.

McMullen, David. *State and Scholars in T'ang China*. Cambridge University Press, 1988.

Meyer, Christian. *Ritendiskussionen am Hof der nördlichen Song-Dynastie (1034–1093): Zwischen Ritengelehrsamkeit, Machtkampf und intellektuellen Bewegungen*. Sankt Augustin: Institut Monumenta Serica, 2008.

Owen, Stephen. *The Great Age of Chinese Poetry: The High T'ang*. New Haven, CT: Yale University Press, 1981.

Tsao, Kai-fu. *The Relationship between Scholars and Rulers in Imperial China: A Comparison between China and the West*. Lanham, MD: University Press of America, 1984.

The Poetry of the Early T'ang. New Haven, CT: Yale University Press, 1977.

Wechsler, Howard J. *Mirror to the Sun of Heaven: Wei Cheng at the Court of T'ang T'ai-tsung*. New Haven, CT: Yale University Press, 1974.

Offerings of Jade and Silk: Ritual and Symbol in the Legitimation of the T'ang Dynasty. New Haven, CT: Yale University Press, 1985.

Japan

Adolphson, Mikael S. *The Gates of Power: Monks, Courtiers, and Warriors in Premodern Japan*. Honolulu, HI: University of Hawai'i Press, 2000.

Brower, Robert H. and Earl Miner. *Japanese Court Poetry*. Stanford, CA: Stanford University Press, 1961.

Brown, Delmer M. and Ichirō Ishida, trans. *The Future and the Past: A Translation and Study of the Gukanshō, an Interpretive History of Japan Written in 1219*. Berkeley, CA: University of California Press, 1979.

Brown, Delmer M., ed. *The Cambridge History of Japan*, vol. 1: Ancient Japan. *Cambridge University Press, 1993*.

Carter, Steven D. *Regent Redux: A Life of the Statesman–Scholar Ichijō Kaneyoshi*. Ann Arbor, MI: Center for Japanese Studies, University of Michigan, 1996.

Hurst, G. Cameron III. *Insei: Abdicated Sovereigns in the Politics of Late Heian Japan. 106–1185*. New York, NY: Columbia University Press, 1976.

Keene, Donald, trans. *Essays in Idleness: The Tsurezuregusa of Kenkō*. New York, NY: Columbia University Press, 1967.

McCullough, William H. and Helen Craig McCullough, trans. *A Tale of Flowering Fortunes: Annals of Japanese Aristocratic Life in the Heian Period*. Stanford University Press, 1980.

Morris, Ivan, trans. *The Pillow Book of Sei Shōnagon*. New York, NY: Columbia University Press, 1967.

trans. *The World of the Shining Prince: Court Life in Ancient Japan*. New York, NY: Knopf, 1964.

Mostow, Joshua, ed. and trans. *At the House of Gathered Leaves: Shorter Biographical and Autobiographical Narratives from Japanese Court Literature*. Honolulu, HI: University of Hawai'i Press, 2004.

Perkins, George W., trans. *The Clear Mirror: A Chronicle of the Japanese Court During the Kamakura Period (1185–1333)*. Stanford, CA: Stanford University Press, 1998.

Piggott, Joan R. *The Emergence of Japanese Kingship*. Stanford, CA: Stanford University Press, 1997.

Shivley, Donald H. and William H. McCullough (eds.). *The Cambridge History of Japan*, vol. II. Cambridge University Press, 1999.

Tyler, Royall, trans. *The Tale of Genji*. New York, NY: Viking, 2001.

Varley, H. Paul, trans. *A Chronicle of Gods and Sovereigns: Jinnō Shōtōki of Kitabatake Chikafusa*. New York, NY: Columbia University Press, 1980.

Yamamura, Kozo, ed. *The Cambridge History of Japan*, vol. III. Cambridge University Press, 1990.

Islamic courts

Abbot, Nabia. *Two Queens of Baghdad: Mother and Wife of Hārūn al-Rashīd*. University of Chicago Press, 1974.

Bennison, Amira K. *The Great Caliphs: The Golden Age of the Abbasid Empire*. London: Yale University Press, 2009.

Bowen, Harold. *The Life and Times of 'Alī ibn 'Īsà, 'the Good Vizier'*. Cambridge University Press, 1928.

Cooperson, Michael. *Al Ma'mun*. Oxford: OneWorld, 2005.

El-Cheikh, Nadia Maria, "Gender and Politics: The Harem of al-Muqtadir," in L. Brubaker and Julia M. H. Smith (eds.), *Gender in the Early Medieval World: East and West, 300–900*. Cambridge University Press, 2004: 147–61.

"Revisiting the Abbasid Harems," *Journal of Middle East Women's Studies* 1 (2005): 1–19.

"Servants at the Gate: Eunuchs at the Court of al-Muqtadir," *Journal of the Social and Economic History of the Orient* 48 (2005): 234–52.

Gutas, Dimitri. *Greek Thought, Arabic Culture: The Graeco-Arabic Translation Movement in Baghdad and Early 'Abbāsid Society (2nd–4th/8th–10th Centuries)*. London: Routledge, 1998.

Lassner, Jacob. *The Shaping of Abbasid Rule*. Princeton University Press, 1980.

Kennedy, Hugh. *The Court of the Caliphs: When Baghdad Ruled the Muslim World*. Cambridge, MA: DaCapo, 2005.

Le Strange, Guy. *Baghdad during the Abbasid Caliphate: From Contemporary Arabic and Persian Sources*. Westport, CT: The Greenwood Press, 1983.

Osti, Letizia. "'Abbasid Intrigues: Competing for Influence at the Caliph's Court," *Al-Masāq* 20(2008): 5–15.

Sabi, Hilal al-. *The Rules and Regulations of the Abbasid Court*, trans. Elie A. Salem. Beirut: Lebanese Commission for the Translation of Great Works, 1977.

Sourdel, Dominique. *Le vizirat 'abbāside de 749 à 936 (132 à 324 de l'hégire)*. Damascus: Institut français de Damas, 1959–60.

Vadet, Jean Claude. *L'Esprit courtois en Orient dans les cinq premiers siècles de l'Hégire*. Paris: Maisonneuve, 1968.

Byzantine courts

Croke, Brian. "Justinian's Constantinople," in M. Maas (ed.), *The Cambridge Companion to the Age of Justinian*. Cambridge University Press, 2005: 60–86.

Maguire, Henry. *Byzantine Court Culture from 829 to 1204*. Washington, DC: Dumbarton Oaks, 1997.

McCormick, Michael. "Analyzing Imperial Ceremonies," *Jahrbuch der Österreichischen Byzantinistik* 35 (1985): 1–20.

"Emperor and Court," in Alan K. Bowman, John B. Bury, and Averil Cameron (eds.), *Cambridge Ancient History*, vol. XIV. Cambridge University Press, 2000: 135–63.

Reiske, Johann Jacob, ed. *De ceremoniis aulae Byzantinae* [Book of Ceremonies, Greek with Latin translation]. Bonn: Eduard Weber, 1829–30.

Vogt, Albert, ed. *Le livre des cérémonies* [Book of Ceremonies, Greek with French translation]. Paris: Société d'édition 'Les Belles lettres', 1967.

Western Europe

Capellanus, Andreas. *The Art of Courtly Love*. Ed. and trans. John Jay Parry. New York: Columbia University Press, 1960.

Barber, Richard, and Juliet Barker. *Tournaments: Jousts, Chivalry and Pageants in the Middle Ages*. Woodbridge: Boydell, 1989.

Bumke, Joachim. *Courtly Culture: Literature and Society in the High Middle Ages*: Woodstock, NY: Overlook Press, 2000.

Cubitt, Catherine, ed. *Court Culture in the Early Middle Ages. The Proceedings of the First Alcuin Conference*. Turnhout: Brepols, 2003.

Fleckenstein, Josef, ed. *Curialitas. Studien zu Grundfragen der höfisch-ritterlichen Kultur*. Göttingen: Vandenhoeck & Ruprecht, 1990.

Hen, Yitzhak. *Roman Barbarians: The Royal Court and Culture in the Early Medieval West*. New York, NY: Palgrave Macmillan, 2007.

Hirschbiegel, Jan and Werner Paravicini (eds.). *Das Frauenzimmer. Die Frau bei Hofe in Spätmittelalter und früher Neuzeit*. Sigmaringen: J. Thorbecke, 2000.

Der Fall des Günstlings. Hofparteien in Europa vom 13. bis zum 17. Jahrhundert. Ostfildern: Thorbecke, 2004.

Jaeger, C. Stephen. *The Origins of Courtliness: Civilizing Trends and the Formation of Courtly Ideals 939–1210*. Philadelphia, PA: University of Pennsylvania Press, 1985.

Jones, Sarah Reese, Richard Marks, and A. J. Minnis (eds.). *Courts and Regions in Medieval Europe*. Rochester, NY: York Medieval Press, 2000.

Kiesel, Helmuth. "Bei Hof, bei Höll." *Untersuchungen zur literarischen Hofkritik von Sebastian Brant bis Friedrich Schiller*. Tübingen: Niemeyer, 1979.

Map, Walter. *De nugis curialium: Courtiers' Trifles*. Ed. and trans. M. R. James. New York, NY: Oxford University Press, 1983.

Paravicini, Werner. *Die ritterlich-höfische Kultur des Mittelalters*. Munich: R. Oldenbourg, 1994.

——— (ed.) *Zeremoniell und Raum*. Sigmaringen: J. Thorbecke, 1997.

Rösener, Werner. *Leben am Hof. Königs- und Fürstenhöfe im Mittelalter*. Ostfildern: Thorbecke, 2008.

Spieß, Karl-Heinz. *Fürsten und Höfe im Mittelalter*. Darmstadt: Primus Verlag, 2008.

Vale, Malcolm. *The Princely Court: Medieval Courts and Culture in North-West Europe, 1270–1380*. Oxford and New York: Oxford University Press, 2007.

8

The age of trans-regional reorientations: cultural crystallization and transformation in the tenth to thirteenth centuries

BJÖRN WITTROCK

The half-century preceding the outbreak of World War I stands out as an era of European economic, political, and cultural dominance never achieved before and no longer possible to sustain at the end of the war. Already in the 1920s speculative works on world history emerged that questioned the viability of continued European dominance, not to speak of hegemony. A few decades later, after yet another world war had shattered the standing of Europe irreversibly, a number of thinkers began to articulate a notion of world history that did not take the history of European antiquity as its point of departure. These scholars, including Karl Jaspers, and later Shmuel N. Eisenstadt and Robert N. Bellah, started out from the observation that in several high cultures of the Old World, in the centuries around the middle of the first millennium BCE, modes of thought emerged nearly simultaneously that displayed greater critical reflexivity and that tended to be premised on a cosmology that made a sharper distinction between a transcendental and a mundane sphere than had earlier philosophies and religions. These modes of thought also involved the articulation of notions of temporality, of agency and of belonging that decisively went beyond those that characterized the kind of mythic thinking that had dominated earlier societies, whether tribal societies or large-scale Archaic societies. This leap in critical reflexivity and the emergence of an intellectual foundation for conceptions of human history, and human interventions aimed at shaping that history, opened up new horizons. In this age, the hinges of history seemed to have opened doors that made previously unimaginable human prospects suddenly become intellectually within grasp. Jaspers termed this period of potential commonality in early world history the *Achsenzeit*, using the German word *Achse*, which means both axis and pivot; in English, this became the Axial Age.

Axial legacies: consequences and antinomies in the first millennium CE

In their conceptualization, the Axial Age – which eventually was understood to encompass the period from 800 BCE to 200 BCE – was characterized by three central developments in five civilizations: ancient Israel, China, Greece, India, and Iran. First, the great world religions emerged and spread, which created new religious ecumenes, that is, imagined realms of community and belonging that encompassed and linked human beings across vast distances. Second, new forms of political order developed, particularly a new conception of empire and rulership, in which kings and emperors might rule with a Mandate of Heaven or the grace of God but could not legitimately claim to be gods. Third, the new imperial orders helped further regional and trans-regional trade networks and directly contributed to the establishment of trade routes.[1]

In the centuries from 200 CE to 800 CE, the transformative force of Axial civilizations became more visible. All of these civilizations contained a potential for heterodox interpretations of the religious texts that articulated relationships between cosmological assumptions and mundane order. In some cases these potentials became so closely circumscribed by links between religious practices and imperial order as to entail a clear subordination. However, in the course of the first millennium CE an intensification of some of the dynamic tendencies inherent in all Axial civilizations occurred. As a result it became more difficult to contain religious practices within the frameworks of existing political institutions. Efforts of rulers to contain and to draw on religious–cultural practices became more pronounced but also more fraught with dilemmas and antinomies.

One reason for this intensification is that a number of composite forms of religious–cultural practices emerged that either drew on elements from different Axial traditions or combined Axial and non-Axial elements in new ways. This is true even in those cases where linkages were particularly strong between imperial rulers and religious elites. For example, developments within the Iranian empire of the Sasanians tended to exhibit a close relationship between religious and political practices. Even so, towards the end of the Sasanian Empire in the seventh century there were tendencies towards religious–cultural realignments that defy notions that such practices should primarily be conceived in terms of their purely instrumental use by the powers-that-be.

---

[1] For a more detailed discussion of the Axial Age, see my essay in vol. IV of the present series.

In China during the Sui and the early years of the Tang dynasties a variety of religious–philosophical–cultural practices generally coexisted that were not only tolerated but often also supported by the political order. However, there were also times of shifting favours and periods of efforts at suppression of some such practices. Thus the Sui dynasty had a tendency to favour Buddhism but also tolerated Daoism and other practices. Much the same can be said for the ensuing Tang dynasty, which in its early history allowed the practice of various Western and Iranian religions, including Zoroastrianism, Manichaeism, and Nestorian Christianity.[2] In the ninth century, however, Nestorian Christianity and Buddhism were suppressed. As a consequence, Nestorian and other forms of Eastern Christianity would henceforth survive not in China itself but at or outside of the western borders of the Chinese Empire. By contrast, the suppression of Buddhism was temporary and could do little to affect the firm grounding of Buddhism in China which had taken place from the fourth century onwards.

In general, imperial rulers in civilizations in which non-deistic religions and philosophies exerted a dominant influence were perhaps less well placed to draw on Axial religions for instrumental purposes than were those where deistic religions flourished. However, they may have been better placed to avoid some of the major tensions and problems involved in such use, as well as less exposed to the violent outbursts of politically focused zeal that were a potential consequence flowing from the articulation of divergent religious standpoints among adherents of deistic Axial religions.

Despite the intensification of religious–cultural practices, however, political practices in the centuries from 200 to 800 CE to a large extent constituted efforts to perpetuate, imitate or replicate classical forms of political order. New forms emerged largely as a consequence of resource restrictions. Towards 1000, however, it became gradually more difficult to contain new societal and cultural dynamics within the framework of these classical forms.[3]

Cultural crystallizations and trans-regional reorientations

This chapter examines transmutations and renovations of complexes of religious–cultural, societal, and political practices that occurred between

---

[2] Mark Edward Lewis, *China's Cosmopolitan Empire: The Tang Dynasty* (Cambridge, MA: The Belknap Press of Harvard University Press, 2009).

[3] For a discussion of political change in the Middle Millennium, see the chapter by Johann Arnason in this volume.

the tenth and the thirteenth centuries in several civilizations. I shall use the term 'cultural crystallizations' to designate articulations of new conceptions of cosmology, temporality, agency, and belonging that come to have deep implications for the emergence of new societal arrangements and institutions. The Axial Age is a period of cultural crystallization – as is the emergence of the modern world in all its varieties and entanglements.

However, the first centuries of the second millennium CE are yet a third major period of cultural crystallization in world history in the course of the last three millennia. In those centuries, the legacies of the Axial Age, as they had become manifested in the civilizations of the great world religions, were being rearticulated. One may perhaps even speak of an age of cultural rearticulation and renaissance in different civilizations. This occurs against the background of increasing global interactions but also a crisis of societal order in the major civilizations of the Old World. As a result, new institutional arrangements emerged, if sometimes only in rudimentary form, which came to shape the institutional landscape of the societies of that world. The Middle Millennium is a period that has a relatively clearly defined beginning, and an end that also marks the beginning of something new in institutional and political terms. It may also be argued, as I shall do in this chapter, that the tenth to the thirteenth centuries CE, i.e. roughly the middle of the Middle Millennium, marks a period of crystallization when different long-term societal trajectories emerge. The reason why we can speak of a relatively clear beginning of the Middle Millennium is that the institutional programmes (to use Eisenstadt's terminology)[4] of the original Axial Age had, if not exhausted themselves, then reached a limit beyond which they could not be pursued without fundamental reformulations. These reformulations became articulated in the centuries that I have chosen to focus on. Conversely, one reason why we can discern such a deeply changed institutional landscape after the Middle Millennium is that the new institutional macro-arrangements, which in rudimentary form emerged in different civilizations in the tenth to the thirteenth centuries, were of formative importance for the set of societal interactions and institutions that have come to be seen as characteristic of the early modern and modern world. Thus the outcome of the transformations of the tenth to thirteenth centuries involved the

---

[4] S. N. Eisenstadt, 'Introduction: Comparative Studies and Sociological Theory – From Sociological Theory to Civilizational Analysis: Autobiographical Notes', in *Comparative Civilizations and Multiple Modernities: A Collection of Essays by S. N. Eisenstadt*, vol. I (Leiden: Brill, 2003): 1–28.

emergence of new societal macro-institutions. The transformations entailed increasing interactions, but also the emergence of different and sometimes diverging paths of development of different civilizations.

As has been pointed out by several observers, including Said Amir Arjomand and Kenneth Pomeranz, until relatively recently 'comparative civilizational analysis' had 'sought to explain the distinctiveness of the Western pattern of development (capitalism and democracy) in terms of the *absence* of certain preconditions', and has involved a focus on 'a parting of the paths of development in the High Middle Ages'.[5] Perhaps the most famous example in the history of social science of a learned and wide-ranging comparative inquiry of the trajectories of different civilizations is that of Max Weber, in his three massive volumes on the sociology of the great world religions first published in 1920–1.[6] In these volumes, full of empirical synthesis and comparative reflections, Weber's declared purpose is, however, not to engage in a broad comparative analysis *per se*, but rather to discover, in the study of non-European contexts, points of comparison to 'our occidental cultural religions'.[7] This has been true of scholars from Max Weber to Benjamin Nelson and Wolfgang Schluchter. Other comparisons in which European categories have been applied beyond Europe – the comparative analysis of 'feudalism' in western Europe and Japan is perhaps the most obvious case in point – do not seem to stand up to the findings of contemporary scholarship. Historians and historical social scientists have thus only taken the first steps in articulating frameworks that might allow for comparative questions to be raised while avoiding the imposition of categories that reflect the European conceptual dominance of the late nineteenth and early twentieth century, which at least indirectly informs hitherto dominant modes of inquiry.

In this chapter, I shall outline some elements of a comparative civilizational analysis that will focus on common patterns of development across civilizations of the Old World and argue that in the early second half of the Middle Millennium profound redefinitions of macro-societal practices occurred in several parts of the Old World that may be fruitfully analysed

---

[5] Said Amir Arjomand, 'Transformations of the Islamicate Civilization: A Turning Point in the Thirteenth Century?' in Johann P. Arnason and Björn Wittrock (eds.), *Eurasian Transformations, Tenth to Thirteenth Centuries: Crystallizations, Divergences, Renaissances* (Leiden: Brill, 2004): 213–45; Kenneth Pomeranz, *The Great Divergence: China, Europe, and the Making of the Modern World Economy* (Princeton University Press, 2000).

[6] Max Weber, *Gesammelte Aufsätze zur Religionssoziologie*. I (Tübingen: J.C.B. Mohr (Paul Siebeck): 1920); II. *Hinduismus und Budhismus* (1921); III. *Das antike Judentum* (1920).

[7] Ibid. vol. I, 15.

in comparative terms.[8] Because these transformations occurred in a number of different world regions, I shall refer to this period as an age of trans-regional reorientations. Transformations taking place in this period can be interpreted as different responses to sets of problems that become acute with near simultaneity in several civilizations of the Old World.

These different reinterpretations came to affect a more extensive part of the world than those that had been formed by Axial religions and philosophies in the preceding period. In the case of Europe, to take but one example, the area of Christendom nearly doubled, although its practices and rituals became affected by earlier non-Axial cultural practices in the newly Christianized lands in the continent's east and north.

Other historians have also pointed to the period from the eleventh to the thirteenth centuries as one of deep-seated change with long-term consequences. Thus in a magisterial work on transformations in western, central, and southern Europe, Thomas N. Bisson focuses on 'lordship' and on processes by which new groupings sought, and often obtained, rights previously reserved for members of an old elite of nobility. These transformations involved extensive and pervasive use of coercive power, and the rights obtained were rights to command and to exercise such power. This was a deeply upsetting process, which broke with customs of the old society and opened it up for new types of governing and government. In Bisson's terminology, this is 'how and why the experience of power became that of government in medieval Europe'.[9] Looking at analogous developments at the other end of the Old World, Pierre François Souyri has described how within a relatively short period of time in the late twelfth century, Japanese society entered 'the Age of the Warriors' which in the end left, to quote the title of his book on medieval Japanese society, 'The World Turned Upside Down'.[10] Scholars looking at developments in China in the Song–Yuan–Ming transition period or at the late 'Abbasid Caliphate have highlighted analogous tendencies towards realignments, if with different long-term

---

[8] Sheldon Pollock has advocated and practised forms of comparative analysis in this vein in a range of publications, including the following ones: Sheldon Pollock, 'The Transformation of Culture-Power in Indo-Europe, 1000–1300', in Arnason and Wittrock, *Eurasian Transformations*, 247–78; Sheldon Pollock, *The Language of the Gods in the World of Men: Sanskrit, Culture, and Power in Premodern India* (Berkeley, CA: University of California Press, 2006): 497–565.

[9] Thomas N. Bisson, *The Crisis of the Twelfth Century: Power, Lordship, and the Origins of European Government* (Princeton University Press, 2009): 17.

[10] Pierre François Souyri, *The World Turned Upside Down: Medieval Japanese Society* (New York, NY: Columbia University Press, 2001).

outcomes.[11] Because the dynamics of the different patterns are so pronounced, in fact, some authors have argued that the use of the term 'early modernities' is justified to designate them.[12]

From the point of view of world history, this period stands out as highly significant. First, even if global interactions were limited by the standards of the twentieth and twenty-first centuries, there was, as argued in the introduction to this volume, an amazing array of long-distance connections across a number of different fields of human activity. Second, the trajectories of different civilizations became more clearly discernible and solidified into premises for macro-societal institutions. These processes involved a reinterpretation and rearticulation of a real or imagined cosmological and cultural heritage and tradition. In this sense it is possible to speak of an age in which profound reorientations of cultural ecumenes in several regions took place. Third, these institutions came to characterize the history of societies in the Old World for most of the rest of the Middle Millennium and beyond. It is possible to view these transformations as processes of deep-seated cultural crystallizations. One element in this type of analysis must be an effort to link conceptual change to processes of sociopolitical transformations and upheavals, and another one to explore different varieties of social formations that emerged.

Indeed, it has been argued that it was only in these centuries at the beginning of the second millennium CE – rather than during the Axial Age and the emergence of the great world religions – that the major civilizations of agro-literate societies were distinctly formed and became clearly demarcated from each other, both in their self-image and in the view of other societies. These were also the centuries when cultural and institutional patterns emerged that were seminal for shaping the later characteristically modern societies.

---

[11] Paul Jakov Smith and Richard von Glahn (eds.), *The Song–Yuan–Ming Transition in Chinese History* (Cambridge, MA: Harvard East Asian Monographs, 221; distributed by Harvard University Press, 2003); Said Amir Arjomand, 'Transformations of the Islamicate Civilization', 213–45. See also Said Amir Arjomand, 'Crystallization of Islam and Developmental Patterns in the Islamicate Civilization', in Said Amir Arjomand (ed.), *Social Theory and Regional Studies in the Global Age* (Albany, NY: State University of New York Press, 2014): 203–20.

[12] Special Issue 'Early Modernities', *Daedalus* 127:3 (Summer 1998); reprinted as S. N. Eisenstadt, Wolfgang Schluchter and Björn Wittrock (eds.), *Public Spheres and Collective Identities* (New Brunswick, NJ: Transaction Press, 2001).

Contexts of change

At the turn of the first millennium CE, the imperial orders that had emerged in the wake of the Axial Age had all withered or been fundamentally transformed. Across the hemisphere, however, processes of challenge and response led to institutional change that involved a questioning as well as a rearticulation of earlier forms of cultural attachment. Leaders in various regions attempted to recreate ecumenical and imperial orders, an attempt often linked to urban and commercial advances. The Song dynasty in China, the Fatimid Caliphate in Egypt, the Ottonian Empire in western Europe, and the revival of the Byzantine Empire under the Macedonian dynasty fall within this pattern. In this hemisphere-wide movement, all the high civilizations were confronted not only by practical challenges but also by challenges to deeply held presuppositions and cosmologies. In this process, the different cultural ecumenes came to articulate and synthesize core components of their political and cultural orders in the face of both expansion and challenge.

Some of the cultures – most prominently perhaps China and the Byzantine world and least prominently perhaps Japan and western Europe – were threatened, if not overwhelmed, by their engagement with peoples of neighbouring areas or nomadic regions. Empires that had emerged in the wake of the Axial Age, including the Roman and the Han Empires, but also the Maurya Empire, had long since succumbed. Even the Sasanian Empire, which had overcome and succeeded the Parthian Empire and successfully withstood incursions of Central Asian nomadic peoples, had itself imploded in the face of the armies of Islam.

In the ninth century the 'Abbasid Caliphate faced a crisis that entailed a long-term weakening, and in the second half of that century even the Tang dynasty, the dynasty that had brought China to its greatest extension so far, succumbed. Its successor, the Song dynasty, was simultaneously challenged and changing. This period witnessed thriving intellectual life, and also new forms of economic activity that eventually brought China to use new energy sources and to reach a stage near that of an industrial revolution in some branches of the economy. While literati elaborated schemes intended to permit a return to governance in the spirit of Confucian virtues, societal forms changed deeply. This new and dynamic China was finally, in the mid-thirteenth century, overwhelmed by Mongol invaders. These new rulers of the Yuan dynasty, however, rapidly came to embrace the habits and cultural features of their new domain; paradoxically, reform proposals elaborated by literati in the Song dynasty were taken up and implemented by the new rulers. Indeed, it seems possible to speak of a series of continuities extending over the successive dynasties of the Song, the Yuan and, a century later, that of a new Chinese dynasty, the Ming.[13] Peter Bol has even made a convincing argument that across the transitions from the dynasties of the Song to Yuan to Ming, Neo-Confucianism managed to establish a degree of intellectual and institutional autonomy for the literati and a position to some extent outside of the immediate domination of the powers that be.[14] Despite continuities during these transitions, however, forms of political, cultural and philosophical practices emerged that make this a period of profound rearticulation of Chinese culture in a distinctly new societal and global context.

In western Europe, the Carolingian Empire had represented an effort to resurrect an element of imperial rule within contexts that differed radically from those of Roman rule in antiquity. However, even if it left a memory that was to be rearticulated time and again in the ensuing centuries, its actual period of rulership was brief and its position in a global context peripheral. Rather than heralding the return of empire, it led instead to an increasing plurality of political forms and entities that with the passage of time gradually came to be perceived as a particularly virtuous Western route to pluralism and innovation. The process by which this was to happen was, however, a complex and largely inadvertent one, in which one element was a series of intense deliberations and controversies about the relationship between the traditions of Latin Christendom and the philosophical and linguistic traditions of classical antiquity.

In China, analogous debates ushered in the Neo-Confucian movement, the reassertion of the virtues of that tradition and, consequently, the preservation of Chinese civilization as a cultural and linguistic ecumene. However, whereas the Neo-Confucian movement and the preservation of an all-encompassing political order in China – and here the interlude of the Yuan dynasty represented a rupture only to a marginal extent – entailed the preservation of a single language across the entire ecumene, western Europe and, along a different trajectory, India, experienced the first steps in a secular shift towards a vernacularization of linguistic practices. Even if ecumenical

---

[13] See Smith and von Glahn, *Song–Yuan–Ming Transition*, and also Paul Jakov Smith, 'Eurasian Transformations of the Tenth to Thirteenth Centuries: The View from Song China, 960–1279', in Arnason and Wittrock, *Eurasian Transformations*, 279–308.

[14] Peter K. Bol, 'Examinations and Orthodoxies: 1070 and 1313 Compared', in Theodore Huters, R. Bin Wong and Pauline Yu (eds.), *Culture and State in Chinese History: Conventions, Accommodations, and Critiques* (Stanford, CA: Stanford University Press, 1987): 29–57; Peter K. Bol, *Neo-Confucianism in History* (Cambridge, MA: Harvard University Asia Center and Harvard University Press, 2008).

and vernacular linguistic practices would coexist for centuries to come, processes of a fundamentally transforming nature had emerged. In Europe the emergence of religious practices tied to new monastic orders entailed closer links to local communities, but they also served as an instrument for homogenizing efforts within the overall framework of the new ecumenical constellation of extended Latin Christendom. The activities of the Cistercian order in the newly Christianized parts of northern and eastern Europe provide one example of this.[15]

In South Asia, the encounter with the cultural and political institutions of Islamic civilization served as one of the sources for reformulations and rearticulations of Hindu traditions before the turn of the first millennium CE. Hindu scholars developed interpretations that entailed claims to universal significance as well as a further strengthening and revitalization of the role of Sanskrit as a language, which formed the basis of a vast array of cultural practices also on the most local level. From the twelfth century onwards a further Islamic expansion occurred across the Indian subcontinent, first involving traders in the south and in Bengal along with Islamic rule in the northwest, and then a consolidation of political rule across northern and central India. The establishment of the Delhi sultanate in the early thirteenth century also created a space in which Islamic and earlier Indian cultures met and intermingled to create forms of Indo-Muslim cultural practices, eventually ushering in the Indo-Muslim world that would flourish in the Mughal Empire from the sixteenth century onwards.[16] Here older linguistic and cultural practices, often but not always Sanskrit-based, would meet with and exert mutual influences on practices of Turkic and Arabic origins, including the high culture and poetry of the Persianite cultures of Iran and Central Asia. In addition, as in western Europe, India experienced a shift towards vernacularization of linguistic practices and a localization of religious practices. In both contexts ecumenical and vernacular linguistic practices would coexist for centuries, but processes of a fundamentally transforming nature had emerged.

---

[15] See e.g. Gábor Klaniczay, 'The Birth of New Europe about 1000 CE: Conversion, Transfer of Institutional Models, New Dynamics', in Arnason and Wittrock, *Eurasian Transformations*, 99–130; and Gábor Klaniczay, *Holy Rulers and Blessed Princesses: Dynastic Cults in Medieval Europe* (Cambridge University Press, 2002).

[16] A wonderfully concise portrait of arguably the greatest Mughal emperor, the sixteenth-century ruler Jalal Ad-Din Akbar, is given by André Wink in his volume *Akbar* (London: Oneworld Publications, 2008).

In Southeast Asia, a cosmopolitan Sanskrit-based cultural ecumene emerged and extended over large areas. It found expression in, to use William McNeill's phrase, 'the Indianized court civilizations',[17] but also in practices where local experiences were inextricably entangled with generalized imaginations in Sanskrit-based culture. These imaginations were based not on conceptions of a centre that influences and is imitated by various peripheries, but rather on the trans-spatial nature of the imagery of Hindu culture. This allowed for the unique fusion between cultural–cosmological imaginations and local sites across large areas of Asia far beyond the subcontinent itself. It also meant that such cultural practices could survive for centuries after Indianized empires and other political entities had been conquered or transformed.

Conditions and causes

Several interlinked processes affected, if in different degrees, civilizations across the Old World during the period from the tenth to the thirteenth centuries, and led to cultural crystallizations and reorientations in many regions. First, there was remarkable demographic growth, more so it appears than in the centuries both before and after this period. This seems to have been true for China, the Indian subcontinent, and Europe. Second, there was pronounced agricultural growth, which resulted from changes in land use but also in production techniques; in Europe these included new types of ploughing and new types of crops.

Third, agricultural growth in turn allowed for the growth of new cities and new types of urban life. Guilds of merchants and artisans appeared, in Chinese cities and in the smaller European cities. Urban developments were furthermore related to efforts at articulating notions of rights both in agriculture and in urban life. Fourth, commerce grew. In South and Southeast Asia such growth could draw on old interlinked networks across the Indian Ocean and beyond. In the European context growth occurred predominantly in local and regional commerce, although, as R. I. Moore has argued, trade routes across the Old World were more important than in the Axial Age.[18]

---

[17] William H. McNeill, *A World History*, 4th edn (New York: Oxford University Press, 1999): 274.

[18] R. I. Moore, 'The Transformation of Europe as a Eurasian Phenomenon', in Arnason and Wittrock, *Eurasian Transformations*, 77–98.

Such growth had as one of its backgrounds a somewhat less restricted sphere of action for commercial activities.

Fifth, in most civilizations, elites formed and were contested, with conflicts between traditional, sometimes clan-like, sometimes aristocratic older elites, often with relationships to imperial courts, and emerging and increasingly influential military and clerical elites. Sixth, new types of institutions for the training of clerical and religious elites emerged, capable of articulating an interpretation of often quasi-judicial rules and laws. The emergence of Neo-Confucian academies in China and the growing support for madrasas in many parts of the Islamic world are examples of this. In Europe the first universities were formed in the eleventh and twelfth centuries, which were integral to the transformation of European societies in this period.

Seventh, the rise of new elites had important implications for the overall social order as well as for the nature and regulation of social interactions outside of the realm of government proper, what might perhaps even be termed new kinds of public spaces. Such spaces arose or were reshaped across the Old World. Eighth, elite contestations tended to focus on what modern social science would describe as processes of state formation but what might better be termed contestation about the nature, rulership and control of political order. In the analysis of Thomas Bisson, for example, European developments should not be thought of in terms of different varieties of government. Rather this was a process whereby efforts were made to create some kind of regulated practices that might serve as a defence against, and in favour of imposing some constraints on, the all-present coercive power inherent in, to use his terminology, lordship. It is out of such efforts that governments and parliaments slowly emerged and were given a form that to some extent could go beyond the immediate expression and exertion of power and coercion of a lord or a king.[19]

Jointly these processes set the stage for long-term trajectories of the agro-literate societies of the Old World, and created some of the conditions for the world of intensified global interactions and encounters that was to follow, although historians view one or more of these as particularly important in different regions. In his analysis of the deep-seated transformations of Song China, for example, Paul Jakov Smith notes, 'The primary engine of this medieval transformation was undoubtedly the shift in the demographic center of gravity' to South China. This stimulated growth and productivity

[19] Bisson, *The Crisis of the Twelfth Century*, 578–81.

in rice agriculture, which in turn led to a stimulus for trade networks. However, he comments that these changes were also linked to 'the collapse of the medieval aristocracy of great clans that had dominated China from the fourth to the ninth centuries. These events were shaped by the sequence of incursions from the steppes in the west culminating in the establishment of the Yuan dynasty in the mid-thirteenth century.'[20]

In his analysis of vernacularization processes in the Sanskrit-based cultural world, Sheldon Pollock also highlights some of the factors identified above. He cautiously argues that 'whereas we can identify some factors that clearly contributed – reinvigorated trading networks in the early second millennium concentrated wealth in local power centers, the expansion of Islam on its western and eastern frontiers offered new cultural stimuli – a unified explanation of the historical origins of vernacularism is improbable'. He concedes, however, that this should not prevent us from using these examples to try to enrich theorizing on culture and power.[21] Analogously, Thomas Bisson argues that in twelfth-century Europe demographic and economic growth created the conditions for 'the multiplication of people with the means and will to coerce others' contrary to an older world in which 'nobles had ruled, and nobles were few'.[22]

Diverging patterns and pathways of transformation

The developments discerned by these and other observers suggest the fruitfulness of a comparative analysis that does not shy away from a study of major historical relocations and reorientations but seeks to avoid the implicit, or sometimes explicit, Eurocentrism of much work in the social and historical sciences. The transformations that form the focus of this chapter have, of course, a longer history, with important influences from the civilizations of the so-called Axial Age. The cultural worlds taken up in this chapter are directly or indirectly successors of the Axial civilizations of antiquity that took form in ancient Israel, Greece, China, India, and Iran, although there were, as already argued, few or no unbroken continuities. Furthermore, Axial transformations originated in only some regions of the Old World, while other parts, including the old civilizations of Mesopotamia and Egypt, were not part of these transformations.

[20] Paul Jakov Smith, 'Eurasian Transformations'.   [21] Pollock, *Language of the Gods*, 30.
[22] Bisson, *Crisis of the Twelfth Century*, 7.

Axial civilizations came to have lasting consequences for wide regions of Eurasia far beyond their places of emergence, however. I will examine some of these in what follows, although it is not possible in one chapter to highlight all the regions in which such influences were a significant factor in shaping the transformations of the tenth to thirteenth centuries. I will first focus on the Indian subcontinent, then China, Japan, and Western Christendom, with a few comments on Byzantium. Because of issues of length, this chapter will similarly leave out Zoroastrianism and Manichaeism, although these also influenced the cultural evolution of the Mediterranean, and the Indian and Chinese worlds over many centuries.

At the beginning of the second millennium CE, all the major civilizations of the Old World were forced to rearticulate notions of power and culture. Sheldon Pollock has noted that 'across much of Eurasia the world abandoned cosmopolitanism and empire in favor of vernacularity and regional polities'. These 'transformations in culture and power that began concurrently in India and Europe around the start of the second millennium were consolidated by its midway . . . the cosmopolitan order in both worlds was almost completely supplanted by the seventeenth century'.[23] In this process, a growing divergence emerged between parts of the Old World, but, as noted by Pollock, there were symmetries and even synchronies in the processes of vernacularization in India and Europe, and even in the societal contextualization of this process, for instance in terms of the role of courtly elites. There were also differences, of course not least in terms of a long, unbroken tradition of 'oral performances on the basis of hand-written texts'.[24] This type of expressivity was one of several features that enabled the existence during virtually all of the Middle Millennium of a Sanskrit-based 'vast ecumene extending over a third of Eurasia', with the others being the trans-local, trans-ethnic and grammatically and lexically stable character of the language.[25] This ecumene extended not only across the Indian subcontinent but also across the mainland and islands of Southeast Asia, creating a cultural community of common outlook and intelligibilities without a political centre and without the type of political orders that started to emerge in Europe in the second half of the Middle Millennium, namely the nascent nation-states, a form of polity 'unlike anything found in South Asia'.[26]

---

[23] Pollock, *Language of the Gods*, 30.   [24] Ibid., 233.   [25] Ibid., 257.

[26] Ibid., 29. See also Sheldon Pollock, 'Cosmopolitan and Vernacular in History', in Carol A. Breckenridge, Sheldon Pollock, Homi K. Bhabha, and Dipesh Chakrabarty (eds.), *Cosmopolitanism* (Durham, NC: Duke University Press, 2002): 15–53.

In China, the parallel developments of the expansion of agricultural production – linked to a demographic shift towards South China – and the growth of urban centres occurred earlier and on a larger scale than elsewhere in Eurasia. China also experienced the decline of an old elite of aristocratic clans with close ties to imperial rule, and even – as mentioned above – elements of an incipient industrial revolution. These social and economic transformations were contemporaneous with the rise of more organized and increasingly threatening political orders at the western and northern borders of China. As a consequence, processes of elite contestation and state formation – or rather the renewal of political order and the search for more efficient means of resource mobilization – interacted and shaped the conditions for social and cultural transformations. One crucial aspect of these transformations was the rise of a clerical elite, based on an ethic that put a premium on service to the political order and on selection via a far more stringent examination than similar groups experienced elsewhere. At the turn of the first millennium, amidst growing territorial threats, this elite of literati came to embrace ever more ambitious and activist policies designed to enact a programme of comprehensive reform.

This so-called Neo-Confucianism, or Learning of the Way (*daoxue*), originated earlier, but at the turn of the first millennium CE it became increasingly related to the crisis and resentment over the loss of Chinese heartlands and dissatisfaction with imperial and ministerial rule. It also – and here it is difficult not to think of analogies with western Europe at roughly the same time – included a focus on family structure and proposals for inheritance and control of property designed to strengthen patrilineal ties and, conversely, to curtail the situation of women. Ironically, these views on women and property, which were largely new but were claimed as an older tradition, only became realizable and institutionalized after the conquest by the Mongol 'barbarians', and they became further strengthened during the Ming dynasty.

During the last years of the Southern Song, what had emerged as a movement of critique and reform came to be embraced, if too late to have any immediate impact, by the political centre, and then, after the fall of the Southern Song, survived at the local level to find a place in schools and academies in Southern China. As an effective ideology of the educated elite, Neo-Confucianism became predominant only after the fall of the Song and during the new Mongol dynasty of the Yuan. By then the Chinese educated elite had achieved sufficient autonomy to serve as a carrier of social and political practices irrespective of dynastic order, and hence also to survive as a ruling stratum under the Ming – and subsequently also under the Qing – thereby providing a unique degree of continuity in the exercise of political and bureaucratic power.

Japanese developments in the beginning of the second millennium CE exhibit many of the features characteristic of both Europe and China during this period. Thus in Japan there was also rapid growth in agricultural production, growth of urban life, increasing commerce both domestically and externally (with China), a movement towards restructuring the basis of traditional elites with less reliance on direct imperial patronage, and a deep-seated restructuring of what might be termed public spaces as well of the nature of political order.

Yet there were, as strongly argued by Mikael Adolphson, continuities in the mutually reinforcing relationship between the imperial political elite and religious elites.[27] The rise of a warrior class out of older elites, more directly tied to the imperial order, was also a gradual development that only in the fifteenth century led to its clear predominance as the ruling class. Rather the persistent pattern is one of continuity between the old imperial order of the Heian period and the power-sharing between imperial political–administrative, religious, and military elites of the Kamakura period (from the late twelfth to the mid-fourteenth centuries). However, rule in the Kamakura period took place within severe financial constraints, and the contributions offered by various elites to the maintenance of the imperial court in Kyoto were on a much lower level than had previously been the case. This reduction in income meant that the expectations of members of the warrior class for rewards, including rewards from service in successfully resisting the two Mongol invasions in the thirteenth century, could not be met. Thus despite a relatively effective and honest system of administration and adjudication, it became gradually more difficult to avoid growing dissatisfaction.

---

[27] See Mikael S. Adolphson, *The Gates of Power: Monks, Courtiers, and Warriors in Pre-modern Japan* (Honolulu: University of Hawai'i Press, 2000); Mikael S. Adolphson, 'Social Change and Contained Transformations: Warriors and Merchants in Japan, 1000–1300', in Arnason and Wittrock, *Eurasian Transformations*, 309–37. To some extent Adolphson's analysis deviates from earlier views which tend to see the transition in the late twelfth century from the imperial order of the Heian period to the Kamakura period as a decisive rupture. An interesting example of such a view is represented in Souyri, *The World Turned Upside Down*. Interesting examples of civilizational analyses of Japan are S. N. Eisenstadt, *Japanese Civilization: A Comparative View* (University of Chicago Press, 1998); and Johann P. Arnason, *The Peripheral Centre: Essays on Japanese History and Civilization* (Melbourne: Trans Pacific Press, 2002).

The new commercial and urban elites, which grew as a result of economic developments, were becoming ever wealthier, but they were also consistently excluded from political power. Even so, the economic needs of society were such that the interests of merchant and commercial interests had to be continuously taken into account as a major variable by the politically dominant groups throughout the second millennium CE, even during the near-absolutist Tokugawa shogunate from the seventeenth century onwards.

The traditional Weberian interpretation of the emergence of a distinctly European trajectory that explains Europe's path to modernity remains suggestive and useful. It emphasizes four coterminous transformations that occurred in the beginning of the second millennium CE.[28] First was the increasing recognition, in the wake of the so-called Papal Revolution, of a de facto separation of ecclesiastical and temporal power. In the political praxis of western Europe, this bifurcation excluded two other forms of political order, theocracy and caesaro-papism. It also set the stage for the institutionalization of forms of contestation and pluralism in matters of the utmost importance to a society. Second was what has come to be termed the Feudal Revolution, involving an articulation of a variety of rights and obligations that could be claimed and upheld in various public fora. Thus we may say an incipient society had been created, in which the rule of law had been transformed from oral adjudication – familiar in many European societies, not least the Scandinavian ones – to one in which the idea had taken root that rights and obligations may be textually inscribed and require interpretation, articulation and competent adjudication by legal scholars. Third was growth of urban life, the Urban Revolution, which not only entailed a stimulus for trade and economic activities, but was also associated with wide-ranging municipal self-government. In some parts of the Holy Roman Empire where effective imperial power had become greatly

---

[28] A sophisticated formulation of the Weberian position is provided by Wolfgang Schluchter in his book *Paradoxes of Modernity: Culture and Conduct in the Theory of Max Weber* (Stanford University Press, 1996), in particular chapter 4, 179–243. In two issues of the journal *Daedalus* – on the themes of *Early Modernities*, Summer 1998, vol. 127, No. 3; and *Multiple Modernities*, Winter 2000, vol. 129, No. 1 – results are reported from a long-term research programme that tried to look at global historical developments and to rethink key concepts in contemporary social theory; both issues have subsequently been reprinted in book format as Eisenstadt, Schluchter and Wittrock (eds.), *Public Spheres and Collective Identities*; and S. N. Eisenstadt (ed.) *Multiple Modernities* (New Brunswick, NJ: Transaction Press, 2002), respectively. See also Johann P. Arnason, *Civilizations in Dispute: Historical Questions and Theoretical Traditions* (Leiden: Brill, 2003).

weakened, such as northern Italy, new forms of urban republican rule took shape. Originally sometimes modelled on an association for common trade purposes, models of urban republican government came to exert a deep influence on notions of political rulership in Europe. This set the stage for the fourth transformation Weber identifies, an intellectual revolution both in scholarly activities themselves and in making possible the existence of multiple fora for intellectual activities, nested in a multiplicity of political and institutional arenas across a Europe that still formed part of one ecumenical order, that of Western Christendom. Thus universities were formed as a particular type of self-governing corporation with at least partial autonomy from the church. Along with the emergence of European universities, this revolution was inherent in the synthesis of the traditions of Western Christendom and the philosophy of classical antiquity, and in the growth of monastic orders as significant institutions.

These processes entailed the emergence of political and intellectual pluralism. They were also related to changes that occurred and that concerned reconceptualizations of notions of cosmology, history, social order and the malleability of worldly existence in terms of human actions. These shifts seem to have been of importance for the economic transformations of Europe, including such shifts as a radical revaluation – or rather devaluation – of the assessment of usury among the mortal sins. In the reading of Douglass North, the institutional changes most of all entailed a reduction in market imperfections.[29]

In Europe in the eleventh to thirteenth centuries, elites that had based their acquisition of power on violent appropriations internally and externally in a context of permeable borders and vaguely defined rules of ownership and inheritance were gradually transforming themselves and seeking to entrench their power more deeply.[30] In the situation of increasing regulation of the rights and borders attached to land and the possibility of an increasing productivity of agriculture, elites transformed themselves into estates with articulated rights. They based their position on extracting revenues from the land and on securing the reproduction of family wealth

---

[29] Douglass C. North and Robert P. Thomas, *The Rise of the Western World: A New Economic History* (Cambridge University Press, 1973): 5ff.

[30] An interesting account that focuses on the intellectual transformations is Marcia L. Colish, *Medieval Foundations of the Western Intellectual Tradition* (New Haven, CT: Yale University Press, 1997). An authoritative overview is Robert Bartlett, *The Making of Europe: Conquest, Colonization, and Cultural Change, 950–1350* (London: Allen Lane, The Penguin Press, 1993).

by laws prescribing primogeniture and patrilineal descent that drastically and suddenly excluded previously legitimate heirs from inheritance, and thereby created a need to tend for daughters and for second and third sons of elite families.

The great geographical expansion of Western Christendom at the turn of the first millennium CE entailed a numerical and spatial enlargement, as well as the pacification of peoples, the Norsemen and Vikings from the north and the Magyars from the east, who had earlier posed a considerable threat to the central and western regions of the continent. It also involved energetic efforts on the part of the papacy to strengthen its relative position through the activities of monastic orders, which were themselves transformed in the process. Similarly and more or less simultaneously, Byzantine Christendom was able to extend its cultural sphere in eastern Europe by conversions of peoples in the Balkans and, perhaps most importantly in the long run, of Kievan Rus'.

In sum, in the Europe of Latin Christendom, a new type of social order emerged, in which landed elites controlled the exercise of violence and in which new rules of marriage, inheritance and chastity guaranteed the preservation of profitable estates over time. One element of this transformation was the emergence of a stratum of professional military men, knights, seeking the favour of greater or lesser lords for shorter or longer times. However an ultimately more profound change was the formation of a new kind of governing class, based on clerical skills. All rulership henceforth depended on the competence of new clerical elites who possessed the necessary abilities to count, record and adjudicate, and the institutions that provide the necessary skills and training for this.

All of these areas – India, China, Japan and western Europe – present both striking analogies and elements of divergence, that came to have radically different consequences. For example, there are striking differences in the formation of collective identities, in the nature of public spheres, and in the development of linguistic practices. In Europe there was a slow but secular growth in the use of vernacular languages and a concomitant shift from imperial towards more nationally conceived forms of political order. In the different parts of the Indian subcontinent, Indologists also identify a growth of secular literature, although this complemented rather than replaced Sanskrit literature. However, as argued by Pollock,[31] there was no emergence of

---

[31] Sheldon Pollock, 'Transformation'.

clearly territorially bounded, not to speak of national, forms of polities, at least in a European sense of the term. In East Asia both classical Chinese and the form and ideal of imperial order were maintained in spite of the vagaries and turmoil over these centuries.

An age of trans-regional reorientations

The period from the tenth to the thirteenth centuries was a time of crisis, but also of the reassertion of cultural legacies in the major civilizations and agro-literate societies of the Old World. In terms of institutional developments, interlinked processes of agricultural expansion, urban and commercial growth and changes in military technology gave rise to elite contestations and efforts at rearrangements of the structure of the political order. These processes tended to be legitimated and interpreted in the light of long-standing cultural legacies within different civilizations. What occurred in these centuries was not a mere shift in ideas, but the articulation and institutional entrenchment of different deep-seated cultural legacies across the Eurasian hemisphere.

The degree of cultural pluralism varied across, and within, civilizations. On the whole the degree of toleration of cultural and religious pluralism was probably lower throughout this period in both Western and Eastern Christendom, than it was in China, Japan or India and later in the Mongol Empire; in the central part of the realm of Islam, toleration diminished under the Mamluks. In China, Confucianism and Daoism had been part of the Chinese cultural ecumene since the Axial Age and in the first half of the first millennium CE were joined by Buddhism in its Mahayana variety and others, not least Lamaism. It is hardly coincidental that the most well-known and popular literary work in the Chinese world up until today is the famous tale from the Tang period about a journey to the West, that is, to India. During some periods – and the Yuan dynasty is one of them – 'Iranian' religions, including Nestorian Christianity, Zoroastrianism and Manichaeism, also played a fully accepted and sometimes prominent role.

Generally, however, what tended to happen towards the end of the first millennium and the beginning of the second millennium CE was that even in the most tolerant contexts, cultural and religious ideas and schools with their roots elsewhere became subject to processes of domestication and integration into the cultural mainstream of a given civilization. In this respect, Japanese developments provide interesting examples of the reinterpretation of Chinese variants of schools of Buddhism and their transposition into forms that appear as distinctly Japanese, of which Zen Buddhism is but one.

In institutional terms, the rise of new types of clerical elites meant that two potential cleavages were of central importance. One had to do with the nature of the relationship between clerical and political elites, in particular the degree of autonomy in the formation of the clerical elites. The other had to do with the relationship between the social and political order, in particular the degree to which social groupings were included or excluded from wielding power in the political arena.

If we compare the major civilizations across Eurasia in terms of the first dimension, it seems clear that western Europe and China were both civilizations in which clerical elites became subject to a demanding formal training and yet enjoyed a high degree of autonomy from political power during their formation. In Constantinople, efforts to train new clerical elites at the beginning of the second millennium CE were tried but seem to have failed largely because ties between these elites and traditional social elites remained too close to allow for a degree of autonomy comparable to what was achieved in the eastern and western parts of Eurasia. Equally important perhaps, the already strained resource base of the Byzantine Empire became drastically limited in the late twelfth century with the loss of most of the mainland of Asia Minor. In Japan, the entourages of the imperial court and of local lords seem to have enjoyed a no more subjugated position than their peers in Europe. However institutionalized autonomy for the formation of clerical elites did not exist to the same degree as in western Europe or in China.

The second dimension concerns relationships between social and political order. In western Europe, there was a real sharing and, to some extent, a spatially defined division of power between different social groupings, including new urban elites and traditional elites, as well as the absence of a long-standing imperial political order. To some extent the church represented the heritage of empire, but it could never assert a generally accepted claim to such a position. Perhaps we can say that western Europe came to represent an institutionalized articulation of what Eisenstadt always saw as the most important characteristic of an Axial civilization, namely a belief in the existence of a chasm between a transcendental and a worldly sphere. In practice such a chasm became institutionally articulated in the division between a domain of the church and another of the secular political order, as well as in a continuing coexistence of institutional pluralism.

The standard view of the European trajectory tends to focus on this emerging pluralism of the western European political order as unique and crucial for the future ascendancy of Europe. However, such accounts tend to overlook vitally important characteristics of other trajectories. In the case of China, to take a prominent counter-example, although the overt position of imperial rule remained paramount, there can be little doubt that the Chinese cultural order had long been characterized by a high, if varying, degree of pluralism and openness towards a range of religious and cultural traditions of different origins but all of which could be accommodated within a Chinese cultural ecumene. Furthermore, even if the Chinese political order was unitary and hierarchical, the cosmological underpinnings of political order were explicitly conditional: while service to the incumbent holder of the Mandate of Heaven was seen as obligatory in Confucian tradition, this Mandate could also be forfeited and an unworthy or inefficient holder of it could invoke no further transcendental legitimacy.[32] What happened at the turn of the first millennium CE is that these elements of conditionality, pluralism and contestability become entrenched in institutional terms through the growing autonomy of the clerical class of literati. In this respect, it is of importance that the Mongol conquest and the establishment of the Yuan dynasty deeply influenced the nature of this basic pattern, but did not come to cause an irreparable rupture in it.[33]

Although the consequences of Mongol conquest may not appear to be so different in the Chinese and the Islamic worlds in terms of the length of conquest – or rather perhaps in the brevity of time before the conquerors had become converted or assimilated into the regional religious and cultural ecumenes – they were significantly different in terms of impact. While both worlds came to preserve their ecumenical cultural languages, it is only in the Chinese context that it is possible to speak also of a continuity in the nature of the political order. One unforeseen effect of the Mongol conquest of Baghdad and central lands of the Islamic world was that the relative benevolence of the Mongols towards the then still substantial Nestorian and Monophysite Christian populations came to engender suspicion and distrust among Muslims. After the collapse of the Mongol Empire, measures to

---

[32] A brief but important discussion about the centrality of political order in Chinese thought is found in Benjamin I. Schwartz, 'The Primacy of the Political Order in East Asian Societies: Some Preliminary Generalizations', in Stuart R. Schram (ed.), *Foundations and Limits of State Power in China* (London: European Science Foundation and SOAS, and Hong Kong: The Chinese University Press, Hong Kong, 1987): 1–10.

[33] See also Bol, 'Examinations and Orthodoxies', 29–57.

encourage conversion or out-migration of Christian populations increased, which led to the numerical decline of Christian minority populations in this region.

Like China, Japan possessed a cultural order with different layers of tradition and religious practice integrated into a coherent unity, but this was characterized at the beginning of the second millennium CE by important shifts in the social and political order. These shifts generally meant that the political order became shaped by contests among three parallel hierarchies, one imperial, another military and a third religious. These hierarchies themselves also become more structured in ways that for some of the classics of social science seemed reminiscent of the structuring of feudal rights in Europe. Another feature that was somewhat reminiscent of Europe was the concomitant emergence of what might be termed a new kind of public space, where commercial and urban interests came to play an important role socially and culturally while – in contrast to Europe – being excluded from real political power for centuries to come.

What happened then about the turn of the first millennium CE was that new articulations emerged in some of the major civilizations of the Old World that made new practices and institutions conceivable. Different conceptualizations of time and belonging ultimately made possible new ways of being and intervening in the world. In many regions of the Old World, these new articulations were directly related to processes of urban and commercial growth and they were linked to the reinterpretation of religious or cosmological accounts. Similarly the emergence of a new clerical class, autonomously formed, was only possible once the interpretability of different textual accounts was seen as a legitimate and institutionalized procedure.

This process in turn was related to the gradual formation of new types of political order. Instead of the imaginations of empire, in Europe these new types of political order emerged out of the realities of city republics, territorial proto-monarchies and assemblies representing the new societal groupings that had emerged. This entailed a need for sustained reflection on the nature and legitimacy of these new forms of domination. In the Sanskrit-based cultural world, the very notion of a close and necessary tie between the political order and religious, much less ethnic, identities came to be seen as increasingly contingent.

Thus some of the most fundamental assumptions behind the conditions for humans living together and ordering their public affairs at the eastern, western, and southern ends of the Old World became distinctly different from one another through separate processes of cultural crystallization and reorientation. However, curiosity and interest in other regions continued and grew. Thus in the early modern period, theorizing about the polity at the western end of Eurasia was deeply influenced by imaginations of how such matters were handled in for instance China and Japan, not to speak of the three great Islamic empires of the Mughals, the Safavids and the Ottomans. Some of the institutional practices and the trajectories of different ecumenes of the world came to diverge in this age of trans-regional reorientations, but the entanglements and encounters of these cultural worlds also became ever closer and were destined to become increasingly so, and in subsequent periods involved far more glaring asymmetries of power and coercion.

FURTHER READING

Adolphson, Mikael S. *The Gates of Power: Monks, Courtiers, and Warriors in Premodern Japan.* Honolulu, HI: University of Hawai'i Press, 2000.

Arnason, Johann P. *The Peripheral Centre: Essays on Japanese History and Civilization.* Melbourne: Trans Pacific Press, 2002.

Civilizations in Dispute: Historical Questions and Theoretical Traditions. Leiden: Brill, 2003.

Arnason, Johann P. and Björn Wittrock (eds.). *Eurasian Transformations, Tenth to Thirteenth Centuries: Crystallizations, Divergences, Renaissances.* Leiden: Brill, 2004.

Bartlett, Robert. *The Making of Europe: Conquest, Colonization, and Cultural Change, 950–1350.* London: Allen Lane, The Penguin Press, 1993.

Bisson, Thomas N. *The Crisis of the Twelfth Century: Power, Lordship, and the Origins of European Government.* Princeton University Press, 2009.

Bol, Peter K. *Neo-Confucianism in History.* Cambridge, MA: Harvard University Asia Center and Harvard University Press, 2008.

Colish, Marcia L. *Medieval Foundations of the Western Intellectual Tradition.* New Haven, CT: Yale University Press, 1997.

Eisenstadt, S. N. *Comparative Civilizations and Multiple Modernities: A Collection of Essays by S. N. Eisenstadt*, vol. I. Leiden: Brill, 2003.

Japanese Civilization: A Comparative View. The University of Chicago Press, 1998.

(ed.) *Multiple Modernities*, New Brunswick, NJ: Transaction Press, 2002: originally published as 'Multiple Modernities', special issue of *Daedalus*, 129:1 (Winter 2000).

Eisenstadt, S. N., Wolfgang Schluchter and Björn Wittrock (eds.). *Public Spheres and Collective Identities*, New Brunswick, NJ: Transaction Press, 2001: originally published as 'Early Modernities', special issue of *Daedalus* 127:3 (Summer 1998).

Klaniczay, Gábor. *Holy Rulers and Blessed Princesses: Dynastic Cults in Medieval Europe.* Cambridge University Press, 2002.

Lewis, Mark Edward. *China's Cosmopolitan Empire: The Tang Dynasty.* Cambridge, MA: The Belknap Press of Harvard University Press, 2009.

Pollock, Sheldon. *The Language of the Gods in the World of Men: Sanskrit, Culture, and Power in Premodern India.* Berkeley, CA: University of California Press, 2006.

Schluchter, Wolfgang. *Paradoxes of Modernity: Culture and Conduct in the Theory of Max Weber.* Stanford, CA: Stanford University Press, 1996.

Souyri, Pierre François. *The World Turned Upside Down: Medieval Japanese Society.* New York, NY: Columbia University Press, Asia Perspectives, 2001.

PART III

★

GROWING INTERACTIONS

9

Trade and commerce across Afro-Eurasia

RICHARD SMITH

In trade and commerce the Afro-Eurasian world was a very different place in 1500 than in 500. A more professional merchant class moved larger cargoes of more varied commodities longer distances to more destinations serving a wider consumer base than could have been imagined at the close of the fifth century. Linkages had become stronger as the Afro-Eurasian world slowly drew together. Nevertheless, interconnectedness was tempered by cycles, waxes and wanes, convergences and divergences, revivals, stagnations, and sometimes collapses. Commercial systems were still fragile, their successes and failures too often determined as much by political and social as economic factors. Production, distribution, and consumption were often linked together in ways not easily determined today, given the range of undetectable variables the historian must deal with. And to complicate matters, the premodern market did not always operate according to the principles of modern trade theory. Finally, most trade and commerce took place on local and regional levels, although long-distance trade was not as marginal as some interpretations have characterized it, and the boundaries between the three levels of trade were often quite porous.

A simple approach to imposing some order on the study of trade and commerce for the Middle Millennium is to divide Afro-Eurasia into three categories of zones: engines, passageways, and cul-de-sacs. Engines were the centers of production, consumption, and exchange and thus the driving forces for long-distance trade in a world where supply never caught up to demand. All zones had some engine qualities, so their impact was relative. Zones were also either passageways or cul-de-sacs depending on location (see Map 9.1).

The engines

The most dynamic engine was China. Fixed at the far end of the land mass, China was a cul-de-sac distanced from the other major zones by the highest

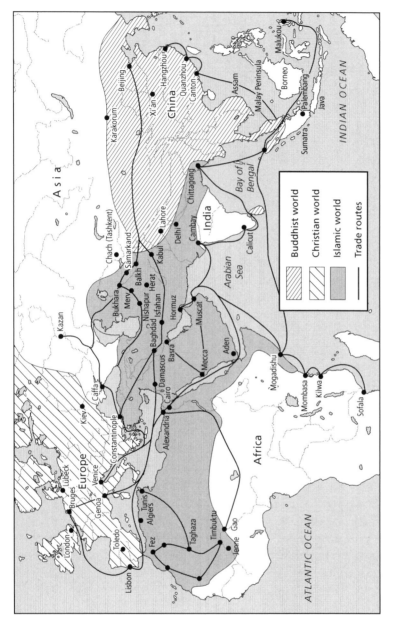

Map 9.1. Major trade routes of Afro-Eurasia 1300 CE

Legend:
- Buddhist world
- Christian world
- Islamic world
- Trade routes

INDIAN OCEAN

ATLANTIC OCEAN

Asia

China
Beijing
Xi'an
Hangzhou
Quanzhou
Canton
Karakorum
Assam
Malay Peninsula
Borneo
Sumatra
Palembang
Java
Malukou

Chittagong
Bay of Bengal
India
Delhi
Lahore
Cambay
Calicut
Arabian Sea

Chach (Tashkent)
Samarkand
Kabul
Balkh
Herat
Bukhara
Merv
Nishapur
Isfahan
Baghdad
Hormuz
Muscat
Basra
Mecca
Aden
Kazan

Caffa
Kiev
Damascus
Cairo
Constantinople
Alexandria
Europe
Venice
Genoa
Lübeck
Bruges
London
Toledo
Lisbon
Fez
Tunis
Algiers
Taghaza
Timbuktu
Gao
Jenne

Mogadishu
Mombasa
Kilwa
Sofala
Africa

234

mountains and some of the most dreadful deserts in the world. Nevertheless, China's assets, beginning with a rich agricultural base, an innovative industrial sector, a productive workforce, and an ample infrastructure of canals, roads, and bridges, more than compensated for location. Between the Tang (618–907) and Song (960–1279) dynasties, China's population doubled. Hangzhou, the Southern Song capital, was the largest city in the world of its time, with more than a million inhabitants,[1] while Quanzhou and Guangzhou were likely the world's busiest ports. The internal Chinese market was of such size and wealth that its commercial energy rippled through much of the rest of Eurasia.

Over the millennium China's population shifted southward, a development that coincided with an equally dramatic change in China's external trade pattern from one based largely on overland routes through the Silk Roads system to one focused more on maritime outlets leading into the Indian Ocean. The Chinese state played a central role in regulating, supervising, taxing, and to varying degrees engaging in foreign exchange. At the imperial court an ongoing debate simmered between advocates of foreign trade and a party of strict Confucians who opposed it, preferring to keep foreign goods, ideas, and people out of China. That the pro-trade party often prevailed was due to the pressing need for revenue. Private trade meant taxes, and direct government involvement sometimes generated profits. The only other reason for countenancing external trade was to obtain exotic luxury goods for the court and elite. Policies favoring trade were not implemented to improve the lot of the common people by providing employment nor to encourage capital accumulation and reinvestment by the entrepreneurial classes. In the Confucian value system, merchants were considered as parasites who produced no real wealth. Although this ideology was often transcended by more practical considerations and some merchants became very rich, as a class they exercised no political power, enjoyed little influence, and were subject to having their assets confiscated if they became too rich or in other ways attracted the official gaze.

Foreign trade became an important element in the overall Chinese economy under the Song and Yuan (1279–1368) dynasties, which together are considered the great age of private commerce. The Ming (1368–1644) instituted more restrictive policies designed to monopolize external exchange through the tribute trade system, which had been practiced in varying

---

1 Jacques Gernet, *Daily Life in China on the Eve of the Mongol Invasion 1250–1276*, trans. H. M. Wright (London: Allen and Unwin, 1962): 28.

degrees by different dynasties since the Han (206 BCE–220 CE). Under this system, exchange was conducted only with official missions arriving from outside China bringing tribute in the form of rare goods to the emperor. In return, they received what were deemed to be "gifts" often worth more in value than what they had brought, the magnanimous gesture of a superior to an inferior. Such exchange sanctified an ideology that confirmed China as the center of the world. Embassies arrived on and off at various times during the Middle Millennium, bringing everything from yak tails and monkey skins to performing elephants and in, one instance, what was listed as "dried scrotum of Pacific seal."[2] For the Chinese, the official intention of tribute trade was not to realize a profit, although this depended to some extent on the dynasty in power: the Song, for example, often benefited while the Ming did not. Embassies were housed, feted, and provided with individual presents. Members of a mission took the occasion to engage in private trade so that often foreign traders not actually from the country offering tribute attached themselves to missions or even contracted the right from a foreign ruler to present themselves as official envoys.

Complementing China in the early centuries of the Middle Millennium as an engine powering Afro-Eurasian commerce was the Islamic heartland, a contiguous stretch of territory from Persia across Iraq, Syria, and Egypt with feeders into Anatolia, across North Africa to al-Andalus (Muslim Iberia), and south to the coasts of the Arabian peninsula. Lying at the intersection of the Eurasian and African land masses and flanked by the Indian Ocean and the Mediterranean Sea, it was the consummate land–sea passageway, custom-made for middlemen. The Silk Roads system provided a direct link from Persia to China, India was a monsoon's sail, Europe was just across the Mediterranean, the Black Sea provided access to the Russian river system, and West Africa was connected by camel caravan. A hub of interlocking, intersecting commercial circuits with multiple points of entry and exit, the Islamic heartland became the great nexus of land and sea systems with much of its wealth generated from transit trade. It had an urban-based economy reaching back four millennia with active and savvy commercial classes, productive handicraft industries based on regional specialization, good ports, an experienced seagoing population, and a wide network of trade contacts already in place. Indeed the peoples of this zone had to rely on trade, since

---

2 Robert M. Hartwell, "Foreign Trade, Monetary Policy and Chinese Mercantilism," in Tsuyoshi Kinugawa (ed.), *Collected Studies on Sung History Dedicated to Professor James T. C. Liu in Celebration of His Seventieth Birthday* (Kyoto: Dohosha, 1989): 454, 469.

huge areas were wastelands and agriculture, still the basis of all large economies, was possible only in select areas. Lack of wood was a perennial problem, and much of the mineral wealth was exhausted. Another resource that had to be continuously supplemented was manpower, as this was a very large zone with a shortage of people in proportion to the role it played economically and geopolitically. To compensate, it sucked in people in a continuous flow of slaves from neighboring areas.

In many ways the Islamic heartland could hardly have been more different from China, yet together the two provided a good balance during the first half of the Middle Millennium. The Chinese economy was larger, with seemingly unlimited human and natural resources, but the Islamic heartland was commercially more diversified, established, and complex. Unlike China, in the Islamic heartland commerce was esteemed a noble profession. The Prophet himself had once been a merchant, many of the founding families of Islam came from mercantile backgrounds, and Islam provided a corpus of commercial law, a commercial language, and an international currency, the Muslim dinar. For much of the first half of the millennium, the Islamic heartland enjoyed political unity under the caliphate. New centers of consumption arose, above all Baghdad, which became, for a while, the commercial center of Eurasia. Beyond the Baghdad Caliphate the larger Islamic world, reaching from the shores of the Atlantic in al-Andalus to the shores of the Pacific at the Muslim trade colony in Quanzhou, tied together the other major zones of the Afro-Eurasia world.

Nor was the Islamic heartland reserved for the exclusive use of Muslim traders. In Baghdad Jews were prominent in finance, and under the early Caliphate an atmosphere of tolerance prevailed. The Radhanites were Jewish merchants who took advantage of the unity provided by the caliphate, traveling from Al-Andalus to India, buying slaves and furs in the west and musk, aloe, camphor, and cinnamon in the east, along with whatever other high-end commodities they happened upon. With their Muslim counterparts, they traveled by sea to South China, at least until 878 when Chinese rebels sacked the port of Guangzhou, massacring a large number of foreign merchants. Thereafter the Radhanites stuck to the overland trunk routes. They enjoyed one great advantage: because they were regarded as neutral in the struggle between Islam and Christianity, they were able to cross hostile religious boundaries. The Radhanites did not comprise a formal association but more a loose network of merchants based in Jewish communities strung along the trade routes.

For the Islamic heartland the good times peaked between the eighth and tenth centuries, before the power of the 'Abbasid Caliphate declined and eventually fragmented. Of the states that emerged from its collapse, the most successful was Egypt under the Fatimids (969–1171) and the Ayyubids (1174–1250). Egypt occupied the most strategic of all positions at the hinge binding the Eurasian and African land masses. Under the Fatimids the western maritime terminus shifted from the Persian Gulf to the Red Sea, in part reflecting the rise of Europe as a market for Asian goods. The government taxed this trade but did not interfere with it. Eventually it came to be controlled by a monopoly under an association of wholesale merchants and shipowners known as the Karimis. Egypt itself produced and exported large quantities of grain, cotton, sugar, linen, and glass. Cairo soon surpassed Baghdad as the hub of world commerce.

Trade through the Red Sea or Persian Gulf led to India, the most complex of the zones, a great commercial engine that was both a cul-de-sac in the north and a maritime passageway in the south. India was actually several places often going in different directions. Northern India had ties to Central Asia and Persia, but its extremities, Bengal and Gujarat, were sea-oriented. In the south, peninsular India was divided between coastal and interior regions that could be strongly interconnected or independent of each other. Coastal peninsular India was separated between west and east, each under its own monsoon wind regime. Malabar and the west coast looked to the Islamic heartland and beyond to Europe; Coromandel and the east coast opened on Southeast Asia and beyond to China. Different groups of merchants dealing in different commodities faced different conditions, opportunities, and challenges.

The complexity is extended by different interpretations of the economy of northern India during the early centuries of the Middle Millennium. In one view, the fall of the Gupta Empire in the late fifth century ushered in political fragmentation; what has been labeled as the great age of "Indian feudalism." Urban market-based economy was replaced by self-sufficient village economy, coinage disappeared, trade routes withered, and the merchant class was reduced to petty peddling.[3] These conditions lasted until the thirteenth century when northern India under the Delhi sultanate was absorbed into the world of Islam. But if Indian feudalism has been a compelling theory, mounting numismatic and archaeological evidence does

---

3 R. S. Sharma, *Urban Decay in India (c. 300–c. 1000)* (New Delhi: Munshiram Manoharlal, 1987): 135–8.

not seem to confirm it. On the matter of money, for example, it is certainly true that northern Indian coinage consisted of base or heavily alloyed metals, but some scholars have seen this not as a sign of decline but instead the opposite. Because northern India lacked sufficient deposits of precious metals and much of what it had was hoarded in temples, they assert, it did not have enough gold and silver to keep up with its vibrant exchange economy.[4] Overall, a mixed picture seems appropriate. Trade shifted and realigned, new patterns emerged, some places suffered, but others prospered. Commercial economy, including long-distance trade, continued and in some places was very brisk. In short, commercial growth and prosperity do not necessarily require political centralization or even stability.

Peninsular India, which had not been a part of the Gupta Empire, went in a different direction. On the Malabar coast the waning of Roman trade had a negative impact on some ports while the trade of Sri Lanka enjoyed a golden age. On the Coromandel coast expansion in the direction of Southeast Asia may have started as early as the seventh century and was thriving by the ninth. For much of this period peninsular maritime India and Southeast Asia formed more of an integrated zone than did southern and northern India. Traffic coming from one side of the Eurasian land mass to the other by sea was almost certain to make landfall somewhere on the Indian coast. In the early centuries pepper and spices remained the most important long-distance, high-value commodities, but the growth market was in cotton textiles, ranging in grade from extremely high quality to mass-produced, all sent seaborne to lands ringing the Indian Ocean. Imports ranged from Chinese porcelain and Southeast Asian tin to Arabian perfume and Mediterranean glassware, while horses in untold numbers were led in from Persia and Central Asia or carried by ship from Arabia for use in warfare and as a symbol of power and status. Overall, India enjoyed a favorable balance of trade that was covered by large imports of gold and silver. India also took the middleman's cut in transit trade, the most lucrative of which involved Chinese silk headed westward.

The passageways

India's connection to China required travel through one or other of the major passageway zones: Southeast Asia at the eastern entrance to the Indian

---

4 John S. Deyell, *Living Without Silver: The Monetary History of Early Medieval North India* (Delhi: Oxford University Press, 1990): 2–5.

Figure 9.1 Bayon temple in Angkor, market scene (photograph by Benjamin Kedar)

Ocean; or Central Asia, the overland tie between China and the rest of Eurasia. Southeast Asia, running between the Malay peninsula and the islands of Sumatra, Java, and Borneo provided some local commodities including spices, incense, and medicinal products that could often be substituted for similar but more expensive items produced farther away (see Figure 9.1). But neither in the production nor the consumption of goods did Southeast Asia have a sufficient impact on other zones to be considered a principal engine. Between the seventh and eleventh centuries the Straits of Malacca were dominated by Srivijaya, variously described as a thalassocracy, empire, or federation of cities or chiefdoms, or dismissed as little more than a figment of Chinese imagination.[5] Its center is thought to have been near Palembang in southeastern Sumatra, from where it levied customs and port fees in return for providing a convenient and safe place for exchange, transshipment, and storage. Srivijaya also assumed control over Southeast Asian products headed into the long-distance network.

Srivijaya's dominance began to unravel after 1025, when a fleet from the Chola kingdom in southern India attacked and plundered Palembang and other Srivijayan cities. The Great Chola Raid has been dismissed as nothing

5 Kenneth R. Hall, *Maritime Trade and State Development in Early Southeast Asia* (Honolulu: University of Hawai'i Press, 1985): 78–93; Janet L. Abu-Lughod, *Before European Hegemony: The World System A.D. 1250–1350* (New York: Oxford University Press, 1989): 304–15.

more than an enormous plundering expedition, or construed as a calculated policy by the Cholas to break Srivijaya's stranglehold over trade between India and China.[6] Srivijaya revived, but in weakened condition, its structure shaken enough to allow for the emergence of a rival centered in eastern Java, which became the dynamo of its own limited but very profitable commercial system. Eastern and central Java constituted one of Asia's most productive rice bowls, capable of generating huge surpluses. The source of all cloves, nutmeg, and mace, the most valuable of spices, was the Malukus, a collection of small islands at the eastern extremity of the Indonesian archipelago, much closer to Java than Sumatra. Land in the Malukus was too valuable for food production, so Javanese traders brought in boatloads of rice along with Indian textiles in return for spices, which they passed on to their Chinese, Arab, and Indian counterparts. The wealth generated from this business stimulated Javanese consumption, resulting in an influx of commodities from China and India. In the late thirteenth century Java became the center for a new power, Majapahit, whose commercial reach extended beyond that of Srivijaya at its peak. The Java trade became one component in a rising maritime system stretching from the South China Sea to the Mediterranean that became prominent between the tenth and thirteenth centuries, a consequence of unhappy events to the north, where China, India, and the Islamic heartland all came under attack by Turkic and Mongol peoples.

The other great passageway zone both paralleled and contrasted with Southeast Asia. Central Asia lay far inland, north of India, west of China, east of the Caspian Sea, and south of the Siberian forests. The climate was cold and dry, and the land consisted mostly of steppe and desert punctuated by great mountain chains. To reach China overland from the Islamic heartland or Europe, few viable alternatives to Central Asia were available. From India an overland passageway started in Assam and ran circuitously up and down rivers, over enormous peaks, and through almost impenetrable jungles across much of mainland Southeast Asia to Yunnan and eventually Sichuan. Shorter routes led over even more difficult paths through Ladakh and Tibet. Although Central Asia held many challenges, most traffic favored it as the best means of getting to China.

The common subsistence activities in Central Asia included oasis and river valley agriculture and nomadic pastoralism, a situation favoring

6 George W. Spencer, *The Politics of Expansion: The Chola Conquest of Sri Lanka and Sri Vajaya* (Madras: New Era Press, 1983): 136–45; André Wink, *Al-Hind: The Making of the Indo-Islamic World*, 1 (Leiden: Brill, 1990): 318–33.

exchange-based symbiotic relationships. Nomadic pastoralists needed grain, cloth, and manufactured goods in return for their surplus animal products. Central Asian nomads were usually eager traders, but resorted to more predatory activities when settled folk shut the door to them. Trade was usually facilitated when all or part of this zone came under the rule of nomadic empires beginning with the Turks in the late sixth century and culminating with the Mongols in the thirteenth. The Uighurs, whose empire succeeded the Turks, were especially trade-friendly. Nomadic pastoralists were not the only traders in Central Asia. On a larger scale, specialized merchants from the settled population did business at convenient commercial intersections. The biggest of the big dealers were the Sogdians, whose homeland lay between the Oxus River and the Pamir Mountains. Noted silk merchants with trade colonies as far east as the Chinese capital of Chang'an, the Sogdians were favored under the Uighurs, who came to adopt many elements of Sogdian culture. After the fall of their empire, the Uighurs established themselves as an important trading people who played a noted role in northern China as moneylenders in long-distance trade.

The major trade arteries across Central Asia intersected in cities, which were also centers of production. Some manufactured commodities were consumed locally, others were sent to the nomads or forest peoples, and some entered the long-distance system for export out of the zone. Cities became widely known for specialized products: Samarkand for paper and brocade; Chach (Tashkent) for leather products, cotton fabrics, and medicine; and Bukhara for carpets and wines. Central Asia remained a major exporter of horses for the armies of China and India and of camels for transport across overland Asia. In the wake of the Arab conquest of the eighth century, the trading economies of the Islamic heartland and Central Asia became so intermeshed as to take on the characteristics of a single zone for a while.

The cul-de-sacs

While all the major zones experienced some degree of disruption at the onset of the Middle Millennium, the most challenging conditions existed in the far west. The Mediterranean basin had served as an important engine under the Roman Empire, but by the sixth century it had been dismembered. The regions of the zone and ultimately the districts within the regions broke off and drifted apart, albeit in a sort of slow motion. With periodic resurges here and there, the overall spin was downward, reaching its nadir in the seventh century. Political division, problems with maintaining order, endemic warfare, deurbanization, and the decline of market-directed agriculture all played important roles. Local products replaced imports as the breakdown in infrastructure led to disruption in the circulation of goods.

Although Europe was relegated to the periphery of Eurasian commerce, long-distance trade never completely died out. Specialized systems arose to address specific needs, two of the most notable originating in the far north beyond former imperial boundaries. Between the seventh and ninth centuries, the Frisians founded a system centered on new emporia scattered across the North Sea that traveled up Rhenish riverain routes into the interior. Trading textiles, weapons, glassware, and wine from Francia, furs and amber from Scandinavia, and silver and bronze prestige items, the Frisians served mostly kings, nobles, and monasteries. The Frisians did not operate past Denmark, but the Baltic did serve as the wellspring of another system. Originating in the late eighth century and reaching its high point in the tenth, this system ran across eastern Europe into the Russian river basins, then south to Transcaucasia, the Caspian Sea, the Byzantine Empire, the caliphate, and Central Asia, carrying slaves, wax, honey, and, above all, furs, the most valuable of which were sable, marten, and miniver to be made into hats or used in the lining of robes. In return, eastern luxury goods and especially silver coins went north. Hoards of dirhams minted in Samarkand, Chach, and Merv, from silver mines in Chach and Pendjir in Afghanistan, have been found in Scandinavia and isolated coins unearthed as far as England and Iceland. Securing the belly of this system were two rival khanates controlled by Turkic peoples, the Bulghars on the Middle Volga and, farther south, the Khazars, whose authority reached north from the Caucasus Mountains and Caspian Sea through the lower Volga and Don basins as far west as the Crimea. The conversion of the Khazar elite to a loose form of Judaism in the mid-eighth century also made their territory a popular transit point on the west-to-east Radhanite route, although the Khazars welcomed all traders so long as they paid a 10 per cent tax. The Khazars fed into the network almost no commodities of their own, nor were they notable as merchants themselves. Nevertheless, the wealth of this system eventually aroused the rapacity of the Rus', an amalgam of Scandinavians, Slavs, and Finnic peoples who controlled the northern stretch of the system and were known to have mixed commerce with plunder. In 965 the Rus' devastated the khanate, and trade shifted westward.

Once the commercial economy of the far west hit bottom it stabilized, and a transformation began taking shape. The ninth century is often seen as a crucial period beginning a trend toward a market-based economy that became more prominent in the tenth and eleventh centuries. This heralded a prolonged period of economic growth culminating in the momentous thirteenth century now touted as the period of the "Commercial Revolution." The fuel for sustained growth came from a demographic explosion during which the population of Europe doubled between 1100 and 1300.[7] Towns became cities that represented concentrated demand and thus increased efficiency in distribution. The rise of centralized authority and the creation of larger integrated political units allowed for increased security in transportation and a more predictable relationship between merchant and political establishment. The cost of doing business dropped.

As the economy became more commercialized, the need for money became more pressing. Silver was discovered in the late tenth century in the Harz Mountains of Saxony followed by other finds in central Europe, the last and greatest being Kutná Hora in Bohemia, which, by the beginning of the thirteenth century, was producing enough ore to mint millions of coins. Much of this was absorbed by the expansion of commerce within Europe, but tons of silver in the form of ingots were shipped to the Levant, Egypt, and the Black Sea to settle trade imbalances Europe accrued in its obsession with Asian luxury products. Nevertheless, silver production never met the demands of the expanding market, and while gold was used in large-scale transactions, metals alone could not satisfy the need. The re-emergence of banking out of currency exchange soon led to the practice of transferring credits on paper from one account to another. New credit instruments were developed, the most important being bills of exchange. Merchants from northern Italian cities led the way, assuming the position of middleman in the transit trade that brought Asian products into Europe and carried silver out. By the end of the thirteenth century, Europe had re-emerged as an engine in Afro-Eurasian commerce, if not yet on the scale of other engines, at least with considerable potential as partner or competitor.

The last of the major zones to connect into the Afro-Eurasian system was West Africa. There an intermesh of local circuits carrying goods of low value, principally foodstuffs and metal products, over short distances eventually merged into inter-regional networks extending from the oases and mines of the southern Sahara to the edge of the rainforests. The different ecological zones running in bands across West Africa provided different commodities for this system. Entrepôts were established at ecotones where transportation

---

7 Jean-Noël Biraben, "Essai sur l'évolution du nombre des hommes," *Population* 34 (1979): 13–25, and the introduction to the present volume, Table 1.1.

modes changed, as in camels for donkeys, donkeys for human head-porterage, and overland for riverain. The middle course of the Niger and its tributaries represented a thousand-mile stretch of navigable waterways.

West African trade connected into the other zones of Afro-Eurasia through the Trans-Sahara. Commerce into and out of the Sahara existed from an early time, but a structured cross-desert system emerged only after the appearance of a high-demand product, which turned out to be gold, and the development of an efficient means of transport, which was made possible by the use of the dromedary as a pack animal. Gold began arriving in North Africa in noticeable amounts perhaps as early as the fourth century and certainly by the eighth,[8] and camel caravans had become common in North Africa by the onset of the Middle Millennium. At the southern edge of the desert, the Trans-Sahara became grafted on to existing West African systems. Other goods going north included animal products, particularly hides and skins, some civet and ivory, and slaves for use as soldiers, concubines, and eunuchs. Goods coming south featured textiles and other manufactured items, warhorses, cowrie shells to serve as currency, and, most importantly, salt from mines in the northern Sahara.

Geography determined that West Africa would remain a cul-de-sac, but other factors limited its overall commercial potential. It exported too many raw materials and imported too many finished products, the type of relationship that builds dependency rather than partnership. Its elite classes were of the warrior-noble variety focused more on raiding and warfare than activities promoting economic development, while its merchant classes, typified by the Wangara (Juula), remained alien in-groups among the customers they served. No banking or credit systems evolved, nor did the economy become monetized: West African states did not use their own gold to mint coins. Cities were essentially commercial centers vulnerable to shifts in trade patterns that proved all too common. Nevertheless, the impact of West African trade on other zones can scarcely be overstated. By the fourteenth century, and probably earlier, West Africa was producing and exporting more gold than anywhere else in the world.[9] This gold together with central European silver undergirded the monetization of Islamic and European economies and provided the lubricant for long-distance trade to India and beyond.

---

8 Timothy F. Garrard, "Myth and Metrology: The Early Trans-Saharan Gold Trade," *Journal of African History* 23 (1982): 447–51; Walter E. Kaegi, "Byzantium and the Trans-Saharan Gold Trade: A Cautionary Note," *Graeco-Arabica* 3 (1984): 95–9.
9 Nehemia Levtzion, *Ancient Ghana and Mali* (London: Methuen, 1973): 132.

The cataclysms

Before the Middle Millennium drew to a close, the Afro-Eurasian world experienced two cataclysmic events that came as calamities in their immediate impact. Viewed from the longue durée, they can be seen as having stimulated complex processes that altered the trajectories of commerce in some places while accelerating existing trends in others. The first was the rise of the Mongol Empire built by Chinggis Khan and his heirs at an appalling cost. Cities were leveled, regions laid to waste, and populations annihilated. The two great engines that had earlier propelled Eurasia's commercial economy along with the land passageway between them suffered the most. North China was ruined, its population decimated, and its wealth plundered. South China, which had held out longer, suffered little damage, and its coastal regions prospered under the Mongol Yuan dynasty. In the Islamic heartland the ancient trade centers of Iraq and Persia were ravaged. Places were sacked often multiple times, and huge swatches of productive land became barren. Baghdad was devastated so thoroughly in 1258 that long-distance trade began to bypass what had once been a hub of the commercial world. In Central Asia the great caravan nexus became the special focus of Mongol wrath. Merv, Herat, Samarkand, and Nishapur were sacked and their populations slaughtered. Balkh was destroyed so utterly that archaeologists later found it difficult to determine its precise location.[10]

Once the conquest was completed, the new system that was imposed, based on exploitation, continued to drive some sectors of the economy downward, especially agricultural production. Trade, however, was another matter. Like most nomads, the Mongols knew that a steadier source of income could be had from taxing than robbing caravans, and thus Mongol policies, chief of which was to provide security, were designed to foster long-distance trade. For merchants, protection costs were usually higher than carriage costs; now in one fell swoop a unified system replaced the hodge-podge of extorting entities that had existed from the Sea of Japan to the Black Sea. For the merchant attempting to calculate his risks and profits, a new degree of predictability became possible. Some of the great caravan cities that had been destroyed were rebuilt, and along the routes way stations and caravanserais were established.

---

10 Luc Kwanten, *A History of Central Asia 500–1500* (Philadelphia: University of Pennsylvania Press, 1979): 120.

Under the Mongols the old network of Silk Roads that circled the Taklamakan Desert, crossed the Pamirs into Transoxania, then ran south-west through Persia to the Mediterranean experienced some rejuvenation. But the big surge took place several hundred miles north, bound for the Mongol capital at Karakorum, which emerged as an enormous center of consumption. This parallel passage, sometimes referred to as the Steppe Road, was an ancient route perhaps first described in Herodotus[11] that ran across open grasslands, skirting the northern edge of the Gobi, crossing the Altai and Urals, and connecting into the Russian river system or Black Sea. The Steppe Road enjoyed many advantages over the Silk Roads, not the least of which was that wheeled vehicles could be used across greater stretches of it. Nevertheless, most of the time it was more open to the depredations of marauders, making it a more dangerous passage than the Silk Roads; thus only in periods of imposed peace as under the Mongols was the Steppe Road extensively used. The Mongol Empire, however, did not last long. Its system of succession was more suited to a division of personal property than the transference of state power, and within a few generations the empire effect-ively became four separate entities. Although all four continued to encourage trade, low-grade warfare increasingly characterized relations between them, as did civil wars within each. Divisions soon became subdivisions, and by the late fourteenth century secure transcontinental travel no longer existed.

For trade and commerce the Mongol interlude was a very mixed bag. From the time the Tang dynasty had started its downward slide, the Silk Roads had been in decline due to unsettled conditions and a growing preference for shipping via the Indian Ocean. While overland trade revived somewhat under the "Pax Mongolica," it did so at a horrible price. The killing off of enormous numbers of people meant a loss in productive capacity that could not be compensated for despite the trade-friendly policies of the Mongols. And the Mongols never favored land over sea traffic. Once in control of South China, the Yuan continued the Song policy of encouraging maritime commerce, from which they received considerable financial bene-fits. When the overland routes subsequently waned, the sea routes continued to boom.

A sad sequel to the Mongol Empire came in the conquests of Timur (Tamerlane), a vain attempt to resurrect the Chinggisid trans-Eurasian world state. Timur had the viciousness of Chinggis without the vision. Between

---

11 Herodotus, *The Histories*, IV.13–32, trans. Robin Waterfield (Oxford University Press, 1998): 239–45.

1370 and 1405 he left a trail of wanton slaughter and ruin, killing a reported 100,000 people in Baghdad and massing towers of severed heads in Delhi, Herat, and Isfahan as he built an empire stretching from northern Syria to northern India. While bestowing wealth and beauty on his beloved capital of Samarkand, elsewhere Timur disrupted trade routes, delivering another blow to the commercial infrastructure. As for the empire itself, Timur was too busy wreaking havoc to consolidate his rule, and after his death it disintegrated.

The second of the late Middle Millennium cataclysms was the spread of the great pandemic known as the Black Death. The origin of this virulent killer may have been a remote area around Lake Issyk-Kul in Central Asia that had easy access to both the Steppe Road and the Silk Roads. People, horses, and pack animals unwittingly carried the vectors of this disease over trade routes through the network of caravanserais into the centers of commerce. Although contemporaries referred to it simply as the "Big Death," most historians and epidemiologists think that the Black Death was bubonic plague, although some scholars dispute this.[12] Whatever it was, the Black Death had the greatest impact on urban areas, especially ports from where it spread inland. It appears to have largely bypassed China and India, inflicting its deadliest havoc on the Mediterranean world. Egypt, Syria, and Iraq were wracked between 1347 and 1349, the plague then reoccurring by one count sixteen separate times in Egypt and fifteen in Syria over the following century and a half.[13] For Europe the traditional account has it brought by ship from the Black Sea port of Caffa in 1347 to Sicily, then to Genoa and Venice, from where it became widespread. The result was a demographic catastrophe. General consensus puts the population of pre-plague Europe at 70–80 million, of which one-third died in the first four years. And the plague was a reoccurring affliction so that by the lowest point in the fifteenth century the population stood at between 50 and 60 per cent of its pre-plague numbers.[14]

---

12 Samuel K. Cohn, Jr, *The Black Death Transformed: Disease and Culture in Early Renaissance Europe* (New York: Oxford University Press, 2003): 1, 247; David Herlihy, *The Black Death and the Transformation of the West* (Cambridge, MA: Harvard University Press, 1997): 6–7, 25–7.

13 Eliyahu Ashtor, *A Social and Economic History of the Near East in the Middle Ages* (Berkeley: University of California Press, 1976): 302; Michael Dols, "The General Mortality of the Black Death in the Mamluk Empire," in A. L. Udovitch (ed.), *The Islamic Middle East, 700–1900: Studies in Economic and Social History* (Princeton: Darwin Press, 1981): 411–17.

14 William H. McNeill, *Plagues and Peoples* (New York: Doubleday, 1976): 149–50.

Recovery from a single disaster, however widespread, could have been effected with little long-term consequence, but waves of recurring plague over a century disrupted the economic order. A smaller population meant a decrease in production, a plunge in demand, and an overall sharp decline in prosperity. Long-distance trade experienced a drop in volume except for slaves, for which the market raged. Nor did the Black Death appear at a time in which the economy was poised to absorb such a shock. Despite a half-millennium of growth, the Afro-Eurasian commercial economy was still a very delicate edifice, still highly vulnerable to dislocation given the wrong set of circumstances. Before the Black Death appeared, such circumstances were already manifest. As the economy had grown, so had the population; often too much, given the available resources and level of technology. In some places in Europe depopulation seems to have already started before the pandemic. Nature soon joined the conspiracy. As early as the thirteenth century, the hitherto mild climate began turning colder with the onset of what has been called the "Little Ice Age," resulting in sporadic crop failures in the fourteenth century and hitting a low in temperature in the fifteenth century.

Problems were compounded by the actions of various governments. Some like the Mamluks (1250–1517) in Egypt became more exploitative, while others took the opportunity to fight long, costly, destructive wars, a prime example being the Hundred Years War between England and France (1337–1453). In China the Yuan dynasty collapsed, to be replaced by the Ming amid much turmoil. In central Europe the silver lodes finally gave out, leading to the Great Bullion Famine of the mid-fourteenth to mid-fifteenth centuries. Many mints debased their coins, resulting in a lack of confidence in the monetary system, while others ceased production altogether. Creditors were unable to repay loans; banks, including some of the largest in Italy, collapsed; and credit dried up. People hoarded even badly debased money. India, often considered as Eurasia's bottomless pit for hoarded precious metals, suffered chronic bullion leakage as armies from beyond the Khyber Pass raked off plunder and tribute. In China paper money, which had been in use under the Song and Yuan, increasingly suffered bouts of inflation until the Ming ceased printing it altogether. By this time engine economies had become heavily monetized, but the money was not there.

Metamorphosis

Parts of the Afro-Eurasian economy did emerge from the abyss, beginning in the late fourteenth and early fifteenth centuries, although some areas and systems had been so badly hammered they did not recover. The days of large-scale overland caravan traffic, for example, had passed. The Steppe Road was permanently defunct, and the Silk Roads resumed their long decline, devolving into a series of connected local units, leaving Central Asia a passageway through which little passed. The Trans-Sahara eventually lost most of its gold trade and the international importance that came with it, but survived on the inter-regional trade in salt. The final triumph of the maritime routes resulted from the culmination of long-term trends rooted in return-to-cost ratios and technological innovations that allowed larger ships to travel more safely in shorter times than ever before. While earlier advances in navigation and maritime technology can be attributed to the Arabs, Indians, and Malays, from at least the twelfth century it was the Chinese who took the lead. They introduced the magnetic compass, pioneered watertight bulkheads, utilized fore-and-aft rigging, built ships employing five or more mainmasts steered by rudders up to 50 feet in length, and greatly enhanced the seaworthiness of their ships by using iron nails instead of coir. With such innovations they were able to build the largest ships ever constructed up to that time, vessels over 400 feet in length, carrying 300 tons of cargo.

Chinese traders aboard Chinese vessels often based in Southeast Asian ports dominated the shipping lanes to southern India where cargoes were trans-shipped and taken on to the Red Sea and Persian Gulf in a segmented system. Under the Song and Yuan, long-distance commerce had been largely in private hands, but this changed under the Ming. On their northern frontier the Ming refused to reach an accommodation with the Mongols, who controlled the overland routes to the west. Henceforth, long-distance trade would have to be done by sea, where early Ming policies, especially under the third emperor, Chengzu (1402–24), reverted to government-controlled tribute trade. Vast quantities of commodities did change hands in this way, but it was not the most efficient system of exchange: in effect a lose–lose situation for the Chinese, since private entrepreneurs were closed out while the government usually ended up giving more and receiving less in its dealings with supposed vassal states. Matters of power and prestige trumped profit.

Chengzu's policy culminated in the voyages of the Treasure Fleets, seven enormous expeditions, under the command of the Muslim–Chinese eunuch Zheng He, that ranged across the Indian Ocean between 1405 and 1433 to visit potential vassal states, enroll them into the tributary system, and ensure their symbolic submission to the universal sovereign. The size of these fleets was staggering, with the first alone containing 62 treasure ships, each with 9 masts and a crew of 500, along with 255 smaller ships. Each fleet carried tons of silk, porcelain, and other goods. Voyages took several years, the early ones calling at all major ports in Southeast Asia, India, and Sri Lanka, the later ones venturing to the Persian Gulf, Red Sea, and East African coast. On the return of the last treasure fleet, the voyages were abruptly terminated. Ships were scrapped, no new ones were allowed to be built, and shipyards were closed. The knowledge of large ship construction was eventually forgotten.

Speculation on the reversal in Ming policy has focused on political and economic factors. The political explanation points to an internal struggle at court between the anti-commercial Confucianist scholar–official bureaucrats and a eunuch faction that was identified with foreign trade and a forward maritime policy. The Confucianists appear to have won. The economic explanation maintains that the voyages were very expensive, and as conditions in China deteriorated due to a series of natural disasters, especially floods – augmented by peasant uprisings, piracy along the coast, an unsuccessful war with Vietnam, and border wars against the Mongols – the emperor could no longer afford the luxury of being recognized as universal sovereign.[15] And a purely practical consideration may have played some role. The huge Chinese ships with their size and seaworthiness are thought to have been originally designed for the trade in Malabar pepper, a commodity that enjoyed a galloping growth market at the time. When a pepper-growing industry developed much closer in Sumatra, the Chinese turned to using smaller, cheaper ships for this trade.[16] The Chinese withdrawal from the Indian Ocean left a vacuum that other traders, particularly Indian Muslims, quickly moved into. Doubtless there was some commercial disruption as the giant Chinese market contracted, although across the waters leading to the Mediterranean, demand was growing. As for the Chinese, they do not seem to have spent much time bemoaning their lost opportunity for maritime global hegemony. Trade on the eastern side of the Straits, both licit and illicit, forged ahead in ports on the South China Sea, the Gulf of Thailand, and the Java Sea. China, the great eastern engine of Afro-Eurasia, was far from spent,

15 Louise Levathes, *When China Ruled the Seas: The Treasure Fleet of the Dragon Throne 1405–1433* (New York: Simon and Schuster, 1994): 174–9; F.W. Mote, *Imperial China 900–1800* (Cambridge, MA: Harvard University Press, 1999): 615–17.
16 Christopher Wake, "The Great Ocean-Going Ships of Southern China in the Age of Chinese Maritime Voyaging to India, Twelfth to Fifteenth Centuries," *International Journal of Maritime History* 9 (1997): 76–81.

and the Chinese commercial economy would subsequently enjoy a resurgence that propelled it far into the early modern period.

On the other side of the Indian Ocean, China's erstwhile partner as the great Western engine of Afro-Eurasian trade, the Islamic heartland, was moving in a different direction. The fragmentation of the 'Abbasid Caliphate did not result in an immediate collapse of trade, but it did signal systemic issues that became amplified over time. Chronic warfare between the dynasties that succeeded the 'Abbasids, compounded by waves of invasions coming out of Central Asia, destroyed cities, dislocated trade, and disrupted production through the forced deportation of skilled craftsmen. Recurrent plague, famine, and impoverishment sustained a long-term trend of depopulation. The most commercially active locations came to be ruled by military castes, mostly slave or mercenary soldiers of Turkish origin, not the optimum form of government for economic development. The main goal of those in charge was to enrich themselves as quickly as possible and to use their wealth to enjoy extravagant lifestyles. Burdensome taxes bordering on extortion, by predatory, rapacious regimes, increased the price of doing business, which raised the cost of merchandise, making zone-produced commodities less competitive on the international market. Private wealth was precarious and outright confiscation by those in power common. In Egypt the Mamluk regime continued to support long-distance trade but dispensed with the Karimi merchants and created its own monopoly. With some exceptions, the military-dominated governments of the Islamic heartland during the late Middle Millennium were not only oppressive, they were incompetent and arbitrary, which made doing business unpredictable. If any single factor accounted for the lack of synergy between politics and economics, it was the failure of the commercial classes to attain some measure of institutionalized political power. Cities often enjoyed considerable autonomy in dealing with local matters, but cities within larger states never became autonomous enough to negotiate with rulers over larger issues. Consequently, in setting priorities and making policies, governments did not have to take the needs of the merchant class or commercial matters in general into consideration.

Bad government was one important ingredient in a larger mix that featured other fundamental issues. A deficiency in natural resources made the Islamic heartland more dependent on trade than other engines. Its role as the ultimate passageway was enhanced by the revival of Europe; after the fall of the caliphate, the growing European economy helped to keep much of the Islamic heartland in business. Egypt, in particular, had been able to offset a steady drain in its balance of trade eastward with income from the West by selling its own products. This changed in the early fifteenth century, when the industries of Egypt and Syria joined in the general collapse that had been evident for much longer in other parts of the zone. This was foremost a matter of technological innovation, or the lack thereof. Industries did not adapt to new technologies and more sophisticated forms of commercial organization, thus becoming less competitive – a legacy, in part, of government monopolies – while in private circles, a conservative business culture still dominated on the highest levels by household enterprises proved resistant to change. European goods became cheaper, allowing Italian exporters to dump products on Syrian and Egyptian markets, ruining local industries. Nor could a decline in manufactured goods be offset by agricultural products. The excessive taxation of an impoverished, poorly producing, and technologically disadvantaged peasantry together with the failure of an entrepreneurial sector to emerge from the ruling classes to champion agricultural interests led to a drop in production. Egypt was still able to export some wheat and Syria some raw cotton, but for many products like olive oil, symbolic because it had been the original staple carried in long-distance trade as an export from this zone by the Phoenicians three millennia earlier, the Islamic heartland became a net importer.[17]

Europe, long the Islamic heartland's bitter political and religious rival, while at the same time close trading partner, emerged from the wreckage of the fourteenth century bound on still another course. Western Europe did not suffer the devastation associated with the Mongol conquest but benefited from the temporary unity the Mongols imposed over other zones. While Europe did not escape the Black Death and the depression that accompanied it, the consequence proved to be more a correction than a *coup de grâce*, a restructuring that led into a long period of growth. Signs of economic recovery are evident as early as the fifteenth century, albeit with considerable regional variation. While overall consumption fell with the drop in population, labor scarcity caused wages to rise, boosting per-capita buying power and charting a new direction in consumerism. Starting in Italy and spreading north and west, population grew, urbanization revived, production increased, commodity prices stabilized, and trade and commerce flourished. The growing political power of the merchant class and its alliance with the state protected and encouraged capital accumulation and investment.

17 Eliyahu Ashtor, "The Economic Decline of the Middle East during the Later Middle Ages," *Asian and African Studies* 15 (1981): 253–86.

Underpinning the revival of trade was the discovery of new sources of silver in central Europe, while advances in mining technology allowed for the reopening of old mines, replenishing the supply of much needed coinage.

The growth of maritime traffic was a favorable trend for Europe perched at the far end of Eurasia, with a coastline far out of proportion to its interior. European sea traffic was itself poised for a shift from the Mediterranean to the Atlantic. In 1434 Gil Eannes sailed past Cape Bojador on the western coast of Africa and returned safely to Lisbon, disproving the commonly held belief that seawater boiled from this point south. In 1471 the Portuguese reached the Gold Coast and began carrying back significant amounts of gold. In 1487 Bartholomew Diaz rounded the Cape of Good Hope, and in 1498 Vasco da Gama landed at Calicut on the Malabar Coast. Despite his shoddy cargo of goods, considerable friction with local authorities, and the loss of two of his four ships, da Gama returned with merchandise worth sixty times the cost of his voyage. Heavily armed, the Portuguese were soon back in the Indian Ocean intent on imposing a commercial monopoly. The world was changing.

Nevertheless, from the vantage point of 1500, European global hegemony was still far in the future. Nor was the commercial world a zero-sum game. The rise of Europe did not necessarily mean that other zones would follow the Islamic heartland and Central Asia into eclipse. Both India and Southeast Asia were on the verge of new commercial expansions, and until at least the end of the eighteenth century, China remained the world's largest economy with a scale of trade still enormous by anyone's standards. If after 1500 the velocity of change began to increase exponentially, it did so within the framework of trends laid down in the Middle Millennium, at least until the Industrial Revolution fundamentally transformed all aspects of world economy.

FURTHER READING

Primary sources

Benjamin of Tudela. *The Itinerary of Benjamin of Tudela: Travels in the Middle Ages*. Trans. Michael Singer, Marcus N. Adler, and A. Asher. Malibu, CA: Joseph Simon/Pangloss Press, 1987.

Chau Ju-Kua. *His Work on the Chinese and Arab Trade in the Twelfth and Thirteenth Centuries Entitled "Chu-Fan Chih."* Trans. Friedrich Hirth and W.W. Rockhill. New York: Paragon Book Reprint, 1966.

Goitein, S. D., trans. and ed. *Letters of Medieval Jewish Traders*. Princeton University Press, 1973.

Goitein, S. D. and M. A. Friedman. *India Traders of the Middle Ages: Documents from the Cairo Geniza (India book)*. Leiden: Brill, 2008.

Hudūd al-'Ālam: 'The Regions of the World,' A Persian Geography 372 A.H.–982 A.D. Trans. V. Minorsky. London: Luzac & Co., 1937.

Ibn Battuta. *The Travels of Ibn Battuta* A.D. *1325–1354*, 5 vols. Trans. H. A. R. Gibb and C. F. Beckingham. London: Hakluyt Society, 1958–2000.

Ibn Hauqal. *Configuration de la Terre (Kitab Surat al-Ard)* 2 vols. Trans. J. H. Kramers and G. Wiet. Paris: Maisonneuve & Larose, 2001.

Ibn Khurdadhbih."Le Livre des Routes et des Provinces par Ibn Khordadbeh" (Kitab al-masalik wa'l mamalik). Trans. C. Barbier de Meynard, *Journal Asiatique* 6/5 (1865): 5–127, 227–80, 446–527.

Levtzion, N. and J. F. P. Hopkins, trans. and ed. *Corpus of Early Arabic Sources for West African History.* Princeton: Markus Wiener, 2000.

Ma Huan. *Ying-yai sheng-lan, The Overall Survey of the Ocean's Shores.* Trans. and ed. J. V. G. Mills. Cambridge: Hakluyt Society, 1970.

Marvazi, Sharaf al-Zaman Tahir. *China, the Turks and India.* Trans. V. Minorsky. London: The Royal Asiatic Society, 1942.

Al-Mas'udi, Abu' l'Hasan 'Ali b. al-Husayn. *Les prairies d'or (Muruj al-Dhahab wa-ma 'adin al-jawhar).* Trans. C. Barbier de Meynard and Pavet de Courteille, revised by Charles Pellat. Paris: Société asiatique, 1962.

Muqaddasi, Shams al-Din Abu Abd Allah Muhammad b. Ahmad. *The Best Divisions for Knowledge of the Regions (Ahsan al-Taqasim fi Ma'rifat al-Aqalim).* Trans. B.A. Colins. Reading: Garnet, 1994.

Polo, Marco. *The Book of Ser Marco Polo* 2 vols. 3rd edn. Trans. and ed. Henry Yule and Henri Cordier. New Delhi: Munshiram Manoharlal, 1993.

Xuanzang. *The Great Tang Dynasty Record of the Western Regions.* Trans. Li Rongxi. Berkeley, CA: Numata Center for Buddhist Translation and Research, 1996.

Yule, Henry and H. Cordier, trans. and ed. *Cathay and the Way Thither, Being a Collection of Medieval Notices of China* 4 vols. London: Hakluyt Society, 1937.

Secondary sources

Abu-Lughod, Janet L. *Before European Hegemony: The World System* A.D. *1250–1350.* New York: Oxford University Press, 1989.

Bentley, Jerry H. *Old World Encounters: Cross Cultural Contacts and Exchanges in Pre-Modern Times.* New York: Oxford University Press, 1993.

Chaudhuri, K. N. *Asia Before Europe: Economy and Civilisation of the Indian Ocean from the Rise of Islam to 1750.* Cambridge University Press, 1991.

Curtin, Philip D. *Cross-Cultural Trade in World History.* Cambridge University Press, 1984.

Franck, Irene and David M. Brownstone. *The Silk Road: A History.* New York: Facts on File Publications, 1986.

Hodges, Richard and David Whitehouse. *Mohammed, Charlemagne, and the Origins of Europe: Archaeology and the Pirenne Thesis.* Ithaca, NY: Cornell University Press, 1983.

McCormick, Michael. *Origins of the European Economy: Communications and Commerce,* A.D. *300–900.* Cambridge University Press, 2001.

McIntosh, Roderick James. *The Peoples of the Middle Niger: The Island of Gold.* Oxford: Blackwell, 1998.

Smith, Richard L. *Premodern Trade in World History.* New York, NY: Routledge, 2009.

Spufford, Peter. *Money and its Uses in Medieval Europe*. Cambridge University Press, 1988.

Thapar, Romila. *Early India: From the Origins to CE 1300*. Berkeley, CA: University of California Press, 2002.

Vaissière, Etienne de la. *Sogdian Traders. A History*. Trans. James Ward. Leiden: Brill, 2005.

Wickham, Chris. *Framing the Early Middle Ages: Europe and the Mediterranean, 400–800*. Oxford University Press, 2005.

Wicks, Robert S. *Money, Markets, and Trade in Early Southeast Asia: The Development of Indigenous Monetary Systems to CE 1400*. Ithaca, NY: Cornell University Press, 1992.

10

European and Mediterranean
trade networks

MICHEL BALARD

Debates on the trade networks in medieval Europe and their ties to neigh-boring geographic regions (Maghreb, Near East, Far East) have produced an immense historiographical literature, from Henri Pirenne[1] to Michael McCormick[2], and from Robert S. Lopez[3] to Peregrine Horden and Nicholas Purcell.[4]

Following Henri Pirenne, scholars have wondered whether there was continuity or rupture in the commercial economy of the late Roman world and that of the High Middle Ages. Did the Arab conquest of the seventh and eighth centuries interrupt trade between the western and the eastern Medi-terranean? Another question in debate: were the Mediterranean commercial networks broken up and unique to the interior sea, or, on the contrary, were they connected with such far-off lands as the Far East and Central Asia, and with the Baltic Sea, the North Sea and the Atlantic Ocean?

To answer these questions, we must highlight merchants and their associ-ations. We must also study their techniques for raising capital, for using diverse monetary modes (scriptural money and metallic coins), for putting to use the ships necessary for their trade, for organizing periodic meetings, fairs, and markets, and for obtaining governmental protection. Our focus will be on the largest sectors of medieval trade from northern Europe to the Muslim

---

1 Henri Pirenne, *Mahomet et Charlemagne* (Paris: Alcan, 1937; new ed., Paris: Presses universitaires de France,1992). For a guide on the debates set off by the Pirenne thesis see Alfred E. Havighurst, *The Pirenne Thesis: Analysis, Criticism and Revision* (Boston: D. C. Heath, 1958). See also the contribution of the archaeological data analyzed by Richard Hodges and David Whitehouse, *Mohammed, Charlemagne and the Origins of Europe* (London: G. Duckworth, 1983).

2 Michael McCormick, *Origins of the European Economy: Communications and Commerce, A.D. 300–900* (Cambridge University Press, 2001).

3 Robert S. Lopez, *The Commercial Revolution of the Middle Ages, 950–1350* (Englewood Cliffs, NJ: Prentice-Hall, 1976).

4 Peregrine Horden and Nicholas Purcell, *The Corrupting Sea. A Study of Mediterranean History* (Oxford: Blackwell, 2000).

world by way of the Mediterranean, and the network of land and sea routes that tie them together, before we turn to commercial goods and their trade.

Merchants and their associations

In western Europe of the Early Middle Ages, references to merchants – the *negociatores* – are rather infrequent in textual sources, so much so that the existence of a commercial economy in the "barbarian" kingdoms was often denied. However, there is no doubt that it existed. The agents of the great monasteries took care of selling the surplus of monastic production or buying what the monks needed. The village markets were centers of transactions that did not need professional merchants. Especially in episcopal cities and in the places of aristocratic residence, the social elite called for luxury goods, spices and precious cloth of the East, which explains the presence of Eastern colonies described as *Syri* – Greeks, Levantines, Egyptians, and Jews – in numerous cities between the Loire and Meuse Rivers.[5] To these were joined native traders: merchants from Verdun enriched by the slave trade; Frisian and Saxon merchants very active in the agricultural and hand-crafted products of the Rhineland destined for England and Jutland; the kings' agents, aristocrats, and abbots, piepowders [*pieds poudreux*] roaming the Frankish countries in order to buy or sell.

In the eighth century, trade activity in the West seems to have occurred on a larger scale. References to *Syri* became rarer, while Jewish quarters prospered in the cities of Gaul's Midi all the way to the entourage of the Carolingian palace. The peak of Frisian merchants' activity took place at the beginning of the ninth century between the trading center of Dorestad, near today's Utrecht, and Haithabu at the southern end of the Jutland peninsula. Textual sources also reveal the existence of Christian merchants in Alsace, Franconia, and the Rhineland who specialized in the grain trade, or as rural market peddlers, going from fair to fair.

It is however mainly in Italy, which had in part remained under Byzantine domination, that groups comprised of merchants begin to appear in the tenth century. Forming small communities established in Constantinople, the Amalfitans and the Venetians replaced Eastern merchants, importing silk,

---

5 Ferdinand Vercauteren, "La circulation des marchands en Europe occidentale du vie au xe siècle: aspects économiques et culturels," *Centri e vie di irradiazione della civiltà nell'alto Medioevo. 11° Settimana di Studio, 18–23 aprile 1963* (Spoleto: Centro Italiano di Studi sull'Alto Medioevo, 1964): 393–411.

spices, precious cloth and objects of art to the West. They were followed by Pisan and Genoese merchants whose numbers increased after the early crusades, the construction of naval shipyards and the ensuing creation of Italian trading posts in the Near East. The viscountal aristocracy, in charge of the collection of custom duties and the sale of agricultural surpluses, formed the backbone of an elite merchant class in the Italian communes of the North, which encouraged a large part of the urban population to engage in trade activities. Because of this, the itinerant merchant of the Early Middle Ages became little by little the sedentary businessman, using the services of factors (i.e. agents) and representatives in the principal commercial centers of Europe.

Among them, such brilliant individuals as Benedetto Zaccaria stand out. Having left for Constantinople in 1259, he obtained from Emperor Michael VIII Palaiologos the alum mining rights of Phocaea, constructed vessels that transported the product to Flanders via Gibraltar, bought grains, hides, and fish in the East, all the while importing woolen cloth and fabric from the West, weapons from Italy, and salt from the western Mediterranean. He ordered his relatives to join his business, made contracts and established proctorships with other families, and fulfilled diplomatic and military missions on behalf of the Commune of Genoa. Admiral of the Genoese fleet, he was victorious over the Pisans at Meloria (1284), came to the king of Castile's aid against the Merinids, obtained in 1304 the concession to the Isle of Chios and the cultivation of mastic – the aromatic resin of the shrub *Pistacia lentiscus*, used as a flavoring and in medicine – before retiring to Genoa where, named constable of the Commune, he died in a fantastic seaside palace in 1307.

As early as the thirteenth century, large merchant companies, family-based and with undefined aims, were constituted. The Lombards of Asti, of Chieri, or of Novara expanded their *casane*, dispensaries of loans and of banking, in numerous Western cities. Such Piacenzans as Alberto Scotto became shopkeepers, lenders, and bankers, intermediaries between the fairs of Champagne and the Mediterranean ports. The Sienese, for example the Bonsignori with their large company, were active in the fairs as bankers, and also specialized in the handling of papal finances. The Milanese sold products from their textile and metal industries, whereas the Florentines created companies with numerous associates and, with the aid of factors, engaged in commerce, banking, and the woolen industry. The Bardi, Peruzzi, Acciaiuoli, and Frescobaldi families dominated finance in the West until their bankruptcy in the 1340s, caused by excessive loans accorded to rulers and not reimbursed.

These failures showed other commercial companies and the individuals who ran them – the Borromeos of Pisa, Dino Rapondi of Lucca, and especially Francesco di Marco Datini, the merchant from Prato who founded partnership companies based in Florence, Pisa, Genoa, Barcelona, Valencia, Ibiza, and Majorca, and who was active in diverse businesses, trade, insurance, banking, and the wool industry – what not to do. All these companies included a large number of businessmen, associates, and factors who, from their Tuscan headquarters, created international networks, developed technical trade innovations, and established an ethical division between capitalist rationalism and the Christian faith. In the fifteenth century, powerful and non-specialized family-based companies were created in Florence, such as those of the Medicis, which prospered in trade, banking and industry under the direction of Cosimo, and which declined at the end of the century under Lorenzo the Magnificent, who was more interested in politics than in business management.

Outside of Italy, trade activity dawned early only in Catalonia. Pierre Bonnassie has highlighted the Jews of Barcelona, who were merchants, smiths, and moneyers in the eleventh century, like such newly rich as Vivas de Provençals and his son Pere Vivas, who took advantage of fertile real-estate holdings and also engaged in commercial transactions, for which the capital, as in other places, came from riches of the soil.[6] The first known commercial companies date to the last decades of the twelfth century, and multiplied in the following century with the Camps and the Banyeres of Barcelona, the Espiells of Tarragona, and in the fourteenth century with Pere de Mitjavila, the Benets, the Casasajas and Guillem Ferrer, who were engaged in trade with the East. In Valencia, Perpignan, Gerona, and Tarragona, a mercantile elite of *mercadores*, wholesale traders who went from *mercadal* to *mercadal*, the weekly markets of growing towns and cities, were rapidly distinguished from shopkeepers and wandering merchants.

In the kingdom of France, the creation of mercantile companies did not occur prior to the twelfth century. The "men of Arras and Flanders" were first named at the fair at Provins in 1137, and those of Hesdin at the fair at Troyes in 1164; this designation suggests the beginning of a collective organization. French merchants remained long focused on the trade of grains and wine for urban provisions, although some (merchants from Bordeaux for

---

6 Pierre Bonnassie, *La Catalogne du milieu du xe à la fin du xie siècle. Croissance et mutation d'une société*, 2 vols. (Toulouse: Association des publications de l'Université de Toulouse-le-Mirail, 1975–6).

wine; merchants from Marseille, Montpellier, and Narbonne for cloth, fabric, and metals) took an interest in exporting to England or the East from the beginning of the thirteenth century. Nevertheless, the few extant French account books from the end of the Middle Ages do not unveil tycoons in the kingdom. The one exception to this was Jacques Coeur (1395–1456), the treasurer of the king, who created subsidiaries in the big cities of France, in Florence and in Bruges, and a port of call for the king's great galley ship in Marseille, but who was obliged to grant loans to nobles from the court and to the king, which caused his downfall.

In the other great economic pole – Flanders, northern Europe, and the Holy Roman Empire – the Frisians gave way to the Scandinavians, the Flemish, the Mosans of Huy, Liège, and Dinant, and the Germans of Cologne who, from 1130, had a house in London. In 1161, the traders of Lübeck formed the "community of the seasonal German merchants of Gotland" on a Baltic island that became the warehouse of Russian and Scandinavian goods. From Visby, the island's major city, German merchants reached Novgorod where Prince Jaroslav allowed them to found the Peterhof, a special merchants' quarter, in 1205–7; they also obtained a quarter in Smolensk in 1229, and then in Polotsk. The expansion toward the North Sea, of German merchants who came from the East – and thus called the *Esterlins* – was just as important as their ventures eastward. In Bruges, they obtained privileges in 1252. In London, they formed three Hanses (merchant associations), those of Cologne, Lübeck, and Hamburg, which merged in 1281 to form the Hanseatic League of Germany, the association created and sworn to protect merchants abroad. Around 1250, the Hanseatic League held a monopoly of the traffic between London and Novgorod; they established a regular liaison between the North and Baltic Seas, and obtained privileges in Flanders in 1252–3. A century later, the Hanse of merchants was transformed into a Hanse of cities, a confederation of nearly 150 cities, united in "three tiers" (Lübeck–Saxonian, Westphalian–Prussian, Gotland–Livonian), which coordinated the defense of their citizens' privileges. Important merchants formed the patriciate, monopolizing urban power. Outside the Hanse, a few commercial companies endeavored to imitate the Italian model. Those of Nuremberg remained fundamentally familial, as did that of the three Veckinchusen brothers from Livonia. The "Great Commercial Company of Ravensburg," on the other hand, founded in 1380, established subsidiaries throughout Europe, from Cologne to Milan and from Vienna to Barcelona. The Fuggers of Augsburg followed this example at the end of the fifteenth century.

In Flanders, the economic center of the woolen cloth industry, merchants who were most often itinerant marketed fabrics from Arras, Ghent, Ypres, Douai, Lille, and Cambrai. The merchants of Ghent were particularly turned toward the Empire, those of Arras toward the fairs of Champagne, and those of Bruges toward England. In the thirteenth century, England did not have a strong merchant oligarchy, even though in London the drapers, smiths, haberdashers, vintners, and merchants of pepper gained access to the sovereigns and wove financial ties with the Cahorsins from southern France and the Italians. In 1363, the king organized the export of English wool, and entrusted this monopoly to a group of merchants, the Merchants Venturers, who explored the English countryside for trade prospects, and assembled the bales of wool at the Wool Staple of Calais, which was both a commercial structure and a financial establishment. Only the Italians exporting wool to Italy evaded this monopoly.

The condition of the merchants in the Mediterranean East was quite different. In Byzantium, they were organized into bodies, or *systèmata*. Among them, the shipowners loaded with the "happy cargo" of the grain tithe held a place of their own in the early Byzantine period, when Constantinople received Egyptian wheat until 619. The Book of the Eparch, a commercial manual composed in 912 during the reign of Leo VI, expresses the Byzantine state's concern for ensuring product quality, avoiding speculation, and limiting concentrations harmful to the free play of competition. The Byzantines divided, for example, the production and the sale of silk fabrics among four professional bodies. The merchants of Constantinople played an important role in the international trade of spices, wood, and precious fabrics. Capital was largely open to foreign merchants, who were welcomed in specific warehouses, the *mitata*; among these were those of the Syrians and the Russians. However, from the eleventh century, the Italians, benefitting from a total or partial exemption from the *kommerkion* (sales tax), established their dominance. They limited the rise of Byzantine businessmen, at least until around 1350. Deprived of their land revenues, the aristocrats turned only later to trade activities with the Latins, whose techniques they adopted: the Palaiologoi, the Angèloi, the Notaras, the Argyroi, the Kantakouzenoi, the Goudèles, the Lascaris, and the ship owners of Monemvasia were in that world of business to which the Ottoman conquest put an end in 1453.

The Muslim world inherited the Byzantine and Sasanian trade traditions. Although they could be grouped together in guilds, subjected to monopoly, and sometimes charged with espionage, Muslim merchants normally exercised a free and individual activity, exempt from any public function. Among them are to be distinguished the small-scale traders (*rakkad*) who went to the sites of production to bring the merchandise to periodic markets; the traveling merchant who went to far-off markets taking orders away with him; and finally the "stationary" merchant (*tajir*), the chief merchant who entrusted sums to traveling partners, and kept up with his business by corresponding with agents established in far-off lands. Some examples will demonstrate the business that they conducted.

The Persian diplomat and geographer Ibn Khurdadhbih describes around 840 the merchant activity of the Slavic Varangians, who brought skins and arms to Baghdad by passing through Itil, the capital of the Khazars, but above all he discusses the activity of the Radhanite Jews (who were probably from Iraq), who were operating all over the world, from Iraq and the Maghreb to the Frankish empire, Russia, and China. Although his narrative contains several unlikely elements, scholars agree (and this is confirmed by coin treasures) that Jews played a leading role in the commercial trade between the Christian world and the Muslim world, whether directly, as occurred in Muslim Spain and the "land of the Franks," or indirectly, as in Egypt and eastern Europe. The list of merchandise they transported included slaves, furs, arms and Spanish silk from the West, spices from the East, and other rare commodities answering the needs of a limited social elite. The Radhanites played an important role in supplying luxury items to the court of Baghdad, and their business was a sign of the sizeable growth in trade in the centuries that were to follow.

The Geniza documents from the ninth-century synagogue of Fustat shed an essential light on the trade networks within the Muslim world and on those who brought it to life. Jewish merchants who spoke Arabic transferred their activity from Qayrawan, Sousse, and Gabès in Tunisia to Egypt following the Fatimid conquest of this country in 969, and yet maintained ties with the ports of the Maghreb and Sicily. These merchants, living in Fustat (Old Cairo), traveled a lot, dominated trade with India, and made the Red Sea the principal axis of exchange with the Far East. Some individuals are highlighted in the letters of the Geniza. Nahray b. Nissim, a native of Qayrawan, whose activity we can follow from 1045 to 1096, was a banker and merchant. He traded everything, traveled from his birthplace to the principal Syrian markets, and kept copious correspondence. Joseph Ibn 'Awkal entrusted to his agents and associates merchandise of great value sent from Alexandria to Mahdiya in Ifriqiya and Mazzara in Sicily. With these important merchants and the brokers (*simsar*) who followed them, Old Cairo was at the confluence of major currents of international trade from around 1050 to 1200, toward the west of the Mediterranean and the Indian Ocean.

At the end of the twelfth century, the intermediary role of the Jews faded away. It is at this moment that the Karimis, spice merchants, came out of the shadows. From the eleventh century, the term referred to ship owners and merchants dealing with the exportation of spices from India to the Near East – not yet an organized company, but a group of ship owners who traveled in a convoy protected by the fleet of the Fatimid Caliphate. In the fourteenth century, it was a heterogeneous group of important merchants not only from Egypt, but also from Iraq, Yemen, or Ethiopia, who traveled to India and sometimes even to China. Protected by the Bahri sultans, the families of Ibn Kuwayk, of al-Kharrubi, and of Muhammad ibn Mussallam acquired an enormous fortune, the last of whom, after his death in 1375, left 200,000 dinars to each of his sons. They determined the price of spices and negotiated fiercely with Western merchants in Alexandria. But in the last decades of the fourteenth century, financial difficulties drove the sultans to impose loans upon the Karimis. In 1426, the sultan Barsbay instituted a sultanate monopoly on the trade of pepper, and then on all spices, which led to the Karimis' ruin. Some went into exile in India, others became "sultanate merchants" while continuing, as did Muhammad ibn al-Muzallik who died in 1444, to conduct some private business.

Commercial techniques

Whether operating alone or in an association, merchants developed and utilized a variety of commercial techniques. These included methods for raising and handling capital, new forms of paper and metal currency, changes in ships and navigational routes, and expanded fairs and markets. Rulers and popes also sought to shape trade through commercial decrees and laws, and sometimes succeeded.

Capital

Gathering together capital is a necessity for a businessman who, before selling his merchandise for profit, must have the funds necessary for purchasing it in the first place. Bartering existed, of course, on the edges of Europe, for example in the trade with Mongol merchants, for which pieces of Western woolen cloth and fabric formed the standard measure for goods brought by trans-Asiatic caravans. The use of *baratare* (=barter) was widespread here; it is found even in well-known commercial markets.

The pursuit of capital in the Mediterranean world could not have occurred without the important intermediary of the notary, who knew how to adapt the legal form of contracts to the requirements at the time. At least in the twelfth and thirteenth centuries, the smallest commercial investment led to the composition of a contract drawn up by a notary, whereas later, the use of the *apodoxia*, a deed of private agreement, expanded imperceptibly, along with the use of account books that recorded the businessman's receipts and expenditures.

The coupling of capital and labor was common in all mercantile milieux, whether Christian or Muslim. It originates from the Roman *societas* of labor and capital. We can distinguish two forms. In the first, bearing the name of *chreokoinônia* in Byzantium, *kirâd* in the Muslim world and *commenda* in the West, an investor entrusted a sum to a merchant for a single voyage to a defined region and for a limited amount of time. The capital risks and possible losses were the responsibility of the lender; the gains were shared according to a variable percentage. However, Islamic *fikh* (law) forbade the lender from placing more merchandise as shares than he could receive in cash from their sale. In the second form of association, the merchant who had a certain amount of capital received a greater amount from the investor, and began selling where he thought it best, in a defined region and for a certain amount of time. The risks were shared proportionally to the amount of capital invested, and the gains split fifty–fifty. This method, called the *shirka* in the Muslim world, is very similar to that of the Genoese *societas maris* or the Venetian *colleganza*. To minimize the risks, the "active merchant" approached several investors, who placed their capital among several part-ners. The resulting nebula of contracts and concentrations of capital gave business a great range. Yet from the fourteenth century these contracts were progressively replaced by the system of commission by which a sedentary businessman sent merchandise to an agent who was established on-site and who received the order to send other merchandise acquired by the proceeds of the sale.

Majority-owned companies brought together several merchants with their capacity for work and their capital for a specific enterprise that was most often limited in time. Potential losses were limited to each one's capital, and the gains were shared on a proportional basis according to the contribution made. Francesco di Marco Datini, the merchant from Prato mentioned above and later renowned for his record-keeping, was in this way the principal associate of nine diverse companies established in the principal commercial markets of the West. He was also engaged in complementary activities including the production of woolen cloth, the English wool trade, supplying the papal curia residing in Avignon, the salt trade on the Rhône River, and the sale of wool hangings and hose in Florence. Very similar to this model are the companies or *comuns* of equal parts of capital that we find in Barcelona in the fourteenth century.

Companies flourishing in Tuscany provide the most fully realized model of this pattern. Under the leadership of a director, they brought together numerous associates who provided social capital, supplemented by the deposits made by the company's personnel and by outside parties who received interest on an annual basis. Most associates in the company were dedicated to business of every type: commerce, banking, insurance, and manufacturing. In these they were assisted by salaried commissioners and by the branch personnel established in the principal commercial centers in the West, not only in Italy, but also in Bruges, Avignon, Barcelona, London, and Paris. The companies also participated in a world economy of sorts; however, they remained fragile because of the rash panics of depositors or the penury of sovereign borrowers. These "idols with feet of clay," as Armando Sapori calls them,[7] that were the Bardi, Peruzzi, and Acciaiuoli families, bankrupt in the 1340s, were replaced by companies with branches such as that of Ravensburg, or those of the Medicis in Florence and the Borromei in Milan.

The development of these large trading companies was accompanied by technical innovations in which the Italians excelled, perfecting the innovations that had come from elsewhere. The diversification of the currencies in circulation gave money changers an irreplaceable role: currency exchange appeared in markets everywhere in the 1200s. The currency exchange contract (*hawāla* in Islam) appeared a century later. The payment of big business was often made on credit, despite the reluctance of the Church regarding such practices. The deed of sale in the West and Byzantium, in which interest was disguised, and the *'aqd* in the Muslim world, provided for this. Muslim merchants used a signed payment order called a *shakk* (from which we derive the check), which first appeared in Pisa at the very end of the fourteenth century. The practice of clearance – settlements made between merchants by playing with their expenses and the entries of deposits they had made – has been attested in Basra in the eleventh century, and became commonplace in the fairs of Champagne a century later. Only Greek businessmen seem to

---

7 Armando Sapori, *Le marchand italien du Moyen Age* (Paris: Armand Colin, 1952).

have lagged behind, although they followed Western models by the four-teenth and fifteenth centuries. The Latins developed maritime insurance, first in the form of fictive sales, and then *alla fiorentina*, that is, insurance with premiums, which remained unknown in the north of Europe. They trans-formed the management of account books by inventing double-entry accounting in the "big book" of important firms, an innovation that the Hanseatics of Lübeck and of Hamburg balked at adopting. Finally, the diversity of weights and measures as well as of the currencies in use in the various commercial markets explain the composition of "merchandise manuals," the most famous of which was that of the Florentine Francesco Balducci Pegolotti (*c.* 1340). A concern for rapid information characterized the world of business, as is attested in the letters of the Geniza, in the *carteggio* of Francesco di Marco Datini, and in the organization by Florentine companies of a true postal enterprise, the *Scarsella*, in the fourteenth century.

Currency

The invention of the bill of exchange was a response to the general shortage of cash money that was required by the increase in business volume. Despite the operation of silver mines in the Harz, in Serbia, and at Iglesias in Sardinia, white metal remained insufficient, especially because the trade between Westerners and the Mongol Khanates required a great deal of silver. Gold came from profitable trade with the Maghreb, from which came the West African *oro di paiola* that contributed to the resumption of gold minting in the West (the florin in 1252, the ducat in 1284). In the Byzantine Empire, the mines of Bithynia, western Anatolia, Armenia, and Georgia provided suffi-cient silver so that it played an essential role in the eleventh and twelfth centuries, whereas the loss of Syria and Egypt in the seventh century forced Byzantium to return to gold washing and to the resources of a few mines in the Balkans. The empire was nonetheless able to maintain a coin of gold (the *nomisma*) of an excellent worth until the eleventh century. The Muslim merchants had currency made of multiple metals: the gold *dinar*, from the mines of Nubia and of sub-Saharan Africa, and also from gold-washing; the silver *dirham*, rare between the eleventh and twelfth centuries, and then more abundant; and a copper penny, the *fals*, for everyday purchases. Fluctuations in the value of these two precious metals, gold and silver, had a clear impact on trade activity, just as did monetary manipulations, which were numerous in the kingdom of France in the fourteenth and fifteenth centuries, and also occurred in Castile during the civil wars of the second half of the fourteenth century, in Byzantium from the eleventh centuries, and in Mamluk Egypt in the fifteenth century.

Ships and navigation

Since antiquity, Mediterranean navigations were based upon the simultaneous use of two principal types of ships: long ships, equipped with oars but also with sails, and round ships, powered solely by sails.

Galleys were the main type of long ship. They had nearly flat decks almost entirely occupied by rowers, whose labor was needed especially in getting in and out of ports, crossing straits, or navigating dangerous passages. For journeys that were straight, galleys used the power of the wind by means of two masts with triangular, lateen sails. Among long ships, the Italian fleet was also made up of ketches, biremes, and light galleys called *saiètes* of various types. The technical innovations at the end of the thirteenth century, which Frederick Lane has called a "medieval nautical revolution,"[8] led to the appearance of light galley ships, which, in addition to their use in piracy and war, were specialized in the transportation of lightweight but expensive merchandise. In order to facilitate transportation and to increase productivity, larger galley ships, able to transport one to two hundred tons of merchandise, appeared in the East around 1340. In the second half of the fourteenth century, they became the only merchant galley ships commonly used, for example, in the convoys organized by the Senate of Venice, the famous *mudae*.

The second type of ship, round ships, were heavy and powered by lateen sails. They were steered by lateral drawbars, and required a crew of more than a hundred men to maneuver the sails properly, which rendered the operating costs onerous. They were used in the transportation of heavy merchandise and raw materials, such as cereals, wine, oil, salt, wool, metal, and alum. We can also include in this category other types of boats: *linhs*, *taridae*, brigantines, *pamphyloi*, *bucii*, *fuste*, *lembi* and barks, capable of carrying both small and medium tonnage, and used for relaying large items across the sea or for the redistribution of goods via coastal navigation. In the fourteenth century, lateen vessels were gradually replaced by cogs (*cochae*) constructed on the model of the *koggen*, ships typical of the Hanseatic fleets. We know their principal characteristics: square rigging (rectangular sails) that made

---

8 Frederick C. Lane, "Progrès technologiques et productivité dans les transports maritimes de la fin du Moyen Age au début des temps modernes," *Revue Historique* 510 (1974): 277–302.

navigation by aft winds easier and saved on labor, and the replacement of lateral drawbars by a sternpost rudder that made maneuvering easier. The cog became the merchant ship *par excellence* in the second half of the fourteenth century. Its use spread rapidly to the whole of the Mediterranean basin except in Barcelona. Italian fleets used this new naval tool for transporting heavy products from the agricultural, pastoral, and mining regions of the countries they visited.

Galley ships and cogs often followed the same itineraries, known since antiquity. An entire system of traffic developed in an extended Mediterranean, a vast space that encompassed the area from Flanders and England to the ends of the Black Sea. A few large port cities were at the heart of this system, and their fortunes rose and fell during the Middle Millennium. Barcelona and Valencia in the Iberian peninsula turned more toward Alexandria and Syria than toward the Byzantine Empire; Marseille was rapidly overtaken by Genoa, Pisa–Florence, Ancona, Ragusa and Venice, all of which endeavored to establish multiple liaisons with the eastern as well as the western Mediterranean. Navigators avoided the shoals and the fogs of southern shores, following the coast as closely as possible, the guidepost *par excellence*. Straight passages across the high sea were rare, and only occurred on itineraries known in advance and practiced with some regularity. Sailors often spent winters in ports on this sea, where strong swells and winter storms were (and are) formidable dangers. But in summer, the season of travels, safety was not necessarily any greater. Piracy, universally practiced in the Mediterranean as in the Baltic, threatened any boat that was alone and defenseless, even one that belonged to the pirates' fellow countrymen.

As a result, merchant cities developed methods very early on to deal with these dangers. The ownership of ships was divided into parts and was transferrable from one person to another, which prevented heavy losses. In Genoa, the first maritime laws from the beginning of the thirteenth century forbade ship captains from navigating alone toward Syria or Romania (that is, the Byzantine Empire), and beyond Majorca. The creation of the so-called *Officium Robarie* allowed the Genoese authorities to reimburse those whose cargos had been stolen by Genoese pirates. In Venice, from the beginning of the fourteenth century, the Senate took care to organize *mudae*, convoys designed to protect merchants. Every year, except in times of war, it offered bids on merchant ships, whose protection it ensured by organizing navigation according to itineraries that were chosen beforehand. In this way, eight routes of navigation were put into place, which were intended theoretically to ensure regular relations across the whole Mediterranean: Romania routes linking Venice to Constantinople and the Black Sea; routes to Cyprus, Alexandria, Beirut, Flanders, Aigues-Mortes, Barbary (North Africa), as well as the Trafego route, which joined the two basins of the Mediterranean.

These *mudae* made the Venetian state an organizing center of trade. Indeed, the Senate determined the number of galley ships to be bid upon, the dates of departures, the itineraries, the required ports of call, and the nature of merchandise to be transported. In addition to armed galley ships, it authorized vessels and cogs to sail in case there was an overabundance of merchandise to transport. This system, which gave Venetian navigation mercantile superiority in the fifteenth century, declined at the end of the Middle Ages for complex reasons: the inability of the giant Venetian shipyard called the Arsenal to provide enough boats in seaworthy state; a sort of disengagement from maritime trade on the part of the Venetian patriciate following Venice's bitter losses of numerous foreign trading posts to the Turks in a series of Ottoman–Venetian wars; technical innovations that made round ships as seaworthy as galley ships, but less expensive; finally, the rivalry with the Ragusans and the Aragonese. The system of *mudae* was thus progressively abandoned over the course of the fifteenth century.

In Byzantium, warships are better known than trade ships. The *dromon*, a term that appeared in the sixth century, was used most often during the Macedonian dynasty (867–1056). This was a monoreme of fifty oars, equipped with triangular lateen sails, which in the twelfth century was replaced by a bireme of a hundred oars. This was in turn replaced in the twelfth century by the lateen galley ship, comprised of two rows of oars. The *chelandia*, often confused with the *dromons*, were used in the transportation of horses; the *pamphyloi* in carrying weapons of war. The *ousia* refers to a sailing ship used in the merchant marine; the *agrarion* and the *sandalion* to small skiffs of the fishing fleet or of coastal navigation. The subdued interest that the Byzantines showed in maritime trade operations clearly explains the relative silence of the textual sources, after the disappearance of the grain transports in 619. All the same, wrecks off the island of Yassi Ada near the city of Bodrum in modern western Turkey, and others recently discovered near Istanbul, attest to Byzantine commercial fleet activity. Before 1204, the Empire kept access to the Black Sea for its citizens, from where Greek shipowners transported wheat, fish, and salt. We find such voyages again in the fifteenth century in the traffic between the Khanate of the Golden Horde and the ports of northern Anatolia.

Men of the desert, the Arabs were not sailors in the seventh century. Conquest forced them to adopt the maritime traditions of the Greeks and the Iranians and to use the ships found in ports of occupied lands, as are attested in the terms for certain ships such as *adrumunun*, derived from *dromon*, and *chalandi*, which comes from *chelandion*. For cargo ships, the Arabs also went back to Byzantine traditions: the *qarib*, a small coastal ship, comes from the Greek *karabos*, whereas the *qunbar*, a heavy round ship with lateral rudders and lateen sails, comes from another ancient Greek word that had disappeared in Greek before the fifth century and was replaced by Byzantine authors by the word *koumparia* to refer to an Arabic merchant ship. As for the word *tharida*, it comes from the name of a reed pirogue used on the Red Sea; it was adopted in Byzantium, Venice, and Catalonia to name a type of round ship able to carry heavy merchandise of little worth. The documents of the Geniza of Cairo cite also the *khinzira*, a round ship attested in Tunis, Tripoli, Egypt and Sicily. Ceramic basins decorating the churches of Pisa and imported from Muslim lands, show two sailing ships, one with a single lateen sail, the other with three masts bearing two lateen sails and a rectangular sail. The Muslim navy made lightning progress, even attacking Constantinople (677, 717–18) and, with the Fatimids, set up a quasi-monopoly on navigation of the Red Sea on the route to India. But in the Mediterranean, from the end of the twelfth century, it was surpassed by the Italian, Provençal, and Catalan fleets; it was strong again only under the Ottomans. The number of Arabic maritime terms that filtered into Western languages also symbolizes the Arabic mastery of the sea: admiral, arsenal, to caulk (*calfater*), and "mahone" (barge; in modern French, *mahonne*] are the best-known examples.

Fairs and markets

Historians have shown great interest in long-distance international trade, but this should not cause one to overlook the very close-knit network of rural markets, where peasants, whether Latin, Greek, or Muslim, came to sell the surplus of their harvest, acquiring by this means a little money that allowed them to pay the land-use fees owed to the landowner, the lord, or the state. Urban areas of more than several tens of thousands of inhabitants required provisions, which came in part from the countryside that surrounded them, but which often came from much further away. In the principal cities of the West that were situated on a waterway, the urban market was not far from the river: the first covered marketplaces in Paris were near the Place de Grève along the bank of the Seine River that flowed through the city. Inside the city, retail trade was hardly separated from the workshop: awnings protected the goods displayed for sale and made in the back of the shop. Food trade held a key place; the retailers were often grouped together by speciality in the same street or the same quarter (e.g. the Boucherie in Paris).

In the Muslim world, urban markets – including a commercial street (*suq*), specialized markets for food commodities, and buildings dedicated to trade (*funduq*, an Arabic word that comes from the Greek *pandokeion*) – coexisted with weekly rural markets, periodic fairs, and occasional markets at caravan stops. In Cairo, for example, the great *suqs* were established along the principal north–south axis of the city, whereas in most Muslim cities the mosques attracted retailers. In Constantinople, the wholesaling of wheat took place outside the imperial walls, all along the Golden Horn, where a large central market, a sort of marketplace building, was located near the port jetties. The shops (*ergasteria*) where retail trade occurred were also set off in specific places, except for the *mangipeia* (bakeries) located in every quarter.

Annual fairs tied to regional agricultural specialities attracted foreign merchants, whose coming encouraged in turn the specialization of regional farming: English wine importers came to Bordeaux and buyers of cheese to the fairs of Apulia. From the eighth century, the Lendit fair at St Denis near Paris brought together Frisian merchants and Saxon cloth salesmen with local merchants selling wine and livestock. Troyes, Lagny, and Provins were at first small regional fairs before becoming in the twelfth and thirteenth centuries the meeting place of all merchants of the West. In England, the wool fairs established at Winchester, Northampton, St Ives, and Stamford constituted a sort of continual market, while in Flanders a cycle of fairs was established for the distribution of wool and woolen cloth at Ypres, Lille, Bruges, Messines, and Thourout.

The fairs of Champagne remained nonetheless the most important in Europe during the twelfth and thirteenth centuries. Created on the site of small local fairs, they developed because of intelligent policies on the part of the counts of Champagne who, by the "fairs' code of conduct" granted merchants complete protection not only on their territory but also on all the routes that led to it. At the fairs themselves, guards reinforced the security of the participants and exercised a jurisdiction that the counts were successful in extending to nearly all of the Christian West. In this way a cycle of six fairs was developed, in four of the count's cities – Provins, Troyes, Lagny and Bar-sur-Aube, where Flemish merchants brought products of the wool industry from the north, which were bought and then sold by Italians throughout the Mediterranean, who then acquired silk and spices from their trading partners. Italians, Provençals, and Languedocians were represented on-site by consuls; the Flemish by a woolen cloth "company of seventeen cities." After 1250, the commercial role of fairs declined, but they became places of currency exchange for all of Europe, a laboratory for new techniques of credit, and a clearing house for international businessmen.

Just as the fairs of Champagne delineated important commercial routes in the twelfth and thirteenth centuries, fairs created in the fourteenth and fifteenth centuries also marked centers of commercial and financial transactions: at the edges of the kingdom of France (Chalon-sur-Saône from the end of the thirteenth century, Geneva at the beginning of the fifteenth, Lyon after 1450, which became chiefly currency exchange fairs in the cities that would become the future important financial centers of the West); in Flanders (Bruges, Antwerp, Berg-op-Zoom); in the Holy Roman Empire (Frankfurt, Leipzig, Nordlingen); in Skänor, Sweden (where a fair specialized in the sale of salted herring took place). All the Hanseatic merchants, and even Flemish, English, and northern French merchants, came to these fairs of the Empire and the Baltic lands, where the trade of wheat, salt, and fish rivaled that of the woolen cloth of the Netherlands, Mediterranean silks, and Russian furs.

The eastern Mediterranean also experienced periodic encounters of merchants, especially as the fair was a recognized pre-Islamic institution. It was set up on pilgrimage routes, and particularly in Mecca. In Alexandria a fair was created that lasted two months when Western businessmen came to visit. In the Byzantine Empire, fairs existed in such provincial cities as Ioannina, Chonai, Skopje, Trebizond, and Thessalonica. Thessalonica, the second largest city of the Empire, the crossroads of the *via Egnatia* (joining Durrazzo to Constantinople) and the route of Vardar, was famous because of the important fair of Saint Demetrius, which, according to the thirteenth-century *Timarion*, attracted Macedonians, Bulgarians, Italians, Iberians (Spanish), Franks, and Greeks from the East, Syria, and Cyprus. Indeed, the city represented an outlet for Bulgarian, Serbian, and Macedonian agricultural products. It also received cloth from Boeotia and the Peloponnese, Egypt and Italy; woolen cloth from Flanders and canvas from Campania; spices from the East; wines from Italy; and soap from Venice. In short, during the month of October, Thessalonica was the meeting place of southern Slavs, Greeks, and Westerners.

To the fairs, we must also add the territorial concessions for purposes of trade obtained by Latin merchants in the Byzantine Empire and in the Muslim world. Over the course of the thirteenth century, Venice and

Genoa were able to create a vast network of foreign trading posts along the principal maritime routes in the Aegean Sea and the Black Sea, which then became centers of commodity exportation, first because of the consequences of the Fourth Crusade, and then because of the Treaty of Nymphaeum in 1261. Venice wielded supremacy in the Ionian Sea with Corfu, in the western part of the Aegean Sea with Coron and Modon, in the south of the Peloponnese at Nafplio and Negroponte, in the duchy of the Archipelago with a colony established by a dynasty of Venetian origin, and especially in Crete, a farming colony *par excellence*, which provided for Venice a large part of its supply in wheat and wine. Genoa established itself at Chios and Phocaea beginning in 1346 and supported the Gattilusios in their possession of Mytilene and the islands in the north of the Aegean. The two maritime republics shared economic supremacy of Constantinople, Trebizond and La Tana, outlets for the Mongolian silk and spice routes, whereas Genoa dominated the Crimean coast with Caffa, Soldaia (Sudak), and Cembalo (Balaklava). The Pisans also established a foreign trading post in Constantinople and another in Porto Pisano, in the Black Sea, about which we know nothing. The Crusades allowed the establishment of significant communities in Syria–Palestine endowed with fiscal advantages (at Antioch, Tripoli, Beirut, Acre, Caesarea), while in Egypt Pisans, Venetians, and Genoese obtained during the thirteenth century *funduqs* at Alexandria without the benefits of extraterritoriality.

In the Baltic world, the "German visitors from Gotland" expelled the Scandinavian confraternity of Visby and rendered that island the warehouse of Russian and Nordic products. The Hanseatic League had four foreign trading posts: London (the Stahlhof), Bruges (the Kontor), Bergen, and Novgorod (the Peterhof), and numerous foreign commission outposts. All these establishments were linked by very busy maritime routes.

State and papal intervention in trade

These concessions of foreign trading posts and colonies were a result of treaties that reduced or eliminated customs duties owed by merchants. In the Byzantine Empire, successive chrysobulls – imperial decrees bearing golden seals – facilitated the establishment of the Latins, first to the benefit of Venice (992 and 1082) and Amalfi, then of Pisa (1111) and Genoa (1115). These treaties were renewed over the last centuries of the Middle Ages, as the Byzantine Empire weakened and called for Western support for its defense. In 1082 the Venetians obtained the rights to free trade in the Empire, the Genoese received exemption from the *kommerkion* in 1261 and the Pisans shortly afterwards, but they all had to struggle to avoid extortion by the *kommerkiar-ioi* – who levied the custom duties – and to obtain the free trade of grains. The other Western nations benefited only from a reduction in custom taxes. Whereas the tax rate for imperial subjects was 10 per cent, it was only 2 per cent for the Catalans, Anconans, and Ragusans; 4 per cent for the Narbonnais; 5 and then 2 per cent for the Florentines.

In the West, customs duties represented a political weapon for rulers, as in the case of England, which had two primary resources for exportation: wool and tin. In 1275 Edward I established an export tax of one half-mark per sack of raw wool payable by foreign merchants. But in 1303, this tax was replaced by the "maltote" tax fixed at three marks per sack. New increases took place in 1311, 1322, and especially in 1342, because of expenses occasioned by the war against France. Cloth exports were taxed less, which helped to support the growing English textile industry, and deprived Flemish markets and Flemish weavers of a part of their supply of raw wool. The creation of the Wool Staple in Calais established a monopoly on exports for the benefit of English merchants. Within one century, the intervention of the English ruler had profoundly changed the circuit of trade. It was the same all over the West.

In the Muslim world, the most well-known intervention by a ruler occurred in Egypt, where the *Minhāj*, a tax treaty drawn up by al-Makhzūmī in the first years of the reign of Saladin, informs us of the organization of foreign trade that fell under the *Diwān al-khums*, the customs bureau, and the *Matjar*, the trade office carrying out purchases and sales on behalf of the state. Importers had to pay an *ad valorem* duty, which varied according to the type of merchandise: iron, wood, pitch and other metals brought by the Italians and indispensable to the Ayyubid sultanate were paid two-thirds in alum. Other taxes were added for the unloading, stocking, and the security of imported bundles. A fixed duty was required on exports, demonstrating the reluctance of authorities to allow merchandise to leave, which would be a sign of impoverishment. Muslims, *dhimmi*, and foreigners were taxed differently. The Ayyubid authorities conceded *funduqs* to foreign merchants, but forbade them from entering the Red Sea, where trade was reserved solely for Muslims. The treaties made with foreign powers and custom duties allowed governments to control trade activity.

Very different was the papal attempt to control trade with the Saracens – that is, the Muslims – promoted from the Third Lateran Council (1179) down to the fifteenth century, the aim of which was to weaken Muslim countries, especially Egypt. The culmination of this occurred on 23 August 1291, when after the fall of Acre, Pope Martin IV forbade all trade with the Saracens. A few years later, however, Pope Boniface VIII was satisfied with simply imposing a fine on violators. These measures were applied in moderation by the Italian maritime republics, but neglected by the King of Aragon, who dealt with the sultan in order to protect the trade relations of his subjects with Egypt. In all the western ports, fraud was ubiquitous. Beginning in 1344, wealthy merchants were able to convince the pope to relax the prohibition, and, for a fee, lower the excise duty and the price of navigation licenses. The pontifical prohibition was thus able only to slow down and reshape trade relations between the West and Egypt without making them disappear, and this too only between 1291 and 1344.

Trade routes and networks

Two important sectors dominated medieval Europe: the Mediterranean and its access routes, the whole of the North Baltic Sea and its interior branches.

The Mediterranean was indisputably the largest center for large-scale international trade from the Early Middle Ages down to the verge of modern times. In the Early Middle Ages, Radhanite Jews established occasional, and sometimes regular, contacts with the Frankish kingdom, Baghdad, and even Central Asia. Beginning in the tenth century, Jewish merchants of the Geniza in Old Cairo expanded their activities into Syria and toward India and Indonesia to the east and in the Iberian peninsula (Almeria), in the Maghreb (Mahdiya), and in Sicily (Mazzara) to the west, which included regular exchanges between al-Andalus and the Maghreb, and between Ifriqqiya and Sicily. With the growth of Italian and Catalan trade beginning in the twelfth century, the whole of the Mediterranean formed a trade network united by navigation lines that brought together Seville, Barcelona, Valencia, Majorca, Montpellier, Marseille, Genoa, Pisa, Naples, Ancona, Venice, and Ragusa with the important port cities of the East, including Alexandria, Acre, Beirut, Candia, Famagusta, Rhodes, Constantinople, Caffa, La Tana, and Trebizond, as well as the transverse routes from Constantinople to Alexandria, for example, or from Caffa to Trebizond. Having originally been linear, trade became polygonal at the end of the Middle Ages, confirming the "connectivity" of the Mediterranean regions underscored by Horden and Purcell.

The sector of the North Sea dominated in the Early Middle Ages by Frisian and Saxon merchants, who were active from Quentovic to Haithabu by way of Dorestad, extended to England, Scandinavia, the Baltic, the Empire, and Russia by the Scandinavians and Germans, especially when the Hanseatic cities came into the mix at the founding of Lübeck in 1158. Their dealings led their merchants to London, the large wool market, to the Atlantic coast of France for the salt of Bourgneuf, to Bergen and in Scania for fish, to southern Germany for the salt and cereals of Lüneburg, to Novgorod for furs, wax, honey, and hides, to Danzig for cereals and wood. In the west, English merchants established the Wool Staple in Calais, sold cloth from Coventry and Ludlow made from the wool of English sheep with long fleece (which made the cloth both stronger and finer than short-fibered fleece), brought tin from Devon and Cornwall that made the people of Bristol rich, and became masters also of the fisheries of Iceland. France remained somewhat at the margins of international trade, in which it participated by way of the Gascons for the wine of Bordeaux, and the Hanseatics for the salt of Bourgneuf. Only Rouen, La Rochelle and Marseille tried to rival Bruges and Antwerp, the large ports of the North.

Between these two important networks flourished multiple river, land, and sea routes, establishing meeting points. On the Seine, "water merchants" had exclusive right to trade with Rouen. On flat-bottomed boats, ferrymen from Po and Brenta distributed Venetian imports inland, and those on German rivers the merchandise of the Hanse. The Ebro and Guadalquivir rivers brought to Barcelona and Seville the agricultural products of Aragon and Andalusia. Land routes were no less important. The Rhône axis joined the fairs of Champagne with Provençal and Italian ports. The route of Saint-Gotthard between Italy and the lands beyond the Alps was developed in the thirteenth century (see Map 10.1). The *via Egnatia* and the trans-Balkan route between Belgrade and Constantinople were the major axes of communication in the west of the Byzantine Empire, as was the Constantinople–Iconium–Antioch route in its east. The archeological finds of money along Russian rivers have revealed a "Nordic arc" from Scandinavia to Constantinople and Central Asia. As for the Mongolian silk and spice routes, they led either to La Tana, at the mouth of the Don River, or to Trebizond. In the Muslim world, the postal relay systems, the khans, and Bedouin surveillance ensured the security of the "sand route" between Egypt, Asia Minor, and Baghdad, from which also went the "royal route" of Khurasan as well as the Nordic route toward Lake Ladoga by way of the Volga, along which treasures of Arab money from the ninth and tenth centuries have been unearthed. The east–west axes of the Maghreb were taken by the pilgrims going to Mecca, whereas the north–south routes tied the port cities of Ifriqiya and Egypt to the towns of the Nigerian Sudan: gold routes, salt routes, and slave routes, on which walked camel caravans.

Maritime routes were innumerable; however, we should nevertheless never underestimate the difficulties of coastal navigation, even when the

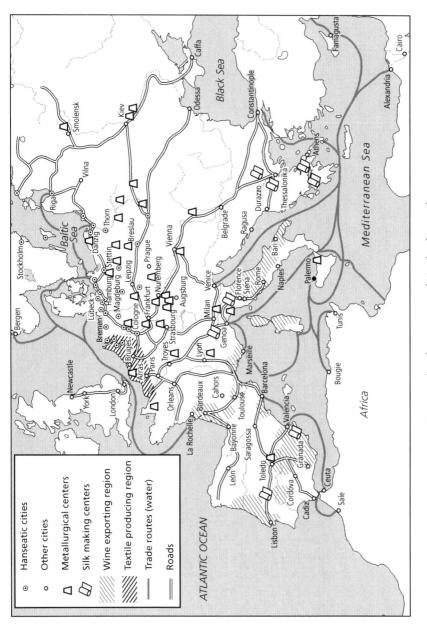

Map 10.1. European/Mediterranean trade in the thirteenth century

circumstances were favorable. Coastal navigation ensured liaisons that land transportation could not provide. From west to east were the royal routes of commerce: the "islands route" for the Catalans, and the route between Italy, Constantinople and the Black Sea for the Italians, dotted with ports of call and foreign trading posts (Coron, Modon, Negroponte, Chios), temporary warehouses and naval repair bases. In the south Aegean, the principal route of the Near East diverged by way of Crete, Rhodes, and Cyprus either toward Acre (until 1291) and Beirut, or towards Alexandria. Under the Ayyubids the Red Sea was an Arab sea, a place of intense coastal navigation long overshadowed by the important route of India, where 'Aydhab (until 1266) and Aden, the principal cities of navigations toward Calicut (Kozhikode), were used for the trans-shipment of goods from the Far East. In the Persian Gulf, after the decline of Shiraz, Hormuz dominated the contacts with Malabar, the crossroads between the Islamic world and the Far East. In the West, the arrival of Genoese vessels at Southampton and Bruges, recorded for the first time in 1277, symbolized the joining of Mediterranean and Atlantic navigation. As for the Nordic route from London to Novgorod, it was from 1250 a Hanseatic monopoly with branches in Bergen and Scania.

On these routes, circumstances were sometimes favorable and sometimes hostile for merchants. The spice route passed by the Persian Gulf and the Fertile Crescent until the middle of the eleventh century; it was detoured toward the Red Sea, 'Aydhab and Qus from 1062 to 1266, making Alexandria the "market between the East and the West"; it then ended up at the Black Sea ports for nearly a century before finding outlets in Egypt and Syria after 1350. On the other hand, the Muslim route of al-Andalus to Egypt ceased to exist in the twelfth century, replaced by the Italian and Catalan route. The only Muslim trade that remained was between the kingdom of Granada and the ports of the Maghreb. In northern Europe, the Frisians and the Scandinavians were pushed aside in favor of the Flemish, Germans, and English. As much in the Mediterranean as in the Baltic, wars slowed or even destroyed trade: the Venetian *mudae* were discontinued during the "colonial" conflicts waged by Genoa and Venice in the fourteenth century; conflicts involving the Danish, Flemish, Hanseatics, and English in the second half of the fourteenth century slowed the course of business (see Map 10.2).

The objects of trade

The businessman of the Middle Ages was not specialized; he traded in everything. Historians have too frequently been interested in the spice trade,

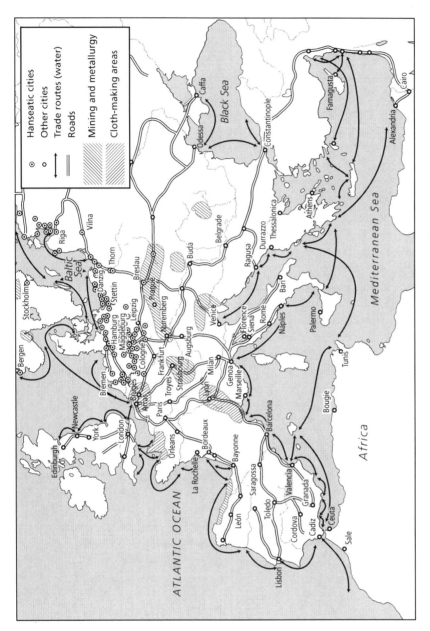

Map 10.2. European/Mediterranean trade in the fifteenth century

considered as the motor of the medieval economy, and have not paid enough attention to more common consumer commodities, especially food products.

Urban growth from the Early Middle Ages onward required subsistence that the near countryside was not always able to provide. As a result, every government attempted to control the grain trade. The grain tithe of Egypt fed Constantinople until 619; the Byzantine capital then had to turn toward the cereal resources of Thrace, the Balkans, or the Russian principalities. The maritime Italian republics were entirely dependent on the outside: Genoa on Maremma, Sicily, and the Black Sea regions; Venice on the Lombard plain, Crete and Sicily, which was the bread basket for all Italy. Barcelona and Valencia sought grains in Sicily, Aragon, and Languedoc, and secondarily in the Flemish hinterlands. The principal currents went from the south toward the north of the Mediterranean. Picardy, Artois, Hainaut, and Cambrai supplied provisions to Flanders and the Netherlands. As for the Hanseatic cities, they relied for their grain supplies on eastern and central Germany. Market instability was the norm.

Wine was the object of intense trade: Bordeaux wines went to England and Flanders; southern Italian wines to the East; Cretan wines to Venice. Oil from Andalusia and Apulia went to the East. The salt that according to Hocquet "paid for the merchandise" in Venice[9] was generally a state monopoly; in the Mediterranean, the primary saltworks were found at Ibiza, in Provence, on the Adriatic coast, in Cyprus and in the north of the Black Sea. Hanseatic merchants went to get salt at Guérande, at Bourgneuf, in Portugal, and at Lüneburg in exchange for Baltic grains. Salt was indispensable for preserving meat and fish, and the principal fishing areas were the sea of La Tana, Norfolk, the Norwegian coast and Scania. The cultivation and production of cane sugar spread toward the west throughout the Middle Ages: from Mesopotamia to Syria–Palestine to Cyprus (with the plantations of the Hospitallers and of the Cornaro family) to Crete (without great success) to Sicily, and then to the coast of Valencia, before going to Madeira in the fifteenth century. Some other food products were also the objects of large-scale trade: cheeses, salted meats, dried fruits, and mastic from Chios, on which the Genoese Mahona had a monopoly of production and sale.

The consumption of spices and silk, considered in the High Middle Ages as luxury goods reserved for a restricted elite, became more generalized: spices

9 Jean-Claude Hocquet, *Le sel et la fortune de Venise, vol 1: Production et monopole* (Villeneuve-d'Ascq: Publications de l'Université de Lille, 1978).

were used for cooking, pharmacopoeia, and craft purposes (alum allowed dyes to be affixed to cloth); silk was at first exclusively produced in the Byzantine Empire (Constantinople, Thebes, Corinth), and then it spread to Sicily, Lucca, Genoa, Venice, Lyon, until King Louis XI (r. 1461–83) tried to create silk factories in Tours. In the fourteenth and fifteenth centuries, spices represented the greatest part of the cargo of Genoese and Venetian galley ships, so much so that the investment necessary for their acquisition in Egypt was never quite as important as on the eve of the Portuguese arrival in India in 1498. Venetian supremacy was complete; the other merchant nations, with the exception of Genoa, came far behind.

Raw materials played a large role in trade. Wood, so rare in the south and east of the Mediterranean with the exception of the forestry resources of Lebanon that were quickly exhausted, was the object of contraband trade from the West to the Muslim world, whereas it was common on the Baltic shores. The exportation of long-fleeced raw wool from England for a long time supplied the Flemish wool industry, before becoming used for the production of high-quality woolen cloth in England over the course of the fourteenth century. Because of the *Mesta* – the organization of Spanish sheep-breeders for the seasonal movement of livestock – Castile supplied merino wool exported to Italy and the north of Europe. In the fifteenth century, the Venetians organized the buying and transportation of cotton from Syria, of which a part went by way of the Fondaco dei Tedeschi in Venice to southern Germany for the production of fustian, a blend of cotton and linen. Linen was one of the major items of exportation from Egypt. Furs from Scandinavia and the Russian principalities were the object of a widespread trade toward the West and the Muslim countries, where they were a marker of social prestige. Among the dyeing products, expensive Eastern coloring agents classified as spices (cocheneal, Brazil wood, and the alum of Phocaea – later of Tolfa – that was used for the dyeing of cloth) are to be distinguished from more accessible and widely distributed Western goods, including saffron from the Midi of France, the Abruzzo region, and Catalonia and woad or pastel from Picardy, Languedoc, and Lombardy. The metal trade was even more widespread. Iron from Sweden and the island of Elba, tin from Cornwall and Bohemia, silver from Harz, and copper from Sweden, Bohemia, Hungary, and Kastamonu (Turkey) supported the complex trade circuits and prosperous metallurgy, such as that for the making of weapons, from which Milan prospered.

Textiles are often considered as the primary currency of medieval trade, along with spices. Flemish woolen cloth from the twelfth century was widely distributed in the Mediterranean world thanks to Genoese and Marseillais intermediaries. The production of Tuscan woolen cloth remained of high quality, and was appreciated in the Eastern world until the end of the Middle Ages. It came in competition with the development of the English woolen cloth industry, which was in the hands of the Merchants Venturers, and also with the lightweight woolen cloth from Normandy and Catalonia, which encroached upon Near Eastern markets and ruined the local production of the Muslim world. It was the same for the canvasses and fustians of Lombardy and southern Germany (Augsburg, Ravensburg).

The slave trade was widely practiced in the Mediterranean world, but its flow varied a great deal. During the Early Middle Ages, Slavic and pagan slaves were sold to Muslim countries. As soon as the Reconquista began in Spain, Saracens captured in the fighting were to be found in the principal commercial marketplaces of Barcelona, Genoa, Venice, Pisa, and Naples. Beginning in the 1270s, slaves from the Black Sea – Circassians, Laz, Abkhaz, and especially Tatars – were sold in Egypt to increase the Mamluk regiments, or were sold in large Western cities such as Venice as servants and sometimes as farmworkers, as in Sicily and Valencia. In the fifteenth century, the slave trade diversified: the Ottoman conquest dried up the Black Sea supplies, which were replaced by the Berbers of Cyrenaica or the Guanches of the Canary Islands. The cargo of "heads" could be bountiful, as is demonstrated by the sale of Greeks after the capture of Heraclea by the Genoese in 1351, or by the business affairs of the Venetian Giacomo Badoer in Constantinople (1436–9). Only at the end of the fourteenth century was a ban progressively established to reduce the sale of Christians into slavery.

Spices and woolen cloth? Examining this pair alone would be to reduce the polymorphous character of the exchanges between the East and the West. However, focusing on this pair allows us to investigate balance sheets in order to determine that the trade deficit the West experienced in the Early Middle Ages had progressively diminished. During the Middle Millennium, the supremacy of the West's maritime powers and its industrial goods – not only woolen goods but also glass, soap, and wrought metal – was asserted, invading Eastern markets and destroying local production. Some historians do not hesitate to see in this competition the origin of the underdevelopment of the countries of the Near East.

Contrary to what Pirenne thought, the impact of the Arab conquest on Mediterranean trade was negligible: the decline occurred before, and lasted until the Carolingian period. A first renaissance in the eighth century was interrupted around 820. Trade networks were then reconstituted from the tenth century, in the Mediterranean as well as in the north of Europe. They were the sign of economies experiencing strong economic growth, tied one to the other by numerous land and sea routes, but affected by the variations of circumstances: at a peak at the end of the thirteenth century, in crisis in the 1340s, with a progressive recovery after 1420, to the point that trade investments in the Mediterranean with the East and the resulting gains (at least 25 per cent on spices, 45–50 per cent on cotton) were the highest they had ever been just before the arrival of the Portuguese in India. In northern Europe at that time, immense fortunes emerged in Lübeck, Nuremberg, and Augsburg, and the English and Dutch rivaled the Hanseatics and were preparing to be in competition with the Italians in the Mediterranean. The development of Western trade had as a counterbalance the decline, at least on the international level, of Byzantine and Muslim businessmen. A first globalization of trade occurred at the end of the Middle Ages, in the West's favor.

Translated by
Michelle Bolduc

FURTHER READING

Ashtor, Eliyahu. *East–West Trade in the Medieval Mediterranean*, ed. Benjamin Z. Kedar, London: Variorum Reprints, 1986.

Ashtor, Eliyahu. *The Levant Trade in the Later Middle Ages*. Princeton University Press, 1983.

Ashtor, Eliyahu. *Technology, Industry and Trade. The Levant versus Europe, 1250–1500*, ed. Benjamin Z. Kedar. London: Variorum Reprints, 1992.

Studies on the Levantine Trade in the Middle Ages. London: Variorum Reprints, 1978

"The Volume of Mediaeval Spice Trade," *The Journal of European Economic History*, 9/3 (1980): 753–63.

Balard, Michel. *La Romanie génoise (xiie–début du xve siècle)*, BEFAR n° 235, 2 vols. Rome-Genoa: École française de Rome, 1978.

"L'impact des produits du Levant sur les économies européennes (xiie–xve siècles)," in Simonetta Cavaciocchi (ed.), *Prodotti e Tecniche d'Oltremare nelle economie europee. Secoli xiii–xviii*, Settimana di Prato (aprile 1997), 1998: 31–57.

et al. "Le transport des denrées alimentaires en Méditerranée au Moyen Age," in K. Friedland (ed.), *Maritime Food Transport*. Cologne: Böhlau, 1994: 91–175.

Bautier, Robert-Henri. "Points de vue sur les relations économiques des Occidentaux avec les pays d'Orient au Moyen Age," in Michel Mollat (ed.), *Sociétés et compagnies de commerce en Orient et dans l'océan Indien (Actes du 8e Congrès international d'Histoire maritime, Beyrouth 1966)*. Paris: SEVPEN, 1970: 263–331; reprinted in his *Commerce méditerranéen et banquiers italiens au Moyen Age*, London: Variorum Reprints, 1992, Study iv.

Borgard, Philippe, Jean-Pierre Brun and Maurice Picon. *L'alun de Méditerranée*. Naples and Aix en Provence: Centre Jean Bérard, 2005.

Carrère, Claude. *Barcelone centre économique à l'époque des difficultés (1380–1462)*, 2 vols. Paris – The Hague: Mouton et Cie, 1967.

Cavaciocchi, Simonetta (ed.). *I porti come impresa economica*. Istituto internazionale di storia economica "F. Datini," Prato. Atti delle Settimane di Studi 19. Florence: Le Monnier, 1988.

(ed.). *Fiere e mercati nella integrazione delle economie europee. Secc. XIII–XVIII*. Istituto internazionale di storia economica "F. Datini," Prato. Atti delle Settimane di Studi 32. Florence: Le Monnier, 2001.

(ed.). *Relazioni economiche tra Europa e mondo islamico. Secc. XIII–XVIII*. Istituto internazionale di storia economica "F. Datini," Prato. Atti delle Settimane di Studi 38. Florence: Le Monnier, 2007.

Coulon, Damien. *Barcelone et le grand commerce d'Orient au Moyen Age. Un siècle de relations avec l'Égypte et la Syrie–Palestine (ca 1330–ca 1430)*. Madrid: Casa de Velázquez; Barcelona: Institut Europeu de la Mediterrània, 2004.

Delort, Robert. *Le commerce des fourrures en Occident à la fin du Moyen Age*, 2 vols. Rome: École française de Rome, 1978.

Del Treppo, Mario. *I mercanti catalani e l'espansione della Corona d'Aragona nel secolo xv*. Naples: Curial, 1972.

Favier, Jean. *Gold and Spices: The Rise of Commerce in the Middle Ages*. New York, NY: Holmes & Meier, 1998.

Goitein, Shelomo D. *A Mediterranean Society*, vol. 1: *Economic Foundations*. Berkeley – Los Angeles, CA: University of California Press, 1967.

Heers, Jacques. "Types de navires et spécialisation des trafics en Méditerranée à la fin du Moyen Age," in Michel Mollat (ed.), *2e colloque international d'Histoire maritime*. Paris: SEVPEN, 1958: 107–17.

"Il commercio nel Mediterraneo alla fine del sec. xiv e nei primi anni del xv," *Archivio storico italiano* 113 (1955): 157–209, reprinted in his *Société et économie à Gênes (xive–xve siècles)*. London: Variorum, 1979, Study 1.

Heyd, Wilhelm. *Histoire du commerce du Levant au Moyen Age*, 2 vols. Leipzig: O. Harrassowitz, 1885–6.

Hocquet, Jean-Claude. *Le sel et la fortune de Venise*, vol. ii: *Voiliers et commerce en Méditerranée (1200–1650)*. Lille: Presses universitaires de Lille, 1979.

Horden, Peregrine and Nicholas Purcell. *The Corrupting Sea. A Study of Mediterranean History*. Oxford: Blackwell, 2000.

Jacoby, David. "Mercanti genovesi e veneziani e le loro merci nel Levante crociato," *Atti della Società ligure di Storia patria*, n.s. 41/1 (2001): 229–56.

"Silk Economics and Cross-Cultural Artistic Interaction: Byzantium, the Islamic World and the Christian West," *Dumbarton Oaks Papers*, 58 (2004): 197–240.

Judde de la Rivière, Claire. *Naviguer, commercer, gouverner. Economie maritime et pouvoirs à Venise (XVe–XVIe siècles)*. Leiden: Brill, 2008.

Kedar, Benjamin Z. *Merchants in Crisis: Genoese and Venetian Men of Affairs and the Fourteenth Century Depression*. New Haven and London: Yale University Press, 1976.

Lopez, Robert S. *The Commercial Revolution of the Middle Ages, 950–1350*. Englewood Cliffs, NJ: Prentice-Hall, 1971.

McCormick, Michael. *Origins of the European Economy. Communications and Commerce A.D. 300–900*. Cambridge University Press, 2001.

Nigro, Giampiero (ed.). *Francesco di Marco Datini. The man, the merchant*. Trans. Isabelle Johnson. Florence: Firenze University Press, 2010.

Oikonomidès, Nicolas. *Hommes d'affaires grecs et latins à Constantinople (xiiie–xve siècle)*. Montréal: Institut d'études médiévales Albert-le-Grand; Paris: J. Vrin, 1979.

Pryor, John H. and Elizabeth M. Jeffreys, *The Age of the ΔΡΟΜΩΝ. The Byzantine Navy ca 500–1204*. Leiden: Brill, 2006.

Renouard, Yves. *Les hommes d'affaires italiens du Moyen Age*. Paris: Colin, 1968.

Tangheroni, Marco. *Commercio e navigazione nel Medioevo*. Bari: Laterza, 1996.

Thiriet, Freddy. *La Romanie vénitienne. Le développement et l'exploitation du domaine colonial vénitien (xiie–xve siècle)*. Paris: E. de Boccard, 1959.

Vallet, Eric. *Marchands vénitiens en Syrie à la fin du xve siècle*. Paris: Association pour le développement de l'histoire économique, 1999.

Verlinden, Charles. *L'esclavage dans l'Europe médiévale*, t. ii: *Italie – Colonies italiennes du Levant – Levant latin – Empire byzantine*. Bruges: De Tempel, 1977.

Trading partners across the Indian Ocean: the making of maritime communities

HIMANSHU PRABHA RAY

The conventional framework of ancient Indian history emphasizes that trading activity proliferated during certain historical periods, and declined thereafter. Implicit in the conventional pattern has been the assumption that maritime trade was dependent on demand from states and empires and was hence sporadic. In terms of the Indian Ocean trading network, the traditional view holds that local trading communities of the Indian subcontinent played a minimal role, especially in the western Indian Ocean, since it was the foreign – European and Arab – demand for luxuries that triggered it.

This view is not supported by the nature of commodities involved in the Indian Ocean network, however, which ranged from salt and cowries at one end of the scale to metals, medicinal plants, aromatics, agricultural produce, costly textiles, silverware and dancing girls, at the other. Such commodities appear in early texts. The *Arthaśāstra*, a Sanskrit treatise on political economy[1] dated between the third century BCE and third century CE provides an interesting array of possibilities for the acquisition of commodities. For example horses could be obtained as gifts, purchased, obtained in war, bred in stables, received in return for help or temporarily borrowed (II.30.I).[2] Other early texts also mention trade. There are references both in early Buddhist literature and in inscriptions to the *śreṇī* or trade associations; the number eighteen is often mentioned, though nowhere are these eighteen enumerated. In the Pali canonical *Jataka* literature, there are frequent references to the chief of the guilds in the retinue of the king (Book II: no. 154) and he is generally revered as a rich

---

1 R. P. Kangle (ed. and trans.), *The Kautiliya Arthaśāstra* (University of Bombay, 1965–72).
2 Himanshu Prabha Ray, 'Inscribed Pots, Emerging Identities: The Social Milieu of Trade', in Patrick Olivelle (ed.), *Between the Empires: Society in India 300 BCE to 400 CE* (New York: Oxford University Press, 2006): 113–43.

and powerful figure. These suggest that local demand played a more important role than the conventional narrative suggests.

André Wink has also stressed continuities, arguing against the decline of Roman trade in the Indian Ocean region in the early centuries of the Common Era because Greek-Byzantine traders again became active in the India trade from the fourth to the sixth centuries.[3] In the fifth–sixth centuries Persian commerce synchronized with the ascendancy of the Sasanian Empire, and with the coming of Islam there was an increase in trading networks in the Indian Ocean. Wink suggested that control of trade was a motivating factor in the Arab conquest of Makran, Sindh, Kathiawar and Kutch and that the tenth century marked the emergence of an integrated Muslim trading empire. In emphasizing the role of Islam in promoting trade, Wink points to the disappearance of Buddhism from India, and contends that, due to restrictions stipulated in the Law Books or *Dharmaśātras* on maritime travel, the Hindu population turned to 'agrarian pursuits and production, away from trade and maritime transport'.[4]

Wink's emphasis on continuity of trading activity in the western Indian Ocean is well taken, but there was also change, with shifts in coastal centres and the emergence of new settlements. For example, Bharuch, Sopara and Kalyan on the western Indian coast were important outlets for trade in the early centuries of the Common Era, but gave way to Valabhi in the Gulf of Cambay around the middle of the first millennium. Subsequently, Arab attacks on Valabhi around the latter half of the eighth century led to its abandonment.[5] There was the consequent rise of Stambhatirtha, or Cambay, at the head of the Gulf of Cambay. Another important coastal settlement was that of Somnath (modern Prabhas Patan) on the Gujarat coast, which continued to play an active role in maritime trade (see Map 11.1).

Trade was also shaped by the presence of Hindu, Buddhist and Jain religious places. Somnath, for example, was the location of an important Hindu temple and site of pilgrimage. At Somnath, archaeological evidence of historical settlement dates to the fourth century BCE, but religious structures, such as temples, emerge only in the fifth–sixth centuries CE. After the tenth century, shops and markets were located in the vicinity of temples and

---

3 André Wink, *Al-Hind: The Making of an Indo-Islamic World* (New Delhi: Oxford University Press, 1990): 45–64.

4 Wink, *Al-Hind*, 72.

5 V. K. Jain, *Trade and Traders in Western India*, A.D. *100–1300* (New Delhi: Munshiram Manoharlal Publications, 1990): 73.

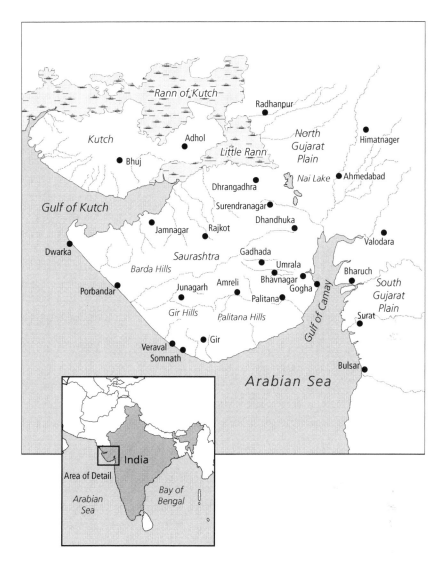

Map 11.1. Gujarat

contributed materials to the performance of rituals and festivities. For example, a thirteenth-century record, inscribed on a long slab of polished black stone from one of the temples at Somnath, refers to the purchase of shops by the benefactor and their donation to the temple.

Kanheri near the present city of Mumbai was the largest Buddhist monastic complex along the west coast of India dating from the first to the eleventh century. Merchants and traders were the major patrons of the monastic site. A six-line inscription in cave 11, dated to 12 September 854, records the visit of a devout worshipper of the Buddha from Gauda or Bengal on the east coast and a permanent endowment made by him of one hundred *drammas* or silver coins for the construction of a meditation room and clothing for monks residing at the monastic complex. This grant also draws attention to the interconnectedness of the two seas, i.e. the Arabian Sea and the Bay of Bengal.

In addition to the varied religious landscape, maritime travel in the medieval period involved a changing array of watercraft. Cargo carriers formed the foundation of trading ventures. Merchants and traders in some cases certainly owned ships and watercraft, but they neither manned nor sailed these. A thirteenth-century inscription from western India (the Anavada inscription of 1291) refers to gifts to a temple by shipowners. More often, goods and cargoes were entrusted to the captain of the vessel, who was then responsible for their sale and profit. Thus maritime activity involved diverse groups, from the owners of watercraft to those who commanded them and still others who sailed them. Hence there can be no simple caste attributions of the communities involved in trading activity. Moreover, the normative rules laid down in the Law Books need to be balanced against the narrative literature in Sanskrit, which provides glowing accounts of maritime travel, by merchants, craftspeople, musicians and others.

Trade also formed an important source of revenue for the state, which continued to be monarchical. From contemporary records in western India, it is evident that tax was collected for use of roads, ferry-crossings and harbour facilities and differed from tax charged on the sale and purchase of commodities in the marketplace. Inscriptions from the fifth century onwards refer to several officials engaged in collecting revenues from trading caravans. The city formed the nucleus of settlement and it is at the city gates that goods were taxed and the king obtained revenue in return for providing protection to local trading communities.

In this chapter I focus on four issues: the communities who participated in the trading networks; the impact of maritime trade on a littoral region, such as that of Gujarat; the organization of trans-oceanic trade in the western Indian Ocean; and finally the interconnectedness of the two sectors of the Indian Ocean, viz. the Arabian Sea and the Bay of Bengal. For each of these issues, I highlight particular sources or examples that provide special insight into maritime trade and its organization in a world historical context.

Local trading communities

Recent research suggests that fishing and sailing communities formed a distinct group and were the crucial component of all sea travel in the Indian Ocean.[6] Fishing was the traditional occupation of coastal groups in several pockets from at least the fifth millennium BCE.[7] These communities adopted numerous occupations associated with the sea: fishing and harvesting other marine resources, salt making, sailing, trade, shipbuilding and piracy.

Fishing and sailing communities formed the foundation of maritime activity in the Indian Ocean and provided a continuum to seafaring throughout history, though no doubt their fortunes fluctuated over time. A common feature of the sewn boats of the Indian Ocean, for example, was the use of coir-rope for stitching. Because coconut palm plantations were restricted to certain parts of the Indian Ocean littoral, coir-rope would have been one of the commodities in demand in the boatbuilding settlements of the coast.[8] Thus, the building of the *dhow*, or traditional watercraft, involved trade and transportation of wood for planking and coconut coir for stitching from different regions of the Indian Ocean, thereby creating networks of interaction and sustaining vibrant exchange across the seas.

The first-century CE *Periplus Maris Erythraei* written by an anonymous sailor in *koine* Greek[9] is unique in that it provides the first detailed description of local boats in the Indian Ocean in the early centuries of the Common Era. It refers to several types that were used from the East African coast to the west coast of India. In the region of the Barbaroi is a small port of trade called 'Avalites, where rafts and small craft put in' (section 7). The island of Menuthias, identified with the island of Pemba on the coast of East Africa, has sewn boats and dugout canoes that are used for fishing and catching turtles (section 15). The name of the southernmost of the towns of Azania,

---

6 K. McPherson, 'Maritime Communities: An Overview', in Himanshu Prabha Ray and Edward A. Alpers (eds.), *Cross Currents and Community Networks: The History of the Indian Ocean World* (New Delhi: Oxford University Press, 2007): 34–49.

7 Himanshu Prabha Ray, *The Archaeology of Seafaring in Ancient South Asia* (Cambridge University Press, 2003), ch. 2.

8 Himanshu Prabha Ray and Jean-François Salles (eds.), *Tradition and Archaeology: Early Maritime Contacts in the Indian Ocean* (New Delhi: Manohar Publishers, 1996).

9 Lionel Casson (ed. and trans.), *The Periplus Maris Erythraei* (Princeton University Press, 1989).

Rhapta, is said to derive from the name of the sewn boats, or *rhapton ploiarion*, found there (section 16). Muza is described as a port teeming with Arabs – shipowners or charterers and sailors who trade across the water and with Barygaza on the west coast of India, using their own outfits (section 21).

Another invaluable literary source for an understanding of the Indian Ocean network is the *Christian Topography* written in the sixth century by an Egyptian monk, Cosmas Indicopleustes ('India-voyager').[10] Cosmas was in all probability of Greek parentage and a native of Alexandria. In the early part of his life, he was a merchant and had travelled widely in the western Indian Ocean. Later he retired from secular life and moved to the cloister, where he devoted himself to the composition of works on geography, cosmography and Scriptural exegesis.

The *Christian Topography* (Book XI: 367–8) refers to a series of coastal centres on the west coast of India, many of which overlap with those mentioned in the *Periplus*. The *Arthaśāstra*, for example, makes a distinction between local trade transacted in fortified cities of the interior, identified as *nagara* or city, and that originating at distant places and exchanged at the *pattana*, located either on sea coasts or on river banks of the interior. The two had a different organization of trade and different administrative structures, with itinerant merchants' organizations being active only at coastal centres. The use of the term *patana* or *pattana* is significant – it is a term that continued to be used in the India letters of the Cairo Geniza dated to the eleventh-twelfth century, which we will discuss later. Thus clearly *pattana* was a market centre with a distinctive administrative structure for the collection of levies that continued from the early centuries CE into the second millennium.

How did the coming of Islam redefine maritime space? Dionisius Agius has shown that with the spread of Islam, Arabic was enriched by borrowings from Aramaic, Persian, Greek, Sanskrit and other Indian languages. He also cautions against equating religious with ethnic identity, as Arabic sources do not make this distinction and thus label as Muslim all non-Arab foreigners who converted to Islam irrespective of their ethnic background.[11] There are nevertheless exceptions. For example, the historian and geographer al-Mas'udi (d. 956–7) states that the Sirafis and Omanis were the leading seafarers of the time, thereby highlighting regional coastal identities.

---

10 *The Christian Topography of Cosmas, an Egyptian Monk*, trans. John Watson McCrindle (Cambridge University Press, 2010).
11 Dionisius A. Agius, *Classic Ships of Islam: From Mesopotamia to the Indian Ocean* (Leiden: Brill, 2008): 10–11.

The Annals of the Tang period (618–907) in China, on the other hand, do not refer to religious affiliations, but make a distinction between Persian and Arab traders, the former termed Po-ssu and the latter Ta-chi or To-che. In contrast, Muslim travellers such as Ibn Jubayr (d. 1217) and Ibn Battuta (d. 1368–9 or 1377) apply the term 'Muslim' in a religious context to distinguish some communities from others that were not Islamic, such as Christians, Jews, Hindus and Zoroastrians. This is an important issue, which has implications not only for understanding the terms used to label medieval trade and the religious or ethnic identities attributed to the seafarers, but more significantly for comprehending emerging religious identities in the Indian Ocean region and the ways in which these were formulated and described.

From the eighth–ninth century onwards, maritime space expanded to include East Asia, and Chinese wares were distributed through the Indian Ocean networks.[12] Excavations at Fustat (Old Cairo) have yielded Chinese ceramics dating from the ninth through the fifteenth century, with the largest concentration from the tenth to the fourteenth century.[13] These need to be used with caution for demarcating the extent and nature of the network, however. For example, the excavations at Siraf in the Persian Gulf yielded a Chinese stoneware fragment bearing two Arabic names – Yūsuf and Mansūr, or Maymūn – incised before glazing the vessel, belonging to a jar probably sent by a merchant resident in China.[14] But who was the owner of this vessel and for what purpose was it used? More broadly: Can the finds of Chinese ceramics, such as Changsha or Yuezhou Celadon Wares, be used to define the nationality of watercraft used in the transportation of the pottery, such as whether these were Chinese ships or Arab ships? Can they be used to determine the direction of the contacts?

A search for Chinese ceramics along the Indian coasts has yielded mainly post-eleventh-century ceramics, a majority belonging to the thirteenth and fourteenth centuries along the Tamil and Malabar coasts.[15] The evidence from Siraf (period II), however, presents a different picture. At the beginning of the ninth century the site reached its maximum extent, covering an area of

12 A. Rougelle, 'Medieval Trade Networks in the Western Indian Ocean', in Ray and Salles (eds.), *Tradition and Archaeology*, 159–80.

13 Katherine Strange Burke and Donald Whitcomb, 'Quseir al-Qadim in the Thirteenth Century', *Ars Orientalis* 34 (2004): 92.

14 Moira Tampoe, *Maritime Trade between China and the West: An Archaeological Study of the Ceramics from Siraf (Persian Gulf), 8th to 15th centuries A.D.* (Oxford: BAR International Series 555, 1989).

15 Noboru Karashima (ed.), *In Search of Chinese Ceramic-Sherds in South India and Sri Lanka* (Tokyo: Taisho University Press, 2004).

over 110 hectares between the seashore and the foot of the mountains. This was also the period of intensive building activity coinciding with the construction of the great Friday mosque. Chinese imports, however, represent less than one per cent of the total amount of excavated ceramics from the site and only one-third of these are from luxury porcelain or Celadon pieces, while two-thirds come from stoneware jars. In contrast to the limited quantities dated to the ninth–tenth century, imports increased in the thirteenth–fourteenth century. In his 1969 survey in southern Iran, A. Williamson picked up about 10,000 Chinese sherds from coastal sites, but no more than ninety from inland centres.[16]

This uneven distribution of Chinese ceramics both temporally and spatially across the western Indian Ocean raises issues of peaks and lows in trading networks in specific regions. Second, the clustering of finds in coastal areas suggests the prevalence of contacts along the coast.

Gujarat: trade and religion in a littoral community

How did this oceanic trade impact centres further inland? The area of Gujarat in western India provides an excellent example of a littoral community where trade and religion combined, as evidenced by a variety of sources. Archaeological investigation in western India has provided information on several long-lasting coastal settlements. For example, after an archaeological exploration conducted in the mid-nineteenth century, the site of Mandvi on the estuary of the Rukmavati River at the entrance to the Gulf of Kutch has been known as a port town with links to both Oman and the East African coast. Dwarka, located on the north coast of Saurashtra, is another contemporary site with a long period of settlement from the first century BCE to almost the present. Its importance stems both from its coastal location as well as the religious significance of its temples and sacred association as a centre of pilgrimage. Other continuously settled sites along the Gujarat coast include Porbandar, Somnath and Valabhi at the head of the Gulf of Cambay as mentioned earlier. Further south, Chaul – referred to as Campavati or Revatiksetra in the *Epics* – is mentioned in inscriptions and literary sources from the early centuries CE to the seventeenth century. In a copper plate record of 1094, three major coastal centres are identified: Chaul, Thane and Sopara, all in western India. Epigraphs dating from the tenth–eleventh

---

16 Rougelle, 'Medieval Trade Networks', 159–80.

centuries refer to these coastal settlements as linked to each other, as well as to settlements in the interior.

In the fifth century CE, Valabhi, located on the Bhavnagar creek in the Gulf of Cambay, emerged not merely as an outlet for maritime trade, but also as the capital of the ruling dynasty of the Maitrakas (493–776) and the core area for religious consolidation.[17] Contemporary Sanskrit literature such as the *Daśakumāracaritam* by Dandin (*fl. c.* 600) describes Valabhi as a prosperous trading centre. One of the stories in the text is set in the city of Valabhi in Saurashtra where the chief of sea traders (*nāvika-pati*) lived. According to the text, he possessed immense wealth, almost like Kubera, the Lord of Wealth.[18] References to Valabhi's wealthy resident and travelling communities of traders (*vaniggrāma*) are found in the copper plate donations from Toramana's reign dating to the late fifth–early sixth centuries. These record gifts made by the trading community of Vadrapalli to the temple of Jayaswami or Narayana belonging to the queen mother. Maharaja Bhuta and Maharaja Matrdas also made donations of certain villages to the temple. The main commodities referred to in the plates are molasses, salt, cotton and grain and a detailed list of revenues transferred is also itemized These revenues were calculated on the basis of vessel-load, donkey-load, and cartload of the produce. Vadrapalli was probably located 8 kilometres to the west of Sanjeli and signatories to the donation included traders from Ujjain, Kannauj, Mathura and perhaps Mandasor. A goldsmith constructed a lake near the temple.[19]

The self-assurance of the trading community is evident from the charter of Visnusena of 592, issued from Lohata in the Kathiawar region, which reiterates the customary practices followed by the group and the acceptance of these by the ruler. This charter is addressed to a list of officials as is usual in Maitraka records. The charter assures protection to the community of merchants (*vaniggrāma*) established in the region and endorses their continued functioning. It provides a detailed list of seventy-two trade regulations or customary laws to be followed. Some of the regulations are of great interest to this discussion, as they indicate not only an active coastal trade,

17 K. J. Virji, *Ancient History of Saurashtra* (Bombay: Konkan Institute of Arts and Sciences, 1952): 245.
18 M. R. Kale (ed.), *Dasakumaracarita of Dandin* (Delhi: Motilal Banarsidass, 1986): 164, 332. An English translation by Isabelle Onians appeared under the title *What Ten Young Men Did* (New York University Press, 2005).
19 R. N. Mehta and A. M. Thakkar (eds.), *M. S. University Copper Plates of the Time of Toramana* (Vadodara: MS University of Baroda, 1978).

but also a lower rate of tax for commodities for religious purposes. For example, it is specified that merchants staying away for a year were not required to pay an entrance fee on their return. Other clauses specify duties that were to be paid. A boat full of containers was charged twelve silver coins, but if the containers were for religious purposes, they were charged only one and a quarter silver coins. In the case of a boat carrying paddy it was half this amount. Other items frequently transported by boat included dried ginger sticks, bamboo, wine, leather, buffaloes, camels and bulls.[20]

Indigo or *nīla* is mentioned as one of the items exported from areas such as Gujarat and the charter of Visnusena mentions a tax on the pressing of the indigo dye. Indigo also figures as one of the items of trade from India westward to Egypt handled by the business house of Ibn 'Awkal between 980 and 1030.[21] One of the three varieties mentioned includes Sindani indigo – Sindan/Sandan being identified with the Konkan coast of the subcontinent.

The variety of taxable commodities mentioned in the charter of Visnusena is an indication of the diverse nature of trade in the region. These included oil mills, sugarcane, wine, cumin seed, black mustard and coriander. The charter also refers to a tax on dyers of cloth, weavers, shoemakers and retailers hawking goods on foot. Others such as blacksmiths, carpenters, barbers, and potters could be recruited for forced labour under the supervision of officers.[22]

This consolidation of economic activity along with expansion of political authority and increasing involvement of brahmanas and Buddhist monastic complexes marks a departure from the trading patterns of earlier periods. Clearly the Maitrakas were attempting to widen their resource base. The inscriptions provide valuable information about the commodities involved in coastal traffic, customary practices adopted by the trading communities, and the differential tax levied on goods required or donated to religious establishments.

It is significant that while archaeological data and distribution networks of ceramics indicate local, regional and oceanic interaction starting from the third–second millennium BCE onwards, inscriptions from Gujarat are largely silent about trading activities until well into the fifth–sixth centuries CE. From

20 D. C. Sircar, 'Charter of Visnusena Samvat 649', *Epigraphia Indica* 30 (1953–4): 163–81.
21 Norman A. Stillman, 'The Eleventh-Century Merchant House of Ibn 'Awkal (A Geniza Study)', *Journal of the Economic and Social History of the Orient* 16 (1973): 15–88.
22 Sircar, 'Charter of Visnusena', 178.

this period onwards inscriptions reflect an increasing complexity in commodities exchanged and in the nature of transactions conducted.

The presence of mosques in several parts of the Indian Ocean littoral and the active role of Muslim merchants and shipowners in the maritime network raise issues regarding cross-cultural interaction especially in Gujarat. On the coast of Kutch in Gujarat, Bhadresvara is an early site, which was also the site of a twelfth-century Jaina temple. The local Muslim community of the Isma'ili sect is said to have built a mosque here with the permission of the Jaina Council, but the most notable structure is the shrine of Ibrāhīm dated on the basis of an *in situ* inscription to 1159–60, i.e. nearly half a century earlier than the Islamic monuments at Delhi or Ajmer.

In Bhadresvara, and at several other sites in Gujarat such as Cambay, Somnath and Patan, there are a number of Muslim tombstones dated between the mid-twelfth and early thirteenth centuries. Many of the architectural features at Bhadresvara are also found in a mosque built by early settlers at Junagarh, where an inscription records that the chief merchant and shipowner Abu'l-Qāsim b. 'Alī al-Idhāji built the mosque in 685 AH (1286–7 CE).[23] Junagarh is an ancient site, as evident by the location of a Mauryan inscription of the fourth–third century BCE, and below the mosque is a Buddhist cave now regarded as a Muslim shrine.

How did this changing religious landscape translate into interactions between communities? Arabic inscriptions and also bilingual epigraphs are important sources for insights into communication between communities after the advent of Islam. The partnership between the *Nākhudā* (master of the ship) and local communities is best exemplified by the Somanath-Veraval inscription of 1264, consisting of two slabs of stone inscribed with a Sanskrit epigraph and, two months later, with an Arabic record. Located at Somanatha-Pattana on the Gujarat coast, the inscription records endowments for the maintenance of a mosque (*dharmasthāna* in Sanskrit) and for providing it other services by *Nākhudā* Nūr al-Dawla wa-l-Dīn Fīrūz, son of Khoja *Nākhudā* Abu Ibrāhīm of Hurmuja-deśa or Hormuz at the mouth of the Persian Gulf, together with the local community leaders (*thākura* in Sanskrit). At that time the king or *rājā* of the coastline (*velākūla*) of Hormuja was *amir śri rukana dina*, that is, Sultan Rukn al-Dīn. The Sanskrit version of the inscription provides a detailed description of the land acquired as a part of

23 Mehrdad Shokoohy, *Muslim Architecture of South India: The Sultanate of Ma'bar and the Traditions of Maritime Settlers on the Malabar and Coromandel Coasts* (London: Routledge Curzon, 2003): 18.

the endowment. This land was located in the vicinity of the city and at least four local residents are listed as providing the land for the endowment. In addition Nūr al-Dīn acquired and donated the products of an oil mill and two shops or marketplaces (*hattas*). The surplus, if any would emanate from these, was to be sent to the holy places of Mecca and Medina.[24] This transaction was witnessed by all the *jamāthas* or groups of Somnath who were also responsible for the upkeep of the property. The groups named are: *Nākhudā-nāvika*; *gamchikas* or oil men along with their preacher; *chūnakāras* or whitewashers; and also *mushalamānas* or Muslims of the town.

It is important that the Arabic version of the inscription contains just twenty-eight lines as compared to the Sanskrit record of forty-three lines. While it agrees in several significant details with the Sanskrit version, it lists the *imām* and the *mu'azzin* of the mosque as beneficiaries. The Arabic version credits Abū Ibrāhīm ibn Muhammad al-'Irāqī, the father of Nūr al-Dīn Fīrūz, with the foundation of the mosque and one of the titles that it attaches to the latter is that of *malik mulūk al-tujjār*, or leader of business-leaders. The Arabic text does not contain details of the land transfer, nor does it mention that the surplus was to be sent to Mecca and Medina. It concludes by quoting from the Quran against tampering with the endowment. It has been suggested that while public inscriptions engraved in Sanskrit were a part of the administrative procedure of the subcontinent, this was not valid for the central Islamic lands, where paper documents were the norm and foundation inscriptions containing basic information about the founder were monumentalized in ornate epigraphs on the buildings. In keeping with the legal requirements of Islamic law the mosque was definable as a *waqf* (i.e. a charitable endowment), and trustees and beneficiaries had to be appointed. The Arabic version is thus crucial to an understanding of the establishment of the institution of *waqf* in western India. The Somanath-Veraval inscription indicates that there were 'two separate registers encoding the interactions between Muslims and their non-Muslim business partners. One was the prescribed register, constituted by Islamic laws defining what was allowable and forbidden in the commercial dealings of its followers. The other was the practical register, evidenced by historical documents.'[25]

24 D. C. Sircar, 'Veraval Inscription of Chaulukya-Vaghela Arjuna, 1264 AD', *Epigraphia Indica*, 34 (1961): 141–50.
25 Alka Patel, 'Transcending Religion', in Grant Parker and Carla Sinopoli (eds.), *Ancient India in its Wider World* (Ann Arbor: University of Michigan Press, 2008): 155–6. See also Z. A. Desai, 'Arabic Inscriptions of the Rajput Period from Gujarat', *Epigraphia Indica: Arabic and Persian Supplement* (1961): 2–24.

This overview of the early history of Gujarat has presented insights into dynamic interactions between merchants, shippers and, most importantly, religious institutions in the coastal regions of the Indian subcontinent. These littoral communities participated in the larger maritime network of the western Indian Ocean.

Trading centres on the Red Sea and trans-oceanic travel

Trading centres on the Red Sea were closely involved in trade with the west coast of India. Interesting evidence for this involvement is provided by more than five hundred paper fragments, written in the Arabic script, recovered during excavations at Quseir al-Qadim on the Red Sea coast about 500 kilometres south of Suez. This evidence is perhaps unique in the Indian Ocean world as, unlike the Cairo Geniza and other contemporary documents, it can be located within an archaeological context. Material remains from the excavations of the shaykh's house at Quseir al-Qadim help provide a cultural milieu to the texts. It is significant that there is no mention of Quseir in the Geniza documents, though they refer to 'Aydhab and Qus frequently.[26] This divergence alerts us to the need to analyse a range of sources rather than a single data base in order to arrive at a holistic picture.

A survey of the fragments from the central area of the town confirms that the majority were addressed to or written on behalf of a certain Shaykh Abū Mufarrij and his son Shaykh Ibrāhīm, and to a lesser extent to other people associated with the family business in the first half of the thirteenth century. Inside the house, several hundred paper fragments, mainly personal and business correspondence written in Arabic, were found along with other small objects. These documents have been studied and translated by Li Guo and the present discussion is largely based on his work. The general pattern was for the letter to be written on the recto, while the verso contained the recipient's address.[27]

Shaykh Abū Mufarrij was the owner of a prosperous transit warehouse in the port of Quseir. His elder son Ibrāhīm worked as a merchant and broker rising to the rank of *rayyis*, or head of trade, and also a *khatīb*, or one who gave the sermon at the local mosque. Thus it is evident that the shaykh and his son were merchants who did not travel themselves, but sent shipments

26 Mordechai A. Friedman, 'Qusayr and Geniza Documents on the Indian Ocean Trade', *Journal of the American Oriental Society* 126 (2006): 402.
27 Li Guo, *Commerce, Culture, and Community in a Red Sea Port in the Thirteenth Century: The Arabic Documents from Quseir* (Leiden: Brill, 2004).

through others. The overlapping responsibilities of being a head of trade and also a *khatīb* in the local mosque underscores the close relationship between economic and religious activities. Pilgrims to Mecca via the Egyptian Red Sea southern route formed an important category of clients. One of the few complete letters requesting supplies written from a ship stuck in Yemen would suggest 'some kind of regular transport of correspondence, supplies, merchandise, and even cash through a kind of maritime shuttle service between Quseir and Yemen'.[28] The coastal centre of al-Qasr al-Yamani, where the ship was stuck, cannot be identified, but it was most likely on the Yemeni side of the Red Sea and the ship was travelling along the Yemeni coast for Hijaz.

Did the warehouse of Shaykh Abū Mufarrij also function as a caravanserai where people stayed overnight? Given the multiple capacities in which the shaykh and his son worked, ranging from merchant, agent and manager to tax farmer, head of trade and market inspector, in addition to the social services the warehouse provided, such as funeral arrangements, medical care and magic practices, the answer should perhaps be positive. It appears also that the shaykh's warehouse functioned as a government agency in charge of grain distribution on the Red Sea and Indian Ocean trade routes, especially for the pilgrims to Mecca.

The Arabic documents from Quseir supplement not only the archaeological data, but also those available in the Geniza papers. These papers, Judeo-Arabic documents preserved in the Cairo Geniza written in Arabic in Hebrew characters and dating to the eleventh and twelfth centuries, also provide insights into the working of trade in the Red Sea and beyond. The 459 documents, comprising 523 shelf-marks related to the India trade, constitute a significant component of the Geniza records. Yemen on the south Arabian coast formed the fulcrum of a network that extended from centres on the Red Sea to the west coast of India, generally designated by the term *diyār al-Yaman wal-Hind*, or the lands of Yemen and Hind.[29] Documents in the Cairo Geniza may be categorized into letters, documents of legal character, and memos accompanying shipments, such as accounts and wage payments of a brass factory in western India.

---

28 Li Guo, 'Arabic Documents from the Red Sea Port of Quseir in the Seventh/ Thirteenth Century', *Journal of Near Eastern Studies* 58 (1999): 181.

29 S. D. Goitein and Mordechai Akiva Friedman, *India Traders of the Middle Ages: Documents from the Cairo Geniza* (Leiden: Brill, 2008).

The second category of documents or deeds of 'partnership according to Muslim law' drawn up before a merchant embarked on a journey are of particular relevance to the present discussion. Invariably a merchant did business not only for himself, but also for others, or acted as an agent for one or several investors. On his return, the merchant was required to make a statement to the local rabbinical or Muslim court and the partners would write out a release indicating that the deed had been concluded to their satisfaction. It should be stressed that whenever possible, merchants preferred sending goods rather than gold, and silk is at times mentioned as a means of payment.

Most large-scale transactions were carried out through partnerships, and merchants preferred to spread out their funds among several partnerships to reduce risks, rather than invest all their funds in a single business venture. Three types of partnerships are evident in the India trade: those between Jewish merchants and their co-religionists; between merchants and shippers; and between Jewish and non-Jewish trading groups. Several prominent Jewish business families are represented in the documents. Joseph b. David Lebdi of Tripoli undertook a voyage from 1094/5 to 1097, which started at al-Mahdiya, Tunisia, and was destined for Nahrwāra (Anahilavada) in Gujarat, the country of lac, textiles, steel and beads.

Lebdi arrived at 'Aydhāb with eighty bales of lac packed in Nahrwāra, Gujarat, and fifty bales of pepper. The overseas venture was in partnership with two other merchants, Abū Nasr and Farah, and was for an amount of 800 dinars. While Lebdi returned to Fustat, after receiving 'governmental prescripts' allowing foreigners and non-Muslims safe passage, he left his two partners at 'Aydhāb to send the lac in installments to Fustat. Unfortunately the two men were murdered, which led to complicated lawsuits.[30] Once the lawsuit was settled, Joseph Lebdi undertook a second voyage in 1099–1101. Lebdi also had dealings with Hasan b. Bundār, representative of merchants in Aden. His son was Madmun b. Hasan b. Bundār, a shipowner and representative of merchants in Aden and *Nagid* or leader of the Jewish community in the land of Yemen.

In contrast to the Lebdi family who travelled to India, Abraham Ben Yijū was resident largely at Mangalore on the south Kanara coast of India. Most of the documents relating to Ben Yijū indicate that his permanent residence in India was at Mangalore (Manjarūr). However he also dispatched shipments

---

30 Goitein and Friedman, *India Traders*, 241–7.

to Aden from Fandaraynā (Pantalāyini) where he must have lived for some time and also from Dahbattan (Valarapattanam) and engaged in business in Fāknūr – all cities on the Malabar coast. On one occasion we are told that his family was in Jurbatan.

Ben Yiju was not only an agent for his partner merchant in Aden, but more importantly he owned a brass factory in India. The Geniza papers provide valuable insights into craft production in the eleventh and twelfth centuries. Customers in Aden provided the materials, i.e. copper and tin as scrap, and paid the artisans per piece according to weight. The Arabic terms *nahās* and *sufr* are used interchangeably to refer to a copper and tin alloy, while 'yellow copper' is often used to designate a higher percentage of tin. The workers included slaves and Jews from Yemen, one of them termed Abram and another called 'Iyār, who was charged with assaying measures and weights. The proprietor provided the workplace and the tools and also procured customers, while the artisans paid for the fuel used, which consisted of rice husks. The artisan was paid according to the weight of the object produced – a system also in use in Yemen.[31]

One further issue regarding Ben Yijū's sojourn in India remains to be addressed. How were goods transported between Mangalore, where Ben Yijū was based, and Aden where his customers lived? Over twenty places on India's west coast are mentioned in the Geniza records, and each ship or convoy had its pre-allocated landing place and was labelled accordingly, such as 'one bound for Broach', or for Tana or Kulam.[32] Indian shipowners were designated as PTN SWMY corresponding to *pattana sami* in one inscription.[33] The term is translated as lord of the mart, or in Arabic *shaykh al-sūq*.[34] Dahbattan or Valarapattanam is mentioned on the Kanara coast where Ben Yijū had his brass factory. An Indian shipowner mentioned several times is PDYĀR who possessed several ships, one of which was commanded by a Muslim.

We have highlighted a range of trading practices in the western Indian Ocean. On the one hand were traders and merchants who did not travel themselves, such as Shaykh Abū Mufarrij and his son Shaykh Ibrāhīm, but who were nevertheless involved in trading networks on account of their ownership of prosperous warehouses at the Red Sea port of Quseir. In

---

31 Goitein and Friedman, *India Traders*, 644–5.   32 *Ibid.*, 24.

33 Arjun Appadurai, *Economic Conditions in South India, 1000–1500 AD*, 2 vols. (Madras University, 1936), vol. I, 385.

34 Goitein and Friedman, *India Traders*, 24.

addition the father and son duo functioned in various capacities ranging from merchant, agent, and manager, to tax farmer; from head of trade and market inspector, to a deliverer of sermons. In contrast is the evidence from the Geniza documents, which trace histories of several families, such as Madmun b. Hasan b. Bundār who represented foreign merchants in local law suits in Aden, the Lebdi family who travelled to India, and Abraham Ben Yijū who was resident largely at Mangalore on the south Kanara coast of India.

While business partnerships and other relationships emerge from these documents, completely absent is any interaction with local rulers or political elites in the Indian subcontinent. This suggests that perhaps coastal centres functioned in a somewhat autonomous fashion and interacted with other littoral settlements, rather than with centres further inland.

Another significant change that emerges from the present discussion relates to legal frameworks for economic activities that were institutionalized in Gujarat from the ninth to the beginning of the fourteenth century. The Sanskrit-written *Lekhapaddhati* is a unique document, dated from 744–5 to 1475–6, that contains a collection of specimen letters and provides rules for drafting a variety of documents, such as rules for drawing up land grants, treaties between rulers, rules of administration and drafts of private letters. It refers to five departments of the state relating to trade and commerce: *vyāpāra karaṇa* (trade and commerce), *velākūla karaṇa* (department of harbours), *jalapatha karaṇa* (department of waterways), *maṇḍapikā karaṇa* (department of customs) and *tanka śālā karaṇa* or mint.[35] What makes the *Lekhapaddhati* invaluable is its close correspondence with the contemporary inscriptions of the Chaulukya kings of Gujarat who ruled from 996 to 1241.

The integration of communities across religious affiliations is further substantiated by information on slave agents and the slave trade. One of the Geniza letters (II, 48) refers to the writer's unsuccessful attempts at purchasing a slave (*wasīf*) from a batch of new slaves brought to Aden, on the occasion of the Jewish festival of Sukkot, from *bilād al-Zanj* or East Africa. There are other references to the purchase of slaves who worked as household servants (II, 56–7). Unlike slaves from Zanj, Ben Yijū had a household retainer – an Indian slave named Bama who helped him in the business and was treated with some respect in the letters. An inscription dated 15 June 1126, discovered at a village about two hundred miles southeast of Mangalore, refers to a servant of warriors named Māsaleya

35 Pushpa Prasad (ed.), *Lekhapaddhati. Documents of State and Everyday Life from Ancient and Medieval Gujarat* (New Delhi: Oxford University Press, 2007): 1–22.

Bamma, while another from the same area records the name of *setti* or trader Bamma from a merchant family.[36]

The earliest document in Ben Yijū's archive, written soon after his arrival in India, is a deed of manumission, done in Mangalore, granting freedom to a slave girl whom he had purchased. Through manumission she became a Jewish convert and was given the name Berakhā (Hebrew for blessing). The manumission deed contains several other phrases that have been identified only in Yemenite Jewish documents. It has been suggested on the basis of a court record written on cloth, but much effaced, that Jewish communities in Broach and Mangalore had some kind of autonomous juridical authority, though they were under the overarching jurisdiction of the rabbinical court of Aden.[37]

After spending eighteen years in India, Ben Yijū returned to Yemen with his family around 1140. He had two sons and one daughter from his wife Ashu, though one son had died as a young child in India (III, 41, line 14).[38] It would seem that Ben Yijū's return to Yemen was not taken kindly by the local Jewish community, especially his marriage to his freed slave. This raised a further question about the legality of this liaison and the inheritance passing on to his son from this marriage. Four letters in the archives in Ben Yijū's handwriting relate to the legal position in the case of a Jewish man having illicit relations with a slave girl before her emancipation.

In contrast to Jewish law and the position of female slaves, the next issue relates to the status of slaves in western India. References to slaves involved in a variety of domestic chores occur in a range of literary sources and the terms *dāsa* and *dāsī* are used for them. The pillar edicts of the Mauryan ruler Aśoka (269–232 BCE), inscriptions written on stone pillars that proclaim his adherence to Buddhism, refer to correct behaviour towards brahmana, sramana, slaves and servants, while the *Jātakas* mention four kinds of slaves: those born slaves; those bought; those who become slaves of their own free will; and those driven by fear. There are scattered references to the import of slaves from India in the Mediterranean world, while the *Periplus* specifically mentions the import of singing boys and female concubines at Barygaza or Bharuch on the west coast. There are references to the exchange of slaves on the island of Socotra, where shippers came from the west coast of India.[39]

36 R. S. Panchamukhi (ed.), *Karnataka Inscriptions* (Dharwad: Kannada Research Institute, 1951), vol. II, 71–3.

37 Goitein and Friedman, *India Traders*, 723.   38 *Ibid.*, p. 727.

39 Casson, *The Periplus Maris Erythraei*, sections 31 and 49.

In this regard the *Lekhapaddhati* is of relevance. The deed of the sale of a female slave dated 30 April 1230/ 19 April 1231 records that King Rana Pratap Singh brought a sixteen-year-old girl named Panuti after attacking another kingdom. She was sold as a female slave at the crossroads after the five leading men of the town were informed, and the merchant Asadhara bought her at a price of 504 Vīsalapriya drammas for doing household work in his house. The deed was signed by residents of the town as witnesses.[40] In another case, the deed refers to the sale of a female who voluntarily chose to become a slave to escape severe famine and harassment by *mlecchas*, that is, those who do not follow the norms of Vedic society. Her duties specified that she was to be employed for household work.

Interconnectedness of the Indian Ocean

From the ninth to the mid-fourteenth centuries, two of the merchant associations that dominated economic transactions in South India were the Manigramam and the Ayyavole. Associated with these were communities of craftsmen such as weavers, basket-makers, potters, leather-workers and so on. As late as the seventeenth century, the Ayyavole seemed to be concentrated in the cotton producing areas of Andhra Pradesh on the east coast of India. Though these two originated independently of each other, from the mid-thirteenth century onward, the Ayyavole association became so powerful that the Manigramam functioned in a subordinate capacity to it. Not only did these merchant associations develop powerful economic networks, but they also employed private armies.[41] The range of their operations extended well beyond the boundaries of the Indian subcontinent into Southeast Asia.

Several clusters of Tamil inscriptions have been found on the eastern fringes of the Indian Ocean from Burma to Sumatra. Of the seven mid-ninth to late thirteenth century inscriptions written in the Tamil or part-Tamil language found so far in Southeast Asia, one has been found near Pagan in Burma, two just south of the Isthmus of Kra in the Malay peninsula, and four in north and west Java. Perhaps the easternmost record is the bilingual Tamil and Chinese language inscription associated with the remains of one of the two Siva temples at Quanzhou in South China. These inscriptions connect merchant associations operating out of South India with the

40 Prasad, *Lekhapaddhati*, 158–9.
41 Meera Abraham, *Two Medieval Merchant Guilds of South India* (New Delhi: Manohar Publications, 1988).

founding or the endowing of temples or other structures for the use of a resident Indian merchant community. In the 1060s and 1070s Chinese records report that the imperial court received missions from the Chola kingdom of South India, as well as from the ruler of Srivijaya located on the island of Sumatra, but by the last decades of the eleventh century, the Chinese court had begun to encourage Chinese traders to venture out to sea.

Perhaps the most relevant example is the Buddhist monastery at Nagapattinam, which was a major landmark on the Tamil coast from the seventh to the nineteenth centuries. A Buddhist temple was erected at Nagapattinam specifically for Chinese Buddhists at the insistence of a Chinese ruler during the reign of the Pallava king Narasimhavarman II (c. 695–722). One of the later Srivijayan kings, Maravijayottunga-varman, is known to have provided for its construction, and the Chola king Rajaraja I granted revenues of a large village, Anaimangalam, for its upkeep in 1006.

In the tenth century, local versions of these merchant guilds named *banigrāma* appeared in the north coast ports of both Java and Bali, especially at Julah on the Balinese coast. There are seven Javanese inscriptions dating from 902 to 1053 that refer to merchant associations called *banigrāma* and to the various tax concessions granted to them. While some foreign merchants may have been included in these groups, these appear largely as indigenous organizations associated with the local economic networks as tax farmers.[42]

At this stage, certain conclusions may be drawn. First, information on seafaring communities from historical and archaeological sources indicates that their composition cut across ethnic boundaries. Second, the role of religions, such as Buddhism, Hinduism or Islam, in motivating and supporting seafaring activity needs to be recognized and accepted. Third, local demand played an important and steady role, and coastal centres frequently interacted with other littoral settlements. Finally, for an appreciation of cultural interchanges across the seas, it is crucial to highlight the diverse channels of communication, which also included oral transmission by priests and pilgrims, traders, wandering storytellers and entertainers. It is only then that a holistic understanding of cultural interaction across the maritime world will emerge.

---

42 Jan Wisseman Christie, 'Asian Sea Trade Between the Tenth and Thirteenth Centuries and its Impact on the States of Java and Bali', in Himanshu Prabha Ray (ed.), *Archaeology of Seafaring: The Indian Ocean in the Ancient Period* (New Delhi: Pragati Publications, 1999): 242–5.

FURTHER READING

Abraham, Meera. *Two Medieval Merchant Guilds of South India*. New Delhi: Manohar Publications, 1988.

Abu-Lughod, Janet L. *Before European Hegemony: The World System A.D. 1250–1350*. New York, NY: Oxford University Press, 1989.

Agius, Dionisius A. *Classic Ships of Islam: From Mesopotamia to the Indian Ocean*. Leiden: Brill, 2008.

Appadurai, Arjun. *Economic Conditions in South India, 1000–1500 A.D.* Madras University, 1936.

Barnett, L. D. 'Bhamodra Mohota Plate of Dronasimha: The Year 183', *Epigraphia Indica* 16 (1921–2): 17–19.

Burke, Katherine Strange and Donald Whitcomb. 'Quseir al-Qadim in the Thirteenth Century: A Community and its Textiles', *Ars Orientalis* 34 (2004): 83–97.

Casson, Lionel. 'P. Vindob. G 40822 and the Shipping Goods from India', *Bulletin of the American Society of Papyrologists* 23 (1986): 73–9.

  (ed. and trans.) *The Periplus Maris Erythraei*. Princeton University Press, 1989.

Christie, Jan Wisseman. 'Asian Sea Trade Between the Tenth and Thirteenth Centuries and its Impact on the States of Java and Bali', in Himanshu Prabha Ray (ed.), *Archaeology of Seafaring: The Indian Ocean in the Ancient Period*. New Delhi: Pragati Publications, 1999: 221–70.

Desai, Z. A. 'Arabic Inscriptions of the Rajput Period from Gujarat', *Epigraphia Indica: Arabic and Persian Supplement* (1961): 2–24.

Fleet, J. F. 'Junagadh Rock Inscription of Skandagupta', *Corpus Inscriptionum Indicarum* 3 (1886): 56–67.

Friedman, Mordechai A. 'Qusayr and Geniza Documents on the Indian Ocean Trade', *Journal of the American Oriental Society* 126 (2006): 401–10.

Goitein S. D. and Mordechai A. Friedman. *India Traders of the Middle Ages: Documents from the Cairo Geniza*. Leiden: Brill, 2008.

Guo, Li. 'Arabic Documents from the Red Sea Port of Quseir in the Seventh/Thirteenth Century', *Journal of Near Eastern Studies* 58 (1999): 161–90.

  Commerce, Culture, and Community in a Red Sea Port in the Thirteenth Century: The Arabic Documents from Quseir. Leiden: Brill, 2004.

Hultzsch, E. 'Palitana Plates of Simhaditya: The Year 255', *Epigraphia Indica* 11 (1911–12): 16–20.

Jain, V. K. *Trade and Traders in Western India, A.D. 100–1300*. New Delhi: Munshiram Manoharlal Publishers, 1990.

Kale, M. R. (ed.). *Dasakumaracarita of Dandin*. New Delhi: Motilal Banarsidass, 1986.

Karashima, Noboru, ed. *In Search of Chinese Ceramic-sherds in South India and Sri Lanka*. Tokyo: Taisho University Press, 2004.

McPherson, K. 'Maritime Communities: an Overview', in Himanshu Prabha Ray and Edward A. Alpers (eds.), *Cross Currents and Community Networks: The History of the Indian Ocean World*. New Delhi: Oxford University Press, 2007: 34–49.

Mehta, R. N. and A. M. Thakkar (eds.). *M. S. University Copper Plates of the Time of Toramana*. Vadodara: M. S. University of Baroda, 1978.

Panchamukhi, R. S., ed. *Karnataka Inscriptions*. Dharwad: Kannada Research Institute, 1951.

Patel, Alka. 'Transcending Religion', in Grant Parker and Carla Sinopoli (eds.), *Ancient India in its Wider World*. Ann Arbor, MI: University of Michigan Press, 2008: 143–64.

Prasad, Pushpa, ed. *Lekhapaddhati. Documents of State and Everyday Life from Ancient and Medieval Gujarat*. New Delhi: Oxford University Press, 2007.

Ray, Himanshu Prabha. *The Archaeology of Seafaring in Ancient South Asia*. Cambridge University Press, 2003.

'Inscribed Pots, Emerging Identities: The Social Milieu of Trade', in Patrick Olivelle (ed.), *Between the Empires: Society in India 300 BCE to 400 CE*. New York, NY: Oxford University Press, 2006:113–43.

Monastery and Guild: Commerce under the Sātāvahanas. New Delhi: Oxford University Press, 1986.

'The Western Indian Ocean and the Early Maritime Links of the Indian Subcontinent', *Indian Economic and Social History Review* 31 (1994): 65–88.

Ray, Himanshu Prabha and Jean-François Salles (eds.). *Tradition and Archaeology: Early Maritime Contacts in the Indian Ocean*. New Delhi: Manohar Publishers, 1996.

Rougelle, A. 'Medieval Trade Networks in the Western Indian Ocean', in Ray and Salles (eds.), *Tradition and Archaeology*, 159–80.

Shokoohy, Mehrdad. *Muslim Architecture of South India: The Sultanate of Ma'bar and the Traditions of Maritime Settlers on the Malabar and Coromandel Coasts*. London: Routledge Curzon, 2003.

Sircar, D. C. 'Charter of Visnusena Samvat 649', *Epigraphia Indica* 30 (1953–4):163–81.

'Veraval Inscription of Chaulukya-Vaghela Arjuna, 1264 CE', *Epigraphia Indica* 34 (1961): 141–50.

Stillman, Norman A. 'The Eleventh Century Merchant House of Ibn 'Awkal (A Geniza Study)', *Journal of the Economic and Social History of the Orient* 16 (1973): 15–88.

Tampoe, Moira. *Maritime Trade between China and the West: An Archaeological Study of the Ceramics from Siraf (Persian Gulf), 8th to 15th centuries CE*. Oxford: BAR International Series 555, 1989.

Vasa, P. N. 'Find of a Late Byzantine Solidus and an Arab Umayyad Dinar from Kutch', *Numismatic Digest* 14 (1990): 30–3.

Virji, K. J. *Ancient History of Saurashtra*. Bombay: Konkan Institute of Arts and Sciences, 1952.

Wink, André. *Al-Hind: The Making of an Indo-Islamic World*. New Delhi: Oxford University Press, 1990.

12

Technology and innovation within expanding webs of exchange

DAGMAR SCHÄFER AND MARCUS POPPLOW

During the Middle Millennium, technology and innovation contributed to the rise and fall of cultures, societies, and empires, in the form of military strength and agricultural development, as well as by the reification of cultural, ritual, and social practice. They often appear as mediating forces between agents, societies, systems, and environments, although contemporaries only infrequently identify them as such explicitly.

Studies with a global perspective on technology and social change during the Middle Millennium are actually quite rare. Historians of this era generally explore narratives of a culture or region.[1] Researchers assert that technologies emerged as phenomena that were recognized and expressed quite heterogeneously across time and space. Innovation was a constantly changing variable, defined and circumscribed by changing desires and needs, and by human interactions with the physical environment. Few general conclusions have therefore been drawn from research on technology in global perspective during the Middle Millennium, while substantial questions of methodology remain.

---

[1] For such comprehensive studies on particular cultures, see Joseph Needham, *Science and Civilisation in China*, vols. I–VII (Cambridge University Press, 1954–2008); Francesca Bray, *Technology and Society in Ming China (1368–1644)* (American Historical Association: Washington DC, 1997); Donald Hill, *Medieval Islamic Technology. From Philo to Al-Jazari – From Alexandria to Diyar Bakr* (Aldershot: Ashgate, 1998); Abdhur Rahman, *History of Indian Science, Technology and Culture AD 1000–1800* (Oxford University Press, 1998); Frances Gies and Joseph Gies, *Cathedral, Forge, and Waterwheel. Technology and Invention in the Middle Ages* (New York: HarperCollins, 1994); Marcus Popplow, *Technik im Mittelalter* (Munich: C. H. Beck, 2010); for studies covering several cultures see Pamela O. Long, *Technology and Society in the Medieval Centuries: Byzantium, Islam, and the West, 500–1300* (Washington DC: American Historical Association, Society for the History of Technology, 2003); James E. McClellan III and Harold Dorn, *Science and Technology in World History. An Introduction* (Baltimore: Johns Hopkins University Press, 2006): 97–201; Thomas Glick, Steven J. Livesey and Faith Wallis, *Medieval Science, Technology and Medicine. An Encyclopedia* (New York, London: Routledge, 2005).

This chapter addresses some major issues and methodological concerns emerging from the socio-historical view of technology and innovation. It tackles some of the 'highlights' of technical ingenuity in different world regions during the Middle Millennium, using identifications such as 'Chinese', 'Indian', 'Islamic' or 'European' to reflect approximations for regionally anchored politically and socially influential groups representing distinct ideals and traditions. The chapter then discusses constitutive factors of cultural frameworks of innovation evident on the global stage, transmission processes, and the relation between ruling powers and technology.

Scholarship on technology

Historical studies of technologies, exchange, and innovation in the Middle Millennium have largely focused on the Eurasian continent, where empires, cultures, and individuals created oscillating spheres of influence and varying contact zones. Africa, the Southeast Asian archipelagos or the peninsulas of northern Europe often function as periphery, while the Americas and Australia are largely ignored. The medieval historian Lynn White Jr substantially shaped the methodology of the history of technology in the 1960s–70s, markedly setting Europe as the framework for any comparative global account.[2] While achievements of Islamic cultures or Chinese traditions have sometimes been foregrounded, they tend to remain the comparative 'other'.

In the post-White era, historians, archaeologists, linguists, and anthropologists have emphasized the European Middle Ages as a period of clear technological development, presaging modern innovative creativity through the production of numerous innovative technologies and inventions. On this basis, the economic historian Joel Mokyr argues that creative medieval European technology forms an integral part of the larger historical narrative of modern economic progress in the Western world.[3] David Landes' account

2 Lynn White, Jr, *Medieval Technology and Social Change* (Oxford University Press, 1962); Lynn White, Jr, *Medieval Religion and Technology* (Berkeley: University of California Press, 1978); For recent critics of White's theses see B. S. Hall, 'Lynn White's Medieval Technology and Social Change after Thirty Years', in Robert Fox (ed.), *Technological Change: Methods and Themes in the History of Technology* (Amsterdam: Harwood Academic, 1996): 85–101; Alex Roland, 'Once More into the Stirrups: Lynn White, Jr, Medieval Technology and Social Change', *Technology and Culture* 44 (2003): 574–85. For White's Eurocentrism see James M. Blaut, *Eight Eurocentric Historians* (New York, London: The Guilford Press, 2000): 31–44.

3 Joel Mokyr, *The Lever of Riches: Technological Creativity and Economic Progress* (Oxford University Press, 1990): 31–56 and 201–8; see also Avner Greif, *Institutions and the Path to the Modern Economy: Lessons from Medieval Trade* (Cambridge University Press, 2006).

of Western cultural supremacy and hegemony during the last millennium also traces modern economic disparities and political power regimes to the Middle Ages.[4] While the works of Landes and Mokyr highlight continuity within European developments, others assert that Europe only began to show distinctive signs of divergence from other world regions after 1500.[5] Arnold Pacey emphasizes that Asian regions surpassed European technological developments for long periods up until 1800.[6]

Global accounts of medieval technology often apply a phenomenological approach, circling around a device such as a plough, an artefact such as paper or a resource such as water. Studies list technological achievements in fields such as mechanical engineering, textile technology, or methods of communication, and compare them in various regions in terms of output and impact, size, production processes and period of origin. Agriculture, architecture and water regulation, military weaponry, textiles, and iron production are employed in unifying approaches to 'technology', and are then compared in terms of features and scales. Many studies are oriented towards large-scale and 'industrial' production schemes, and relate to the employment of tools and machines, with development measured in terms of spectacular engineering achievements. In contrast, everyday practices such as the production of shoes, or the technologies of heating, cooking, sewing, or tanning are depicted as local, basic and interchangeable with negligible global impact. Knowledge flows in such commonplace practices are difficult to reconstruct, since they took place below the radar of state or elite written recognition, but a more thorough integration of archaeological research might help to overcome such a skewed perspective in the future.[7]

The global view has revealed that many of the elements attributed to European industrialization and 'modern' global structural developments emerged in other regions first. For example, the Chinese Song (960–1279)

Michael Mitterauer, *Warum Europa? Mittelalterliche Grundlagen eines Sonderwegs* (Munich: C. H. Beck, 2003) compares particularities of medieval European developments to other world regions, including those on the technological level.

4 David Landes, *The Wealth and Poverty of Nations: Why Some are so Rich and Some so Poor* (New York: W.W. Norton, 1999) see esp. Chapter 4.

5 K. N. Chaudhuri, *Asia before Europe: Economy and Civilisation of the Indian Ocean from the Rise of Islam to 1750* (Cambridge University Press, 1990): 297–337.

6 Arnold Pacey, *Technology in World Civilization: A Thousand-Year History* (Boston: The MIT Press, 1990), viii, 51.

7 For Europe, see James Graham-Campbell and Magdalena Valor (eds.), *The Archaeology of Medieval Europe, Eighth to Twelfth Centuries AD* (Aarhus University Press, 2007); Martin Carver and Jan Klápste (eds.), *The Archaeology of Medieval Europe, Twelfth to Sixteenth Centuries* (Aarhus University Press, 2011).

and Ming (1368–1644) dynasties both produced ceramics and textiles through large-scale, state-owned manufacturing that – similar to the private workshops – implemented sophisticated labour segmentation processes.[8] The porcelain city of Jingdezhen is one example of a regional manufacturing centre with good global trade links since at least the thirteenth century.[9] Manufacturers and factories of a comparable size or complexity did not appear in European countries such as Britain until the eighteenth century. A global view of technology thus reveals the nonlinear character of technological change.

Historians of the Asian Middle Millennium who approach technology and innovation often highlight use and consumption, since state and elite interests and trade are the most visible historical interfaces of technological knowledge diffusion. For example, during the Tang dynasty (618–907), elite interests in horses, spices and herbs, and products made by foreign goldsmiths fostered trade and cultural exchanges.[10] In contrast, Song literati attempting to strengthen their 'culture' (*wen*) invested in refined local styles. Researchers have shown that aside from changing taste, patterns of consumption and use were affected by the availability of materials, and the ways in which people learnt to process them. For example, as access to silver from Yunnan improved and trade with Bengal increased during the late Tang, Chinese elites began to favour silver ware over ceramics.[11] Silver workshops flourished into the Song period, while at the same time potters developed kiln technologies and learnt to fire porcelaneous wares at a higher temperature. The porcelain now known as 'china' emerged in northern China before production accelerated in the south.[12]

Histories of changing tastes and design demonstrate that political rulers and socially dominant elites shape technological developments, often lastingly and subtly through financial or social support rather than through overt exertion of power. In chronologies of consumption, moral, political, and social issues converge with economic concerns or ideas about the value of

---

8 For a discussion of the idea of modular design, see Lothar Ledderose, *Ten Thousand Things: Module and Mass Production in Chinese Art* (Princeton University Press, 2001).

9 Anne Gerritsen, 'Ceramics for Local and Global Markets: Jingdezhen's Agora of Technologies', in Dagmar Schäfer (ed.), *Cultures of Knowledge: Technology in Chinese History* (Leiden: Brill, 2012): 161–84.

10 Edward H. Schafer, *The Golden Peaches of Samarkand: A Study of T'ang Exotics* (Berkeley and Los Angeles: University of California Press, 1985).

11 Yang Bin, 'Horses, Silver, and Cowries: Yunnan in Global Perspective', *Journal of World History* 15,3 (2004): 281–322.

12 Nigel Wood, *Chinese Glazes: Their Origins, Chemistry and Recreation* (Philadelphia: University of Pennsylvania Press, 1999).

materials, and the larger context is revealed. In contrast, historians of medieval technology in Europe have paid more attention to production, showcasing the impact of labour and materials on changing technological repositories.

Change and continuity

European Renaissance humanists established the idea that technological inventions stood at the heart of periodic developmental leaps. For them, the European invention of gunpowder, printing, the compass and subsequent voyages of discovery (and colonization) impelled a new age of human endeavour which, in stark contrast to the localized, 'dark', Middle Ages, operated at a global scale. The modern historiography of China has identified a climax during the Song dynasty, when scholars increasingly discussed and recorded earlier and contemporary technological innovations. Illustrated catalogues or state documents account for hydraulic, agricultural, astronomical, and military change: textile manufacture, printing, dyeing, transportation, and building technologies were modified.

Recent historical research has emphasized that technological development is rarely sudden or unprecedented, but evolutionary in nature. 'If technology', as George Basalla commented, 'is to evolve, then novelty must appear in the midst of the continuous', which suggests that old technologies should be studied in as much depth as more spectacular innovations.[13] Hydraulic engineering, astronomy, and medicine continued from the Koryŏ (918–1392) to the Chosŏn dynasties (1392–1897) in what is now Korea, with no sudden ruptures.[14] Starting from such a perspective, innovation is shown to be transient within long-term processes of knowledge accumulation, where the new can only take root if it is founded on a fading old technology. Maintenance and repair of existing technologies led to as many innovations as did unique moments of ingenuity.

In fact, numerous studies have demonstrated that technologies emerging after 500 were strongly related to pre-500 experiences, and achievements of the early modern period rooted in developments of the Middle Millennium. Heavy ploughs and mills, for example, had evolved in Europe slowly and

---

13 George Basalla, *The Evolution of Technology* (Cambridge University Press, 1988), viii.
14 See John B. Duncan, *The Origins of the Chosŏn Dynasty* (University of Washington Press, 2000): 204–28 on issues of stability, change, and reforms.

continuously since Roman antiquity.[15] Texts record the progression of milling technology in China as equally continuous pre- and post-500. The Song developed sugar crushing and woodblock printing based on knowledge that had come to their region earlier from South Asia.

Discontinuities evolved in the diversification of basic grain-mill technologies, which were also employed to drive bellows of iron furnaces and run water-lifting devices. Researchers intensively debate the extent to which these machines were in fact employed for such purposes in medieval Europe or Asia. Earlier claims that their employment allows us to speak of an 'industrial revolution' in the European Middle Ages have proven to be exaggerated.[16] In England, for instance, 10,000 or so mills existed in 1300, but these provided only 6 per cent of all required kinetic energy, while animals supplied 75 per cent and the rest came from humans.[17]

In China, mills developed differently not because of different attitudes towards mechanical technology, but simply because the most populated southern regions relied mainly on rice that does not require milling. Conversely, during the eleventh century, Song scholars described large and complex machines for silk-reeling and weaving, and water-driven bellows through which blast furnaces could reach temperatures high enough to allow the direct casting of iron products instead of having first to produce wrought iron.[18] In addition, the ways in which the same device was used were open to change: Wang Zhuo (1081–1161) notes that Chinese monasteries and farmers had already used an edge runner for oil processing before they applied it to the crushing of sugar cane.[19]

Such examples demonstrate that any era's attitude towards innovation and technology is the result of complex social and cultural processes. Evidently, people identified technologies as much from the political and social power regimes within which they were embedded as through actual use. As a general rule, contemporary commentators seem to have identified

---

15 John Langdon, *Mills in the Medieval Economy: England 1300–1540* (Oxford University Press, 2004); Adam Lucas, *Wind, Water, Work: Ancient and Medieval Milling Technology* (Leiden: Brill, 2006).

16 Jean Gimpel, *La Révolution industrielle du Moyen Age* (Paris: Éditions du Seuil, 1975).

17 John Langdon, *Horses, Oxen, and Technological Innovation: The Use of Draught Animals in English Farming from 1066 to 1500* (Cambridge University Press, 1986): 117–18.

18 Donald B. Wagner, *The Traditional Chinese Iron Industry and Its Modern Fate* (Richmond: Curzon Press, 1997): 12–14.

19 Wang Zhuo (twelfth century), *Tang shuang pu* [Tract on sugar frosting, +1145]. Wenyuan ge siku quanshu edition-online database, preface, 1a; see also Sucheta Mazumdar, *Sugar and Society in China: Peasants, Technology, and the World Market* (Boston: Harvard Yenching Institute, 1998): 172–6.

technological innovation as an agent of change in the military field more than any other. In medieval Europe, for example, the crossbow and longbow affected combat strategies. Clearly many factors had to come together to make such a singular technical innovation effective. Training as well as heavy financial investment paved the way for new types of military equipment such as the gunpowder weapons that were soon used across Eurasia.[20] Artefacts like the heavy plough, the water mill, and the horse-collar could only boost agrarian change in medieval Europe because they were combined with three-field crop rotation, the introduction of specific grains (especially rye and oats) and because they could be accommodated in the yearly labour cycle of peasants.[21] Technologies were interdependent forces that had to be developed in correlation to allow for a leap. Contemporary commentators rarely took notice of such complex implications, however, and instead discussed the relevance of innovations mainly within their own region and remit.

A deliberate balance of the old and new stabilized cultures during times of peace, whereas war, disease, and environmental catastrophe often shed a new light on everyday technologies. Both in war and peace, technological knowledge got lost, resurfaced or was transformed. The sophisticated managerial knowledge in architecture and irrigation of the Khmer Empire of Southeast Asia disappeared when the fourteenth century brought periods of war. After substantial growth in the High Middle Ages, central European mining regions collapsed in the wake of the Black Death (*c.* 1347–51). In the fifteenth century territorial rulers took over mining administration and new techniques enabled workers to extract silver from deposits previously considered not worthy of exploitation. With the collapse of the Roman Empire, long-distance infrastructure deteriorated, but competitive medieval rulers continued to use streets and aqueducts locally.

New sociopolitical structures often spurred technological changes. In China, women who had raised sericulture to new economic heights in household production during the Song dynasty were de-skilled and pushed back into the private sphere as the Ming dynasty built up its network of state-owned weaving and dyeing workshops.[22] Political shifts stimulated new

20 Peter Lorge, 'Development and Spread of Firearms in Medieval and Early Modern Eurasia', *History Compass* 9,10 (2011): 818–26.
21 Grenville Astill and John Langdon (eds.), *Medieval Farming and Technology: The Impact of Agricultural Change in Northwest Europe*, Technology and Change in History, vol. 1 (Leiden: Brill, 1997).
22 Francesca Bray, *Technology and Gender: Fabrics of Power in Late Imperial China* (Berkeley and Los Angeles: University of California Press, 1997): 248.

methods of defence, ideas of communication, and routes of contact that went as far as Central Asia.[23] Northern tribes compelled Song dynastic inhabitants during the twelfth century to migrate south. They adapted plants and animals from the north and cultivated new plants. Exchanges from completely different environments could have a broad effect, stimulating cultures to consider new agricultural schemes and new technological equipment, which then in turn spurred new infrastructures and new political and social forms. Contemporary commentators recognized such complex implications, drawing with great mastery on local sources and means.

In many cases, attention turned to what we now identify as technology when cultures struggled to find methods of recruiting larger amounts of energy, and worked to expand resources of food and materials for use in producing the arts and crafts.[24] Population density, urbanization and the accrual of artisanal processes increased the demand for energy, food, water and shelter, and limitations had to be overcome.[25] While mechanization, slowly increasing during the Middle Ages, indeed powered European industrialization in the eighteenth and nineteenth century, Chinese and Indian textile production and agricultural processes advanced, based on intensive labour schemes, small-scale family businesses, and diversification. In the cotton industry that prospered over long periods on the Indian subcontinent, productivity relied on a multitude of minor organizational and managerial innovations, in contrast to modern industrialization that depended on the mechanization of labour.[26]

Workshop owners and state officials innovated sectors with a concern about the availability of materials, funds, and skills. Actors were concerned about simple and resource-saving solutions and rarely fancied new equipment or complex machinery in their developmental strategies. In the Near East, for example, qanats, i.e. underground channels, irrigated fields over several kilometres efficiently without additional pumping, functioning reliably through an inbuilt downhill gradient.[27]

23 Kenneth Chase, *Firearms: A Global History to 1700* (Cambridge University Press, 2003).

24 Elizabeth B. Smith and Michael Wolfe (eds.), *Technology and Resource-Use in Medieval Europe: Cathedrals, Mills, and Mines* (Aldershot: Ashgate, 2004); Mark Elvin, *The Retreat of the Elephants: An Environmental History of China* (New Haven: Yale University Press, 2004).

25 Paolo Malanima, *Pre-modern European Economy: One Thousand Years (10th–19th Centuries)* (Leiden: Brill 2009): 49–94.

26 Giorgio Riello and Prasannan Parthasarathi (eds.), *The Spinning World: A Global History of Cotton Textiles* (Oxford University Press, 2009): 360–6.

27 Edmund Burke III, 'Islam at the Center: Technological Complexes and the Roots of Modernity', *Journal of World History* 20,2 (2009): 165–86.

The motivations for innovation were manifold and hence structures also differed substantially or subtly. The Ming, for instance, standardized silk-weaving production, targeting improved quality and a diversification of patterns and textures. Consequently technical solutions in silk differed from those developed later in cotton, which in the nineteenth century emphasized quantity and standardized mass production that later spurred on mechanization.[28]

Inventions had diverse local impacts. Asian cultures employed gunpowder, printing, and compasses for centuries before these inventions reached Europe. The impact of printing on European notions of society, the state, and the self has been widely discussed. Much less recognized is that the emergence of printing also – and earlier – caused substantial social and political change in Asia and particularly in dynastic China. In the seventh century, woodblock printing emerged and prospered in the course of Buddhist proselytization. The increasing availability of printed matter was one of many factors that explains this era's changing attitudes towards religion, learning, and history, as well as social developments that came from changing attitudes towards the usage, consumption, and production of 'things (wu)', a Chinese category that embraced artefacts, the human, natural and supernatural, processes and materials alike. The increased application of representational media that occurred as a result of the printing press stabilized forms of technical knowledge and their transmission within statecraft and elite culture. Individual technical knowledge and specialized skills, flexibly and innovatively attuned to local or regional conditions, also found scant attention in such media-based systems of knowledge.

Some technical innovations can be directly related to political events. During the Middle Millennium, when the Khitan Liao (907–1125) and Jurchen Jin dynasty (1115–1234) forced the Han-Chinese Song dynasty into the South of Asia, Asian shipbuilders improved designs and enabled the traverse of large distances without touching land, effectively reshaping regional networks of power and trade in the 'Asian' Mediterranean.[29] European voyages of discovery in the fifteenth century appear much less dramatic when we envisage the dense networks of seafaring that connected the Islamic world with the coasts of East Asia during the eleventh and twelfth century.

---

28 Dagmar Schäfer, *Des Kaisers Seidene Kleider: Staatliche Seidenmanufakturen in der Ming-Zeit (1368–1644)* (Heidelberg: edition forum, 1997): 20–3.

29 Sally K. Church, 'The Colossal Ships of Zheng He: Image or Reality?' In Claudine Salmon and Roderich Ptak (eds.), *Zheng He: Images and Perceptions / Bilder und Wahrnehmungen* (Wiesbaden: Harrassowitz, 2005): 155–76.

Technologies often continued or even prospered in spite of political change. The Mongol occupation of Baghdad in 1258 did not permanently harm the highly skilled artisanal and agricultural production of this region – in fact, it remained prosperous.[30] Even though Byzantium fell in 1453, technical expertise in the region continued, enhancing the Ottoman Empire's quick rise to economic and military strength. The only cultures where technological ruptures can be seen in 1500 are the Aztec and Inca where urban planning, water management with extended irrigation systems, transportation, and mining collapsed, alongside the emergence of colonialism. As European diseases and warfare decimated the indigenous population in these regions of the world, lines of transmission were cut off.

From a birds-eye perspective, technological development during the Middle Millennium appears as a series of knowledge continuities, accumulations and losses with as many major breakthroughs as setbacks. Change occured though, so that by the sixteenth century most regions in Europe, Asia, and Africa deployed a technological apparatus remarkably different from that available around 500.

Discourses of technology

Gaps between modern and historical categories are a ubiquitous concern in the daily work of the historian. In terms of technology, the problem starts when 'attitudes' or 'ideologies' towards technology are identified for epochs in which technical objects were generally discussed separately from human technical expertise, instead of being fused in one word as they are in the modern notion of technology. Systematic research on the terminologies and discourses of pre-industrial cultures is scanty, in all world regions. Issues such as differences from modern discourses on technology have not even been discussed as a methodological problem among historians and philosophers of technology. The emic – or insiders' – perspective on discourses about innovation is thus still missing.[31] In general, scribal cultures discussed technical abilities as part of evaluations of human work or artisanal expertise in comparison with various forms of scholarship, whereas they discussed innovations and inventions as part of all sorts of material objects new to a given cultural setting. Textual recording during the Middle Millennium was

---

30 Denise Aigle, 'Loi mongole vs loi islamique: entre mythe et réalité', *Annales. Histoire, Sciences Sociales* 59, 5/6 (2004): 971–96.
31 Marcus Popplow, *Neu, nützlich und erfindungsreich: Die Idealisierung von Technik in der frühen Neuzeit* (Münster, New York: Waxmann, 1998).

clustered in political and religious centres that shaped notions and visual representations of technical innovation.

The relationship between actual innovations and their written documentation is complex and ambiguous and none used classifications such as 'innovation', 'invention', and 'technology' in the same sense that we understand these terms today. Instead, scholars during this period debated the impact of innovations on the human mind, the moral value of work or the consumption of luxury goods for personal or ritual usage.[32]

Contemporaries labelled issues purposefully as new or old to situate tools, weapons and machines, large-scale technical projects, and practical and managerial production methods within complex ethical, social, or individual concerns. In the *Wujing zongyao* (Collection of the most important military techniques, 1044) compiled by Zeng Gongliang (998–1078), Ding Du and Yang Weide (n.d.), military tactics were endorsed with references to ancient times, classical studies, and the idealized Zhou state (fifth–seventh centuries), but the text also promoted the use of novel improved weaponry. In many places, soldiers actually engaged in war employed the latest products and most innovative technologies, while the civilian elites claimed to have superior knowledge about military principles, drawing on examples from history.

References to the past in this era both in the West and East bestowed gravitas on new ideas or products. In philosophical debates on *wuyuan*, the 'origin of things', however, Chinese scholars gave novelties a past primarily to substantiate their cultural relevance. Thus, Lü Bi in the seventeenth century explained the south-pointing chariot – a mechanism that was meant to keep pointing south whichever direction the vehicle turned – as the product of a long process of knowledge accumulation and successive subtle and substantial innovations by sages who had invented the wheel, the chariot, and the needle that again were based on earlier developments such as the bi-disc, or the spear. Lü recalled this nexus as a reminder for rightful and moral rulership in full awareness that the knowledge to construct this machine was in fact already lost.[33]

---

32 Themes such as the value of work were anchored in Chinese classics of the pre-imperial period like the *Li ji* (Book of Rites) or the *Kaogong ji* (Artificers Record). For Europe, see George Ovitt, *The Restoration of Perfection: Labor and Technology in Medieval Culture* (New Brunswick: Rutgers University Press, 1987).

33 Lü Bi (seventeenth century), *Shiwu chulüe* (Preliminary Summary of Things and Affairs). Siku quanshu cunmu congshu, zibu 98 (Ji'nan: Qi lu shushi chubanshe 1995 [reprint of 1637 edition]), ch. 33, 13a.

Within these debates on the 'origin of things' Chinese scholars pondered technologies and innovation as admonitions and chances for human development.[34] Imperial historiography often invoked technological innovations within a rhetoric of political and cultural dominance. Mythical figures such as the Yellow Emperor gave the civilized inhabitants of Chinese culture the implements and methods to write, print, and construct a boat or cart, while barbarians clothed themselves with furs and feathers, hunted for food or collected wild berries. Similarly, European scholars situated artisans' knowledge within general accounts of human understanding and endeavour.[35]

In China, artisanal communities informed such discourses even though historiography has highlighted the scholarly role. As a general rule, craftsmen seem to have disguised their original trade when rising into higher ranks. Artisans participated in and affected literati thought; natural philosophers brought new developments and patterns of thought into the mainstream, pondered practices and legitimized new utensils.

Technical treatises, visual representations, and scale models

Since the time of Michael Polanyi, numerous studies have indicated the role of practice and explained how 'tacit' knowledge plays an important role in the recognition of technological development and historical reflections on it. Historians of technology have not yet studied the diverse forms of artisanal expertise systematically. However, even if codification in everyday activities embedded in the diverse traditions of local family communities or regional expert communities might not be as visible as knowledge codified in writing or drawing, it doubtless secured the application and transmission of technical knowledge in various world regions. Stunning works of art produced from a wide range of materials such as metals, stone, glass, wood, and ceramics resulted from this kind of expertise. Technical instruction based on imitation rather than on specialized vocabulary and teaching institutions could cross language borders, as long as the persons involved agreed on the transmission of the expertise.

34 Martina Siebert, 'Making Technology History', in Schäfer, *Cultures of Knowledge*, 253–81, here 268.
35 Elspeth Whitney, *Paradise Restored: The Mechanical Arts from Antiquity Through the Thirteenth Century* (Transactions of the American Philosophical Society, 80[1]; Philadelphia: American Philosophical Society, 1990).

Between 500 and 1500, the makers and creators of technologies conveyed their knowledge within collaborative networks. They learned from each other and through the interchange of samples, tools or products, stabilizing their trade with ritual, social and cultural practices. Across Eurasia technical procedures were also shared through text and images, a development that formed part of the far-reaching changes in communication induced by the spread of paper from China over to the Islamic world to Europe during the Middle Millennium. Textual scripts aimed to preserve and transmit practical knowledge within a scholarly realm and elite context. To what extent texts and images also served to instruct, or were directly employed in the realization of technical projects, is still open to debate.

Across cultures, elites demonstrated a keen interest in the circulation of agricultural expertise. In China rulers pondered the documentation of farming techniques, along with spinning and weaving, as issues of societal and individual moral development in state and philosophical contexts, making agronomy a 'science of the state'.[36] In the Islamic world, officials of the Muslim caliphates equally attempted to advance new cultivation methods.[37] In Europe, by contrast, treatises on agronomy, closely linking to Roman antiquity, portrayed ideals and did not ponder practical application.

From the ninth century, scholars writing in Arabic also produced illustrated treatises on mechanical contrivances, automata, and water-lifting devices. Such works brought attention to individual expertise and ability. Rulers commissioned compilations on technical issues to substantiate their own mandate over a field of knowledge. Fifteenth-century Italian authors addressed elites in treatises on architecture and civil and military mechanical engineering. European monks described the material properties, formulae, and procedures of crafts that artisans had previously only transmitted orally and visually from father to son, or from master to disciple. In the twelfth century the German Benedictine priest known by the pseudonym 'Theophilus' provides in a work called *Diversarum artium schedula* (List of various arts) instructions for religious decorative art including painting, metalwork,

---

36 For a discussion of agricultural treatises and their content, see Francesca Bray, *Science and Civilisation in China*, vol. vi, Part 2: *Agriculture*, ed. Joseph Needham (Cambridge University Press, 1984).

37 Karl W. Butzer, 'The Islamic Traditions of Agroecology: Crosscultural Experience, Ideas and Innovations', *Cultural Geographies* (January 1994): 7–50; Michael Decker, 'Plants and Progress. Rethinking the Islamic Agricultural Revolution', *Journal of Global History* 20 (2009): 187–206.

stained glass windows, organ-building, and casting bells. The author justifies his interest as a form of worshipping God, probably responding to contemporary critics who condemned such superfluous luxuries. In China, such works were written by scholars and artisans advancing into officialdom. Liu Ji (1311–75) in *Duoneng bishi* (The many doings of vulgar affairs) gave an encyclopaedic overview of dyeing procedures, medicinal mixtures, and cooking recipes, alongside instructions for divination, farming, and the use of utensils.

Authors and states that promoted texts as a way of disseminating technical information were well aware of their audiences. Their rhetoric expressed a keen concern for openness, and at other times emphasized secrecy for ideological or marketing reasons. Works that stressed the need for open access still silently withheld crucial information that would have enabled the reader to put the process into practice.[38] The privileges for (mostly mechanical) inventions granted by territorial powers north of the Alps in mining regions and Italian city-states of the late fifteenth century are one example, highlighting the growing importance of written documents for the legal institutionalization of innovative activity that scholars usually situate in the early modern era.[39]

In general, technical instruction remained firmly rooted in the arts and crafts, and was not yet dependent on the study of mathematically formulated natural laws and curricula in institutions of higher technical learning.[40] Many cultures employed basic rules of practical mathematics, often supported by simple means such as ropes and templates, most frequently to determine the sizing of technical objects or in architecture. Small groups of scholars in all cultures reflected on basic mechanical phenomena, most notably those connected to the relation of weight, time, and force in the application of simple machines like the lever and the balance. Related theoretical developments featured most prominently in texts of Arabic-writing scholars extending the mechanical knowledge of their Greek and Hellenistic predecessors. In the Late Middle Ages, a few European scholars recognized these works, which by the sixteenth century became one of the cornerstones of

---

38 Pamela O. Long, *Openness, Secrecy, Authorship: Technical Arts and the Culture of Knowledge from Antiquity to the Renaissance* (Baltimore: Johns Hopkins Press, 2001).

39 Carlo Belfanti, 'Guilds, Patents, and the Circulation of Technical Knowledge', *Technology & Culture* 45 (2004): 569–89.

40 Bert De Munck, Steven L. Kaplan and Hugo Soly (eds.), *Learning on the Shop Floor: Historical Perspectives on Apprenticeship* (New York, Oxford: Berghahn, 2007).

pre-classical mechanics. But innovation in medieval technology was nowhere dependent on such theoretical or scientific reflections.

When knowledge had to be made available across large areas or time-spans, artisans and elites functionalized texts within a variety of media such as sketches, models, or plans. Sometimes, elite actors involved in technical enterprises decided that models or migrating artisans would be more effective than texts. For example, Song officials favoured the dissemination of models (*yang*) over written instruction when asked to promote the rather basic tool of the foot plough. The first Ming ruler Zhu Yuanzhang (1328–98), believing in person-to-person contact, obliged artisans to travel and exchange their skills within state-owned manufactures.[41] In a quite different environment, European guilds in the Late Middle Ages fostered journeymen's travel as a means of acquiring foreign knowledge.[42]

Beyond Europe, the role of modules, templates, and scale models has only been scantily studied. Generally, the use of such media increased with the size of technological sites, or where technical expertise met courtly demands. European masons, for example, made drawings directly onto building stonework, tracing floors and setting out lines and curves to guide the cutting and placing of individual components. At the Dunhuang grottoes in Central Asia, artisans systematically employed templates and plans to copy and reconfigure wall paintings and plaster sculptures. In the fifteenth and sixteenth centuries, Ottoman architecture used model books to advertise and realize ornamental building decorations with very complex mathematical and geometrical structures.

In China, Europe, and the Islamic world actors employed scale models in hydraulic works, building construction, or astronomical instruments.[43] Whenever investment was high and the outcome needed to be secured, individuals and state actors ordered the construction of models prior to production, as the high court official and polymath Shen Kuo (1031–95) attested: 'The assistant official of the imperial Yanhe palace oversees the production of a wooden model for the armillary sphere.' The source commented 'according to the *Tianwen zhi* (Record on astronomy) a wooden

41 For example, see the set-up of state-owned silk manufacture: Schäfer, *Des Kaisers Seidene Kleider*, esp. chs. 2 and 3.
42 Reinhold Reith, 'Circulation of Skilled Labour in Late Medieval and Early Modern Central Europe', in Stephan R. Epstein and Maarten Prak (eds.), *Guilds, Innovation, and the European Economy* (Leiden: Brill, 2008): 114–42.
43 Klaas Ruitenbeek, *Carpentry and Building in Late Imperial China: A Study of the Carpenter's Manual Luban Jing* (New York: Brill, 1993): 49–67.

model has to be produced so that mistakes can be corrected.'[44] In about 1158, the provincial governor Zhang Zhongyan, who was then in the service of the Jurchen Jin, 'began to build ships. The artisans did not know how. So Zhongyan personally made a small boat several thumb-widths long, fitting it all together perfectly from bow to stern without using glue or lacquer and calling it his demonstration model. The astonished artisans showed him the greatest respect.'[45] Italian sources increasingly mention architectural and machine models around 1400 and their use has been closely linked to Renaissance court culture and new developments in the organization of large-scale building processes.[46] Ottoman architects at the same time also seem to have built on a tradition of planning using both drawings and models.

By the Song era, Chinese scholar–officials regularly drew sketches or commissioned samples. The high minister and polymath Su Song (1020–1101) listed all elements of his new clock tower in the *Xin yixiang fayao* (New design for an armillary [sphere] and [celestial] globe, printed in 1094) (see Figure 12.1). A later edition shows meticulously illustrated gears, wheels, and axles to evince the expertise that went into this project and justify the substantial investment. Su Song's apparatus was built, but then the Jurchen conquered the Song capital, and dismantled the clock tower for transportation to their capital Kaifeng. They were not able to restore it to functionality again.[47]

In the printing boom of the Song the relation of illustrations and textual means for the communication, construction, and memorization of knowledge became a matter of scholarly debate.[48] State managerial literature on crafts and technologies compiled during this era achieved model character for later eras. The prime example is the Chinese classic text of architectural writings, the *Yingzao fashi* (Building Standards) of the Song dynasty that standardized building methods, terminology and construction elements within imperial

44 Tuo Tuo, *The History of the Song*, ch. 162, 952.

45 Tuo Tuo, *Jin shi* (History of the Jin [Dynasty 1125–1234]) (Beijing: Zhonghua shuju, 1975 [1343]), ch. 79, 9a.

46 Marcus Popplow, *Models of Machines: A 'Missing Link' between Early Modern Engineering and Mechanics* (Berlin: Max Planck Institute for the History of Science, Preprint 225, 2002).

47 For a discussion of Su Song's efforts see Joseph Needham, *Heavenly Clockwork: The Great Astronomical Clocks of Medieval China* (Cambridge: Published in association with the Antiquarian Horological Society at the University Press, 1960).

48 Francesca Bray, Vera Dorofeeva-Lichtmann and Georges Métailié (eds.), *Graphics and Text in the Production of Technical Knowledge in China: The Warp and the Weft* (Leiden: Brill, 2007).

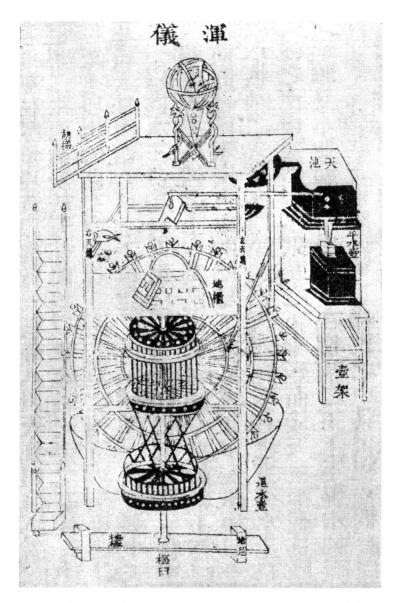

Figure 12.1 Design for a Chinese water clock, by Su Song, 1088 CE (School of African and Oriental Studies, London, UK / Bridgeman Images)

architecture, based on earlier handbooks (such as the *Mujing* [Classic on Carpentry]).[49] Published during the Song era, the *Yingzao fashi* functioned as a managerial rather than a technical guide, working with illustrations and texts. Translating craftsmen skills into the poetic language and concepts of a literati world, this book subtly demonstrates how learned and non-learned cultures intermingled in the building trade. In contrast, the famous notebook of Villard de Honnecourt (*c.* 1220), whose sketches include construction details of several French cathedrals, is of a more informal nature (see Figure 12.2).[50] More elaborate architectural treatises, following the ancient role model of the Roman architect Vitruvius, were not composed until the fifteenth century in Europe.

Much of what we know about technology originates from the products of technical processes, i.e. works of art, religious paraphernalia, or everyday objects. Archaeologists have unearthed on-site technical changes in house building, oven construction, metalworking, and textile production that are not evident in contemporary texts or illustrations. These objects are another avenue into histories of technology, even though their interpretation is difficult. Remnants demonstrate a diversification of loom technology in the European Middle Ages; they shifted from vertical to horizontal forms, while the frame size expanded, possibly following the silk looms employed by Arab artisans in al-Andalus and Sicily. Today, anonymous technical achievements that have actually survived, such as the water-supply system of Machu Picchu, and the famous eighth-century bridge equipped with iron chains in China, are respected and admired. Such artefacts give us another view, although their contextualization within a process of change is difficult. In contrast, attaching a named expert to technical achievements usually secures attention to projects whose realization is difficult to substantiate. Engineer–authors such as the Musa brothers (Banu Musa) or al-Jazari are known in the Islamic world and beyond, although their machines have not survived.

In sum, writing enhanced the role of practical knowledge and the practitioner's social status, and practical knowledge and practitioners contributed to the value of writing. Artisans deliberately identified themselves as scholars, whilst scholars substantiated their practical abilities by writing about them. Before 1500 technical instructions were based on imitation and

---

49 Feng Jiren, *Chinese Architecture and Metaphor: Song Culture in the Yingzao fashi Building Manual* (Honolulu: University of Hawai'i Press, 2012).
50 Carl F. Barnes (ed.), *The Portfolio of Villard de Honnecourt* (Aldershot: Ashgate, 2009).

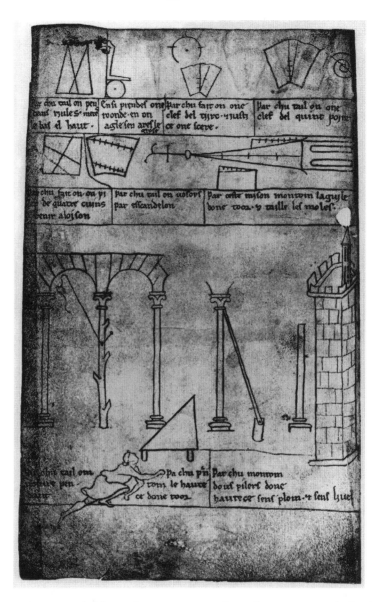

Figure 12.2 Geometrical figures for construction, arches and man measuring the height of a tower (facsimile copy, pen & ink on paper), Villard de Honnecourt (*fl.* 1190–1235) (Bibliothèque Nationale, Paris, France / Giraudon / Bridgeman Images)

not formal teaching institutions; practical knowledge cultures combined social memory systems, and various media. Written documents played various roles.

Transmission processes

Although models of centre and periphery, transfer and resistance have been brought into question, global histories of knowledge and technological change still remain grounded in the identification of distinct, separate units of culture interacting in contact zones, that is social spaces where cultures, represented by individuals or groups, meet, and connect with each other. Power relations, and mechanisms of trust, truth and morality affect the exchange, appropriation, or rejection of knowledge. Political, religious and social powers shaped major directions.

In terms of webs of technological exchange, the world of the Middle Millennium was still one of land masses: connections were made by land or along coastal lines. Before 1500, the peoples of the Americas employed sets of technological tools, techniques, and expertise largely independent of those of Afro-Eurasia, as did the people of Australia. This era therefore contrasts with the era after 1500, in which technology spread by seafaring and colonialism on a global scale.

For a long time, historians of technology equated transmission processes with the rise of European power at the end of the sixteenth century. More recently, they have acknowledged the reciprocity of exchange, and the focus of studies has moved from transmission to circulation and the processes of mediation, adaptation, and translation. Considerable exchange of merchandise and technical ideas over large distances across Eurasia marks the Middle Millennium, but mostly the exchange happened from one neighboring power to the next. Regions fostered close linkages informed by diverse ideas and products, then developed quite autochthonous technological cultures. Northern European, Mediterranean, Near Eastern, East or Southeast Asian, African, and North or South American cultures each produced distinctive forms of coastal ships with specific features that existed nowhere else. Chinese shipbuilders built large ships with watertight sealed compartments that allowed long-distance trade and explorations to Arabia and the East African coasts. Such exchanges were still extraordinary, and thus, while building technologies travelled, most shipyards continued to produce ships for distinctive regional purposes and conditions and thus local styles were maintained. Towards the end of the period the Portuguese started to mix

European traditions of shipbuilding, creating caravels and carracks that enabled journeys across the Indian Ocean and eventually to the Americas.

Transmission happened by chance within trade contexts, through individuals, or through political initiatives.[51] Territorial powers attracted and recruited foreign technical experts for civil and military purposes. Courts and communal administrations offered privileges to artisans with desired skills. Periods of unified political administration such as the Pax Mongolica facilitated the rapid travel of gunpowder expertise. Qubilai Khan (1215–94), enforced mobility on experts of all regions of Eurasia through patronage and slavery. The caliphs exchanged hydraulic experts, moving them between regions as distant as the Levant and al-Andalus.[52] The medieval Mediterranean was another contact zone of diverse cultures of southern Europe, Byzantium, and the Islamic world, drawing on the material and cultural remains of Roman, Hellenistic, or Egyptian times. Spanish irrigation techniques were a legacy of Rome and previous exchanges with North Africa.[53] Technological exchange was therefore multidirectional and multifarious, embedded in the transfer of material culture, from luxury to everyday goods, works of art and commodities such as silk and rice. Times of war could disrupt channels of knowledge transmission but they could equally open up new ones. Political ruptures such as the crusades have been discussed as important catalysts for intercultural knowledge transmission. Crusaders imported traits of Near Eastern fortress architecture to Europe.

Technologies usually migrated together with the people who used them, who crossed cultural and geographic boundaries with political or religious incentives. These people often attempted to maintain coherence and continuity across regions and time, whilst being forced to compromise because of a lack of locally available materials, skills, or financial resources. Religious communities, for instance, fostered the development of such technical expertise. The Cistercian order in Europe trained monks in hydraulic works, advanced agriculture, and ironworking, and then disseminated these skills through its dense monastic network. Religious institutions promoted technologies also for financial incentives. Buddhist monasteries during the Tang

---

51 Liliane Hilaire-Perez and Catherine Verna, 'Dissemination of Technical Knowledge in the Middle Ages and the Early Modern Era', *Technology & Culture* 47 (2006): 536–65.

52 Yassir Benhima and Pierre Guichard, 'Quelques aspects des échanges techniques en Méditerranée occidentale à la fin du Moyen Âge', in *Mélanges Halima Ferhat* (Rabat: Institut des Études Africaines, 2005): 73–112.

53 Andrew I. Wilson, 'Classical Water Technology in the Early Islamic World', in Christer Bruun and Ari Saastamoinen (eds.), *Technology, Ideology, Water: From Frontinus to the Renaissance and Beyond* (Rome: Institutum Romanum Finlandiae, 2003): 115–41.

era, for example, engaged their staff systematically in the production of oils and silk.[54] New illusionary painting techniques and items such as the eternally burning lamp circulated and the chair was introduced to China and then onwards to Goguryeo Korea and Heian Japan (794–1185). The effect was dramatic. Tiered seating orders, from the mat and squatting to an elevated position, became indicators of social status throughout Asia.[55] The elevation of the human body impacted ideas about the body itself, the universe, and the order of the cosmos. How these developments in turn affected technological matters is still barely understood.

Ruling powers and technological innovation

Territorial powers and their political infrastructure between 500 and 1500 created, selected, documented and preserved historical records about technologies, artefacts, and implements. Hence, even though developments in fact often occurred bottom-up, we know more about the political rhetoric of technologies and individuals who were said to have created, discovered or recorded technologies or brought innovations to effect, than actual practitioners and production. European historiography for a long time tended to emphasize the creative genius. The nature of the available sources in Asia is such that communal issues and state activity are highlighted. In both cases, courts and courtiers are the protagonists who spurred technological changes within hegemonic structures or through financial incentives, rights of settlement, or social security and status. Elite fashions and desires had both local and far-reaching impact. Elites in the Muslim world, for example, initiated the local development of delicate mechanisms and sensitive control systems for water clocks, fountains, toys and automata as well astronomical instruments like the astrolabe, which prompted similar aspirations in Europe.[56] A demand for gold among the European ruling classes or copper in the Muslim realm stimulated mining activities as far afield as Africa.

In the Near East, Africa, Europe, and Asia, imperial and religious patronage systems existed, through which subtle shifts in material culture as well as

---

54 Jacques Gernet, *Buddhism in Chinese Society: An Economic History from the Fifth to the Tenth Centuries*, trans. Franciscus Verellen (New York: Columbia University Press, 1995): 192–3.
55 For the chair and everyday culture during the Tang see Charles D. Benn, *Daily Life in Traditional China: The Tang Dynasty* (Westport, CT: Greenwood Press, 2002): 85. For the spread to Japan see Fabio Rambelli, *Buddhist Materiality: A Cultural History of Objects in Japanese Buddhism* (Stanford University Press, 2007).
56 For an overview of sources see Hill, *Medieval Islamic Technology*, 167–86.

daring technical projects were realized. In the seventh century, religious leaders promoted bronze workshops in Sotlaniganj in Bihar and the monastic centres of Nalanda or Antichak to boost the size of their bronze statues.[57] Excavations and artefacts found in present-day Nigeria from the fourteenth century attest to the large-scale exploitation of copper resources, the development of bronze casting and smelting techniques for the production of coins, ritual and decorative items, and trade in resources.[58] Gothic cathedrals,[59] Indian mausoleums, temples, tombs, rulers' palaces and ritual sites – in Mesoamerica, Cambodia and China – were places where materials and their properties were tested in new contexts. Palaces and monasteries, once built, were constantly repaired, or modified. Like arsenals, wharfs and mines, construction sites constituted centres of innovation where aristocratic, religious, and military elites, scholars, traders and artisans interacted, debating old and new techniques.[60]

State or elite interests brought technologies into effect through administrative control. Muslim rulers promoted irrigation schemes along the Mediterranean coasts and the Near East within state-organizational frameworks. The Tang, Jin, Liao, Song, Yuan and Ming dynasties in China planned waterways and dykes, sometimes locally and then again in central state institutions, on a scale that would have been unimaginable within the politically fragmented landscape of medieval Europe.[61] The Grand Canal, whose oldest parts date back to the seventh century, provided an inland route for transporting the annual grain taxes from Hangzhou to the capital Kaifeng, once it was provided with pound locks in the tenth century. The Song preferred the Grand Canal as a long-term solution to recurring costly military campaigns against the pirates that hampered sea trade.[62] Technological choices thus rested on a multitude of considerations.

57 Niharranjan Ray, Karl J. Khandalavala and Sadashiv Gorakshkar, *Eastern Indian Bronzes* (New Delhi: Lalit Kala Akademi, 1986): 96.

58 P. R. Schmidt, *Iron Technology in East Africa: Symbolism, Science, and Archaeology* (Bloomington: Indiana University Press, 1997).

59 Lynn T. Courtenay (ed.), *The Engineering of Medieval Cathedrals* (Aldershot: Ashgate, 1997).

60 See Pamela O. Long, *Artisan/Practitioners and the Rise of the New Sciences, 1400–1600* (Corvallis: Oregon State University Press, 2011), ch. 4.

61 For water-management in medieval Europe see P. Squatriti (ed.), *Working with Water in Medieval Europe: Technology and Resource-Use* (Leiden: Brill, 2000); R. Magnusson, *Water Technology in the Middle Ages: Cities, Monasteries, and Waterworks after the Roman Empire* (Baltimore: Johns Hopkins University Press, 2001).

62 In the *Ru Shu ji* [Record of a Trip to Shu] Lu You (1125–1210) recounts 153 days of a 157-day-long travel along the Grand Canal and the Changjiang river. For an English

Huge technological projects such as the Chinese Grand Canal also took place during times of turmoil. Anxieties concerning food, shelter, and life led elites to concern themselves with practical matters or try out new ways. In the fragmented Song dynasty, when the Chinese state was weak and threatened by tribes in the north, a meritocratic elite became increasingly interested in technological change and thus documented it. Social and political pressures were at the heart of the ferocious struggle among late medieval Italian cities and city-states that fostered their interest in military and civil engineering and led to splendid, innovative architectural works.

Between 500 and 1500 state-directed technical projects can only be understood by examining the social, political, and ideological concerns that motivated them. The large-scale hydraulic projects of the Song and Yuan dynasties helped to transform swamps and wilderness into cultivated fields, but dyke and canal construction, in constant need of labour, could also provoke social unrest from potentially hazardous groups such as immigrants and exploited farmers. The high chancellor of the Song dynasty, Ding Wei (962–1033), thus explicitly described hydraulic projects with military rhetoric, as forming ramparts against intruding Northerners, contextualizing such projects as an issue of political stability.[63]

A comparison between written and artefactual evidence often shows that elites overemphasized the local adoption and regional expansion of what an era defined or used as its significant technologies. In the case of China, studies of sites have helped to deconstruct the myth of omnipresent state power, demonstrating that localities adjusted technologies to suit their own purpose, rather than adhering to imperial styles, and elite ideologies or methods. The local aim was to make things work. Despite their rhetoric of control, the Song and Ming elites in fact often kept a loose rein on local developments.[64] Even with a unified rule and centralized administration, the landscape of Chinese technologies was probably as scattered and diverse as it was in the fragmented political scene of Europe. Meso- and South American rulers did not apply standardized territorial power in the realm of

translation see Philip Watson, *Grand Canal, Great River: The Travel Diary of a Twelfth-Century Chinese Poet* (London: Frances Lincoln, 2007).

63 Christian Lamouroux, 'From the Yellow River to the Huai: New Representations of a River Network and the Hydraulic Crisis of 1128', in Mark Elvin and Liu Ts'ui-jung, *Sediments of Time: Environment and Society in Chinese History* (Cambridge University Press, 1998): 554.

64 Peter Bol, 'The Rise of Local History: History, Geography, and Culture in Southern Song and Yuan Wuzhou', *Harvard Journal of Asiatic Studies* 61,1 (2001): 37–76.

technology, and the Islamic world relied on the cooperation of a number of ever-shifting local or intermediary actors.

Diverse agents of local or regional power played a role in technical innovation through measures such as water and waste management, and by investing in material equipment to achieve cultural supremacy. In Europe, mechanized clockwork spread in the fourteenth century not primarily because of monks' or merchants' needs for more precise time-keeping, but because towns became enthusiastic about an artefact that signalled the time acoustically and visually, turning clocks rapidly into a status symbol. Clerical communities invested in astronomical clockworks as visualizations of the fascinating regularities of the universe created by God.[65] Su Song's much earlier monumental astronomical clock of 1088 instead manifested a dynastic effort to legitimate Chinese rulership. Within a tradition of manufacturing acoustic bells, Su Song developed his mechanism as a way to harmonize the universe's visible and invisible realms and find order. The clock demonstrated to the populace, through sound and sight, that their ruler was in charge of time, and knowledgeable about how to attune the human to the heavenly realm.

Only occasionally do sources allow a glimpse of non-elite groups such as village inhabitants who came together to carry out large-scale works, including settlers in late medieval Holland who organized land reclamation at the local or regional level.[66] But these non-elites must be understood as the basis of complex organizational schemes that linked territorial powers, local entrepreneurs, and advanced technical expertise, for example, in central European mining regions. In the end, the historically visible figures were often those who managed to bring an innovation to effect or to set the standards in a particular location or region by selecting from what others had already developed, or by imposing their individual tastes through social or political means.

Elites often acted as the catalysts for innovation, but practitioners implemented them. Much depended on pragmatic considerations of economic benefit such as the fact that medieval English peasants accepted horses as working animals. In this regard research has proven that less highly educated groups in pre-industrial Europe were *not* necessarily hostile to innovation.

---

65 Gerhard Dohrn van Rossum, *History of the Hour: Clocks and Modern Temporal Orders*, trans. Thomas Dunlap (University of Chicago Press, 1996).

66 William TeBrake, 'Hydraulic Engineering in the Netherlands during the Middle Ages', in Squatriti, *Working with Water in Medieval Europe*, 101–27.

From the High Middle Ages onwards craft guilds actually fostered or sustained technological development.[67] In fact, most artisanal gatherings in any culture, whether organized along communal rules or by way of kinship, dealt pragmatically with novelty or traditional techniques and products, seeing which best protected their trade and secured individual survival. Clearly for contemporaries of the Middle Millennium novelty was not 'global', but locally distinct and ephemeral. New developments lingered for a while, or were even invented several times, before they took root, turned into traditions – and eventually gained historical attention.

Environmental factors

As historians of technology have come to explore the social construction of technology, environmental historians have started to consider the physical and natural conditions affecting human technological endeavour. Changes in environmental circumstances or human migration into areas that required different equipment were at least as important as political and institutional frameworks in stimulating technological innovation. Due to energy needs in the porcelain industry, urbanization, shipbuilding or husbandry, whole regions were deforested. Cattle and horses accelerated trade and communication channels, although this also meant that large areas of arable land had to be relinquished for grazing or the growing of fodder crops.

The Middle Millennium is mainly depicted as a phase of slowly accelerating regional shifts in land usage, food-production methods, and patterns of energy and resource consumption. People are seen as having ambivalent roles, being both affected by nature and reacting to or being conditioned by their physical environment whilst also impacting their physical environment through their own intervention. Technology and environment were directly linked, affecting each other often immediately and within a local or regional, rather than global scale. One of the most notable environmental events of this era was the Medieval Climate Optimum – a period of favourable natural conditions for agriculture in parts of the northern hemisphere between the tenth and the thirteenth centuries. The increase in food resources led to accelerated population growth in both Europe and Asian regions such as Song China. By the fourteenth century, average temperatures dropped again and plague ravaged through much of Eurasia, slowing the demographic accretion.

67 Epstein and Prak, *Guilds*, Introduction.

The relation between environmental change, crisis and technology in this period is far from understood: which came first and which afterwards? As Radkau notes in this volume, people reacted to local weather, not to global climate; they pondered local crop failure, and water shortage, but rarely noticed desertification or deforestation in regions far away. In many cases, attention is turned to what we now identify as technology when cultures struggled to find methods of recruiting larger amounts of energy, and worked to expand resources of food and materials for use in producing the arts and crafts.[68] The limited availability of energy, food, water, and shelter set limits to population density, urbanization, and the increase of artisanal processes.[69] In some cases, ritual and social constraints set in, or people moved. In other cases technological change was brought about. Most cultures around the world used non-fossil fuels such as wood, dung or peat for fire and heat up until the eighteenth century and far beyond. One exception is Song China, where coal was employed to process iron for weaponry and, as people attempted to get rid of impurities in the coal and improve energy output, coke production developed. After the Mongol invasion in the thirteenth century, coal exploitation stopped, and was not taken up again on a large scale until the nineteenth century.

In historical discourse, the environment plays a role as the grid along which technologies circulated. Monsoon winds, sea currents, valleys, and mountains directed the flow of the human race. Rivers were major thoroughfares, because water transportation was often the cheapest and fastest way to move goods and people. Humans pushed the environmental limits by technological means, building channels into rivers to redirect their flows or enable new connections. To counter floods, rulers initiated the construction of dykes, while other communities installed hydraulic systems to provide arid zones with water for agriculture. In this era, humans were strongly bound to local environmental conditions in their use of resources. Building practices evolved from the qualities of locally available building materials, yet when people moved, they took materials, plants or techniques to a new locale. In this way, porcelain spread and the red dye called sappanwood was transmitted from India and Malaya throughout Asia and northern Europe.[70]

---

68 Smith and Wolfe (eds.), *Technology and Resource-Use*, 464.
69 Malanima, *Pre-modern European Economy*, 49–94.
70 Regula Schorta and A. D. H. Bivar, *Central Asian Textiles and their Contexts in the Early Middle Ages* (Riggisberg: Abegg-Stiftung, 2006): 44.

The soil itself influenced technological change. Imported new crops, such as fast-ripening Vietnamese varieties of Champa rice in eleventh-century China, brought about dramatic changes, affecting the balance of nature as well as food production and consumption. Economic historians and theorists have intensely debated the causes and consequences of the different organizational responses made by China and Europe to the population pressures they faced during the Medieval Climate Optimum, when the Chinese developed a labour-intensive method of irrigated agriculture and Europeans a capital-intensive form of 'dry' agriculture. Nevertheless, similar tools and mechanisms were sometimes applied in quite different environments. The mouldboard plough was effective both for working heavy European soils and for preparing underwater rice paddies in China. Once in use, such technology could stimulate distinct forms of social cooperation. For example, because turning ploughs in heavy soil was difficult, in Europe land was ploughed in long strips with no barriers between them, and villagers decided as a group what crops to plant.

Historians of technology and the environment contend with issues of cause and effect. In global cross-cultural comparisons, environmental factors can explain technological choices. Camels proved to be an advantageous form of transportation in the arid and semi-arid zones of Africa, Arabia and Central Asia, because they could survive despite water shortages and did not require any investment in infrastructures such as roads. Beginning around 500, a new kind of saddle allowed them to be used for transporting heavy loads and in military battles, changing the pace and scope of communication in Northern Africa and Central Asia. Considering their suitability to specific environmental circumstances, camels were thus not technologically inferior to carts.

Conclusion

Technological innovation was a ubiquitous global phenomenon between 500 and 1500, yet its appearances and impact varied greatly in different world regions and cultures of knowledge. Most scholars of global history today agree that the 'great divergence' in the sense of a particular European development into industrialized modernity was not yet visible in 1500. Regions manifested diverse modes of technological prowess, and competed primarily with their neighbours in terms of engineering achievements, artisanal knowledge, and agricultural production. Regions acted on a global scale through linkages with their neighbours rather than direct interchange.

Many changes appear gradual when examined close up, yet clearly technology in 1500 differed remarkably from that employed around 500 across Eurasia. By 1500, technologies often developed through the merging of several regional traditions, which were adopted and adapted to each locale's economic, social, and environmental conditions.[71] Political or religious structures framed the activity, but artisanal experts and practitioners held the basis of technical knowledge and stabilized its circulation. Future research should attempt to write a history of technological knowledge that integrates the diverse cultural discourses on forms of knowledge representation, ideas about innovative forces, and historical choices of technologies.

If we accept that technology and innovation are historically contingent and that cultures employed them in many different ways, it becomes difficult to maintain the idea that certain cultures were hostile towards technology or ignorant of it, as has been argued for Christianity and occasionally also for Asian or African cultures in this era. In technological terms, the world of the Middle Millennium was dynamic and multifarious and people dealt with technology and innovation both deliberately and playfully. Sometimes they praised what was novel, and sometimes they invoked an ideal past. It was therefore an age that paradoxically used innovation for both reform and the continuation of traditions. People considered technological development not as a value in its own right, but as an agent of their daily life and thought.

FURTHER READING

Adas, Michael. *Machines as the Measure of Men: Science, Technology, and Ideologies of Western Dominance*. Ithaca and London: Cornell University Press, 1989.

Astill, Grenville and John Langdon, eds. *Medieval Farming and Technology: The Impact of Agricultural Change in Northwest Europe. Technology and Change in History*, vol. 1. Leiden: Brill, 1997.

Basalla, George. *The Evolution of Technology*. Cambridge University Press, 1988.

Benn, Charles D. *Daily Life in Traditional China: The Tang Dynasty*. Westport, CT: Greenwood Press, 2002.

Bray, Francesca. *Technology and Gender: Fabrics of Power in Late Imperial China*. Berkeley and Los Angeles, CA: University of California Press, 1997.

Bray, Francesca, Vera Dorofeeva-Lichtmann and Georges Métailié, eds. *Graphics and Text in the Production of Technical Knowledge in China: The Warp and the Weft*. Leiden: Brill, 2007.

Burke, Edmund, III. 'Islam at the Center: Technological Complexes and the Roots of Modernity', *Journal of World History* 20,2 (2009): 165–86.

71 Feza Günergun and Dhruv Raina, *Science between Europe and Asia: Historical Studies on the Transmission, Adoption and Adaptation of Knowledge* (New York: Springer, 2011).

Chaudhuri, K. N. *Asia before Europe: Economy and Civilisation of the Indian Ocean from the Rise of Islam to 1750.* Cambridge University Press, 1990.

De Vries, Kelly. *Guns and Men in Medieval Europe, 1200–1500.* Aldershot: Ashgate, 2002.

Feng Jiren. *Chinese Architecture and Metaphor: Song Culture in the Yingzao Fashi Building Manual.* Honolulu, HI: University of Hawai'i Press, 2012.

Gernet, Jacques. *Buddhism in Chinese Society: An Economic History from the Fifth to the Tenth Centuries,* trans. Franciscus Verellen. New York, NY: Columbia Press, 1995.

Gies, Frances and Joseph Gies. *Cathedral, Forge, and Waterwheel: Technology and Invention in the Middle Ages.* New York, NY: HarperCollins, 1994.

Glick, Thomas, Steven J. Livesey and Faith Wallis. *Medieval Science, Technology and Medicine: An Encyclopedia.* New York and London: Routledge, 2005.

Han Qi, Zhang Xiumin. *Zhongguo yinshua shi,* 2 vols. Hangzhou: Zhejiang guji chubanshe, 2006. Translated into English by Chen Jiehua et al. *The History of Chinese Printing.* Paramus: Homa & Sekey, 2009.

Hill, Donald. *Medieval Islamic Technology: From Philo to Al-Jazari – From Alexandria to Diyar Bakr.* Collected Studies Series, 555. Aldershot: Ashgate, 1998.

Khan, Iqtidar Alam. *Gunpowder and Firearms: Warfare in Medieval India.* Oxford University Press, 2004.

Lucas, Adam. *Wind, Water, Work: Ancient and Medieval Milling Technology.* Leiden: Brill, 2006.

Ledderose, Lothar. *Ten Thousand Things: Module and Mass Production in Chinese Art.* Princeton University Press, 2001.

Long, Pamela O. *Technology and Society in the Medieval Centuries: Byzantium, Islam, and the West, 500–1300.* Washington DC: American Historical Association; Society for the History of Technology, 2003.

Needham, Joseph. *Heavenly Clockwork: The Great Astronomical Clocks of Medieval China.* Cambridge: Published in association with the Antiquarian Horological Society at the University Press, 1960.

Pacey, Arnold. *Technology in World Civilization: A Thousand-Year History.* Boston: The MIT Press, 1990.

Popplow, Marcus. *Technik im Mittelalter.* Munich: C. H. Beck, 2010.

Rahman, Abdhur. *History of Indian Science, Technology and Culture CE 1000–1800.* Oxford University Press, 1998.

Schäfer, Dagmar, ed. *Cultures of Knowledge: Technology in Chinese History.* Leiden: Brill, 2012.

Schmidt, P. R. *Iron Technology in East Africa: Symbolism, Science, and Archaeology.* Bloomington, IN: Indiana University Press, 1997.

Siebert, Martina. *Pulu: Abhandlungen und Auflistungen: zu materieller Kultur und Naturkunde im traditionellen China.* Wiesbaden: Harrassowitz, 2006.

Sivin, Nathan. *Granting the Season: The Chinese Astronomical Reform of 1280. With a Study of its Many Dimensions and an Annotated Translation of its Records.* Sources and Studies in the History of Mathematics and Physical Science. New York, NY: Springer, 2009.

White, Lynn Jr. *Medieval Technology and Social Change.* Oxford University Press, 1962.

13

The transmission of science
and philosophy

CHARLES BURNETT

This chapter concentrates on the theoretical sciences: man's reasoning concerning the world that he lives in; about the visible and the invisible; about causes and beginnings; sciences that can be pursued without any practical aim in mind beyond the elevation of the human spirit, though there can be practical applications. For the West they can characterized as the subject matter of Aristotle's natural science and metaphysics, plus the mathematical sciences of the *quadrivium*. They would all be embraced under the terms *philosophia* and *scientia*. In Arabic the terms would be *falsafa* and *'ilm*. (In India and China one might characterize the non-deistic religions as 'philosophies': Buddhism, Confucianism and Taoism.) The Western tradition appealed to the Book of Wisdom, one of the deuterocanonical writings of the Old Testament, that God arranged everything by measure, number and weight (Wisdom 11:21), and it was incumbent on man to discover this disposition, as Galileo was to emphasize in *Il Saggiatore* (1623):

> Philosophy is written in that great book which ever lies before our eyes –
> I mean the universe – but we cannot understand it if we do not first learn the
> language and grasp the symbols in which it is written. This book is written in
> the mathematical language, and the symbols are triangles, circles and other
> geometrical figures, without whose help it is impossible to comprehend a
> single word of it; without which one wanders in vain through a dark labyrinth.[1]

Diffusion from one source or
independent discoveries

If one is considering the spread of such science on a global level, a basic question is whether there is diffusion from one centre, or traditions deriving

---

[1] Galileo, *Il Saggiatore* (The Assayer), translated by Stillman Drake, *Discoveries and Opinions of Galileo* (New York: Doubleday & Company, 1957): 237–8.

from different sources. Some scholars, like Joseph Needham and Nayef al-Rodhan, would see the spread in terms of streams of scientific invention flowing together into the common pool of modern science. In respect to alchemy, for example, Needham writes that 'neither the Chinese nor any other culture can usefully be thought of in total isolation. But do we yet know enough to demonstrate, or even to suggest, that the great intellectual adventure of proto-chemistry and alchemy, aurifiction, aurifaction and the elixir, was really one single movement, even with separate foci of origin, during the past three thousand years?'[2] And Lawrence Picken can write, in respect to music,

> It is our view that the musics of Asia and Europe constitute a single, historical continuum; the processes of development and evolution observable in one region are relevant elsewhere; that musical evolution in Europe is not to be understood in isolation from that of Asia, any more than evolution in East Asia is to be understood in isolation from processes in Central or Western Asia, in the Ancient Middle East, and more recently in Europe; that throughout Eurasia, the social context of music, indeed, the sociology of music, can only be adequately explored on a supranational basis.[3]

Other scholars would see different civilizations having their distinctive sciences – or scientific point of view – one of which is not necessarily 'better' or more correct than another; of which Seyyed Hossein Nasr is an example.[4]

Sometimes the similarity of an idea or technique can be explained by historical evidence of transmission, at other times that similarity is used as an indication that there must have been such contacts, even if they are now difficult to trace. Migrations, trade and travel over the land mass of Eurasia can account for the spread of ideas and techniques between the most northern and western lands of Europe to the most eastern and southern lands of Asia, and to the offshore islands of the British Isles and Iceland at one end, to those of Japan and the Spice Islands at the other. The continent of Africa, whose Mediterranean shores bound it to Europe, and whose eastern seaboard opened it up to West Asian, Indian and Far Eastern contacts, can

---

2 Joseph Needham, *Science and Civilisation in China* (Cambridge University Press, 1954–2008), vol. v, pt. 4 (1980): 323. For Nayef al-Rodhan, see his *The Role of the Arab–Islamic World in the Rise of the West* (London: Palgrave Macmillan, 2012).

3 Laurence Picken, Foreword to the first volume of *Musica Asiatica* (London: Oxford University Press, 1977), v.

4 Seyyed Hossein Nasr, *An Introduction to Islamic Cosmological Doctrines* (Cambridge, MA: Belknap Press of Harvard University, 1964).

also be brought into the global network. But contacts with the New World, and with Australia and New Zealand, are more difficult to ascertain until the voyages of discovery that began in the fifteenth century.[5]

In Central America, therefore, we find peoples who had discovered, independently of their contemporaries in the eastern hemisphere, mathematical principles in the ordering of the universe, and the Maya invention of a sophisticated kind of writing (hieroglyphs denoting syllables) and of numerical symbols.[6] But their separation from Eurasia also allowed their conception of the universe to develop along different lines. The Aztec, Maya and others built up the idea of a layered universe rather than a universe consisting of concentric circles, and gave prominence to the planet Venus (whose period of 260 days approximated to the human period of gestation).[7]

Historically within Eurasia one tradition of thought has regarded all knowledge as originating in the East and flowing West. This is a leitmotif in both Islamic culture and European science, and is also expressed in a previous 'History of the World' – that of Sir Walter Raleigh (1614):

> And if we look so far as the Sun-rising, and hear Paulus Venetus [1368–1428] what he reporteth of the uttermost Angle and Island thereof, wee shall finde that those Nations have sent out, and not received, lent knowledge and not borrowed it from the West. For the farther East (to this day) the more civill, the farther West the more savage.[8]

This has been given flesh in modern times, in which there is a move to provide a counterbalance to the spread of structures of state and society through the European colonialism of the nineteenth century and the American dominance in the twentieth, and the subsequent Eurocentric view of the universe. Thus publications have appeared such as Joseph Needham's *Science and Civilisation in China*, Roshdi Rashed and Régis Morelon's *Encyclopedia of the History of Arabic Science* and Helaine Selin's *Encyclopaedia of the History of*

---

5 Not that these connections have not been attempted: see R. A. Jairazbhoy, *Ancient Egyptians and Chinese in America* (London: George Prior, 1974), and in respect to Central Asia and North America, Peter Kingsley, *A Story Waiting to Pierce You: Mongolia, Tibet and the Destiny of the Western World* (Point Reyes, CA: Golden Sufi Center Publishing, 2010).

6 Stephen Chrisomalis, *Numerical Notation: A Comparative History* (Cambridge University Press, 2010): for Maya systems see Chapter 9, 284–308.

7 The cosmological ideas of the western hemisphere are put into the context of the rest of the world by John North in *Cosmos: An Illustrated History of Astronomy and Cosmology* (Chicago and London: The University of Chicago Press, 2008): 161–70.

8 Sir Walter Raleigh, *History of the World* (London, 1652; first edition, 1614), pt. 1, bk. 1, ch. 7, paragraph 10, section 4, 98. Quoted in Needham, *Science and Civilisation in China* (1980): vol. v, pt. 4 iii.

Science, Technology and Medicine in Non-Western Cultures. In the period with which we are concerned Edmund Burke III would argue for Islam being the centre, from which perspective the rest of Eurasia should be viewed.[9] The idea of a spread of civilization from Africa is a more recent phenomenon,[10] but the passion that this thesis has given rise to shows just how important questions of cultural origins are perceived to be.

Legends about the diffusion of science

Within the historical period we are concerned with, there were several accounts about how one's own nation or people acquired scientific knowledge, often motivated by national pride or political reasons, but usually rooted in some historical basis. The Chinese had no doubt that all their sciences had been invented by the Yellow Emperor in the mists of time past. Schäfer and Popplow, in this volume, draw attention to Lü Bi's seventeenth-century explanation of the south-pointing chariot as the rhetorical rediscovery of ancient wisdom.[11] For the Greeks, and many medieval traditions deriving from them, Hermes is the originator of the sciences. Invention myths were gathered together in Isidore of Seville's aptly named *Etymologiae* (the 'true accounts of derivations of words'). A genealogy is common to prefaces to many of the arts and sciences. In Islam we find the 'chain of tradition' (*isnad*) which bestowed authority, usually applied to the sayings of the Prophet, transferred to science: such as the chronological parade of authorities in the preface to 'Ali ibn al-'Abbas al-Majusi's *Kitab al-malaki*,[12] and the derivation of Arabic geomancy through a series of Berber authorities.[13] This carries over into Latin texts. Petrus Alfonsi, an Andalusian Jew who converted to Christianity in the early twelfth century, claimed that his astronomical tables were

---

9 Cf. Edmund Burke III, 'Islam at the Center: Technological Complexes and the Roots of Modernity', *Journal of World History* 20 (2009): 165–86.

10 Martin Bernal, *Black Athena: The Afroasiatic Roots of Classical Civilization*, 3 vols (New Brunswick: Rutgers University Press, 1987–2006); for the reaction, see Mary Lefkowitz and Guy M. Rogers (eds.), *Black Athena Revisited* (Chapel Hill: University of North Carolina Press, 1996).

11 See p. 319.

12 Danielle Jacquart, 'Le sense donné par Constantin l'Africain à son œuvre: les chapitres introductifs en arabe et en latin', in Charles Burnett and Danielle Jacquart (eds.), *Constantine the African and 'Ali ibn al-'Abbas al-Maǧusi: the Pantegni and Related Texts* (Leiden: Brill, 1994): 71–89 (significantly, Constantine, in his translation, omits the Arabic stage of the *isnad*, and passes directly from the ancient doctors to his own work).

13 Carra de Vaux, 'La géomancie chez les arabes', in Paul Tannery, *Mémoires scientifiques*, ed. Johan Ludvig Heiberg (Toulouse and Paris: Edouard Privat and Gauthier-Villars, 1920), IV, 299–317 (at 300–1).

'taken from' those of the Arabs, Persians and Egyptians.[14] The authority of the science derived from the authority of the nations from which it originated. Sa'id al-Andalusi, writing his *Categories of Nations* in Toledo in the late eleventh century, considered that certain nations had a predisposition to scientific learning, including Indians, Persians, Chaldeans, Egyptians, Greeks, Byzantines, Jews and especially the Western Arabs, to whom he belonged.[15]

Prominently displayed in the *Fihrist* of Ibn al-Nadim (written in the late tenth century) is a text by the Persian Abu Sahl al-Fadl ibn Nawbakht (*c.* 800 CE), deriving the sciences from Alexander the Great and through Iran, which may be summarized as follows:

> The many varieties of science descended from Babylon to Egypt and India. A knowledge of astronomy and astrology is especially associated with Jam, the son of Awanjhan. Afterwards there ruled Dahhak ibn Qay in the period of Jupiter and he built a city named after that planet. In this city he constructed twelve palaces named after the twelve signs of the zodiac, and installed in each a library and a group of scholars. Eventually, the greatest of these scientists – Hermes – abandoned the city and went to Egypt, where he became king; he brought with him much learning, though most of the wisdom remained behind. When Alexander invaded Persia, he raised al-Mada'in and destroyed the stones and pieces of wood bearing inscriptions. However, he had the Persian manuscripts in the Treasure Houses and Archives of Persepolis, including one on astronomy, medicine, and physics entitled *al-Kashtaj*, translated into Greek and Coptic before being burned; the translations were sent to Egypt. But, on the advice of their prophets, Zaradusht and Jamasb, earlier Persian kings had concealed copies of those books on the confines of India and China, where they escaped the ravages of Alexander. Iraq, then, was without learning until the reign of Ardashir ibn Babak, who sent to India, China and Rum [Byzantium] for copies of the lost books and had them translated back into Persian; Ardashir's son Sabur continued this task. Among the books of Babylonian origin translated at this time were the works of Hermes the Babylonian, who had ruled over Egypt, of Dorotheus the Syrian, of Cedros the Greek from the city of Athens, which is famed for its science, and Ptolemy, the Alexandrian, and of Farmasb the Indian. In later times Khosro Anushirwan worked on these texts.[16]

---

14 Prologue to the astrological tables of al-Khwarizmi, edited in Charles Burnett, 'The Works of Petrus Alfonsi: Questions of Authenticity', *Medium Aevum* 66 (1997): 42–79 (66–7).

15 *Science in the Medieval World: 'Book of the Categories of Nations' by Said al-Andalusi*, transl. Semaan I. Salem and Alok Kumar (Austin: University of Texas Press, 1991).

16 This is the summary in David Pingree, *The Thousands of Abu Ma'shar* (London: The Warburg Institute, 1968): 9–10. The full text is provided with a helpful commentary in Kevin van Bladel, 'The Arabic History of Science of Abû Sahl ibn Nawbaht (*fl. c.* 770–809) and its Middle Persian Sources', in Felicitas Opwis and David Reisman (eds.),

As an Iranian himself, Ibn Nawbakht was likely to support an Iranian tradition for the transmission of science. This includes some grains of truth, in that, thanks to Alexander the Great's conquests, Greek science did form part of the learning of the Seleucid Empire, and that there was a revival of learning under Khosro I Anushirwan.[17] Moreover, there were Persian scholars in Egypt, such as Ostanes.

A Jew, however, would claim that the Jews were the proprietors of wisdom. For example, Berakhya ha-Naqdan, the late twelfth-century Norman Jew who translated Adelard of Bath's *Questions on Natural Science* from Latin into Hebrew, wrote in his preface: 'I was worried about translating these subjects, since I found them in non-Jewish writings. But they were originally translated from Hebrew ... and I wished to cleanse the subjects from the defilement of the Gentile and restore them to the Holy Language'.[18] Similarly, many Chinese scholars over the centuries argued that Buddhism, and, later, the Western ideas brought to China by the Jesuits, had originally been Chinese.[19]

Even the most banal text could be elevated in importance by claims of a venerable tradition. A text on prediction by thunder, of early medieval Irish origin, prefixes each prediction with a reference to sage authorities, described in an imaginative variety of ways: 'philosophers who, by physical speculation with an almost prophetic enunciation according to the flourishing knowledge of excessive sagacity, declare what indications of things signify in a mystical way, predict'; 'authors of outstanding intelligence, who have described by speculation throughout the night the prefigurations of all things, and all the mystical things, according to the capacity of human intelligence'.[20]

Hubs of scientific knowledge

But legends of the transmission of science also reflect reality. When we survey the Middle Millennium, certain courts or cities stand out as hubs of learning and intellectual exchanges:

Islamic Philosophy, Science, Culture, and Religion: Studies in Honor of Dimitri Gutas (Leiden: Brill, 2012): 41–62.

17 See p. 345 below.

18 Hermann Gollancz, *Dodi ve-Nechdi (Uncle and Nephew) of Berachya Hanakdan* (London: Humphrey Milford and Oxford University Press, 1920), iv.

19 See the broad chronological survey of Michael Lackner, 'Ex Oriente Scientia? Reconsidering the Ideology of a Chinese Origin of Western Knowledge', *Asia Major*, 3rd series, 21 (2008): 183–200.

20 These are phrases from a text edited by David Juste and Hilbert Chiu, 'The *De tonitruis* Attributed to Bede: An Early Medieval Treatise on Divination by Thunder Translated from Irish', *Traditio* 68 (2013): 97–124. Here p. 115.

1. At the beginning of the sixth century Alexandria still retained much of the glory of its past, as a centre of intellectual activity, drawing together the philosophy and theology of Jews, Christians, Gnostics, followers of Hermes Trismegistus, Buddhists and Zoroastrians. The leading intellectual figure of the time was John Philoponus (490–570), who commented on the works of Aristotle as a Christian, and was, in turn, espoused by Arabic philosophers after Alexandria fell into the hands of the Arabs in the 640s.

2. The court of Khosro I Anushirwan, the Sasanian emperor (r. 531–79). When Justinian closed the Athenian Academy in 529, the Greek philosophers who taught there were welcomed by Khosro. Among these philosophers were Priscianus Lydus (who wrote a set of questions on natural science for Khosro: *Solutiones ad Chosroem*), and Simplicius and Damascius, both commentators on Aristotle. Translations were made into Pahlavi both from Greek and from Sanskrit. The translation of the Indian tales of *Panchatantra*, which was subsequently translated into Arabic and thence into most of the languages of the Mediterranean region,[21] was made by a doctor in Khosro's court, Burzoy, while to another court official, Buzurjmihr, several works on astrology were attributed.[22]

3. The emperors of the Tang dynasty. This dynasty came into being in 618 CE and achieved its first glorious period just at the time when Muhammad was establishing Islam. Its capital, Chang'an, was the most populous city in the world, and marked the eastern end and destination of the Silk Road, a large part of which the Tang controlled (the 'first period' of the Silk Road). Thus Chang'an benefited from the arrival of people of different races with a wealth of ideas. Persian astronomers and musicians arrived at the court, and the Indian astronomers Qutan Luo and Gautama Siddhartha were directors of the astronomical bureau.[23]

4. Tokharistan (Bactria) with its capital at Balkh. This was an important crossroads of culture. It is referred to in Arabic documents as the 'Mother of Cities' – *umm al-bilad*. Its Nava Vihara ('New College') – Nawbahar in

---

21 Regina Forster, 'Fabel und Exempel, Sprichwort und Gnome. Das Prozesskapitel von ,Kalīla wa-Dimna', in Hugo O. Bizzarri and Martin Rohde (eds.), *Tradition des proverbes et des exempla dans l'Occident médiéval / Die Tradition der Sprichwörter und exempla im Mittelalter* (Berlin: de Gruyter, 2009 = Scrinium Friburgense 24): 191–218.

22 François de Blois, *Burzōy's Voyage to India and the Origin of the Book of Kalīlah wa Dimnah* (London: Royal Asiatic Society, 1990).

23 North, *Cosmos*, 149–50.

Arabic – was directed by the 'Barmak', whose son, Khalid, took part in the 'Abbasid revolution, which drew its strength from this region (Khorasan, the larger area, including Tokharistan, by its Arabic designation). His grandson, Yahya ibn Barmak, was the tutor of Caliph Harun al-Rashid (786–809), and facilitated a major translation enterprise from Sanskrit to Arabic, including the Indian medical classics, of the *Susruta*, the *Astangahrdaya samhita* of Vagbhata and the *Siddhasara* of Ravigupta. If one follows Beckwith one would attribute to the influence of the Nawbahar the introduction of a distinct type of argumentation into the Arabic world.[24] Balkh was also a goal for Chinese scholars seeking Buddhism (as is detailed elsewhere in this book), as is witnessed by the Buddhist monk Xuanzang, who travelled there in the mid-seventh century.

5. 'Abbasid Baghdad in the ninth century. After the establishment of the 'Abbasid Caliphate (749/50) and the foundation of its new capital at Baghdad (762) Arabic was made the official language for the whole Islamic realm, and a concerted attempt was made to translate the cultural heritage of those within the realm (Persian, Syriac and Greek) into the one Arabic language. Hence Arabic became the language of bureaucracy and of science from one end of the Mediterranean to the other.[25] In the ninth century sponsored campaigns were made to translate Greek corpora in philosophy, mathematics and medicine into Arabic.

6. Mosul in the tenth century. Mosul was the bridgehead on the Tigris, on the opposite bank to ancient Nineveh, commanding the west–east route to Persia and India. It achieved its greatest importance under the Hamdanids, who effectively governed the central Islam realms from 890 to 1004. But in the early thirteenth century Kamal al-Din ibn Yunus (1156–1242) was teaching science and philosophy there, and expounding the Torah to Jews and the Gospels to Christians.

7. Cordova in the tenth century. When 'Abd al-Rahman III, the ruler of Islamic Spain from 915–961, declared himself caliph (929), his kingdom

---

24 See Kevin van Bladel, 'The Bactrian Background of the Barmakids', in Anna Akasoy, Charles Burnett and Ronit Yoeli-Tlalim (eds.), *Islam and Tibet. Interactions along the Musk Routes* (Farnham: Ashgate, 2011): 43–88, and Christopher Beckwith, *Warriors of the Cloisters: The Central Asian Origins of Science in the Medieval World* (Princeton University Press, 2012).

25 Dimitri Gutas, *Greek Thought, Arabic Culture: The Graeco-Arabic Translation Movement in Baghdad and Early 'Abbasid Society (2nd–4th/8th–10th centuries)* (London and New York: Routledge, 1988). For another account of how Arabic became the official language of science, see George Saliba, *Islamic Science and the Making of the European Renaissance* (Cambridge, MA: MIT Press, 2007).

rivalled that of Baghdad. The mixture of the population encouraged cultural exchange. Aside from pure Arabs – themselves divided into Yemenis and Mudaris (Syrians) – the population included Berbers, Spanish Christians, who adopted Arabic customs and language but remained Christians (Mozarabs), and Spaniards who converted to Islam (Muwalladun), Jews, black Africans and Slavs (*saqalabun* – slaves from northern Europe and Slavic lands). Cordova became the centre of a Talmudic school and Hebrew poetry flourished. The Bible was translated into Arabic (the Psalter twice). Cordova had half a million inhabitants, seven hundred mosques, three hundred public baths. It was the most cultured city of Europe, boasting street lighting and sanitation.

7. Toledo in the twelfth century. While other places in Spain, as well as in Sicily, southern Italy and the Crusader States were centres for cultural exchange between Arabic and Latin (as well as Greek, in the case of Sicily and the Crusader States), Toledo from the mid-twelfth century until the mid-thirteenth century was undoubtedly the principal centre for Arabic–Latin translations. It is difficult to identify an official policy on the part of the Christian rulers, or the ecclesiastical authorities. Rather, the incentive appears to have come from scholars themselves, who were able to benefit from the presence of Arabic libraries and the linguistic help of Jewish scholars and Arabic-speaking local Christians (Mozarabs).

8. Constantinople in the mid- to late twelfth century, under Manuel I Comnenos (1118–80, r. 1143–80). Already the emperor's daughter Anna Comnena (1083–1153) had documented the intellectual standing of the city in the mid-twelfth century.[26] In the discussions led by bishop Anselm of Havelberg and Metropolitan Niketas of Nikomedia in the Pisan quarter of Constantinople in 1136, James of Venice, Burgundio of Pisa and Moses of Bergamo were all present as interpreters, and in turn translated philosophical and theological texts from Greek into Latin. A copy of Ptolemy's *Almagest* was brought from Constantinople to Palermo by the ambassador and scholar Henricus Aristippus, and the Pisan brothers Hugo Eterianus (d. 1182) and his brother Leo Tuscus, the 'famous interpreter of the unconquered prince' (*invicti principis egregius interpres*) ensured contacts between Constantinople and Tuscany.[27]

26 Robert Browning, 'An Unpublished Funeral Oration on Anna Comnena', in R. Sorabji (ed.), *Aristotle Transformed: The Ancient Commentators and Their Influence* (London: Duckworth, 1990): 393–406.

27 Charles Homer Haskins, *Studies in the History of Mediaeval Science*, 2nd edn. (Cambridge, MA: Harvard University Press, 1927): 213–18.

9. Tabriz at the turn of the thirteenth to fourteenth centuries. After the Mongols, through their conquests from China to the borders of Europe, established a Pax Mongolica and the Silk Road enjoyed a second period of activity, Tabriz became a cultural centre of great importance. Rashīd al-Dīn (1247–1318), a vizier for the Ilkhanid Khan stated that

> in these days, when, thank God, all corners of the earth are under our control and that of Chinggis Khan's illustrious family, and philosophers, astronomers, scholars, and historians of all religions and nations – Cathay [northern China], Machin [southern China], India, Kashmir, Tibet, Uyghur, and other nations of Turks, Arabs, and Franks – are gathered in droves at our glorious court, each and every one of them possessing copies of the histories, stories, and beliefs of their own people.[28]

Among these scholars was a Chinese astronomer, Fu Mengchi, known as *singsing* (Taoist master), whom Hulegu, the Ilkhan, ordered to explain what he knew about the Chinese calendar and astrology to Nasir al-Din al-Tusi and, in turn, to learn astronomy from Nasir al-Din. In two days, Nasir al-Din acquired whatever he knew in this field and incorporated it into the *Zij i-Ilkhani* that he compiled.

10. Gao and Timbuktu in the late fifteenth century. Under its first emperor, Sonni Ali (r. 1468–92), Songhay became the largest kingdom that has ever existed in Africa. It owed its wealth to trade in gold, salt, ivory and slaves. Askia Muhammad the Great (1493–1529) transferred the capital to Timbuktu, and promoted both Islam and scientific learning, encouraging scholars to come from Egypt and Morocco.

Methods of transmitting science

The spread of science was accomplished through books, artefacts and, above all, through the mobility of practitioners. The beginnings of Arabic astronomical theory resulted from an Indian embassy coming to the court of Caliph al-Mansur in Baghdad in 754–5, with a copy of the Sanskrit astronomical tables, which an Arabic court astrologer, al-Fazari, translated as the *Zij al-Sindhind al-kabir* – indicating by its title its origin in Sindh (present-day southern Pakistan) and Hind (India).[29] In the case of the Western

---

28 Rashīd al-Dīn, *Rashiduddin Fazlullah's Jami'u't-tawarikh: Compendium of Chronicles. A History of the Mongols*, trans. Wheeler M. Thackston, vol. 1 (Cambridge, MA: Harvard University Press, 1998): 6.

29 Van Bladel, 'The Bactrian Background', 83.

transmission, we have examples of books being among diplomatic exchanges, such as the copy of Dioscorides' *De materia medica*, the foundation of Western pharmacology, sent to the Muslim court in Cordova from Constantinople in the early ninth century,[30] or the copy of Ptolemy's *Almagest*, the corresponding foundation of Western astronomy, brought again from Constantinople to Palermo by Henricus Aristippus, acting as ambassador for King William I of Sicily, shortly before 1160.[31]

But scholars were needed to interpret the contents of books or the workings of scientific instruments. Nobody in Cordova could understand the Greek of Dioscorides, and so the caliph, 'Abd al-Rahman III, asked the Byzantine emperor to send a Greek speaker, a monk called Nicolas, who collaborated with Andalusian scholars to produce a revision of Dioscorides' work which would provide a stimulus for subsequent pharmacological research in al-Andalus. The Irish *computus* tradition for calculating the Christian calendar traces its origin to Mo-Sinnu moccu Min, abbot of Bangor, who in the late seventh century wrote down a *computus* that he had learnt orally from a certain Greek. Where this encounter took place is not clear, but at the time there is considerable evidence for exchange between Ireland and the eastern Mediterranean.[32] Oral, too (*apo phônês*) was the commentary on astronomical tables, by Shams al-Bukhari, put down in writing by Gregory Chioniades (d. 1302). Shams was orally translating from Arabic into Persian, and Chioniades was then writing down this translation in Greek. The importation of astronomy by the converted Jew, Petrus Alfonsi to Walcher, prior of Great Malvern, could only have been by word of mouth, if we believe his word that he had left his books on the other side of the English Channel.[33]

---

30 Juan Vernet and Julio Samsó, 'The Development of Arabic Science in Andalusia', in Roshdi Rashed and Régis Morelon (eds.), *Encyclopedia of the History of Arabic Science*, 3 vols (London: Routledge, 1996), I, 243–75 (at 251–2).

31 Haskins, *Studies*, 143.

32 See Daibhí Ó Cróinín, 'Mo-Sinnu Moccu Min and the Computus of Bangor', *Peritia* 1 (1982): 281–9.

33 In 'Sententia Petri Ebrei, cognomento Anphus, de dracone quam dominus Walcerus prior Malvernensis ecclesie in Latinam transtulit linguam', edited in José Maria Millás-Vallicrosa, 'La aportación astronómica de Pedro Alfonso', *Sefarad* 3 (1943): 87–97. In the transmission of knowledge from Arabic into Latin, Jews often provided oral interpretations in the vernacular language, which Christian scholars then wrote down in good Latin; later intermediate vernacular interpretations were also written down. A comprehensive list of these translations is provided in Mauro Zonta, 'The Jewish Mediation in the Transmission of Arabo-Islamic Science and Philosophy in the Latin Middle Ages. Historical Overview and Perspectives of Research', in Andreas Speer and

But while Petrus Alfonsi had left his books behind, he did have his astrolabe with him. Already in the late tenth century, Gerbert of Aurillac was well known for using instruments and models in teaching a new curriculum in the seven liberal arts in the cathedral school of Rheims.[34] In twelfth-century England, the games of rhythmomachy and chess were used as recreational activities to help the learning of arithmetic and geometry respectively.[35]

With the rise of universities in the West, teaching took the form of lecturing on a curriculum of set texts, and exploring the validity of arguments through dialectical reasoning which took a set format: the 'Scholastic method'. Christopher Beckwith has argued that a scholastic method of teaching, developed in the *viharas* of Buddhist Central Asia, was carried over both into Tibetan Buddhist disputation, and also into the teaching method of the Islamic madrasas which originated in Central Asia, and often took over the buildings of the *viharas*.[36] From Islam it was able to spread to western Europe, through translations of Arabic works that exemplified the method, which coincided with the time of the establishment of European universities.[37]

The establishment of curricula goes hand-in-hand with institutionalized teaching. In the European context, the choice of texts to translate from Arabic in the twelfth century was determined partly by the perceived need to fill in gaps in the curricula (at first, the seven liberal arts, and later, the Peripatetic curriculum of natural science, metaphysics and ethics), and partly

---

Lydia Wegener (eds.), *Wissen über Grenzen: Arabisches Wissen und lateinisches Mittelalter*, Miscellanea Mediaevalia 33 (Berlin and New York: De Gruyter, 2006): 89–105.

34 Richer, *Histoire de France*, ed. and trans. Robert Latouche (Paris: Les Belles Lettres, 1964), 2 vols.; Book III, chapters 43–54, 50–65. Arianna Borrelli, in her *Aspects of the Astrolabe: 'architectonica ratio' in tenth- and eleventh-century Europe*, Sudhoffs Archiv 57 (Stuttgart: Franz Steiner Verlag, 2008), provides very convincing evidence for the early texts on the astrolabe to be notes on how the instrument-models were to be used.

35 Charles Burnett, 'The Instruments which are the Proper Delights of the Quadrivium: Rhythmomachy and Chess in the Teaching of Arithmetic in Twelfth-Century England', *Viator* 28 (1997): 175–201. For the Persian text that was at the origin of European chess, and for its symbolism of the movement of the stars and of military tactics, see Antonio Panaino, *La novella degli scacchi e della tavola reale: un antico fonte orientale sui due giochi da tavoliere più diffusi nel mondo euroasiatico tra Tardoantico e Medioevo e sulla loro simbologia militare e astrale* (Milan: Associazione Culturale Mimesis, 1999).

36 Beckwith, *Warriors of the Cloisters*.

37 That the modelling of the college system in European universities itself mirrors, and derived from, the Arabic *waqf* system is the argument of George Makdisi, *The Rise of Colleges: Institutions of Learning in Islam and the West* (Edinburgh University Press, 1981). Both Makdisi's and Beckwith's theses are thought-provoking; they draw undeniable parallels between Western institutions and methods and those of the East, but they have not received universal acceptance.

by the texts available and studied in the source language.[38] A translation of a text, however, does not ensure its reception,[39] and even if information is transmitted, it may have no practical use, as pointed out by the tenth-century pharmacologist Ibn Juljul, who wrote 'an article on the drugs not mentioned in Dioscorides' book, but divided those that are used in medicine and are beneficial and those that are not used and were noted just for the sake of the record'.[40] It is also valid to ask why certain knowledge was not transferred from one culture to another, such as the works of Plato which were passed over in favour of those of Aristotle, both in the transference of philosophy from the Late Antique to the Islamic world, and in the translations (of both Arabic and Greek philosophy) into Latin in the Middle Ages.[41] Plato was regarded as more of a poet than a philosopher, and his dialectical way of arguing was not sufficiently systematic.

The politics of communicating science

If scientific knowledge has such a premium, one must be careful that it does not fall into the wrong hands. There is a statement by Ibn 'Abdun, who presided over the market traders of Seville in the early twelfth century, that they should not sell books concerning science to the Jews or Christians, because they translate them and attribute them to their co-religionists and

---

38 The first is emphasized in Charles Burnett, 'The Coherence of the Arabic–Latin Translation Programme in Toledo in the Twelfth Century', *Science in Context*, 14 (2001): 249–88, reprinted with corrections in *Arabic into Latin in the Middle Ages: The Translators and their Intellectual and Social Context* (Farnham: Ashgate, 2009), Article vii; the second in Dimitri Gutas, 'What was there in Arabic for the Latins to Receive? Remarks on the Modalities of the Twelfth-Century Translation Movement in Spain', in Speer and Wegener, *Wissen über Grenzen*, 3–21.

39 One can point to several works which have survived in only one manuscript (usually close in date to the translator), and show no sign of being read, such as the translation of Ibn al-Haytham's *On the Configuration of the World* included in the *Liber Mamonis* of 'Stephen, the disciple of philosophy' (fl. 1127), and the earliest Arabic–Latin translation of Ptolemy's *Almagest* ('the Dresden *Almagest*'), both works being the subject of Dirk Grupe, 'The Latin Reception of Arabic Astronomy and Cosmology in Mid-twelfth-century Antioch: The Liber Mamonis and the Dresden Almagest', unpublished PhD thesis, University of London, 2013.

40 Joan Vernet in Charles C. Gillispie (ed.), *Dictionary of Scientific Biography* (New York: Charles Scribner's Sons, 1973), vii, 187.

41 For the first see Dimitri Gutas, 'The Absence of Plato in the Medieval Graeco-Arabic Transmission: Mechanisms of Non-Transfer of Knowledge', in the *Proceedings of the Conference on the Globalization of Knowledge in the Mediterranean World*, October 26–27, 2012, Berlin-Dahlem, forthcoming; for the latter see Charles Burnett, 'Plato Amongst the Arabic–Latin Translators of the Twelfth Century', in Francesco Celia and Angela Ulacco (eds.), *Il Timeo, Esegesi greche, arabe, latine* (Pisa: Studi, 2012): 269–306.

their bishops.[42] In the late thirteenth century the Byzantine scholar who visited Tabriz in search of knowledge, Gregory Chioniades, was told that he could have access to all the sciences except astronomy, since the Persians feared that their king would be overthrown by the Byzantines through using astronomy which they had taken from Persian sources.[43] In Tang China an Indian astronomer accused Yi Xing of stealing from the Indians when making his new calendar, which had important implications for the state.[44]

If one was stealing knowledge from another race, one had to use subterfuge to do so. Chioniades learnt Persian so thoroughly that he inveigled himself into the Ilkhanid king's court and was able to obtain the privileges that other Persians had, gain access to Persian astronomical tables and translate them into Greek. Hugo of Santalla's patron, Michael, bishop of Tarazona in the mid-twelfth century, was able to enter 'the secret depths of the library' (*secreta bibliotece penetralia*) of the Islamic petty kings of the Banu Hud and, again, take a work on astronomy, which Hugo translated into Latin.[45]

One must be wary of the knowledge of foreigners, for it could be used to one's own disadvantage. Ibn 'Abdun followed up his interdiction against selling books to Christians and Jews by another statement: that Jewish and Christian doctors should not be trusted: they may deliberately harm their Islamic patients.[46]

But, if one might incur the wrath of one's enemies, one might also meet with suspicion from one's own people. The man who knew too much, especially of 'foreign sciences', was held in suspicion. In the Muslim context, he could be accused of being a *zindiq* – a freethinker.[47] The first scholar to introduce the Arabic astrolabe and the abacus into Europe was accused of having been taught by devils.[48] Toledo, the most significant locus for the

---

42 Alejandro García-Sanjuán, 'Jews and Christians in Almoravid Seville Through the Hisba Treatise by Ibn 'Abdun', *Medieval Encounters* 14 (2008): 78–98 (at 98).

43 Raymond Mercier, 'The Greek-Persian *Syntaxis* and the *Zij-i Ilkhani*', *Archives internationales d'histoire des sciences* 34 (1984): 35–6 (at 35): the prologue is edited in Joseph Gerard Leichter, 'The Zij al-Sanjari of Gregory Chioniades: Text, Translation and Greek to Arabic Glossary', PhD dissertation, Brown University, 2004.

44 North, *Cosmos*, 150.   45 Haskins, *Studies*, 73.

46 García-Sanjuán, 'Jews and Christians', 98.

47 Sara Stroumsa, *Freethinkers of Medieval Islam: Ibn al-Rawandi, Abu Bakr al-Razi, and their Impact on Islamic Thought*, Islamic Philosophy and Theology 35 (Leiden: Brill, 1999).

48 According to Michael Scot (early thirteenth century) Gerbert of Aurillac 'was the best necromancer in France, whom the demons of the air readily obeyed in all that he required of them by day and night, because of the great sacrifices he offered them': quoted in Lynn Thorndike, *Michael Scot* (London: Nelson, 1965): 93–4.

transmission of Arabic science and philosophy to the West also had the reputation for being the centre for the magical arts.[49] A whole genre – the *ars notaria* – developed in the West, at the height of the Scholastic period, in order to instruct students how they could acquire knowledge in each of their university subjects in a miraculously short period of time – thus enforcing the association of learning and magic.[50] In China, too, Yi Xing, the greatest astronomer of the Tang dynasty, had a reputation for magic. The emperor had complained that the head of the Astronomical Bureau had found that the constellation of the Great Bear was missing. Yi Xing said that the only way a disaster could be averted was for the emperor to grant a general amnesty. And, indeed, when he had done so, the stars returned to their proper places.[51]

New ideas could be viewed with suspicion. The scholar who introduced novelties had to act with caution. Adelard of Bath complains, in his dedicatory preface to his *Questions on Natural Science*, that his contemporaries think that nothing should be accepted which is discovered by the 'moderni'.[52] Hence he attributes his own ideas to the Arabs. In Europe, as in China, innovation was a tricky business.[53]

With whom should science be shared?

What is important is to make sure the knowledge gets into the right hands. Ahmad ibn Yusuf (Cairo, late ninth to early tenth century) had said in the preface to a book on advanced geometry, claiming the authority of Plato, that one should not reveal the contents of a science irrespective of the student and the occasion, but rather only to an intelligent student in whom the rational power of the soul is dominant.[54] Hugo of Santalla, in turn, regarded his transmission of Hermetic learning from the Arabs as a privilege only of an intellectual elite. In his preface to Pseudo-Ptolemy's *Centiloquium* he exhorts his patron, Bishop Michael 'not to commit the secrets of such

49 Jaime Ferreiro Alemparte, 'La escuela de nigromancia de Toledo', *Anuario de Estudios Medievales* 13 (1983): 205–67.
50 Julien Véronèse, *L'Ars notaria au moyen âge* (Florence: Edizioni del Galluzzo, 2007).
51 North, *Cosmos*, 144.
52 *Quaestiones naturales*, in Adelard of Bath, *Conversations with his Nephew*, ed. Charles Burnett et al. (Cambridge University Press, 1998): 82–3.
53 See Schäfer and Popplow above, 319 (on Lü Bi).
54 MS Paris, BnF, lat. 9335, fol. 64rb. The full passage about the perfect pupil is provided in Charles Burnett, 'Dialectic and Mathematics According to Ahmad ibn Yusuf: a Model for Gerard of Cremona's Programme of Translation and Teaching?' in Joel Biard (ed.), *Langage, sciences, philosophie au XIIe siècle* (Paris: Librairie Philosophique J. Vrin, 1999): 82–92 (at 87–8).

wisdom into the hands of any unworthy individual, or to allow anyone to share in the secrets who rejoices in the number of his books rather than delights in their teaching'.[55] His contemporary, Hermann of Carinthia, expresses a similar concern about revealing Arabic learning. Like an initiate into mysteries he is afraid to divulge the secret knowledge that he and his collaborator, Robert of Ketton, have learnt from the Arabs.

> You [Robert] remember, I think, that, while we went forth from our inner sanctuaries into the public festival of Minerva, the multitude of people milling around were gaping at us with open mouths, not valuing us so much as individuals as admiring the trappings and decorations which long vigils and our most zealous labour had acquired for us from the depths of the treasuries of the Arabs. At that time I began to have a very deep sense of pity concerning those men who were so impressed by these outward appearances. How much they would value the undergarments, if it were lawful for them to look at them!

But he is persuaded in a dream by Minerva, the goddess of wisdom, to impart this knowledge to students, for 'our wealth increases when it is given freely'.[56]

In order to ensure standards in the transmission of knowledge, official controls could be used. In Song China in the eleventh century, Su Song, a scientist and councillor, and inventor of a very advanced astronomical clock tower, directed 'a vast imperial plan to amalgamate medical writings and print the ancient medical classics'.[57] In the Islamic world there was a system of 'testing' (imtihan), for the professions of doctors, engineers and astronomers. For example, al-Qabisi wrote a 'Letter for testing those who call themselves astrologers' for his patron, Sayf al-Dawla, the Hamdanid emir of Aleppo from 945 to 967, to enable him, through a set of questions, to separate those who truly knew their art from charlatans and pretenders.[58]

The Chinese examination system for recruitment into the civil service, based on the Confucian classics, ensured a unity of official knowledge passed on from generation to generation. But side-by-side with this, one had the Buddhist canon (Tripitaka), which included within it texts on

---

55 Haskins, *Studies*, 70.
56 Hermann of Carinthia, *De essentiis*, ed. Charles Burnett (Leiden: Brill, 1982): 71–3.
57 North, *Cosmos*, 141.
58 Anne Regourd, 'L'Epître ayant pour objet la mise à l'épreuve de ceux qui n'ont d'astrologue que le nom d'al-Qabisi (ıve/xe s.)', *Politica Hermetica* 17 (2003): 24–53.

scientific subjects, including Greek astronomy as conveyed through Indian conduits.[59] The preservation and transmission of science, however, belonged to the 'bureaus', in which different traditions were kept apart. For example, the Islamic astronomical bureau, which was founded in the Yuan period by the Mongols in 1271 and sponsored translations of Islamic astronomy and astrology, such as the *Huihui li* ('Western tables') and Kushyar ibn Labban's *Introduction to Astrology* (both translated by a team with Muslim names in 1383), continued to function alongside the Chinese astronomical bureau for four centuries, until it was displaced by new Western astronomy introduced by the Jesuits.[60] Like two religions, these two systems, one based on ecliptical coordinates (demarcated by the path of the Sun), the other on equatorial coordinates (demarcated by the equator), existed alongside each other. Thus, in spite of the characterization of astronomy as an 'exact science', different traditions can be observed, both in the West and the East, in the same way as different medical traditions could coexist.

The Unani (literally 'Greek') traditional medicine of modern India and South Asia can be traced back, through Arabic intermediaries, to ancient Greek medicine.[61] But India also cultivated Buddhist and Hindu (Ayurvedic) medicine, based on ancient Sanskrit sources. These have coexisted in spite of fundamental differences, such as that Greek-Islamic medicine is based on a four-humour system, Ayurvedic on that of three.[62] Both the Buddhist and the Greek-Islamic tradition (symbolized by the alleged arrival of a doctor called 'Galen') reached Tibet,[63] and Tibetan medicine (with its mix of Islamic and Indian) arrived in China.[64]

---

59 Kristina Buhrman, 'The Stars and the State: Astronomy, Astrology and the Politics of Natural Knowledge in Early Medieval Japan'; PhD diss., University of Southern California, 2012.

60 Michio Yano, *Kusyar Ibn Labban's Introduction to Astrology* (Arabic and Chinese versions, with an English translation) (Tokyo: Institute for the Study of Languages and Cultures of Asia and Africa, 1997).

61 The name 'Unani' is derived from the Arabic term for the ancient Greeks which, in turn, is a transliteration of the Greek 'iônios'.

62 Dominik Wujastyk, *The Roots of Ayurveda* (London: Penguin Books, 1998).

63 See Dan Martin, 'Greek and Islamic Medicine's Historical Contact with Tibet: A Reassessment in View of Recently Available but Relatively Early Sources on Tibetan Medical Eclecticism', in Akasoy et al., *Islam and Tibet*, 117–43.

64 Paul D. Buell, 'Tibetans, Mongols and the Fusion of Eurasian Cultures', in Akasoy et al., *Islam and Tibet*, 189–208. In this article the Tibetan influences on the Chinese *Huihui yaofang* ('Muslims' Medicinal Recipes') and the imperial dietary manual of Mongol China, the *Yinshan zhengya* ('Proper and Essential Things for the Emperor's Food and Drink') are explored.

Science and religion

One would expect the transmission of science and philosophy to transcend religious boundaries. Hermann of Carinthia, as a translator of Arabic science, scorns Muslims for not believing in the divinity of Christ, but on the other hand praises Arabic authorities for providing scientific evidence which is independent of religion and has always been available (such as the arrangement of the stars in the sign of Virgo, which indicate that a child will be born to a Virgin).[65] Tommaso Giunta, in publishing the Latin translations of the commentaries of Averroes on Aristotle in Venice in 1550, contrasts the inimical and treacherous Ottoman Turks, with the pure wisdom of Averroes, whose Muslim faith is not even mentioned.[66]

The transformation of science

In the course of transmission, whether by teaching, or through the translation of texts, ideas become transformed, and appropriated to new situations and cultures.[67] Sometimes, certain ideas were always considered foreign, whereas others from the same source were assimilated into the learning of the new culture.[68] The transformation of knowledge in respect of the Islamic and Mediterranean tradition has been the subject of a series of projects and conferences in recent years.[69] The circulation of knowledge during the Middle Millennium on a global level, which includes at least the whole of Eurasia and Africa, is a subject which will continue to engage scholars for many years to come.

65 Hermann, *De essentiis*, 80–3.
66 *Aristotelis Stagiritae omnia quae extant opera... Averrois Cordubensis in ea opera omnes...commentarii...* (Venice: Giunta, 1550–2).
67 This is the subject of Abdelhamid I. Sabra's 'The Appropriation and Subsequent Nationalization of Greek Sciences in Medieval Islam: a Preliminary Statement', *History of Science* 25 (1987): 223–43, reprinted in F. Jamil Ragep, Sally Ragep and Steven Livesey, *Tradition, Transmission, Transformation. Proceedings of Two Conferences on Pre-Modern Science Held at the University of Oklahoma* (Leiden: Brill, 1996): 3–27.
68 This is demonstrated in respect to the Indian attitude towards foreign science by Kim Plofker in '"Yavana" and "Indian": Transmission and Foreign Identity in the Exact Sciences', *Annals of Science* 68 (2011): 467–76, and by David Pingree in 'Indian Reception of Muslim Versions of Ptolemaic Astronomy', in Ragep et al.,*Tradition, Transmission, Transformation*, 471–85 (see 471: 'some Indians attempted to make the Muslim interpretation of Ptolemy palatable to their fellows, who frequently dismissed it as foreign rubbish').
69 A summary of recent work is provided by Benno van Dalen in 'Between Orient and Occident: transformation of knowledge', *Annals of Science* 68 (2011): 467–76.

FURTHER READING

Akasoy, Anna, Charles Burnett and Ronit Yoeli-Tlalim, eds. *Islam and Tibet: Interactions along the Musk Routes*. Farnham: Ashgate, 2011.

al-Rodhan, Nayef. *The Role of the Arab–Islamic World in the Rise of the West*. London: Palgrave Macmillan, 2012.

Beckwith, Christopher. *Warriors of the Cloisters: The Central Asian Origins of Science in the Medieval World*. Princeton University Press, 2012.

Burke, Edmund, III. 'Islam at the Center: Technological Complexes and the Roots of Modernity', *Journal of World History* 20 (2009): 165–86.

Burnett, Charles. *Arabic into Latin in the Middle Ages: The Translators and their Intellectual and Social Context*. Farnham: Ashgate, 2009.

Chrisomalis, Stephen. *Numerical Notation: A Comparative History*. Cambridge University Press, 2010.

Gutas, Dimitri. *Greek Thought, Arabic Culture: The Graeco-Arabic Translation Movement in Baghdad and Early 'Abbasid Society (2nd–4th/8th–10th Centuries)*. London and New York: Routledge, 1988.

Haskins, Charles Homer. *Studies in the History of Mediaeval Science*, 2nd edn. Cambridge, MA: Harvard University Press, 1927.

Kingsley, Peter. *A Story Waiting to Pierce You: Mongolia, Tibet and the Destiny of the Western World*. Point Reyes, CA: Golden Sufi Center Publishing, 2010.

Lackner, Michael. 'Ex Oriente Scientia? Reconsidering the Ideology of a Chinese Origin of Western Knowledge', *Asia Major*, 3rd series, 21 (2008): 183–200.

Makdisi, George. *The Rise of Colleges: Institutions of Learning in Islam and the West*. Edinburgh University Press, 1981.

Nasr, Seyyed Hossein. *An Introduction to Islamic Cosmological Doctrines*. Cambridge, MA: Belknap Press of Harvard University Press, 1964.

Needham, Joseph. *Science and Civilisation in China*. Cambridge University Press, 1954–2008.

North, John. *Cosmos: An Illustrated History of Astronomy and Cosmology*. The University of Chicago Press, 2008.

Picken, Laurence. *Foreword to the first volume of* Musica Asiatica. London: Oxford University Press, 1977.

Ragep, F. Jamil, Sally Ragep and Steven Livesey, eds. *Tradition, Transmission, Transformation. Proceedings of Two Conferences on Pre-Modern Science Held at the University of Oklahoma*. Leiden: Brill, 1996.

Rashed, Roshdi and Régis Morelon, eds. *Encyclopedia of the History of Arabic Science*, 3 vols. London: Routledge, 1996.

Saliba, George. *Islamic Science and the Making of the European Renaissance*. Cambridge, MA: MIT Press, 2007.

Selin, Helaine, ed. *Encyclopaedia of the History of Science, Technology and Medicine in Non-Western Cultures*. Dordrecht and Boston: Kluwer Academic Press, 1997).

Science in the Medieval World: 'Book of the Categories of nations' by Said al-Andalusi. Trans. Semaan I. Salem and Alok Kumar. Austin, TX: University of Texas Press, 1991.

Speer, Andreas and Lydia Wegener, eds. *Wissen über Grenzen: Arabisches Wissen und lateinisches Mittelalter*. Miscellanea Mediaevalia 33. Berlin and New York: De Gruyter, 2006.

Tischler, Matthias M. and Alexander Fidora, eds. *Christlicher Norden – Muslimischer Süden: Ansprüche und Wirklichkeiten von Christen, Juden und Muslimen auf der Iberischen Halbinsel im Hoch- und Spätmittelalter*. Frankfurt: Aschendorff, 2011.

van Dalen, Benno and Charles Burnett, eds. 'Between Orient and Occident: Transformation of Knowledge', *Annals of Science* 68 (2011), Special Issue.

Wujastyk, Dominik. *The Roots of Ayurveda*. London: Penguin Books, 1998.

14

Pastoral nomadic migrations and conquests

ANATOLY M. KHAZANOV

In the period under consideration, large-scale pastoral nomadic migrations, invasions, and conquests were much more common than in previous and later times. For the purposes of this chapter migrations may be defined as a one-way ticket, "a simultaneous and permanent movement of substantial numbers of people."[1] Migration should be distinguished from pastoral mobility. Regular mobility is intrinsically connected with pastoralist production cycles, with the maintenance of herds all year round on natural pastures, which implied periodic movements within the boundaries of specific grazing territories or between them.

One may agree with those scholars who admit that there is little point in attempting to find an essentialist characterization of migrations that would fit every historic or cultural context.[2] Various explanatory theories and models of migrations related to the modern and contemporary periods are hardly applicable to the nomadic migrations of previous times, except for the "push" (negative conditions in the home region) and "pull" (better conditions in other region or regions) theory in the most general terms.[3] On the other hand there are some general patterns. Although individual nomadic migrations and conquests were caused by particular historical circumstances, both internal and external, the main reasons for them were peculiarities of pastoral nomadic economy and sociopolitical organization,

---

1 W. Adams, D. van Gerven and R. Levy, "The Retreat from Migrationism," *Annual Review of Anthropology* 7 (1978): 486.

2 Leslie Page Moch, *Moving Europeans: Migration in Western Europe since 1650* (Bloomington: Indiana University Press, 1992): 58–9; John Chapman and Helena Hamerow, "On the Move Again: Migrations and Invasions in Archaeological Explanation," in John Chapman and Helena Hamerow (eds.), *Migrations and Invasions in Archaeological Explanation* (Oxford: BAR International Series 664, 1997): 2.

3 E. S. Lee, "A Theory of Migration," *Demography* 3 (1966): 47–57; G. J. Lewis, *Human Migration: A Geographical Perspective* (New York: St Martin's Press, 1982): 100.

and the specifics of the nomads' relations with the outside sedentary world as well as with other nomads.[4]

This chapter first analyzes some general causes for pastoral nomadic migrations in this period, and then examines three parts of Afro-Eurasia: the Eurasian steppes, semi-deserts and deserts; the Near and Middle East and North Africa; and India. It ends with a discussion of the economic, sociopolitical, and institutional effects of the nomadic migrations and conquests.

Causes

Pastoral nomadism as an economic system was characterized by permanent instability. It was based on dynamic balance between three variables: the availability of natural resources, such as vegetation and water; the number of livestock; and the size of the population. All of these were constantly oscillating. The situation was further complicated because these oscillations were not synchronic, as each of the variables was determined by many factors, temporary and permanent, regular and irregular. Thus, even annual productivity of pastures varied significantly because it was connected to microclimatic and ecological conditions. The simplest and best-known case of temporary imbalance was periodic mass loss of livestock and consequent famine, due to various natural calamities and epizootic diseases. In other cases, stock numbers and population size sometimes outgrew the carrying capacities of available pastures. This pressure often pushed the nomads to extend or change their pasturelands.

However, by the middle of the first millennium BCE there were no unutilized and unclaimed pastures anywhere in Eurasia. Thus, migrations by nomads aimed at acquiring new pasturelands were almost always accompanied by the ousting of others (and sometimes also of cultivators in the fringe areas, where both forms of economic activities were possible). Moreover, such replacements often resulted in a domino effect and initiated chain migrations. As a rule, this process was rife with military conflicts.

The main reasons for nomadic subjugation and conquest of sedentary countries and peoples were connected with the non-autarkic character of pastoral nomadic economy, which had to be supplemented with products of cultivation and crafts procured from the sedentary world, and the peculiarities of the sociopolitical organization of the nomads. In terms of economics,

---

4 Anatoly M. Khazanov, *Nomads and the Outside World*, 2nd edn. (Madison: The University of Wisconsin Press, 1994): 15.

they depended on sedentary, farming and urban societies much more than the latter depended on the nomads, and they strove for the acquisition of their products by all means possible. This had already been noticed by Ibn Khaldun (1332–1406), who wrote about the North African nomads:

> The desert civilization is inferior to urban civilization, because not all the necessities of civilization are to be found among the people of the desert . . . While they [the Bedouins] need cities for their necessities of life, the urban population needs [the Bedouins] for convenience and luxuries. Thus, as long as they live in the desert and have not acquired royal authority and control of the cities, the Bedouins need the inhabitants of the latter.[5]

With regard to the sociopolitical organization of nomads it is important to take into account that power in their societies was to a large extent diffused. Correspondingly, the composition of their polities was fluid; they were loose and short-lived. A number of factors limited the development of strong and permanent social stratification amongst nomads, except in the cases when they underwent transformation as a result of their specific relations with the outside, sedentary world. In other words, internal requirements for political integration in nomadic polities were too weak to bring on an irreversible structural change. Their societies lacked a strong machinery of coercion. In the final analysis, only the benefits from the exploitation of sedentary societies strengthened the positions of the nomads' political elites.

In all, the nomads had to adapt not only to a specific natural environment but also to external sociopolitical, economic, and cultural environments. Their interrelations with sedentary societies varied: some were direct exchange, trade, trade mediation and other services, including mercenarism; some involved blackmailing, raids, looting, and receiving occasional payments; some were more or less institutionalized subsidies and regular tribute extraction; and last but not least, some were direct conquests, amounting to an extreme form of submission. Non-economic ways, in particular the various forms of subjugation of sedentary groups, societies and states, were the most advantageous modes of acquiring products the nomads were unable to produce themselves. A striking peculiarity of nomadic states consisted in the fact that they emerged and existed only when nomads maintained asymmetrical relations with sedentary societies and states, i.e. when they were able to exploit them in one way or another.[6]

---

5 Ibn Khaldun, *An Introduction to History: The Muqaddimah*, trans. Franz Rosental, abridged and ed. N. I. Dawood (London: Routledge and Kegan Paul, Secker and Warburg, 1967): 122.
6 Khazanov, *Nomads and the Outside World*, 228; Nicola Di Cosmo, "State Formation and Periodization in Inner Asian History," *Journal of World History* 10 (1999): 1–40.

Thus, there were two main causes of nomadic migrations, invasions, and conquests: economic and political, and in many cases they were intertwined. The "push–pull" theory implies that transportation costs should be affordable and that migrating groups should have sufficient information about routes and destinations of migrations. In this regard, the nomads were at an advantage because of their mobile way of life and sufficient number of riding and transport animals. Many common cultural characteristics shared by all nomads of the Eurasian steppes, since the beginning of the first millennium BCE, or by the nomads of the Arabian peninsula, indicate intensive information and human flows in corresponding regions. Besides, when information about natural and sociopolitical environments in the regions destined for migrations and conquests was considered insufficient, the nomads resorted to scouting expeditions and/or raids.

One may wonder why for many centuries the nomads with their limited human resources[7] and less complex culture and sociopolitical organization often had a military edge on their sedentary counterparts. In general terms, the explanation is connected with three main factors.[8] First, with but few exceptions, in sedentary states the military realm was a specialized and professionalized sphere of activities. It was the occupation of only a small sector of the general population. This was not accidental, since all non-modern states faced many financial and other difficulties with recruiting, training, and maintenance costs of their troops. By contrast, in nomadic societies, with their relatively undeveloped division of labor and wide social participation, every commoner had sufficient material resources to be a pastoralist in peaceful times and a warrior in times of war. The ratio of warriors to general population in nomadic societies was 1:5, and sometimes even 1:4. This allowed them to mobilize sufficiently large armies to match, or at least to minimize, the numerical strength of their sedentary adversaries.

Second, the nomadic way of life consisted simultaneously of equestrian and military training. To a large extent these were conducted from a very early age within families, lineages, and clans, and did not require special expenditures by the society at large. Every adult nomad was a battle-ready

---

7 For example, the number of nomads in the territory of contemporary Mongolia during the period of the early medieval Turkic khaqanates, or in the early thirteenth century at the time of Chinggis Khan's ascendancy to power, was a little less than one million people, while the population of China at those times numbered dozens if not hundreds of millions of people.

8 Anatoly M. Khazanov, "Nomads of the Eurasian Steppes in Historical Retrospective," in N. N. Kradin, D. M. Bondarenko and T. J. Barfield (eds.), *Nomadic Pathways in Social Evolution* (Moscow: Center for Civilizational and Regional Studies, 2003): 31–2.

cavalryman. In terms of individual military skills, only the medieval European knights and the Middle Eastern mamluks were a match for nomadic mounted warriors. However, the European knights were ill-suited for disciplined, collective actions after an initial charge was over; and as for the mamluks, their training and military equipment sometimes reflected nomadic military traditions.[9]

Third, the pastoral nomads of Eurasia never experienced a shortage of mounts, having horses and dromedaries. However, in this respect the nomads of the Eurasian steppes enjoyed a marked advantage over all other nomadic and sedentary populations, since they possessed the largest number of horses, and the horse is the riding animal best suited for military actions. A camel is inferior to a horse in this regard. Many sedentary states such as China, the states of the Indian peninsula and others, continually experienced a shortage of military horses, and keeping them was quite expensive. In the nomadic societies of the Eurasian steppes, the situation was quite different. Their horses were kept all year round on natural pastures, and a nomadic warrior usually took the field with a string of horses.

In all, the relative economic and social backwardness of the Eurasian nomads and their mobile way of life turned out to be a military advantage in interrelations with their sedentary counterparts. Up to modern times, this advantage often allowed them to transfer these interrelations from purely economic or cultural planes onto a political one. Their military superiority provided them with the leverage for political domination. This was particularly true for the nomads of the Near and Middle East, and especially of the Eurasian steppes, who were capable of the large-scale intrusions and conquests so numerous in medieval history.

Regional developments

The Eurasian steppes, semi-deserts and deserts

In the Eurasian steppes, the most common migrations of the nomads were in the westward direction, inasmuch as the steppe belt that stretched from the Hungarian *puszta* (grassland) all the way to North China, was more fertile in its western, Ponto-Caspian part, than in its eastern one. At the same time, the most important wars of subjugation and conquest were aimed at China, the

---

9 J. D. Latham, "Notes on Mamluk Horse-archers," *Bulletin of the School of Oriental and African Studies* 32 (1969): 257; Reuven Amitai-Preiss, *Mongols and Mamluks: The Mamluk-Ilkhanid War, 1260–1281* (Cambridge University Press, 1995): 218.

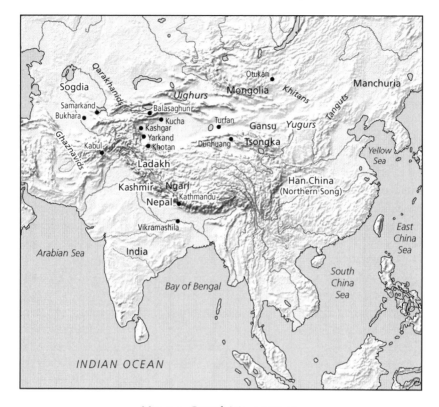

Map 14.1. Central Asia, *c.* 1000 CE

sedentary countries of Central Asia and the Middle East, and, to a lesser degree, at the Slavic lands.

On a theoretical level it is worthwhile to distinguish between migrations and subjugations, including direct conquests. Nomadic migrations, especially within the steppe zone, were most often connected with inter-nomadic and internecine fighting and the vicissitudes of nomadic statehood in the region. For that reason, large-scale migrations, as a rule, were accompanied by or had been preceded by, military and political actions. By contrast, subjugations and conquests were mainly connected with interrelations between nomadic and sedentary societies. Furthermore, some forms of subjugation of sedentary populations and societies by nomads, though usually achieved by military force or the threat of its use, were not necessarily accompanied by large-scale migrations into their territories. This was especially true for the cases in which these territories were located in the zones ill-suited for

364

pastoral nomadism. In such cases dependent populations and states retained their own political organization.

Thus, in the period of the Turkic khaqanates or nomadic empires (552–742), the Turks subjugated many oasis states in Central Asia, yet mainly continued to roam in the steppes remote from these states. In the ninth to the first half of the tenth century, East Slavic tribes and the state of Volga Bulgaria paid tribute to the Khazar khaqanate, but the Khazars inhabited the steppe zone only. Likewise, much later the Russian principalities paid tribute to the Golden Horde, but the location of these principalities in the forest and forest steppe zones prevented nomadic migrations into their territories. The Muscovite state began its career as a fiscal agent of the Golden Horde, with the Moscow princes being loyal vassals of its khans. More than any other factor, their obedience and collaboration allowed the Moscow princes eventually to be able to take the upper hand over the other Russian princes.

However, when nomadic invasions and conquests resulted in significant political changes, such as the destruction of existing states and the creation of new ones, this was often connected with, or followed by, the migrations of the nomads into conquered countries. During the Middle Millennium, there were three major waves of nomadic migration in the Eurasian steppes and adjacent regions.[10] Remarkably, all of them were connected with events in Inner Asia, with the rise and/or fall of the successive nomadic states that emerged in the territory of contemporary Mongolia. The first major movement had begun with the disintegration of the Hsiung-nu state and the emergence of new nomadic polities in the region. These events set in motion chain-migrations over the entire belt of the Eurasian steppes, which lasted for several centuries. One of the outcomes was the movement of Hunnic tribes into the East European steppes, and then into Pannonia.[11] Since most of these migrations had taken place in the first centuries CE, they will not be dealt with in this chapter. Suffice it to mention that no later than by the mid-fifth century, and perhaps even earlier, some Turkic-speaking nomadic groupings had already appeared in the Pontic region. The second major movement of the nomads was set in motion by the rise and fall of the Turkic khaqanates and their successor states.[12] In 552, the

---

10 Peter B. Golden, *An Introduction to the History of the Turkic Peoples: Ethnogenesis and State-formation in Medieval and Early Modern Eurasia and the Middle East* (Wiesbaden: Otto Harrassowitz, 1992): 57.

11 O. Mänchen-Helfen, *The World of the Huns* (Berkeley, CA: University of California Press, 1973); D. Sinor, "The Hun period," in D. Sinor (ed.), *The Cambridge History of Early Inner Asia* (Cambridge University Press, 1990): 177–205.

12 S. G. Kliashtornyi and D. G. Savinov, *Stepnye imperii drevnei Evrazii (The Steppe Empires of Ancient Eurasia)* (St Petersburg: St Petersburg State University, 2005): 73.

Turks, a group dependent on the Joan-Joan nomadic state, successfully revolted against their overlords and established their own state, the First Türk khaqanate (552–630 in the east, lasting until 659 in the western parts of the empire). In the next few decades the new state extended its power over most of the nomads of the Eurasian steppes and the sedentary territories to the north of the Amu-Darya River. It even temporarily conquered Bosphorus in the Crimea, in around 579. Thus, the Turks created the first pan-Eurasian nomadic empire. This unprecedented expansion had a certain economic motivation, a desire to acquire lucrative control over the Great Silk Road. This desire, as well as diplomatic activities of the Türk rulers, was encouraged and facilitated by their new sedentary subjects, the Sogdians, who were involved in the international silk trade and played an important commercial and cultural role in the Türk realm.

One of the consequences of the political changes in distant Inner Asia was the conquest of Pannonia by the Avars, in the second half of the sixth century. Their relation to the defeated Joan-Joan is unclear; however, the data of physical anthropology indicate an Inner Asian origin, at least of their ruling strata. During their flight from the East the Avars incorporated into their polity many Turkic and, possibly, other nomadic groups. After the conquest of Pannonia they subjugated some sedentary Slavic populations, but in many important respects their state was built upon the previous Inner Asian model of nomadic statehood. In addition to a dominant tribe, or tribes, it embraced subordinated nomadic tribes. Just as the Hsiung-nu and other nomadic states in Inner Asia forayed into China and strove to extract gifts, subsidies and even regular payments without attempting to conquer the country, the Avars pursued a similar policy towards Byzantium. Their state existed until the late eighth century, when it was destroyed by the Franks.

In the East, the Turkic khaqanate successfully exploited the weakness and disunity of China and, in addition to plundering, extorted numerous gifts and tributes from it. In Central Asia, its overlordship over local states was limited to extracting tribute. In addition, some Central Asian states were ruled by dynasties of Turkic origin. However, while China soon afterwards became united under the Sui (581–618) and later under the Tang (618–907) dynasties, the Türk khaqanate began to disintegrate due to overextension, revolts of subordinated tribes, and the dynastic instability within the royal clan so characteristic of nomadic states lacking strictly fixed rules of succession. The empire was divided into the western and eastern khaqanates. Further revolts, splits, internecine strife, and often unsuccessful wars with China followed. Some eastern Turks migrated to China and were brought into

Tang military service as a border security force against other nomads. Soon afterwards they revolted and managed to restore their state, the Second Eastern Türk Khaqanate (682–742), until, in 742, it was finally destroyed by a coalition of its former nomadic vassals, Basmils, Qarluks, and Uighurs.

Meanwhile, the Uighurs established their hegemony in Inner Asia, which lasted from 744 until 840.[13] This development had set the stage for a series of new migrations. Thus, the Qarluks were forced to move to Central Asia and became masters of the Western Türk lands in Semirechie. In 840, the Uighur khaqanate was destroyed by its former vassals, the Qirghiz, whose lands were located on the Upper Yenisei River. The defeated Uighurs fled in different directions, some of them moving to eastern Turkestan.[14] There they subjugated the local sedentary Iranian or Tokharian population, which in time resulted in its Turkicization. However, in eastern Turkestan opportunities for leading a pastoral nomadic way of life were rather limited. The Uighurs began to settle in towns and to engage in agriculture.[15]

There was another important consequence of these events. For many centuries, Mongolia was the heartland of the Turkic nomads. However, in the second half of the first millennium, and perhaps even earlier, many began to migrate westwards into Central Asia, or still further, to the East European steppes. In the tenth century, pressure from the Mongolian-speaking Khitans drove most of the remaining Turkic groups out of the region. The vacuum was filled by Mongolian nomads migrating from Manchuria. Since that time and up to the present day, Mongolia became their new homeland.

By the end of the ninth century the Turks constituted a vast majority of the nomads in the Eurasian steppes, from Pannonia to Mongolia and Tibet. In the far west, one group of the Bulghar tribes defeated by the Khazars migrated to the Balkans (c. 679), subjugated some sedentary Slavic tribes, and established a state there, eventually assimilating to their more numerous subjects.[16] Another group of Bulghars withdrew to the north, settled in the

13 Colin Mackerras, *The Uighur Empire According to the T'ang Dynastic Histories: A Study in Sino-Uighur Relations, 744–840* (Canberra: Australian National University Press, 1972).
14 G. Maliavkin, "K voprosu o rasselenii uigurov posle gibeli Uigurskogo kaganata" ("On the Settling of the Uighurs after the Downfall of Uighur Khaqanate"), *Izvestiia Sibirskogo otdeleniia Akademii Nauk SSSR*, No 1. Seriia obshchestvennykh nauk, vyp. 1 (1972): 27–35.
15 A. von Gabain, *Das Leben im uigurischen Königreich von Qočo (850–1250)* (Wiesbaden: Otto Harrassowitz, 1973), vol. 1.
16 G. G. Litavrin, "Formirovanie i razvitie bolgarskogo rannefeodal'nogo gosudarstva" ("Formation and Development of the Early Feudal Bulghar State"), in G. G. Litavrin (ed.), *Rannefeodal'nye gosudarstva na Balkanakh VI–XII vv.* (Moscow: Nauka, 1985): 144.

Middle Volga region and coalesced with the local, sedentary, Finnic-speaking tribes into another state.[17] In this case, the Turkic language prevailed.

The only exception to the almost complete predominance of Turkic nomads in the East European steppes in the second half of the first millennium were the Magyars (Hungarians). Their language belongs to the Ugorian branch of the Finno-Ugric linguistic family. The location of their original homeland is far from resolved.[18] It is well known, however, that in the eighth–ninth centuries they lived in the Pontic steppes and were within the political orbit of the Khazar state. Under pressure from the Pechenegs advancing from the East, they crossed the Carpathians in 895 and conquered their new homeland in the Danubian basin that later came to be known as Hungary. In the beginning, they behaved in Europe in the traditional way of their nomadic predecessors. For six decades they raided and extracted "gifts" and tribute, until, in 955, they sustained a crushing defeat at Lechfeld, near Augsburg, at the hands of united German forces under Otto I. Eventually the Hungarians converted to Christianity and sedentarized; their kingdom was integrated into the general European trajectory. They also assimilated some Turkic and Slavic groups in the region. But, most remarkably, they managed to retain their unique language, which today is an island surrounded by a sea of the German, Romance, and Slavic languages.[19]

However, it was the Khazar khaqanate that emerged *c.* 650, which became for several centuries the major force in East Europe, including the Ponto-Caspian steppe lands and the North Caucasus. The historical role of this state was especially significant in three respects. First, in the prolonged Arabo-Khazar wars, in the period 642–737, the Khazars, despite suffering some setbacks, managed to stop the penetration of the Arabs to the Pontic area and from there to East Europe. This happened just at the time when the Arab drive into West Europe was stopped, in 732, by the Franks of Charles Martel on the field of Tours. Were it otherwise, the whole history of Europe might have taken quite a different direction, since at that time there was no other political and military force in East Europe capable of preventing the Arab invasion. Second, in the eighth to the mid-tenth centuries, the Pax Chazarica served as the bulwark that protected Byzantium from the nomadic

---

17 V. F. Genning and A. Kh. Khalikov, *Rannie bolgary na Volge* (*The Early Bulghars in the Volga Region*) (Moscow: Nauka, 1964): 100.

18 I. Fodor, *In Search of a New Homeland: The Prehistory of the Hungarian People and the Conquest* (Budapest: Corvina Kiadó, 1982).

19 Fodor, *In Search of a New Homeland*; András Róna-Tas, *Hungarians and Europe in the Early Middle Ages* (Budapest: Central European University Press, 1999).

invasions. Third, the Khazar state facilitated the development of the Dnepr–Black Sea and Volga–Caspian trading networks. Controlled by the Khazars in the late eighth to tenth centuries, it was an important channel of 'Abbasid trade with East Europe. It is also worth noting the Khazars' conversion to Judaism – a unique event in medieval Eurasian history.

With regard to the sedentary populations, the Khazar khaqanate was not much different from other nomadic states of the early medieval period. The Khazars avoided or were incapable of direct conquests of sedentary states. In addition to raiding, they were quite satisfied with their vassalage and/or various forms of tribute extraction. The Khazar state was destroyed in 965 by the combined forces of the Rus' and Oghuz nomads.[20] It was the last nomadic state created by the nomads in East Europe. The next one, the Golden Horde, emerged only during the Chinggisid conquests.

The westward migrations of the Turkic nomads in the steppe zone continued almost uninterrupted until the Mongol period. Not infrequently, pressure from one nomadic grouping pushed others to move to new territories, and thus initiated a kind of chain-migration during which some groupings were displaced and/or incorporated into the polities of new-comers. By the end of the ninth century, the Oghuz, pressed from the East by the Kimeks and Qipchaqs, forced the Pechenegs to move from the Volga-Ural and Syr-Darya steppes into the Pontic ones, where they displaced the Hungarians. In their turn, in the eleventh century, the Pechenegs were ousted by the western Oghuz, driven thither by the Qipchaqs; and soon afterwards the Qipchaqs became the dominant force in the western steppe zone, from Khwarazm to the Danube.[21]

Meanwhile, a new type of statehood, the Islamic Turco-Iranian states, emerged in Central Asia and the Middle East. These were states of the conquest-type, in which the nomadic or formerly nomadic elites, who had converted to Islam, ruled over the conquered sedentary countries with the assistance of Iranian bureaucracy. The first such state was the Qarakhanid one, named after the ruling dynasty, which lasted from 992 to 1214.

The Qarakhanid conquest of Maveraunnahr (territories between the Amu-Darya and Syr-Darya rivers, otherwise known as Transoxiana) and the

---

20 On the Khazars see D. M. Dunlop, *The History of the Jewish Khazars* (Princeton University Press, 1954); M. I. Artamonov, *Istoriia khazar* (*A History of the Khazars*) (Leningrad: Izdatel'stvo Gosudarstvennogo Ermitazha, 1962); Peter B. Golden, *Khazar Studies: An Historico-Philological Inquiry into the Origins of the Khazars* (Budapest: Akadémiai Kiadó, 1980), vol. I.

21 Golden, *Introduction to the History of the Turkic Peoples*, 264.

overthrow of the previous Iranian Samanid dynasty at the end of the tenth century entailed neither the destruction nor the resistance of the conquered sedentary population. This was facilitated by the conquerors' previous conversion to Islam.[22] Although many Qarakhanid khans led a semi-nomadic life,[23] they preserved some Samanid administrative and bureaucratic institutions, saw to the flourishing of towns and made sure that nomads did nothing to offend cultivators, sometimes to the dissatisfaction of the former.[24] However, in the ruling class of the new state the military aristocracy of nomadic origin played the major role. The Qarakhanid rulers confiscated landed properties that belonged to the most influential members of the old sedentary aristocracy and distributed them amongst their followers on condition of their military service.

A new type of conquest-state also emerged at that period in Inner Asia. The previous Turkic states in the region had been satisfied with raiding, looting, and extracting payments, subsidies and tribute from China without conquering the country. But the nomadic Khitans seized their chance when the central authority in the country had collapsed. The Khitan state, which took the Chinese dynastic name Liao (907–1125), included Manchuria and some districts of northern China, as well as Inner Mongolia and significant parts of Outer Mongolia. The Khitans were followed by another Manchurian people, the Jurchens, who practiced a mixed economy with a strong pastoralist component. In the early twelfth century, the Jurchens defeated the Liao, forced some Khitans to move to Central Asia,[25] and founded their own dynasty, the Jin (1115–1234) that ruled over all of North China. Whereas the ratio of Chinese to Khitans had been around 3:1 in the Liao state, the Chinese outnumbered the Jurchens 10:1.[26]

When discussing the Khitan and Jurchen conquests of China and their statehood there,[27] one should take into account one important consideration.

22 O. Pritsak, "Die Karachaniden," *Der Islam* 31 (1953–4): 16–68.
23 V. V. Barthold, *Sochineniia, vol. 1: Turkestan v epokhu mongol'skogo nashestviia* (*Turkestan in the Times of the Mongol Invasion*). (Moscow: Izdatel'stvo vostochnoi literatury, 1963), vol. I, 378.
24 A. M. Belenitsky, I. M. Bentovich and O. G. Bol'shakov, *Srednevekovyi gorod Srednei Azii* (*The Medieval Town in Central Asia*) (Leningrad: Nauka, 1973): 348–9.
25 Michal Biran, *The Empire of the Qara Khitai in Eurasian History: Between China and the Islamic World* (Cambridge University Press, 2005).
26 Thomas J. Barfield, *The Perilous Frontier: Nomadic Empires and China* (Cambridge, MA: Basil Blackwell, 1989): 180.
27 Karl A. Wittfogel and Chia-sheng Feng, *The History of Chinese Society: Liao, 907–1125* (Philadelphia: American Philosophical Society, 1949); Barfield, *The Perilous Frontier*, 164; Denis Twitchett and Klaus-Peter Tietze, "The Liao," in Herbert Franke and Denis

In the tenth century, the economic center of the country shifted to South China, ruled by the Song dynasty. Although the Khitans and Jurchens were unable to conquer that part of the country, they managed to extract significant tribute from the Song; but in order to do this they had to move to its borders.

The third major wave of migrations of the Eurasian nomads was set in motion by the creation of the Mongol Empire and its conquests. These conquests proceeded with remarkable speed. In 1205–27 the Mongols destroyed the Hsia (Tangut) state; in 1211–34 they conquered North China and put an end to the Jin dynasty; in 1218 they established their supremacy in eastern Turkestan; in 1219–24 they conquered Central Asia; by 1236–8 they gained control over of the Transcaucasian countries; Volga Bulgaria and the Russian principalities were subjugated in 1237–40; by 1243 the Seljuks of Rum became vassals of the Empire; in 1258 the Mongols accomplished the subjugation of Iran and captured Baghdad; the last Song emperor capitulated in 1276.[28]

Along with the conquests of sedentary countries, the Mongols subjugated and incorporated into their armies all nomads of the Eurasian steppes, mainly the most numerous Turkic ones, but also the Khitan, Tungus and Tangut. By the mid-thirteenth century this process was accomplished. Chinggis Khan and his immediate successors deliberately broke up the old tribal nomadic unions, shuffling and scattering their parts to different armies and relocating them to different parts of the Empire. The same happened to the Mongol tribes. Still, it seems that the number of Turkic nomads actually relocated to the conquered countries far exceeded the Mongol ones.

After the disintegration of the single Mongol Empire, in the Golden Horde the vast majority of nomads continued to abide by their pastoralist way of life in the steppe zone.[29] Many other nomads migrated to the Chagatay state in Central Asia. At the *quriltay* (the diet of the Chinggisid princes and the nobility) of 1269, on the banks of the Talas River, it was decided that the nomads should live in the steppes and mountains, move along specific routes and not allow their herds to trespass on arable

Twitchett (eds.), *The Cambridge History of China* (Cambridge University Press, 1994), vol. VI, 43–153; Franke, "The Chin Dynasty," in Franke and Twitchett (eds.), *The Cambridge History of China*, vol. VI, 215–320.

28 S. L. Tikhvinsky (ed.), *Tataro-mongoly v Azii i Evrope (The Tataro-Mongols in Asia and Europe)* 2nd edn. (Moscow: Nauka, 1977).

29 G. A. Fedorov-Davydov, *Kochevniki Vostochnoi Evropy pod vlast'iu zolotoordynskikh khanov (The Nomads of Eastern Europe under the Rule of the Khans of the Golden Horde)* (Moscow: Izdatel'stvo MGU, 1966).

lands.[30] But in practice the devastation of agricultural territories continued right up to the ascent to power of Timur in about 1370.

However, in China the situation was different. In order to rule the Yuan state, Qubilai (r. 1260–94) and his successors had to bring to the country many Mongol nomads; others were later called up into the army or for permanent garrison duty. To a large extent, they had to abandon their traditional way of life. At the end of the Mongol rule, there were more than 400, 000 Mongols in China.[31] Most of them were never able to return to Mongolia.

The nomadic movements of the Mongol period had another important consequence. In the Middle East, Central Asia, and the Eurasian steppes – with the exception of Mongolia – the less numerous Mongol nomads were invariably Turkicized. The end result of tribal displacements and reconfigurations of the Mongol and, later, of the Timurid eras was the emergence of new and subsequently retribalized ethnic units, some of which eventually crystallized into many of the Turkic peoples of today.[32]

The Near and Middle East and North Africa

For ecological and historical reasons, in the Islamic heartland nomads and sedentaries were more closely linked to each other than in some other regions like China, India, or East Europe. It is worth distinguishing between nomadic migrations that took place within this region and those that brought nomads there from the Eurasian steppes. The Bedouins were never empire-builders. With few and incomplete exceptions – such as the short-lived Almoravid Empire in which the Sanhaja nomads, pressed by the Zenata, were temporarily united by a reformed Islamic leadership – the same can be said about the North African Berbers. Interestingly, the creation of the Almoravid Empire was not followed by a mass Berber migration into the conquered lands. In these respects, the Turks and Mongols were quite different.

The creation of the Islamic Caliphate resulted in numerous Bedouin migrations, which continued throughout the whole period. Already in the seventh century a large number of them moved into Mesopotamia. One of the latest large-scale Bedouin migrations was the Hilalian invasion of North

---

30 V. V. Barthold, *Dvenadtsat' lektsii po istorii turetskikh narodov Srednei Azii (Twelve Lectures on the History of Central Asia)* (Moscow: Izdatel'stvo vostochnoi literatury, 1963), vol. II, 69.

31 Lubsan Danzan (trans.), *Altan Tobchi ("Zolotoe skazanie" (Altan Tobchi (The Golden Legend))* (Moscow: Nauka, 1973): 252.

32 Golden, *An Introduction to the History of the Turkic Peoples*, 292; Peter B. Golden, *Ethnicity and State Formation in Pre-Činggisid Eurasia* (Bloomington: Indiana University Press, 2001): 45–6.

Africa in the eleventh century. It is worth noting, however, that the victorious Banu Hilal never attempted to create their own state. Their various tribes just became allies of local dynasties and occupied privileged positions in their states. In addition, there were numerous Berber migrations within the North African region. However, unlike many migrations of the nomads of the Eurasian steppes, the migrations of Bedouins from Arabia in the early Islamic period were often organized, encouraged and directed by the central sedentary powers.[33] Many were persuaded or forced to settle in garrison towns, cities or villages; others continued to maintain the nomadic way of life.

During the Middle Millennium, the invasions and migrations of great masses of nomads from Arabia, and especially from the Eurasian steppes, led to the territorial expansion of nomadism and to a significant increase in the number of nomads in Anatolia, Iran, and Afghanistan. The most important role in these processes was that of the Eurasian steppe nomads. The Bedouins could not penetrate the Anatolian plateau because its climate was too cold for their dromedaries. In Iran, Bedouins who continued to pursue a nomadic life occupied only the southern province of Fars and a part of Khuzistan.[34]

The first mass migration of the Turkic-speaking nomads to the Middle Eastern countries took place after the Seljuk conquests.[35] The Seljuk Empire was another Turco-Iranian state, and its creation was unexpected even by the Seljuks themselves. In the first half of the eleventh century, some rebellious Oghuz nomads, originally from the Syr-Darya region, fled under the leadership of the Seljuk dynasty to Khurasan and began to pillage the province. The attempts of Mas'ud, the ruler of the Ghaznavid state, to pacify them failed, and in 1040 he was defeated in the battle at Dandanqan. Soon after this

---

33 Fred McGraf Donner, *The Early Islamic Conquests* (Princeton University Press, 1981): 228, 248.

34 Xavier de Planhol, *Les fondements géographiques de l'histoire de l'Islam* (Paris: Flammarion, 1968): 73; Claude Cahen, "Tribes, Cities and Social Organization," in R. N. Frye (ed.), *The Cambridge History of Iran* (Cambridge University Press, 1975), vol. IV, 310.

35 On the Seljuks and their state see V. . Gordlevsky, *Gozudarstvo Sel'dzhukidov Maloi Azii (The State of the Seljuks in Asia Minor)* (Moscow: Izdastel'stvo vostochnoi literatury, 1960), vol. I; Barthold, *Turkestan*; Ann K. S. Lambton, "The Internal Structure of the Saljuq Empire," in J. A. Boyle (ed.), *The Cambridge History of Iran* (Cambridge University Press, 1968), vol. V; C. E. Bosworth, "The Political and Dynastic History of the Iranian World (A.D. 1000–1217)," in Boyle (ed.), *The Cambridge History of Iran* (Cambridge University Press, 1968), vol. V, 1–202; S. G. Agadzhanov, *Ocherki istorii oguzov i turkmen Srednei Azii IX–XII vv. (Essays on the History of the Oghuz and Turkmen in Central Asia in the IX–XII Centuries)* (Ashkhabad: Ylym, 1969); S. G. Agadzhanov, *Der Staat der Seldschukiden und Mittelasien im 11.-12. Jahrhundert* (Berlin: Reinhold Schletzer Verlag, 1994); Andrew C. S Peacock, *Early Seljük History: A New Interpretation* (London: Routledge, 2010); C. Lange and S. Mecit (eds.), *The Seljuks: Politics, Society and Culture* (Edinburgh University Press, 2011).

decisive historical event, the Seljuks became masters of Central and Western Iran and some parts of Transcaucasia. In 1055 their ruler, Toghrul, entered Baghdad and was honored by the caliph as the champion of Sunni Islam. In 1071, in another historically decisive battle at Manzikert, the Seljuks defeated the Byzantines. Thenceforth the penetration of the Turkic nomads into Asia Minor, and especially Iran, began and continued during the whole Seljuk period.[36]

In the Seljuk state, the ruling class consisted primarily of members of the dynasty and the nomadic aristocracy. The latter benefitted from the widely practiced institute of *iqta'*. These allotments of land in compensation for military service did not entail proprietary rights over land, but allowed the new ruling class to extract taxes and dues, and to establish its superiority over the Iranian peasantry without abandoning their nomadic way of life. However, nomadic traditions and institutions were ill-fitted for governing a state in which the majority of people were sedentary. The Seljuk sultans had to rely on the Iranian bureaucracy and to retain the governmental institutions of the previous Middle Eastern states, although in a somewhat modified way. Once they began to rely on an old social foundation, they sought to relegate ordinary nomads to the level of sedentary subjects. But nomadic commoners insisted that they were entitled to privileged positions in the state that had been created with their participation. They did not want to pay taxes and submit to the governing Iranian bureaucracy. In the eleventh century, nomads continued to play an important role in the army, but efforts were made to send them to the borders of the state and to use them in raids and struggles with Christian sedentary states. In the twelfth century, bellicose nomads actively participated in internecine wars, tended to be less and less obedient to the central power, and sometimes revolted against it. This contributed to the disintegration of the Seljuk state.

The Mongol conquest of Iran in the thirteenth century brought to the region many more nomads from the Eurasian steppes.[37] In all, between the twelfth and fourteenth centuries nomads made up about one quarter of the population of Iran,[38] much more than in previous times.

---

36 Ann K. S. Lambton, *Landlord and Peasant in Persia: A Study in Land Tenure and Land Revenue Administration* (London: Oxford University Press, 1953): 59; Bosworth, "The Political and Dynastic History of the Iranian World," 79.

37 John Mason Smith, "Mongol Manpower and Persian Population," *Journal of the Economic and Social History of the Orient* 18 (1975): 271; Thomas T. Allsen, *Mongol Imperialism: The Policies of the Grand Qan Möngke in China, Russia, and the Islamic Lands, 1251–1259* (Berkeley: University of California Press, 1987): 203–7.

38 Leonard M. Helfgott, "Tribalism as a Socioeconomic Formation in Iranian History," *Iranian Studies* 9 (1977): 36.

The nomadic migrations during the Seljuk period, and particularly during the ensuing invasions of the nomads of the Eurasian steppes, infiltrated the local population and affected their pastoralism. Some nomads were crowded out by others. Thus, the Seljuks pushed the Baluch out of Khurasan and Kirman into Makran and further east.[39] In the thirteenth and fourteenth centuries, some dissident groups of the Turco-Mongol nomads known as the Hazara and the Nögödaris moved into the territories west of Kabul.[40] Only in that period did nomadism in Afghanistan assume its now-traditional forms.

India

Nomads migrated into the Indian subcontinent over many centuries and even millennia. In the fifth century, the Joan-Joan nomadic state became dominant in Mongolia, and soon afterwards in many other regions of Inner Asia. Under its pressure, a nomadic group known in the Byzantine sources as the Kidarite Huns, apparently of mixed ethnic origin, moved into northern and central India and defeated the Gupta state in the first half of the sixth century.

At the same time, nomads of mixed ethnic composition known as the Heftalites (apparently after the name of their dynasty) controlled vast sedentary territories in northwestern India from their center in Afghanistan, until the joined forces of Sasanians and Turks destroyed them in 557. Remarkably, the official language in their realm was the Bactrian tongue belonging to the Iranian group. This reliance on the professionals from the sedentary population for the governance is a characteristic of many later nomadic states.

However, due to climatic conditions, those nomads who remained in India had to abandon their pastoralism. The large-scale nomadic migrations and conquests that had been set in motion by the Turks in the late tenth century, reached their climax with the Mongols in the thirteenth century, and ended with Timur's raids and the sacking of Delhi in the late fourteenth century, albeit that his short-lived empire can hardly be considered a nomadic one. The Turco-Mongols in India, just like their predecessors, had to leave their pastoral nomadism behind. However, they brought about new ways of warfare and military technique that allowed them to impose new

39 André Wink, "On the Road to Failure: The Afghans in Mughal India," *Cracow Indological Studies* 9 (2009): 277–81.
40 Herbert Franz Schurmann, *The Mongols of Afghanistan: An Ethnography of the Moghôls and Related Peoples of Afghanistan* (s'-Gravenhage: Mouton, 1962): 45–6.

patterns of political mobilization and resource allocation. André Wink calls these developments a successful "fusion" of nomadic frontier elements and sedentary society.[41]

Effects

The impact of the nomadic migrations and conquests on the historical development of the sedentary world was manifold and sometimes contradictory. Also, it varied a great deal from region to region. No wonder that scholars have different opinions on these issues.[42] Still, it is desirable to avoid the extremes in this regard.

Histories written by the defeated may be as one-sided and biased as histories written by the victors. Claims that the nomads were always cold-blooded predators, despoilers, and butchers, and that they resorted to destruction and slaughter more enthusiastically than their sedentary counterparts, are still rather widespread,[43] but largely unsubstantiated. It is true that many, though far from all, nomadic conquests of sedentary countries were devastating; but sometimes these devastations were exaggerated by contemporary sedentary historians and their modern followers.

The thesis of the destructive consequences of all nomadic intrusions and conquests should be treated with a certain caution, especially if one discusses economic processes of long duration. Too often the nomads are made scapegoats for the economic decay and contemporary backwardness of some countries and regions. Thus, the desolation of certain areas of Central Asia, like Khwarazm, was explained by Soviet scholars as the result of the destruction of the irrigation networks by invading nomads; while in fact the salinization of the soil played a more important role in this gradual process than the nomads.

Contrary to still widespread opinion, the Iraqi irrigation system had already been in decline since the tenth century, i.e. long before the Mongol invasion.[44] It is true that the Bedouins contributed to the decline of

41 André Wink, "India and the Turko-Mongol Frontier," in Anatoly M. Khazanov and André Wink (eds.), *Nomads in the Sedentary World* (Richmond, Surrey: Curzon Press, 2001): 219–23.

42 Khazanov and Wink (eds.), *Nomads in the Sedentary World*.

43 For one of the most recent claims of this sort see Thomas Sowell, *Conquests and Cultures: An International History* (New York: Basic Books, 1998): 3–4.

44 Robert M. Adams, *Land behind Baghdad. A History of Settlement on the Diyala Plains* (Chicago University Press, 1965): 71–89; Dominique Sourdel and Janine Sourdel, *La civilisation de l'Islam classique* (Paris: Arthaud, 1968): 272 ff.

agriculture in northern Syria and Iraq in the seventh to tenth centuries, but over-taxation played at least as important a role in the general regression of sedentary life there as did nomadic pressure.[45]

In North Africa, the destruction and ruin caused by the Hilalian invasion, which Ibn Khaldun called "a swarm of locusts," apparently was exaggerated not only by that Muslim scholar but also by his followers amongst the French historians of the old school.[46] The decline of the Tunisian economy was the result of many factors, and the nomadic invasions were only one of them. Moreover, the destruction was not total. The coastal regions survived, and agriculture continued to flourish in many regions of North Africa.[47] One should also take into account that as soon as the conquests were accomplished, new nomadic rulers often made serious efforts to restore agricultural and urban life in the conquered countries.

Still, some conclusions are incontrovertible. It is obvious that the impact of nomads on the linguistic and ethnic history of the Old World during the Middle Millennium was very great. In particular, language shifts and the spread of Turkic languages from East Siberia (Yakutia) to the Middle Volga region and to the Balkans were directly connected with the migrations, conquests, and/or political dominance of the nomads.[48] Apparently no later than in the sixth century, at the time of the West Türk khaqanate, if not even earlier, processes of ethnic mingling of the Turkic-speaking nomads with the Iranian-speaking ones had started, along with the gradual linguistic Turkicization of the latter.[49] These processes continued for many centuries, and accelerated markedly in the eleventh and twelfth centuries (the Qarakhanid period), when the nomads were migrating into and settling in the agricultural areas of Central Asia in considerably larger numbers than in previous periods.[50] The Seljuk conquests and the subsequent migrations of the nomads into the conquered territories initiated a gradual Turkicization of Anatolia. Azerbaijan was already largely Turkicized during that period.

45 Ira M. Lapidus, *A History of the Islamic Societies* (Cambridge University Press, 1988): 136.
46 J. Poncet, "Le mythe de la catastrophe hilalienne," *Annales. Économies, Sociétés, Civilisations* 22 (1967): 1099–120; H. J. Fisher, "The Eastern Maghrib and Central Sudan," in Roland Olivier (ed.), *The Cambridge History of Africa* (Cambridge University Press, 1977), vol. III, 244–5.
47 Lapidus, *A History of the Islamic Societies*, 371–2.
48 Golden, *An Introduction to the History of the Turkic Peoples*, 15.
49 S. G. Kliashtornyi, *Drevnetiurkskie runicheskie pamiatniki kak istochnik po istorii Srednei Azii (Ancient Turkic Runic Inscriptions as a Source in the Study of the History of Central Asia).* (Moscow: Nauka, 1964): 174.
50 V. V. Barthold, *Ocherk istorii Semirechia (An Essay on the History of Semirechie)* (Frunze: Kirgizgosizdat, 1943): 213.

By the thirteenth century, the migration of the Oghuz and Qipchaq nomads to Khwarazm had resulted in the almost complete disappearance of the Iranian Khwarazmian language and its replacement with the Turkic one.[51] The dissemination of the Turkic languages was facilitated by the fact that they became languages of ruling elites and also served as a lingua franca.

The dissemination of Arabic from Iran to Sudan was partly connected with the numerous and various migrations of Bedouins. Thus, the Banu Hilal contributed to the spread of the vernacular Arabic in the countryside of North Africa and to the retreat of the Berber language into the hills and mountains.[52] The Arabic language itself was conceived by medieval philologists as having a close relationship with Bedouin patrimony.[53]

However, this was not always the case. Numerous migrations of pastoralists from Mongolia and Manchuria into North China always resulted in the eventual assimilation of those who remained there. In Iran, the Arabs were largely assimilated to the Persian milieu.

The role of nomads in facilitating and stimulating transcontinental information, knowledge flow, and cultural exchange, not infrequently connected with long-distance continental and transcontinental trading, was also very great. Such trade was always linked first and foremost with the political situation in a wide area that sometimes comprised several historical regions. It was not a coincidence that all the great overland trade routes of the Middle Ages flourished when nomadic states created a *pax* that provided security and transportation facilities. The Great Silk Road was only the best-known case. When Mongol rule in China collapsed, overland trade came to a halt and the price of Chinese silk and certain spices doubled in Europe.[54] Besides, the nomadic states stimulated trade though an increased demand for luxury commodities and prestigious goods with important symbolic meaning.[55] In their turn, they were the main suppliers of slaves and horses to their sedentary counterparts. With regard to trade, information flow, and cross-cultural contacts and exchange, however, no nomadic state could surpass the

---

51 Barthold, *Dvenadtsat' lektsii*, 77.
52 M. Brett, "The Central Lands of North Africa and Sicily, Until the Beginning of the Almohad Period," in Maribel Fierro (ed.), *The New Cambridge History of Islam* (Cambridge University Press, 2010), vol. II: 56.
53 Stefan Leder, "Nomadic and Sedentary Peoples – A Misleading Dichotomy? The Bedouin and Bedouinism in the Arab Past," in Stefan Leder and Bernhard Streck (eds.), *Shifts and Drifts in Nomad-Sedentary Relations* (Wiesbaden: Ludwig Reichert Verlag, 2005): 401.
54 Jack Goody, *The East in the West* (Cambridge University Press, 1996): 57.
55 Thomas T. Allsen, *Commodity and Exchange in the Mongol Empire: A Cultural History of Islamic Textiles* (Cambridge University Press, 1997): 103–4.

Mongol Empire. Under Mongol auspices various commodities, technologies, and knowledge, as well as human, animal, and plant populations were disseminated and displayed across Eurasia.[56] On the negative side, one should mention the plague pandemic of the fourteenth century, which was possibly connected with the intensification of transcontinental trade.[57]

The enormous role of the nomadic conquests in the political history of Asia, Europe, and even Africa also seems to be quite clear. Not infrequently their outcomes were radical border changes, the destruction of some states and emergence of others. But not all nomadic conquests resulted in profound cultural, socio-economic, and political change of long duration. It is important to note that in only a few cases did they lead to irreversible political reconfigurations of entire historical regions. It is true that the Seljuk conquest of Anatolia and related migrations, or the Arab conquests, eventually brought corresponding regions into quite different political constellations. But it is also true that when the dust of the Mongol conquests settled, the main historical regions that had preceded them, such as China, India, Central Asia, Iran, Turkic Anatolia as a core of the Ottoman Empire, and the Russian lands, resurfaced once again.

The consequences of nomadic conquests were often mainly limited to dynastic changes and to more-or-less serious changes in the composition of the ruling class.[58] The circulation of political elites caused by the nomads in North Africa is well described by Ibn Khaldun. In many conquered countries and in different historical periods, the nomadic aristocracies strove to become landed elites. This often happened in Iran, Central Asia, and China.

But even the turnover of the ruling and privileged elites was far from always complete. Very remarkable in this regard is the old aphorism repeated by the Sinicized Khitan councilor Yelü Chucai to the Great Khan Ögödei, son and successor of Chinggis Khan: "Although you inherited the Chinese Empire on horseback, you cannot rule it from that position."[59] It was relatively easy and expedient for the victors to replace the old military elites. But in order to rule the conquered countries with a modicum of efficiency, they needed bureaucrats; and the latter could be recruited only from the

---

56 Thomas T. Allsen, *Culture and Conquest in Mongol Eurasia* (Cambridge University Press, 2001).
57 William H. McNeill, *Plagues and Peoples* (New York: Anchor Press, 1976).
58 Anatoly M. Khazanov, "Nomads in the History of the Sedentary World," in Khazanov and Wink, *Nomads in the Sedentary World*, 3.
59 N. Munkuev, *Kitaiskii istochnik o pervykh mongol'skikh khanakh. Nadgrobnaia nadpis' na mogile Eliui Chu-tsaia (A Chinese Source about the First Mongol Khans. The Epitaph on the Tomb of Yehlü Ch'uts'ai)*. (Moscow: Nauka, 1965).

subjugated sedentary population. In China, the literati officials proved to be indispensable to all conquerors. Even the Yuan eventually had to revive the old Confucian examination system.

In the Muslim countries, the religious nobility survived as well in cases when the nomads had already converted to Islam by the time of their conquests. In Central Asia and Iran, a series of conquests destroyed the *dihqans*, the land-owning Iranian aristocracy. But neither the Qarakhanids nor the Seljuks, nor other conquerors for that matter, ever considered encroachment upon the privileges of the *'ulama* and the Sufi *shaykhs*.

When nomadic rulers tried to make serious changes in the structures of conquered sedentary societies and to impose upon them their own socio-political norms, these attempts, as a rule, were not particularly successful, at any rate not in the long run. For example, the system of apportioned lands that was practiced in the Chinggisid Empire was disruptive of local patterns of landholding, and was abandoned after the end of Mongol rule.[60]

The nomads of the Eurasian steppes had their own centuries-old and quite sophisticated polyethnic political culture.[61] However, the mere necessity of governing over conquered sedentary countries eventually forced the nomadic rulers to find ways to accommodate their new subjects and, when necessary, to legitimize their rule in terms acceptable to them. From North Africa to India, those who already had been Muslims strove to stress their bona fide Islamic credentials. When the Mongols conquered Central Asia and Iran, they were still pagans, but afterwards they converted to Islam, and in 1295–1335 the Mongol rulers of Iran consistently sought to promote their image as the ideal Islamic rulers, the defenders and propagators of the faith.[62] At the same time, the Mongol ruling elite in China converted to Buddhism. They soon discovered that it was impossible to rule the country by applying their own customary law and had to accommodate themselves to Chinese legal concepts and institutions.[63] The Khitan (Liao), Jürchen (Jin), and the Mongol (Yuan) emperors accepted Chinese court

---

60 Thomas T. Allsen, "Sharing Out the Empire: Apportioned Lands Under the Mongols," in Khazanov and Wink, *Nomads in the Sedentary World*, 172–90.

61 Igor de Rachewiltz, "Some Remarks on the Ideological Foundations of Chingiz Khan's Empire," *Papers on Far Eastern History* 7 (1973): 21–36; Peter B. Golden, "Imperial Ideology and the Sources of Political Unity Amongst the Pre-Chinggisid Nomads in Western Eurasia," *Archivum Eurasiae Medii Aevi* 2 (1982): 37–76.

62 Thomas T. Allsen, "Changing Forms of Legitimation in Mongol Iran," in Gary Seaman and Daniel Marks (eds.), *Rulers from the Steppe: State Formation on the Eurasian Periphery* (Los Angeles: Ethnographics Press, University of Southern California, 1991): 235.

63 Paul Heng-chao Ch'en, *Chinese Legal Tradition under the Mongols: The Code of 1291 as Reconstructed* (Princeton University Press, 1979).

ritual, although the Khitans and Mongols to a lesser extent than the Jürchens.[64]

One may conclude that nomadic conquests nowhere, or almost nowhere, drastically changed sociopolitical structures of historical–cultural regions. The nomadic rulers had to adopt or adjust to the pre-existing institutional infrastructure, administrative models, religious situation, and legitimation patterns of the conquered states. A certain, and sometimes temporary, permutation within the existing social order was more frequent than its irreversible transformation. It seems that the nomadic factor was nowhere a single, or even the most important one, among those many factors that defined long-duration historical development.

Anyway, by the sixteenth century, with the advent of the early modern period, the age of great nomadic migrations and conquests was over. The great geographic discoveries and the shift of trade routes were a serious blow to long-distance overland trade. Caravels defeated caravans. The centralized empires of Russia, Ottoman Turkey, and China created massive regular armies, which increasingly employed firearms with ever-growing lethal power. Against such armies, the irregular cavalries of the nomads were ineffective.

FURTHER READING

Agadzhanow, S. G. *Der Staat der Seldschukiden und Mittelasien im 11.–12. Jahrhundert*. Berlin: Reinhold Schletzer Verlag, 1994.

Allsen, Thomas T. *Culture and Conquest in Mongol Eurasia*. Cambridge University Press, 2001.

Mongol Imperialism: The Policies of the Grand Qan Möngke in China, Russia, and the Islamic Lands, 1251–1259. Berkeley, CA: University of California Press, 1987.

Amitai-Preiss, Reuven. *Mongols and Mamluks: The Mamluk-Ilkhanid War, 1260–1281*. Cambridge University Press, 1995.

Barfield, Thomas J. *The Perilous Frontier: Nomadic Empires and China*. Cambridge, MA: Basil Blackwell, 1989.

Barthold, V. V. *Turkestan v epokhu mongol'skogo nashestviia (Turkestan in the Times of the Mongol Invasion)*. Moscow: Izdatel'stvo vostochnoi literatury, 1963.

Biran, Michal. *The Empire of the Qara Khitai in Eurasian History: Between China and the Islamic World*. Cambridge University Press, 2005.

---

64 Herbert Franke, *From Tribal Chieftain to Universal Emperor and God: The Legitimation of the Yüan Dynasty* (Munich: Bayerische Akademie der Wissenschaften, philosophisch-historische Klasse. Sitzungsberichte, fasc. 2, 1978); Peter K. Bol, "Seeking Common Ground: Han Literati under Jurchen Rule," *Harvard Journal of Asiatic Studies* 47 (1987): 461–538; Elizabeth Endicott-West, "Aspects of Khitan Liao and Mongolian Yüan Imperial Rule: A Comparative Perspective," in Seaman and Marks, *Rulers from the Steppe*, 199–222.

Bosworth, C. E. "The Political and Dynastic History of the Iranian World (A.D. 1000–1217)," in J. A Boyle (ed.), *The Cambridge History of Iran*, vol. v. Cambridge University Press, 1968: 1–202.

Brett, M. "The Central Lands of North Africa and Sicily, Until the Beginning of the Almohad Period," in Maribel Fierro (ed.), *The New Cambridge History of Islam*, vol. ii. Cambridge University Press, 2010: 48–65.

Cohen, Claude. *Pre-Ottoman Turkey*. New York: Taplinger Publishing Company, 1968.

Donner, Fred McGraf. *The Early Islamic Conquests*. Princeton University Press, 1981.

Dunlop, D. M. *The History of the Jewish Khazars*. Princeton University Press, 1954.

Endicott-West, Elizabeth. "Aspects of Khitan Liao and Mongolian Yüan Imperial Rule: A Comparative Perspective," in Gary Seaman and Daniel Marks (eds.), *Rulers from the Steppe: State Formation on the Eurasian Periphery*. Los Angeles, CA: Ethnographics Press, University of Southern California, 1991: 199–222.

Fisher, H. J. "The Eastern Maghrib and Central Sudan," in Roland Olivier (ed.), *The Cambridge History of Africa*, vol. iii. Cambridge University Press, 1977: 232–330.

Golden, Peter B. "Imperial Ideology and the Sources of Political Unity amongst the Pre-Chinggisid Nomads in Western Eurasia," *Archivum Eurasiae Medii Aevi* 2(1982): 37–76.

An Introduction to the History of the Turkic Peoples: Ethnogenesis and State-formation in Medieval and Early Modern Eurasia and the Middle East. Wiesbaden: Otto Harrassowitz, 1992.

Khazar Studies: An Historico-Philological Inquiry into the Origins of the Khazars Budapest: Akadémiai Kiadó, 1980.

Khazanov, Anatoly M. *Nomads and the Outside World*, 2nd edn. Madison, WI: The University of Wisconsin Press, 1994.

"Nomads in the History of the Sedentary World," in Khazanov and Wink (eds.), *Nomads in the Sedentary World*, 1–23.

Khazanov, Anatoly M. and Wink, André, eds. *Nomads in the Sedentary World*. Richmond, Surrey: Curzon Press, 2001.

Kliashtornyi, S. G. *Drevnetiurkskie runicheskie pamiatniki kak istochnik po istorii Srednei Azii (Ancient Turkic Runic Inscriptions as a Source in Study of the History of Central Asia)*. Moscow: Nauka, 1964.

Kliashtornyi, S. G. and D. G. Savinov. *Stepnye imperii drevnei Evrazii (The Steppe Empires of Ancient Eurasia)*. St Petersburg State University, 2005.

Mackerras, Colin. *The Uighur Empire According to the T'ang Dynastic Histories: A Study in Sino–Uighur Relations, 744–840*. Canberra: Australian National University Press, 1972.

Peacock, Andrew C. S. *Early Seljūk History: A New Interpretation*. London: Routledge, 2010.

Poncet, J. "Le mythe de la catastrophe hilalienne" ("The Myth of the Hilalian Catastrophy"), *Annales. Économies, Sociétés, Civilisations* 22 (1967): 1099–120.

Róna-Tas, András. *Hungarians and Europe in the Early Middle Ages*. Budapest: Central European University Press, 1999.

Tikhvinsky, S. L. (ed). *Tataro-mongoly v Azii i Evrope (The Tataro-Mongols in Asia and Europe)*, 2nd edn. Moscow: Nauka, 1977.

Wink, André. "India and the Turko-Mongol Frontier," in Khazanov and Wink (eds.), *Nomads in the Sedentary World*, 211–33.

PART IV

★

EXPANDING RELIGIOUS
SYSTEMS

15

The centrality of Islamic civilization

MICHAEL COOK

"Islamic civilization" is not a term calculated to endear itself to anyone with a systematic preference for splitting rather than lumping. For one thing, it commits us to the view that, in spite of a large amount of regional and local diversity, there is an overarching unity to be discerned in the lifestyles of Muslim peoples. For another, it entails that the phenomenon of Islamic civilization is itself a member of a larger set – one civilization among others, sharing basic features with its peers. Both implications are correct, but both invite a measure of caution. With regard to the balance of unity and diversity, that caution will have its place throughout this chapter. With regard to the parity between Islamic and other civilizations, a look at some of the features that set the Islamic case apart from its peers is a good place to begin this survey.

Perhaps the most obvious of these features is the sheer extent of the civilization by the end of our period, around 1500. The emergence of what by neolithic or bronze-age standards were very large human communities is a phenomenon familiar from the last three thousand years of human history in the Old World, but in no earlier case had such a community extended over so vast a territory – from West Africa to Southeast Asia, from East Africa to the bend in the Volga. Only the spread of European civilization across the globe since 1500 has eclipsed the Islamic expansion.

Another unprecedented feature of Islamic civilization is best approached by noting that earlier instances of very large human communities had taken one of two forms. They might involve the emergence of relative cultural homogeneity in particular regions, as with the spread of Hellenism in the eastern Mediterranean and Western Asia, the extension of northern Indian culture to the south, or the similar southward expansion of northern Chinese

I would like to thank Patricia Crone, Anatoly Khazanov, and the editors of this volume for their comments on a draft of this chapter, W.W. Norton for permission to reproduce the map, and Alan Stahl for help with scanning the coins.

culture; in other words, they could be what we call civilizations. Alternatively, they might take the form of what we refer to with some exaggeration as "world religions," so called because they came to extend beyond the boundaries of particular cultural regions, as with the spread of Buddhism to China, or of Christianity to Ethiopia or Central Asia. What was unprecedented about the Islamic case was the fact that it was a civilization and a world religion combined. Indeed this combination remains unparalleled even today: our current world civilization is not a world religion.

Islamic civilization is also unusual in the relatively late date of its emergence. The major civilizations of the Old World typically took shape many centuries before the beginning of our era; Islamic civilization stands apart from its peers by virtue of the fact that it emerged well over a millennium later. It thus appeared at a time when most parts of the Old World with the requisite economic resources had already filled up with civilizations or equivalent cultural formations.

This last feature had significant implications for the interaction between Islamic and other civilizations. For one thing, it meant that the new civilization often superseded earlier ones. Such supersession was not unprecedented, nor was it total – earlier civilizations did not vanish without trace. And of course the expansion of Islamic civilization did not involve supersession everywhere. Being also a world religion, and one that originated in a region that was largely desert, Islam was well suited to spread among peoples whose limited economic resources or relative isolation placed them beyond the frontiers of existing civilizations; it did so in several parts of the Old World, such as West Africa and northern Eurasia. But overall, the supersession of older civilizations bulked unusually large in the history of Islamic civilization.

The theme of interaction is also central to the origins of Islamic civilization. Typically a civilization has its beginnings in a region that possesses the economic resources to support one but is not currently doing so: either it has never done so, as in the case of northern China in the second millennium before our era, or an earlier civilization has succumbed to the hazards of history, as in northwestern India in the same period. The Middle East, the region with the longest history of civilization anywhere on earth, had ceased to contain such regions long before the seventh century. It was not that all of the Middle East was civilized. Geographically speaking, much of Arabia is in effect an eastern extension of the Sahara Desert, and whatever its links to the civilizations that prevailed in the wider region, the constraints of the Arabian environment largely precluded its adoption of them. But if the Middle East was made up on the one hand of a region that already possessed well-established civilizations, and on the other of a region that lacked the resources to support one, where was a new civilization to take shape? There is a puzzle here; at the very least, we can say that the formation of Islamic civilization was not a development that anyone living prior to the seventh century had reason to anticipate.

But for the moment, in fact until near the end of this chapter, let us leave aside the puzzle of the emergence of Islamic civilization. Instead, let us start with a survey of the territories that made up the domain of this civilization – the Islamic world – as it was towards the end of our period. In the process we will also see how these varied regions had come to be part of this world (see Map 15.1).

The regions of Islamic civilization around 1500: the new lands

A glance at the map, showing the extent of the Islamic world around 1500, serves to underline two things. The first is the sheer size of the territory involved, a point we have already noted. The second is the central location of this territory: it is tempting, and to an extent correct, to divide the Old World into a Muslim core on the one hand, and a set of non-Muslim peripheries on the other. The most notable of these peripheries are located in East Asia, sub-Saharan Africa, and Europe. Of course just where we place the boundaries of the Islamic world depends on how we define it. Thus if we exclude from our definition areas in which, despite Muslim political dominance, the bulk of the population remained non-Muslim, then we can add to the peripheries most of India together with southeastern Europe. Yet in crude geographical terms the sense of an Old World made up of a vast Islamic core and a set of dispersed peripheries would remain. In one respect, however, this way of looking at things is misleading: it does not take into account the considerable disparities of economic and demographic weight that distinguished the various regions of the Old World. Once we bring them into the picture, a rather ominous fact emerges: the three areas of the Eurasian land mass with the greatest density of resources and population were located in the non-Muslim peripheries, not in the Muslim core. China was one, India another, and Europe the third. But this imbalance, though of great geopolitical significance for the future, was not yet particularly salient at the end of our period.

The process by which the Islamic world came to be so large can conveniently be divided into three unequal phases. The first was the lifetime of

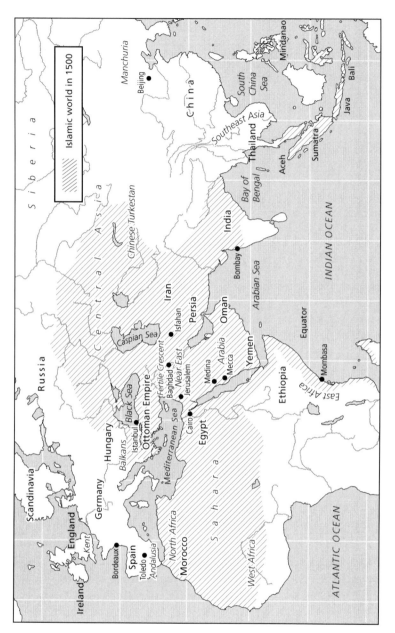

Map 15.1. The Islamic world

Muhammad, the Prophet of Islam, and more particularly the decade from 622 to his death in 632, during which he established and ruled a state in western Arabia that played an increasing role in Arab affairs. The second phase was the military expansion of this state in the century after his death: by the 720s it had come to rule a territory extending from Spain and Morocco in the west to Transoxania (roughly modern Uzbekistan) and Sindh (in modern Pakistan) in the east. The third phase lumps together the subsequent territorial gains that expanded the Muslim world on a variety of fronts during the rest of our period; these gains were also accompanied by occasional losses, most notably those of Muslim Spain and Sicily. Unlike the expansion of the first two phases, that of the third phase was not directed from any one centre.

Let us begin our survey with the territories added in the third phase. We can conveniently start in the far north among the Bulghars, and then proceed roughly clockwise.

The far north

The Bulghars were a Turkic people living around the bend in the Volga. Their case is not of major historical significance, but it is instructive.

In the early tenth century the Bulghar ruler was showing interest in adopting Islam and instituting diplomatic relations with the Caliph in Baghdad. The Caliph duly dispatched an embassy that included a certain Ibn Fadlan, who left a detailed account of his experiences which has fortunately survived. He found the Bulghar ruler ill-informed about Islam but anxious to learn. For example, he was making mistakes in connection with the ritual of Muslim prayer, including the Friday prayer, the major public ritual of the Muslim polity in which the ruler is mentioned by name and title. Ibn Fadlan accordingly coached him in the proper way to do things. Yet it is clear from the account of the mission that the ruler's openness to Islam was not just a matter of religious conviction. Like the emperor Constantine who had converted to Christianity six centuries earlier, the Bulghar ruler had other things on his mind. In his case a major concern was the Khazar threat. Between his country and the caliphate lay the empire of the Khazars, a rival Turkic people and the lords of a powerful nomadic state of the kind familiar in the history of the Eurasian steppes. Since the Khazars were a threat to both the Bulghars and the caliphate, an alliance between the Bulghar ruler and the Caliph made sense. Articulating that alliance in religious terms was likewise an apt move: the political elite of the Khazars had converted to Judaism, itself an imaginative solution to the geopolitical problem of maintaining their distance from both the Muslim caliphate and the Christian Byzantine Empire. The Bulghar ruler was thus looking for more from the caliphate than just to be coached in the proper performance of the Friday prayer. He wanted an alliance, he wanted military technology to help him construct a fort to defend his territory against the Khazars, and he wanted financial support – something Ibn Fadlan, despite good intentions on the part of the Caliph, had unfortunately arrived without. When the Bulghar ruler realized this, he suspected Ibn Fadlan of having embezzled the funds he should have been sent with; tellingly, he expressed his displeasure by deliberately reverting to one of the ritual practices that Ibn Fadlan considered erroneous.

The Bulghar conversion extended beyond the ruler to the people at large. Ibn Fadlan was heartened by the signs he encountered of their willingness to adopt Islam. Yet their adherence was no more unconditional than that of their ruler. Thus Ibn Fadlan, a punctilious and puritanical Muslim, was deeply disturbed by the way in which the Bulghars would bathe in the Volga: they did so in the nude, and worse yet in mixed company. Tellingly, his attempts to put an end to this distressingly un-Islamic practice were a failure.

And yet there is no question that Islam took root among the Bulghars. For later centuries we have nothing as vivid as Ibn Fadlan's account, but we do have unquestionably Muslim tombstones inscribed in the Bulghar language that date from the fourteenth century. What we see in the Bulghar case is thus an example of a people who converted to Islam without being exposed to any military threat from a Muslim source, let alone a Muslim conquest; as the ruler remarked pointedly to Ibn Fadlan, there was no way the Caliph could project military power as far as the lands of the Bulghars. The factor most visibly at work in this conversion was geopolitical calculation, but to this we can add a couple of further factors that are surely relevant. One is the role of the fur trade in ensuring that the Bulghars already possessed some awareness of Islam, despite having no Muslim neighbours; this transit trade was based on the high level of demand in the Muslim world for the fur of animals hunted in the Arctic forests to the north. The other factor is the frequent readiness of pagan populations – and especially their rulers – to convert to a world religion when given the opportunity.

Meanwhile Islam had achieved some success among other elements in the western steppes. One by-product of this was that Hungary, the Christian country located at the far western end of the steppes, had a Muslim minority, though it had disappeared by the end of the fourteenth century; the hostility these Muslims encountered from the church tended to be balanced by the support they received from the rulers of the country, who regarded their Muslims as people who could perform useful services for the state. In cultural terms they seem to have been a rather assimilated minority. Some Hungarian Muslims were zealous enough to travel all the way to Aleppo and Jerusalem for a Muslim education. But these students described their community to a Muslim geographer as dressing like Christians, and even shaving their beards – a practice almost as un-Islamic as mixed bathing.

The thirteenth century, however, saw a major upheaval in the western steppes thanks to the arrival of the pagan Mongol conquerors. The result was a Mongol state, the Golden Horde, that lasted in some fashion into the sixteenth century. The Golden Horde was in fact one of several Mongol states established in the wake of the Mongol conquests, and all of them sooner or later converted to one of the world religions; in the first half of the fourteenth century the Golden Horde chose Islam. It is this conversion that lies behind the adoption of Islam by the Tatars, the Turkic-speaking Muslim populations that replaced the Bulghars around the bend in the Volga and also settled in the Crimea. There was even an isolated Muslim Tatar population far to the northwest, known as the Lithuanian Tatars. In many ways they assimilated to their Christian environment: they had coats of arms, spoke Polish or White Russian, and developed the view that for a thirsty man to down a drink or two is not actually forbidden so long as he does not get drunk. Yet they remained Muslims, and produced a religious literature composed in Polish or White Russian but written in the Arabic script.

The Turks

On his way to visit the Bulghars, Ibn Fadlan passed through the lands of yet another Turkic people, the Oghuz – often known simply as the Turks. Living on the fringes of Muslim Central Asia, these nomads were just beginning a process of Islamization that proved to be of major historical importance. Ibn Fadlan found them in general to be pagans, but with an interest in Islam that could lead to occasional conversion. Thus one Oghuz tribesman embraced Islam, only to renounce it when his fellow-tribesmen refused to accept him as their chief unless he did so. Over the next century Islam must have made major inroads among the Oghuz, for by the time they went on to invade Muslim Iran in the eleventh century they were either already Muslims or quickly became so. Though we have little information about the process, this too was clearly a case in which a pagan population was in no danger of being conquered by Muslims, but was nevertheless aware of Islam. This was perhaps due as much to proximity as to trade; the "silk route" between Iran and China may have played a large part in the eastward spread of Buddhism, Christianity, and Manichaeism, but it does not seem to have done much for Islam. Another difference between the Bulghar and Oghuz conversions is that among the Oghuz no one appears to have played the role of the Bulghar ruler.

Thanks in part to this conversion, the invasion of Iran by the Oghuz – or let us simply say the Turks – was far less traumatic than the arrival of the pagan Mongols two centuries later. Indeed one of the main effects of the Turkish conquest was to boost the military strength of the eastern Islamic world against its non-Muslim neighbours.

Thus to the west of Iran, it was the now Muslim Turks who ended the power of the Christian Byzantine Empire in Anatolia, which by the fifteenth century they had largely transformed from a land of Greek-speaking Christians to one of Turkish-speaking Muslims. Already in the fourteenth century, one of the Turkish dynasties of Anatolia, the Ottomans, had expanded the frontiers of Islam yet further, crossing the Dardanelles and invading the Balkans. The result was to establish a Muslim dominion over southeastern Europe that lasted into the nineteenth century, and at its height extended far into Hungary. But unlike the Turkish invasion of Anatolia, the Ottoman conquest of the Balkans did not lead to the conversion of the population at large; today Albania is the only Balkan nation with a Muslim majority.

A parallel expansion took place to the southeast of Iran. Here the extension of Muslim rule beyond Sindh had been begun by a Turkish dynasty that antedated the Oghuz invasion of Iran, the Ghaznawids. But the arrival of the Oghuz certainly boosted the process. By the end of our period Muslim rule was the norm in northern India, and was rapidly expanding southwards. Yet here, as in the Balkans, Islam was not adopted by a majority of the population. The exception in this case was the territory that is now Pakistan (in Bengal mass conversion seems to have taken place only after the end of our period). Elsewhere the Muslim population remained a minority, no more than the salt in a dish as one Muslim ruler put it; and after the twelfth century it was rare for Muslim rulers with possessions in India to have a base outside it. The result was that these rulers often had strong pragmatic reasons to accommodate their Hindu subjects, and this sometimes resulted in a degree of cultural and religious syncretism among the elite that we do not find in the Balkans. But the fact that Muslims were a minority wielding political power could also lead to fanatical Muslim intransigence.

Before we leave the Eurasian interior there is one other extension of the Islamic world that we should note: the conversion of the Uighurs of Chinese

Turkestan. North of the Indian Ocean this was the easternmost case of a large Muslim population. Still further to the east, China had a significant Muslim minority from the time of the Mongol conquest; like the kings of Hungary, the Mongol rulers of China found Muslims to be useful people, particularly as tax-collectors, and many arrived from the West in response to this opportunity. Their descendants became Chinese in language and to a large extent in culture, while retaining their Muslim faith; from the seventeenth century, the Chinese-educated Muslim elite in southern and eastern China was producing a literature in Chinese that sought to reconcile Islam and Confucianism.

The Indian Ocean

Around the Indian Ocean, far more than in the Eurasian interior, the spread of Islam was linked to long-distance trade routes that had already developed centuries before the time of Muhammad. With the rise of Islam we soon find Muslim merchants playing a prominent part in this commercial scene. As early as the eighth century we know that they were sailing all the way to the ports of southern China; in 758 they sacked Canton and then escaped by sea, thereby attracting the notice of the Chinese historians. In 869 a major rebellion of slaves from East Africa broke out in Iraq, thereby securing the attention of the Arabic historians, and providing indirect but powerful evidence of large-scale commercial relations with East Africa, almost certainly conducted by Muslim merchants. East Africans, doubtless slaves, also appear in ninth-century Java – no surprise since they had already reached southern China in the eighth century. Given this pattern of long-distance Indian Ocean trade, it was only a matter of time before a combination of Muslim commercial settlement and local conversion in response to it would lead to the spread of Islam around the rim of the Indian Ocean.

Since those who chronicle historical events give much more attention to the doings of rulers than to those of merchants, we have little direct information about this maritime spread of Islam. But we know the outcome. To the east, Muslim populations appeared along the coasts of India and Ceylon, and on the Arakanese coast of northern Burma. To the south, a similar ribbon development took place down the coast of East Africa, where it is likely that Muslim settlement and interaction with the native populations had issued in the formation of the lingua franca known as Swahili well before the end of our period.

The spread of Islam around the shores of the Indian Ocean also initiated the Islamization of a large part of island Southeast Asia, together with the

Malay peninsula. Here the arrival of Islam was manifestly the result of Indian Ocean commerce, though once established, the new religion often spread further through conquest. In Java especially, the incoming Islamic civilization superseded an older culture of Indian origin, but not without a degree of admixture of the two cultural traditions that went beyond anything we find further west. For example, one seventeenth-century Javanese court adopted a calendric reform whereby the year was now defined as the Muslim lunar year – and yet they continued to count these lunar years according to their traditional Indian era, not the Muslim era one might have expected them to adopt.

What this maritime spread of Islam across the Indian Ocean did not do was to generate large Muslim populations in the continental interiors. This was as true of East Africa as it was of India and Southeast Asia. Only in the desert lands of the Horn of Africa did such a development take place; and in the highlands behind them Ethiopia itself was able to remain Christian, though it only just escaped Muslim conquest in the early sixteenth century.

The African interior

Further west, however, conquest proved effective in spreading Islam up the Nile valley. The seventh-century Arab conquest of Egypt had stopped short of Nubia, where independent Christian kingdoms held out for several centuries more. But a combination of harrying by warlike Arab tribes and full-scale military expeditions launched by the Mamluk rulers of Egypt meant that by the end of our period Islam had spread far to the south; this is the source of the Arab Muslim population that is the core of northern Sudan today. To the west of the Nile valley, Islam was sooner or later adopted by all the tribal peoples of the Sahara, though elements of their pre-Islamic cultures often survived. Thus in the eleventh century, the Berber nomads of the western Sahara still maintained some conspicuously un-Islamic practices (such as marrying more than four wives), though they were Muslim enough to serve as the vehicle of a puritanical Muslim reformer whose followers, the Almoravids, conquered Morocco and Muslim Spain. Even today the Touareg nomads retain the use of a script derived from the Phoenician alphabet as it was used by the Carthaginians.

In the agricultural belt south of the Sahara – the Sahel – our best evidence comes from the lands along the northern course of the River Niger. Archaeology gives us reason to believe that there were states in this part of West Africa long before the rise of Islam, but it provides no indication that they came under the influence of the civilizations and religions that prevailed to the north of the Sahara. The rise of Islam ended this isolation, a development that must bear some relation to the familiarity of the Arabs with desert conditions. By the ninth century the Sahara had become sufficiently transparent for us to learn from an Arabic author the name of an African kingdom in the Sahel: Ghana. A detailed account of Ghana dating from the eleventh century reveals a pagan kingdom with a significant Muslim commercial presence. There was a separate Muslim city a few miles from the pagan capital. Our account makes it clear that the rulers of Ghana regarded the Muslims as useful people, no doubt in part because of the goods they brought from the lands to the north of the Sahara, and in part because they possessed a skill of literacy that had no native counterpart. The king thus made use of Muslims as ministers, one of them having charge of the royal treasury. What is not clear from this account is whether there were any indigenous African converts to Islam in Ghana.

Just how Islam spread to the mass of the native population we do not know, but by the fourteenth century the account of the Moroccan traveller Ibn Battuta describes a Muslim state in this region, that of Mali, that had been in place since the previous century. In some ways he found the inhabitants of Mali commendably zealous in their practice of Islam; for example, they would encourage their children to memorize the Quran by putting them in chains till they did so. But in other ways he was as shocked as Ibn Fadlan among the Bulghars; for example, he noted court rituals that struck him as absurd, and described how young women would walk around naked. This latter practice was still current in the late fifteenth century, when a pious ruler of Mali was sufficiently perturbed by it to consult a Moroccan religious scholar on the subject. Since then things have changed in the region, though the prominence of women in the marketplace continues to distinguish West African societies from those of the Muslim heartlands.

The Atlantic

The original Arab conquest had brought Islamic civilization to the western coasts of Morocco and the Iberian peninsula. But here, in contrast to the Indian Ocean, there was to be no maritime spread of Islam. Even the Canary Islands, not far off the coast of Morocco, remained outside the Islamic world, eventually to be colonized and Christianized by the Spanish in the fifteenth century. The Arab conqueror of Morocco in the later seventh century is reputed to have ridden his horse out into the Atlantic, telling God that only the sea prevented him from taking the fight further. In the very different conditions prevailing in 1600, a Moroccan ruler wanted to set up a joint venture with the English to acquire territory in the Americas – a plausible alliance, since Spain, the major power in the New World, was their common enemy. But nothing came of this initiative. Even in the Old World, there was no maritime spread of Islam down the west coast of Africa to mirror what was happening in East Africa; still less was there a coastal spread of this kind in western Europe north of Muslim Spain.

Indeed, the Christian lands of western Europe as a whole were remarkable for the absence of a Muslim commercial diaspora; instead it was the Europeans – mainly the Italians – who established trading outposts along the Muslim coastlands of the Mediterranean. This fits with the fact that while three of the five larger Mediterranean islands came under Muslim rule at one time or another – including Sicily from the ninth to the eleventh century – only Cyprus retains a significant Muslim population at the present day, one dating from the Ottoman conquest of the sixteenth century.

The regions of Islamic civilization around 1500: the old lands

The five coins shown in Figure 15.1 are at first sight hard to tell apart. All five share the same aniconic design and are inscribed in the same Arabic script; indeed the inscriptions are largely identical. Minor features of design apart, they differ only in two particulars, contained in one of the inscriptions: the name of the mint and the date of minting. From these we learn that the first coin was minted in Muslim Spain in 725–6, the second in Tunisia in 729–30, the third in Syria in 738–9, the fourth in Iraq in 739–40, and the fifth in what is now northern Afghanistan in 733–4. Thus all were minted within a 15-year period, but in places spread out over a distance of some four thousand miles. The coordination that is evident here could only be the work of a state imposing a uniform monetary system over the whole expanse of its territory, and the state in question was in fact the Umayyad Caliphate (661–750), the first hereditary dynasty of Islamic history.

Remarkable as this uniformity was, it was superimposed on tremendous diversity. In the first wave of expansion, in the 630s and 640s, the Muslim state had conquered the entire Persian Empire and the southern provinces of the Byzantine Empire. In later decades the conquests were extended westwards across North Africa to Spain, passing beyond the limits of former Byzantine rule; at the same time they were extended eastwards to Transoxania and Sindh, moving beyond the limits of former Persian rule. The Muslim state that minted the five coins was thus ruling over an unprecedented assortment of territories.

Figure 15.1 Islamic coins, obverse and reverse (photographs by Alan Stahl)

Figure 15.1 (cont.)

The former Persian Empire

The Persian Empire under the rule of the Sasanian dynasty (224–651) represented a geopolitical synergy of some antiquity: it combined the military
manpower of the Iranian plateau with the fiscal resources of the lowlands of
Mesopotamia – or to use the Arabic term, Iraq. This pattern first appeared
with the Achaemenid dynasty in the sixth century before our era, and was
revived for a century or so in Islamic times by the early rulers of the 'Abbasid
dynasty (749/50–1258); it worked well as long as Iraq retained its agricultural

wealth. One result was that the Persian Empire was inevitably a cultural hybrid. There were the traditions of the plateau, which at least at an elite level enshrined a proud Iranian identity; this identity was associated with languages such as Persian and Parthian, with memories of empire projected back onto mythical rulers antedating even the Achaemenids, and with the Zoroastrian religion and its sacred text, the Avesta. The realities at ground level, to the extent that we know about them, were rather different and more diverse. Alongside these traditions of the plateau were those of Mesopotamia, where there was no shared sense of an ancient political identity, but rather a variety of religious traditions each associated with a literature written in a different dialect of Aramaic. The culture of the Mesopotamian lowlands was thus more fragmented, though also more cosmopolitan and sophisticated, than that of the Iranian plateau.

That the disorganized tribes of Arabia should conquer the Persian Empire would have struck any political analyst of the sixth century as highly improbable – as improbable as the formation of a new civilization. But the first wave of Arab conquest coincided with a low point in Persian political and military fortunes: the Persians had ended up the losers in a prolonged war with the Byzantines, and while the victors made no attempt to annex the defeated empire, they left it politically unstable and devoid of effective leadership. Moreover the Persian capital was located at Ctesiphon in the Mesopotamian lowlands, territory similar to what the Arabs were accustomed to in Arabia; once they had taken the capital city, the chances of coordinated resistance on the plateau were poor. The last Persian "King of Kings," Yazdagird III, held out till his death in 651, but thereafter the Arabs enjoyed more or less undisputed possession of the former Sasanian territories. Their most formidable enemies in this quarter were now the Khazar state to the north of the Caucasus and a Turkic empire in Central Asia (ruled by a pagan Turkic people, nomads like the Khazars, but distinct from the Oghuz whom we met above).

What then became of the former Sasanian territories under the new Islamic dispensation? In one respect Iraq and Iran were no different: in the long run – perhaps by the year 1000 or so – the great majority of the population of both regions converted to Islam, predominantly in its Sunni form (it is only in recent centuries that the majority of the population in Iraq and Iran has shifted to Shi'ite Islam). In another respect the two regions fared very differently. In Iraq, over roughly the same period, conversion was accompanied by a linguistic change whereby Arabic replaced Aramaic, even among the non-Muslim population; whereas in Iran Persian held out as the spoken language, and spread at the expense of other Iranian languages. This disparity was matched by a larger cultural contrast. The Muslims of Iraq knew very little about the pre-Islamic past of their land, and had no sense that this past was part of their heritage; for them, the coming of the new religion and the formation of the new civilization had more or less wiped the slate clean. The Muslims of Iran, by contrast, did not just continue to use Persian as their spoken language; from the ninth or tenth century onwards they also wrote it, albeit in the Arabic script and with many Arabic loanwords (a precedent later followed by the Turks and others). The result was the emergence of an elaborate literature in Persian. Some of this literature invoked the memory of the pre-Islamic past; for the last thousand years Persian-speakers have been in proud possession of an epic account of the pre-Islamic history of Iran, the "Book of Kings" (*Shahnama*), composed by the poet Firdawsi. Yet Muslim Iran was still very much part of the wider Islamic civilization; indeed many of the most famous works of Arabic literature, history, scholarship, and science were written by men whose vernacular was Persian or some other Iranian language, and the idea of using a Persian translation of the Quran in a ritual context never made much headway. Iran nonetheless maintained a cultural continuity with a pre-Islamic past that it persisted in regarding as its own.

It is not hard to suggest a couple of reasons for the differing outcomes of the Arab conquest in Iraq and Iran. One is the contrast between the cultures of the two regions, with Iran conspicuously high on identity and Iraq notably low on it. The other is the fact that the Arabs came from Arabia: Iraq was a region at a similar elevation and with similar climatic conditions, a land in which not just Arabs but whole Arab tribes could readily make themselves at home. The Iranian highland with its frigid winters was a very different environment, unlikely to attract large-scale Arab settlement, which in any case was militarily unnecessary given the rapid collapse of resistance. The strongest Arab presence in Iran was in the northeast, near the Turkish front, and even these Arabs had a marked tendency to become Persian-speaking – though scattered pockets of Arabic-speakers survived into modern times.

The former Byzantine provinces

Unlike the Persian Empire, the Byzantine Empire was fortunate in having its capital city located far away from Arabia. To reach Constantinople the Arabs had either to cross the Anatolian plateau – a territory as geographically alien to them as the Iranian plateau – or to develop sufficient naval power to reach the city by sea. They did both, though only twice, and each time the formidable defenses of Constantinople saved the day for the Byzantines. The result was that while Anatolia became a war-zone, consolidated conquests on this front were limited. The Byzantine Empire thus survived the Arab onslaught in a reduced form. But if the Arabs found it hard to push north, they had little difficulty expanding to the west. Egypt was taken in the first wave of conquest, which also saw a venture into Tunisia; the definitive conquest of Tunisia came in the later seventh century, at a time when the Arabs were extending their reach in North Africa further to the west than Byzantine rule had ever extended.

What this meant was that the Arabs had annexed a set of Byzantine provinces, entities more like Iraq than Iran, with no counterparts of the features that enabled Iran to retain its distinctiveness. Beyond that, each case was different. In cultural terms Syria was a western Iraq: its population spoke Aramaic, and was divided into a variety of religious groups that might base their written languages on different Aramaic dialects. Here too, both Islam and Arabic prevailed among the majority of the population by sometime around the year 1000. Egypt was set apart by geography (the Nile valley was insulated on both sides by desert) and language (the population spoke Coptic, a late form of ancient Egyptian), but the outcome was essentially the same. In Tunisia too, conversion to Islam was overwhelming, and Arabic equally successful; after the twelfth century we hear little of the indigenous Christians, and today they have entirely disappeared.

The second wave of conquests

Finally we come to the lands that became part of the Islamic world during the second wave of conquests in the early eighth century. Here, as already indicated, the Arabs were moving beyond the frontiers of the former Persian and Byzantine Empires, though into territories that had historical and cultural links with one or other of them.

Transoxania in the early Islamic period was inhabited by people speaking Sogdian, an Iranian language very different from Persian; they were divided among a number of small principalities, and adhered to a variety of religions – Zoroastrianism, Buddhism, Christianity, and Manichaeism. The Arab conquest led to the spread of an Arabic elite culture, but also, more paradoxically, of Persian as a spoken and eventually written language. In addition it brought about some contact with China, where remnants of the Sasanian elite had taken shelter after the Arab conquest of Iran; but there was no significant interaction with Chinese culture.

Where there was interaction with an alien civilization was in Sindh. Though this northwestern corner of India had experienced Persian rule, it was culturally Indian, and its conquest marked the earliest phase of conflict and accommodation between Islam and Hinduism. However the Arabic historiographical tradition, while deeply interested in the conquest of Transoxania, regarded that of Sindh as a side-show, and the interaction with Hinduism seems to have remained of largely local interest. It is not till the time of the Ghaznawids that we get a real sense of the clash of civilizations on this front; and by then the Muslim conquerors were Turks rather than Arabs. It was in this Ghaznawid context that the polymath Biruni visited India, and learnt Sanskrit the better to understand its elite culture.

On the western front, when the Arab conquerors went beyond Egypt they were entering territory largely inhabited by the Berbers. Like the pre-Islamic Arabs, the Berbers were a tribal people with limited tolerance for centralized government; west of Tunisia they put up a fierce resistance to Arab conquest, and frequently rebelled thereafter. But they seem to have found Islam itself attractive. Many Berbers, eventually all of them, converted to Islam, though at first often to heretical forms of the religion that were at odds with the Umayyad and 'Abbasid Caliphs. In the early centuries we also hear of new religions appearing among the Berbers that mimicked Islam. Thus until the eleventh century the Berber tribesmen of the Atlantic plains of Morocco followed a faith brought to them by a Berber prophet; they had a scripture like the Quran, but composed in Berber, and celebrated a weekly communal prayer, but on Thursday rather than Friday. The one thing we do not hear about is any long-term survival of Berber pagans or Christians. On the other hand, their conversion to Islam, like that of the Iranians, does not seem to have been accompanied by the adoption of Arabic. But in the long run their fate diverged considerably from that of the Iranians. In the first place, they had no memory of a glorious past when the Berbers had ruled the world; there was no Berber Firdawsi. In the second place, the North African lowlands, though not the mountains, were the kind of territory in which Arab tribes felt at home; by the end of our period the westward and eventually southward spread of these tribes had laid the foundations for the present-day status of Algeria, Morocco, and Mauritania as Arab countries, albeit with significant Berber minorities in Algeria and Morocco.

The original Arab conquest, however, did not continue to the south of Morocco. It did continue into Spain, despite the barrier posed by the Straits of Gibraltar. Here the Arabs – and their Berber converts – encountered a solidly Christian population made up of Romance-speakers ruled by a

Visigothic monarchy and aristocracy. The conquerors seized some two thirds of the country and put an end to Visigothic domination; but Christian political power survived in the north, and eventually played a large part in the Christian reconquest that was completed shortly before the end of our period. By then Muslims in Spain were a persecuted minority, soon to be forcibly converted to Christianity and finally, in 1609–14, expelled from the country. In the late seventeenth century a Moroccan ambassador to Spain met people who still remembered nostalgically that their ancestors had been Muslims; but for all their interest in hearing about Islam, they were no longer Muslims themselves.

All these regions were far from the centre of the Islamic world – which is why they were conquered only in the second wave. But they differed considerably in how they related to the the central lands. Transoxania, with northeastern Iran, was effectively part of the metropolitan cultural scene in pre-Mongol times. Sindh was not. Nor was North Africa west of Tunisia for most of our period, though by the fifteenth century Morocco had produced a Sufi writer who would be read as far east as Southeast Asia. Muslim Spain was known mainly for the care with which it imitated the culture of the central Islamic world; a tenth-century Iranian vizier who procured a copy of a literary anthology composed in Spain was disappointed to see that the book was "just our own goods they're sending back to us." But by the eleventh century some Spanish scholars were repackaging eastern goods so well that their books became standard works in the central Islamic lands.

The Arabian homeland

Our survey of the Islamic world is now complete with the exception of Arabia, where it all began. The Arabs of pre-Islamic times were not in fact confined to the peninsula; Arab nomads were already present in the Syrian desert, the Sinai peninsula, and the eastern desert of Egypt, thus foreshadowing the Islamic expansion. But Arabia was their homeland, and it was here that Islam had its origins.

The fundamental feature of the Arabian environment was aridity. There was some rainfall in the southwestern corner of the peninsula, and to a lesser extent in the southeast, in each case thanks to the presence of mountains; but elsewhere the water supply, such as it was, mostly took the form of oases. Nowhere in Arabia was there a river like the Tigris, the Euphrates, or the Nile. This aridity imposed a low ceiling on the economic, social, and political life of the region. The population was overwhelmingly tribal and to a large extent nomadic. Commercially it had little to offer the outside world in the period that concerns us: the incense trade was over before the rise of Islam, the Yemeni coffee trade did not begin till after our period was over, and Saudi oil was of course far in the future. It is therefore unsurprising that the tribes of Arabia lacked the steep social stratification common among the tribes of the steppes, where nobles and commoners were distinct social groups. Such states as there were in Arabia tended to be located on the fringes of the peninsula, where the supply of rainfall was greater (as in Yemen and Oman) or imperial subsidies more generous (as on the borders of the Persian and Byzantine Empires).

Within this generally arid environment, the interior of western Arabia with its scattered oases – the land known as the Hijaz – hardly seemed particularly promising. But it was here that Muhammad proclaimed his religious message – a monotheism that unlike Judaism or Christianity was customized to resonate with Arab identity. Moreover, he went on to use his message to found a state that extended its influence over Arabia, and after his death far beyond it. Yet once the power of the Muslim state was firmly established outside Arabia, the brief exposure of the peninsula to the geopolitical limelight came to an end. The center of power shifted to the richer lands of the Fertile Crescent – Iraq and Syria – in the civil war of the later 650s, and it never returned to the arid soil of Arabia.

The impact of Islam on the peninsula was nonetheless profound. The Arabian population converted early and easily to Islam; it was *their* religion, in a way in which it was not for the conquered peoples outside Arabia. Yemen and Oman continued to matter owing to their combination of relatively greater agricultural resources and commercial frontage on the Indian Ocean; merchants from both regions were active in the trade with East Africa. Despite its lack of productive resources, the Hijaz was now able to join these relatively favored regions thanks to its possession of two of Islam's holiest sanctuaries: Mecca where Muhammad was born, and Medina where he built his state and was buried. This assured the Hijaz a flow of resources from the economically more privileged regions of the Muslim world. Elsewhere Islam showed its unusual ability to generate and maintain networks of religious scholars, even in desert environments where the full panoply of Islamic civilization was unsustainable. This made a real difference in Arabia, as it also did in such parts of the Sahara as Mauritania. But it was not till the coming of oil that Arabia was once again to achieve geopolitical prominence.

The components of Islamic civilization

To speak of Islamic civilization is to say that Islam is more than just a part of a larger package; rather, it is the core around which the civilization is built. That we do not readily speak in the same way of Christian or Buddhist civilization implies that Islam is unique in performing this role. This is a large claim, but a plausible one.

By way of illustration, consider the coins we looked at earlier. They have to be seen against the background of the standard model of coinage that had previously predominated in the Old World west of China: a round, flat piece of metal with the ruler's head on one side and a religious symbol on the other. Our Islamic coins diverge sharply from the standard model in two obvious ways. The first is that they are aniconic, reflecting the Islamic prohibition of images of living beings. The second concerns the substance of the inscriptions. With the exception of the one that states where and when the coin was minted, they consist entirely of Quranic material selected to proclaim God's message to mankind, with no ruler or governor so much as mentioned. They are still round, flat, metallic objects, and immediately recognizable as coins; but their content has been radically Islamized.

Our assignment now is to glance at some other aspects of Islamic civilization in a similar perspective. For convenience, let us look first at institutions and then at culture.

Institutions

What are the central institutions of Islamic civilization, and how do they relate to Islam? Let us start with what the religion prescribes. In the first place, it requires an Islamic political order: the Muslim community is to be under the authority of a single Muslim ruler, the Caliph – a title understood to refer to his role as either deputy of God or successor of the Prophet. Eligibility for this office is governed by certain rules, for example that the Caliph should belong to Quraysh, the Arab tribe into which Muhammad was born; at the same time there are procedural rules about how the Caliph is to be chosen – there is nothing like a rule of dynastic succession in Sunni Islam. The duties of the Caliph are both domestic and foreign. On the domestic side, he is to see to the performance of the basic public rituals of Islam, notably the Friday prayer; this involves building and maintaining suitable mosques in urban centers. At the same time he is to establish and maintain an Islamic legal order; this entails appointing judges whose learning and integrity qualifies them to give judgment according to Islamic law. But unlike most rulers, he does not have the power to make new law: God is the only legislator. On the foreign side, the Caliph's primary responsibility is military. He has to defend the frontiers of the Muslim world against any invasion by unbelievers from outside, and to attack these unbelievers from time to time with a view to extending the frontiers of Islam. Alongside this political order there must also be an Islamic social order, that is to say a Muslim society conducting its affairs in accordance with Islamic law. Here two characteristic features are worth mentioning. One is that there must be a group of people learned in Islamic matters, the scholars. The other feature is that women are subject to certain norms of subordination and segregation that limit their interaction with males outside the family and restrict their role in public space. There is much we could add to extend and refine this simple account, but for our purposes this outline suffices.

All this, of course, is prescription, so we should now ask how far it corresponds to historical reality even in the central lands of Islam. For simplicity, we can think in terms of three possibilities.

One possibility was that historical practice would more or less ignore Islamic prescriptions, leaving the scholars to save the appearances as best they could. A case in point is the principle that the Muslim community should form a single state ruled by the Caliph. This was still a realistic requirement in the first decades after Muhammad's death, and one message of our five coins is that as late as the first half of the eighth century this unity was still intact. But an empire stretching from Spain to Afghanistan was in geopolitical terms unsustainable: such a configuration had never existed before, and was never to be reconstituted. Already in the second half of the eighth century the Islamic world was beginning to break up into a number of regional states, and by the tenth century the political disintegration was complete; there were still contacts between Muslims from distant parts of the Islamic world, especially in the context of the pilgrimage to Mecca, but they now paid their taxes to many different rulers. What then was to become of the office of Caliph in the absence of a unitary state? One could have a shadow caliphate, a solution best represented by Egypt towards the end of our period; here an 'Abbasid Caliph went through the motions of reigning while a Turkish or Circassian sultan actually ruled. Or one could bestow the caliphate on all Muslim rulers, or on none. Or the ruler of the largest and most powerful state in the Muslim world might claim the caliphate, and receive some degree of recognition outside his own lands; from the sixteenth century this came to be the case with the Ottoman sultan, despite the awkward fact that he did not descend from the tribe of Quraysh.

Meanwhile the prime concern of the scholars was to construe the political realities of the day in such a way as to avoid the distressing conclusion that a legitimate Islamic order no longer existed; they did not usually take the drastic step of seeking to change the realities on the ground in order to bring them into line with the principles enshrined in the religious tradition.

Another possibility was that Islamic institutions could exist side-by-side with non-Islamic ones. An obvious case of this was the administration of justice. Rulers did indeed appoint judges, and the judges did indeed apply Islamic law in one or other of its recognized forms. But while this was part of the story, it was not the whole story. A large part of the population, especially those living outside the major cities, conducted their legal affairs in accordance with whatever system of customary law was accepted locally. The difference mattered: for example, in cases of inheritance Islamic law assigned shares to women, whereas customary law regularly excluded them. At the same time rulers might infringe on God's legislative monopoly by making laws of their own; for a long time the Ottoman sultans did this, producing an elaborate body of law that was known as Qanun (an Arabized form of the same Greek word that gives us the English "canon"). This too could make a substantive difference: for example, Qanun frequently imposed fines as punishments, something Islamic law does not do. We can easily find parallels to this situation in other aspects of Islamic civilization. One clear-cut example concerns the calendar. The formal calendar of Muslim societies was the Islamic calendar; its unique feature was that it defined a year as consisting invariably of twelve lunar months, thus making it some ten days shorter than the solar year, with the result that it was not in phase with the seasons. But in real life the Islamic lunar calendar regularly coexisted with some solar calendar, typically one inherited from the pre-Islamic past of the region in question. Another example takes us back to the prohibition of images. Though the law made no such distinction, the tendency was for the prohibition to be observed in public contexts and disregarded in private ones. But there was no hard and fast boundary: in the period following the Turkish invasion of the Middle East, there was a remarkable efflorescence of coins with images on them.

The third possibility was that Islamic principles might be more-or-less honored in practice. For example, most Islamic societies really did contain groups of Islamic scholars learned in the religious tradition.

Two points are worth adding to this reality check. The first is that the Islamic prescriptions often left much undefined. For example, they required rulers to build and maintain mosques in which the Friday prayer could be performed. But they did not tell them what these mosques should look like, for example by prescribing that all mosques should be built on the model of Muhammad's mosque in Medina. As a result, no serious tensions arose over the fact that different regions of the Islamic world developed very different traditions of religious architecture (no one would mistake an Ottoman mosque for a traditional North African one). Likewise there had to be scholars, but the law made no institutional provision for their education. In the early Islamic period they received it by joining informal study circles around individual teachers; from the tenth century onwards, this pattern tended to give ground to a new religious institution, the madrasa or college, which was endowed by the rich and powerful, paid salaries to its teachers, and provided support for its students. The madrasa thus became a widespread feature of Islamic civilization, but it was not the only way to arrange things. In the same way Islamic norms did not tell Muslim rulers how their armies should be organized, nor did they say much about how Muslim societies should be stratified.

The second point relates to the way in which the non-Islamic elements we have noted presented themselves. It was one thing for a non-Islamic practice to coexist quietly with Islamic norms, but another for such a practice to flaunt itself in some flagrantly un-Islamic fashion. For example, rulers who were not Caliphs, or claimed the caliphate merely as an add-on, might go by a variety of titles; but if they had the temerity to include the title "King of Kings" (the historic title of the pre-Islamic rulers of Iran) in the ritual of the Friday prayer, this could put them on a collision course with pious Muslims. Likewise if rulers made law and called it by the rather colourless term "Qanun," this was less likely to raise objections than if they called it "Yasa," a Mongolian word closely associated with the pagan Mongol conqueror Chinggis Khan. In the same way, Muslim societies were regularly seen as divided into the elite and the masses, but any assertion of formal caste divisions was open to challenge as un-Islamic.

Culture

Let us now shift our attention from institutions to culture, with particular reference to the high culture of the pre-modern Islamic world. We can best begin with the tradition of religious learning created and transmitted by the scholars, though the fact that our surviving sources were written mainly by these scholars means that their activities are likely to loom larger in hindsight than they did in real life (indeed the scholars themselves were given to complaining that no one paid any attention to what they said). The starting point of this tradition was of course divine revelation: the precisely bounded corpus of God's speech, the Quran, and the less well-defined corpus of authentic reports of Muhammad's inspired sayings and doings. As might be expected, the meaning of these texts, and their implications for the lives of subsequent Muslims, were not always transparent, leading to elaborate commentarial genres that proceeded verse by verse, report by report. But the scholars were not confined to following the thread of the revealed texts. They also composed systematic works that were arranged thematically. Thus they wrote treatises on substantive law, treatises on the theory of law, treatises on dogma, and so forth, while the mystics among them wrote works on Sufism. The scholars also wrote abundantly about themselves: collections of biographies of scholars are a stock-in-trade of Islamic scholarship.

At the same time, the scholars wrote on fields of knowledge less intrinsic to the religious tradition. For example, they collected and commented on poetry, including that composed in pre-Islamic Arabia, and they wrote poetry themselves. Such pursuits could be denounced by the pious as frivolous, but they could also be defended in terms of the benefits they offered to properly religious scholarship: a pagan poet's use of a word could illuminate its meaning in a Quranic verse, since the scripture was revealed in the language of the Arabs of Muhammad's day. What is clear is that whatever validity this rationale might possess, those who wrote and read such works liked poetry for its own sake. Historical writing was a somewhat analogous case. Writing the history of Muhammad and his immediate, authoritative successors was a contribution to properly religious scholarship; but the religious justification for continuing the story down to one's own day was more tenuous, and the bottom line is that people in Muslim societies found history interesting to read about. The case for belles-lettres was weaker still, but a man who was ignorant of the genre could not pass for educated in polite society. By no means all those who wrote poetry, history, or belles-lettres were at the same time scholars of the religious tradition, but many were.

Rather different was the case of scholarly genres that manifestly originated outside the Arabic and Islamic tradition. Such was the case with philosophy, by which is meant in this context the philosophical tradition of ancient Greece, translated into Arabic by Christians for the ninth-century Muslim elite. This tradition came to be an established component of Islamic civilization, but its alien origin was not forgotten and could always be held against it. Something similar can be said of the sciences, which came to the Muslims largely from Greek sources, but also from Middle Persian and Sanskrit. One example is the Greek medical tradition identified with Hippocrates and Galen. This became the standard medical tradition of Islamic civilization, but like philosophy it was open to challenge for its alien origins. Some pietists thus preferred a rival tradition, the remedies reported to have been prescribed by Muhammad, and there was contention about this; one might hold such remedies to be a part of God's revelation, or one might dismiss them as mere folk medicine that Muhammad had picked up from his environment. Indirect support for such dismissal was available in a report describing how Muhammad once gave advice regarding the cultivation of date-palms. The cultivators duly followed his advice, with disastrous results; he then told them that anything he said on such matters was just his own human opinion, and carried no stamp of divine approval. Astronomy was another science that could be contentious. The astronomers believed the earth to be spherical, and had no regard for those who considered it flat; but their view was in awkward tension with the literal sense of revealed texts. Moreover astronomers often doubled as astrologers, protagonists of a set of beliefs about the influence of the heavenly bodies on earthly events that was horribly un-Islamic, though very widespread in Muslim, as in other, societies.

Islamic civilization as we find it in the core lands of Islam was thus a tense but rather stable mixture of fully Islamic elements, quasi-Islamic elements, and transparently un-Islamic elements. Outside the core, it was some version of this mix that was spread by the later expansion of Islam. The outcome in any given region depended on a number of factors: the precise version of Islamic civilization in play, the force with which it arrived, and the strength of local traditions antedating its arrival. An obvious example of the importance of version is the fact that the new lands dependent on Iran received Persian literary culture as part of the package; this applies to Anatolia, Central Asia, and India, but not to Southeast Asia or Africa. As to the role of force, the limited part played by conquest in Southeast Asia and West Africa is surely related to the persistence in both those regions of Muslim societies retaining systems of matrilineal inheritance from the pre-Islamic past. Finally, a clear example of the part played by the strength of local traditions is the admixture of Islamic and indigenous elite culture that we find in some measure in India, and to a much greater extent in Java and among the Muslim minority in southern and eastern China; significantly, both Java and China were lands in which Muslims not only used the indigenous languages, but wrote them in the indigenous scripts.

Against such diversity we can set a striking linguistic unity in one key respect. Religions that spread widely have to decide whether to confer on translations of their foundational texts the same ritual standing as the originals possess. Both Buddhism and Christianity did this at some points in their pre-modern history but not at others. Islam, with one still-born exception, did not do it at all.

The origins of Islamic civilization

It would be easy to imagine a counterfactual history in which the outcome of the Arab expansion was the absorption of the conquerors by the peoples they had conquered; such an outcome would have been favored by the disparity of numbers, and has many historical parallels. But instead it was the conquering Arabs who were the assimilators, ultimately spreading their language from Mauritania to Iraq, and their religion over an even wider area. Nor was this all: as we have seen, in the wake of the Arab conquests a new civilization took shape. The paradox is that the key role in this drama should have been played by conquerors coming from the least civilized part of the Middle East. How do we resolve this paradox?

Part of the answer must have to do with the character of the peoples the Arabs conquered in the Fertile Crescent. It was here that Arab settlement was densest, and here that the new Arab rulers had their capital cities, notably Damascus under the Umayyads and Baghdad under the 'Abbasids. So it stands to reason that this was the crucial region for the formation of Islamic civilization. As we have seen, the native inhabitants of Iraq and Syria were speakers of varieties of Aramaic, which like Arabic was a Semitic language. Many of them readily joined the conquerors and adopted Arabic. Culturally they had much to bring with them: they possessed elaborate literary traditions of a kind that Arabia lacked. But a millennium of foreign rule had long ago eroded any strong identity of the Iranian type, at once ethnic, religious, and political.

The other half of the answer must relate to the character of the Arab conquerors. In contrast to the peoples of the Fertile Crescent, they were low on elite culture but amply endowed with just the kind of identity that the Aramaic-speakers lacked. Like the Iranians, the Arabs were now in possession of an identity that was at once ethnic, religious, and political. The ethnic component was an old sense of Arab identity, the religious component was the Islamic customization of monotheism that highlighted this identity, and the political component was participation in the immensely rewarding enterprise of extending the sway of the Islamic state far beyond the borders of Arabia.

There was thus a certain complementarity between the conquered and the conquerors. The Arabs brought such things as their language, their traditions of poetry and public speaking, their consuming interest in genealogy, and their as yet uncanonized scripture. But the process that turned all this into a comprehensive literary culture surely owed more to the non-Arab converts of the Fertile Crescent. And yet it has to be emphasized that any account of the way in which Islamic civilization emerged is likely to remain in large measure speculative. In the end we cannot say much more than that this civilization was not yet there at the beginning of the seventh century, and had crystallized by the end of the eighth. Nor does it help that we are dealing with an event to which we have no historical parallel. In short, the dramatic changes that issued in the formation of the new civilization can fairly be seen as one of the great black-swan events of history: utterly unlikely in prospect, and immensely consequential in retrospect.

FURTHER READING

1. General historical surveys and reference

Encyclopaedia Iranica, ed. Ehsan Yarshater. London: Routledge & Kegan Paul, 1985–.

The Encyclopaedia of Islam, second edn. Leiden: Brill, 1960–2009.

Humphreys, R. Stephen. *Islamic History: A Framework for Inquiry*, revised edn. Princeton University Press, 1991.

Kennedy, Hugh. *The Prophet and the Age of the Caliphates: The Islamic Near East from the Sixth to the Eleventh Century*, second edn. Harlow: Pearson Longman, 2004.

Lapidus, Ira M. *A History of Islamic Societies*, second edn. Cambridge University Press, 2002.

The New Cambridge History of Islam, 6 vols. Cambridge University Press, 2010, vol. I: *The Formation of the Islamic World, Sixth to Eleventh Centuries*, ed. Chase F. Robinson; vol. II: *The Western Islamic World, Eleventh to Eighteenth Centuries*, ed. Maribel Fierro; vol. III: *The Eastern Islamic World, Eleventh to Eighteenth Centuries*, ed. David O. Morgan and Antony Reid.

2. Regional historical surveys

Asher, Catherine B. and Cynthia Talbot. *India before Europe*. Cambridge University Press, 2006.

Berend, Nora. *At the Gate of Christendom: Jews, Muslims, and "Pagans" in Medieval Hungary, c. 1000 – c. 1300*. Cambridge University Press, 2001.

The Cambridge History of Africa, 8 vols. Cambridge University Press, 1975–84; vol. II: *From c. 500 BC to AD 1050*, ed. J. D. Fage; vol. III: *From c. 1050 to c. 1500*, ed. Roland Oliver.

The Cambridge History of Egypt, 2 vols. Cambridge University Press, 1998; vol. I: *Islamic Egypt, 640–1517*, ed. Carl F. Petry.

The Cambridge History of Iran, 7 vols. Cambridge University Press, 1968–91; vol. IV: *The Period from the Arab Invasion to the Saljuqs*, ed. R. N. Frye; vol. V: *The Saljuq and Mongol Periods*, ed. J. A. Boyle; vol. VI: *The Timurid and Safavid Periods*, ed. Peter Jackson and Lawrence Lockhart.

Golden, Peter B. *An Introduction to the History of the Turkic Peoples*. Wiesbaden: O. Harrassowitz, 1992.

Holt, Peter. *The Age of the Crusades: The Near East from the Eleventh Century to 1516*. London and New York: Longman, 1986.

Imber, Colin. *The Ottoman Empire 1300–1481*. Istanbul: The Isis Press, 1990.

The Ottoman Empire, 1300–1650: The Structure of Power. Basingstoke and New York: Palgrave Macmillan, 2002.

Kennedy, Hugh. *Muslim Spain and Portugal: A Political History of al-Andalus*. London and New York: Longman, 1996.

Levtzion, Nehemia. *Ancient Ghana and Mali*. London: Methuen, 1973.

Lewis, Bernard. *The Middle East: A Brief History of the Last 2,000 years*. New York, NY: Scribner, 1995.

Morgan, David. *Medieval Persia*. London and New York: Longman, 1988.

Soucek, Svat. *A History of Inner Asia*. Cambridge University Press, 2000.

3. Aspects of Islamic culture

Alam, Muzaffar. *The Languages of Political Islam: India 1200–1800*. University of Chicago Press, 2004.

Berkey, Jonathan P. *The Formation of Islam: Religion and Society in the Near East, 600–1800*. Cambridge University Press, 2003.

Blair, Sheila S. and Jonathan M. Bloom. *The Art and Architecture of Islam, 1250–1800*. New Haven and London: Yale University Press, 1994.

The Cambridge History of Arabic Literature, 6 vols. Cambridge University Press, 1983–2006.

Crone, Patricia. *Medieval Islamic Political Thought*. Edinburgh University Press, 2004.

Ettinghausen, Richard, Oleg Grabar, and Marilyn Jenkins-Medina. *Islamic Art and Architecture, 650–1250*, second edn. New Haven and London: Yale University Press, 2001.

Grunebaum, Gustave E. von. *Medieval Islam: A Study in Cultural Orientation*, second edn. University of Chicago Press, 1953.

Hillenbrand, Robert. *Islamic Architecture: Form, Function and Meaning*. Edinburgh University Press, 1994.

Karamustafa, Ahmet T. *Sufism: The Formative Period*. Edinburgh University Press, 2007.

The New Cambridge History of Islam, 6 vols. Cambridge University Press, 2010, vol. IV: *Islamic Cultures and Societies to the End of the Eighteenth Century*, ed. Robert Irwin.

Robinson, Chase F. *Islamic Historiography*. Cambridge University Press, 2003.

Rosenthal, Franz. *A History of Muslim Historiography*, second edn. Leiden: Brill, 1968.

Rypka, Jan. *History of Iranian Literature*. Dordrecht: D. Reidel, 1968.

Ullmann, Manfred. *Islamic Medicine*. Edinburgh University Press, 1978.

Walther, Wiebke. *Women in Islam*. Princeton and New York: Marcus Wiener, 1993.

4. Primary sources in translation

Frye, Richard N., trans. *Ibn Fadlan's Journey to Russia*. Princeton, NJ: Markus Wiener, 2005.

Hopkins, J. F. P. and N. Levtzion, ed. and trans. *Corpus of Early Arabic Sources for West African History*. Cambridge University Press, 1981.

Lewis, Bernard, ed. and trans. *Islam from the Prophet Muhammad to the Capture of Constantinople*, 2 vols. New York and Oxford: Oxford University Press, 1987.

16

Christendom's regional systems

MIRI RUBIN

The religion born among the Jews of Palestine under Roman imperial rule some 2,000 years ago is now a global religion characterized by great diversity among its constituent groups.[1] This chapter will study Christianity's regional systems over a thousand years, 500 CE–1500 CE, during which it was the official religion of the Byzantine Empire and spread throughout Europe, much of Asia and parts of Africa. In Europe it reached west and north to become the hegemonic religion of the continent through a process that in northeast Europe ended only in the fourteenth century. In Syria, North Africa and Spain, Christianity ceded in the seventh and eighth centuries to Islam's progress, and lost to it in the fourteenth and fifteenth centuries control of almost all parts of what had been the Byzantine Empire. In Africa, Christian rule survived in Ethiopia alone, in the kingdom of Axum, and Christians lived within the Islamic states of North Africa.[2] In Asia, from Syria to Persia two countervailing processes unfolded: the adaptation of Christian life to Islamic rule, and the spread of Christianity beyond the caliphate into neighbouring regions of Central Asia, India and China. The last decades of our period see the implantation of new forms of Christian life on the northwest coast of Africa in Portuguese mercantile colonies. The 1490s saw Vasco da Gama reach western India and the arrival of European Christians in the Caribbean.

---

1 I am most grateful to Michal Biran for suggesting extremely useful reading on Christianity in China, and to Yossef Rapoport for reading a draft of this paper and helping me learn more about Coptic Christianity.

2 On Axum, G. W. Bowersock, *The Throne of Adulis. Red Sea Wars on the Eve of Islam* (Oxford University Press, 2013). On North African Christianity, see Mohammed Talbi, 'Le Christianisme maghrébin de la conquête musulmanne à sa disparition: une tentative d'explication', in Michael Gervers and Ramzi Jibran Bikhazi (eds.), *Conversion and Continuity: Indigenous Christian Communities in Islamic Lands Eighth to Eighteenth Centuries* (Toronto: Pontifical Institute of Medieval Studies, 1990): 313–51.

Amidst great diversity, one major aspect of Christian cultures that may have been familiar and reassuring to those travelling throughout Byzantium, into Europe or the lands of Rus', further east, or south to Ethiopia, was the presence of the figure of the Virgin Mary. Here two main models prevailed, different yet not unrecognizably so. One type, the product of Byzantine imperial Christianity, was Mary as *Theotokos*, the one who gives birth to God: enthroned, attended by angels, facing the viewer with her solemn son in her lap facing the viewer too. The other type depicted Mary as an active mother much like other women, who read, prayed, cooked, knitted; she interacted lovingly with her son as an infant, or lamented his crucifixion as an adult man.

At the beginning of our period, Byzantine prestige as the foremost Christian polity was displayed in great building projects as well as in the widespread presence of coins, all imprinted with Christian symbols. These defined a visual style. Images of the Virgin Mary disseminated from the imperial capital dominated the style of representation for centuries, in icons, mosaics, and ivories throughout Christian regions, such as the Syriac Bible of the sixth century, the image of Mary in the Irish Book of Kells of *c.* 800, the Russian icon associated with the protection of Novgorod in 1170, Our Lady of the Sign, or images produced in Italy throughout our period.

This chapter begins with a consideration of some of the characteristics of Christian life and its implications for polities, communities, and individuals. It proceeds to examine life in areas of the world governed by Christian rulers – the borders of which were always shifting – then to the Islamic world, and finally to polities further east. The chapter ends with a consideration of some movements – trade, crusading, mission – which encouraged links between the Christian regions.

The characteristics of Christian institutions

Around 500, Christian life officially dominated the areas that had been part of the Roman Empire. In the provinces of Spain and Gaul, Italy and the Balkans, Asia Minor, Syria and Palestine as well as Egypt and the coast of North Africa, Christian communities were supported and protected by the Byzantine Empire around the Mediterranean, and by Christian kingdoms that succeeded the Western Roman Empire (see Map 16.1). Further afield, there was Christian life in Ireland and Scotland to the north and west, as well in the Sasanian Empire to the east, whose state religion was Zoroastrianism. While in 500 most Christian communities in Europe were of recent conversion,

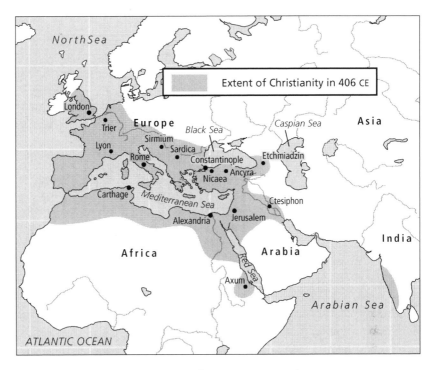

Map 16.1. Christianity in 406 CE

those in the East were ancient, born from the conversion of members of ancient pagan and Jewish communities, and who used Syriac – eastern and western – for liturgical purposes.

Christianity based its claim to universal truth on the belief that it embodied the fulfilment of biblical prophecies realized in the incarnation, life, crucifixion, resurrection and ascension of Jesus Christ. Its sense of history, defined by the Christian bishop and historian Eusebius (c. 263–339), saw a succession of world powers – from the Chaldeans to the Romans – destined to culminate in a future apocalyptic time. Augustine (354–430), bishop of Hippo in North Africa, established an historical view whereby the new covenant between God and his people was described in the narratives of Christ's life, written down by his disciples the evangelists, and combined with the prophecies of the Hebrew Bible into Christian scripture. A chain of succession was created by Jesus in his lifetime, a bond cemented by the offering of his body at a meal shared by Jesus and his disciples before his death that became known as the Last Supper, and reiterated through the bestowal of authority to the apostles. By the beginning of our period, the bishops of Rome claimed superiority to the other episcopal sees because their see was founded – according to tradition – by St Peter, the leader of the disciples. The authority to interpret, translate and explicate scripture and the authority to determine which enunciations would become part of the growing Christian canon was, and remained, disputed. Control of access to scripture and to the sacraments – rituals understood to convey saving grace – became a prime ecclesiastical preoccupation, periodically and regularly challenged by laypeople and clergy alike. In Europe at the end of our period, this was the issue that brought about the profound critique and rupture with the past associated with the Protestant Reformation.

Christian life was organized in communities, and these were overseen by bishops from great churches situated in cities such as Poitiers, Milan, Lyon, Toledo, Hippo and Antioch. Some bishops were considered more exalted than others because of the apostolic foundation, antiquity, and dignity of their sees, and were designated as patriarchates: Antioch, Alexandria, Constantinople, Rome, and Jerusalem. By 500 bishops provided the backbone of Christian administration, building where this existed upon the bureaucratic infrastructure of the Roman Empire. They often assumed functions of state when imperial provision failed, supplying cities with grain and water, repairing city walls, and negotiating treaties with Barbarian leaders. Bishops also set the standards for religious instruction and true belief: they supervised the training of priests, managed church property, ordered the content and rhythm of liturgy, authorized versions of scripture, maintained church courts, distributed alms, and oversaw the teaching of orthodoxy. Each bishop – or metropolitan in the Church of the East – traced the foundation of his see to an apostle or a martyr, whose cult provided the core of local identity and a uniting theme for regional life alongside the great universal truths of Christianity. By the beginning of our period, such cults celebrated St Martin in Tours, St Peter in Rome, St Vitale in Ravenna, St Thomas on the Malabar Coast. Constantinople adopted the Virgin Mary, Jesus' mother, as its special protector, and there she soon was addressed as *Theotokos*.

Regional affinities and styles reflected the missionary effort that had led to conversion. Christians in India still claimed their ancestry from St Thomas the Apostle and used Syriac as their liturgical language until this was expunged in the sixteenth century by European Christians. In Syria and Mesopotamia, Christianity had grown among the vast pagan, Zoroastrian and Jewish communities; converts from the latter retained a deep-rooted biblicism and a cautious attitude to the use of images in worship.[3] When St Augustine (d. 604) – later to be named 'of Canterbury' – was sent by Pope Gregory I from Rome to convert the people of England, he imported the Roman calendar and liturgy. The mission to the Slavs of Great Moravia in the ninth century was led by the brothers and future saints Cyril and Methodius, who devised the Glagolitic alphabet from which Cyrillic – the alphabet used by the people of Rus' – was derived. Be it under imperial Christian rule, in European dynastic kingdoms or under non-Christian rule, Christian life always exhibited a commitment to Christian universality, but also the telling marks of local histories and the circumstances of diverse presents.

In the analysis of Christian life, whether in Christian polities or under Sasanian, Muslim or Central Asian rule, it may be useful to apply the concepts of charisma and institution as developed by the social theorist Max Weber (1864–1920) in his discussion of the formation of institutions and bureaucracies. The process by which Christian churches emerged may be interpreted as an attempt to routinize the legacy of Jesus' charisma, to make it enduring and repeatable. One example would be the office of bishop, which we have already encountered: heir and successor to the role of apostles as teachers, and guardian of grace to be transmitted to believers through the sacraments. Their eminence was incorporated in certain European Christian kingdoms – including England, France, and Poland – into a close relationship with dynasts, the charisma of lineage joining that of episcopal office in interdependence.

Churchmen – educated and competent in Latin, and in central and western Europe after the eleventh century, required to live in celibacy – provided rulers with a wide range of expertise in law, diplomacy, science and communication. They assisted rulers in projecting a credible and legitimate figure of rule, and helped enhance them above other landed magnates. Both in European polities and in the Byzantine Empire, a coexistence of mutual benefit – though not without tension – evolved between dynastic and ecclesiastical bearers of authority and the bureaucratic structures they endorsed. European kings and the rulers of the Holy Roman Empire accepted bishops as great vassals, with vast estates, areas of jurisdiction and an autonomous system of ecclesiastical courts. While the boundaries of these spheres were

---

3 See the discussion in Jules Leroy, *Les Manuscrits syriaques à peintures conservés dans les bibliothèques d'Europe et d'Orient* (Paris: Librairie orientaliste Paul Geuthner, 1964). See also Sebastian P. Brock, *The Bible in the Syriac Tradition* (Piscataway, NJ: Gorgias Press, 2006).

often contested – especially over issues of taxation and legal competence – the fundamental arrangement was not: state and church were both involved in establishing order and maintaining social hierarchy within the general framework of Christian ethics. Kings and emperors were understood to rule by the grace of God. They were charged with supporting the church in the work of salvation and were expected to allow the sphere of ecclesiastical law to prevail in a wide range of areas – marriage, testamentary bequests, identification and persecution of heresy, and discipline of the clergy. In Europe, towards the later Middle Ages, rulers became less dependent on the clergy for essential services because secular bureaucracies of professional elites developed in many areas of administration and then grew in ambition and competence.

Life in Christian polities

The routinization of charisma within the institutions of the church and the beneficial coexistence of church and state bureaucracies in Europe and in the Byzantine Empire invited perennial critique. Those who fashioned lives of ascetic spirituality were believed to possess the authority born of the virtue exhibited in their lives. There were usually holy men, whose lives and influence have been evoked so powerfully by the historian Peter Brown.[4] They called believers to penance and devoted their lives to the heroics of asceticism. In the deserts of Syria, Palestine, and Egypt, in the hills of Armenia and northern Persia, they inspired a powerful genre of hagiography, and drew adherents to shrines. One of these ascetics was St Simeon the Stylite (389–459), who lived for decades upon a stone pillar, encouraging villagers to repent, and drawing pilgrims from as far as North Africa and Europe to Qal'at Sim'an, his shrine some 60 kilometres northeast of Antioch.[5] Such 'living saints' could also challenge the power of the state to lay down orthodox belief. When the monk and theologian Maximus the Confessor (580–662), challenged the imperial formulation on the will of Christ he was mutilated – his tongue and right hand cut off – and sent into

---

4 Peter Brown, *Society and the Holy in Late Antiquity* (London: Faber, 1982).
5 Gary Vikan, '"Guided by Land and Sea": Pilgrim Art and Pilgrim Travel in Early Byzantium', in Gary Vikan, *Sacred Images and Sacred Power in Byzantium* (Aldershot: Ashgate, 2003): 74–92. On stylites, Brandie Ratliff, 'The Stylites of Syria', in *Byzantium and Islam: Age of Transition 7th–9th Century* (New York: Metropolitan Museum of Art, 2012): 94–7, and on pilgrimage more broadly, see Brandie Ratliff, 'Travel to the Holy', in *Byzantium and Islam*, 86–93.

exile in Thrace in the Caucasus.[6] Yet soldiers who guarded him were appalled at being forced to incarcerate the holy man.

Christian political hegemony offered many benefits to Christian communities, in the legal protection of churches and clergy, in the support of church courts, in munificent benefactions, and the incorporation of Christian content into court rituals. The Byzantine emperors since Constantine presided over the councils that determined matters of faith, and used the power of the state to enforce that orthodoxy by persecuting dissenters. Heresy was tantamount to treason. Yet such support for the church came at a price; in Byzantium and later in European polities, rulers sought to codify belief and define orthodoxy, and also persecuted those who dissented from the mainstream. Life outside the protection of Christian rulers could sometimes provide space for more autonomous expression of religious life, and especially of the non-bureaucratic, charismatic type. When the authority of the Patriarchate of Jerusalem declined after the Muslim conquest of Jerusalem in 638 and the separation from the imperial Byzantine church that resulted from it, monastic life in the region flourished. The monasteries of the Judean desert became the sole local repositories of Christian scholarship, and produced important scholars, influential for their exemplary – charismatic – teaching, and for their actions outside an enabling official framework.[7]

Wise rulers attempted to harness the power of charisma. For example, Pope Innocent III was forced to decide what was to be done with Francis of Assisi (1181–1226) and his following. Francis had given up the privileged life of a merchant's son and sought to live the apostolic life of poverty and preaching.[8] Pope Innocent did not treat him as just another enthusiast preaching poverty without licence, but rather embraced him. Francis and his followers were turned into a vanguard in the service of the church, with the privilege to preach anywhere in order to turn lukewarm Christians into committed ones. Some Franciscans turned their intellectual and oratorical energies towards polemic against Jews and to missionary efforts far beyond Christian Europe: in Tunis, Egypt and as far as China.

6 Robert Louis Wilken, *The Spirit of Early Christian Thought: Seeking the Face of God* (New Haven, CT: Yale University Press, 2003): 113–18.

7 Brouria Bitton-Ashkelony and Aryeh Kofsky, 'Monasticism in the Holy Land', in Ora Limor and Guy G. Stroumsa (eds.), *Christians and Christianity in the Holy Land: From the Origins to the Latin Kingdoms* (Turnhout: Brepols, 2006): 288–9.

8 André Vauchez, *Francis of Assisi: The Life and Afterlife of a Medieval Saint* (New Haven, CT: Yale University Press, 2012).

Our emphasis so far has been on the workings of charisma and institutions in Christian regions. These were reflected in the continuous tension between the authority invested in bishops who organized Christian life through the provision of education, ritual and law, on the one hand, and that unmediated authority earned by adored holy people, on the other. The fundamental challenge faced by ecclesiastical institutions, both within and without Christian polities, was in providing believers with a compelling narrative that made sense of their lives, based on authoritative texts and disseminated in the vernacular. Alongside such teaching was the rich ritual world that re-enacted the Christian narrative, and which also marked meaningful points of the life cycle. None of this was easily achieved or uniformly practised, but everywhere Christian rituals incorporated pre-existing – pre-Christian – traditions and robust symbols of the Christian faith. Christian rituals, including baptism and the Eucharist, were often enactments of episodes in Jesus' life. No ritual of the life cycle was left untouched, so for example, by the seventh century the Franks possessed a Christian ritual for the marking of an adolescent boy's first facial shaving, the *barbatoria*. More significantly, the religion that announced the coming of an incarnate God, who was enmeshed in exemplary practices of asceticism and physical purity, came to sanction marriage and sexuality.[9] In Europe, from the twelfth century a rich cultural sphere came to surround marriage as a sacrament of love. The religion which offered eternal life also dealt expertly with the end of life. It solemnized death by claiming it was not the end, and offered ideas and practices – like the concept of purgatory elaborated in Europe – which allowed the living to communicate with the dead and to act in piety on their behalf.[10]

The ritual world marked the human life cycle and celebrated above all the life of Jesus, his mother and apostles, martyrs and saints (see Figure 16.1). By the year 500 a rich world of legend enhanced the life-narratives of Jesus, Mary and Joseph, filling in the gaps in the Christian story and rendering these figures compelling and familiar figures of purity and faith. Peter Brown has described this system as the incorporation of dead humans into the ritual practices of the living.[11] Thus were created in a

---

9 Peter J. Payer, *The Bridling of Desire: Views of Sex in the Later Middle Ages* (Toronto: University of Toronto Press, 1993); Christopher N. L. Brooke, *The Medieval Idea of Marriage* (Oxford University Press, 1989).

10 Frederick S. Paxton, *Christianizing Death: The Creation of a Ritual Process in Early Medieval Europe* (Ithaca: Cornell University Press, 1990).

11 Peter Brown, *The Cult of Saints: Its Rise and Function in Latin Christianity* (London: SCM Press, 1981): 177.

Figure 16.1 Ivory plaque with the Adoration of the Magi, Early Byzantine, early sixth century (©The Trustees of the British Museum. All rights reserved)

variety of languages – Greek, Latin, Armenian, Coptic, Syriac – the narratives of Jesus' childhood, the stories which imagined the ends of Mary and Joseph.[12] In subsequent centuries and in Europe above all, this world of legend – considered by some Christian thinkers to be of doubtful authority, and ever lampooned by Jews – reached heights of elaboration. The prevailing cultural trend in Europe favoured the mediation of religious narratives through eliciting identification: Jesus was portrayed after the year 1200 either as a sweet baby or as a suffering man, and his mother as a doting parent or as a bereaved one, in the European medieval image *par excellence*, the *pietà*. These images were available in Christian regions very widely and publicly: a Madonna on every street corner, a cross in every market square (see Figure 16.2).

Christians were organized in communities for collective worship, under the guidance of a priest – sometimes a monk allocated to the task – and these parishes often overlapped with already cohesive groups of neighbourhood, work and sociability. Parishes often reflected the underlying economic and social structures: they overlapped with villages and urban neighbourhoods, reinforcing interactions within and between families. This was not only the case in Europe, but in Egypt and Syria under Muslim rule too. From the eve of the Crusades and throughout the Latin presence in West Asia (1099–1291), Melkite Christians – followers of Greek Orthodox Christianity – still lived in large parts of Samaria in villages, each with its small church in Byzantine style, first built probably in the fifth or sixth century.[13] Where Christians lived in nucleated villages and densely populated cities, provision of pastoral care was probably the most effective, benefitting from the underlying networks of work, security and bureaucracy. In areas more sparsely populated, or where pastoral or nomadic lifestyles prevailed – as in large parts of Ireland, the Jura Mountains of today's France and Switzerland, or much of Central Asia – provision of pastoral care was less regular and was often disrupted for lack of churches, priests or a sufficiently large congregation. The Franciscan William of Rubruck (c. 1220–c. 1293) was bemused to find (what he considered to be only so-called) Christians among the Naiman people of Central Asia, served

---

12 Lucette Valensi, *La Fuite en Égypte. Histoires d'Orient et d'Occident; essai d'histoire comparée* (Paris: Seuil, 2002); Stephen J. Shoemaker, *Ancient Traditions of the Virgin Mary's Dormition and Assumption* (Oxford University Press, 2002).
13 Ronnie Ellenblum, *Frankish Rural Settlement in the Latin Kingdom of Jerusalem* (Cambridge University Press, 1998).

Figure 16.2 The Holy Family, Joos van Cleve, c. 1485–1540/41, Antwerp (Metropolitan Museum of Art / © SCALA)

by 'a certain Nestorian, a mighty herdsman and the ruler over a people called the Naiman, who were Nestorian Christians'.[14]

Whatever the terrain and the conditions of subsistence, Christian life always combined elements of the local and predictable with those that were more unusual, even exotic. The local church stood for centuries, maintained and adorned as far as communities could manage and the surroundings allowed. Within it unfolded familiar chants and ritual acts guided by old books, with the participation of the congregation of young and old, male and female, committed and less-committed Christians. Christian life was embedded within family and work, but alongside these rhythms there were less predictable, enriching and sometimes baffling, experiences: the visit of a specialist religious, monk or preacher; an encounter with a hermit living in a forest or a cave in the hills south of Siena or those of Tur 'Abdin in northern Iraq; the arrival of a church tribunal – like that which appeared repeatedly to examine the villagers of Montaillou in the early fourteenth century; pilgrimage to a shrine nearby or perhaps the return of a pilgrim, merchant or crusader from further afield with tales to tell and souvenirs to show and share.

When and where Christian kingdoms appeared to be in serious threat – confronting conquest, raids, loss of sovereignty, or exaction of tribute – in those zones of war some of the most creative cultural processes took place, often forging unique patterns of identity.[15] As the Muscovite kingdom of Rus' (1238–1480) evolved after the Mongol conquests, church writers and secular authorities combined in creating myths of Christian resistance, martyrdom and heroism. In fact, the Grand Duchy of Moscow was established within the sphere of the Khanate of the Golden Horde. The Grand Duchy represented sedentary Christian order, but even after the decline of the Golden Horde it still retained a formative attachment to the dread of the Other – the enemy to the East. It now invested this in the Cossacks – settlers of the steppes who mingled Russian heritage with the life-style and military skills of the nomads – despite the fact that the Cossacks were Christians.[16]

Christian life was vastly varied even within the lands where it was the majority religion and the rulers were Christian. As we shall see, it developed

---

14 *The Mission of Friar William of Rubruck: His Journey to the Court of the Great Khan Möngke 1253–1255*, trans. Peter Jackson, ed. Peter Jackson and David Morgan (London: Hakluyt Society, 1990), vol. XVII, 122.

15 This argument is developed for Europe in Robert Bartlett, *The Making of Europe: Conquest, Colonization, and Cultural Change, 950–1350* (London: Allan Lane, 1993).

16 Moshe Gammer, 'Russia and the Eurasian Steppe Nomads: An Overview', in Reuven Amitai and Michal Biran (eds.), *Mongols, Turks, and Others: Eurasian Nomads and the Sedentary World* (Leiden: Brill, 2005): 483–502.

particular variations where Christians lived as large, tolerated indigenous communities, as was the case under Islam.

Christian life in the Sasanian and Muslim polities

At the beginning of the Middle Millennium, Christianity was already well established within the Mediterranean basin, although it was only beginning to spread northwards in Europe. Under the Emperor Justinian (527–65), Byzantine hegemony was asserted over most of the Mediterranean basin, suppressing the Christian kingdoms of Vandals, Visigoths and Ostrogoths, in which an Arian version of Christianity prevailed. This belief, named for the fourth-century Alexandrian priest Arius, emphasized the separate, created nature of Jesus as Son of God within the Trinity, and it was repeatedly denounced by the Byzantine church councils. To the east of the Empire there was the Christian kingdom of Armenia, with an independent Christian tradition that varied in matters of Christology from the formulations of the Council of Chalcedon of 451. Byzantium and Armenia also bordered the Sasanian Empire, from which Christians often fled to Armenia and Georgia in periods of persecution.

Christianity of the East can be characterized by three main historic groupings, which contained different denominations, some of which have survived until today. There were (1) the Church of the East, the name later applied to those dissident 'Nestorians' who broke away from imperial Christianity in 431, whose liturgical language was East (classical) Syriac and whose adherents have survived in Iraq and Iran but have also migrated to Europe, Australia and the United States; (2) Syrian followers of imperial Orthodoxy, Melkites and Maronites, whose liturgical language was Greek; and (3) the Syriac Orthodox Church (or the Church of the West, or Jacobite), which separated from Greek Orthodoxy over theological issues in 451, whose liturgical language was Greek and which maintained close ties with other non-Chalcedonian groups such as the Copts, as well as the Nubians and Ethiopians who depended upon the Copts hierarchically. Despite a recognition that there was great variety, certain aspects of Christian practice still amazed travellers: the Coptic priest and traveller Abu al-Makarim (1205–73) described with disapproval the use by Ethiopians of vinegar for communion, just as he marvelled at the sumptuous gilt of a Christian church in San'a, Yemen.[17]

---

17 *The Churches and Monasteries of Egypt and Some Neighbouring Countries Attributed to Abû Sâlih, the Armenian,* trans. B. T. A. Evetts (Oxford: Clarendon Press 1895): 289 and 300.

Early Christian communities developed within the Byzantine (325–1453) and Sasanian Empires (224–651) and they included – among others – many converts from among the long-established urban Jewish communities. This explains some of the distinctive cultural traits of the region's Christian culture: a liturgy that was highly scriptural, and a theology to which Greek Platonic concepts were all but foreign in these early, formative stages. The cultural centre of Syriac Christianity was Edessa, which was also an important economic centre to which many Persian Christians had escaped during Sasanian persecutions. Edessa's distinctive theology was exegetical in emphasis and it rejected the formulations made in Constantinople about a God in whom divinity and humanity were fully combined. Theodore of Mopsuestia (c. 350–428) taught of Jesus the Man, who offered a 'habitation' for the Word of God. From this also followed that the Virgin Mary was not the mother of God – *Theotokos* – bearer of God, the appellation accepted at the Council of Ephesus (431), which became the core of imperial liturgy. Rather, she had given birth to the man Christ, and was thus to be addressed as *Anthropotokos* or *Christotokos*. Such understandings are also called Nestorian, after Nestorius, the Syrian Patriarch of Constantinople, who promoted them, until his condemnation at that council. So alien were these beliefs to official imperial Christianity that the school at Edessa was closed by imperial mandate in 489, and a new centre for the Church of the East emerged further east – in Nisibis on the river Tigris – whose school guided Christian thought within the Persian sphere for centuries to come.[18]

The Church of the East was led by the *catholicos*, whose province ranged from Lake Van in the north to the Persian Gulf in the south, and whose seat was in the city of Seleucia/Ctesiphon up to 780, when it moved to Baghdad. Besides settled communities, Christians of the East supported in this period some hundred and fifty monasteries, many in the northern borderlands between Byzantine and – up to 651 – Sasanian control. The *catholicos* supervised Christian worship in all these areas, but in comparison with Europe or Byzantium provisions for believers were sparse. In 820 there were some nineteen metropolitans (equivalent to archbishops), which by the

---

18 Sebastian Brock, 'The "Nestorian" Church: A Lamentable Misnomer', *Bulletin of the John Rylands Library* 78(1996): 23–35; Sergey Minov, 'The *Cave of Treasures* and the Formation of Syriac Christian Identity in Late Antique Mesopotamia', in Brouria Bitton-Ashkelony and Lorenzo Perrone, *Between Personal and Institutional Religion: Self, Doctrine and Practice in Late Antique Eastern Christianity* (Turnhout: Brepols, 2013): 155–94; Dietmar W. Winkler, 'The Age of the Sassanians: until 651', in Wilhelm Baum and Dietmar W. Winkler, *The Church of the East: A Concise History* (London: Routledge, 2003): 7–41.

fourteenth century had increased to twenty-five, with some two hundred bishops under them. The growth of Christian communities was followed by institutional provision: the bishop's see of Kashgar on the Silk Road, for example, was elevated in the late twelfth century to a metropolitan see. Missionaries of the Church of the East reached as far as southern India, Malaya and China, easily travelling with the merchants of the southern Silk Road. As was the case in other Christian regions, the metropolitan – equivalent to an archbishop elsewhere – appointed bishops and headed synods. By the early sixth century, metropolitans were appointed for the Christians of India, some sedentary and some itinerant; in the next century one metropolitan was castigated for the neglect of his duties to the Indian churches 'which extend from the borders of the Persian Empire to the place they call *Qalah'*.[19] Beyond the boundaries of the Sasanian world, then, following the travels of merchants who had traded with the Malabar coast at least since Roman times, Christians settled in the rich spice-trading ports, and drew local people to their religion. For the next millennium or so, Christians of southern India spoke Malayalam in daily life, used Syriac for their liturgy and hagiographical writings, and insisted on the antiquity and apostolic origin of their church.[20]

The spread of Muslim power affected Christians dramatically in their many and diverse communities. Following the teachings of Muhammad, Jews and Christians were termed People of the Book (*ahl al-kitab*), and were treated as corporate groups defined by their scripture-based religion. Christians and Jews were deemed to be in error, and thus inferior subjects, but their affinity to the shared history of prophecy and scripture set them apart from other conquered people, whom Muslims regarded as pagans and stargazers. Jews and Christians lived as protected people (*dhimmi*) so long as their dependence on the magnanimity of the caliph was recognized through payment of a poll tax and the submission to some civic limitations. One treaty incorporated into a Coptic chronicle shows how this may have worked. It reports that when 'Amr ibn al-'As, conqueror of Egypt, entered a treaty of surrender with Cyrus, Melkite patriarch of Alexandria, he

19 Adolf Heuken, 'Christianity in Pre-Colonial Indonesia', in Jan Sihar Aritonang and Karel Steenbrink (eds.), *A History of Christianity in Indonesia* (Leiden: Brill, 2008): 3–7. *Qalah* was Arab geographers' name for an island, renowned as a centre of trade in the Indian Ocean. It has been variously identified with Malaka or with an island off the coast of modern Sri Lanka.

20 Susan Bayly, *Saints, Goddesses and Kings: Muslims and Christians in South Indian Society, 1700–1900* (Cambridge University Press, 1989): 241–7; on the commercial basis for the spread of Christianity further east see Kenneth McPherson, *The Indian Ocean: A History of People and the Sea* (Delhi: Oxford University Press, 1998), 76–122.

promised not to intervene in Christian affairs. During the Umayyad period (661–750), the law of Islam replaced Byzantine and Sasanian law, but it left local administrations intact. The jurisprudence that developed during the 'Abbasid period (749/50–1258) aimed to harmonize the teaching of the Quran with local traditions through development of Islamic law.

The prevailing understanding of the link between community (*ummah*) and religion, which characterized Islam, when applied to Christians and Jews, allowed them to live according to their respective sacred laws, as long as these did not insult Islam.[21] There were, of course, points of meeting and conflict, for which Muslim law provided guidelines: a Christian could not own a Muslim slave, nor own copies of the Quran or collections of *hadith* – the sayings of the Prophet Muhammad that were collected and that guided legal deliberations.[22] There was no universal agreement between Muslim jurists on the extent of legal autonomy for Christians, but in practice they enjoyed it except in cases involving public order and respect for Islam: highway robbery, apostasy and blasphemy. Even given these restrictions, some Christians of the East, whose understanding of Christianity differed from that of their Byzantine rulers, welcomed the advent of the Arab conquerors as liberators.[23]

Christians of the East were burdened with one anxiety that did not weigh on those in Europe and Byzantium, the fear of apostasy: the conversion of sons and daughters, relatives and neighbours to Islam and away from their shared faith. So they produced tracts aimed at defending their faith and criticizing the tenets of the triumphant one around them. For Christians living in Islamic polities this was a real concern. Conversion to Islam was relatively easy, and it opened opportunities, while conversion from Islam to Christianity was deemed to be apostasy, and was punishable by death. Christians nonetheless lived and prospered alongside Jewish communities that shared many of their living conditions. While the general policy was one of toleration, as the united caliphate turned quickly into a vast array of independent states, Christians lived at greater risk from occasional reversals of policy, and periods of heightened fervour that disturbed the status quo.

21 Benjamin Z. Kedar, *Crusade and Mission: European Approaches toward the Muslims* (Princeton University Press, 1984): 9–14.
22 Néophyte Edelby, 'The Legislative Autonomy of Christians in the Islamic World', in Robert Hoyland (ed.), *Muslims and Others in Early Islamic Society* (Aldershot: Ashgate, 2004): 49, 64–5.
23 Raymond Le Coz, *Histoire de l'Eglise d'Orient: Chrétiens d'Iraq, d'Iran et de Turquie* (Paris: Cerf, 1995): 135.

This was the case at the northern borders of the caliphate, in the early and mid-eleventh century with the rise to hegemony of the recently converted Seljuks, just as it was in twelfth-century al-Andalus, when it was conquered by the North African Almohad dynasty.

A telling example of a Christian's personal struggle with the attractions of Islam is imagined in the hagiographical account of the life of the Coptic martyr Joannes of Phanijoit. The *Life* of *c*. 1211 describes the ways in which a good Christian might be lured by Islam, here appearing in the form of an exoticized Muslim woman, who leads him astray:

> Joannes also mixed
> with these ones in this way, and he
> learned their ways, for he was
> a flax merchant to the women from the
> avenue of [St Sergius?] in Old Cairo.
> Satan deceived him with the
> lust of a Saracen woman.[24]

Joannes became a Muslim, but when he grew old he returned to his village and was slowly drawn back to Christianity. He sought advice, both spiritual and legal, but there was no way in Ayyubid Egypt for a Muslim to renounce his faith. Joannes thus became a martyr, inspired by the examples of Coptic martyrs during Emperor Diocletian's persecutions in the early fourth century.[25]

A particularly intense period of violence against Christians and their churches is associated with the arrival of wandering Sufi reformers to Upper Egypt, and their encounter with the ancient Coptic settlements there.[26] Large Christian communities thrived in Upper Egypt with a network of monasteries endowed and supported by wealthy merchants and by respected and well-connected Christian administrators in service of the Ayubbid sultans.[27] In the

24 *The Coptic Martyrdom of John of Phanijōit: Assimilation and Conversion to Islam in Thirteenth-Century Egypt*, ed. and trans. Jason R. Zaborowski (Leiden: Brill, 2005): 58–61.

25 The sultan – like other Muslim rulers under similar circumstances – did his best to save Joannes' life, as was also told in the case of the ninth-century martyrs of Cordova. On both cases see Sidney H. Griffith, *The Church in the Shadow of the Mosque: Christians and Muslims in the World of Islam* (Princeton University Press, 2008): 151–5.

26 Tamer el-Leithy, 'Sufis, Copts and the Politics of Piety: Moral Regulation in Fourteenth-Century Upper Egypt', in Richard J. A. McGregor and A. Sabra (eds.), *Le développement du soufisme en Égypte à l'époque mamelouke* (Cairo: Institut français d'archéologie orientale, 2006): 75–119. On Coptic Christianity and its monastic culture, see *Byzantium and Islam*, 69–86.

27 On the central role played by Copts in Egypt, see Leslie S. B. MacCoull, 'Three Cultures under Arab Rule: The Fate of Coptic', *Bulletin de la Société d'Archéologie Copte* 27(1985): 61–70.

early fourteenth century, anti-*dhimmi* pamphlets were composed by the Sufis, similar in tone to the invective against the Jews of Europe at the same time. Christians were accused of being rich and haughty, of enjoying privileges from rulers who depended upon their services. Reformers like Ibn Taymiyya (1263–1328) inveighed against monks in particular, as perverters of religious truth who sought monastic status in order to be free from the poll tax that applied to Christians.

The primacy of Islam was not only embedded in its political rule, but also in the transformation of space. Since Islam was to be recognized as the true religion, the symbols of Christian worship – above all the places of worship – were kept smaller, lower, and less magnificent than mosques. In the decades of conquest and settlement, Muslim governors accommodated the need for new administrative headquarters, combined with the desire to leave local populations undisturbed, by erecting twin cities. This meant that new settlements were built alongside existing ones, like the building of Ramla only four kilometres from Lydda. With the establishment of Umayyad rule in 661 and the associated systems of finance, big building projects were undertaken, such as the construction of the Dome of the Rock in Jerusalem in 691/2, the great Mosque of Damascus in 715, and that of Aleppo a decade later.

Christian communities in Muslim polities retained many of the cultural attributes of their pre-Islamic life. For ritual purposes they continued to use Coptic in Egypt, versions of Syriac in Syria, Mesopotamia and Persia, Greek in Palestine and Asia Minor, and Armenian and Georgian in their respective regions. Yet by the late seventh century, Christian writers were using the Muslim dating system that reckoned time from 622, the year Mohammed migrated from Mecca to Medina, alongside the Byzantine chronology that combined the year from the creation of the world and the imperial tax year. Christians brought to the newly established Muslim polity their traditions of local knowledge and administrative experience, while benefitting from Muslim medical and scientific knowledge. The dependent *dhimmi* status of Christians – as of Jews – meant that Muslim rulers also expected them to be loyal.

It is striking to note just how deeply Muslim rulers relied on Christians at the highest echelons of prestigious service. Christians were mediators of important and useful knowledge, including astronomy, medicine, science and commerce. Theophilus of Edessa, for example, was astronomer to Caliph al-Mahdi (r. 755–85), and a historian as well. As we have seen, Copts were central to the administration of Egypt. Some Christians were able to offer Muslim courts the practical arts of astronomy, which combined the classical heritage and Persian science.[28] The earliest mentions of the Arab conquests were made by Syriac Christians who were at work in all areas of learning and administration; they even wrote the histories of Muslim countries in Arabic, a practice that continued into the eleventh century.[29] Historiographical writings, like the Eusebian scheme of world history, were translated for Caliph al-Mansur (reigned 745–55), and Orosius' *Historia* of *c.* 417 was translated in al-Andalus in the tenth century as *Kitab Harushiyush*, an authoritative history of the Roman Empire, the age that had preceded Islam.[30]

The Christian contribution to the administration of Islamic rule did not mean that Christians were incapable of developing a critique of that emergent order, although the earliest reactions by East Syrian authors to the advent of Islam display 'greater awareness that a new empire had arisen, [rather] than that a new religion had been born'.[31] The religious confrontation with Islam was slow to come, for its most tangible impact on the life of Christians was political. Thus there was a relatively slow emergence of polemical literature, and this was often based on pre-existing texts written against Jews and Judaism.[32] The rise of Islam would eventually challenge a whole conception of salvation and world history, however. A late seventh-century Armenian historian saw the 'Ishmaelites' as the fourth beast of Daniel's prophecy; others turned their hopes to a saving Byzantine emperor, while still others blamed that Empire for its failure in the face of Islam.[33] The emergent Christian historiographical tradition maintained that Muhammad was a trickster, even a lunatic. Why did Islam prosper? Christian authors came to view this as a punishment for the sins of Christians. To those Muslims who saw in Islam's

---

28 On the impact of Central Asian science, often mediated by Asian Christians, both on Arabic and Latin intellectual cultures, see Christopher I. Beckwith, *Warriors of the Cloisters: The Central Asian Origins of Science in the Medieval World* (Princeton University Press, 2012).

29 Chase Robinson, *Islamic Historiography* (Cambridge University Press, 2002).

30 Christian C. Sahner, 'From Augustine to Islam: Translation and History in the Arabic Orosius', *Speculum* 88(2013): 905–931.

31 Sebastian P. Brock, 'Syriac Views of Emergent Islam', in G. H. A. Juynboll (ed.), *Studies on the First Century of Islamic History* (Carbondale-Edwardsville: Southern Illinois University Press, 1982): 13

32 G. J. Reinink, 'The Beginnings of Syriac Apologetic Literature in Response to Islam', *Oriens Christianus* 77(1993): 165–77.

33 Brock, 'Syriac Views', 11 and 19; G. J. Reinink, 'Ps.-Methodius: A Concept of History in Response to the Rise of Islam', in A. Cameron and L. Conrad (eds.), *The Byzantine and Early Islamic Near East 1: Problems in the Literary Source Material* (Princeton: Darwin Press, 1992): 156–8.

remarkable military successes the sign of divine favour, Christians answered: 'Do prophets come with a sword?'[34]

Christian communities assimilated large areas of social practices prevalent within Islam. So, for example, the Coptic Church in Egypt came to legitimize divorce in the thirteenth century, within the environment of Mamluk society in which divorce was very common. In general, patterns of family life of Christians – and Jews – came to resemble very closely those of the Muslim population.[35]

Just as in Europe and Byzantium, Eastern Christians who lived ordinary lives of work and family admired and supported the unique few who pursued religious perfection through lives of asceticism, mysticism and scholarship. The Church of the East was intellectually lively and active in pastoral provision for its members. Its bishops were not land-holding, political and military figures, as they were in Europe. Some were even known to move between the city and an ascetic life-style. Isaac, bishop of Nineveh (d. c. 700) is a good example. Born in the province of Qatar, he was an ascetic called to the office of bishop who clearly struggled with the responsibilities, and finally abdicated to seek solitude in a monastery in the mountains of Huzistan. The impact of his writings was felt for centuries, with translations into Greek and Georgian, the version that survives. At the centre of Isaac's world was belief in God 'Creator and Guide of the universe', God as boundless love: 'How with a love that cannot be measured he arrived at the establishment of the world at the beginning of creation . . . in love is he going to bring it to that wondrous transformed state, and in love will the whole world be swallowed up in the great mystery of him.'[36] Another remarkable figure is Joannes of Dalyatha (c. 690–c. 780). Born in a village in the mountains of Kurdistan, Joannes learned the basics of faith there, and then entered a monastery in the mountains of Qardu. After seven years he became a solitary in those mountains. Building on a rich mystical tradition in that region, Joannes wrote letters about the inner life, and prayer: like the fourth-century poet and theologian Ephrem, he contemplated God's glory as light and wonder

---

34 Robert G. Hoyland, *Seeing Islam as Others Saw It: A Survey and Evaluation of Christian, Jewish and Zoroastrian Writings on Early Islam* (Princeton: The Darwin Press, 1997): 523; K. B. Wolf, *Conquerors and Chroniclers in Early Medieval Spain* (University of Liverpool Press, 1990): 30.

35 Yossef Rapoport, *Marriage, Money and Divorce in Medieval Islamic Society* (Cambridge University Press, 2005): 3–5.

36 Isaac of Nineveh, *The 'Second Part', Chapters IV–XLI*, ed. and trans. Sebastian P. Brock (Louvain: Peeters, 1995), II, 10, XXXVII, 1–2.

in a distinctively Syriac fashion.[37] Syriac intellectual life flourished over centuries not only in civic urban schools, but also in remote places of seclusion. Prayer rather than sacraments animated these men, in Joannes' words: 'Continual prayer is wonder before God ... Truly, I incline my head in shame, I am silent and I take refuge in mercy. Help me by prayer.'[38] Such works were disseminated and copied, spreading the fame of even an enclosed monastic. Monks and others translated many works in all religious genres; the seventh-century *Life of Mary*, for example, written in Greek by Maximus the Confessor, was translated into Georgian in the tenth, and that is the version that has survived to our day.

Just as local political traditions and the circumstances of rule, including such issues as security and fiscal burdens, determined the quality of life for Muslims, so they did for Christians as well. Local arrangements could change dramatically under the influence of large-scale challenges, such as the recurrent famines of the eleventh century or the advance of Mongol power westwards under the leadership of Chinggis Khan. Yet despite these challenges, Christians developed and maintained networks of trade, pilgrimage, and scholarship, made possible by the placement of crucial facilitators in positions of administrative capacity.[39] This sphere was served by the Syriac language, even in areas where it was not spoken; it is remarkable just how many Syriac texts were translated into Coptic. One might even say that something like a Syriac *cosmopolis* developed, to build on a term created by Sheldon Pollock for the Sanskrit sphere.[40]

A new dynamic affected Christians in the course of the eleventh century with the military initiative led by Seljuk tribes who sacked Baghdad in 1055 and continued to move westward. A new war-zone emerged in Syria and Asia Minor, with the conquest of large parts of Byzantine Anatolia and northern Syria, culminating in the defeat of the Byzantine army at Manzikert in 1071. The region was further destabilized by the advent of European warriors, their conquest of the Holy Land, and their settlement in parts of

---

37 On Ephrem's powerful contribution to Syriac spirituality, see Sebastian P. Brock, *Luminous Eye: The Spiritual World Vision of Saint Ephrem* (Kalamazoo, MI: Cistercian Publications, 1992).

38 *The Letters of John of Dalyatha*, trans. Mart T. Hanbury (Piscataway, NJ: Gorgias Press, 2006), vii–xii.

39 On pilgrimage and commerce seen through material remains, see *Byzantium and Islam*, 124–99.

40 Sheldon Pollock, *The Language of the Gods in the World of Men: Sanskrit, Culture, and Power in Premodern India* (Berkeley and Los Angeles: University of California Press, 2006). I have also benefited from Ronit Ricci, *Islam Translated: Literature, Conversion, and the Arabic Cosmopolis of South and Southeast Asia* (University of Chicago Press, 2011).

West Asia for the next two centuries. The Crusades – as they came to be known in various European languages in the course of the thirteenth century – in turn inspired a political and military mobilization in northern Syria and Egypt which saw the ousting of most Christian rule by 1187, and all by 1291. The engagements of this period transformed forever European understandings of Asia and its Christians. The Crusades created new patterns of pilgrimage and mission, led to the creation of military orders inspired by monastic rigour, and also facilitated trade links that were to endure to the end of our period and beyond.

The encounter between Western and Eastern Christians produced some mutual recognition and a great deal of bafflement, even distrust. When the European scholar and bishop of Acre, Jacques of Vitry (c. 1170–1240), encountered the Christians of Palestine, he described their cultural habits as follows: 'The Syrians use the Saracen language in their common speech, and they use the Saracen script in deeds and business and all other writing, except for the Holy Scriptures ... in which they use Greek letters; wherefore in Divine service their laity, who know only the Saracenic language, do not understand them.'[41] Even in Holy Scripture there was an occasional use of Arabic, as the stunning Coptic manuscript of the Gospels, made in Damietta around 1179/80, shows: on the sumptuous full-page image of the Marriage at Cana, titles in Coptic indicate the figures of Mary and Jesus, and an Arabic inscription entitles the whole scene 'When he changed the water into wine at the Marriage in Cana of the Galilee'. Even more distinctive is the inspiration for the adornment of Gospel books taken from geometrical designs used in the decoration of Qurans. The maker of the carpet-like decoration of a page from a 1205 Coptic manuscript embeds nine crosses into its intricate pattern.[42] Within the lands of Islam, each with its own distinctive political and economic infrastructure, its own idioms and aesthetics, Christians of the East developed ecclesiastical structures and cultural production that sustained their identity. These qualities often recommended them as useful mediators and administrators, and even inspired them with confidence to spread the word further east, beyond that familiar world.

---

41 *Jacques de Vitry's History of Jerusalem* (London: Palestine Pilgrims' Text Society, 1896): 68–9.

42 Jules Leroy, *Les Manuscrits coptes et coptes-arabes illustrés* (Paris: Librairie orientaliste Paul Geuthner, 1974): 113, 140, and plate D, 64–5. Similar interpenetration of influences took place in Europe between Jewish and Christian manuscript makers as discussed in Sarit Shalev-Eyni, *Jews Among Christians: Hebrew Book Illumination from Lake Constance* (Turnhout: Brepols, 2010).

Christian life outside the Abrahamic sphere

So far we have considered life within Christian polities, in Europe, Byzantium and Ethiopia, and Christian life in established communities after the advent of Islam. Christian communities also existed in regions far from the heartlands of the Abrahamic religions. They were usually established as the result of trading contacts that saw the settlement of Christians in trading colonies, followed by missionaries intent on spreading the faith. The Christian communities on the Malabar Coast claimed association with the apostle Thomas, and were most probably created by Christian merchants and priests from Persia in the fifth century.

At the edges of the Muslim political sphere, to its north, the political order was far more volatile than it was in the realm of Islam. The regions from the Black Sea to northern China were inhabited by nomadic tribes that only in the thirteenth century came to be united under Mongol hegemony. Contact with the supernatural for these nomadic people was mediated by spiritually adept individuals later called shamans, who were bound together by strong kinship ties. Not unlike nomadic peoples who encountered Christianity at the beginning of our period, such as the Franks, Goths, and Avars, leaders of steppe nomads often decided on religious conversion for good political reasons and carried their tribe with them. A famous example of this process is the conversion of the upper classes of the Khazars to Judaism in the eighth century, and others are the conversion of the Kerait and Naiman tribes in the Mongolian plateau to Christianity, which happened by about 1000. While most nomads of Central Asia ultimately converted to Islam, there were also communities of Christians, Buddhists, Manicheans and Jews in the cities that they ruled. When nomads conquered sedentary people they usually tolerated local customs and left religious practices intact.[43]

Missionaries of the Church of the East had left their mark along the Silk Road already before the advent of Islam, as an early iron cross from Jiangxi attests.[44] Nestorian Christianity also spread north from the edge of the Persian Empire into Central Asia in the sixth century, through the mediation of Sogdian horse merchants, inhabitants of the Ferghana Valley, who traversed the steppes. By 650 there was a metropolitan in Samarkand, who

---

43 Amitai and Biran, 'Introduction', in *Mongols, Turks, and Others*, 1–11; Yehoshua Frenkel, 'The Turks and the Eurasian Steppes in Arabic Geographical Literature', in Amitai and Biran, *Mongols, Turks, and Others*, 219–20.

44 Johann Ferreira, 'Tang Christianity: Its Syriac Origins and Character', *Jian Dao: A Journal of Bible and Theology* 21(2004): 129–57.

oversaw tens of bishops in the region. With the coming of Islam, the nomads of the steppes were attracted to the emergent empire to their south and to the opportunities it offered, especially through military service.

Christianity was introduced along the Silk Road, where communities of merchants developed in Turfan, Dunhuang, Wuwei, Lingwu and in Chang'an (modern Xi-an), the gateway to the Silk Road since the Han dynasty (206 BCE–220 CE) (see Map 17.1, p. 449). These merchants were Persian speaking, and many came from Sogdia, the northwest region of the Persian sphere. Sogdian Nestorians lived in a complex in the capital, in family groups attested by tombstones. In northern China Christian learned men and priests interacted with Tantric Buddhists in the eighth and ninth centuries CE. Both groups were adapting to China, translating their scriptures into Chinese. Christians and Buddhists interacted in the favourable atmosphere of the Tang court, the former borrowing Buddhist terms to assist in the translation of scripture into Chinese. In turn, Nestorians brought sophisticated astronomical knowledge, and the planetary week was adopted as well as Persian systems of divination.[45]

A Syrian mission, led by the Nestorian priest Alopen, brought Christianity to China during the Tang dynasty (618–907) and was allowed to establish a Christian presence in the capital Chang'an. Soon the *Jesus Sutras*, writings on Christian history and thought, were produced, beginning in *c.* 640–60 and into the next century. They tell of the history of the Church of the East with confidence, and see Christian life in China both as part of a wider Christian universe and as one of a variety of local religions, which also included shamanism, Confucianism, Taoism, and Buddhism.[46] The oldest of the *Jesus Sutras* that survives is a tablet of 781 inscribed in Chinese and Syriac, which similarly records Christian history in northern China. Christianity is here portrayed as the Luminous Religion of a triune God who 'divided his Godhead and the illustrious and adorable Messiah, veiling his true majesty, appeared in the world as a man. Angels proclaimed the glad tidings. A Virgin brought forth the Holy one'.[47]

---

45 Chen Huaiyu, 'The Encounter of Nestorian Christianity with Tantric Buddhism in Medieval China', in Dietmar W. Winkler and Li Tang (eds.), *Hidden Treasures and Intercultural Encounters: Studies on East Syriac Christianity in China and Central Asia* (Vienna: LIT Verlag, 2009): 195–213.

46 Martin Palmer, *The Jesus Sutras: Rediscovering the Lost Religion of Taoist Christianity* (London: Judy Piatkus, 2001).

47 James Legge, *The Nestorian Monument of Hsî-an Fû in Shen-hsî, China* (London: Trübner and Co., 1888): 5–7; Erica C. D. Hunter, 'The Persian Contribution to Christianity in China: Reflections in the Xi'an Fu Syriac Inscriptions', in Winkler and Tang, *Hidden Treasures and Intercultural Encounters*, 71–86.

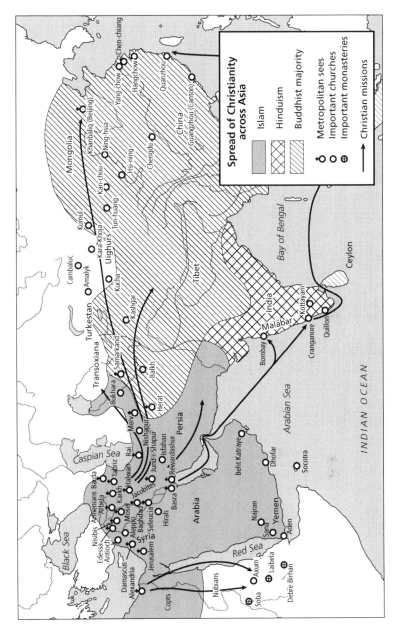

Map 16.2. Spread of Christianity across Asia

Outside the Muslim sphere Christians vied for a place among a multitude of religions, and their freedom to worship depended greatly on the favour of rulers. From the mid-twelfth century nomadic groups controlled vast territories under a sole ruler, in polities often called empires. One of these was the Qara Khitai Empire founded by the Khitan leader Dashi, which stretched from China to Transoxania and encompassed powerful nomadic people like the Liao. The battle of Qatwan in 1141 sealed Qara Khitai hegemony over the Turkic – now Muslim – Seljuks. It also gave birth to one of the greatest myths about eastern Christianity: the legend of Prester John.[48] The belief that a Christian kingdom prospered in the east periodically inspired expectations in Christians about Asia, and also about Africa, as the kingdom of Prester John was sometimes thought to be in Ethiopia: he was a hoped-for saviour, an ally in areas dominated by Islam.

The next stage of growth in Christian presence in China was during the Yuan dynasty (1271–1368) established by the Mongols. Under Mongol rule China opened its territories to trade and allowed missions to operate. All established priests were understood by the Mongols to possess charisma and magical powers, and so Chinggis Khan (r. 1206–27) and his heir Ögödei were reported to have exempted most clergy – Christian alongside Buddhist, Daoist and Muslim – from payment of some taxes, with the expectation that they use their powers of prayer and blessing to benefit Mongol leaders.[49] The Mongols retained Muslim and Christian bureaucrats, and this led to continuity in local administration and inspired a related continuity in toleration of the religions of the local population. This toleration was particularly evident in the Ilkhanid state in Persia.[50]

Interesting information about Christian life in Central and East Asia in the Mongol period comes from accounts of travellers, traders and missionaries, who now included many from Europe. The earliest account of the Church of the East was written by the Franciscan friar Giovanni da Pian del Carpine (c. 1182–1252) who travelled through Rus' and Central Asia as papal emissary to the court of the Great Khan. He arrived there in 1246 and witnessed the

---

48 Charles F. Beckingham and Bernard Hamilton (eds.), *Prester John, the Mongols and the Ten Lost Tribes* (Aldershot: Variorum, 1996), and L. N. Gumilev, *Searches for the Imaginary Kingdom: The Legend of the Kingdom of Prester John*, trans. R. E. F. Smith (Cambridge University Press, 1987).

49 Peter Jackson, 'The Mongols and the Faith of the Conquered', in Reuven Amitai and Michal Biran (eds.), *Mongols, Turks, and Others: Eurasian Nomads and the Sedentary World* (Leiden: Brill, 2005): 267–8.

50 D. O. Morgan, 'Who Ran the Mongol Empire?', *Journal of the Royal Asiatic Society of Great Britain and Ireland* (1982): 124–36.

enthronement of Güyük, Chinggis Khan's grandson. In 1254 the Franciscan friar William of Rubruck debated Christian faith at the court of the Great Khan Möngke: his interlocutors – whom he sometimes found loquacious and baffling – were Buddhists, Muslims and Nestorians. With Peter Lombard's *Sentences* and a statuette of the Virgin Mary in his bags he aimed to share the quintessence of Christianity; he consulted Nestorians on strategy and hoped for support from the monotheistic Muslims when debating with the Buddhists.[51] The finest descriptions of all are, of course, those of the Venetian merchant Marco Polo.

The Franciscan friars were particularly committed to the project of conversion: Giovanni di Monte Corvino (1246–1328), for example, spent thirty-four years in Beijing, during which he assumed overall ecclesiastical authority. Functioning as an archbishop, he consecrated priests and bishops, and converted thousands. Such friars also acted as papal emissaries, and supervised efforts of mission further afield. Three Franciscan missionaries – Gerardo Albuini, Pellegrino da Città di Castello and Andrea da Perugia – followed one another as bishops of the important river-port-city of Quanzhou (known in Arabic as Zayton). The last of them died in 1332; his tombstone is engraved in Latin, and resembles in its iconography some of the Zayton Christian tombstones inscribed in Syro-Turkic.[52]

Conclusions

With all its diversity of beliefs, rituals, languages and vast geographical reach, in what sense was Christianity indeed a single religion? Did it induce cooperation between Christian monarchs? Such affinity was a rhetorical trope that could become beneficial when interests converged, but just as often they did not. Differences in language and culture produced highly unflattering reports from diplomats, like the embittered Lombard Liutprand, bishop of Cremona, who summarized his legation to Constantinople in 968 on behalf of Emperor Otto I: 'The Greeks cannot be trusted. Don't trust them, Latins; heed not their words. How piously does a Greek perjure himself, providing that he

---

51 Bartlett, *The Making of Europe*, 260; Benjamin Z. Kedar, 'The Multilateral Disputation at the Court of the Grand Qan Möngke, 1254', in Hava Lazarus-Yafeh, Mark R. Cohen, Sasson Somekh, and Sidney H. Griffith (eds.), *The Majlis: Interreligious Encounters in Medieval Islam* (Wiesbaden: Harrassowitz, 1999): 162–183.

52 On the tombstone see Ken Parry, 'The Iconography of the Christian Tombstones from Quanzhou', in S. Lieu, I. Gardner, and K. Parry (eds.), *From Palmyra to Zayton: Epigraphy and Iconography* (Turnhout: Brepols, 2005): 230–1 and plate 18, and for comparison with Syro-Turkic tombs, see plates 4 and 5.

can win by so doing!'[53] Christian institutions and teaching possessed the potential for inclusion and exclusion, for accommodating diversity as well as encouraging polities to become persecuting societies.[54] So, for example, in the thirteenth century a coalition of the king of France, the pope and the Dominican order produced an onslaught – a veritable crusade followed by a campaign of inquisition and intensive preaching – against those Christians of southern France who adhered to dualist beliefs, usually called the Cathars or the Albigensians.[55] In fifteenth-century Ethiopia, political unity was promoted through the dissemination of state-sponsored devotional themes and images for worship. Christian polities saw periods of aggressive expansion in the name of Christianity, such as the Crusades in western Asia or the northern crusades against pagans in the Baltic region.

In order to promote political expansion and state-led conversion, intellectuals developed theories of just war, and criteria by which crusades against Christians and non-Christians might be deemed acceptable. Such theories were always a subject for debate and disagreement, and approaches to conversion divided Christian leaders from the very beginning of Christianity. Beyond the realm of theory, however, both the beginning and the end of our period see concerted efforts by Christian dynasts to extend their territories and make them Christian, with the support – moral and sometimes financial too – of church institutions. Yet only Christians living within Christian polities were able to put these theories into practice.

We may end our analysis of Christian regions over one thousand years with a consideration of those activities that brought them into contact with each other and then exemplify their diversity by dwelling on the visual depictions of the Virgin Mary in various regions. A lively tradition of pilgrimage meant that Christians visited Jerusalem throughout our period; some left interesting travelogues, others brought relics back to share with their communities back home.[56] The Crusades brought many more European Christians into contact with Eastern Christendom and, in the

---

53 *Liutprandi relatio de legatione Constantinopolitana*, ed. and trans. Brian Scott (Bristol Classical Press, 1993): 21 and 52.

54 This is a gesture towards R. I. Moore's influential book, *The Formation of a Persecuting Society* (Oxford University Press, 1987) which deals with Christianity in Europe between 950–1250.

55 Jonathan Sumption, *The Albigensian Crusade* (London: Faber, 1978), and Mark Gregory Pegg, *The Albigensian Crusade and the Battle for Christendom* (Oxford University Press, 2008).

56 Rodney Aist, *The Christian Topography of Early Islamic Jerusalem. The Evidence of Willibald of Eichstätt (700–787 CE)* (Turnhout: Brepols, 2009).

Kingdom of Jerusalem and the other Frankish states of West Asia, generated a modus vivendi with them that has no parallel elsewhere; also, the spread of knowledge about them, and attempts at religious union. The cohabitation of the various Christian groups in the Frankish Church of the Holy Sepulcher in Jerusalem epitomizes this new reality, as the pilgrim Theoderich noted in his travelogue of *c.* 1170, and as the Franciscan pilgrim Francesco Suriano appreciated again in the 1460s.[57] The possibilities of trade made Europeans travel east in search of spices and silk, and south in search of gold and domestic slaves. Trade attracted Christians to travel east along the Silk Roads mediating between China and India, and along the roads and sea lanes that led to West Asia and Egypt. Emissaries were particularly frequent during the heated period of diplomacy and expectations that brought the Mongols and Europeans in touch with one another. Part of the description of Christian life in West Asia and Europe penned by the Beijing-born Nestorian Christian monk, Rabban Sauma (*c.* 1225–94), has survived. This pious and linguistically adept religious and his companion were sent in 1287 by the Mongol ruler of Iran, the Ilkhan Arghun, to seek contact with the Byzantine emperor and the pope.[58] Their travelogue sometimes shows just how impressed they were by the rich and varied forms of Christian life they encountered:

> Having lost the greater part of what they had on the road, they went on to the monastery of Saint Mâr Şehyôn, which was in the neighbourhood of the city of Ṭûs [the capital of Khôrâsân], and they were blessed by the bishop who lived therein and by the monks. And they thought that they had been born into the world anew.[59]

In the early part of our period, when there were few Europeans in Asia, Jews offered their services of trade between Asia and Europe, often through Sicily and Italy. With the rallying of the European economy after 1100, and the establishment of European states in the eastern Mediterranean, by the twelfth century there were large European merchant colonies in Constantinople and the Black Sea; a Venetian presence from the thirteenth century in the Chinese court of the Yuan, which has given us Marco Polo and his testimony. Where there was some regular contact through trade, merchants

57 On awareness of eastern Christianities among Europeans, see Jonathan Rubin, 'Benoît d'Alignan and Thomas Agni: Two Western Intellectuals and the Study of Oriental Christianity in Thirteenth-Century Kingdom of Jerusalem', *Viator* 44 (2013): 189–200.

58 Morris Rossabi, *Voyager from Xanadu. Rabban Sauma and the First Journey from China to the West* (Tokyo: Kodansha International, 1992).

59 E. A. Wallis Budge (ed.), *The Monks of Kûblâi Khân Emperor of China* (London: Religious Tract Society, 1928): 139–40.

were accompanied by religious, intent on exploring lands for conversion; above all by friars, unencumbered by parish duties or by the rules of monastic seclusion. Such men were free to join journeys to the East, like the Crusade of King Louis IX to the Holy Land in 1250, which saw the beginning of William of Rubruck's long trip through the Qipchaq Khanate.

Contact between Christian communities did not eradicate diversity, however. Nowhere is this more evident than in the diverse treatments accorded to the figure of the Virgin Mary. Although the Byzantine visual style was highly influential, it also interacted with local traditions and tastes. Within the Egyptian sphere the Virgin Mary resembled greatly the ancient goddess Isis: centuries before Europeans became enamoured with the scene, Christians in Egypt comfortably observed Mary offering her breast to the Child Christ. Ethiopian images traditionally adhered to the Byzantine style, as can be seen in the wall-painting of the Annunciation of *c.* 1200 from St Mary's church in Lalibela. Yet contacts with Europe, as well as with India and China towards the end of our period, are also evident in the art of Ethiopia, as in the icon made for King Lebnä-Dengel (1508–40) with Mary as a blond woman, or the panel of a diptych of 1480–1530, in which Mary and her son have distinctly oriental features.[60]

The further east we travel in the Christian regions, the more constrained is the use of religious imagery. For Christians living under Islam, word and rhyme seem to have filled the affective role played by images in Byzantium and Europe. There Mary is omnipresent too, however, in place-names and church dedications. The Coptic traveller Abu al-Makarim, in his compilation on the churches of Africa and Asia, described the city of Fahsur on the south Indian coast (Travancore): 'Here there are several churches and all the Christians are Nestorians ... It is from this place that camphor comes; and this commodity (is a gum which) oozes from the trees. In this town there is one church named after our Lady, the Pure Virgin Mary.' The vast majority of churches in Ethiopian Tigray were also dedicated to the Virgin Mary.[61] When Rabban Sauma reached Constantinople he was surely amazed by the sheer size of Hagia Sophia, and within it of the gleaming majesty of mosaics of the *Theotokos*. Nothing so monumental and triumphant could be made further east in the Christian regions.

60 Jacques Mercier, *Vierges d'Éthiopie* (Montpellier: L'Archange Minotaure, 2004): 38, 66–7.
61 Claude Lepage and Jacques Mercier, *Art éthiopien: les églises historiques du Tigray* (Paris: ERC, 2005.

Sometimes vastly differing in core beliefs, other times indistinguishable from the Muslims or Mongols around them, Christian regions had a sufficient element of family resemblance, to make them a force – among others – in world history.

FURTHER READING

Angold, Michael. *Eastern Christianity.* Cambridge University Press, 2006.

Baum, Wilhelm and Dietmar W. Winkler. *The Church of the East: A Concise History.* London: Routledge, 2003.

Brock, Sebastian. *Luminous Eye: The Spiritual World Vision of Saint Ephrem.* Kalamazoo, MI: Cistercian Publications, 1992.

Brown, Peter. *Society and the Holy in Late Antiquity.* London: Faber, 1982.

Byzantium and Islam: Age of Transition 7th–9th Century. New York: Metropolitan Museum of Art, 2012.

Beckingham, Charles F. and Bernard Hamilton, eds. *Prester John, the Mongols and the Ten Lost Tribes.* Aldershot: Variorum, 1996.

Beckwith, Christopher, I. *Warriors of the Cloisters: The Central Asian Origins of Science in the Medieval World.* Princeton University Press, 2012.

Cohen, Mark R., Sidney H. Griffith, Hava Lazarus-Yafeh, and Sasson Somekh. *The Majlis: Interreligious Encounters in Medieval Islam.* Wiesbaden: Harrassowitz, 1999.

Ellenblum, Ronnie. *Frankish Rural Settlement in the Latin Kingdom of Jerusalem.* Cambridge University Press, 1998.

Griffith, Sidney H. *The Church in the Shadow of the Mosque: Christians and Muslims in the World of Islam.* Princeton University Press, 2008.

Kedar, Benjamin Z. *Crusade and Mission: European Approaches toward the Muslims.* Princeton University Press, 1984.

Lawrence, C. H. *Medieval Monasticism: Forms of Religious Life in Western Europe in the Middle Ages.* Harlow: Longman, 2001.

Le Coz, Raymond. *Histoire de l'Eglise de l'Orient. Chrétiens d'Iran et de Turquie.* Paris: Cerf, 1995.

Limor, Ora and Guy G. Stroumsa, eds. *Christians and Christianity in the Holy Land: From the Origins to the Latin Kingdoms.* Turnhout: Brepols, 2006.

Logan, F. Donald. *A History of the Church in the Middle Ages.* London: Routledge, 2002.

Moore, R. I. *The Formation of a Persecuting Society.* Oxford University Press, 1987.

Noble, Thomas F. X. and Julia M. H. Smith. *Early Medieval Christianities, c. 600-c. 1100.* Cambridge University Press, 2008.

Payer, Peter J. *The Bridling of Desire: Views of Sex in the Later Middle Ages.* University of Toronto Press, 1993.

Riley-Smith, Jonathan. *The Crusades: A History.* London: Continuum, 2005.

Rossabi, Morris. *Voyager from Xanadu: Rabban Sauma and the First Journey from China to the West.* Tokyo: Kodansha International, 1992.

Rubin, Miri. *Mother of God: A History of the Virgin Mary.* London: Allen Lane, 2009.

Rubin, Miri and Walter Simons, eds. *Christianity in Western Europe c. 1100-c.1500.* Cambridge History of Christianity vol iv, Cambridge University Press, 2009.

Shinners, John R., ed. *Medieval Popular Religion, 1000–1500: A Reader*. Toronto University Press, 2006.

Shoemaker, Stephen J. *Ancient Traditions of the Virgin Mary's Dormition and Assumption*. Oxford University Press, 2002.

Swanson, Robert N. *Religion and Devotion in Europe, c. 1215–c. 1515*. Cambridge University Press, 1995.

Winkler, Dietmar W. and Tang, Li, eds. *Hidden Treasures and Intercultural Encounters: Studies on East Syriac Christianity in China and Central Asia*. Vienna: LIT Verlag, 2009.

Tanner, Norman P. *The Church in the Later Middle Ages*. London: I. B. Tauris, 2008.

Wilken, Robert Louis. *The Spirit of Early Christian Thought: Seeking the Face of God*. New Haven, CT: Yale University Press, 2003.

17

The spread of Buddhism

TANSEN SEN

Several factors facilitated the spread of Buddhism over vast distances after its establishment in the Gangetic region of northern India in the fifth century BCE. First, the encouragement of missionary work, attributed to the Buddha himself, resulted in the travels of monks and nuns through perilous land and sea routes into regions that were far away from the Buddhist heartland in South Asia. Second, the intimate relationship between merchants and Buddhist communities gave rise to a symbiotic association that not only helped the long-distance spread of Buddhist ideas, but also created a mechanism through which religious paraphernalia could be easily supplied to the emerging centers of Buddhism. Third, rulers and polities in various parts of Asia supported the diffusion of Buddhism through their patronage. While the actions of King Aśoka (*c.* 268–232 BCE) of the Mauryan Empire (324/ 321–187 BCE) contributed to the rapid spread of Buddhism in South Asia in the third century BCE, some of the later polities in Southeast and East Asia found it useful to employ Buddhist doctrines to legitimize their political power and authority, resulting in state support for Buddhist activities and exchanges.

The transmission of Buddhism is often described as a linear process, spreading from ancient India to other parts of Asia. This is illustrated in maps with arrows from the Buddhist heartland in South Asia to Central and Southeast Asia and then from those regions to East Asia. In reality, the process was more complex and the transmission was not necessarily in one direction. Buddhist monks from South Asia, for example, went to China not only to transmit the doctrine, but also to pay homage to Buddhist divinities purportedly living on Chinese mountains. Similarly, ideas formulated by Japanese monks seem to have influenced Buddhist schools in China, considered to be the main source of Buddhism in Japan. In some cases Buddhist doctrines might have evolved internally without any stimuli from foreign regions or monks. Indeed, the spread of Buddhism was a complex process, with ideas sometimes filtering back to places that were the original transmitting centers.

It should also be noted that although the Buddha might have emphasized missionary activity, the transmission of the doctrine outside South Asia was never undertaken in an organized way or through forced conversion. Buddhist teachings, texts, and images spread in fragmented forms, frequently along the major trade routes and often carried by itinerant monks and merchants. Consequently, in several places different schools and doctrines of Buddhism coexisted and mingled with each other, without the followers making a clear distinction between the diverse traditions. The spread of Buddhism, therefore, was not a systematic process. Rather, multiple strains of Buddhist doctrines originating in different regions circulated in Asia from the middle of the first millennium BCE to the twentieth century (see Map 17.1).

Within this long history of the transmissions and evolutions of Buddhism, the fifth–sixth century CE was an important watershed. Prior to this period, Buddhist ideas had spread to most regions of the Indian subcontinent and made significant inroads into Han and post-Han China. After the fifth century, places such as Sumatra, Japan, and Korea were also incorporated into the Buddhist realm. Additionally, new networks of Buddhist exchanges were established and diverse forms of Buddhist teachings and schools emerged throughout these regions. By the tenth century, the Buddhist world spanned from the western regions of Central Asia to the towns and mountains of Heian Japan. The tenth century marked another turning point for Buddhist exchanges. The long-distance networks of Buddhist interactions between South Asia and what is present-day China began unraveling. What emerged after the tenth century were multiple centers of Buddhism, with their own spheres of influence and connections. These centers and the associated spheres formed distinct Buddhist worlds unto themselves, usually featuring a major Buddhist tradition.

This chapter focuses on the above two turning points in the history of the spread of Buddhism. However, since Buddhist exchanges after the fifth century were grounded in the networks and modalities of transmission that developed prior to this period, the first part of the chapter deals with some of the key elements of the early diffusion of the doctrine. The aim, on one hand, is to demonstrate the reasons and methods of the initial spread of the doctrine within South Asia and from South Asia to Han and post-Han China; and on the other hand, it is to argue that the pre-fifth century networks continued to have significant impact on the later transmissions of Buddhist doctrines across Asia.

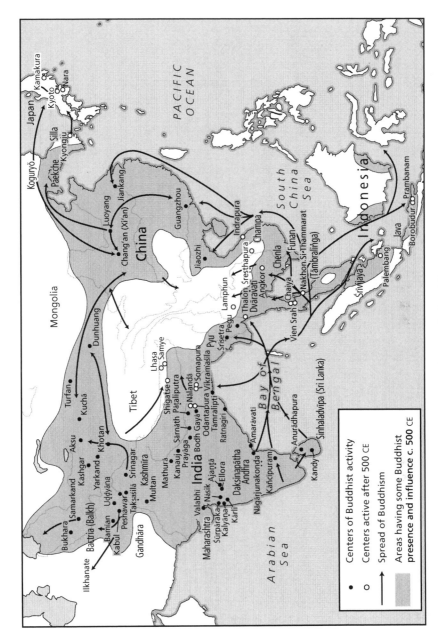

Map 17.1. The spread of Buddhism in Asia

449

The early spread of Buddhism

Gautama Siddhartha, who became known as the Buddha ("the enlightened one"), lived in around the fifth century BCE during a period that had witnessed urban growth and flourishing commercial activity. Buddhist biographical works, which were composed several centuries after the Buddha's death, suggest he was born in an upper class, ruling family. He is said to have "renounced" his family and wealth after witnessing for the first time, in his late twenties, some of the most visible and disconcerting aspects of urban life (old age, sickness, death, and ascetic life). After attaining enlightenment, at a place called Bodhgayā (in the present-day Bihar state in India), the first people whom the Buddha met were merchants called Tapussa and Bhallika. The story of them becoming the first two lay disciples of the Buddha underscores the close relationship between the Buddhist and merchant communities that would develop during the subsequent periods.

The Buddha lived until the age of eighty. His death, termed as *mahāparinirvāṇa* (the final or eternal extinction, indicating a state from which there is no rebirth), was also an important element of the early spread of Buddhist doctrines, especially through the development of the relic cult. Early Buddhist works speak of eight rulers of India vying for the bodily remains of the Buddha. Eventually it was decided that these relics were to be distributed equally among the eight rulers, each of whom took the remains to their kingdoms and had them enshrined. In the third century BCE, King Aśoka reportedly exhumed these relics and redistributed them throughout his empire and also as gifts to foreign polities. Many local Buddhist legends credit the initial transmission of Buddhist doctrines to their regions to this pious act of King Aśoka. The most important of these was Sri Lanka (Ceylon), where the Mauryan ruler is recorded to have sent his son Mahinda with a sapling of the Bodhi Tree, the Sacred Fig tree under which the Buddha is understood to have received enlightenment. This was presented to the Sri Lankan ruler Devānaṃpiya Tissa, who shortly after receiving the gift is said to have established the first Buddhist monastic institution in his kingdom. For his contributions, Aśoka was portrayed in Buddhist literature as the ideal king with the laudatory title *chakravartin* or "Universal Ruler."

While it is generally accepted that King Aśoka played an important role in the spread of Buddhism within his empire and in surrounding regions, the process was more complicated than simply a state-sponsored propagation. By the third century BCE, an intimate relationship between the monastic community and trading networks had developed in South Asia.[1] These networks connected the Gangetic regions, where the Buddha had dwelled and preached, to the regions in central and southern India. The early Buddhist sites were mostly located near urban centers along the trade routes. Thus the northwestern town of Taxila (in present-day Pakistan), the Gangetic cities of Śrāvastī (near present-day Benares) and Pāṭaliputra (modern-day Patna), and the central and southern urban centers of Sāñcī (in present-day Madhya Pradesh) and Amarāvatī (in present-day Andhra Pradesh) became closely connected through the intertwined networks of trade and Buddhism. Inscriptions by King Aśoka, highlighting teachings associated with Buddhism, have been found near many of these urban centers.

The spread of Buddhism along the trading networks within South Asia continued after the death of Aśoka. The two succeeding empires, the Śātavāhanas (c. first century BCE – c. third century CE) in the Deccan region of India and the Kuṣāṇas (c. 30 CE – c. 230) ruling in northern India, were instrumental in this regard, and also played a significant role in the diffusion of Buddhism outside South Asia. The Śātavāhana court emerged as one of the leading supporters of Buddhism in India, although the rulers themselves may not have converted to the religion. Their patronage of Buddhism can be discerned from the inscriptions that report sponsorship of monasteries, rock-cut temple complexes, and donations to Buddhist institutions in the Deccan region.[2] Also evident in epigraphical records from western and eastern regions of Deccan is the thriving relationship between traders and Buddhist institutions. Places such as Amarāvatī, Nāgārjunakoṇḍa and others in the eastern part of the Deccan suggest intimate connections not only between Buddhism and the local trading communities, but also with merchant guilds engaged in overseas maritime commerce.[3]

The Kuṣāṇas, who originated in the eastern part of Central Asia, formed their empire during the first century CE. Expansion under King Kaniṣka (c. 127 – c. 140) in the second century CE stretched the empire from Central Asia to the Gangetic plains of eastern India. Trade routes connecting the oasis states of Central Asia with the maritime world of Bay of Bengal became more

1 James Heitzman, "Early Buddhism, Trade and Empire," in Kenneth A. R. Kennedy and Gregory L. Possehl (eds.), *Studies in the Archaeology and Palaeoanthropology of South Asia* (Calcutta: Oxford University Press, 1984): 124.
2 D. K. Chakrabarti, "Buddhist Sites Across South Asia as Influenced by Political and Economic Forces," *World Archaeology* 27. 2 (1995): 199.
3 See Himanshu P. Ray, *Monastery and Guild: Commerce under the Satavahanas* (New Delhi: Oxford University Press, 1986).

extensive and integrated during the Kuṣāṇa period. Similar to King Aśoka and the Śātavāhana rulers, the Kuṣāṇa kings supported Buddhist institutions through donations and sponsorships. Taxila, for example, consolidated its position as a leading center for Buddhist learning in southern Asia under the Kuṣāṇas. More importantly, the itinerant merchant communities from Central Asia expanded their trading networks into Southeast and East Asia. Some of these merchants, the Sogdians in particular, played a leading role in introducing Buddhist teachings and images to Han China, which also was witnessing a period of urbanization and commercial expansion.

Buddhism had undergone noteworthy doctrinal changes by the time it entered the urban centers and port towns of Han China. The most important of these was the emergence of the Mahāyāna (Great Vehicle) school. The teachings of Mahāyāna Buddhism, appearing mostly in texts written in Sanskrit, allowed the laity to pursue the Buddhist path without the need to renounce society and join the monastic community. Some of these people could also become *bodhisattvas*, enlightened beings who delayed entering Nirvāṇa in order to help others. The Mahāyāna Buddhists developed their unique philosophical traditions, texts, and images, which became popular in Central Asia, China, Japan, and Korea. The Theravada school, with its distinct texts, teachings, rules of personal conduct, and the primary use of Pāli language, eventually became dominant in Sri Lanka, Myanmar (Burma), and Thailand. This does not imply, however, that people in these regions exclusively practiced one specific form of Buddhism. As noted above, in many of these places one could find texts and images belonging to multiple forms of Buddhism, including those from the later Tantric/esoteric or Vajrayāna (Thunderbolt Vehicle) tradition, which developed in the seventh century. Also evident in these regions is the incorporation of local beliefs into Buddhist teachings and practices.

The route of transmission of Buddhism to China has been debated extensively during the past century. The argument has focused on whether the doctrine was initially transmitted through the overland roads or maritime routes. Erik Zürcher has questioned the long-accepted view that the transmission of Buddhist doctrines to China through the overland route was staged from Central Asian oasis states. He argues that the evidence for Buddhism in China predates the evidence for the presence of monastic institutions in eastern Central Asia. While textual and archeological sources make it clear that Buddhism spread to China by the second century CE, the earliest Buddhist remains from places such as Kucha and Khotan in eastern Central Asia date from the fourth century. In other words, Buddhism seems to have penetrated Chinese society at least two centuries before it was established in regions that were considered to be the key staging sites for the diffusion of Buddhism to China. Thus Zürcher contends that the spread of Buddhism from southern Asia to China was through "long-distance" transmission rather than a result of "contact expansion."[4]

No matter through which route Buddhism first reached China, it is clear that there was some presence of the doctrine and Buddhist monks in the Han capital Luoyang around the year 65 CE. A popular legend associates the spread of Buddhism to China with a dream of the Han Emperor Ming (r. 58–75 CE). In his dream, the Chinese ruler is said to have seen a "golden man." Upon enquiring, the court officials told him that it might have been the foreign god called the Buddha. Learning this, the emperor sent two envoys to the "Western Regions" to seek more information about the foreign deity. Three years later, the envoys are said to have returned with two Buddhist monks, who were housed at the "first" Chinese Buddhist monastery called the Baimasi (White Horse Monastery) and asked to translate Buddhist texts. The history of Buddhism in China usually begins with this story of official introduction of the doctrine. While it is clear that this story is a later fabrication, meant to link the introduction of Buddhism with the Chinese court and legitimize the presence of a foreign doctrine in China, there are other reliable records to indicate the existence of Buddhist ideas and followers in Han China during the reign of Emperor Ming.[5]

By the beginning of the sixth century, over two thousand Buddhist texts (known as *sutras*) were translated and cataloged in China. The rendition of Buddhist texts into Chinese may have been one of the important factors for the successful establishment of the doctrine in China. Often more than four people collaborated in the translation of a single Buddhist sutra. The first person recited the text, either from memory or from a manuscript, the second translated it orally into Chinese, the third wrote down the Chinese translation, and the fourth edited the written version of the Chinese translation. This method of translation of Buddhist texts, due to the lack of bilingual specialists, continued through to the tenth century. Initially, the translations consisted of basic Buddhist teachings and the *Jātaka* tales (stories of the

---

4 Erik Zürcher, "Han Buddhism and the Western Regions," in W. L. Idema and Erik Zürcher (eds.), *Thought and Law in Qin and Han China: Studies Presented to Anthony Hulsewé on the Occasion of his Eightieth Birthday* (Leiden: Brill, 1990): 158–82.

5 On this and other similar stories, see Erik Zürcher, *The Buddhist Conquest of China: The Spread and Adaptation of Buddhism in Early Medieval China*, third edn. (Leiden: Brill, 2007): 19–23.

Buddha's previous births). Gradually, more philosophical works belonging to various schools of Buddhism were rendered into Chinese. Several other genres of Buddhist literature, ranging from the biographical accounts of famous monks to apocryphal texts that placed Buddhist teachings within the Chinese socio-cultural framework, were composed in China. Also, by this time, Chinese monks, starting with Faxian (337/342–c. 422) in the fifth century, were traveling to South Asia to procure new texts and make pilgrimages. In other words, networks of Buddhist exchanges between China and South Asia were firmly established by the sixth century. During the subsequent centuries, these networks and the Buddhist centers in China facilitated the further spread of Buddhism to other parts of Asia.

The spread of Buddhism between the fifth and tenth centuries

The fifth and sixth centuries witnessed several developments across most of Asia that resulted in the spread of Buddhism to places that either had no prior encounter with the doctrine or were marginally in contact with it. While Korea and Japan fall into the former category, the maritime polities of Southeast Asia can be associated with the latter. The brisk networks of exchange between South Asia and China, mentioned above, augmented Central and Southeast Asia's participation in the flow of Buddhist monks, merchants, and paraphernalia from one region to another. In the seventh century, these networks had also integrated Korea and Japan. Additionally, many of these regions outside South Asia started developing their own unique schools and traditions of Buddhism to address local needs and situations. This process, sometimes referred to as "domestication" or "localization," intensified Buddhist interactions, created multiple centers of Buddhism, and transformed Buddhism into the first pan-Asiatic religion.

Buddhism across Asia

Established in the middle of the fifth century, the Nālandā Mahāvihāra in the present-day Bihar state of India rapidly developed into the leading center of Buddhist learning. By the seventh century, this institution was not only attracting students from across Asia, it was also actively sending monks to propagate the doctrine. The monastery also received donations from local and foreign rulers. Indeed, the establishment of Nālandā seems to have had significant impact on cross-regional Buddhist exchanges during the second half of the first millennium. Two other developments also contributed to the rapid spread of Buddhism during this period. First, new dynasties and polities that emerged in China, Japan, and Korea, as well as in Central and Southeast Asia, started employing Buddhism to legitimize their political authority. Their aim was often to create a distinct identity for the newly established regime through the use of Buddhism. Links with existing Buddhist centers were essential for these political entities to import texts and other paraphernalia in order to further the cause of the doctrine in their lands. Second, the intensification of long-distance commercial activity in the fifth and sixth centuries reinforced the association between merchants and monastic communities and contributed to the spread of Buddhism to new sites of interactions.

Between the fall of the Han Empire in 220 CE and the formation of a new unified empire by the Sui in 589, several contending kingdoms and dynasties rose and fell in China. Some of these, the Liang dynasty (502–557) in southern China for instance, employed Buddhism in unprecedented ways. The founding ruler of the dynasty, Emperor Wu (r. 502–49), not only propagated Buddhist doctrines and rituals within his state, but also established connections with Buddhist centers in South Asia, and took steps to transmit the doctrine to Korea. After ascending to the throne, Emperor Wu dispatched a delegation of eighty-two people to bring an image of the Buddha from central India. This delegation returned in 511 by the maritime route with the image especially made for the Chinese emperor. Emperor Wu is also reported to have sent envoys to the Funan polity in Southeast Asia to fetch Buddhist relics. This interest in Buddhist artifacts by Emperor Wu seems to have triggered various embassies from South and Southeast Asian polities that presented Buddhist relics and other paraphernalia to the Chinese court. The polity of Panpan, for example, presented Buddhist relics to Emperor Wu in 528 and 534, Dandan offered a tooth relic and a Buddha image in 528, and in 540 Funan gave an image of the Buddha and Buddhist texts.[6] All these polities were located in the maritime regions of Southeast Asia and were encountering Buddhism more intensely due to the upsurge in long-distance mercantile activity in the Bay of Bengal and South China Sea regions.

Similarly, in northern China, under the Northern Wei dynasty (386–534), established by the Tuoba migrants from the steppe region in Central Asia, Buddhism was favored and propagated by several rulers. With the support and sponsorship of these rulers, construction of a large number of Buddhist

---

6 Panpan and Dandan were most likely located on the east coast of the Malay peninsula.

Figure 17.1 Buddhist figures, Longmen Caves, Henan Province (Private Collection, Leemage / Bridgeman Images)

temples and monuments took place in the major towns of northern China. Also noteworthy was the building of the cave complexes at Longmen (near the city of Luoyang, Henan Province) and Yungang (near the city of Datong, Shanxi Province), which required the introduction of various kinds of religious paraphernalia, including relics, sculptures, and texts, and created a demand for artists and craftsmen familiar with Buddhist style and practices (see Figure 17.1). The Chinese monk Falin (572–640) reports that in northern China during the Northern Wei period there were 47 "great state monasteries," 839 monasteries built by the royalty and the elites, and more than 30,000 Buddhist temples constructed by commoners.[7] In the south, on the other hand, there were 2,846 monasteries and 82,700 monks.[8]

7 Jacques Gernet, *Buddhism in Chinese Society: An Economic History from the Fifth to the Tenth Centuries*, trans. Franciscus Verellen (New York: Columbia University Press, 1995 [1956]): 4.
8 Kenneth Ch'en, *Buddhism in China: A Historical Survey* (Princeton University Press, 1964): 136.

The impressive growth of Buddhism in China during the fifth and sixth centuries seems to have had considerable impact on the development of Buddhism in regions of Central and Southeast Asia. The demand for Buddhist paraphernalia and artisans in China and the corresponding emergence of Nālandā as a center for Buddhist learning and propagation greatly increased the Buddhist traffic between South Asia and China. All the regions in between, as a consequence, came into contact with Buddhist preachers, pilgrims, artifacts, and artisans more frequently and in larger numbers than in any previous periods.

Indeed, while Buddhist doctrines had already penetrated the oasis states of Central Asia before the fifth century, the increased traffic between South Asia and China continued to foster Buddhism in areas such as Kucha, Khotan, and Dunhuang. These places were vital stopovers for Buddhist monks travelling overland between South Asia and China and benefited from doctrines and goods moving along these so-called Silk Roads. In the late fifth century, Kocho (Chinese: Gaochang) emerged as a new polity in the present-day Turfan area of Xinjiang Autonomous Region. Buddhism flourished under some of the rulers of Kocho, who sponsored the translation of Buddhist texts, conducted grand religious ceremonies, and constructed temples and cave complexes. Textual and archaeological evidence suggest that the doctrine was widespread in the Kocho society, both among elites and commoners.

The fifth and sixth centuries were especially important for the spread of Buddhism to the maritime regions of Southeast Asia. In areas of mainland Southeast Asia, such as Myanmar and Thailand, Buddhist doctrines might have entered prior to the fourth century. Some scholars have pointed to the architectural influences of Nāgārjunakoṇḍa and Amarāvatī on the design of stupas (mound-like structures containing sacred relics) in the Pyu (in present-day Myanmar) and Mon (in present-day Thailand) areas, as well as the discovery of Mauryan-style Buddhist inscriptions (known as *dharmacakra* and *ye dharma*) in these regions, to suggest the transmission of Buddhism to mainland Southeast Asia by the second century CE.[9] The Pyu site Śrīṣetra (in the lower Irrawaddy river) and the Mon site Dvāravatī (in the Chao Phraya basin) also revealed the earliest Pāli inscriptions in inland Southeast Asia dating from the fifth to seventh centuries and sixth to eighth centuries respectively, indicating, for some, the presence of Theravada doctrines.[10]

9 Prapod Assavavirulhakarn, *The Ascendancy of Theravada Buddhism in Southeast Asia* (Bangkok: Silkworm Books, 2010): 68.
10 Peter Skilling, "The Advent of Theravāda Buddhism to Mainland South-east Asia," *Journal of the International Association of Buddhist Studies* 20 (1997): 93–107.

The earliest concrete evidence for the presence and practice of Buddhism in maritime regions of Southeast Asia, on the other hand, dates to the fourth–fifth century. One of these is a fifth-century Sanskrit inscription found in Kedah in present-day Malaysia. Commissioned by a sea captain named Buddhagupta, the inscription also has an engraved image of a stupa. The three-line inscription offers prayers to the Buddha and records of Buddhagupta as the "great sea captain" and a resident of Raktamṛttika, which most scholars identify as the Southeast Asian polity called Chitu (on the eastern coast of the Malay peninsula) in later Chinese sources. Other early Buddhist inscriptions in maritime Southeast Asia were also found in the Kedah region (see Map 17.2).[11]

Excavations in Kedah and its vicinity have also revealed several Buddha statues and sculptures from the same period. While some of these images stylistically resemble Gupta art forms and may have been imported from South Asia, others seem to have been made locally. Buddhist statues made of stone and bronze, votive tablets and stupas dating from the fifth to the seventh centuries have also been discovered on the east coast of the Malay peninsula. Made in different styles, these objects indicate links between Southeast Asia and several regions of South Asia, including the present-day Indian states of West Bengal, Odisha, Andhra, and Tamil Nadu, and the presence of distinct traditions of Buddhist doctrines.

The above evidence for the presence of Buddhism in maritime Southeast Asia coincided with the decline of Funan, a polity centered in the present-day Cambodia–Vietnam region, and in the formation of new polities in it. To legitimize their authority, the rulers of some of these new polities opted for Buddhism instead of the Brahmanical doctrines that might have prevailed in Funan. The fact that almost at the same time Chinese dynasties were also using Buddhism for political legitimization would have been apparent to these rulers. The emergence of the powerful Śrīvijayan polity centered in Sumatra in the seventh century, as noted below, further stimulated the spread of Buddhism in maritime Southeast Asia.

The use of Buddhism to legitimize or project political power was also instrumental in the establishment of the doctrine in Korea and Japan. The development of Buddhism in these areas was closely associated with diplomatic, commercial, and religious connections to China. According to a twelfth-century Korean work called *Samguk sagi* (Historical Records of the

---

11 Michel Jacq-Hergoualch'h, *The Malay Peninsula: Crossroads of the Maritime Silk Road (100 BC – 1300 AD)*, trans. Victoria Hobson (Leiden: Brill, 2002): 207–21.

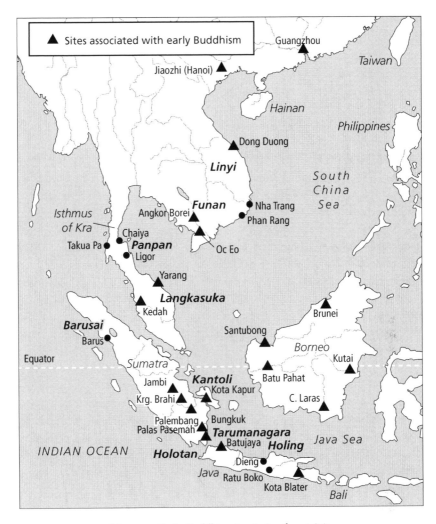

Map 17.2. Early Buddhist sites in Southeast Asia

Three Kingdoms), Buddhism was introduced to Korea during the Three Kingdoms period, to the kingdom of Koguryŏ in 372, the kingdom of Paekche in 384, and the kingdom of Silla in 528.[12] While contacts with Chinese kingdoms are credited with the transmission of the doctrine to the

---

12 On the spread of Buddhism to Korea, see Lewis R. Lancaster and C. S. Yu (eds.), *Introduction of Buddhism to Korea: New Cultural Patterns* (Berkeley: Asian Humanities Press, 1989).

former two kingdoms, monks from Koguryŏ are said to have brought Buddhist teachings to Silla.[13] The spread of Buddhism to Japan, on the other hand, is attributed to Buddhist teachers from Paekche. The *Samguk sagi* and other sources also suggest that the transmission of Buddhism to the region was intimately connected to the larger networks of Buddhist interactions across Asia. In both Paekche and Silla, for example, the two earliest monks, named Maranant'a (Mālānanda?) and Mukhoja respectively, seem to have come from Central Asia.[14]

Textual sources from the sixth and seventh centuries indicate intense interactions between Buddhist communities in East Asia. The Liang dynasty in China, which, as outlined above, fostered Buddhist linkages with South and Southeast Asia, also facilitated Buddhist exchanges in East Asia. Not only did monks from the Korean kingdoms travel to Liang China to study, but Emperor Wu is also known to have sent Buddhist delegations and relics to Korea. In fact in 527, the ruler of Paekche built a Buddhist temple called Taet'ong-sa (Chinese: Datong si) in honor of Emperor Wu's contribution to the spread of the doctrine to his kingdom.[15] Additionally, within a few decades of the introduction of the doctrine, the rulers of the Silla kingdom, similar to Emperor Wu, were using the symbolism of the *chakravartin*, associated with King Aśoka, to portray themselves as powerful and pious Buddhist monarchs.[16]

Monks from Korea also started traveling to South Asia in the sixth century to study and procure Buddhist texts. One of the earliest monks to make this journey might have been Kyomik from Paekche who went to India by the sea route.[17] It was also through the maritime networks that monks from Paekche introduced Buddhist doctrines to Japan. After the initial transmission of Buddhism to Japan in 552 by a monk named Norisach'igye,[18] several other Buddhist missions were sent from Paekche to Japan. Monks from Koguryŏ were active in Japan during the sixth century as well and are known to have established the

---

13 Some sources credited an official mission from the Liang court in China for the transmission of the doctrine to Silla.

14 Ahn Kye-hyŏn, "A Short History of Ancient Korean Buddhism," in Lancaster and Yu (eds.), *Introduction of Buddhism to Korea*, 1–27.

15 Jonathan Best, *A History of the Early Korean Kingdom of Paekche: Together with an Annotated Translation of the Paekche Annals of the Samguk Sagi* (Cambridge, MA: Harvard University Asia Center, 2007): 135–6.

16 Richard D. McBride II, *Domesticating the Dharma: Buddhist Cults and the Hwaŏm Synthesis in Silla Korea* (Honolulu: University of Hawai'i Press, 2008).

17 On the early Korean monks who reportedly traveled to South Asia, see Jonathan Best, "Tales of Three Paekche Monks who Traveled Afar in Search of the Law," *Harvard Journal of Asiatic Studies* 51, 1 (1991): 139–97.

18 Ahn, "A Short History," 13.

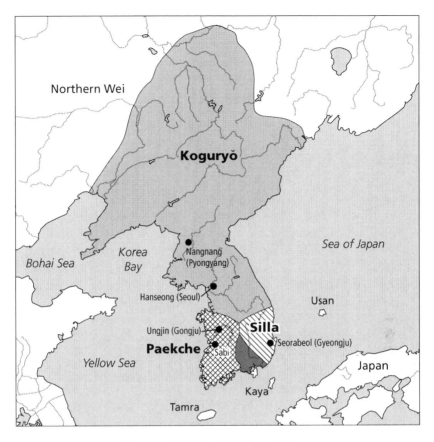

Map 17.3. The Three Kingdoms in Korea

first order of nuns in the island. In 594, Koguryŏ and Paekche monks, Hyeja and Hyech'ong respectively, were instrumental in explaining the Buddhist doctrines to Prince Shōtoku, who became one of the first members of the royalty in Japan to advocate Buddhism.[19] Aware of the importance of China as a center of Buddhism, Shōtoku sent an envoy to the Sui court (581–618) in 607 to bring, among other things, Buddhist texts. By the time of Prince Shōtoku's death in 622, Buddhist doctrines had penetrated the easternmost region of Asia.

19 On the transmission of Buddhism from the Korean peninsula to Japan, see Kamata Shigeo, "The Transmission of Paekche Buddhism to Japan," in Lancaster and Yu (eds.), *Introduction of Buddhism to Korea*, 143–60.

Buddhist networks and exchanges

The spread of Buddhism across Asia triggered vibrant cross-cultural exchanges during the seventh and eighth centuries. This is manifested in the increased number of monks traveling between various regions of Asia, the growth in the exchange of Buddhist paraphernalia, and the creation of new networks of Buddhist transmissions. This period also witnessed the formation of several localized schools of Buddhist thought, the establishment of unique pilgrimage sites and the creation of new art motifs throughout the Buddhist realm (see Figure 17.2). The latter developments eventually contributed to the emergence of multiple centers of Buddhism that would gradually form their own spheres of influences.

The travels of the Chinese monks Xuanzang (600?–664) and Yijing (635–713), the pilgrimage of the Korean Buddhist Hye'cho (c. 700–c. 780), the missionary work of the South Asian Tantric masters Vajrabodhi (671–741) and Amoghavajra (705–774), and the Japanese monk Kūkai's (774–835) sojourn in China are indicative of the highly connected and interactive nature of Buddhist exchanges during the seventh and eighth centuries. The travels of Xuanzang, which were later fictionalized by Chinese writers, are perhaps the best known of these cross-regional interactions that sustained the diffusion of Buddhist ideas, images, and paraphernalia.

Xuanzang seems to have come to know about Nālandā from a South Asian monk named Prabhākaramitra, who reached Tang China in the early seventh century. He set out on his journey through Central Asia sometime around 629, with the intention to learn about Yogacara teachings. During his stay in South Asia, Xuanzang had audiences with two powerful rulers, King Harṣa of Kanauj (located in northern India) and King Bhāskarvarman of Kāmarūpa (in eastern India). After staying at Nālandā for about ten years, Xuanzang returned to Tang China in 645 with over 600 Buddhist texts and many Buddhist images. Xuanzang continued to maintain contacts with his teachers and fellow students at Nālandā and may have even played some role in fostering diplomatic exchanges between the Tang court and kingdoms in South Asia.[20]

A few decades after Xuanzang's return, another Chinese monk called Yijing also travelled to Nālandā and observed the ways in which Buddhist practices in South Asia differed from those in China and Southeast Asia.

---

20 Tansen Sen, *Buddhism, Diplomacy, and Trade: The Realignment of Sino-Indian Relations, 600–1400* (Honolulu: University of Hawai'i Press, 2003).

Figure 17.2 Pensive Bodhisattva, Three Kingdoms period (57 BCE–668 CE), mid–seventh century, Korea (Metropolitan Museum of Art / © SCALA)

Yijing wrote about several other monks from East Asia who went to Nālandā in the seventh century, making their journeys either by the sea or the land route. More importantly, Yijing's activities indicate an intimate networking between the Buddhist learning centers in Tang China, Southeast Asia, and South Asia. Before reaching Nālandā, Yijing studied Sanskrit in Śrīvijaya for about half a year. On his way back, he lived in the Southeast Asian polity again to write his accounts of travels and undertake, in collaboration with other Chinese monks, translation work. In fact, in one of his translations, Yijing recommends that Chinese monks planning to visit South Asia should first study Sanskrit in Śrīvijaya.

Yijing also mentions several Korean monks who made (or attempted to make) pilgrimages to South Asia. This included the monks Hyeŏp, Hyeryun, Hyŏnʻgak, Hyŏnjo, Hyŏnyu, and Hyŏntʻae. Some of these monks lived and died in Nālandā. There were others who, according to Yijing, passed away on their way to South Asia. The most famous Korean monk to travel to Nalanda was Hyechʻo, who reached there in the early eighth century. This monk from the Silla kingdom studied in Tang China under the Indian Tantric master Vajrabodhi before making his pilgrimage to the sacred sites in India. After his pilgrimage, Hyechʻo returned to China and continued to work under Vajrabodhi and his disciple Amoghavajra. He is credited with writing a memoir called *Wang ocheonchukguk jeon* (Memoir of a Pilgrimage to the Five Indias), which also vividly demonstrates the linkages that existed between various Buddhist learning centers and pilgrimage sites in South and East Asia.

The two South Asian masters under whom Hyechʻo studied in Tang China were part of the larger movement to transmit new doctrines of Buddhism associated with Tantric practices. Tantra is defined as

> that body of beliefs and practices which, working from the principle that the universe we experience is nothing other than the concrete manifestation of the divine energy [or teaching/enlightened consciousness, in the case of Buddhism] of the godhead that creates and maintains that universe, seeks to ritually appropriate and channel that energy, within the human microcosm, in creative and emancipatory ways.[21]

Spells, chants, and ritual ceremonies were key elements of this tradition which developed in South Asia in the seventh century and influenced both Brahmanism and Buddhism.

Between the second half of the seventh and the late eighth century, Tantric Buddhist doctrines spread rapidly to all parts of the Buddhist realm. Tantra gained favor among the Pāla rulers in the Bihar–Bengal region of South Asia, with some of the Tang emperors in China, and also influenced monastic institutions in Sri Lanka, Southeast Asia, Korea, and Japan. It made

---

21 David Gordon White, "Introduction, Tantra in Practice: Mapping a Tradition," in David Gordon White (ed.), *Tantra in Practice* (Princeton University Press, 2000): 9.

the most significant impact in Tibet, where Buddhist doctrines entered in the eighth century.

Tantric Buddhism introduced new styles of religious paraphernalia into the existing networks of exchange. The activities of Tantric masters Vajrabodhi and Amoghavajra, and one of their predecessors, a South Asian monk named Śubhakarasiṃha (d. 735), reveal the vitality of these expanded networks. The three monks were closely associated with the Tang rulers and performed various rituals and ceremonies for the protection of the state, translated numerous Tantric texts, and trained Chinese and other East Asian monks. The Japanese monk Kūkai studied with one of Amoghavajra's Chinese students named Huiguo and returned to his homeland in 806 to promote Tantric doctrines in Japan by establishing the school known as Shingon. The Japanese emperors Kammu (r. 781–806) and Junna (r. 823–33) were his leading patrons.[22] Huiguo also had a student from Java named Bianhong, who, after returning from China, may have contributed to the designing of the temple of Borobudur.[23]

Not far from Borobudur, in central Java, is a site called Ratu Boko, where an eighth-century Sanskrit inscription indicates the presence of Sri Lankan monks. The architectural features of the Buddhist monastic site in Ratu Boko also show similarities to the Abhayagiri monastery in Sri Lanka.[24] In 741, Amoghavajra visited the Abhayagiri monastery and passed through Java on his way from Tang China to South Asia. He and his Chinese disciples are known to have stayed in Sri Lanka for several months and brought back Tantric Buddhist texts and artifacts to China. It is clear from textual records and archaeological evidence that Sri Lanka was an integral part of the Tantric networks of the seventh and eighth centuries.

The Tantric masters in China were also responsible for furthering the cult of Mañjuśrī, the bodhisattva of compassion. Mount Wutai, perceived as an abode of the bodhisattva Mañjuśrī, was perhaps the most important Buddhist pilgrimage site outside South Asia. Starting from around the sixth century, Chinese Buddhist texts started promoting the mountain in central China as the site where one could encounter and venerate Mañjuśrī. The legends

---

22 Ryūichi Abé, *The Weaving of Mantra: Kūkai and the Construction of Esoteric Buddhist Discourse* (New York: Columbia University Press, 1999).

23 Hiram W. Woodward, "Bianhong, Mastermind of Borobudur?," *Pacific World: Journal of the Institute of Buddhist Studies* 11 (2009): 25–60.

24 Jeffrey Roger Sundberg, "The Wilderness Monks of the Abhyagirivihāra and the Origins of Sino-Javanese Esoteric Buddhism," *Bijdragen tot de Taal-, Land- en Volkenkunde* 160 (2004): 163–88.

associated with the presence of the Buddhist divinity at the mountain became so popular that even monks from South Asia began making pilgrimages to the site. Vajrabodhi was one such monk who, after reaching China, frequently organized ritual and ceremonies on the mountain. The Mañjuśrī cult associated with Mount Wutai also spread to Tibet and later became an important part of the diplomatic intercourse between the rulers in China and Lhasa.[25]

Tibet was the last major region of Asia where Buddhist doctrines penetrated. Although some sources suggest that Buddhist ideas spread as early as the reign of King Songtsen Gampo (Srong btsan sgam po, r. c. 614–650), it was only under King Tri Songdetsen (Khri srong lde btsan, r. 754–797) that they gained popularity. King Tri Songdetsen is said to have converted to Buddhism and employed it not only to consolidate his political power, but also in Tibet's diplomatic relations with foreign polities.[26] The process through which the doctrine spread to Tibet reveals the existence of multiple centers of Buddhism and the diverse array of Buddhist ideas that had developed throughout Asia by the eighth century.[27]

During Tri Songdetsen's reign, several Indian and Chinese monks were active in Tibet. This included Indian monks belonging to the Madhyamikā school, represented by Śāntarakṣita and his disciple Kamalaśīla, the Kashmīri Tantric master Padmasambhava, who is credited for establishing the first Buddhist monastery in Tibet known as Samye (Bsam yas) in 779, and the Chinese Moheyan, who headed the local Chan school. Shortly before the death of Tri Songdetsen, a great debate is reported to have ensued between the followers of Madhyamikā and Chan, represented by Kamalaśīla and Moheyan respectively, to determine the true nature of enlightenment. Tibetan sources hold that Moheyan was defeated and banished from Tibet. It was then decided that the Madhyamikā school would be followed in Tibet.[28]

Buddhist exchanges between Tibet and other regions of the Buddhist world grew considerably during the reigns of Tri Songdetsen and his

---

25 Sen, *Buddhism, Diplomacy, and Trade*, 76–86.

26 The spread of Buddhist ideas to Tibet is outlined in Donald S. Lopez, Jr, *Religions of Tibet in Practice* (Princeton University Press, 1997): 5–25.

27 See for example Matthew T. Kapstein, "The Treaty Temple of Turquoise Grove," in Matthew T. Kapstein (ed.), *Buddhism between Tibet & China* (Somerville, MA: Wisdom Publications, 2009): 21–71.

28 Paul Demiéville, *Le Concile de Lhasa: une controverse sur le quiétisme entre bouddhistes de l'Inde et de la Chine au viiie siècle de l'ère chrétienne* (Paris: Imprimerie Nationale de France, 1952).

successor Ralpajen (Ral pa can, r. c. 815–835). Tri Songdetsen was interested in Buddhist pilgrimage sites in both India and China, including Mount Wutai. On one occasion, he is recorded to have sent a diplomatic mission to the Tang court to request a painting of Mount Wutai. Under Ralpajen, on the other hand, several translation academies were established in Tibet to translate Indian Buddhist texts and study Sanskrit. Military expansion into Dunhuang also gave Tibetans access to Buddhist texts and artifacts from Central Asia. These exchanges and interactions were interrupted in 838, when the King Langdarma (Glang dar ma) persecuted Buddhist monks and suppressed monastic institutions. Langdarma may have been eventually assassinated by a Buddhist monk, which, while ending the persecution of Buddhism, also led to the disintegration of the Tibetan empire. It was only in the eleventh century that Buddhist exchanges between Tibet and other Buddhist centers started to revive.

The multiple worlds of Buddhism, 1000–1500

By the eleventh century, three distinct "worlds" of Buddhism seemed to have emerged across Asia: the India-Tibet world, centered on the monastic institutions in the Bihar–Bengal region; the East Asian world, with multiple centers in China, Korea and Japan; and the Sri Lanka–Southeast Asia world, connected through the Theravada/Pāli Buddhist networks. This does not imply, however, that the contacts and exchanges across and between the various Buddhist regions ceased. The travels of the South Asian monk Atīśa (982–1054) are indicative of the persistent Buddhist connections across Asia. Also known as Dīpaṃkara Śrījñāna, Atīśa traveled to Sumatra in the early eleventh century and studied under a local monk named Dharmakīrti. After spending about eleven years in Southeast Asia, he returned to India and settled at the Vikramaśīla Monastery. In 1040, on an invitation from the Tibetan royalty, Atīśa went to central Tibet to teach Tantric Buddhist doctrines.[29] There was also a monk named Dhyanabhadra (Ch. Chanxian/ Zhikong, 1225–1363), who in the thirteenth century was ordained at Nālandā and then traveled from India to Beijing and subsequently to the Korean peninsula.[30] Indeed, despite the fact that the contours of the three Buddhist

---

29 For details about Atīśa's life see Alaka Chattopadhyaya, *Atīśa and Tibet: Life and Works of Dīpaṃkara Śrījñāna in Relation to the History and Religion of Tibet* (New Delhi: Motilal Banarsidass, 1996).

30 See Duan Yuming, *Zhikong: Zuihou yiwei lai Hua de Yindu gaoseng (Zhikong: The Last Eminent Monk from India to Travel to China)* (Chengdu: Bashu shushe, 2007).

worlds became more distinct with regard to doctrinal practices, the connections between them continued through to the twentieth century.

The India-Tibet Buddhist world

The Vikramaśīla Monastery where Atīśa lived before accepting the invitation to go to Tibet emerged as one of the leading Buddhist centers in South Asia. The Pāla ruler Dharmapāla (r. 770?–810) built the monastery in the late eighth or early ninth century, and it continued to prosper under the patronage of the later rulers of the dynasty. Located not far from Nālandā, the monastery was a key site for interactions between local Tantric clergies and those visiting from Tibet. Until its decline in the twelfth century, Vikramaśīla played an important role in the spread of Tantric Buddhism to Nepal and Tibet. Another monastic institution that flourished and engaged in the transmission of Buddhist Tantric doctrines during the Pāla period was Odantapurī, also located in the modern state of Bihar. Although Nālandā received less attention from the Pāla rulers than either Vikramaśīla or Odantapurī, it nonetheless remained an important destination for foreign monks and attracted donations from polities as far away as in Sumatra.[31]

The above three monasteries were not only involved in the transmission of Tantric doctrines, but they were also instrumental in the spread of new Buddhist art forms that developed under the Pālas and other smaller kingdoms located in the Bihar–Bengal region between the eighth and twelfth centuries. Often represented in black stone or metal, with images that incorporated Brahmanical deities, the Pāla Tantric art dispersed across Asia, even though the reception and impact was not always comparable. Nepal, Tibet, Yunnan, Java, and Myanmar seem to have been the main regions that were influenced by Pāla art forms.[32]

Other art forms produced during this period suggest serious rivalries between the followers of Buddhism and Brahmanism in several regions of India. In the seventh century, when the Chinese monk Xuanzang visited northern India, he had witnessed the decline of several urban centers and monastic institutions. It seems that the decline of urban centers, which were important for the initial spread of Buddhism, and the conflict with Brahmanism had considerable impact on Buddhism, despite the strong patronage of

---

31 On the monastic institutions sponsored and patronized by the Pāla rulers, see Puspa Niyogi, *Buddhism in Ancient Bengal* (Calcutta: Jijnasa, 1980).
32 Susan L. Huntington and John C. Huntington, *Leaves from the Bodhi Tree: The Art of Pāla India (8th–12th centuries) and its International Legacy* (Seattle: University of Washington Press, 1990).

the Pāla rulers.[33] Eventually, in the thirteenth century, the invasions by Turco-Mongol pillagers led to the decline of almost all major Buddhist monastic institutions in northern India, including the three mentioned above.

In many ways, Tibet was the inheritor of the Tantric Buddhist traditions developed during the Pāla period. Similar to the other regions, Tibet also added its own unique features to the doctrine, including the belief in reincarnating lamas (Buddhist teachers), which may have derived from the teachings of Atīśa. Several other schools of Buddhism developed in central, western, and eastern parts of Tibet due to the distinct interactions each of these places had with other parts of the Buddhist realm that included Kashmīr, Central Asia, and China. There were also famous Buddhist monks, such as 'Brog-mi (992–1072) and Milarepa (Mi-la-ras-pa, 1012–96), who founded their own traditions that were centered at a specific monastery in Tibet. Consequently, different indigenous schools of Buddhism emerged in Tibet, some of which competed with each other for religious and political clout.[34]

The major Buddhist schools in Tibet that evolved through these cross-regional interactions and individual introspections included the Sakyapa (Sa-skya-pa), established by 'Brog-mi, who had studied at Vikramaśīla Monastery and translated one of the main Tantric texts known as the Hevajra tantra; the Karmapa (Karma-pa), members of which negotiated the surrender of Tibet to Chinggis Khan; and the Gelukpa (Dge-lugs-pa), which, founded in the fourteenth century, emphasized monastic discipline and is associated with the traditions of Dalai and Panchen lamas. The latter two schools were often in conflict with each other and tried to gain favor from the Mongol and later rulers of China. Many of these Tibetan schools of Buddhism also contributed to the diffusion of Tantric Buddhist traditions. Their impact can be discerned, for example, from the religious practices of the Mongols in Mongolia and the present-day Inner Mongolia Autonomous Region of China. In the eighteenth century, some of these teachings even spread to Buryatia in the southern Siberian region of Russia.[35]

The East Asian Buddhist world

The persecution of Buddhism by the Tang Emperor Wuzong (r. 840–46) in 845 – often termed the Huichang Persecution, as Huichang is the name given

---

33 Giovanni Verardi, *Hardships and Downfall of Buddhism in India* (New Delhi: Manohar and Institute of Southeast Asian Studies, 2011).

34 See Lopez, "Introduction," in Lopez (ed.), *Religions of Tibet in Practice*.

35 John Snelling, *Buddhism in Russia: The Story of Agvan Dorzhiev, Lhasa's Emissary to the Tsar* (Shaftesbury: Element, 1993).

to Wuzong's reign period – used to be viewed as a watershed in the history of the doctrine in China, but the belief that Buddhism declined in China after this event is no longer accepted. Recent studies have demonstrated that the doctrine had already penetrated deep into Chinese society by this time. They also note the fact that Buddhism continued to play a significant role in China's interactions with the neighboring region during the subsequent periods. Under the first three rulers of the Song dynasty, for example, Buddhism seems to have recovered from the persecution in 845 and developed into an integral part of Song China's diplomatic and commercial exchanges with neighboring societies. Translation activity and doctrinal discourse also revived during the late tenth and eleventh centuries.

The Huichang Persecution was one of the most severe measures launched by the state to address the impact of Buddhist monastic institutions on the Chinese economy. Due to their large land ownership and soaring number of tax-exempted clergy, Buddhist monasteries were a significant drain on state revenue. This issue had resulted in at least two earlier suppressions of Buddhism in China. The one under Wuzong in the ninth century, however, was the most brutal. According to a report presented to Emperor Wuzong after the persecution, 4,600 monasteries were destroyed, 260,500 monks and nuns were defrocked and subjected to tax, and a large amount of fertile land belonging to Buddhist institutions was confiscated by the state.[36]

Neither Emperor Wuzong nor the Tang dynasty survived very long after the Huichang Persecution. When the Song dynasty reunified China in 960, not only did Buddhist monastic institutions recover, but networks of Buddhist exchanges were re-established with Japan, Korea, and the nomadic states emerging at the northern and western borders of the Chinese Empire. Several factors were responsible for the survival and resurgence of Buddhism in Song China. The penetration of Buddhist ideas deep into Chinese society, as noted above, was perhaps the most important. Ideas associated with Pure Land Buddhism, for instance, which advocated possible rebirth in the paradise of the celestial Buddha called Amitabha, became immensely popular among lay Buddhists and spread to Korea, Japan, and Vietnam. Similarly, the Chan tradition that became widespread in China had a significant impact on East Asian societies.[37] The destruction of monastic institutions and defrocking of monks and nuns during the Huichang period did not seem to have had a

36 Ch'en, *Buddhism in China*, 232.
37 Nguyen Cuong Tu, *Zen in Medieval Vietnam: A Study and Translation of the Thiền uyển tập anh* (Honolulu: University of Hawai'i Press, 1997).

dire impact on these practices and beliefs that were already ingrained among the common people.

During the tenth and eleventh centuries, commercial networks and state formations continued to stimulate and sustain Buddhist exchanges in East Asia. A new catalyst to this was the invention of movable-type printing that contributed to the increased circulation of Buddhist texts and canons. The Song court's policy to promote internal and external commerce had a tremendous impact on its economy. New networks and markets developed throughout China, which gradually became integrated with the larger Eurasian commercial exchanges. Buddhist monasteries in Song China became part of this commercial revolution by providing loans to merchants and space for fairs and markets. Trade in Buddhist paraphernalia witnessed rapid growth, although the involvement of Buddhist monks (and merchants pretending to be such) became a concern for the Song court.

The growth in demand for Buddhist paraphernalia was not only connected to the expansion of trade during the Song period, but also to state formation among some of the nomadic tribes in Central and East Asia, particularly by the Khitans and Tanguts, who established the Liao (907–1125) and Xixia (1038–1227) dynasties respectively. Similar to the polities in East and Southeast Asia discussed above, the Liao and Xixia, and later the Mongols, also used Buddhism to create state identities and legitimize political authority.[38]

Another important development that led to increased trade in Buddhist artifacts had to do with the apocalyptic prophecies credited to the Buddha himself. It was prophesied that at a certain point in future, the exact time for which varied from text to text, invasion of India by foreigners, the ensuing destruction of Buddhist monuments, or corruption within the monastic organization would lead to the disappearance of Buddhist doctrines. The world would be rampant with greed, chaos, disease, and starvation until the Buddha of the future, Maitreya, would descend to earth and restore order and revive Buddhism. Reports about the decay of monastic centers in India and the popularity of apocalyptic ideas found in Buddhist texts seems to have influenced Buddhist communities throughout East Asia. This perception amplified the demand for relics and texts, which were to be stored for the future regeneration of the doctrine.[39]

---

38 Ruth W. Dunnell, *The Great State of White and High: Buddhism and State Formation in Eleventh-Century Xia* (Honolulu: University of Hawai'i Press, 1996).

39 The apocalyptic prophecies in Buddhism are discussed in detail by Jan Nattier, *Once Upon a Future Time: Studies in a Buddhist Prophecy of Decline* (Berkeley: Asian Humanities Press, 1988).

Within the above contexts, the Chinese Buddhist canon that could be rapidly copied and distributed became an object of high demand in East Asia. This demand contributed to an increase in the need for new Buddhist texts and translators and the establishment of official translation bureaus. The Song translation bureau is known to have employed Indian and Chinese monks, who translated a record number of Buddhist texts and printed several copies of the Buddhist canon. In fact, it seems that the number of Buddhist texts translated during the reign of the first three Song emperors was greater than in any of the previous dynasties. However, the aim to either produce or distribute these canons was not always related to the propagation (or preservation) of the doctrine as such. The Song court in China and the Koryŏ kingdom (918–1392) in Korea, for example, competed with each other to donate Buddhist canons to neighboring regions as part of their diplomatic maneuverings.[40]

Buddhism in Korea had developed and diversified significantly under the Silla kingdom, which unified the region politically in the seventh century. Buddhist schools and cults entering Korea from China were synthesized and domesticated by monks including Wŏnhyo (617–689) and Ŭisang (625–702). Some Korean monks, such as the monk Ch'egwan belonging to the Tiantai school, were even invited to China for doctrinal input. The Buddhist clergy in Korea, similar to their counterparts in China, also transformed several sites in their region into leading pilgrimage centers. This included the establishment of a Mount Wutai-like pilgrimage site at Mount Odae, where the devotees could encounter the Mañjuśrī cult without the need to travel to China.[41]

Many of the accomplishments attained during the Silla period contributed to the growth of Buddhism under the Koryŏ rulers. Teachings related to Sŏn Buddhism in particular became popular during this period, and state-sponsored Buddhist rituals were common. A cordial and mutually beneficial relationship between the Buddhist community and the Koryŏ state was established during the reign of T'aejo (r. 918–43), the founding ruler of the kingdom. And while restrictions were imposed on the ordination of monks, Buddhism in general and Sŏn monks in particular received state support during most of Koryŏ period. The Buddhist monasteries were also prosperous, with large land holdings, private donations, and state support. In fact, it is estimated that Buddhist monasteries in Koryŏ controlled one-sixth of all arable land.[42]

40 Sen, *Buddhism, Diplomacy, and Trade*, 118.   41 McBride, *Domesticating the Dharma*.
42 See Vermeersch, *The Power of the Buddhas: The Politics of Buddhism During the Koryŏ Dynasty (918–1392)* (Cambridge, MA: Harvard University Asia Center, 2008).

The Korean pattern of domestication of Buddhism and the continued links to Buddhist centers and institutions in China also took place in Japan. Monks from Japan frequently visited Tang China to study with either Chinese or Indian teachers. Ideas associated with Tiantai, Tantric, and Chan Buddhism entered Japan mainly through these channels. These three traditions developed into what are known as the Tendai, Shingon, and Zen schools during the Heian (794–1185) and Kamakura (1185–1333) periods. While the monk Saichō (767–822) is credited with establishing the Tendai school, Kūkai, as noted above, was instrumental in introducing Tantric teachings in Japan. The monks Honen (1133–1212) and Shinran (1173–1262), on the other hand, are associated with propagating Pure Land Buddhism in Japan. Each of these schools, although originally imported from China, went through evolution in Japan, sometimes leading to the establishment of new branches. The most pertinent example is that of the Nichiren school, which emerged when the Japanese monk Nichiren (1222–82) decided to reform the ideas of the Tendai school by emphasizing the *Lotus Sutra* as the only true text of Buddhism.

Under the Kamakura shogunate, Buddhism enjoyed state support, the expansion of monastic economic prowess, and the widespread popularity of Buddhist rituals and ceremonies. Similar to other parts of East Asia during this period, the relics of the Buddha became prized items of monastic institutions and the state itself. As a consequence, a number of Buddhist ceremonies during the Kamakura period revolved around the veneration of the relics. The relics housed in the Tōji temple in Kyoto, for instance, were considered to be the "spiritual jewels" of India, China, and Japan, and described as the "spiritual treasures of the realm and protectors of the imperial family."[43]

By the time Qubilai Khan established the Yuan dynasty (1271–1368) in China, Korea and Japan had created their own Buddhist worlds, with their own unique doctrinal and ritualistic emphases. For the clergy and lay followers of Buddhism in these regions, the necessary monastic institutions, learning centers, and pilgrimage sites had all been established. Despite these localizing developments, however, linkages and exchanges continued within the larger Buddhist realm. In fact, because of the acceptance of Tibetan Buddhism by Qubilai in China and Hulegu in Iran, pan-Asiatic Buddhist

---

43 Brian D. Ruppert, *Jewel in the Ashes: Buddha Relics and Power in Early Medieval Japan* (Cambridge, MA: Harvard University Asia Center, 2000): 274.

networks, spanning from Japan to the Persian Gulf, persisted during the thirteenth and fourteenth centuries.

The Sri Lanka–Southeast Asia Buddhist world

After the eleventh century, networks associated with Theravada Buddhism drew together Sri Lanka and different mainland and maritime polities of Southeast Asia more closely than in the previous periods. With links to various regions of India, the monastic sites in Sri Lanka, and influences from southern and southwestern regions of China, Buddhist practices in Southeast Asia were diverse and multifaceted. They included doctrines and art forms originating from the Andhra region in India, Theravada and Tantric teachings transmitted from Sri Lanka, and the influx of Chan and other schools of Buddhism from China. There were also various cults and ideas that developed locally and spread to several regions of Southeast Asia. After the tenth century the Theravada linkages became much stronger, primarily due to political changes taking place in Sri Lanka, Myanmar, and Thailand.

In the second half of the eleventh century, Vijayabāhu I (1055–1110) ended the rule of the Coḷas from southern India and consolidated his power in Sri Lanka. The Sinhalese political hold over the island grew stronger during the reign of Parākramabāhu I (1153–1186), who reportedly launched military offensives against South Indian kingdoms and revitalized the maritime networks connecting Sri Lanka to the regions in the South China Sea. Buddhist institutions flourished under the patronage of Vijayabāhu I and Parākramabāhu I.[44]

During his battles against the Coḷas, Vijayabāhu I is known to have asked Aniruddha (1044–1077), the ruler of the newly established Pagan polity in Myanmar, to preserve the Buddhist tradition and paraphernalia during the period of chaos and warfare in the island. Even before this, the Pagan ruler seems to have decided to use ideas associated with Theravada Buddhism, which had entered Myanmar previously, to legitimize his political authority. Monks from Myanmar are reported to have visited Sri Lanka after Vijayabāhu I's victory and assisted in the re-establishment of Buddhism on the island. The collaboration between the Pagan rulers and the Sinhalese kings during the succeeding periods resulted in frequent Buddhist exchanges between the two regions, including gifts of relics and texts. One of the most famous Buddhist monks from Myanmar to visit Sri Lanka was

---

44 For details, see R. A. L. H. Gunawardana, *Robe and Plough: Monasticism and Economic Interest in Early Medieval Sri Lanka* (Tucson: The University of Arizona Press, 1979).

Uttarajīva, who reached the island during the reign of King Parākramabāhu I. Chapaṭa, a member of Uttarajīva's delegation, remained behind to study in Sri Lanka. After returning to Myanmar in 1181 or 1182, Chapaṭa established a Sinhala Buddhist center, which, according to R. A. L. H. Gunawardana, not only played a significant role in the spread of Sinhalese Theravada Buddhism in Myanmar, but also to other parts of Southeast Asia.[45] It should be noted, however, that several other schools of Buddhism, deriving from specific local teachers, monastic institutions and regions of origin, also existed within the Pagan polity.

Patronage of Buddhism by local rulers, diplomatic interactions with Sri Lanka, and the exchanges between monastic communities were also the reasons for the gradual dominance of Theravada Buddhism in Thailand during the Sukhothai period (1238–1438). Under King Rāma Khambaeng (r. c. 1279–99) and his successors, Sinhalese Theravada doctrines and monastic traditions spread throughout the Sukhothai-controlled regions of Thailand. Similarly, rulers in the Chiangmai region developed their own links with Sri Lanka, leading to the diffusion of Sinhala Theravada Buddhism to almost all regions of present-day Thailand.[46]

Even in regions that were not dominated by the Sinhala Theravada tradition, Buddhist interactions between Sri Lanka and Southeast Asian were also boosted by the popularity of the relic cult. The tooth and other remains and relics of the Buddha found in Sri Lanka attracted monks, envoys, and donations from almost all regions of Southeast Asia. A ruler from Tāmbralinga named Candrabhānu is said to have even attacked Sri Lanka on two occasions, in 1247 and 1262, to obtain Buddhist relics.[47] The popularity of relics may have also enticed Qubilai Khan in China to procure the Buddha's alms bowl by sending a special envoy in 1284. It is also possible, furthermore, that the conflict between the Ming admiral Zheng He and the Sri Lankan ruler Alakéswara in 1410–11, which led to the arrest and removal of the latter to China, took place over the sacred remains of the Buddha preserved on the island.[48]

45 Gunawardana, *Robe and Plough*, 276–7.
46 Donald K. Swearer, "Buddhism in Southeast Asia," in Joseph M. Kitagawa and Mark D. Cummings (eds.), *Buddhism and Asian History* (New York: Macmillan, 1987): 116–18.
47 W. M. Sirisena, *Sri Lanka and South-East Asia: Political, Religious and Cultural Relations, A.D. c. 1000 to c. 1500* (Leiden: Brill, 1978): 36–57.
48 Louise Levathes, *When China Ruled the Seas: The Treasure Fleet of the Dragon Throne 1405–1433* (New York: Simon & Schuster, 1994): 116–18.

The interest of the Yuan and Ming (1368–1644) courts in Sri Lanka reflects the entry of China-based trading and diplomatic networks into the Indian Ocean region. By the end of the thirteenth century, Chinese diasporic communities had been established at ports in South and Southeast Asia. As noted above, Buddhist ideas from China had previously spread to Vietnam, Myanmar, and perhaps also Java. With the formation of Chinese diasporic networks, popular forms of Buddhism carried by the migrants also began spreading to various regions of Southeast Asia. The cult of Guanyin, for example, became widespread in maritime Southeast Asia, especially at sites where Chinese diasporic communities had been established. During the later periods, these communities also erected temples and shrines dedicated to Guanyin in South Asia. Indeed, the maritime networks of the Sri Lankans, Southeast Asians, and the Chinese continued to link the Buddhist worlds in Asia during much of the colonial period.

Concluding remarks

The spread of Buddhism was not simply the diffusion of religious doctrines. It included the transmission of art forms, literary genres, ritual items, geographical knowledge, and technologies and scientific ideas. The cultural, political, and social lives of numerous people living across most of Asia were transformed because of these transmissions. The worldviews, belief systems, and even self-perceptions of settled societies, nomadic tribes, and island dwellers were fundamentally changed as they encountered and accepted Buddhist teachings. At the same time, however, each of these regions contributed to the adaptations of Buddhist ideas and teachings based on local needs and values. Indeed, the pan-Asiatic nature of Buddhism was remarkable not only because of its geographical spread, but also due to the input each of these regions made to the doctrine itself.

Closely linked to the mercantile communities and networks, the spread of Buddhism also had a significant impact on economic activity and cross-regional commercial interactions. Monastic institutions were sometimes large landowners and accumulators of substantial wealth. While some of these aspects led to instances of state interventions and suppressions of Buddhism, they also promoted economic activity. Temple fairs, investment in commercial ventures, and provision of lodging facilities for itinerant traders were conducive to commercial exchanges. Merchants, as noted above, also facilitated the movement of monks, supplied ritual items, and helped establish and sustain monastic institutions through donations. They were also key transmitters of Buddhist ideas from one region to another.

For almost two millennia, the above aspects related to the spread of Buddhism had a significant impact on Asian history. First, Buddhism integrated various regions of Asia, from Iran to Japan, through cultural, diplomatic, and commercial exchanges. Missionary and pilgrimage activities of Buddhists, as well as their attempts to seek new teachings and texts, bonded distant towns, ports, oases, and sacred sites more intimately than perhaps mercantile networks alone. Second, common interest in the teachings of the Buddha, no matter in what form they actually manifested in a local region, led to the circulation of a wide range of ideas among Asian societies. Third, Buddhism shaped economic activities, statecraft, the formation of political / cultural identities, and the creation of sacred landscapes throughout most of Asia. In fact, in the late eighteenth and early twentieth centuries, when Asian intellectuals started formulating the idea of pan-Asianism, Buddhist connections prior to European colonization were at the core of their vision.

Beyond Asia, however, Buddhism seems to have made very little impact before the sixteenth century. It is possible that some Buddhist ideas may have filtered into the Mediterranean region, transmitted perhaps by the same networks that introduced some Greek and Roman imagery and art forms into Buddhism.[49] Substantial European, and subsequently American, encounter with Buddhism took place after the sixteenth century. During the past two centuries, the American Henry Steel Olcott (1832–1907), the Ukrainian Helena Petrovna Blavatsky (1831–1891) – the two founders of the Theosophical Society – the Sri Lankan monk Anagarika Dharmapala (1834–1933), and eventually the fourteenth Dalai Lama were instrumental in transforming Buddhism into a global religion.

FURTHER READING

Benn, James A. *Burning for the Buddha: Self-Immolation in Chinese Buddhism.* Studies in East Asian Buddhism. Honolulu, HI: University of Hawai'i Press, 2007.

Birnbaum, Raoul. *The Healing Buddha.* Revised edn. Boston, MA: Shambhala, 1989.

Bogel, Cynthea J. *With A Single Glance: Buddhist Icon and Early Mikkyō.* Seattle and London: University of Washington Press, 2009.

49 On the possible spread of Buddhist ideas to the West and the issue of their failure to have similar impact as in Asia, see Erik Seldeslachts, "Greece, the Final Frontier? – The Westward Spread of Buddhism," in Ann Heirman and Stephen Peter Bumbacher (eds.), *The Spread of Buddhism* (Leiden: Brill, 2007): 131–66.

Chen, Jinhua. *Monks and Monarchs, Kinship and Kingship: Tanqian in Sui Buddhism and Politics*. Kyoto: Italian School of East Asian Studies, 2002.

Chou, Yi-liang. "Tantrism in China," *Harvard Journal of Asiatic Studies* 8 (1944–5): 241–332.

Davidson, Ronald M. *Indian Esoteric Buddhism: A Social History of the Tantric Movement*. New York, NY: Columbia University Press, 2002.

Fontein, Jan. *Entering the Dharmadhātu: A Study of the Gandavyūha Reliefs of Borobudur*. Leiden: Brill, 2012.

Gregory, Peter N. and Daniel A. Getz, Jr, eds. *Buddhism in the Sung*. Honolulu, HI: University of Hawai'i Press, 1999.

Kieschnick, John. *The Eminent Monk: Buddhist Ideals in Medieval Chinese Hagiography*. Honolulu, HI: University of Hawai'i Press, 1997.

The Impact of Buddhism on Chinese Material Culture. Princeton University Press, 2003.

Kohn, Livia. *Laughing at the Tao: Debates among Buddhists and Taoists in Medieval China*. Princeton University Press, 1995.

Lamotte, Étienne. *History of Indian Buddhism: From the Origins to the Śaka Era*. Transl. Sara Webb-Boin. Louvain: Institut Orientaliste, 1988.

Li, Rongxi, trans. *A Biography of the Tripitaka Master of the Great Ci'en Monastery of the Great Tang Dynasty*. Berkeley, CA: Numata Center for Buddhist Translation and Research, 1995.

trans. *Buddhist Monastic Traditions of Southern Asia: A Record of the Inner Law Sent Home from the South Seas*. Berkeley, CA: Numata Center for Buddhist Translation and Research, 2000.

trans. *The Great Tang Dynasty Record of the Western Regions*. Berkeley, CA: Numata Center for Buddhist Translation and Research, 1996.

trans. "The Journey of the Eminent Monk Faxian," in *Lives of Great Monks and Nuns*, Berkeley, CA: Numata Center for Buddhist Translation and Research, 2002, 155–214.

Linrothe, Rob. *Ruthless Compassion: Wrathful Deities in Early Indo-Tibetan Esoteric Buddhist Art*. Boston, MA: Shambhala, 1999.

Liu, Xinru. *Ancient India and Ancient China: Trade and Religious Exchanges, A.D. 1–600*. Delhi: Oxford University Press, 1988.

Luce, Gordon H. "The Advent of Buddhism to Burma," in L. A. Cousins, A. Kunst, and K. R. Norman (eds.), *Buddhist Studies in Honour of I. B. Horner*. Dordrecht: D. Reidel Publishing Company, 1974, 119–38.

Mollier, Christine. *Buddhism and Taoism Face to Face: Scripture, Ritual, and Iconographic Exchange in Medieval China*. Honolulu, HI: University of Hawai'i Press, 2008.

Neelis, Jason. *Early Buddhist Transmission and Trade Networks: Mobility and Exchange within and beyond the Northwestern Borderlands of South Asia*. Leiden: Brill, 2011.

Orzech, Charles D. *Politics and Transcendent Wisdom: The Scripture for the Humane Kings in the Creation of Chinese Buddhism*. Pennsylvania State University Press, 1998.

Prazniak, Roxann. "Ilkhanid Buddhism: Traces of a Passage in Eurasian History," *Comparative Studies in Society and History* 56.3 (2014): 650–80.

Reichle, Natasha. *Violence and Serenity: Late Buddhist Sculpture from Indonesia*. Honolulu, HI: University of Hawai'i Press, 2007.

Sharf, Robert H. *Coming to Terms with Chinese Buddhism: A Reading of the Treasure Store Treatise*. Honolulu, HI: University of Hawai'i Press, 2002.

Shuhaimi, Nik Hassan. "Art, Archaeology, and the Early Kingdoms in the Malay Peninsula and Sumatra: c. 400–1400 CE". Unpublished PhD thesis, University of London, 1976.

Strong, John S. *Relics of the Buddha*. Princeton University Press, 2004.

Teiser, Stephen F. *The Ghost Festival in Medieval China*. Princeton University Press, 1988.

Trainor, Kevin. *Relics, Rituals, and Representation in Buddhism: Rematerializing the Sri Lankan Theravāda Tradition*. Cambridge University Press, 1997.

Yü, Chün-Fang. *Kuan-yin: The Chinese Transformation of Avalokiteśvara*. New York, NY: Columbia University Press, 2001.

Williams, Paul. *Mahāyāna Buddhism: The Doctrinal Foundations*, 2nd edn. London and New York: Routledge, 2009.

PART V

★

STATE FORMATIONS

18

State formation and empire building

JOHANN P. ARNASON

This chapter focuses on states and empires, and more precisely on imperial trends and turns in processes of state formation, political developments that lend support to the idea that the mid-first to mid-second millennium was a distinct period. That period coincides roughly with the conventional definition of the Middle Ages, a periodization that is often dismissed as Eurocentric, unduly levelling, and laden with value judgments that now seem unfair to the long epoch in question. This periodization also has a history of coming back, however, reinvigorated by new evidence from outside its original context, although those who want to avoid 'medieval' connotations may prefer to speak of the Middle Millennium or of an 'intermediate age'.[1] Views on the events, episodes and restructurings that mark the beginning and the end of this period depend on thematic choices; the approximate dates to be preferred will therefore vary from one regional setting to another. As will be seen, the main patterns at work in imperial turns in state formation intertwine with religious cultures and institutions.

The political landmarks defining
the Middle Millennium

To begin with Western Christendom, the inaugural chain of events links the fifth and the sixth centuries CE. The decomposition of the Roman Empire was followed by the rise of two Germanic kingdoms aspiring to great power

---

1 The term 'intermediate ages' was coined in S. E. Finer, *The History of Government from the Earliest Times* (Oxford University Press, 1997), vol. II: *The Intermediate Ages*. The framework for the present chapter grew out of a critical response to Finer's model. For a recent example of world historians applying the mid-first to mid-second millennium periodization in a global context, see Johannes Fried and Ernst-Dieter Hehl (eds.), *WBG Weltgeschichte* (Darmstadt: Wissenschaftliche Buchgesellschaft, 2010), vol. III: *Weltdeutungen und Weltreligionen, 600 bis 1500*.

status: the Ostrogoths in Italy and the Franks in Gaul. The destruction of the Ostrogoths by Justinian's counter-offensive did not lead to imperial reunification, and the definitive failure of that project, together with the survival and strengthening of the papacy, set the scene for further geopolitical developments. As for the final episode, the grand but failed strategic project pursued by Charles V is the most salient landmark. This was an attempt to put the wealth and prestige derived from trans-oceanic conquest at the service of older aspirations to imperial supremacy in Europe; its failure and the consequent change to geopolitical conditions make the mid-sixteenth century an obvious turning point.

A slightly different chronology seems required for the Byzantine world. Here we can begin with the last decades of the sixth century. The critical state of the empire after Justinian's bid to reconquer the West, aggravated by plague and culminating in a struggle for survival against threats from north and east, may be seen as the beginning of the transition from an East Roman to a Byzantine Empire; this process then took a more decisive turn when Islamic expansion changed the regional balance of power. The Byzantine trajectory came to an end with two major but contrasting geopolitical shifts. The post-imperial state system that had – with active involvement of Western invaders and rivals from within the Byzantine world – taken shape in southeastern Europe after 1204 was absorbed by the Ottoman Empire, whose background reflects the last great wave of Inner Eurasian expansion. The Russian periphery, long subject to an Inner Eurasian power, gained the upper hand against its former overlords and embarked on a multi-secular expansion across northern and Inner Eurasia.

With regard to the Islamic world, there can be no doubt about the point of departure. But the emergence of Islam is not to be understood as an abrupt leap into a new religious universe. The sixth-century geopolitical upheaval in the Arabian peninsula, in which Sasanian Persia participated directly and the East Roman Empire indirectly through its Axumite allies, is an important part of the story, and so are the troubles preceding the late seventh-century consolidation of an Islamic realm. At the other end of our period, the formation of the early modern Islamic empires (Ottoman, Safavid and Mughal) represents a major historical divide; after the ninth- and tenth-century fragmentation of the 'Abbasid Empire, this was the first stable reorganization of the Islamic world along imperial lines. The foundation of the Mughal Empire in 1526 may therefore be seen as the beginning of a new epoch. This chronological framing also has an obvious bearing on Indian history. In the South Asian subcontinent, the sixth-century downfall of the

Gupta dynasty is the most decisive mid-first millennium landmark. But soon afterwards, at the very beginning of the eighth century, Islamic expansion gained its first foothold in India with the conquest of Sindh. There are thus good grounds to regard Islamic expansion as a co-determinant of Indian history during most of the period in question, unfolding through successive stages and taking its most decisive turn with the foundation of the Mughal Empire.

China and the broader East Asian region pose specific problems. It is relatively easy to construct an opening phase. The late sixth-century reunification of the Chinese Empire, carried out by the Sui dynasty and consolidated by their Tang successors, was accompanied by the rise of unified states in Korea and Japan. The mid-second millennium is a more difficult case. Historians of China often work with the model of a late imperial period beginning in the mid-sixteenth century; the middle imperial stage is most frequently equated with the Tang dynasty and the ascendant phase of Song rule (before the loss of North China). The idea of a Song–Yuan–Ming transition, from the early twelfth to the late fifteenth century, has been used to bridge the gap between the two periods. From the present point of view, focusing on changing imperial regimes, there is much to be said for a periodization stressing the Manchu takeover in 1644 and the establishment of the Qing dynasty.

As for other parts of the East Asian regional core, the rise of the Qing roughly coincided with changes that are now generally seen as the beginning of an early modern epoch in Japanese history: unification under the Tokugawa regime (1603–1868) and withdrawal from interstate relations. There are both contrasts and parallels between the Tokugawa settlement and the seventh- to early eighth-century developments that brought core regions of the archipelago under the control of a reformed central state. In both cases, intensified reception of Chinese cultural models went hand in hand with strategic withdrawal; the main contrast is that the state created in the wake of the mid-seventh-century Taika reform drew on Chinese institutional patterns, whereas the Tokugawa regime grew out of more indigenous trends. Korean history calls for a different approach; here the main landmark of the second millennium was a late fourteenth-century combination of dynastic change, political restructuring and ideological reorientation, often described as a Neo-Confucian transformation. The chronological discrepancy is, however, less important than the lasting results. In East Asia, the period in question ends with a regional bifurcation that was to have a major impact on the roads to modernity. On the one hand, a new wave of Chinese cultural influence on the outlying countries (the Neo-Confucian turn) coincided with a definitive parting of political ways. Japan abandoned all political contact with China and all political ambitions on the mainland, and after the Mongol interlude, no Chinese dynasty exercised direct control over Korea. On the other hand, the Qing conquests brought China into political union with an Inner Eurasian periphery where its cultural reach was much more limited.

It is more difficult to draw chronological boundaries for Southeast Asian history; but it seems reasonably clear that the sixth century saw the decline and disintegration of the first known powerful political centre in the region (the state known from Chinese sources as Fu-nan), and that both its demise and its legacy were important for later developments. A good case for a closure and a new beginning in the mid-second millennium can be made on the basis of Anthony Reid's work.[2] As he sees it, the modern phase of Southeast Asian history begins with the fifteenth-century resurgence of Islamic expansion and the durable division of the region between a predominantly Islamic archipelago (including the Malay peninsula) and a predominantly Theravada Buddhist mainland.

Finally, the Middle Millennium history of Inner Eurasia is very clearly demarcated from earlier and later stages. The sixth-century rise of the Turkic Empire (khaqanate) brought the eastern and western parts of this region into closer contact than before. The Turkic imperial formation was the first to extend across Inner Eurasia and leave a cluster of successor states – from the Avars in Europe and the Khazars on the South Russian steppe to the Tibetan and Uighur empires on the eastern frontier. The era of large empires and lesser successors came to an end with the very transformations already noted in the East Asian and Russian context.

The focus of this chapter is the Eurasian macro-region (including the southern shores of the Mediterranean), but a brief comment on other parts of the world is in order. The history of state formation in sub-Saharan Africa is a long and variegated one, and includes cases of rapid rise and fall as well as more sustained development. This vast regional field and its internal divergences are beyond the scope of our discussion. But when it comes to the more specific question of imperial trends and traditions in Africa, connections to the broader Eurasian context are more important, and the main ones have to do with the dynamics of Islamic expansion. In the region later known as the Horn of Africa, the Axumite kingdom had by the sixth century grown

2 Anthony Reid, *Southeast Asia in the Age of Commerce* (New Haven, CT: Yale University Press, 1988), vols. I–II.

into an imperial centre that 'united under its rule ... all the civilizations to the south of the Roman Empire, between the Sahara in the west and the Rub' el-Khali desert in the east'.[3] Among the three imperial formations surrounding the birthplace of Islam, it was most directly involved in the peninsular upheaval that preceded Muhammad's mission, and the Islamic impact on its history differed from the two other cases. Sasanian Persia was conquered; Byzantium survived as a diminished but genuine empire; Axum was marginalized without direct confrontation, but a shrunken imperial tradition – Christianized roughly at the same time as the Roman Empire – seems to have survived and left its mark on the later trajectory of the Ethiopian state under successive dynasties. At the other end of the period, the failed Islamic assault on Ethiopia in the first half of the sixteenth century sealed geopolitical and geo-religious divisions for a long time to come. In West Africa, the ramifications of Islamic expansion were very different, but important to the course of state formation. Here the main example of regional power centres with imperial reach is the sequence of three formations with core areas gradually shifting from west to east: Ghana, Mali and Songhay. The beginnings of this story are obscure, and no convincing reconstruction has gone back to a mid-first millennium date. The terminating event is closer to our time frame: the late sixteenth-century Moroccan conquest of Songhay (a more visibly imperial power than its predecessors) changed the geopolitical profile of West Africa.

As for the Americas, the sixteenth-century destruction of Mesoamerican and Andean states and civilizations by Spanish conquerors was part of a broader geopolitical upheaval at the end of the Middle Millennium. It is more difficult to find parallels to the beginnings of our period. The most significant historical divides before the conquest have to do with collapses of political and cultural centres, not always markedly imperial in character: Teotihuacan and the classical Maya city-states in Mesoamerica during the second half of the first millennium, Wari and Tiahuanaco in the Andean zone around and after 1000.

Interactions between Inner Eurasia and adjacent civilizations

Interaction between inner and outer parts of Eurasia was of particular importance for the history of states and empires during the Middle

---

3 Yuri M. Kobishchanov, 'Axum', in Henri J. M. Claessen and Peter Skalník (eds.), *The Early State* (The Hague: Mouton, 1978): 152.

Millennium. It is now generally agreed that the interactive process was too complex and too formative on both sides to be reduced to being understood as outbreaks of barbarian aggression. Specific aspects of the relationship between the two historical complexes are more disputed. This problem begins with varying labels for historical and geographical regions; and here I make a distinction between Inner Eurasia, broadly defined, and a more narrowly demarcated Central Asian part of that region. The Inner Eurasian region is to be identified with the whole area between the Siberian Arctic and the shifting borders of settled civilizations in the European, Iranian, Indian and Chinese worlds; in terms of west-to-east, it reaches from the Russian steppe to Manchuria. Central Asia proper is a zone of deserts, oases, mountains and valleys. The typical political pattern in the larger part of this region was the oasis-state with long-distance trade connections. There was, however, one case of a larger Central Asian state flourishing from the early seventh to the middle of the ninth century: the Tibetan Empire. It was based in the agricultural south, but drew on the historical experience of empires with a nomadic pedigree.[4] The conversion to Buddhism may be seen in that light: as a strategic and limited change of religious orientations, comparable to earlier cases of conquest dynasties in Northern China. But if the initial conversion was part of an empire building strategy, it also paved the way for a post-imperial re-appropriation of Buddhism more original than anything developed elsewhere in Central Asia, and capable of spreading further afield. This indirect legacy of the Tibetan Empire has overshadowed its geopolitical record.

However, the main impetus to empire building across the great civilizational divide came from further north. Popular notions of 'nomad conquerors' may suggest a simple equation of nomadism and Inner Eurasian dynamics. In fact, the interaction of nomadism with agricultural and urban modes of settled social life is a precondition, not just a result of imperial expansion. These interconnections developed through several levels. In the first place, the Inner Eurasian world is best understood as an 'entire spectrum from intensive cultivation to strict steppe pastoralism',[5] and the continuum between these extremes allowed for varying balances. Not all empire-builders were primarily nomads. At more advanced stages of state formation,

---

4 Christopher Beckwith, *The Tibetan Empire in Central Asia* (Princeton University Press, 1993): 11–12.
5 Joseph Fletcher, 'The Mongols: Ecological and Social Perspectives', *Harvard Journal of Asiatic Studies* 46 (1986): 12.

the incorporation of urban-based societies in Central Asia was crucial to further growth of nomad-ruled empires; the role of the Uighurs in the Mongol Empire is a classic case. Finally, the economic dependence of nomads on the more productive economies of sedentary neighbours did not necessarily lead the former to embark on conquest; but when it did, and when the conquerors maintained their rule without assimilating to domestic elites, the resulting combination could become a strategic basis for new imperial projects. It was the Mongol takeover of such innovations in northern China, as well as the very different symbiosis between nomadic and settled cultures in eastern and western Turkestan, that provided foundations and incentives for the building of an unprecedentedly cross-Eurasian empire.

There are nevertheless good reasons to stress a strategic role of nomadism within a more complex configuration. Peter B. Golden argues that 'given their tribal organization, continual training for war and the executive talents needed to move herds and people some distance, the state was latent in most Eurasian nomadic societies'.[6] This generalized disposition to state formation could be activated by a variety of factors. But a more unitary view is suggested by Nicola Di Cosmo: the nomadic state is typically a 'social response to a state of crisis' and to the accompanying 'endemic, low-level violence'.[7] The particular crisis-proneness of nomadic societies is due to ecological and geographical conditions: the vulnerability to environmental change, even on a small scale, and the high mobility of ethnic groupings, often forced to compete for scarce resources, led to periodic destabilization. Not that the emergence of state structures was an automatic response – the history of steppe societies contains episodes of long-drawn-out disintegration as well as cases of durable organization halfway between tribe and state. It is a basic fact about Inner Eurasian history that states were more likely to form in the eastern than in the western part of the steppe, and that invaders or refugees from the east often set the course in the west. But state formation is frequent enough for recurrent basic mechanisms to be identified. Two internal transformations were decisive. Social stratification gave rise to a hierarchy of tribal groupings and identities. This process was combined with – and counterbalanced by – the decimal military organization, in which armies were arranged into inter-ethnic units of ten and commanded to be

6 Peter B. Golden, *An Introduction to the History of the Turkic Peoples: Ethnogenesis and State Formation in Medieval and Early Modern Eurasia and the Middle East* (Wiesbaden: Harrassowitz, 1992): 9.
7 Nicola Di Cosmo, 'State Formation and Periodization in Inner Asian History', *Journal of World History* 10 (1999): 14.

loyal to all, regardless of tribe or ethnic group. The decimal military system seems to have been invented at an early stage and transmitted with remarkable continuity to later nomad states. But since these changes imposed further demands on a fragile resource basis, they only prefigured a more ambitious solution to the problem.

The process that led to the formation of states and empires with nomads in key roles was no mere reaction under pressure; it had a cultural framework, continuity and vision of its own. In this regard, the Turkic Empire that stands at the beginning of our epoch was – despite its brief duration – a paradigmatic achievement. It entered the cultural memory of later states and shaped their self-understanding. The Turkic rulers had not attempted any large-scale conquest of sedentary regions, but their claim to supreme dignity, inherited by later contenders, appears to have been easily translatable into visions of universal domination, most effectively in the case of the Mongols. This imperial ideology was rooted in a religious imaginary well attested for the imperial Turks, and clearly of older origin; the core notion was a celestial pedigree of royal power, defined in terms that indicate a Mandate of Heaven.

The ideological continuity noted above was compatible with a wide variety of strategies applied in relations with sedentary societies and powers. Inner Eurasian states were, even more than the tribal groupings from which they emerged, dependent on resources provided by more complex economies in southern and eastern Eurasia. Recent scholarship distinguishes four solutions to the problem: raiding, trade, tribute, and territorial conquest followed by direct taxation. If the accumulation of military means and the extraction of resources are key factors in state formation, the Inner Eurasian pattern was thus marked by a problematic relationship between them: internal conditions enabled rapid and spiralling militarization (through ongoing incorporation of tribes), but the resources needed to sustain this process had to come from elsewhere. In favourable circumstances, the dynamic thus generated could lead to self-perpetuating expansion. Whether the history of states built on this basis reveals cumulative or evolutionary trends is a more complex question. A glance at the overall trajectory suggests not so much a cumulative trend as a renewable but, in the very long run, self-cancelling pattern. The Turkic Empire did not expand into sedentary zones, but its reach from east to west and its control over trade zones were unprecedented. Its successor states on the eastern and western sides of Inner Eurasia varied widely in terms of strength, structure and relations with neighbouring civilizations. Conversions to marginal or even persecuted religions from the sedentary world (Judaism among the Khazars, Manichae-ism among the Uighurs) represent the highest point of a cultural demarcation strategy that was not adopted by later arrivals in the borderlands of Inner and Outer Eurasia. But although these political formations retained links to the Turkic imagery and nomenclature of power, none of them could aspire to imperial rule on a corresponding scale. The second wave of imperial expan-sion across Inner Eurasia (and this time beyond its borders on all sides) came with the Mongol conquests.

There is some justification for seeing the first stages in the rise of the Mongols as shifts in the balance of power within a China-centred constel-lation. The marginal society within which Chinggis Khan rose to power appears to have been a decomposing former tributary of the Jin dynasty that had ousted the Liao from power in North China in 1125 and inherited from them a distinctive mode of rule, known to historians as dual adminis-tration. It is worth noting that this innovative technique of expansion – maintaining the separate identity of the conquerors and their ultimate control over territories and resources, while making use of indigenous governmental traditions – was first developed by the Liao outside China proper, when in 926 they conquered Bohai, a Korean kingdom beyond the borders of the unified Korean peninsula. The whole process can thus be seen as a dynamic unfolding between a Chinese regional order and its Inner Eurasian neighbours, and Chinggis Khan's enterprise as a new beginning favoured by particularly unsettled conditions on a distinct but potentially strategic periphery. As the Mongol expansion gathered momen-tum, it resulted in conquests of sedentary regions far beyond all earlier limits. The thirteenth-century Mongol Empire is often described as the largest contiguous one in human history, but it should also be emphasized that this phase of Mongol power – an east-to-west Eurasian realm ruled from a single centre – was very short-lived. The conquest of Iran and adjacent regions almost coincided with an intra-dynastic conflict that marked the beginning of the end for imperial unity; the most enriching and empowering conquest (that of Song China, completed in 1279) was carried out by a North China branch of the empire, with only symbolic claims to universal sovereignty.

This is not to suggest that the Mongol Empire began to fall apart as a result of overstretch. It seems more likely that the extremely effective power-maximizing strategies of the Mongols could have sustained further growth. The centralized military machine, the eclectic but highly extractive taxing methods, and the systematic gathering and redistribution of 'human talent and skill as a form of booty'[8] added up to an unequalled supra-regional dominance. The once widely accepted view that the Mongols imposed a universal law code (*yasa*) has been questioned; but the alternative model of context-dependent modifications of existing legal traditions underlines the adaptive strengths of the regime. The halting of the Mongol advance in various places at successive junctures is probably to be explained in specific terms for each case. But it can be argued that some distinctive features of Mongol empire building constituted both strengths and weaknesses, and that their mutually reinforcing impact also led to disintegrative pressures. Chinggis Khan's ascent to unchallenged power gave rise to an extreme version of dynastic charisma, strong enough to survive the empire as well as the first generation of successor states and leave its mark on the later history of the Inner Eurasian heartland; but this incentive to continuity proved inseparable from the regional tradition of intra-dynastic struggle as a test of legitimacy. On all fronts of expansion, the Mongols also drew on more specific methods and experiences of nomadic or nomad-dominated precursors. Seen as a whole, this pattern represents a synthesis of previously separate developments, rather than a culmination of general trends. But the combination also posed new problems. The adoption of diverse precedents led to adaptive processes that pulled the main regions of the empire further apart. Finally, the mixing of civilizational traditions, especially in administrative affairs, reflects the reach of the empire and the pragmatism of its rulers, but it also provoked resistances that fed into the decomposing process; Chinese objections to Muslim influence, and vice versa in West Asia, exemplify this point. Given all these background factors, it is not surprising that the division of the empire into separate states 'was almost as bloody and as tortuous a business as was the expansion of the empire itself for those powers and peoples that were its victims'.[9] The 'largest contiguous empire in history' was a fleeting formation, unduly magnified and sometimes romanticized by later historians.

The sequel to the Mongol Empire is best understood as a three- or four-generation series of successor states, with some regional variations. The first separate realms were domains (*ulus*) of imperial family members, hardly to be described as states, but gradually transformed into more clearly

---

8 Thomas T. Allsen, *Culture and Conquest in Mongol Eurasia* (Cambridge University Press, 2001): 210.

9 Peter Jackson, 'From *Ulus* to State: The Making of the Mongol States', in Reuven Amitai-Preiss and David O. Morgan (eds.), *The Mongol Empire and its Legacy* (Leiden: Brill, 2000): 36.

demarcated entities under dynastic rule and with power bases in pre-existing regions (China, Central Asia, Iran and the western steppe). A third phase saw the further partition of these imperial fragments into shifting mixtures of dynastic centres and tribal formations reverting to earlier ways. Timur's vast raids, perhaps best described as 'plundering tourism',[10] were the most destructive episode of this intermediate stage. Their spectacular character has led to misconceptions of a culminating Inner Eurasian empire; in fact, they did not result in state-building on an imperial scale, and closer analysis of Timur's strategy[11] suggests a balancing act between tribal basis and despotic conquest. The only long-term upshot was a charismatic aura without institutional anchor, transferable to those who could claim a genealogical connection and embark on other ventures elsewhere, most notably in India.

State, empire and religion in Outer Eurasia

A conception of state formation as a long-term process, indeed a set of such processes, is needed to make sense of connections between early medieval backgrounds and early modern outcomes. The most seminal argument of that kind is to be found in Norbert Elias' work on the civilizing process as a long-term dynamic with durable trends and cumulative consequences, and constellations that impose their logic on historical actors and channel their projects in specific directions. This explanatory framework highlights the twin monopolies of violence and taxation as links between the strategic and structural levels in state formation.[12] To summarize a complex discussion, three main themes have emerged as necessary correctives to Elias' approach. The twin monopolies have been subsumed under the more general and interconnected imperatives of control and mobilization, applying to human and non-human resources. More attention must be paid to contextual factors, affecting the long-term processes in significant ways. To mention only European examples, the Eliasian model does not do justice to the role of the Catholic Church, nor to the reactivation of Roman law. Finally, the cultural frameworks of state formation call for closer analysis.

With these perspectives in mind, a few basic points about the imperial versions of state formation should be added before discussing particular

---

10 Peter B. Golden, *Central Asia in World History* (Oxford University Press, 2011): 95.
11 See Beatrice Forbes Manz, *The Rise and Rule of Tamerlane* (Cambridge University Press, 1989).
12 See Norbert Elias, *The Civilizing Process* (Oxford and Malden, MA: Blackwell, 2000 [1939]).

cases. Given the enormous variety of imperial regimes, and the unsatisfactory state of comparative research, we cannot begin with a general definition of empire as a category. It seems more useful to treat imperial turns as specific episodes within processes of state formation, and to allow for a range of patterns and developments that tend to accompany such turns in widely varying degrees and combinations. Imperial regimes are thus linked through 'family resemblances', rather than constant defining features. The starting point for comparative analysis would then be the very transition to imperial rule, i.e. the attempt to unite separate processes of state formation – or their outcomes – under a single centre. A recurrent but unequally developed trend leads to the transfiguration of imperial power into a higher order; in the most pronounced cases, this culminates in visions of world domination. Higher-order interpretations of power give rise to institutionally and ideologically eminent centres and correspondingly elevated notions of rulership. How the imaginary meaning of ultimate sovereignty translates into practical terms is a more complex issue. Imperial power favours autocratic rule, but other factors may turn this form into a facade for more oligarchic regimes.

With the above comments on states and empires in mind, the main paths of outer Eurasian history during our period should now be compared in broad outlines, with due allowance for the fact that here the interrelations of religious and political dynamics were more significant than on the Inner Eurasian side. If we begin with the Western Christian world, it is certainly not being suggested that this region was central to the whole scene. The key point is, rather, the long-drawn-out transition, from a fragmented and marginal condition to the early modern field of consolidated states in quest of empire, that opened a new chapter of history. Also, as analyses and theories of state formation have mainly drawn on the western European experience, there are valid reasons to deal first with that part of the world.

Western Christendom

For much of our period, the western Eurasian periphery – in civilizational terms, Western Christendom – was geopolitically marginal, highly fragmented, and limited to expansion on separate and narrowly circumscribed frontiers. But around the middle of the second millennium, a small group of states emerged from the long-fragmented European field and embarked on overseas conquest. They included the unified Spanish state, the economic and cultural powerhouse of the Netherlands, as well as the English and French monarchies. But a historical interpretation of early modern European ascendancy must take note of preconditions emerging at much earlier stages.

Such aspects include political factors, and recent scholarship tends to put the state back into times and places where earlier approaches had tended to dissolve it into networks of ritualized interpersonal relations.[13]

A glance at the history of medieval Western Christendom will highlight not only political fragmentation, but also the qualitative diversity of political centres. This civilization was not durably dominated by an imperial centre, yet a ruler and a realm with claims to imperial dignity were, for most of the time, present as key components of the civilizational complex. The emperor as an institution was a model of supreme rulership, intermittently translated into aspirations to more effective and extensive power, but also imitated by lower-ranking rulers who wanted to enhance their legitimacy; the empire as a geopolitical entity brought together more diverse communities than other states of the times, but this was a double-edged asset that could both serve to elevate the centre and – in the long run more decisively – to enable the creation of autonomous power structures at lower levels. Within Western Christendom, the position of the empire was defined by its relationship to the papacy. The latter was the civilizational institution *par excellence*, a potential rival to the empire – on the basis of claims to ultimate authority over Christian rulers – and an active player in political conflicts and alliances on multiple levels. But in the very long run, the most sustainable setting for state formation was a changing number of kingdoms with shifting territorial boundaries, typically defined with some reference to ethnic identity and stabilized – in varying degrees – by dynastic continuity. Finally, the urban transformation that gathered momentum from the eleventh century onwards gave rise to autonomous legislation, self-government and a republican political tradition. Whether the quest for autonomy resulted in a revolutionary challenge to authorities, and whether self-government came to involve a claim to sovereignty, are more specific issues that should not be conflated with the general question of the city as a political innovator. These urban communities represented an alternative line of state formation; they flourished within a geopolitical setting that blocked the road from city-state to empire, with one limited exception: the expansion of Venice.

These various forms of political power were also different versions of the religio-political nexus. The conflict between empire and papacy was not simply a clash of secular and sacred authorities. A mixture of the two was invoked by both sides, and the relative weights changed over time: eleventh-century

---

13 See Walter Pohl and Veronika Wieser (eds.), *Der frühmittelalterliche Staat: Europäische Perspektiven* (Vienna: Verlag der österreichischen Akademie der Wissenschaften, 2009).

emperors made more emphatic claims to sacral rulership than their successors, and the twelfth-century successes of the papacy markedly increased its influence on the level of power politics. As for the urban communities, the religious background to their history manifested itself in multiple ways. Urban centres shrank during the transition from antiquity to medieval times, but without a basic continuity the whole subsequent pattern of growth would have been unthinkable. The Church, and particularly the position of bishops as holders of social power, gave institutional support to this enabling legacy. The High Medieval breakthrough to urban autonomy was, in significant measure, achieved against local Church powers and related to new currents in religious culture. The eleventh-century rise of the northern Italian communes – the most radical version of a civilization-wide, though not uniform, change – is instructive in both regards. The devolution of Carolingian power in Italy had strengthened episcopal authority in the cities; the communes established themselves in conflict with this offshoot of the weakening alliance between Church and Empire, and more generally as a rejection of 'aristocratic–oligarchic reality', to which they opposed the 'idea of brotherly unity'. In short, 'the foundation of the commune is, in the last instance, a religious idea'.[14]

The geopolitical patterns evolving on this complex basis underwent major changes. If we regard the post-Roman centuries of fragmentation and fluctuating hegemonies as a transitional stage, the formative turn was the rise of Carolingian power and its imperial expansion. The conquests and the close relationship with the papacy made it possible to revive the idea of imperial rulership and claim equality with the surviving Byzantine Empire. Empire and Church were intertwined on ideological, institutional and administrative levels; efforts to develop cultural centres and resources were attuned to this power structure, and the intellectual revival, although limited to a narrow circle, was important enough to justify the notion of a Carolingian Renaissance as the first of such transformative turns in the medieval West. For all these reasons, the Carolingian Empire deserves to be described as a civilizational matrix, even though it did not incorporate the whole area of Western Christendom. In the shorter run, however, it gave way to a more diverse and fragmented pattern. The Ottonian revival and relocation of empire in

---

14 On all this see Hagen Keller, 'Der Übergang zur Kommune: Zur Entwicklung der italienischen Städteverfassung im 11. Jahrhundert', in Bernhard Diestelkamp (ed.), *Beiträge zum hochmittelalterlichen Städtewesen* (Cologne and Vienna: Böhlau, 1982): 55–72 (at 62).

962 was a landmark. The imperial institution was transferred to a frontier of the Carolingian world and superimposed on pre-existing power centres and ethnic identities in formation, over which it had only limited and precarious control. The efforts to strengthen the Roman – and more generally Italian – connection were meant to compensate for these weaknesses. But if the Holy Roman Empire was to a high degree an imaginary institution, this does not mean that its historical impact was minor or illusory. Visions of statehood and/or empire enter into the pursuit of power and the resultant long-term processes; in this particular case, the presence of the empire influenced various paths of state formation. The imperial institution as such was capable of reforms that consolidated state structures, and the need to accommodate multiple centres gave a constitutional twist to this trend; such projects became more ambitious towards the end of our epoch. Territorial units within the empire moved towards statehood, both in connection and in rivalry with the centre. Distinctive political developments on the periphery of the empire led to lasting results (for example in the territories that later became Switzerland and the Netherlands).

During the later half of the Middle Millennium, new political centres proliferated through civilizational and military expansion. But this was also the age of pioneering state-strengthening measures in key centres of the older civilizational core, notably the English and French kingdoms, and of emerging city-state cultures in rapidly developing regions, especially northern Italy and the northwestern corner of the continent. The pluralism of political centres thus reached its highest level; so did the divergence of regional trajectories, and that aspect became more salient during the last centuries of our period. The 'new monarchies' of the Atlantic seaboard became exemplary cases for analyses of state formation, but they also gave rise to a somewhat misleading perspective. England, France and the Spanish kingdom created by the dynastic union of Castile and Aragon represented new levels of control and mobilization, and their experience came to be seen as a decisive turn towards the modern conversion of monarchies into nation-states. This supposedly paradigmatic path of state formation obscured the variety of historical trajectories, and in particular the continuing presence of empires. The type of statehood represented by the new monarchies was, on the larger European and incipiently global scene, intertwined with imperial trends in two different ways. On the one hand, the seaboard kingdoms became pioneers of trans-oceanic empire building. The united Spanish state – the most traditional and, in the longer run, least transformative of the new monarchies – was the first to acquire major overseas possessions. On the other hand, composite states were a key element of late medieval geopolitics, and this trend sometimes took imperial turns. The composite state may be seen as a more stabilized version of purely dynastic unions, and was in some cases accompanied by dynastic change. It is common in late medieval Europe (Portugal is the main exception), but more dominant in some regions than elsewhere. Even the new monarchies had composite backgrounds. France is an outstanding case of a centralizing monarchy gradually prevailing over the component principalities; the fourteenth- and fifteenth-century career of the Burgundian state exemplifies the chances then still open to the principalities. England was in part a composite state, but the late medieval and early modern push to strengthen the centre kept this pluralistic aspect in check. Spain was the most durably composite of the key states, but this was for some time counterbalanced by a succession of strong rulers and by gains from conquest. Elsewhere the composite character of state formation was more pronounced. The Kalmar Union (1389–1523) that brought the Nordic kingdoms under one ruler was an exemplary composite state, and even after its downfall the Danish kingdom retained this character. Another prominent case is the Polish–Lithuanian commonwealth, whose ruling dynasty briefly came to power in other central European states, but without personal union; here it seems justified to speak of an uncompleted imperial upgrading. Finally, the Holy Roman Empire restructured itself as a more formally institutionalized composite state, with the specific feature of a centre endowed with higher dignity but confined to more limited political options than the rulers of the rising monarchies.

East Asia

Comparisons with the Western Christian constellation are easier to envisage in some regions than in others, and are particularly revealing in the Chinese case. Chinese institutions, cultural orientations and geopolitics were – to a higher degree than those of any other civilization during the Middle Millennium – embedded in older patterns. In the first place, state formation in China had a head start on other regions. Rival centres competing for hegemony raised their capacities of control and mobilization; the result was a unified imperial regime, durably identified with the Han dynasty (206 BCE–220 CE). The core institution was a very strong version of sacral rulership, operating through a close integration of ritual, political and administrative practices. The staying power of this sacral–imperial centre prevented developments comparable to Western Christian institutional and territorial division. But the model that endured was also a source of variations within its framework. The imperial centre, relying on its own sacral legitimacy, could emphasize and privilege different parts of a composite tradition which also came to include Buddhism. On the other hand, the sovereignty of the emperor, enhanced by his autonomously sacral status, could serve to impose autocratic rule.

Alongside the cultural legacy and the imperial model, a third aspect of the Chinese pattern also emerged during the formative phase that preceded our period. As noted above, the beginnings of Inner Eurasian state formation on imperial scale go back to the early Han period, and smaller conquest states with a more sedentary social background came to the fore in the aftermath of Han decline. Both kinds of frontier formations became permanent presences in Chinese history, but in the first phase of the Middle Millennium their role was more marginal than later. The Turkic origins of the dynasties that united and consolidated the empire, Sui (581–618) and Tang (618–907), did not translate into any institutional fusion or combination of traditions. The Tang dynasty built on Sui foundations and stayed in power long enough to develop more variations within the received model. Religious pluralism and regional influence have often led historians to describe the Tang Empire as the most cosmopolitan in Chinese history, but there are good reasons to emphasize another side. The application of Chinese models to autonomous state-building in Korea and Japan during the early Tang era completed the formation of an East Asian region, made up of three main political centres within a cultural *koine*. On the other hand, Tang expansion did not result in an enlarged empire. Korea resisted conquest, and Japan was never within reach; on the continental side, the Tibetan Empire became a serious threat, and warfare in the Turkic zone ended in a stalemate conducive to fragmentation on both sides.

The three dynastic regimes following the tenth-century fragmentation after the Tang collapse – Song, Yuan and Ming – cover more than the second half of our period; they are crucial for China's place in world history, not least in relation to Inner Eurasian empires and their trans-regional dynamic. This was an intermediate phase between the Tang empire, widely regarded by later generations as a paradigm of cultural and political achievement, and the late imperial stage that began with the Manchu conquest in 1644. From one point of view the whole period appears as a long-drawn-out withdrawal (not without backlashes) of the imperial state from direct involvement in social life, accompanied by urban growth and a progressive empowerment of local elites. On this view, the eleventh- and early twelfth-century contest between statist reformers and advocates of a more decentralized regime was a turning point. The centralizing drive led by Wang Anshi (1021–86) was closely linked to plans for a military offensive against northern neighbours seen as usurpers of imperial territory and threats to Song power. The outcome appears as an irreversible defeat on both fronts: Inner China was divided between Song emperors and conquest dynasties from the north, later followed by Mongol rule over the whole realm (and thus by a reconstitution of the imperial domain that had previously been divided between a Chinese core and peripheral states with expansionist ambitions), and on the internal side, social power shifted from the imperial centre to a broadly based and regionally diversified gentry that combined access to offices with landed property and local authority. The focus is thus on connections between a changing geopolitical situation in continental East Asia, a resumption of state formation on an imperial scale, and a redistribution of social power. This is a useful reminder of broader contexts. But in the long run and the overall picture, the resilience of the imperial state seems more important than the restructuring of its social basis. The ascendancy of the gentry under the Song can also be seen from this angle, and in contrast to aristocratic power during the Tang era: from the beginning of the second millennium to the nineteenth century, 'there were no challenges to the emperor by elites with independent bases of authority'.[15] Access to office was crucial to the position of the gentry, and this institutional link to the imperial centre was reinforced by ideological changes. Neo-Confucianism, gradually established as a dominant school of thought, was not simply an ideology of gentry power; it also served to integrate the latter into the imperial order, and in that capacity, it may be seen as an adaptation of the religio-political nexus. Moreover, the whole regime of education and indoctrination, centred on Neo-Confucianism, represents 'efforts by a state to influence belief and behaviour patterns of the general population well before such activities were imagined, let alone pursued, in Europe'.[16] This highly developed cultural framework could compensate for shortcomings of state structures, but it was also conducive to underestimation and neglect of structural problems that became acute when the empire faced external challenges. The Ming dynasty that ousted the Mongols in 1368 inherited their reunified realm, but its founder also attempted to restore a comprehensive Chinese order with strongly nativist overtones, a shifting preference for particular traditions within the Chinese civilizational complex, and an extremely autocratic model of rulership. The restoration seems to have been marked by a lasting dissonance between

---

15 R. Bin Wong, *China Transformed* (Ithaca: Cornell University Press, 2000): 92.
16 Wong, *China Transformed*, 97.

cultural–political patterns and economic development, and this flaw helps to explain the seventeenth-century collapse. The mobilizing capacity of the imperial centre was tried and found wanting.

To conclude, a comparison of Western Christendom and China will not simply contrast a failure of empire in the former case with its continuous presence in the latter. Imperial ventures and aspirations were also involved on the Western side; but the staying power, the cultural reach and the exclusive status of the Chinese imperial centre had no Western parallel. There was no Chinese analogy to the Western split between empire and papacy, but a core conflictual relationship of another kind affected the course of events: the mutually formative rivalry of Chinese and Inner Eurasian claimants to empire. A further feature of the East Asian scene is the transfer of the Chinese imperial model to outlying countries (Korea, Japan, Vietnam) where it became a framework for state formation on a significant scale but without any impact on the geopolitics of the Chinese heartland and its northern frontier. No such separation of centre and periphery occurred in the West.

India and Southeast Asia

Certain aspects of the Indian experience suggest affinities with China. In both cases, Inner Eurasian invasions were a defining feature of our period, whereas their impact on Western Christendom was minimal. But the Indian conquest dynasties differed from the Chinese ones in that they were converts to a universal religion and heirs to its empire building tradition, and their impact on the subcontinent was correspondingly more radical. Further contrasts and parallels have to do with the spread of Chinese and Indian models in East and Southeast Asia. A common feature of the two regional configurations was the transfer of state-building strategies, traditions and ideologies from centres to peripheries, without military conquest, and some-times – as in seventh- and eighth-century Japan vis-à-vis China – with a view to mimetic rivalry. But there were also major differences. Korean and Japanese adaptations of Chinese models resulted in a remarkably stable geopolitical constellation of one major and two minor centres, modified only by intermittent waves of Inner Eurasian conquests. Southeast Asia saw the emergence, flowering and fall of numerous states, often loosely demarcated and sometimes barely present in the historical record. Despite these diver-gences, the two regional examples of derivative statehood share a contrast with European trends. State formation along the lines of borrowed models was certainly not unknown in medieval Western Christendom, but in the upshot, military conquest played a much greater role in the medieval making of Europe than in the corresponding East and Southeast Asian processes.

A closer analysis should link developments on the Indian subcontinent to the record of insular and continental Southeast Asia. This expanded cultural orbit is best approached from a vantage-point often taken to mark the end of classical Indian civilization, but now more plausibly seen as the onset of a new phase. In the subcontinent, the beginning of the Middle Millennium was an imperial aftermath; this resembles the situation of Western Christendom, but differs from imperial renewal in China and imperial succession in the Islamic and Byzantine worlds. The Gupta dynasty, collapsing in the early sixth century under the pressure of internal tensions and invaders from the northwest, was the last indigenous contender for pan-Indian empire. But it also developed a pattern of statehood that could be adopted by later rulers, albeit on a smaller scale and in mutual contest. Variously described as concentric, segmentary or galactic, this type of regime combined a domain of central power with less effective control over local rulers and subaltern allies. Control over trade routes was essential, and so was the ritual integration of the rulers' domains achieved through cooperation with priests and temples; the historical alliance of rulers and Brahmins was perfected in that context. But this form of the religio-political nexus also allowed for mutual interference and rivalry. The deification of kings combined with the refiguration of gods as kings or sovereigns of the realm in question. Finally, this new paradigm of the post-Gupta state stresses a process that was repeated and replicated in successive phases and shifting regional settings (one of the characteristics of this period was the cultural and geopolitical integration of the whole subcontinent). Beginning with local lordships in pursuit of power and moving on to kingdoms with more expansive aims, the trend culminated in large regional states with imperial ambitions. None of them established the kind of dominance that the Gupta rulers at their strongest had enjoyed, but a sequence of pre-eminent powers can be reconstructed. While historians disagree on some cases, they seem to agree that the last one before the eleventh-century turning point (marked by a new wave of Islamic invasions) was the Chola kingdom based at the southern end of the subcontinent. The Cholas sent military expeditions to the Northern Indian plains as well as Southeast Asia, and entered into diplomatic relations with China.[17]

---

17 See especially Hermann Kulke, 'The Early and the Imperial Kingdom: A Processural Model of Integrative State Formation in Early Medieval India', in Hermann Kulke (ed.), *The State in India: 1000–1700* (Delhi: Oxford University Press, 1997): 233–62;

The Southeast Asian political formations that took shape in the course of a multi-secular process varied widely in time and space, and in individual cases, their strength and size seem to have fluctuated. On the whole, however, it seems clear that Southeast Asian patterns of rulership never shifted to the unconditional Brahmin primacy posited in the most ideological constructions of the Indian model, and where Buddhist religious culture predominated, it remained – during the first half of our period – more syncretic than the elite versions of Indian Buddhism. Both these historical features seem related to indigenous notions of sacral power and their continuing active role in shaping the course of Indianizing developments.

Given the overall context, it is not surprising that Southeast Asian trajectories of state formation have proved difficult to trace, and boundaries between minor or middle-range states more elusive than in most other places. During the first half of our period, two very different and unequally known cases stand out against a blurred background; both have been labelled as empires, although it is hard to pinpoint a transition to that level. In the western part of the Malay-Indonesian archipelagic zone, the kingdom of Srivijaya became a power centre with far-flung contacts and control over trade routes, but no continuous history of it can be written. Much better known is the Khmer kingdom on the mainland, whose beginnings can with reasonable certainty be dated to the early ninth century; this was, at least in its culminating twelfth-century phase, a genuinely imperial formation, and its basis was control over a key agricultural region. But in contrast to the East Asian region, no stable geopolitical pattern crystallized during the first half of our period. It was only during the second half that the outlines of such a configuration began to emerge, and this was also the time of the most significant extension of East Asian models to Southeast Asia: the rise of an expansionist Vietnamese state that continued to develop its own versions of Chinese institutions. Burmese and Tai states based in western and central reaches of the area emerged during the same period.[18] Towards the end of the Middle Millennium, their trajectories culminated in large unified states on both sides; more specifically, the sixteenth-century expansion of the Burmese kingdom made it – for a short time – one of the most markedly imperial formations in Southeast Asian history. Burmese and Tai directions

Brajadulal Chattopadhyaya, 'Political Processes and the Structure of Polity in Early Medieval India', in Kulke (ed.), *State in India*, 195–232; and André Wink, *Al-Hind: The Making of the Indo-Islamic World* (Leiden: Brill, 2003), vols. I–III.

18 To avoid confusion with the modern Thai nation, the term "Tai" refers to a cluster of peoples associated with earlier processes of state formation.

of state formation were characterized by a new and more firmly structured relationship between religion and politics. The shift to Theravada Buddhism, now seen as a gradual process rather than an outright conversion, led to closer connections between the ruler, idealized in more distinctively Buddhist terms, and the monastic community; in a more general sense, it strengthened control and discipline.

The Islamic world

After the eleventh century, Islamic conquest dynasties became the dominant factor in Indian history, and this situation must be seen against the background of Islamic expansion as a long-term process. In the context of the Middle Millennium, Islam stands apart from other civilizations in several ways. As argued above, its emergence marks the beginning of our period; it represents the closest ever union of religious and imperial expansion; but it also exemplifies a uniquely thoroughgoing fusion of religion and politics, and reinterpreted memories of this origin could later be invoked as a corrective against the drifting apart of the two component forces. Yet no retrospective idealization could suppress a problem built into Islamic approaches to power and authority. The founder who embodied the perfect union of religious and political leadership was canonized as the last of the prophets, and hence irreplaceable; on the other hand, some kind of succession was needed to keep the community intact. The response to this dilemma was the institution of the caliphate, initially conceived as a strong version of sacral rulership. Whether the definition of the caliph as God's deputy was fully established is a matter of debate, but it could certainly be activated in times of crisis in response to internal conflicts and a later slowdown of expansion. On the other hand, it was vulnerable to erosion. The ruler could neither inherit nor re-establish the status of prophet, and this flaw prefigured further retreat. But the process was never linear: periodic efforts to reclaim the religious authority of the caliphate left their mark on Islamic history. At the same time, the succession problem was complicated by another divisive factor. Claims could be made on the basis of a kinship-based connection to the Prophet, or from a position of strength and authority within the community of his followers. That kind of dispute was the original trigger of the split between Sunnis and Shi'ites; but in a situation where the relationship between religion and politics had to be restructured, further constructions developed on both sides. When a strong and temporarily successful bid for dynastic rule by descendants of the Prophet was made (by the Isma'ilis and their Fatimid leaders in the tenth century), it was combined with a highly elaborate paradigm of spiritual authority (the imamate), complementary to prophecy rather than a substitute for it.

The Islamic trajectory thus began with a very distinctive form of the religio-political nexus. But this was a disputed field of issues and interpretations, not a consistent model, and it had to do with ways of dignifying and sacralizing power, rather than organizing it on the level of state structures or imperial domination. Further development, and more specifically the path from peninsular unity to all-round expansion, was shaped by the encounter with two imperial monarchies, Byzantium and Sasanian Persia, but the circumstances of these two cases differed, and so did the effects upon Islamic modes of rule. The Sasanian kingdom was obliterated by rapid conquest, but this initiated a long process of adapting Persian statecraft and experience to the successive phases of Islamic empire building and post-imperial state formation. The Persian connection was also crucial in another regard: this was where the problem of integrating non-Arab converts became most acute, and its repercussions unfolded on two levels. It was a major factor in the mid-eighth-century change of caliphal dynasty, often described as the 'Abbasid revolution, and the ensuing restructuring of the empire; but in a more diffuse fashion, the interaction between Islam and local communities surviving the conquest gave rise to sectarian rebellions on the border between heterodoxy and secession; although they did not lead to political transformations, they seem to have paved the way for the ninth-century erosion of caliphal power. By contrast, the Byzantine Empire survived, and even in its massively weakened state it became an enduring challenge to Islamic power as well as an inducement to maintain the claim to imperial universality.

In short, early Islamic expansion confronted two separate worlds of monarchy, empire and civilization, with unequal success and different consequences. But the very fact of conquest on both sides reinforced the universal and unifying ambitions of the emerging power. After the troubled transition from peninsular state to Near Eastern empire, the first clearly defined Islamic polity (consolidated under 'Abd al-Malik, 685–705) resumed expansion on all fronts and relied on a combination of invented and adapted institutions to support it. It was the coincidence of stalled expansion in several regions and pressures for a more inclusive imperial order that triggered a regime crisis and a change of dynasty in 750. The 'Abbasids became the main state-builders of early Islamic history. A new capital became the most metropolitan city in the history of the Near East and the centre of a complex bureaucracy organized for taxation on an imperial scale; but the bureaucratic structures were intertwined with local elites and clientelistic ties, and to sum up, 'the degree of control varied from highly centralized administration to loosely held suzerainty'.[19] The ascendant phase of 'Abbasid power also saw a major effort to restore the religious authority of the caliph (under al-Ma'mun, 813–33). This attempt to upgrade the religio-political nexus took place at a stage when the differentiation of schools and trends had progressed beyond the initial pattern, and ideological power was to a decisive degree held by religious and legal scholars; the controversy provoked by caliphal policies was correspondingly sharp, and their failure bound to have broader effects.

Seen in the long-term context of Islamic history, two aspects of 'Abbasid decline – beginning in the ninth century – seem especially noteworthy. On the one hand, the loss of central control and geopolitical weight set in very soon after the retreat from religious interventionism. The record thus highlights the interdependence of the various aspects of caliphal power. On the other hand, the caliphate as an institution proved very resilient. Its migrations and metamorphoses included rival versions set up in opposition to or at least defiance of the 'Abbasid one (the tenth- and eleventh-century Fatimid caliphate in Egypt and the more remote one in the Iberian penin-sula), as well as the latter's shadow in exile and out of power, surviving as a paradigm of political order (in the final phase, it was appropriated by the Ottoman Empire and used to back up a claim to pre-eminence). The endur-ing civilizational significance of the caliphate – as a vision, not as a renewable project – was also reflected in limits to the alternatives that emerged in the course of its decline. New ethnic communities were integrated into the Islamic world, but contrary to trends in the post-Roman West, there was no turn to ethnic definitions of statehood. The main contenders during the middle centuries of our period, separated by a geopolitical divide, were the Fatimid counter-caliphate in the western and a changing constellation of militarized local or regional regimes in the eastern lands of Islam. The Fatimid state, of imperial dimensions at its strongest and backed up by a schismatic vision of Islamic history as well as (at a more esoteric level) an ambitious reinterpretation of the Quranic message, failed to develop a political model capable of refounding the caliphate. The military elites that gained the upper hand in provinces escaping central control paved the way for a power structure commonly seen as a new type of state: 'not a direct expression of Islam, but a secular institution whose duty it was to uphold

19 Ira M. Lapidus, *Islamic Societies to the Nineteenth Century: A Global History* (Cambridge University Press, 2012): 97.

Islam'.[20] But this ambiguous status also meant that the militarized mode of government remained in the shadow of the caliphate. Even when bereft of power, the latter could still function as a source of legitimacy. On the other hand, the very construction of the military regimes, and *a fortiori* their expansion, depended on two factors from outside the Islamic orbit: tribal groupings from Inner Eurasia, migrating into the Near Eastern heartland and converting more or less at the same time, and borrowings from Persian statecraft. Both these sources could serve to upgrade the image of rulership and claim some kind of divine sanction; the doctrine of two unequal powers, prophecy and kingship, could in turn be invoked to contain such trends.

As we have seen, two major inter-civilizational encounters – with Byzantium and Persia – affected the course of early Islamic history. By contrast, the contact with Western Christendom – seen from the Islamic side – did not develop into a significant encounter during the Middle Millennium (that stage only began with the sixteenth-century Mediterranean expansion of the Ottoman Empire). But the final centuries of the Middle Millennium were marked by two other encounters: with Inner Eurasia through the Mongol conquests and their aftermath, and with the Indian world through Islamic advances into the subcontinent. In both cases, significant long-term effects resulted, but along different lines, not least in regard to the destinies of states and empires. The Mongol impact began with massive destruction inflicted by unbelievers and was then muted by conversion, but this did not mean that the whole episode was absorbed into an ongoing Islamic trajectory. Apart from lasting changes to the interrelations of nomadic and settled populations in the Islamic heartland, converted elites of Mongol and Turkic origin transmitted key elements of political culture to the Islamic world. This complex of operative notions included visions of empire, revitalized by the Mongol example; an exceptionally strong dynastic charisma attached to Chinggis Khan's descendants; and, to use Marshall Hodgson's term, a more systematic version of the military patronage state already adumbrated by the Turks.[21] The Indian encounter did not give rise to that kind of generalizable pattern, but it produced an expanding state based on a more stable and regulated coexistence with another civilization than any comparable power structure in the earlier history of Islam. Conversion seems to have been most effective in areas marginal to Hindu society, not at the centre of Islamic

---

20 Ira M. Lapidus, 'State and Religion in Islamic Societies', *Past & Present* 151 (1996): 19.
21 See Marshall G. S. Hodgson, *The Venture of Islam* (University of Chicago Press, 1974), vol. II, 402–10.

domination; there was, admittedly, no appropriation of Indian thought that could be compared to earlier engagement with Hellenic traditions, but in institutional and practical regards, the imperial power that grew out of Islamic expansion into India rested on an inter-civilizational basis.

Byzantium

Among the regional and civilizational formations discussed here, the Byzantine trajectory stands out as most nearly coextensive with the Middle Millennium. It was also the one whose destinies were most decisively affected by forces and processes generated elsewhere (more precisely within Western Christendom and Islam). The end of the Byzantine state was one of the most salient terminating events, although aspects of the Byzantine legacy survived within the Islamic empire of the Ottomans and as elements of the composite imperial tradition that took shape in Russia. The beginning of Byzantine history is more controversial, but as we have seen, it can be equated with a concatenation of major conflicts that also involved other civilizations and led to massive territorial losses. Internal transformations of the seventh and eighth centuries – affecting Byzantine state structures, society, worldview and identity – were in large measure due to the geopolitical downsizing and re-centring of the erstwhile East Roman empire.

The formation that emerged from these upheavals is perhaps best described as an 'amalgamation of faith-zone, imperial idea and state apparatus'.[22] To call it an amalgam is to underline the less-than-complete unity of the component parts, and that is doubly important. The relationship between the three factors was flexible enough to allow for significant changes; it also enabled the diffusion of cultural and institutional models beyond imperial borders, with some variations in the relative weight and visibility of separate aspects. Historians have widely used the term 'Byzantine Commonwealth' for the cluster of neighbouring states – from Bulgaria to Kiev Rus' – that developed autonomous versions of Byzantine patterns on all three above-mentioned levels.

The imperial idea, inseparable from the affirmation of continuity with the Roman past, was an enduring and defining feature. More precisely, the core imaginary institution of Byzantium linked the imperial status of the ruler to the imperial sovereignty of the state and the imperial eminence of its urban centre (the last was more important for Byzantine civilization than for

---

22 Jonathan Shepard (ed.), *The Cambridge History of the Byzantine Empire, c.500–1492* (Cambridge University Press, 2008): 9.

any other). There was, for much of the time, an imperial substance behind the idea, but this is no longer sustainable for the period from 1204 to 1453. During this final phase, the Byzantine world came to resemble a state system with a symbolic but gradually disempowered centre. One consequence of this was a loosening of the links between empire and faith. But even for the much longer, genuinely imperial period, it is now widely accepted that the long-held notion of Byzantine caesaro-papism is untenable. This is one of the most fundamental reappraisals in Byzantine studies, and it has led to better understanding of the religio-political nexus in question. There is no doubt that the Byzantine imperial institution had more power over the Church than its Western counterpart could ever claim. But the emperor was the protector of the Church, not its head; the power balance between the two summits of authority, however asymmetric in principle, could vary in practice, and disagreements could develop. Some notable imperial interventions in religious matters ended in failure; there was, in Dagron's terms, no successful fusion of imperial and priestly roles.[23]

Another reappraisal, not unrelated to the first, has to do with the state apparatus underpinning the empire. Contrary to earlier views, the changes triggered by Islamic expansion now appear as multiple long-drawn-out processes, rather than a grand design coordinating the infrastructures of state power; and the complex interrelations between sociopolitical forces, variously affected by successes and setbacks on external fronts, are central to present debates on Byzantine history.[24] For one thing, it seems well established that the Komnenoi dynasty, in power from 1081, was not an embodiment of feudal decline. Its state-building capacities were far from negligible.

Concluding remarks

The main conclusion from our survey is that imperial patterns – as distinct from more basic or common forms of statehood – are present in all Eurasian civilizations, but on very different levels. Imperial formations may be intermittent episodes in a longer civilizational trajectory, as in the Inner Eurasian case, or become durable components of a civilizational complex, as in the Chinese and Byzantine worlds (less successfully in the latter). In the

---

23 See Gilbert Dagron, *Emperor and Priest: The Imperial Office in Byzantium* (London: Cambridge University Press, 2003).

24 For a classic formulation of the earlier view, see George Ostrogorsky, *History of the Byzantine State* (New Brunswick, NJ: Rutgers University Press, 1986 [1963]).

particular context of Western Christendom, where the absence of a unifying empire was important for long-term developments, the imperial dimension of power was embodied in two centres: the Holy Roman Empire and the papacy. A minimal version of the imperial factor, evident in the ambitions and brief overlordships of regional dynasties, seems to have marked Indian history at least for the first half of our period. The simultaneous expansion of empire and religion was an Islamic invention, but the union was not perpetuated on a civilizational scale; later imperial ventures were of more modest size.

Several new imperial constellations emerged in the transition from the Middle Millennium to the early modern era. The Islamic world was more durably divided between empires than ever before; the Qing dynasty established the most balanced and lasting synthesis of Chinese and Inner Eurasian imperial traditions; Russian expansion across Siberia brought much of Inner Eurasia under the control of a power based northwest of the steppe; and the states of the western European seaboard acquired the first overseas empires. This last-named innovation was by no means a direct path to world domination, but it foreshadowed more radical changes to world affairs than the others.

FURTHER READING

General

Finer, S. E. *The History of Government from the Earliest Times,* vol. II: *The Intermediate Ages.* Oxford University Press, 1997.

Fried, Johannes and Ernst-Dieter Hehl, eds. *WBG-Weltgeschichte, vol. III: Weltdeutungen und Weltreligionen, 600 bis 1500.* Darmstadt: Wissenschaftliche Buchgesellschaft, 2010.

McNeill, William H. *The Rise of the West,* especially 'Eurasian cultural balance', 247–562. University of Chicago Press, 1963.

Inner Eurasia and its neighbours

Allsen, Thomas T. *Culture and Conquest in Mongol Eurasia.* Cambridge University Press, 2001.

Amitai-Preiss, Reuven and David O. Morgan, eds. *The Mongol Empire and its Legacy.* Leiden: Brill, 2000.

Beckwith, Christopher. *Empires of the Silk Road: History of Central Eurasia from the Bronze Age to the Present.* Princeton University Press, 2011.

Di Cosmo, Nicola. 'State Formation and Periodization in Inner Asian History', *Journal of World History* 10:1 (1999): 1–40.

Golden, Peter B. *Central Asia in World History.* Oxford University Press, 2011.

Morgan, David O. *The Mongols.* 2nd edn. Oxford and Malden, MA: Wiley-Blackwell, 2007.

Western Christendom

Barber, Malcolm. *The Two Cities: Medieval Europe 1050–1320*. London: Routledge, 2004.

Bartlett, Robert. *The Making of Europe: Conquest, Colonization, and Cultural Change 950–1350*. London: Penguin, 1994.

Elias, Norbert. *The Civilizing Process*. Oxford and Malden, MA: Wiley-Blackwell, 2000 [1939].

Jones, Philip. *The Italian City-State: From Commune to Signoria*. Oxford: Clarendon Press, 1997.

Le Goff, Jacques. *Medieval Civilization*. Oxford and Malden, MA: Wiley-Blackwell, 1990.

McKitterick, Rosamond. *Charlemagne: The Formation of a European Identity*. Cambridge University Press, 2008.

Seibt, Ferdinand. *Glanz und Elend des Mittelalters*. Hamburg and Munich: Orbis Verlag, 1999.

Wickham, Chris. *The Inheritance of Rome: A History of Europe from 400 to 1000*. London: Penguin, 2010.

China

Cambridge History of China, 13 vols. Cambridge University Press, 1979–2009, vol. III: *Sui and T'ang China, 589–906 CE, pt. 1*, ed. Denis C. Twitchett; vol. V: *The Sung Dynasty and its Precursors, 907–1279, pt. 1*, eds. Denis C. Twitchett and Paul Jakov Smith; vol. VI: *Alien Regimes and Border States, 710–1368*, eds. Denis C. Twitchett and Herbert Franke; vol. VII: *The Ming Dynasty, 1368–1644, pt. 1*, eds. Frederick W. Mote and Denis C. Twitchett; vol. VIII: *The Ming Dynasty, 1368–1644, pt. 2*, eds. Denis C. Twitchett and Frederick W. Mote.

Lewis, Mark Edward. *China's Cosmopolitan Empire: The Tang Dynasty*. Cambridge, MA: Belknap Press of Harvard University, 2012.

Mote, Frederick W. *Imperial China 900–1800*. Cambridge, MA: Harvard University Press, 2003.

Smith, Paul Jakov and Richard von Glahn, eds. *The Song–Yuan–Ming Transition in Chinese History*. Cambridge, MA: Harvard University Press, 2003.

Wong, R. Bin. *China Transformed. Historical Change and the Limits of European Experience*. Ithaca, NY: Cornell University Press, 2000.

India and Southeast Asia

Kulke, Hermann. *Kings and Cults: State Formation and Legitimation in India and South-East Asia*. Delhi: Manohar, 2008.

Kulke, Hermann. ed. *The State in India 1000–1700*. Delhi: Oxford University Press, 1997.

Ricklefs, M. C., Bruce Lockhart, Albert Lau, Portia Reyes and Maitrii Aung-Thwin. *A New History of Southeast Asia*. New York, NY: Palgrave-Macmillan, 2010.

Singh, Upinder, ed. *Rethinking Early Medieval India*. Delhi: Oxford University Press, 2011.

Wink, André. *Al-Hind: The Making of the Indo-Islamic World*, vol. I: *Early Medieval India and the Expansion of Islam, 7th–11th Centuries*; vol. II: *The Slave Kings and the Islamic Conquest, 11th–13th Centuries*; vol. III: *Indo–Islamic Society, 14th–15th Centuries*. Leiden: Brill, 1991–2003.

The Islamic world

Crone, Patricia. *Slaves on Horses: The Evolution of the Islamic Polity*. Cambridge University Press, 1980.

Feldbauer, Peter. *Die islamische Welt 600–1250: Ein Frühfall von Unterentwicklung?* Vienna: Promedia, 1995.

Garcin, Jean-Claude, et al. *États, sociétés et cultures du monde musulman médiéval*, vols. I–III. Paris: Presses universitaires de France, 1998–2000.

Hodgson, Marshall G. S. *The Venture of Islam*, vols. I–III. University of Chicago Press, 1974.

Kennedy, Hugh. *The Prophet and the Age of the Caliphates: The Islamic Near East from the 6th to the 11th Century*. London: Routledge, 2004.

Lapidus, Ira M. *Islamic Societies to the Nineteenth Century: A Global History*. Cambridge University Press, 2012.

'State and Religion in Islamic Societies', *Past & Present* 151 (1996): 3–27.

Byzantium

Dagron, Gilbert. *Emperor and Priest: The Imperial Office in Byzantium*. Cambridge University Press, 2003.

Shepard, Jonathan, ed. *The Cambridge History of the Byzantine Empire c. 500–1492*. Cambridge University Press, 2008.

Treadgold, Warren. *A History of the Byzantine State and Society*. Stanford University Press, 1997.

19

State formation in China from the Sui through the Song dynasties

RICHARD VON GLAHN

The demise of the long-lasting Han and Roman empires marked the defini-tive end of the ancient world, but aspirations to restore a universal empire lived on. The decisive failure of Emperor Justinian's project of imperial reunification in the sixth century – ultimately thwarted by wars with the Slavs, Persians, and Avars, the devastation sown by the plague epidemic, and the abrupt new challenge of the Islamic Empire – set the stage for the rise of a new multi-polar geopolitical order in the Mediterranean world. In East Asia, however, after four centuries of political fragmentation and foreign invasion, Yang Jian – the upstart founder of the Sui dynasty – succeeded in restoring imperial rule over nearly all of the former Han territory in 589. From this time onward the unified empire prevailed in China as both the political ideal and – with fairly brief interruptions – the historical reality. Despite the continuity of the Chinese Empire across successive dynasties, however, its ideological principles, institutional structure, and relations with neighboring polities underwent dramatic changes.

Political legacy of the Northern Wei

Both the short-lived Sui dynasty (581–618) and the succeeding Tang dynasty (618–907) were products of the political consolidation achieved in North China by the foreign-ruled Northern Wei (386–534). The Sui and Tang emperors sprang from the hybrid Taghbač-Chinese aristocratic elite fostered by the Northern Wei and saw themselves as heirs to both the sedentary civilization of China and the nomadic traditions of the Eurasian steppes. In contrast to earlier (and later) Chinese empires, the Sui–Tang ruling class also embraced the cosmopolitan and multicultural society that flourished under the Northern Wei.

The Taghbač rulers of the Northern Wei descended from the Xianbei nomads who had occupied much of the eastern steppe after the demise of the

Xiongnu confederation. The Taghbač pioneered the use of heavily armored cavalry – made possible in part by the introduction of the stirrup – to build up formidable military strength. In 386 the Taghbač unveiled their ambition to conquer China by adopting the Chinese-style dynastic name Northern Wei. From 430, when they captured the former Han capital of Chang'an, down to the 530s the Taghbač dominated a wide swath of Inner Eurasia from Manchuria to Bactria, including most of China north of the Yangzi River.

Unlike the Xiongnu, who merely sought to extract booty, the Taghbač developed enduring institutions for governing agrarian China, most notably the state-administered land allocations known as the Equal Field (*juntian*) system. The Equal Field system provided an economic footing for farming families beleaguered by invasion and war and ensured stable revenues – collected in grain, cloth, and labor service – for the state. The Northern Wei emperor Xiaowen (r. 471–99) encouraged intermarriage between the Taghbač nobility and the leading Chinese aristocratic clans as well as adoption of Chinese language, dress, and customs. Xiaowen sought to create a hybrid ruling class that would combine the martial heritage of the steppe with the cultural prestige and administrative acumen of imperial China. The relocation of the Northern Wei capital from Pingyang, at the edge of the Great Wall frontier, to the traditional imperial capital of Luoyang in 494 testified to Xiaowen's ambition to rule in the style of a Chinese emperor. However, his policies provoked hostility and civil war between the Northern Wei leaders and the Taghbač tribes in the steppe grasslands, who staunchly resisted Chinese habits and values. In 534 the Northern Wei split into two rival states, which in turn were wracked by internal conflict. Although the incessant warfare caused much misery and devastation, it also further enhanced the military might of the northern states. One of the innovations of this era was the creation of farmer–soldier militias known as *fubing*, which reduced the logistical costs of a standing army. The political and military institutions of the Northern Wei and its successors laid the foundations for the Sui reunification.

The Sui–Tang reunification

Yang Jian (Emperor Wendi, r. 581–604) proclaimed his Sui dynasty in 581 after a bloody coup in which he seized power from a child-ruler – his own seven-year-old grandson. Once securely enthroned, Yang launched a multi-pronged invasion of southern China that toppled the Chinese-ruled Chen dynasty there, and completed the project of reunification in 589. Yang moved swiftly to assert his supreme authority as emperor. He rebuilt the former Han capital at Chang'an on an even grander scale – the largest imperial capital in Chinese history, encompassing eighty-four square kilometers, although much land within the walls remained vacant. Yang revived the authority of the central government, distributing executive and legislative responsibilities among three principal organs: the Department of State Affairs, the Chancellery, and the Secretariat. At the same time he acted decisively to curtail the independence of local officials, stripping them of military forces and subordinating them directly to the central state. Yang also voided the hereditary rights to office that aristocratic clans enjoyed during the period of disunion. As in the Han, local officials recommended candidates for appointment to the civil service, but the Sui instituted written examinations for some nominees – the first sprouts of the civil service examination system that would dominate Chinese government, society, and culture during the late imperial era. Nonetheless, the Sui emperors recruited their senior officials and closest advisers from the hybrid aristocracy cultivated by Emperor Xiaowen of the Northern Wei, which came to be known as the Guanzhong aristocracy.

Steeped in the steppe traditions of the Taghbač and their warrior arts of hunting, archery, and falconry, Yang Jian had scant regard for the moral dictates of Confucian political philosophy and the restraints it imposed on autocratic rule. Instead Yang found a more appealing model of pious rulership in the supreme and unchallengeable authority of the Buddhist *chakravartin* (the ideal universal ruler who turns the wheel of Dharma), especially as exemplified by Aśoka, emperor of the Maurya dynasty in India in the third century BCE. Declaring himself a "bodhisattva Son of Heaven" dedicated to the propagation of the Buddhist faith, Yang imitated Aśoka by commissioning the construction of Buddhist monuments and monasteries in all major cities of the empire. Yang's conspicuous patronage of Buddhism was meant to impress his subjects, but also to redeem himself from the burden of sin – and the prospect of karmic retribution in his next lifetime – accumulated during his violent usurpation of power.

By the sixth century, Buddhist beliefs, rituals, and social practices had become deeply implanted throughout the Chinese world. Both the Northern Wei and Chinese rulers in the south had lavishly patronized the Buddhist religion and its clergy. Luoyang reportedly had 1,367 Buddhist shrines and monasteries at the time the Northern Wei fell in 534. Ruling over a multitude of subjects of diverse ethnic origins, Yang Jian consciously strove to instill political and social unity through this common cultural core of Buddhist faith.

Yang Jian's successor, Yang Guang (Emperor Yangdi, r. 604–18), continued his father's project of imperial consolidation. Yangdi's most notable achievement was the construction of the Grand Canal, which became the vital transport link connecting the rapidly developing rice economy of the Yangzi River Delta to the capitals (Chang'an and Luoyang) located in the arid northwest. But Yangdi also entertained quixotic ambitions of restoring Chinese rule over the Korean peninsula. The catastrophic failure of Yangdi's military campaigns in Korea in 612–14 ignited a political crisis at home. In 618 Yangdi was murdered, and shortly afterward Li Yuan, another scion of the Guanzhong aristocracy, declared the founding of a new dynasty, Tang.

In some respects, the establishment of the Tang dynasty in 618 can be seen as one in a series of *coups d'état* instigated by military leaders among the close-knit aristocratic clans that had ruled North China since the Northern Wei. Like the Sui, the Tang rulers preserved the basic political institutions developed by the Northern Wei and its successors such as the Equal Field landholding system and the *fubing* militias. The early Tang emperors also retained the cosmopolitan cultural orientation of the Sui court. The second Tang emperor, Li Shimin (Emperor Taizong, r. 626–49), seized power by killing his older brother, the heir apparent, and forcing his father to abdicate. Yet Taizong embraced both the warrior heritage of the steppe nomads and the civil virtues of the Confucian monarch. Taizong projected Tang military power over much of the eastern steppe, forcing into submission the Eastern Turks – who acknowledged Taizong as "lord of the steppe" (*khaqan*) – and imposing colonial rule over many of the Silk Road oasis towns. At the same time Taizong cultivated the support of the rank-and-file bureaucrats imbued with Confucian traditions of statecraft and cultural refinement. By the mid-seventh century the Tang had become the dominant political, military, and cultural force in eastern Eurasia (see Map 19.1).

The genesis of East Asia

The reunification of China under the Sui and Tang dynasties was the catalyst for the formation of a common East Asian civilization and the shaping of East Asia's political order. The power and majesty of the Sui–Tang empires deeply impressed China's neighbors and inspired them to emulate the Chinese model, developing more centralized "national states" and avidly patronizing the Buddhist religion and clergy. By the end of the seventh century, Korea, Japan, and Tibet all had become unified under a single

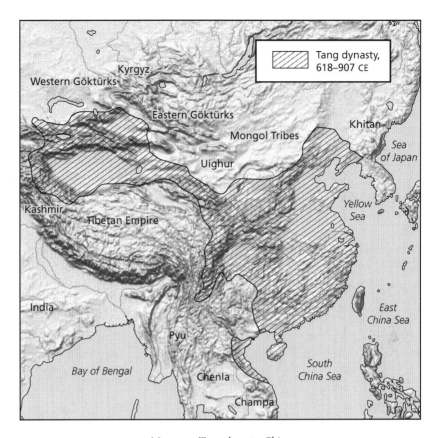

Map 19.1. Tang dynasty China

paramount ruler, establishing a multi-state political order that has persisted down to modern times.

The Han Empire had extended its suzerainty over portions of the Korean peninsula and the Red River Delta of northern Vietnam. After the final withdrawal of Chinese colonial governors from Korea in the early fourth century CE, three independent Korean kingdoms emerged. Koguryŏ, the earliest and most powerful, dominated the northern peninsula and much of Manchuria. Koguryŏ combined military might based on the heavy cavalry of the steppe nomads with the trappings of Confucian monarchy and bureaucratic government. Paekche, located in the southwestern peninsula, cultivated cordial diplomatic relations with the southern dynasties in China and the nascent Yamato regime in Japan. Silla, in the remote southeastern corner of the peninsula, coalesced as a monarchal state somewhat later, but quickly achieved parity in military and political strength thanks to its ample resources of iron and gold. Constant warfare propelled warrior elites to dominance in each of the Korean states.

Beginning *c.* 400 BCE a wave of immigrants from the Korean peninsula had swept into the Japanese islands, introducing wet-rice farming, sericulture, metallurgy, cattle, and horses. This technological infusion stimulated rapid population growth and the formation of regional chiefdoms. In the third century CE a mysterious female ruler known as Himiko – perhaps a theurgic queen – dispatched the first diplomatic mission from Japan to the court of the Wei kingdom in China. The movement of people, goods, and technologies between Korea and Japan intensified in the fourth and fifth centuries, and contingents of Japanese warriors became embroiled in the strife among the Korean kingdoms. Over the course of the fifth–sixth centuries the Yamato "Great Kings" established their rule over much of the Japanese archipelago. Korean monks – principally from Paekche – became the conduit for the transmission not only of the Buddhist religion, but also of vital knowledge about Chinese kingship, statecraft, ritual culture, and administrative expertise. In 604, upon the return of an embassy to the Sui court, Queen Suiko and her nephew and co-ruler Prince Shōtoku reconfigured the Yamato court, creating (in imitation of Korean practice) a formal ranked nobility subordinated to the supreme authority of the monarch and establishing official patronage of the Buddhist church.

Although Emperor Yangdi's disastrous invasion of Korea was instrumental in the downfall of the Sui, the Tang rulers continued to harbor imperialist designs on Korea. Silla forged an alliance with Tang against its rivals, and in 660 the combined Silla–Tang forces overwhelmed Paekche and deposed its king. After a restoration effort aided by a Yamato naval expedition failed in 663, the remnants of the Paekche court fled to Japan. In 668, the Silla-Tang armies conquered Koguryŏ. The Tang sought to reduce Silla to a mere client regime, but the Silla kings successfully resisted Tang encroachment and for the first time established a unified state on the Korean peninsula.

The rout of Yamato naval forces by the Tang fleet in Paekche in 663, and subsequent demands that the Japanese recognize Tang overlordship, sent tremors through the Japanese ruling class. In the shadow of this looming threat from China, the Yamato rulers won the acquiescence of the nobility to construct a more centralized state based on the Chinese model of a universal sovereign presiding over a bureaucratic administration with strong fiscal and legal powers. By 700 the Yamato had rechristened themselves as *tennō* ("heavenly sovereigns"), formally adopted the Chinese name "Japan" (Nihon, or "Land of the Rising Sun"), and issued a law code that strengthened their control over land revenues, the clergy, and defense. A Chinese-style royal capital was laid out at Nara in 710, followed by the building of an even more elaborate imperial metropolis at Kyoto beginning in 794. At the same time the Japanese court promoted its own distinctive ideology of legitimacy centered on the unique ritual purity of an unbroken line of *tennō* descended from the Sun Goddess.

By 700, then, unified states that borrowed heavily from Chinese political institutions had emerged in both Korea and Japan. Yet neither the Silla kings nor the Japanese *tennō*, confronted by entrenched aristocratic classes that retained formidable power at the local level, matched the centralized political control of the Chinese empires. The Buddhist clergy and religious institutions also acquired far greater wealth and political clout in Korea and Japan than in China. Moreover, the waning of Tang power after 750 damaged its reputation in the eyes of its neighbors, and Korea and Japan increasingly diverged from the Sui–Tang political model. Nonetheless, this period witnessed the genesis of East Asia both as a coherent cultural identity and as a stable multi-state political order.

Perhaps the most powerful force for the creation of an East Asian cultural identity was the use of Chinese as the common written language. The dissemination of Chinese philosophy, ritual, poetry, law codes, historical writing, and the Buddhist religion – especially in its distinctively Chinese forms, such as the Pure Land and Chan/Zen traditions – created a shared cultural vocabulary across East Asia. To be sure, the ideas and values transmitted through texts written in Chinese were remolded in light of indigenous traditions, and eventually Japanese and Koreans developed their own vernacular writing systems (the Japanese *kana* script in the tenth century, and the Korean *han'gŭl* script in the fifteenth century). Nonetheless, Chinese writing enjoyed greater prestige than vernacular languages, and China's philosophical and literary traditions continued to exert a profound impact on the intellectual cultures of its neighbors.

Internal challenges and the decline of Tang power

Despite its peerless supremacy within the East Asian international order in the seventh century, the Tang Empire faced challenges from within that ultimately sapped its power and prestige. The first major challenge was the seizure of the mantle of imperial authority by Wu Zhao (629–705), one of the most controversial figures in Chinese history and the only woman ever to reign as emperor of China. Wu Zhao came to the Tang court in 655 as a consort to Taizong's successor, Emperor Gaozong (r. 649–83), and soon wielded decisive influence over her sickly and compliant husband. A wily politician, Wu Zhao overcame the fierce opposition of the Guanzhong aristocracy through strategic political maneuvers and ruthless use of espionage and violence. Wu openly presided over the Tang court after her husband's death, and in 690 she boldly set aside the Tang dynastic house and proclaimed herself emperor – under the name Wu Zetian ("Modeled on Heaven") – of her own Zhou dynasty. Wu's usurpation opened deep rifts within the ruling elite, but the empire enjoyed domestic prosperity during her reign as well as continued success against its Turk and Tibetan adversaries. In an effort to outflank her aristocratic enemies Wu elevated the stature and power of bureaucratic officeholders by enhancing the use of meritocratic civil service examinations and delegating important decision-making powers to the secretariat and the heads of ministries. But opposition to her rule never abated. In 705, shortly before her death, the elderly empress was forced to relinquish her throne and the Tang dynasty was reinstated.

The full restoration of the Tang house under Emperor Xuanzong (r. 712–56) inaugurated a period of imperial splendor and cultural efflorescence with few equals in Chinese history. But Xuanzong's favoritism toward the Guanzhong aristocracy, which supported the emperor's desire for strong imperial rule, aggravated the examination-bred literati officials cultivated by Wu Zetian and fanned the flames of factional strife. Economic prosperity and commercial growth increasingly came into conflict with the rigid principles of the Equal Field landholding system and threatened to undermine the fiscal foundations of the central government. The *fubing* militias also atrophied as effective fighting forces and were superseded by large permanent standing armies stationed along the Inner Eurasian and Korean frontiers. In order to insulate the military from the struggle between the aristocrats and the literati officials, Xuanzong entrusted the major military commands to generals of non-Chinese ancestry whom he deemed non-partisan and apolitical.

Chief among these foreign generals was An Lushan, a Sogdian who enjoyed the full confidence of Xuanzong. The Sogdian merchant network dominated the Silk Road caravan trade at this time, and soldiers-of-fortune like An as well as many Sogdian merchant families settled in the Tang capital of Chang'an. In 755, with the aging emperor enfeebled and An's political enemies in ascendancy at the Tang court, An rallied other frontier generals to launch an armed insurrection against the Tang. In 756 An's armies captured

Chang'an, forcing Xuanzong to flee to Sichuan in the southwest, where he abdicated and died in exile. The attempt to overthrow the Tang foundered, however, when An Lushan was murdered by his son in 757. Nonetheless the rebellion lasted for eight years (755–63) before loyalist forces, with the aid of Uighur Turk mercenaries, could suppress the insurgents and restore Tang rule.

The post-An Lushan transformation of Chinese government and society

Although the Tang dynasty survived, the An Lushan Rebellion had devastated North China and permanently crippled the authority of the central government. The post-rebellion transformation of Chinese government, society, and economy constituted one of the key watersheds in Chinese history.

First, the rebellion triggered the final collapse of the fraying institutional order inaugurated by the Northern Wei. The Equal Field landownership system disintegrated, resulting in the emergence of *de facto* private land ownership. The *fubing* militias – already greatly deteriorated as fighting forces – likewise were abandoned. Power gravitated into the hands of military strongmen who entrenched themselves as regional governors and exercised considerable freedom from the central government. The sharply diminished power of the court dealt a fatal blow to the aristocratic clans that had dominated Chinese government and society since the Han dynasty, and the Guanzhong aristocrats in particular. Examination success and administrative expertise displaced aristocratic pedigree as the crucial criteria for appointment to political office. Over the next several centuries the aristocracy lost its identity as a coherent social class, and most aristocratic clans faded into obscurity.

Second, the rebellion unleashed a backlash against the cosmopolitan spirit of the early Tang, and especially the Buddhist religion. Confucian critics such as the noted poet and polemicist Han Yu (786–824) vehemently denounced the eclectic multiculturalism of the Tang court. Many of Han's contemporaries were persuaded by his claims that the other-worldly orientation of Buddhism had unraveled the moral fiber of the Chinese people and deflected the imperial state from its true mission of providing for the moral and material welfare of the people. With the rise of the new examination-based political elite, Confucianism regained its former primacy as the fount of political, cultural, and intellectual values. Moreover, Confucianism itself was transformed by the revival of an idealist tradition derived from the ancient philosopher Mencius, a revision sufficiently far-reaching to merit the name Neo-Confucianism. Neo-Confucian philosophy achieved its full flowering in the eleventh–twelfth centuries and dominated the Chinese intellectual world down to the late nineteenth century.

Third, the An Lushan Rebellion gave major impetus to a long-term shift in the economic center of gravity of the Chinese Empire, from the traditional heartland in the North China Plain to the Yangzi River Delta. Millions of farming families abandoned war-torn North China and fled to the fertile plains of the Yangzi Delta and the inland valleys of the Yangzi River basin, still a largely virgin frontier. As immigrants settled in the south, they began to tap the region's rich economic resources. The highly productive rice agriculture of South China accelerated population growth, which in turn generated the labor power required for intensive irrigated rice cultivation. Landholding was no longer subject to the constraints of the Equal Field system, and land became a commodity freely bought and sold. Most aristocratic estates were broken up. Some local powermongers and nouveaux riches families built up sizable landholdings, but most land was held by smallholder households. Private enterprise flourished in both trade and agriculture. The abundant navigable waterways of South China facilitated commercial and urban growth, while a host of new industries – including tea, porcelain, paper, sugar, and shipbuilding – emerged. However, the full development of a monetary economy was constrained by the state's inability to expand the money supply. Since the founding of the first empires in the third century BCE the Chinese state solely recognized state-issued bronze currency as legal tender, but because of the low value of these bronze coins the economy suffered from perennial shortages of currency.

The fiscal structure of the Tang state likewise underwent dramatic changes. The demise of the Equal Field landholding system spelled the end of the taxation system (which combined uniform in-kind payments of grain and cloth with labor service) based on it. In its place the Tang created the Twice-a-Year Tax, a progressively scaled tax levied on the wealth (chiefly measured by landholding) of households. But direct taxes occupied a much reduced place in the fiscal system. Instead, the central government's revenues increasingly were drawn from indirect taxation, including a range of commercial taxes and above all the revenues of the salt monopoly. At the same time specialized branches of government – notably a new Finance Commission that controlled the bulk of the new revenues – eclipsed the secretariat and the regular ministries as the centers of state power.

The Five Dynasties interregnum (907–960)

The final demise of the Tang dynasty was ushered in by the Huang Chao rebellion (774–84), which raged unchecked across China for a decade and left the imperial government crippled and bankrupt. In 907 the last Tang emperor, a mere child, was deposed by a turncoat follower of Huang Chao with his own imperial aspirations. But the fall of the Tang was followed by the dissolution of the empire into a panoply of rival regimes incessantly at war with each other. In sharp contrast to the expansive, cosmopolitan empires of Sui and Tang, the rulers of this era focused on building a political base at the local and regional levels. In the north, a series of praetorian coups led to the rise and fall of five dynastic houses in quick succession within the span of a half-century. Amid this political turmoil, actual power devolved to dozens of local warlord regimes. In the south however, a more stable multi-state system of seven regional kingdoms emerged that largely corresponded to the main geographic macro-regions. The multi-state system of South China was preserved in the structure of the Song dynasty's territorial administration and later in the provincial units of the Ming and Qing dynasties.

The pattern of military rule that prevailed during the late Tang continued in the Five Dynasties period. The decay of the *fubing* soldier-farmer militias had forced the Tang to rely on professional armies to defend its frontiers. The rulers of the Five Dynasties likewise mustered large standing armies. Provisions of food and clothing and pay (in coin) for several hundred thousand troops consumed the lion's share of state revenue.

Political disunity invited new incursions from aggressive steppe-based states. The Khitan rulers of Manchuria created their own powerful military regime and occupied the territories around modern Beijing. By the 930s the Khitan wielded paramount influence in North China. In 947, after a military triumph over the Kaifeng-based Later Tang dynasty, the Khitan were poised to seize the entire North China Plain. Although the Khitan leaders asserted their imperial dignity by adopting the Chinese-style dynastic title of Liao, they ultimately decided against annexing the rest of North China. In the northwest, another nomad regime, the Tangut kingdom of Xia (later Xixia), sat astride the old Silk Road corridor leading to Inner Eurasia.

Despite the constant political struggles and warfare, South China continued to enjoy robust economic growth. Intense competition among the southern kingdoms prompted resort to mercantilist fiscal and monetary policies and intensive exploitation of mineral and forest resources. Regional specialization in the production of tea, salt, timber, paper, copper, silver, and textiles intensified as the various states sought to capitalize on their comparative advantages in resources. Although political fragmentation and rivalry posed obstacles to inter-regional trade, the rulers of these states also depended on commerce to obtain vital supplies – notably iron, salt, sulfur, and alum – as well as now indispensable consumer staples such as tea. The southern regimes eagerly promoted trade with the remote foreign states on the northern frontier, Liao and Xia, principally based on the exchange of tea for warhorses. The coastal kingdoms of Wu-Yue, Min, and Southern Han actively pursued overseas trade with the Liao, the newly established Koryŏ kingdom in Korea, and Japan as well as Southeast Asia.

At the same time rulers adopted mercantilist strategies intended to strengthen their national economies and prevent the drain of currency – bronze coin and uncoined silver and gold – to neighboring rivals. Like the post-An Lushan Tang central government, the states of the Five Dynasties period relied heavily on indirect taxation for their revenues. The northern states, lacking domestic supplies of copper, suffered from critical shortages of money. A proscription against Buddhism enacted by the Northern Zhou in 955 was a thinly disguised ruse to seize bronze statues and other religious ornaments held by monasteries and private devotees for use as raw material for coinage. Even states with ample copper supplies such as Wu-Yue and Southern Tang ultimately resorted to minting iron coins to discourage the export of coin abroad. Other southern states such as Min, Southern Han, and Chu issued even cheaper lead coins. These monetary policies contributed to a pattern of regional economic autarky that persisted into the Song period.

Prosperity and crisis under the Song Empire
(960–1279)

The restoration of a unified empire emerged from the struggle for supremacy among the military strongmen of the north. In the 950s the Northern Zhou regime regained the upper hand against its Liao adversaries. Zhao Kuangyin, head of the palace army, overthrew the Northern Zhou ruler and declared the founding of his Song dynasty in 960, but it took twenty years before the Song defeated the last of the regional states. The new geopolitical order was reflected in Zhao's decision to establish his capital at Kaifeng, centrally located along the Grand Canal, rather than at the traditional capitals of Chang'an or Luoyang farther west. Scholars have characterized the Song as a "lesser empire," hemmed in by the powerful steppe-based states of Liao and Xia that had breached the Great Wall barrier. Throughout its existence the Song repeatedly suffered setbacks when it tried to establish more secure borders along its northern frontiers. Under the terms of the Treaty of Shanyuan, imposed on the Song in 1004 after a humiliating defeat at the hands of the Liao, the Song emperor was forced to accept the Liao ruler as his equal. The treaty obligated the Song to pay substantial tributes of silver and silk to the Liao, but the cost of these indemnities was recouped through lucrative cross-border trade and customs revenue.

The Song emperors, mindful of the disunity fostered by military leaders since the An Lushan Rebellion, strongly championed civil governance. Zhao Kuangyin famously disarmed and retired the generals who had assisted his rise to power, and the Song armies remained subordinated to civilian command. The Song emperors patronized the resurgent Neo-Confucian movement, and established examinations based on Confucian classical learning and political ideology as virtually the sole avenue of recruitment to government office. The fiercely competitive civil service examinations effectively precluded the re-formation of a closed political caste like the old aristocratic clans.

Domestic peace and stability – along with an array of technological advances – accelerated the economic trends set in motion by the An Lushan Rebellion, resulting in steady improvement in agricultural productivity, expanding markets for both consumer goods (e.g. silk textiles and tea) and producer goods (e.g. iron and steel), monetization of the economy, and the growth of cities. Mining and metallurgical industries boomed. The Song state greatly expanded coinage, and by the 1070s mint output was nearly twenty times greater than the peak level reached during the Tang. The Song also introduced the world's first viable paper currency, initially (in 1024) as a regional currency in Sichuan and on an empire-wide basis in the late twelfth century. The technical requirements of wet-rice agriculture favored small, intensively cultivated family farms over large landed estates. Most farming families owned at least some land of their own. Thus the economic benefits of rising productivity were widely distributed. The population of the empire doubled, reaching 100 million by 1100, with two-thirds of the population concentrated in the rice-growing regions of South China. As in the late Tang, the Song state depended heavily on indirect taxes; levies from commercial taxes, maritime customs, and monopoly commodities such as salt, liquor, and tea generated substantial cash revenues.

The Arab conquest of Sogdia in 712 and the downfall of the Uighur confederation in the mid-ninth century had disrupted commercial exchange across the Silk Road. With the overland routes largely barred by hostile states

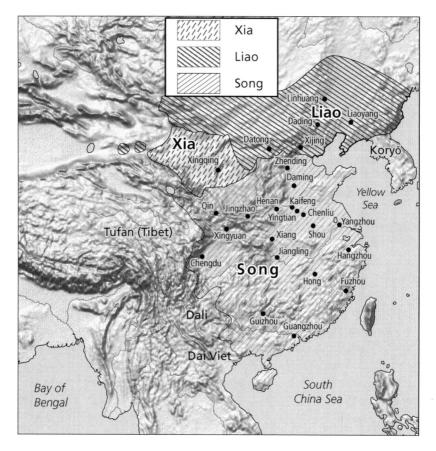

Map 19.2. Xia, Liao, and Song Empires

to the north, China's foreign trade became reoriented to the maritime world. Overseas trade with Japan, Southeast Asia, and the Indian Ocean world boomed throughout the Song period, and the ports of Guangzhou and Quanzhou on China's southern coast became home to large communities of Arab, Persian, Malay, and Tamil traders.

Although the income of the Song state rose sharply during its first century, soaring military expenses continually outran revenues. After a disastrous war with the Tangut Xia kingdom in the 1040s the Song was forced to maintain a standing army of more than a million soldiers to defend its borders. The military threat posed by the steppe-based states and the burden of defense costs severely tested the strategic, organizational, and logistic capacities of the Song state.

The new policies of Wang Anshi

Military setbacks and fiscal exigencies prompted repeated appeals for reform. Confucian scholar–officials, who tended to view all political problems as questions of proper moral leadership, concentrated their reform efforts on the character and qualifications of officials, beginning with school curricula and the civil service examinations. In the early 1040s a cadre of young officials pushed through a reform agenda focused on reducing the privileged access to government appointment granted to relatives of high officials, increasing state investment in public schools, and strengthening military preparedness. But in 1045, conservative opponents succeeded in ousting the reformers and rescinding their initiatives.

An opportunity for more radical reform came two decades later with the ascension of a young monarch, Emperor Shenzong (r. 1067–85), who swiftly promoted an ambitious and brilliant statesman, Wang Anshi (1021–86), to chief minister. Wang sought to circumvent a sclerotic bureaucracy by creating a host of new, task-oriented state agencies headed by upstart officials liberated from many of the constraints of civil service protocols – a political style dubbed "bureaucratic entrepreneurship" by Paul J. Smith in 1991. Wang also proposed a new examination curriculum centered on public policy and current affairs that de-emphasized literary skills such as poetry composition. Above all, Wang implemented far-reaching changes in fiscal policy, seeking to free up productive energies in an economy undergoing rapid monetization by converting labor services to cash payments, investing state resources in agricultural improvement (the central government initiated over 11,000 irrigation projects), and pumping vast amounts of currency into the economy.

Under Wang Anshi's leadership, fiscal management became the defining feature of the art of government. But Wang also feared that market exchange created imbalances in the distribution in wealth and was vulnerable to manipulation by merchant cartels. To forestall such inequities he advocated state intervention in commerce and moneylending. Wang created new state agencies to manage wholesale trade at the capital and provide credit for retail businesses, turned private brokers into government agents, tightened the state's control of foreign trade, and extended the existing monopoly on salt production to include much tea cultivation as well. The most controversial – and most reviled – of Wang's fiscal innovations was the so-called "Green Sprouts" program, through which the state offered direct loans to farmers. Intended to provide relief from usurious private lending, the Green Sprouts loans degenerated into a form of confiscatory taxation whereby local officials compelled farming households to assume loans regardless of their ability to repay them, worsening the problem of indebtedness. Under the aegis of Wang's "New Policies" cash payments climbed to 72 per cent of central government revenues, compared to 43 per cent *c*. 1000.

The majority of Song officialdom stridently denounced Wang's activist agenda, and especially its intrusions into the private economy, as a corruption of time-honored Confucian values. Intellectual opposition to the New Policies coalesced around the Dao Learning circle, which prized ethical knowledge and personal moral integrity as the wellsprings of correct governance. Wang was forced into permanent retirement in 1076, but his allies continued to direct court policy until Shenzong's death in 1085.

Wang Anshi's New Policies pitched China into a half-century of incessant partisan struggle in which the reform measures were repeatedly done and undone. This factional conflict paralyzed the Song government and left it vulnerable to the invasions launched by the rising Jurchen state of Jin (1115–1234), which displaced the Liao regime in Manchuria. In 1127 Jin armies captured the northern half of the empire, including the capital at Kaifeng, forcing the Song court to flee to the south and reconstitute itself at the "provisional capital" of Hangzhou in the Yangzi Delta. Many blamed the loss of North China on the misgovernment of Wang and his reform-minded successors. Although the causes of the military debacle were far more complex, during the "Southern" Song Chinese statesmen spurned the New Policies programs and Wang Anshi's vision of the central state as the engine of positive social and economic change (see Map 19.3).

The "localist turn" in the Southern Song

The Southern Song (1127–1276/9) period, too, was defined by perennial military threats. An uneasy truce with the Jin was achieved in 1161, but renewed war with the Jin, combined with the outbreak of civil war in 1205–7, precipitated grave military and fiscal crises. The Jin itself was beset by Mongol invasions and finally was conquered by the Mongols in 1234, leaving the Song confronted with an even more formidable adversary. From the inception of the Southern Song period, the state raised revenues by resorting to expedient fiscal policies widely condemned as parasitical by contemporaries. The four regional Military Commissariats created to manage defense logistics largely eclipsed the central government's ministry of revenue, initiating a trend that led to the formation of province-level governments under subsequent dynasties. Local magistrates found

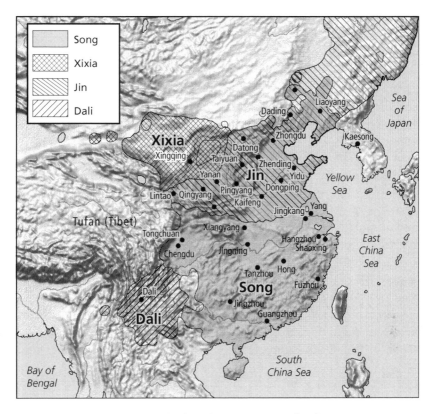

Map 19.3. Southern Song, Xixia, Jin and Dali

themselves caught between the proliferating demands of the central government and rapid socio-economic changes beyond their capacity to control.

By the end of the twelfth century the Dao Learning movement attained paramount influence in Chinese intellectual life, a dominance that would last for the remainder of the imperial era. The philosopher Zhu Xi (1130–1200) codified the Dao Learning teachings in a systematic body of philosophical doctrines, commentaries on the canonical Confucian texts, historical interpretation, behavioral norms, and ritual practices. In 1241 the Song court inducted Zhu Xi and other leading Dao Learning figures into the official Confucian pantheon, and in 1315 the Mongol Yuan dynasty made Zhu's philosophical and political views the "correct" standard for the civil service examinations.

Dao Learning luminaries like Zhu Xi rejected the state-centered activism espoused by Wang Anshi in favor of community-based initiatives in local governance and social welfare (e.g. famine relief, credit associations, and communal ritual assemblies). Although these programs had a negligible impact on social life, they remained enduring ideals celebrated by all Neo-Confucians as the proper institutions for fulfilling Confucian social ideals. The "localist turn" in Confucian statecraft marked a major reorientation in Chinese conceptions of the relationship between state and society, paving the way for the Confucian-educated local elite to assume the leading role in public affairs – in some cases overshadowing the authority of the state-appointed magistrates.

Nonetheless, the Southern Song state remained a robust presence in most regions. Even more striking, however, was the vibrant economic growth and expansion of the market economy. During the Southern Song the Yangzi Delta region flourished not only as the vital economic heart of the empire, but also as the center of intellectual and cultural life.

The Song weathered the military crises of the first decade of the thirteenth century, but in the late 1250s Mongol armies under the leadership of Qubilai Khan (r. 1260–94) mounted sustained attacks against Song territories, culminating in the conquest of Hangzhou and the fall of the Southern Song in 1276. Both contemporaries and later historians identified various scapegoats to blame for the Mongol conquest, which resulted in all of China falling under foreign rule for the first time. But the supremacy of Mongol military logistics, rather than the failings of Song political leadership, provides a more credible explanation for the Mongols' success.

Long-term trends in state–society relations

During the period 500–1300, Chinese governance underwent dramatic changes that redefined the imperial institution, transformed the relationship between the state and its subjects, and engendered a new international political order in East Asia.

First, a revitalized Confucian model of imperial sovereignty displaced the Sino–nomad synthesis created by the Northern Wei and continued by the Sui–Tang states. The Northern Wei, the most powerful of the post-Han successor regimes, had joined the militarized rulership of the steppe nomads with the Buddhist ideal of the "wheel-turning" universal ruler. Under this conception of monarchy the ruler wielded virtually limitless authority as the defender of the faith, even though his power was constrained by the presence of a strongly entrenched nobility and manorial landholding. The Equal Field system and the *fubing* militias restored some degree of central control over revenues, labor resources, and military power. But it was the rebuilding of a civil bureaucracy drawn from the learned classes in the Tang and Song that shifted the balance of power back to the central government. Neo-Confucian political ideology rested on the ideal of a transcendent emperor who embodied civil virtue but also entrusted actual government to officials schooled in Confucian ethics and statecraft and chosen through highly competitive examinations. In the wake of Wang Anshi's failed reform movement, however, faith in the transformative potential of the central state waned. The Dao Learning agenda of literati leadership within local society became the main inspiration for social reform.

Second, the revival of the bureaucratic state altered the relationship between the state and the individual. In contrast to the static socio-economic order on which the Equal Field system was premised, Song leaders sought to mobilize resources through bureaucratic interventions in a surging market economy. The Twice-a-Year tax system – which persisted largely intact throughout the late imperial era – replaced uniform exactions assessed in goods and labor service with a progressively indexed levy on wealth. Military and labor service occupied a much diminished role in the state's system of extraction: the Song relied on paid standing armies rather than military conscription, and many labor services were commuted to money payments. In addition, the state's income increasingly derived from indirect taxes levied on commerce rather than direct taxes on agricultural production. The co-resident household (in essence, the conjugal family) became firmly entrenched as the fundamental economic unit in both the private economy and the state fiscal system.

The household also superseded larger kin groups or village communities as the object of legal and social control. Legal changes erased the distinction between aristocrats and commoners. The growth of the market economy fostered a new social hierarchy defined by wealth rather than ascriptive status. Although families of officials enjoyed some legal and fiscal privileges, "good subjects" (liangmin) – the vast majority of the population – enjoyed equality before the law.

Finally, this period witnessed the emergence and consolidation of an enduring multi-state political order in East Asia. The Sui–Tang model of national unification under centralized government provided a powerful impetus for state formation among China's neighbors, including Korea, Japan, Tibet, and later Vietnam as well. But strong centralized government failed to take root elsewhere in East Asia. In Japan, the imperial court steadily relinquished control of land, population, and resources to a resurgent landowning class comprised of aristocrats, religious institutions, and the imperial clan itself. In Tibet, a strong monarchy rooted in the Buddhist conception of the "wheel-turning" king collapsed in the mid-ninth century and political authority devolved to local monastic leaders. Monarchical authority also ebbed in Korea, but from *c.* 1400 Korean and Vietnamese rulers launched "Neo-Confucian revolutions" modeled upon Chinese political values and institutions.

In contrast to the stability of China's frontiers and foreign relations with its sedentary neighbors, the steppe-based states remained a constant menace to the Chinese Empire. After 900, nomad confederations vulnerable to the whims of shifting tribal allegiances were supplanted by more durable forms of "dual government" pioneered by the Khitan Liao state that established separate administrations for the nomadic and settled populations. The Jin state and later the Yuan Empire of Qubilai Khan also adopted many features of Chinese bureaucratic government. Ultimately, however, Qubilai's attempt to apply the dual government model to the entire Chinese Empire failed, due in no small part to the predatory exactions of the Mongol rulers and their merchant clients as well as to internecine feuding among the Mongol nobles.

The restoration of Chinese rule under the Ming dynasty (1368–1644) completed the Neo-Confucian revolution. The Ming founder embraced the Neo-Confucians' atavistic yearning to restore the autarkic agrarian livelihood and communal village society idealized by Mencius. The Ming state expropriated the large landholdings accumulated by entrepreneurial landowners, stifled commercial enterprise and overseas trade, and reverted to in-kind payments of goods and labor services in place of monetized taxes. These policies devastated the thriving market economy of Song–Yuan times. Only in the sixteenth century, with the original Ming fiscal institutions in ruin, did the Chinese economy regain its earlier dynamism.

FURTHER READING

Adshead, S. A. M. *T'ang China: The Rise of the East in World History.* London: Palgrave Macmillan, 2004.

Beckwith, Christopher. *Empires of the Silk Road: A History of Central Eurasia from the Bronze Age to the Present.* Princeton University Press, 2009.

Bol, Peter K. *Neo-Confucianism in History.* Cambridge, MA: Harvard University Area Center, 2008.

Elman, Benjamin A. *A Cultural History of Civil Examinations in Late Imperial China.* Berkeley, CA: University of California Press, 2000.

Hartwell, Robert M. "Demographic, Political, and Social Transformations of China, 750–1550," *Harvard Journal of Asiatic Studies* 42.2 (1982): 365–442.

Holcombe, Charles. *The Genesis of East Asia, 221 B.C.–A.D. 907*. Honolulu, HI: University of Hawai'i Press, 2001.

Hymes, Robert P. and Conrad Schirokauer, eds. *Ordering the World: Approaches to State and Society in Sung Dynasty China*. Berkeley, CA: University of California Press, 1993.

Kuhn, Dieter. *The Age of Confucian Rule: The Song Transformation of China*. Cambridge, MA: Harvard University Press, 2009.

Lewis, Mark Edward. *China's Cosmopolitan Empire: The Tang Dynasty*. Cambridge, MA: Harvard University Press, 2009.

Mote, Frederick W. *Imperial China, 900–1800*. Cambridge, MA: Harvard University Press, 1999.

Rossabi, Morris, ed. *China among Equals: The Middle Kingdom and its Neighbors, 10th–14th Centuries*. Berkeley, CA: University of California Press, 1983.

Sen, Tansen. *Buddhism, Diplomacy, and Trade: The Realignment of Sino–Indian Relations, 600–1400*. Honolulu, HI: University of Hawai'i Press, 2001.

Smith, Paul J. *Taxing Heaven's Storehouse: Horses, Bureaucrats, and the Destruction of the Sichuan Tea Industry, 1074–1224*. Cambridge, MA: Harvard Council on East Asian Studies, 1991.

Smith, Paul J., and Richard von Glahn, eds. *The Song–Yuan–Ming Transition in Chinese History*. Cambridge, MA: Harvard University Asia Center, 2003.

Wright, Arthur F. *The Sui Dynasty*. New York: Knopf, 1978.

20

The Mongol Empire and inter-civilizational exchange

MICHAL BIRAN

In the early thirteenth century, Chinggis Khan and his heirs built the largest contiguous empire the world has ever seen, an empire that at its height stretched from Korea to Hungary, from Burma and Iraq to Siberia. The Chinggisids not only conquered the whole Eurasian steppe, the home of the nomads, but they also subsumed under their rule three other civilizations: the Chinese, whose centre and hinterland came under their rule by 1279; the Islamic, whose erstwhile centre, Baghdad, was conquered in 1258, after a large share of the eastern Islamic lands had already fallen; and since 1241, the Orthodox Christian outer realms, though not its centre, Byzantium itself. Moreover, as the only superpower of the thirteenth century, the Mongols had a noticeable impact on regions and civilizations outside their purview, such as Japan, Southeast Asia, the Indian subcontinent, the Muslim Middle East, and much of Europe.

The Mongols, a group of demographically marginal nomads, were able to create such a huge empire only by fully mobilizing the resources – both human and material – that they extracted from the regions under their control. More specifically, the formation of the empire, its continued expansion, and the establishment of its administration entailed a vast mobilization of people, goods, techniques, institutions, texts and ideas throughout its territory and farther afield. This process constituted the first step towards a robust inter-civilizational exchange.

Unprecedented human mobility informed the unified and constantly growing empire (1206–60). It continued on a smaller yet highly significant scale when the polity was divided into four khanates, each a regional empire headed by Chinggis Khan's descendants. The Khanate of the Great Khan, later known as the Yuan dynasty (1271–1368), ruled over China, Mongolia,

I would like to thank Tom Allsen for his valuable comments.

Tibet and Manchuria, and enjoyed a nominal, though not uncontested, primacy over its counterparts. The Ilkhanate (1260–1335), literally 'the empire of the submissive khans', ruled in modern Iran, Iraq, Azerbaijan, Turkmenistan, parts of Anatolia, and the Caucasus. The Chaghadaid Khanate held power in Central Asia, from eastern Xinjiang (China) to Uzbekistan, until Timur's rise to power in 1370, and over eastern Central Asia through the late 1600s. The Golden Horde (1260–1480) governed the northwestern Eurasian steppe, from the eastern border of Hungary to Siberia, as well as the Russian principalities. Despite the many, often bloody, disputes between the four polities, they retained a strong sense of Chinggisid unity. In the mid-fourteenth century all four khanates were embroiled in political crises that led to the collapse of the Ilkhanate (1335) and Yuan China (1368), while considerably weakening the steppe khanates. The fall of the Yuan is generally deemed to be the end of the Mongol period, although from a Muslim vantage point, the 'Mongolian moment' sometimes extends until the Timurids' demise in 1500 (see Map 20.1).

Although the Mongol era was relatively short in imperial terms, the Chinggisids' impact on world history has been much more enduring. The primary reasons for this were their active promotion of inter-civilizational contacts and the transformations – not always intended – of religious and ethnic identities that were triggered by their population movements. Moreover, it is hard to ignore the imperial legacy that the Mongols bequeathed to ambitious dynasties across Eurasia, and a host of functioning institutions. This contribution holds true both for empires that paid homage to the Chinggisids (Timurid and Uzbek Central Asia, Qing China and Mughal India) and for those that ardently denied any such debt (Ming China, Muscovy and the Ottomans).

Running the gamut from the "Tatar Yoke" to the Pax Mongolica, the question of the empire's influence on world history has been debated for centuries in a discourse that is often freighted with strong nationalist undertones. The merciless destruction that the Mongols left in their wake is still what most people associate with the empire, and there is no reason to pretend it did not happen. Nevertheless, their legacy is much more complex, as they also triggered a long-lasting cultural effervescence; a thriving artistic and scientific exchange; booming international trade; new and abiding forms of legitimacy, jurisprudence and imperial culture; and a host of religious, ethnic and political changes. What is more, the Mongols integrated Eurasia on an unprecedented scale, a globalization of the Old World that contributed to the discovery of the New World and helped shape the early modern period.

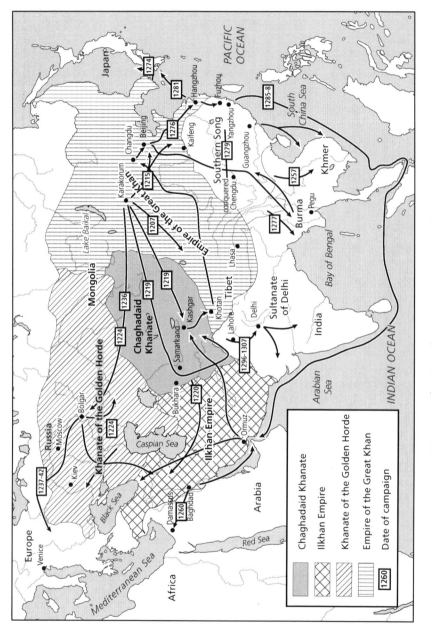

Map 20.1. The Mongol conquests and the Four Khanates

The focus of this chapter is on the Mongols' promotion of cultural, religious and economic exchange. In addition, it will discuss the legacy that they bequeathed to future empires. Before we proceed, though, let us set the stage with a sketch of the Mongols' imperial enterprise.

Empire building

In 1206, when Temüjin united the Mongolian tribes after more than two decades of in-fighting and was enthroned as Chinggis Khan, he had no intention of conquering the world. However, the ensuing spate of victories convinced both Chinggis Khan and everyone else around him that he was destined to rule the planet. The political fragmentation of Eurasia in the centuries that preceded the Mongols' rise and the emergence of post-nomadic states in eastern, central and western Asia were contributing factors, but Chinggis Khan's policies – above all the creative use of the Inner Asian cultural legacy and his pragmatic willingness to learn from others – merit the lion's share of credit behind the Mongols' success.

The basis for supra-tribal unity in Mongolia was the legacy of the prior steppe empires, most notably the Turks (c. 552–743), as these polities bequeathed a religio-political ideology and templates for military organization. Steppe ideology centred around the belief in Tengri (Heaven), the supreme sky god, who conferred heavenly charisma (suu) and the right to rule on earth to a single clan, each of whose members could be elevated to the khaqanate – the supreme office of the ruler. As Tengri did not bestow his mandate on every generation, its possession by the khaqan was confirmed by triumph on the battlefield and by the shamanic apparatus. The sovereign had certain shamanic functions, and his legitimacy was reinforced by controlling the sacred territory of the Orkhon River in Central Mongolia, where the Turks etched the Orkhon inscriptions and the Mongols built their capital, Qara Qorum, some four hundred years later. Following the demise of the Turks' successors, the Uighurs in Mongolia (744–840) and the Khazars in the western steppes (c. 618–965), no khaqan had tried to unite the steppe. However, the ideology was merely held 'in reserve', waiting to be put to fruition by future unifiers like Chinggis Khan.

More practical means behind the conquest's success was the organization of the army: Chinggis Khan retained the typical decimal unit that was characteristic of former Inner Asian empires, in which armies were arranged into units of ten and larger units based on powers of ten, but abolished its linkage to the tribal system: the new Mongol units often combined people from different tribes and were led by Chinggis Khan's *nökers* (personal allies), rather than tribal chiefs. Chosen on the basis of merit and loyalty, this new elite provided the Mongols with a most professional military leadership. Moreover, the khan could confidently assign troops to fight on the extremities of Eurasia without fear of treason. Since every Mongol was a soldier (women offered logistical support), this reorganization begat social revolution: The soldiers' loyalty was transferred from tribe to commander and, higher up the chain, to the Chinggisid family. Moreover, allegiance was further buttressed by draconian disciplinary measures and booty. The rules governing the behaviour in these units, together with the growing body of legal precedents that Chinggis Khan ordered to register from 1206 onwards, were probably the basis for the famous *Jasaq* (Turkic: *Yasa*) – the ever-evolving law code ascribed to Chinggis Khan, which remained valid throughout the empire in conjunction with local laws.

The decimal organization was also a convenient means for incorporating new soldiers: During their campaigns, the Mongols eliminated existing nomadic elites and reorganized their troops into units headed by their loyal followers. This enabled them to impose a single, centralized authority across the whole steppe and mobilize its chief military resource – mounted archers. In turn, this system was broadened to include soldiers from the sedentary population. As a result, the more the Mongols conquered, the more manpower they had for their next conquests. As the troops advanced, the Mongols built roads and bridges and seized arms, thereby laying the groundwork for further expansion. In the process, they collected arms along with artisans who were transferred eastward in the service of the empire.

Chinggis Khan also retained the Inner Asian institution of the Royal Guard (*keshig*) that became the incubator of the military and administrative elite. The guard was responsible for the khan's personal security and general well-being: its ranks included officers who were responsible for his food and drink, garments, weapons, and herds; others were charged with writing his decrees and recording his deeds. The *keshig* also carried out police functions and served as the imperial crack troops. Its men were recruited from the decimal units, as commanders were instructed to assign both their sons and top warriors – regardless of their genealogy – to the elite guard. Consequently, the *keshig* served as both a reservoir of potential hostages (to which sons of subject rulers and high officials were later added) and a training centre for future Mongol commanders.

This organization, the quality of the commanders, the loyalty of the troops and their skill in mobile warfare, combined with meticulous operational planning, were among the keys to the Mongol success. Another factor was the devastation and massacres on an unprecedented scale that accompanied the conquests. This violence should not be interpreted as wanton cruelty, for it was a strategic ploy that went beyond psychological warfare. The destruction was a brutal yet effective means of compensating for the Mongols' numerical inferiority and preventing future resistance: More specifically, the empire ravaged much more territory than it kept, thereby creating a wide belt of destruction around its borders. This buffer protected Mongol territory from future incursions, facilitated the Mongols' continuous expansion and increased their pasture lands. At later stages of the conquest (e.g. South China), the devastation was substantially reduced, as by then the conquerors had realized that their subjects were more useful alive. In some areas, the restoration was as potent as the wreckage.

Another major reason for the Mongol success was their willingness and capacity to learn from others. A case in point was the Chinese and Iranian siege engineers whose skills were used by the empire. For the campaign in South China, it even built a navy. However, the Mongols' eye for talent and innovation was most conspicuous in the field of administration, where they lacked not only numbers but experts and skills. As early as 1204, Chinggis Khan adopted the Uighur script for writing Mongolian, thereby creating a literate staff. Afterwards, he drew on experienced subjects to administer the conquered territories.

The administration evolved with the empire's growth and was systematized, first and foremost, by two of Chinggis' heirs, the khans Ögödei (r. 1229–41) and Möngke (r. 1251–9). While the bureaucracy's lower echelons were manned primarily by the subjected population, Mongols played a major role in its upper levels, which were inherently patrimonial. The Central Secretariat, a sort of Mongol government, evolved out of the *keshig* and its members were personally loyal to the khan. The Secretariat was based in Qara Qorum, the Mongol capital, which Ögödei erected in 1237. Its chief priority was to secure resources for the empire's functioning and continued expansion.

For the most part, Mongol rule was direct. This was partly because many of the elites were eliminated during the conquests. That said, former steppe empires usually settled for indirect administration, leaving former elites to govern their own lands. Mongol direct rule was administered by mobile secretariats (*xingsheng*) that branched off from the central government. The *xingsheng* indeed governed North China, Turkestan, and Northern Iran, eventually serving as the nucleus for Yuan China, Ilkhanid Iran and the

Chaghadaid administrations. Led by experienced non-Mongol administrators, such as the Khwarizmian merchants Mahmud Yalawach and his son Mas'ud Beg or the Khitan Yelü Chucai, their main duties were census taking and tax collection. The census, which was adopted from the Chinese, was the key element in Mongol efforts to harvest their domains, as it was used to impose taxes, recruit troops and labour and identify natural and human resources. The Mongols usually retained existing taxes, but also tacked on the *Qubchir* (contributions), a special levy to meet the rulers' immediate needs, and later the *Tamgha*, a commercial tax. The nomads also paid taxes and were rewarded, above all, from the centrally collected and then redistributed booty.

The Mongol administration had a dual character in several respects: From Ögödei's time onwards, the military and civil administrations were mostly separated. In addition, the Mongols often preferred double-staffing administrative posts, frequently pairing together home-grown and foreign officials. This method is well-documented in the Yuan dynasty, but was apparently also employed in the Ilkhanate. The idea was to have the two officials keep each other in check, a technique that the Mongols were indeed very fond of. Since the empire viewed the administration of all the sedentary lands – whether in China, Turkestan or Iran – as basically the same (despite local variants), they often exchanged administrative personnel.

In a number of cases, though, local dynasts were permitted to remain in place and govern with the empire's stamp of approval and under the supervision of Mongolian-appointed imperial residents known as *darughachi*, *basqaq* or *shiḥna* – a post inherited from the Qara Khitai. These officials also served in directly administered territories. This indirect administration existed mainly in regions north of the steppe: most prominently the Rus' principalities, but also the northern tribes of Manchuria and Siberia and various kingdoms on the khanates' margins, such as Armenia, Georgia, Anatolia, Tibet and Korea. These polities had to pay tribute to the Mongol treasury, participate in the census, provide military units when required, and send their leaders' relatives to the imperial guards.

Communication across the vast empire was maintained by the *Jam*, the mounted postal courier system. Though perhaps based on Khitan precedent, the *Jam* was systematized by Ögödei: Each station was located about every 33 to 45 kilometres from the next, and provided horses, fodder and couriers for authorized travelers who were able to cover about 350–400 kilometres a day. This network enabled the khan to transmit his orders efficiently, acquire information from the far reaches of the empire, and secure the roads for ambassadors and merchants.

The khan's attempts at centralization were balanced by the nomadic conception of the empire as the common property of all the Chinggisids, whereby the ruler was but *primus inter pares*. A prime example of this mindset was the appanage (*Qubi*). During the conquest period, vast territories were parcelled out to various Chinggisids, including women. While the central government administered the appanages, their revenues were forwarded directly to their owners. In a similar vein, the mobile secretariats were staffed with appointees of both the khan and the different princes, so that the interests of the entire Chinggisid clan were taken into account. Reforms to the administration were usually implemented in tandem with new waves of expansion. One reason for this timing was that the government had then secured funds for new campaigns, but it also stemmed from the need for further expansion in order to gain the traditional Mongol elites' consent for increased centralization. The empire's expansion and centralization reached their peak under Möngke, although even he failed to abolish the appanages. The dismantlement of the united empire after Möngke's death in 1259 – due to succession struggles, the sheer girth of the polity and the fact that it had reached the steppe's ecological borders – appreciably curtailed the resources that each khanate could muster for further expansion. Apart from South China, where the area's wealth and prestige justified the great effort needed for conquest, there was no significant Mongol expansion after the empire's dissolution. With respect to administration, local strategies became more important to the four successor states, but Mongol institutions (such as the *keshig, Jam*, and tax apparatus) were retained and the khanates continued to exchange administrators.

Cross-cultural exchange

The immense size of the Mongol Empire encouraged cross-cultural ties both within and beyond its borders, as no polity had hitherto commanded such a large portion of Eurasia's talent pool. However, as adeptly illustrated in the seminal works of Thomas T. Allsen,[1] the Mongols were not simply a passive medium that enabled such contacts to take place. Instead, they were the main agents who promoted and directed such contacts. What is more, they served as a filter that determined which particular cultural elements would be diffused across the continent. As a result, the Mongols' nomadic culture

---

[1] Especially Thomas T. Allsen, *Culture and Conquest in Mongol Eurasia* (Cambridge University Press, 2001). See also Allsen's other works in the further reading.

had an enormous impact on what the sedentary civilizations exchanged. This connection was initiated by the Mongols' invasion of Turkestan in the 1220s, which drew on the human and material resources of northeast Asia. Following this campaign, the Mongols returned home with talent and material goods from the Muslim world. In fact, the process of empire building, which as aforementioned involved a massive flow of human and material resources, was often the first stage of cross-cultural ties. Since the Chinggisids regarded skilled individuals as a form of booty to be distributed across the empire and amongst the family, myriads of people were transferred across Eurasia to provide for the empire's needs – military, administrative and cultural.

The first and most potent catalyst for this mobilization was the army, as the Mongols appropriated the defeated and submitted populations – both nomad and sedentary – and organized them into decimal units, which were sent to wage war across the continent. In turn, the advance of this formidable army instigated a mass flight of people, as throngs of refugees from all classes and professions sought to escape the approaching storm. Furthermore, the empire transferred thousands of farmers and artisans to repopulate and revive the devastated areas. The Mongols also looked for experts in fields as varied as administration, military technology, trade, religion, craftsmanship, science and entertainment. The recruitment of professionals was systematized as early as the late 1230s by means of a census in which people were classified according to vocational skills. Later on, the different khanates competed for and exchanged specialists for the purpose of optimizing their sedentary lands' economic and cultural wealth and enhancing their kingly reputation. Additionally, the Mongols' reputation for rewarding loyal retainers, their encouragement of trade, and their religious pluralism attracted many gifted people to Chinggisid courts.

Dating back to the time of Chinggis Khan, the Mongol administration's recruitment of foreign specialists encouraged further mobilization and exchange. This policy was fine-tuned in Yuan China (where the demographic imbalance between rulers and ruled was far greater than in other regions), as a special category of *semuren* ('people of various kinds', i.e. non-Mongols and non-Chinese) was created for the many foreigners who played a significant role in the bureaucracy. With respect to privileges, the *semuren* outranked the local Chinese subjects and were second only to the Mongols themselves. The empire preferred immigrants from nomadic and post-nomadic empires such as those of the Khitans, Uighurs, or Khwarazmians because they were not only well-versed in the laws of the cities, but had connections to the steppe.

That said, the case of Marco Polo epitomizes the fact that other talented people were also welcome. For the purpose of winning over the loyalty of these newcomers, the Mongols sought to give them 'a taste of home', importing foreign (mostly Muslim) food, medicine and entertainment to, say, Yuan China. While the situation in China is far better-documented than in other khanates, there is evidence of a certain presence of Far Eastern food, medicine, knowledge and entertainment in Mongol Iran and apparently the steppe khanates.

Most of what was conveyed throughout the empire was not the Mongols' own culture, but rather elements from that of their sedentary subjects. However, it was the Chinggisids who initiated the bulk of these exchanges. The prime movers of this culture were imperial agents, including diplomats, merchants, administrators, artisans, soldiers and hostages. The particular cultural goods that diffused across Eurasia were those compatible with Mongol norms and beliefs, such as medicine (i.e. healing), astronomy and divination (reading of the heavens), geography and cartography (reading of the earth), and thus the Mongols also promoted scientific transfers. In short, the flow of people, ideas, and goods across Eurasia was determined to a large extent by the Mongols' affinities and needs.

The extensive mobilization along with growing trade (discussed below) elicited a constant and voluminous movement of people, objects and ideas throughout Eurasia. These developments not only encouraged integration, but also inspired the creation of tools such as maps, multilingual dictionaries and travel literature that facilitated further contacts both within and outside the empire. For example, in the thirteenth and fourteenth centuries, multilingual dictionaries could be found not only in Iran and China, but also in Armenia, Korea, North India, Egypt, Yemen and Crimea. Likewise, the two most famous travelogues, those of Marco Polo and of Ibn Battuta, were compiled by natives of Venice and Tangier (in North Africa), respectively. The broadening of intellectual horizons under the Mongols finds expression in, among other works, the first true history of the world, which was compiled for the Ilkhans in Persia by their vizier Rashīd al-Dīn (d. 1318) – a polymath of Jewish origin whose diverse interests included medicine, theology, cooking, agriculture, history and geography. His *Compendium of Chronicles* (*Jāmi' al-tawārīkh*) offered not only a detailed history of the Mongols from the pre-Chinggisid period to the reign of Qubilai's successor, Temür Öljeitü (r. 1307–1311), but also sections dedicated to the annals of China, India, the Muslim world, the Jews, and the Franks, as well as comprehensive genealogical and geographical appendixes (see Figure 20.1).

Figure 20.1 The Birth of the Prophet Muhammad, miniature from the *'Jāmi' al-tawārīkh* of Rashīd al-Dīn, *c*. 1307 (vellum) (Edinburgh University Library, Scotland. With kind permission of the University of Edinburgh / Bridgeman Images)

Like the official histories in China, this tome was compiled by a team of research assistants under the direction of Rashīd al-Dīn. The result was that more information about the world (especially East Asia) became available in the Muslim Middle East. Produced in the 1330s with the help of Muslim cartographers, maps showing, inter alia, over a hundred places in western Europe and over thirty in Africa, also increased knowledge about the world in Yuan China. Correspondingly, the Europeans expanded the limits of their own knowledge to Central, East, South and Southeast Asia, and Mongols and Tatars were extolled in European literary works from *The Canterbury Tales* to *The Divine Comedy*.

The main axes of Mongol cross-cultural exchange ran between the Sinitic and Islamic civilizations, whereas the Christian Orthodox were a relatively marginal partner. This was mostly because China and the Muslim world, roughly equivalent in terms of culture, had much more to offer the Mongols than did the hinterlands of Orthodox Christianity that came under the empire's control. Although the Russians supplied soldiers and artisans to the far corners of Eurasia, they lacked both administrative personnel with experience in serving nomadic rulers, and scientists – astronomers, geographers, mathematicians – of the stature of their prestigious Chinese, Central Asian or Iranian counterparts. Furthermore, the Mongols shared the same territory with their sedentary subjects in Iran, Central Asia and China, a fact that encouraged all the parties to share economic resources and enhance collaboration between their specialists. Conversely, the Mongols in the Golden Horde remained on the steppe, at a distance from their Russian subjects who were allowed to retain their own leaders. In addition, the political alliance between Yuan China and Ilkhanid Iran encouraged mutual exchange.

Another facet of cross-cultural exchange was the direct impact that Mongolian culture had on the Mongols' subjects and neighbours. The unparalleled success of the Chinggisids spawned imitation throughout Eurasia in all that concerned Mongolian names, clothes, hair style, diet and music. For instance, elements of 'Tatar dress' (the medieval equivalent of blue jeans), including fabric with small patterns, vests, and fur trim were adopted in fourteenth-century England, in Yuan and Ming China, Ilkhanid and post-Ilkhanid Iran, Chaghadaid and Timurid Central Asia, Mamluk Egypt and North India. Tent furnishings such as rugs and tapestries, which the Mongols used to make their palaces resemble tents, became high fashion among ruling elites from the Pacific to the Adriatic. Pasta, originating in the Middle East and favoured by the Mongols, spread into both China and Italy. Additionally, Eurasian elites became well-versed in Chinggisid lore. Mongol social norms also penetrated their subjects' lives. For instance, levirate marriages, condemned by both Islamic law and Confucian ethics, were not rare in Ilkhanid Iran and Yuan China. Lastly, following in the footsteps of their Mongol counterparts, Persian and Korean princesses attained an elevated status and became intimately involved in politics.

What were the ramifications of these cross-cultural ties in the post-thirteenth century world? It appears as though not all the imported knowledge was received with open arms or had a lasting impact. A case in point is intellectual property, such as medical theories. These sorts of goods did not travel well, for they were closely linked to particular worldviews. Technologies disseminated more easily: the Mongols introduced gunpowder from China to the West (at this stage, though, it was far from a military 'game changer'), while the art of distilling sugar arrived East from the Muslim world. Material culture, especially art, was often well-received and adapted to local conditions and tastes. The enduring influence of Chinese painting on Persian art is a well-documented legacy of the Mongol period, which even left its mark in Italy. Chinese-inspired Ilkhanid paintings and attendant new methods surfaced throughout the lands of Islam, where they became the standard for quality painting from the Ottoman Empire to Mughal India. In sum, Mongol policies fostered Eurasian integration on an unprecedented scale.

Religious exchange

The Mongols neither preached nor tried to force their indigenous faith – a complex polytheistic religion featuring Tengri, the sky God, and shamanic practices – on their subjects. However, their policies and inclinations culminated in substantial religious transformations throughout Eurasia, most notably the appreciable expansion of Islam and the flourishing of Tibetan Buddhism.

Even the empire's harshest critics have praised its 'religious tolerance'. In fact, the Chinggisids sprang forth from a multi-religious environment where no religion was considered exclusive. Moreover, they drew a distinction between the purview of their own indigenous beliefs and that of world religions: the former, now generally termed Shamanism, influenced the conditions in this life; and world religions stressed the afterlife. These faiths were not seen as competitors of Mongol Shamanism, but as another path to Tengri, the supreme god who is revered by all religions, each in their own way. Spiritual leaders who impressed Chinggis Khan, such as Changchun (1148–1227), the Daoist priest he summoned to reveal the secret of longevity – received tax exemptions and other privileges, in return for which they were supposed to pray for the leader's well-being. Under Chinggis' heirs, this policy was broadened to include experts from all the dominant faiths (Buddhism, Daoism, Confucianism, Islam and Christianity). However, the privileges were not extended to the clergy of religions without state power, such as Judaism, Manichaeism or Zoroastrianism. The Mongols also quickly realized the benefit of securing acquiescence through spiritual leaders and freedom of worship. As such, their relative religious tolerance was a component of their *realpolitik*. In other words, it was not only meant to soothe the deities, but to shore up their rule in the subjugated lands. Chinggis Khan was ready to let everyone observe their own rite, so long as it neither contravened the Mongol faith nor posed a threat to his political standing. If it did pose a threat, as in the case of the shaman Teb Tengri, who tried to divide Chinggis Khan's family, he immediately had him killed. Similarly, the Mongols did not hesitate to exploit religious sensitivities: when Jebe and Sübetei reached Armenia in the 1220s, they painted crosses on their troops' shields as a tactical ploy against their Christian enemies. When the Armenians lowered their guard upon seeing the holy symbol, the Mongol generals immediately launched their attack.[2]

2 Peter Jackson, 'The Mongols and the Faith of the Conquered', in Reuven Amitai and Michal Biran (eds.), *Mongols, Turks, and Others: Eurasian Nomads and the Sedentary World* (Leiden: Brill, 2005): 245–90.

As an imperial elite, the Mongols were a coveted prize for missionaries of various creeds. So long as the empire was united, Tengri remained the sole god of the ruling class. However, after its dissolution, each khanate adopted a world religion either to ingratiate itself with the local population or, conversely, to accentuate its ideological independence. Muslim civilization, by far the most mobile, mercantile and cosmopolitan society in the empire, had already amassed considerable experience assimilating people, including many nomads, and was the great winner in the conversion race: Adopted by three out of the four Mongol khanates, Islam also expanded into other regions, such as China, India, Southeast Asia, and Africa. Its unbridled expansion, which began even before the Islamization of the khanates, was one of the unintended ramifications of Mongol population movements.

The Islamization of the Mongol khanates – the Ilkhanate in 1295, and the Golden Horde and Chaghadaids over the next fifty or so years – was a gradual and complex process, stemming mainly from the deep ties between the Chinggisids and their Muslim subjects, notably the Turkish officers and soldiers comprising the bulk of the Mongol armies. Conversion stories suggest that Mongol Islamization began with a royal conversion and then spread downward. However, at least in the case of the Ilkhanate and the Chaghadaids, the process seems to have started with the military's rank and file, primarily due to acculturation, intermarriage and charismatic preachers. While spirituality's role in conversion dynamics cannot be denied, political motives must also be factored into the equation, at least with respect to the leadership: For example, the Ilkhan Ghazan (1295–1304) embraced Islam during his struggle for the crown, thereby winning the support of Muslim segments in the army, not least a senior Mongol commander. Furthermore, the annihilation of the caliphate meant that there was no longer a universal leader of Islam (as the pope purported to be for Western Christendom). For this reason, the Mongols were immediately in the running for the position upon converting to Islam. Furthermore, they instantly merited a degree of legitimacy in the eyes of their Muslim subjects that was beyond the reach of any 'infidel'. This may have been another incentive behind, or at least a favourable by-product of, the conversion of the Ilkhanids. In contrast, the Islamization of the Golden Horde's rulers set them apart from their Christian Russian subjects, while drawing them closer to the area's Turks.

Another factor that promoted conversion was the Sufis. By dint of their emphasis on respect for other religious traditions and their capacity for 'magic' (i.e. healing), Sufis were the impetus behind many royal conversions, and have maintained their position as leading agents of Islamization ever since. Royal conversions and the campaigns against non-believers that usually ensued (such as the persecution of Buddhism in Iran during Ghazan's reign) further consolidated Islam's position in the Mongol khanates. While most of the population in the Ilkhanate was already Muslim, the conversion of the Chaghadaid and Golden Horde's khans enabled Islam to penetrate the steppes of Central Asia and eastern Europe. By the mid-1300s, the Islamization of the Chinggisids gave rise to a new Turco-Mongolian elite between the Tian Shan mountains (in Kyrgyzstan and China) and the Volga. This group practised Islam, spoke Turkish, and honoured the traditions of the Mongol Empire. It is difficult to recall another era in which such a vast expanse of land shared so much in terms of language, religion, and culture.

Mongol China never embraced Islam, but the Muslim presence therein expanded considerably during this period. Muslims arrived both as conscripts, not least the thousands of relocated artisans, and of their own volition, mainly merchants or experts who often found jobs in the Yuan administration. Prominent officials, such as Sayid Ajjal (d. 1283), Qubilai's governor of Yunnan, attracted many co-religionists to the region. Lastly, a few Mongol princes and their troops converted to Islam as well.

Although less directly, the Mongols also pushed Islam into the Indian subcontinent, mostly in the form of several waves of Central Asian refugees fleeing the army of Chinggis Khan and later upheavals in the Chaghadaid Khanate. Taking a page out of the Mongol attitude towards human talent, several Delhi sultans actively enticed Muslim religious scholars, scientists, merchants and soldiers into their realm. These immigrants enhanced the religious prestige of the newly established Delhi sultanate and bolstered its expansion into southern India. The growth of maritime trade also led to the establishment of sizeable Muslim communities in Indian ports, especially along the Gujarat coast. Some of these communities later played a key role in the conversion of other regions.

More indirectly still was the Mongols' part in the Islamization of Southeast Asia and Africa. Since the main catalysts were traders, the thriving commerce in the Mongol Empire galvanized this process. Marco Polo observed that the kingdom of Perlak in northern Sumatra 'is so much frequented by the Saracen merchants that they have converted the natives to the law of Muhammad'. As in China and India, the Muslim faith began to thrive in Africa long before the Mongol period, especially in Mali, Zanzibar and Zimbabwe. The Islamization of these regions was far from complete in the thirteenth century, but Islam continued to make strides in most of them.

The Mongol period was also fecund in terms of Muslim relations with members of other faiths, as the empire brought together experts on Islam, Buddhism, Christianity and Shamanism. 'Ala' al-Din al-Simnani (d. 1336), a famous Sufi who was raised in the Ilkhanid guard, recorded his conversations with Buddhist monks and Mongol shamans in the court of the Ilkhan Arghun (r. 1284–91). He even concluded that the Dharma, Buddhist law, is tantamount to shari'a law. Sufi analogies between various religions and water in different colours (i.e. essentially the same) are also reminiscent of the above-mentioned Mongol outlook.

A fascinating manifestation of these interfaith contacts can be found in Ilkhanid and Timurid art. For the first and last time in the history of Muslim art, we find visual representations of Muhammad (and other prophets). In these renderings, Muhammad is placed in Buddhist or Christian models. For instance, the Prophet's birth in the *Compendium of Chronicles* is based on the Christian Nativity scene (see Figure 20.1). These portraits must have appealed to the Chinggisids' taste, as they surface in competing Sunni and Shi'ite works aimed at proselytizing the Mongols. Put differently, the missionary use of visual culture that is characteristic of Buddhism was adopted in Muslim Iran, where religious art merged Buddhist, Christian and Chinese elements.[3]

Another example of a royal conversion took place in China: Qubilai's adoption of Tibetan Buddhism under the influence of Phags Pa (1235–80), a brilliant Tibetan monk. This religion, which was quite popular among Ilkhanid and Chaghadaid rulers before their Islamization, further legitimized Qubilai's rule. Like many outside rulers of China before him, Qubilai was presented as *chakravartin* – the ideal universal Buddhist king who turns the wheel of Dharma. The specific attraction of Tibetan Buddhism, aside from its political nature and shamanic magic and colours, was that it conspicuously distinguished the Mongols from their Chinese subjects, while appealing to the Tibetan and Uighur populace. Unlike the Mongols' adoption of Tibetan Buddhism in the sixteenth century or their conversion to Islam, embracing Buddhism at this stage was a highly elitist phenomenon that won few souls among the Mongol rank and file. In any event, the Chinggisids' favourable attitude towards Buddhism and tolerant outlook brought together Buddhists of different cultural backgrounds and streams. For example, the description of the faith in the *Compendium of Chronicles* includes elements of Chinese, Tibetan, Uighur, and Kashmiri Buddhism. In Yuan China, Korean and

3 Johan Elverskog, *Buddhism and Islam on the Silk Road* (Philadelphia, PA: University of Pennsylvania Press, 2010): 167–74.

Japanese Buddhists also took part in this intra-faith exchange. Multiple translations of Buddhist texts (mainly from Tibetan to Mongolian, Uighur and Chinese) appeared in China and Central Asia. Furthermore, the artistic and architectural forms of Tibetan Buddhism became integral components of Yuan palaces. The Mongols oversaw the completion of Tibet's unseating of India as the centre of Buddhism, and the beginning of theocratic rule in Tibet. Tibetan Buddhism remained an imperial cult even in Ming China (1368–1644), and its standing only improved under the Manchu Qing dynasty (1644–1911), which presented its emperors as incarnations of Chinggis Khan and Qubilai. The main spiritual competition on the steppe during the post-Mongol era pitted Islam against Tibetan Buddhism.[4]

In contrast, plagued by doctrinal schism, stressing exclusivity, less adept in magic and expecting the khans to accept the pope's superiority, Christianity failed, despite intensive missionary efforts, to translate the freedom and access into new territories under the Chinggisids into durable achievements.

Economic exchange

Similar to the cultural sphere, the Mongols cultivated economic ties that extended well beyond the empire's borders. They inherited, invigorated, and extended various trade routes as well as sundry means for resource extraction and exchange, including plunder, asset redistribution, taxation or tribute, and gift giving. Not only did the Mongols provide security and transportation infrastructure, but they were also active participants in trade as both investors and consumers.

Trade had long been essential to nomads, as their own resources did not always cover all their needs and nomadic political culture requires leaders to redistribute wealth among their followers. The very formation of nomad states heightened the demand for precious metals, gems, and especially fine cloth, for the newfangled regime needed these items to assert its authority. Chinggis Khan was certainly aware of the benefits of commerce, which was the premise behind his expansion into Central Asia. Likewise, Muslim and Uighur merchants were among his earliest supporters. As the empire grew, systemic plunder was the major source of luxury goods. Redistributed among the Mongol elite, the khans and princes often chose to invest these considerable fortunes in international trade. Consequently, they entrusted

---

4 Elverskog, *Buddhism and Islam*, 145–62.

their capital to agents, *ortoqs* (partners), most of whom were Muslims and Uighurs. The *ortoq* was a trader (or trading company) acting on behalf of or financed by a Mongol or other notable, in return for a share of the profits. To a large degree, the revenues were expended on the lavish consumption that typifies the nouveau riche. The establishment of Qara Qorum also induced trade, for the resources of Mongolia could hardly support a city that was large by steppe standards and the Chinggisids were ready to pay handsome sums to enjoy the best of the sedentary world while remaining on the steppe. Many traders eagerly exploited these opportunities, benefiting from the safe roads and access to imperial post stations. As a result, international trade in both luxury and bulk goods resumed soon after the conquests.

The slowing of Mongol expansion after the empire's division accelerated the expansion of trade. As taxation replaced booty as the main source of revenue, the different Mongol governments continued to advance both local and international commerce, which provided taxes, markets, profits, and prestige. The khanates competed for commercial specialists, established the infrastructure for transcontinental travel and played a significant role in both trans-civilizational (East–West) and trans-ecological (North–South) exchanges. In the far north, furs were obtained from Siberia and Manchuria by dint of traditional barter arrangements and tributary relationships. At the centre, Chinggisid royal courts were undergirded by redistribution, namely rulers lavishing goods that they extracted from the sedentary populace on their retinues and collaborators. Mongol capitals in Azerbaijan, the Volga region and North China became the hubs of international markets, so that trade routes shifted northwards. New urban centres of exchange materialized along the Silk Roads in Central Asia, and particularly in the Volga region.

The overland routes flourished during the united empire period, and picked up again in the first half of the fourteenth century, after the 1304 peace between the Mongol khanates. Yet the maritime routes also thrived, especially from the 1280s onward, due to the Mongol takeover of the Song dynasty, not least its busy ports, and the enmity between the Yuan and the Mongol princes in Central Asia, which encouraged the shift from land to sea. South China's ports, notably Quanzhou (in modern Fujian), became centres of international trade that reached far beyond the empire's borders, attracting merchants from India, the Muslim world, Southeast Asia and Europe. The main axes of exchange were between South China – the terminus for goods from East and Southeast Asia – and India; and between the latter and the Persian Gulf or Red Sea. From there, the cargos continued either by land to Iran, Iraq, Anatolia and Europe (both eastern and western) or via the maritime routes through Egypt and the Mediterranean to Europe or from Aden to the shores of East Africa. Shorter sea routes catered to the lively slave trade between the Golden Horde's ports on the Black Sea and Egypt, involving Muslim, Italian and Byzantine traders. The maritime and overland routes were often closely linked: the Black Sea ports serviced luxury goods arriving from the East over continental routes and caravans headed inland from the Indian coast during seasons unsuited for sailing. This extensive network, indeed, connected the entire Old World. Furthermore, sophisticated market-driven exchange prevailed in the more developed economies of the south. For example, Yuan workshops imported cobalt from northern Europe in order to produce blue and white porcelain, which was in high demand throughout the Muslim world. Likewise, the Ilkhanid court's fiscal policy took into account currency exchanges and bullion flows that ranged from the Indian Ocean to the Mediterranean. Yuan paper money was backed by silver, and much of the Song dynasty's silver reserves reached westwards through the *ortoqs*. In fact, the period spanning the 1280s and 1360s – from the conquest of Song China to the fall of the Yuan – bore witness to a sharp rise in the use of silver across Eurasia, from England to Bengal and North Africa. Uncoined silver became the standard unit for pricing transactions throughout Eurasia, even when paid by other means.[5]

The key non-Mongol players in this global network were the Indian kingdoms and the Italian city-states. The latter established permanent, government-backed colonies in Caffa and Tana on the Black Sea and in Ilkhanid Tabriz, while many Italian adventurers and entrepreneurs (the best known of whom is Marco Polo) embarked on private ventures further east.

Apart from commerce, taxation and booty, several other institutions underpinned economic exchange both within and outside the empire. The Mongol system of appanages linked up the various khanate economies: After the empire's dissolution, most princes had appanages in other Chinggisid realms. The proceeds from these estates were collected by the local khanate, sometimes under the supervision of the owner's representatives, and transferred to the beneficiary. However, the revenues were frozen in the event of a war between the two domains. For instance, when Chapar b. Qaidu, the Ogedeid prince, ended a forty-year conflict by submitting to the Yuan in 1310, he received the dormant profits from his father's Chinese appanages.

5 Kuroda Akinobu, 'The Eurasian Silver Century, 1276–1359: Commensurability and Multiplicity', *Journal of Global History* 4 (2009): 245–69.

Another form of exchange was gift giving, an integral part of any diplomatic mission. These sort of embassies, which Chinese sources viewed as tributary delegations, brought their hosts exotic items (e.g. jewellery, hunting cheetahs, and beautiful slaves), frequently combining statecraft with business, private and/or governmental. In 1297–8, for example, the Ilkhan Ghazan dispatched Fakhr al-Din al-Tibbi, a merchant from Kish (an island in the Persian Gulf), to Yuan on a threefold mission: to advance diplomatic objectives; to collect the ruler's appanage revenues; and to invest 100,000 gold dinars. Needless to say, Fakhr al-Din concomitantly pursued his own business opportunities.

The thriving international exchange survived the fall of the Ilkhanate (1335), as the trade routes merely shifted to the Golden Horde. However, the Yuan collapse (1368) on the heels of the Black Plague in Europe and the Middle East, which coincided with upheavals in the Golden Horde, seriously undermined the Mongol international system of trade.

The legacy of Mongol statecraft

Until a few decades ago, even scholars commonly viewed the Mongol period as a short and bloody interlude that either left no impact on Eurasian history or was responsible for all the troubles that befell the empire's conquered civilizations from that period on. It was easy to overlook the Chinggisids' impact because they did not leave behind an ethnic culture, language, or religion of their own, but a complex and heterogeneous imperial culture. Moreover, they bequeathed a different institutional legacy to each of the various civilizations that they encountered. The deepest imprint was on regions where they ruled the longest and those without a strong indigenous tradition of a centralized state, namely Central Asia and Russia. A certain institutional imprint is also perceptible in China, Iran and even beyond the empire's limits, primarily in the Muslim world. Finally, a distinction must be drawn between the practical use of Mongol institutions and embracing Chinggisid political ideology.

Mongol imperial rule left its mark on subsequent Eurasian empires, both steppe and sown, that is, both nomadic pastoralists and settled agriculturalists. Creative manipulations notwithstanding, the Chinggisid principle, the basic tenet of Mongol ideology according to which only descendants of Chinggis Khan were eligible for supreme rulership, remained valid in Central Asia until the eighteenth century, influencing monarchical behaviour and social hierarchies in Qing China, Mughal India, Muscovy and even the

Ottoman Empire. The ever-evolving *Yasa* played a significant role in the Muslim world, despite various glaring contradictions with Islamic law. The Mongol institution of the postal system was adopted in Ming and Qing China, Safavid Iran and Muscovy; the empire's military organization was adhered to in Ming China and Muscovy (up to the rise of firearms); Chinese provincial borders date back to Yuan times; and the empire's commercial taxation and monetary policies continued to be implemented in Russia, Iran and Central Asia.

Geopolitically, the Mongols relocated the capitals of the khanates towards the northeast, perhaps on account of the nomads' preference for residing closer to the steppe: the Chinese capital was transferred from Kaifeng and Hangzhou to Beijing; in the eastern Islamic world, it moved from Baghdad to Tabriz (in Azerbaijan); Kiev first gave way to Saray (southeast of Kiev) and ultimately to Moscow (northeast yet again); and in Central Asia, Balasaghun (in Kyrgyzstan) ceded to the Almaliq region (in northern Xinjiang). While Azerbaijan retained its importance up to the end of the sixteenth century and Samarkand superseded Almaliq in Central Asia by the late 1300s, the pre-eminence of Beijing and Moscow remains unchallenged.

Furthermore, the Mongols revived the notion of Iran as a distinct political entity within the Muslim world. In China, they created a unified entity that remained undivided throughout the later imperial period and laid the foundation for a multi-ethnic polity, which also controlled large swaths of nomadic lands. Similarly, they turned a group of city-states into the nucleus of a huge Russian empire. With respect to Central Asia, the main effect of the Mongol period was a major ethnic reconfiguration: Mongol population movements led to the disappearance of various established steppe people, such as the Khitans, Tanguts, Uighurs and Qipchaqs, and the emergence of new collectivities, such as the Uzbeks, Qazakhs and Tatars, who became the modern Central Asian Muslim peoples.

Conclusion

The nomadic Mongols embarked upon an unprecedented mobilization of peoples, goods and ideas to forge the largest contiguous empire the world has known. In so doing, they bolstered Eurasian integration and broadened the horizons of their subjects and neighbours. Mongol nomadic culture had an enormous impact on Eurasian exchange under their auspices. While adhering to the legacy of former nomadic empires, the Chinggisids faced a much more complex set of problems, for they not only ruled over the steppe, but over centres of the sedentary civilizations as well. Taking advantage of personnel, institutions and imperial concepts from both East and West, the Mongols developed an imperial administration and culture that merged their indigenous norms with various elements of their subjects' cultures, especially those of the Muslims and Chinese, thereby creating sophisticated means for ruling both steppe and sown. These means continued to stand at the disposal of large Eurasian political units well into the early modern era, and eventually led to the division of the steppe between Muscovy and Qing China at the expense of the nomads.

That said, the Chinggisids' legacy transcended the continental empires. By advancing long-distance commercial and financial exchanges, improving its maritime prowess, forming new collectivities, and ratcheting up the 'connectivity' between different regions, the Mongol Empire ushered in the early modern period. As Samuel Adshead puts it, 'if Europe came to dominate the world, it was because Europe first perceived there was a world to dominate'.[6] When Columbus set out on his first voyage in 1492, his principal objective was to find the land of the 'Great Khan' that emerges from the Book of Marco Polo, whom he ardently admired. Against this backdrop, our globalized world can be viewed as a progeny of the Mongols' imperial enterprise.

FURTHER READING

Adshead, Samuel A. M. *Central Asia in World History*. New York, NY: St Martin's Press, 1993.

Aigle, Denise, ed. *L'Iran face à la domination mongole: Études*. Teheran: Institut Français de Recherche en Iran, 1997.

Akasoy, Anna, Charles Burnett and Ronit Yoeli-Tlalim, eds. *Islam and Tibet: Interactions along the Musk Routes*. Farnham: Ashgate, 2011.

Allsen, Thomas T. *Commodity and Exchange in the Mongol Empire: A Cultural History of Islamic Textiles*. Cambridge University Press, 1997.

Culture and Conquest in Mongol Eurasia. Cambridge University Press, 2001.

Mongol Imperialism: The Policies of the Grand Khan Möngke in China, Russia, and the Islamic Lands, 1251–1259. Berkeley, CA: University of California Press, 1987.

Amitai, Reuven. *The Mongols in the Islamic Lands: Studies in the History of the Ilkhanate*. Aldershot: Ashgate, 2007.

Amitai, Reuven and Michal Biran, eds. *Mongols, Turks, and Others: Eurasian Nomads and the Sedentary World*. Leiden: Brill, 2005.

6 Samuel A. M. Adshead, *Central Asia in World History* (New York: St Martin's Press, 1993): 77.

eds. *Eurasian Nomads as Agents of Cultural Change*. Honolulu, HI: University of Hawai'i Press, 2015.

Amitai-Preiss, Reuven. *Mongols and Mamluks: The Mamluk-Ilkhanid War, 1260–1281*. Cambridge University Press, 1995.

Amitai-Preiss, Reuven and David O. Morgan, eds. *The Mongol Empire and its Legacy*. Leiden: Brill, 1999.

Atwood, Christopher P. *Encyclopedia of Mongolia and the Mongol Empire*. New York, NY: Facts on File, 2004.

Bentley, Jerry H. *Old World Encounters: Cross-Cultural Contacts and Exchanges in Pre-Modern Times*. Oxford University Press, 1993.

Biran, Michal. *Chinggis Khan (The Makers of the Islamic World)*. Oxford: Oneworld, 2007.

'Kitan Migrations in Eurasia (11th–14th centuries)', *Journal of Central Eurasian Studies* 3 (2012): 85–108.

'The Mongol Transformation: From the Steppe to Eurasian Empire', *Medieval Encounters* 10 (2004): 338–61.

Qaidu and the Rise of the Independent Mongol State in Central Asia. Richmond, Surrey: Curzon, 1997.

Birge, Bettine. 'Levirate Marriage and the Revival of Widow Chastity in Yüan China', *Asia Major* 8 (1995): 107–46.

Blair, Sheila S. *A Compendium of Chronicles: Rashid al-Din's Illustrated History of the World*. London: Nour Foundation in Association with Azimuth Editions and Oxford University Press, 1995.

Broadbridge, Anne F. *Kingship and Ideology in the Islamic and Mongol Worlds*. Cambridge University Press, 2008.

Brose, Michael C. *Subjects and Masters: Uyghurs in the Mongol Empire*. Bellingham, WA: Center for East Asian Studies, Western Washington University, 2007.

DeWeese, Devin. *Islamization and Native Religion in the Golden Horde: Baba Tükles and Conversion to Islam in Historical and Epic Tradition*. Philadelphia, PA: Pennsylvania State University Press, 1994.

Di Cosmo, Nicola. 'Black Sea Emporia and the Mongol Empire: A Reassessment of the *Pax Mongolica*', *Journal of the Economic and Social History of the Orient* 53 (2010): 83–108.

Di Cosmo, Nicola, Peter B. Golden, and Allen J. Frank, eds. *The Cambridge History of Inner Asia*. Cambridge University Press, 2009.

Elverskog, Johan. *Buddhism and Islam on the Silk Road*. Philadelphia, PA: University of Pennsylvania Press, 2010.

Endicott-West, Elizabeth. 'Merchant Associations in Yuan China: The *Ortogh*', *Asia Major* 2 (1989): 127–54.

Mongolian Rule in China: Local Administration in the Yuan Dynasty. Cambridge, MA: Council on East Asian Studies, Harvard University, 1989.

Fletcher, Joseph F. 'The Mongols: Ecological and Social Perspective', *Harvard Journal of Asiatic Studies* 46 (1986): 11–50.

Fragner, Bert G. et al., eds. *Pferde in Asien: Geschichte, Handel und Kultur = Horses in Asia: History, Trade and Culture*. Vienna: Verlag der Österreichischen Akademie der Wissenschaften, 2009.

Franke, Herbert. *China under Mongol Rule*. Aldershot: Variorum, 1994.

von Glahn, Richard. 'Monies of Account and Monetary Transition in China, Twelfth to Fourteenth Centuries', *Journal of the Economic and Social History of the Orient* 53 (2010): 463–505.

Halperin, Charles. *Russia and the Mongols: Slavs and the Steppe in Medieval and Early Modern Russia*. Bucharest: Editura Academiei Române, 2007.

Jackson, Peter. *The Delhi Sultanate: A Political and Military History*. Cambridge University Press, 1999.

The Mongols and the West, 1221–1410. New York, NY: Pearson Longman, 2005.

'The State of Research: The Mongol Empire, 1986–1999', *Journal of Medieval History* 26 (2000): 189–210.

Kadoi, Yuko. *Islamic Chinoiserie: The Art of Mongol Iran*. Edinburgh University Press, 2009.

Kauz, Ralph, ed. *Aspects of the Maritime Silk Road: From the Persian Gulf to the East China Sea*. Wiesbaden: Harrassowitz, 2010.

Kim, Hodong. 'The Unity of the Mongol Empire and Continental Exchange over Eurasia', *Journal of Central Eurasian Studies* 1 (2009): 15–42.

Komaroff, Linda, ed. *Beyond the Legacy of Genghis*. Leiden: Brill, 2006.

Kuroda, Akinobu. 'The Eurasian Silver Century, 1276–1359: Commensurability and Multiplicity', *Journal of Global History* 4 (2009): 245–69.

Lambton, Ann K. S. *Community and Change in Medieval Persia: Aspects of Administrative, Economic and Social History, 11th–14th Century*. London: I. B. Tauris, 1988.

Lane, George. *Early Mongol Rule in Thirteenth Century Iran: A Persian Renaissance*. London: Routledge Curzon, 2003.

Langlois, John D., ed. *China under Mongol Rule*. Princeton University Press, 1981.

Larner, John. *Marco Polo and the Discovery of the World*. New Haven, CT: Yale University Press, 1999.

Laufer, Berthold. 'Columbus and Cathay, and the Meaning of America to the Orientalist', *Journal of the American Oriental Society* 51 (1931): 87–103.

Manz, Beatrice F. 'The Rule of the Infidels: The Mongols and the Islamic World', in David O. Morgan and Anthony Reid (eds.), *The Eastern Islamic World Eleventh to Eighteenth Centuries*. Cambridge University Press, 2010: 128–68.

May, Timothy. *The Mongol Art of War*. Yardley, PA: Westholme, 2007.

Melville, Charles. *The Fall of Amir Chupan and the Decline of the Ilkhanate, 1327–37: A Decade of Discord in Mongol Iran*. Bloomington, IN: Indiana University Research Institute for Inner Asian Studies, 1999.

Morgan, David O. *The Mongols*. Oxford: Blackwell Publishing, 2007.

Ostrowski, Donald G. *Muscovy and the Mongols: Cross-Cultural Influences on the Steppe Frontier, 1304–1589*. Cambridge University Press, 1998.

Pochekaev, Roman, Iu. *Khanyĭ Zolotoi Ordy*. St Petersburg: Eurasia, 2010.

Prazniak, Roxanne. 'Siena on the Silk Roads: Ambrogio Lorenzetti and the Mongol Global Century, 1250–1350', *Journal of World History*, 21 (2010): 177–217.

de Rachewiltz, Igor et al., eds. *In the Service of the Khan: Eminent Personalities of the Early Mongol – Yuan Period*. Wiesbaden: Harrassowitz, 1993.

Ratchnevsky, Paul. *Genghis Khan: His Life and Legacy*. Trans. and ed. Thomas N. Haining, Oxford: Basil Blackwell, 1991.

Robinson, David M. *Empire's Twilight: Northeast Asia under the Mongols.* Cambridge, MA: Harvard-Yenching Institute; Harvard University Press, 2009.

Rossabi, Morris. *Khubilai Khan: His Life and Times.* Berkeley, CA: University of California Press, 1988.

Schottenhammer, Angela. *The East Asian Mediterranean – Maritime Crossroads of Culture, Commerce, and Human Migration.* Wiesbaden: Harrassowitz, 2008.

Silverstein, Adam J. *Postal Systems in the Pre-Modern Islamic World.* Cambridge University Press, 2007.

Smith, Paul J. and Richard von Glahn, eds. *The Song–Yuan–Ming Transition in Chinese History.* Cambridge, MA: Harvard University Asia Center, 2003.

Vásáry, István. *Cumans and Tatars: Oriental Military in the pre-Ottoman Balkans 1183–1365.* Cambridge University Press, 2005.

Wink, André. *Al-Hind: The Making of the Indo-Islamic World.* Leiden: Brill: 1997, 2004, vols. II and III.

Winkler, Dietmar W. and Li Tang, eds. *Hidden Treasures and Intercultural Encounters: Studies on East Syriac Christianity in China and Central Asia.* Berlin: Lit Verlag, 2011.

21

Byzantium

JEAN-CLAUDE CHEYNET

The Roman Empire in the East that we call Byzantium is the only European or Mediterranean state formed in antiquity that survived into the dawn of the modern era by metamorphosing itself repeatedly.[1] This demonstrates its capacity for adaptation despite tremendous challenges, since its geographic position meant that it was located on the path of every people on the move from the steppes of Central Asia to the hot deserts of the Arabian peninsula. The Empire experienced multiple transformations. It was the continuation of the Roman Empire in the East, at one time extending again to almost all the Mediterranean shorelines. Then, after the barbarian and Muslim conquests, it was a state reduced to Asia Minor, a few islands and coastal territories, before becoming around the year 1000 once again the primary power of the Mediterranean world. The arrival of the Turks progressively pushed back Byzantine power in two stages, and eventually the Turks were able to prevent an Aegean Greek state from surviving.

Over its long history, Byzantium faced three primary challenges. The first was to push back enemies on borders that stretched for a long time over several continents; the second, to create a political system that put the right leader as the head of the state; the third, to find a balance between support for its central institutions and the necessary room for local elites and populations to have autonomy so as to overcome the natural causes of division – ethnic and linguistic diversity and religious rivalries.

The rulers of Byzantium had major advantages as they faced these challenges. First, they had the Roman legacy of a government that adapted

---

1 For an event-based history of the Empire, see Warren T. Treadgold, *A History of the Byzantine State and Society* (Stanford University Press, 1997). For its structures, see the recent general study by Elizabeth Jeffreys, John Haldon and Robin Cormack (eds.), *The Oxford Handbook of Byzantine Studies* (Oxford University Press, 2008), and Jean-Claude Cheynet, Angeliki Laiou, and Cécile Morrisson (eds.), *Monde byzantin*, 3 vols. (Paris: Presses universitaires de France, 2004–11).

to the circumstances of its time. On the borders where it encountered organized adversaries, such as Persia, the Roman Empire endeavored to establish a network of states under its influence, as in Armenia or in the Arabian peninsula. Expeditions of religious missionaries contributed to strengthening this network also toward Ethiopia in the south. The Byzantines continued this policy, which allowed them to save time and to be on alert for new invasions.

A second advantage was that one religion, Christianity, allowed the hope of religious unity centered on the sovereign. By about 500, Christianity was the religion of the majority of the population, and it served the sovereign, the lieutenant of God on earth. But the faithful were divided into branches, some of which had been rejected as heretical at the Council of Chalcedon in 451. One of these was the Monophysites, who held that Christ had only one nature – divine – rather than the two natures – divine and human – accepted by the majority of the church and the emperor. The Monophysites hoped for a long time to join with the emperor, and in 500 Emperor Anastasius (r. 491–518) was favorably disposed toward them. But from the time of Justinian in the mid-sixth century on, and despite the sentiments of the empress Theodora, orthodox Chalcedonians controlled the official Church. In the second half of the sixth century, the Monophysites formed autonomous churches, including the Coptic Church and the Jacobite (Syriac Orthodox) Churches. The emperors were constantly concerned with attaining religious unity, a pipedream that was pursued in vain as long as the eastern provinces were a part of the Empire. The highest of the Chalcedonian hierarchy favored the imperial ideology of Constantinople, but this did not mean that the Monophysites envisioned or wished for the disappearance of the Empire.

The bishop of Constantinople was at the head of a patriarchate after the Council of Chalcedon in 451 and the only rival to the pope of Rome following the Arab conquest of the eastern provinces. He directed a vast ecclesiastical administration whose jurisdiction was long interwoven with that of the Empire. The Saint Sophia church, neighbor to the Great Palace, was in the eyes of its Christian visitors a spectacular building without equal. With the conversion of the Bulgars and Russians in the ninth and tenth centuries, the Byzantine Church expanded its influence to the vast stretches of Russia while strengthening its specific features relative to the Latin Church. When the relics from Jerusalem, and especially those of the True Cross, arrived in Constantinople in the seventh century, it became a major center of pilgrimage, even for the Latins, who tried to bring back to their home countries relics acquired during their stay in the imperial capital. After 1204, Latin pilgrims, who had abundantly pillaged the relics and sent them massively to the West, were fewer in number than the faithful of the patriarchate, especially Russians, who continued to visit Constantinople as a holy city. When the Empire weakened under the Palaiologoi (1261–1453) and was progressively absorbed by the Muslim state of the Ottomans, the patriarchate remained dynamic because of the Bulgar, Serbian, and Russian churches, an advantage that allowed not only the patriarchate to survive following the fall of Constantinople in 1453, but also the Balkan subjects of the Ottomans to preserve an identity that became national in the nineteenth century.

A third advantage of the Empire was a well-defended capital. The foundation of Constantinople gave the eastern part of the Roman Empire an admirably situated capital. On the Bosphorus between Asia and Europe, the city was easy to defend once the question of provisions of water and grain had been solved. Walls erected under the emperor Theodosius effectively protected a population that could number nearly 500,000 inhabitants, but which numbered only 60,000 to 100,000 inhabitants in the eighth century and fewer than 50,000 in the fifteenth. The city housed an administration that underwent great changes over the course of the Byzantine millennium, but whose continuity was ensured, except for the period of the Latin occupation between 1204 and 1261.[2] (This episode was brief, but bore grave consequences for the future.) Constantinople offered an impressive background for imperial ceremonies, and the halls of the Great Palace were arranged so as to highlight the providential power of the sovereign.

A fourth advantage was the emperors' ability to keep the public treasury more or less filled and secure. Other than in 1204, the treasury did not fall into enemy hands and even then a large part had been carried away ahead of time. The tax administration never ceased to be efficient, even when it could not rely upon the network of cities inherited from Rome that were ruined by Persian invasions and economic decline, and had to look to villages, the sole stable element during the ruralization of the Empire that began in the sixth century. The stability of the gold currency created by Constantine, the *nomisma*, contributed to the prestige of the Empire over seven centuries,

2 Cyril Mango, *Le développement urbain de Constantinople (ive–viie siècles)* (Paris: De Boccard, 1990); Paul Magdalino, *Constantinople médiévale: Études sur l'évolution des structures urbaines* (Paris: De Boccard, 1996); and Raymond Janin, *Constantinople byzantine: Développement urbain et répertoire topographique* (Paris: Institut Français d'Études Byzantines, 1964).

until the eleventh century. Because the populations of Arab-ruled Egypt and Syria had confidence only in the *nomismata* of the Byzantine emperors, the first caliphs were constrained to mint imitations of these Byzantine coins. *Nomismata* have been found throughout western Europe and also in China.

The stable treasury allowed the army to be continually paid, as long as it made adjustments to its account balances and the number of troops. This funding also supported a policy of prestige, implemented through the distribution of imperial dignities, a powerful factor of cohesion. These dignities were not only eagerly and long sought-after by the elites at the heart of the Empire, but also appreciated outside the Empire, and they served to promote alliances. Imperial munificence furnished such concrete advantages as the payment of an annual *roga* (salary) and gifts of precious clothing, which were often accompanied by pieces of high-quality silk.

These four major advantages – Roman traditions, an influential religious hierarchy, a well-defended capital, and a relatively stable financial system – allowed Byzantium to adapt to many of the challenges it faced in the Middle Millennium. Ultimately the three primary challenges – enemies on the borders, instability in the succession to the emperorship, and challenges by local elites – led the Empire to collapse, but this would be nearly a millennium after the end of the Roman Empire in the West.

Upheaval, adaption, and stability from 500 to 750

Toward 500, the Western Empire had dissolved, to the benefit of the great Germanic kingdoms that considered themselves the successors to Rome and therefore shared values with the Roman East that had remained intact: the Frankish king Clovis (r. 481–511), for example, liked the title of patrician given him by the emperor Anastasius. To a certain extent, the law also remained a link between the provinces of the Empire that were from this point on divided. Constantinople dominated a vast territory, but this generally included only two prefectures, those of the East and Illyricum. Under Justinian's rule, the reconquest of Africa and Italy allowed at least a partial recovery of at least two other prefectures (see Map 21.1). But the arrival of the plague in 541, and the economic and especially demographic decline it caused, damaged imperial ambitions. The number of troops was not the same as at the time of Constantine.

On the economic level, trade in the Mediterranean took on a more markedly regional character even prior to the invasions of the seventh century. All the same, the assessment of the Justinianic reconquest is not

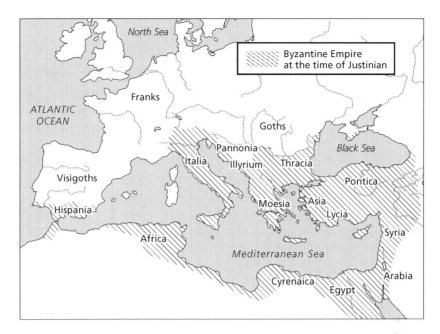

Map 21.1. Byzantine Empire at the time of Justinian, 555 CE

entirely negative, since the possession of the richest part of Africa and especially of prosperous Sicily contributed in the seventh century to the Empire's survival.[3] Between 580 and 641, the date of the death of the emperor Heraclius, the Empire progressively became a reduced state, as much from a territorial point of view as from the point of view of financial resources, leading to a change in its structure.[4]

The collapse was so sudden that the population was unable to measure its significance for a long time. In Syria, Palestine, and in Egypt, the inhabitants, despite having been for the most part Monophysites, long maintained the hope for a return of the Byzantine emperor and the re-establishment of Rome's eternal power, especially because the local administration had not changed, even if the taxes were now sent to a Muslim ruler. In 641, the

3 John F. Haldon, *Warfare, State and Society in the Byzantine World 565–1204* (London: UCLA Press, 1999) and John F. Haldon, *State, Army and Society in Byzantium* (Aldershot: Variorum, 1995).

4 On the Byzantine tax system see Wolfram Brandes, *Finanzverwaltung in Krisenzeiten: Untersuchungen zur byzantinischen Verwaltungsgeschichte* (Frankfurt am Main: Löwenklau, 2002), and Nikolaos Antōniu Oikonomidès, *Fiscalité et exemption fiscale à Byzance (ixe–xie s.)* (Athens: Institut de Recherches Byzantines, 1996).

Empire was spread out over three continents and still had strongholds in Italy and in Africa. However, no obstacle stood in the way of its new adversary, the caliphate of Medina, that was about to seize the eastern provinces and was in the process of absorbing the Empire's old rival, Persia, thereby combining the best of the resources of the ancient world, the valley of the Nile and Mesopotamia. The threat was accentuated when the Umayyad caliphs, who were dependent primarily upon the Syrian army, settled in Damascus, a simple stopover place on the route to Constantinople.

The Armenian plateau had traditionally constituted a place of strategic importance. Even though the Armenians were Christians, their princes sealed a pact with the Arabs, which allowed them an autonomy long sought-after at the price of very moderate concessions. Such emperors of the second half of the seventh century as Constantine IV (r. 668–85) or Justinian II (r. 685–95 and 705–11) endeavored in vain to recover control of the region. When the Armenians came to understand that the Umayyad caliphs' demands – both of men and taxes – would increase, it was too late.

Between the death of Heraclius in 641 and the first great land victory over the Arabs at Akroinon in 741, the Empire was threatened with destruction. The Balkans had been long invaded by the Slavs, and then by a formidable people of nomadic warriors, the Avars, who were the first to besiege Constantinople in 626. From the end of the sixth century, the Slavs had penetrated all the way to the Peloponnese. The Byzantines no longer held anything but the islands and the coasts of the Aegean Sea, and the *Via Egnatia*, leading from Dyrrachion (Durrazzo, Durrës) on the Adriatic Sea to Constantinople, was cut off for several centuries. This rendered communication with Italy even more difficult, as it depended on maritime routes subject to the vagaries of climate and the threat of pirates. Africa and Italy, far removed from Constantinople, were governed from the sixth century by exarchs who had the freedom to take emergency measures in civil and military matters as required by the local situation.

In the eastern Mediterranean Cyprus was quickly neutralized, and the Cilician plain in Asia Minor became the strategic site of a bitter struggle that, in the first decades of the eighth century, ended with the victory of the Arabs, who fortified such cities as Tarsus that served as bases for raids on the Anatolian plain. The caliphs twice tried to take possession of Constantinople, around 670 and in 717–18, but the walls proved impregnable, and the Arab fleet suffered heavy losses due to the use of Greek fire, an incendiary fluid shot out of pressurized nozzles. Finally, toward the middle of the eighth century, a certain balance was established when the 'Abbasid caliphs, who had driven out the Umayyads, re-centered their empire in Mesopotamia, a shift symbolized by the foundation of Baghdad in 763. The border moved, in short, away from the Taurus and Anti-Taurus mountains, from Seleucia to Trebizond, and remained stable for two centuries after the creation of a sort of no-man's-land that protected each state's lands from raids. From the time of Constantine V (r. 741–75), the emperors had in effect begun to counter attack, aiming at the cities on the caliphate's border.

To come to such a point, the emperors had had to make progressive adjustments that profoundly transformed the organization of the Empire. The nature of these reforms is still under debate, especially regarding the most important reform, that of the army. How could the Empire have at its disposal a greater number of troops, when it had undoubtedly lost two-thirds of its fiscal resources and, with the exception of modest regional trade, its commerce had collapsed? One of the great unknowns is the demographic impact of the wars, epidemics, and natural catastrophes. One thing is certain, for it has been confirmed by archeology: cities had almost entirely disappeared, except for Constantinople and a few towns that had strong garrisons such as Amorium. The others were reduced to a fortified perimeter that no longer protected anything but a modest part of the ancient section of the town, as at Angora or Pergamum, or even more dramatically at Ephesus.[5] On the other hand, we do not know what the situation was in the countryside. We no longer believe in the theory of a Balkan revitalization by a Slavic influx, but we do not know if the number of peasants declined in the same proportion as that of city-dwellers. The situation was undoubtedly different depending on whether the province was affected or not by the plague, or located on the route of an enemy raid. It seems that the regions close to Constantinople (Thrace and Bithynia) were relatively spared, and that, besides episodes of siege, the prefecture of Asia escaped serious damage.

The financing of the army is also a subject of debate, because it is tied to issues regarding the organization of themes [*themata*]. One part of the army, once stationed in the far-off eastern provinces, was pulled back into Asia Minor where it progressively settled and recruited its soldiers.[6] They were organized into new military–civilian administrative divisions of the Empire called themes, which over the course of the eighth and ninth centuries

5 Clive Foss, *Cities, Fortresses and Villages of Byzantine Asia Minor* (Aldershot: Variorum, 1996).

6 Constantin Zuckerman, "Learning from the Enemy and More: Studies in 'Dark Centuries' Byzantium," *Millennium: Jahrbuch zu Kultur und Geschichte des ersten Jahrtausends n. Chr.* 2 (2005): 79–135.

replaced the provinces inherited from the Roman period. Each theme was under the leadership of a *strategos*, a general who also often assumed civilian responsibilities of governance. Resources were adjusted by reducing the cash paid out and instead requiring peasants to provide supplies for men and beasts because of a shortage of monetary currency.

What saved the Empire in this moment of distress was the maintenance of a central power. It was, of course, sometimes feeble. For instance, between 695 and 717 multiple *coups d'état* led to a series of short-lived emperors. However, the Empire was always able to count on the loyalty of the provinces that remained within its borders, including far-off Sicily, the only bright spot in terms of monetary and economic health. The provinces provided the expected taxes and recruits despite successive defeats, and for this reason, the Arabs were not able to gain a long-term foothold on the Anatolian plain.

The Empire's reorganization and recovery, 750–1000

From the middle of the eighth century, when the epidemics of the plague had ceased and the Arab pressure had lessened somewhat, the militarization of the Empire and a succession of military emperors from the Isaurian dynasty onward ensured the Empire's survival. This occurred despite serious failures, like the death of emperor Nikephoros I (r. 802–11) in 811 on the battlefield against the Bulgars, or the defeat in 838 which allowed Caliph al-Mu'tasim to seize Amorion, capital of Anatolia, the first theme of the Empire.

Society was transformed, because the former senatorial elite disappeared, except at Constantinople, where it remained protected. A new aristocracy was founded on those faithful to the emperor, who amassed the principal military and fiscal offices and, in Anatolia, on families who distinguished themselves in the struggle against the Arabs.[7]

The victorious resistance in Asia Minor came at a price for the West. In 751, the exarchate of Ravenna disappeared as a result of the Lombard attacks, and the pope, who traditionally had relied upon the Byzantines to repel Lombard raids, was obliged to turn toward the rising power in the West, the Carolingians. The Byzantines only kept isolated positions. Venice,

---

7 Michael Angold (ed.), *The Byzantine Aristocracy, IX to XIII Centuries* (Oxford: B.A.R, 1984), and Jean-Claude Cheynet, *The Byzantine Aristocracy and its Military Function* (Aldershot: Ashgate, 2006).

a former Byzantine duchy, became independent in the ninth century, even though its leader, whom we call the doge, continued to receive Byzantine titles for centuries. The Empire was maintained in southern Italy as well as in Sicily until the emirs of Africa slowly took possession of these areas during the ninth century. Byzantine diplomacy endeavored to maintain within its sphere of influence the Lombard principalities of the South and the duchies of Gaeta, Naples, and Amalfi, which allowed the Empire to keep a close eye on the Western powers. The distribution of titles further helped to maintain links between some members of the foreign elite and the Empire.

Assured of survival and endowed with an effective military administration, the Empire recovered on all levels (demographic, economic, military) in the ninth through the eleventh centuries, reaching its maximum expansion in the eleventh century. At that time, the sovereign of Constantinople controlled territory that stretched from southern Italy to the Caucasus and from the Danube River to northern Syria. The sovereigns no longer relied on municipal elites as in antiquity, but on the local aristocracy. The officers of the armies of the themes came from this milieu. The most fortunate obtained important positions of command, such as the *strategoi* (military governors) of the Anatolic theme in Central Asia Minor or the *domesticos* of the *Scholai*, superior officers who commanded the army in the absence of the emperor. They were obliged to go to court, where they received promotions and the *roga* that corresponded to the offices they held and titles they bore.[8] These important figures were surrounded by family members and servants who benefitted from the imperial favors conferred upon their leader. The leader intervened on their behalf, and they obtained either money or positions from the emperor. A solid although indirect connection was thus made between the local elites and Constantinople.

A similar policy of patronage and seduction was applied to the princes of states that were on the periphery of the Empire by the emperors who wanted to integrate them into their zone of influence. The titles conferred upon these rulers were often elevated, superior to those that imperial subjects were able to obtain. The ruler of Caucasian Iberia (in present-day Georgia), for example, until the middle of the eleventh century traditionally held the title of curopalate, which was normally reserved at that time for the imperial family. When they were paid, the *rogai* granted to these dignitaries consisted

8 Paul Lemerle, "'Roga' et rente d'État aux xe–xie siècles," *Revue des études byzantines* 25 (1967): 77–100; repr. in Lemerle, *Le monde de Byzance: histoire et institutions* (London: Variorum, 1978).

of large quantities of cash and numerous pieces of silk, which the beneficiary redistributed among his followers, creating a type of pressure favorable to good relations with the Empire. By this means the Empire created a network of rather faithful allies in Italy, Armenia, and the Muslim world, and was able to exercise an influence far from its frontiers throughout the Mediterranean world and the Latin West. The Fatimid sovereigns scrupulously recorded the gifts sent by the emperors of Constantinople. Greatly sought after, the Byzantine silks that were offered to Western sovereigns or to bishops are still preserved in numerous church treasuries, where they cover precious relics – which had themselves sometimes come from Constantinople, because they were widely distributed there to important visitors, who appreciated them greatly.

This evolution of the Empire did not go without consequences for society. During the "Dark Ages," the army was idealized as the means of popular defense, and it is true that its social base was made of small and medium landowners. All the same, the great landowners were not entirely absent in this period. The old senatorial aristocracy, composed of rich absent land-owners, had undoubtedly suffered a severe setback with the loss of the Eastern provinces and the ravages of war in Italy. The fate of the aristocracy residing at Constantinople is more uncertain, because there was no rupture as in the East and West. In the eighth century, the emperor, the tax department, the monasteries and even such important private landowners as the mythic Saint Philaretos of Amnia – whose later hagiography empha-sized his boundless generosity – possessed vast domains. We also see a concentration of ownership that increased after the harsh winter of 927/28. Suffering peasants sold their fields to great landowners, public or private, becoming *paroikoi*, peasants bound to their tenure of their own lands. However, the tax system depended upon the solidarity of the landowners of the same village, which had become the administrative district *par excellence*. The destruction of this balance threatened the number of recruits and the financing of the armies.

The emperors reacted by promulgating a series of increasingly severe new laws in order to safeguard small estates. This was in vain, for the peasants were no longer interested in serving in the military, and many of them preferred paying a monetary tax, even selling their arms, rather than enlisting in person. The failure was predictable, despite terrible confiscatory measures taken by Basil II (976–1025).

The possibility given to the peasants to buy back their land was an unrealistic arrangement, because it presupposed that they had the funds with which to do so. Byzantine *strategoi* did not really miss soldiers who were not very motivated. Money, which came from making the *strateia* (here, military service) subject to tax, went to pay professional soldiers, Byzantine or foreign, who were more and more numerous in the central army of the *tagmata*, the elite regiments of the guard first reconstituted by Constantine V, formed in great part of the cavalry.[9]

The army of the themes also underwent transformations. Troops were recruited locally, and the larger themes were broken up, so as not to concentrate too much power in the hands of a single *strategos*. Several times the *strategoi* of the Anatolics rebelled, and some even seized power, such as Leo III the Isaurian (r. 717–41) or Leo V the Armenian (r. 813–20). The early great themes of the Anatolics, Armeniacs, and Opsicians were greatly reduced in size, even if in the *Taktika* – treatises on court protocol – their rank was not called into question.[10] Reconquest in the Balkans and in Anatolia noticeably increased the number of themes. At the end of the tenth century, small themes, often peopled by Armenians, were created on the eastern frontier, sometimes around a simple fortress. It is unclear whether after the phase of conquest these strongholds were still staffed with a *strategos* and a garrison. In order to avoid a splintering of power, these frontier themes were often grouped into large districts in the hands of a duke or another officer called a *catepan*; these districts included the duchies of Antioch, Iberia, and Italy. In the century that followed, all the frontiers had been reorganized based on this model.

In the Balkans, the navy, organized on the model of the land army with provincial squadrons, and then enlarged by a central fleet,[11] was maintained on the Aegean coasts and a few coastal fortresses of Epirus and of Dalmatia, chief of which was Dyrrachion, the beachhead of the *Via Egnatia*. The interior of the Balkans was inhabited in the south by Slavic tribes and in the north by a powerful state ruled from the seventh century on by the khagan of the Bulgars. Regaining control of the Balkan peninsula required more than three centuries. The reoccupation of Hellas and of the Pelopon-nese happened rather easily over the course of the ninth century through a

9 John Haldon, *Byzantine Praetorians: An Administrative, Institutional, and Social Survey of the Opsikion and Tagmata, c.580–900* (Bonn: Habelt, 1984).

10 Nikolaos Antōniu Oikonomidès, *Les listes de préséance byzantines des ixe et xe siècles* (Paris: Éditions du Centre national de la recherche scientifique, 1972).

11 Hélène Ahrweiler, *Byzance et la mer. La marine de guerre, la politique et les institutions maritimes de Byzance aux viiᵉ-xvᵉ siècles* (Paris: Presses universitaires de France, 1966), and Elizabeth M. Jeffreys and John H. Pryor, *The Age of the Dromon: The Byzantine Navy ca 500–1204* (Boston: Brill, 2006).

mixture of military pressure and the standard policy of patronage and seduction, in which leaders in semi-autonomous territories, the *sklavinies*, were introduced into the Byzantine administrative system. The scaling-back of the Bulgarian state was much more difficult. This warrior people inflicted tremendous losses upon the Byzantine army; and their leaders, Krum and then Simeon, even besieged Constantinople, although this was in vain.

Expansion and its limitations in the East and the West

The effectiveness of armies and Byzantine gold was reinforced by missionary activity. The emperors favored the expansion of Christianity in the pagan world, in the hopes of seeing the religion inculcate in the newly faithful the respect due to the universal sovereign chosen by God.[12] Such a policy was unthinkable with regard to the Muslims. In the Balkans, the reoccupation of the Peloponnese and Hellas was accompanied by the restoration of the network of bishoprics that had been constituted during the proto-Byzantine period, but which had been lost when the pagan Slavs invaded. In 865, the Bulgar khagan Boris converted, taking the name of his godfather, the emperor Michael III (r. 842–67). The Bulgar sovereign, however, did not feel at all subject to the emperor or regard him as the "father" of Christian nations. After several decades of conflicts, independence ended only in 1018, when Emperor Basil II succeeded in overcoming the last remaining resistance among the Bulgars by promising titles and offices to the noble boyars who had been won over.

In the East, the Byzantine advance was slow in taking shape, because the balance of power evolved slowly. The 'Abbasid Caliphate, capable of organizing large expeditions, began to break apart in the second half of the ninth century. Compared to the Empire, it suffered an organizational weakness in its tax system. In fact, the provincial governors who collected taxes paid their civil service and troops before sending the surplus to Baghdad, whereas in the Empire provincial civil servants sent the tax revenues paid in gold first to Constantinople. The tax administration in the capital, in the person of the logothete of the *génikon* and of the *stratiôtikon,* then sent back the salaries of the provincial civil servants and soldiers. This system had a significant drawback, since a lot of gold circulated, and there are many references in

---

12 On the missions, see the special issue of *Harvard Ukrainian Studies* 12–13 (1988–9).

the sources to the *roga* of a theme being captured by the enemy. The advantage for the central authority, however, was that it remained in control of the movement of funds. The governors of large provinces of the caliphate such as Iran or Egypt, by contrast, simply ceased sending the surplus, and in this way easily became autonomous.

The decline of the caliphate was in part counterbalanced by the emergence of emirates at the Byzantine frontier, those of Melitene, Tarsus, and Aleppo, which concentrated the efforts of *jihad*. These emirates no longer had the capacity to threaten the heart of the Empire on a long-term basis, but, after grave losses, they reconstituted their troops by making an appeal for volunteers to the *jihad* and for money to combat the infidels. Over more than a century, at passes in the Taurus mountains the thematic armies, sometimes reinforced by contingents from the central army, clashed with the troops of emirs, whose numbers were increased by volunteers. The goal was no longer conquest, but enrichment by means of pillaging and selling prisoners captured in raids. The exploits of Sayf al-Dawla, the Hamdanid emir of Aleppo, were answered by the exploits of the brothers Nicephoros and Leo Phokas, both powerful and wealthy Byzantine generals. On both sides of the frontier two societies were formed, but sharing one way of life, often termed "acritic" from the Greek word *akritai,* meaning border guards. Both sides shared common values: to fight for the salvation of co-religionists by exalting the soldiers fallen in combat, who were considered martyrs by both the Byzantines on the frontier and their Muslim adversaries across the border. An admiration for battle exploits was common to both: the poetry of Abu-Firas and Mutanabbi exalting the victories of the Hamdanid Sayf al-Dawla is matched by the popular songs celebrating the Digenis Akritas, a hero born of the union of a Byzantine noblewoman and an Arab emir.[13]

This advance in the East was accompanied by the recovery of ecclesiastical centers, of which the most famous was that of Antioch. New sees were reorganized. During the reconquest, the emperors called on the Syriacs (Monophysite Christians living under the authority of Muslim princes), to repopulate the zones taken back from the Arabs, and they left on-site important Armenian garrisons. A network of Armenian or Syriac bishoprics was formed, and at first the emperors supported the foundation of great

---

13 On the fascination of the spirit of *jihad* in Anatolian society, cf. Gilbert Dagron, "Byzance et le modèle islamique au xe siècle: à propos des *Constitutions tactiques* de l'empereur Léon VI," *Comptes rendus de l'Académie des Inscriptions et Belles-Lettres* 2 (1983): 219–43.

Syriac monasteries, some endowed with *scriptoria*. This religious diversity created conflicts, but nothing indicates that non-Chalcedonians would have preferred living under the authority of the Turkish invaders.

The Empire did not mark the same success on the Latin side. In the West, Byzantium managed to retain only the province of Apulia in southern Italy, which it used as a base for observation and later intervention. The Western monarchies reorganized, and twice sovereigns claimed that they were bringing the Empire back to life in the West: Charlemagne in 800, and then Otto in 962. Besides a rather secondary quarrel over rank, concerning the use of the imperial title, when the sovereigns of Constantinople preserved the monopoly of the Roman *basileia*, the only point of contention was the possession of Italy and Rome. The Western sovereigns had not forgotten the division of 395, which placed all of Italy and a part of Dalmatia under the authority of the Western emperor, but Byzantine ambitions were limited to preserving their positions in the south of the peninsula and to preventing any other power from dominating all of Italy and especially Rome.

Developments of the eleventh century

The eleventh century has fascinated historians, because it shaped the final centuries of the Empire. At the height of its power in 1025, the Empire seemed in agony by 1081 (see Map 21.2). This century was also marked by the awareness of the Latin world's renewed power. This brutal subsidence was not due to a demographic decline, because Byzantium continued to be a part of the slow but steady population growth in Europe and the Mediterranean world, except in regions temporarily exposed to invasions. The failure has been attributed to the progressive disappearance of the thematic armies, at least as effective combat units, although these survived until the second half of the eleventh century.

The demographic growth in Europe that revived trade circuits, especially in Italy, produced a sustained increase in trade in the Mediterranean that benefited Constantinople, which became again a megalopolis of perhaps 300,000 inhabitants under the Komnenoi dynasty in the eleventh century. It was a major center of consumption that attracted merchants from the whole Mediterranean. They came seeking luxury goods that the craftspeople of the capital furnished in abundance: silks, bronze doors, ivories, mosaics, precious icons. However, contrary to the deep-rooted image, Byzantine merchants did not simply wait for clients, comfortably seated in their shops in the capital, but instead they braved the sea in order to gain riches abroad. They

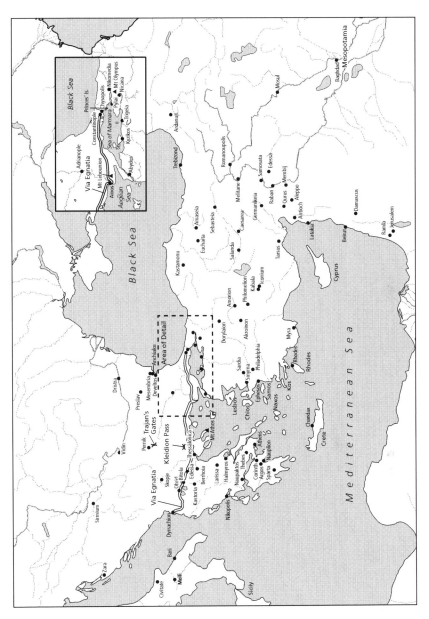

Map 21.2. Byzantine Empire in the eleventh century

573

undoubtedly no longer visited the Red Sea, Ethiopia, and perhaps India as they had in the time of the famed merchant and geographer Cosmas Indicopleustes in the sixth century; however, many of them, notably provincials, visited Mediterranean ports, in particular Alexandria, and entered by way of land routes beyond the Euphrates. In the Middle Ages, perfumes and precious wood from India arrived in the markets near the Great Palace, where Latin merchants came to buy supplies for their own commerce.[14] The Byzantine state was hardly interventionist in terms of the economy, although it did control the activities of certain professions of Constantinople, notably those that concerned precious materials, such as money changers and smiths, or those that involved the capital's food security, such as bakers and butchers, because these were a matter of public order.

As regards foreigners, the emperors tried at first to limit the exportation of the most precious silk cloth, forbidding even the export of purple dyes because this color was reserved for the emperor. The treaties made with the Bulgars and the Russians in the ninth and tenth centuries should be seen in this light, for these peoples were avid purchasers of Byzantine luxury goods. In the eleventh century, the emperors granted to Italian cities even greater privileges in exchange for the use of their military fleet. Venice was the first to benefit from this in 1082, and then Pisa and Genoa followed, under conditions a little less favorable. These agreements had as a consequence an increased circulation of Byzantine goods, but also an eventual weakening of Byzantine merchants, who were placed in an unfavorable position relative to their Italian rivals. Under the Palaiologoi dynasty that ruled from the thirteenth to the fifteenth centuries, the emperors lost trade revenue to the Italians, notably to the Genoese, solidly established at Galata, across the inlet of the Golden Horn from Constantinople.

The poet Tzetzes, a contemporary of Manuel I Komnenos (1143–80), heard and commented on all the languages spoken in Constantinople by the merchants and others who came to the city. At the same time, a major fair in Thessalonica, held during the feast of Saint Demetrius, the patron saint of the city, brought together for a few weeks merchants from all of Europe and the Caucasus.

---

14 On the mobility of merchants and the place of Byzantine merchants in Mediterranean trade, see the numerous articles of David Jacoby, notably those assembled in the volume, *Latins, Greeks and Muslims: Encounters in the Eastern Mediterranean, 10th–15th centuries* (Farnham-Burlington, VT: Ashgate, 2009).

Economic expansion and territorial growth, notably the annexation of cities of great commercial dynamism such as Melitene, Antioch, and Edessa in the East, increased the financial resources of the state. Additionally, the emperors had learned the lesson from the failure of the Macedonian legislation to preserve medium-sized property, and they reorganized the tax system.

From this point on, the tax administration maintained and cultivated the estates obtained in great number from conquest, confiscations, and the abandonment of land by peasants who resettled elsewhere for tax reasons. The traditional offices of the tax administration disappeared, replaced by the office of *oikeikôn* (private property).

The provincial military aristocracy formed the backbone of the army, but it could become dangerous for the emperor because its regiments were made up of a network of family members and supporters who were more loyal to each other than to him.

In the tenth century, the Empire experienced great danger when it was almost taken over by a rebellion of the noble Phokas family, the military commanders who dominated central Anatolia.[15] Although one of the Phokas clan did briefly become emperor, the revolt was put down, and under Basil II the empire began the reconstruction of the military aristocracy by incorporating such *homines novi* as the Komnenoi family and numerous foreigners, notably from the Caucasus. At the same time, the emperors promoted the settling of aristocrats in Constantinople, and it was increasingly necessary to be present at court there in order to have a career. This evolution had two consequences. First, the power of important families was harnessed, except for those living in Adrianople, a town that is rather near Constantinople. Second, the elites at least partially abandoned their provinces; a situation that proved to be dangerous during later invasions, because the inhabitants no longer had leaders to encourage them to resist fiercely, as they had in the time of the Arab assaults.

The new professional army in which foreigners were more numerous, combined with the traditional support of the Armenians and the arrival of the Varangian Guard and then the Franks as troops, did allow the reconquest of northern Syria and Bulgaria, followed by the annexation of Armenian principalities.[16] But the Empire still experienced a setback in the middle of the

15 Jean-Claude Cheynet, *Pouvoir et contestations à Byzance (963–1210)* (Paris: Publications de la Sorbonne, 1990).
16 Hélène Ahrweiler and Angeliki E. Laiou (eds.), *Studies on the Internal Diaspora of the Byzantine Empire* (Washington, DC: Dumbarton Oaks, 1998).

eleventh century because of weakness in the imperial succession. Under normal conditions, the son succeeded his father. However, a victorious usurper at times seized power, which often improved the quality of the government because a dynamic emperor took the place of a less competent one, but still created instability. The Macedonian dynasty had ruled Byzantium from 867, but from 1028 it was clear that that dynasty was going to fade away, although two daughters of Constantine VIII were named official successors – called *Porphyrogenitoi*, literally "born in the purple," from the purple room in the palace in which they were born – and the choice of a new dynasty was momentarily postponed.

Over the next half-century, successive coups occurred at a time when threats on the border were multiplying. The combination of the two was fatal. The events surrounding the battle of Manzikert in August 1071 are representative. The emperor at the time, Romanos Diogenes (r. 1068–71), had come to power by marrying the widowed reigning empress, a situation that was not without precedent. Chosen for his military expertise, he was supposed to protect the Empire until Michael VII Doukas (r. 1071–8), the son of the previous emperor, was ready to rule. The Byzantine army was still operational, and the number of troops remained considerable. By chance, Diogenes and his army met the army of the Seljuk sultan Alp Arslan, whose aim in fact was to combat the Fatimids, the Muslim rulers of Egypt. Diogenes refused to negotiate, because he needed a military triumph to cement his power as emperor. The interests of the leader of the rear-guard, Andronikos Doukas, the cousin of Michael VII, were the exact opposite. Andronikos Doukas' desertion from the field appears to have allowed the Turks to win the battle and to encircle and capture Romanos Diogenes. He was held only a short while, and released with the promise of a large ransom payment, but civil war, intrigue over the throne, and revolts by generals followed, which opened up Asia Minor to the Turks.

The attempt at balance under the Komnenoi

Struggles for imperial power lessened when Alexis I Komnenos (r. 1081–1118), a member of a prominent noble family who had married into the ruling Doukas dynasty, took power. He found a different Empire than had been the case under Basil II half a century earlier, and he adapted his administration to the new circumstances. Asia Minor was largely lost, even if the Byzantines were able to take the rich plains of western Asia Minor from the Seljuks of Nicaea. In the Balkans, however, Alexis defeated the Pecheneg nomads, a

Turkic people who had threatened Byzantium, and the Balkans became the economic heart of the Empire. Administrative units were concentrated, and the most important – and least numerous – positions, especially those of army commanders, were conferred upon the emperors' supporters, most often family members.[17] The administration of finances was in the hands of two officials called *megas logariastes* (grand accountant); one in charge of the central fiscal offices of the Empire (the *sékréta*) and the other in charge of religious foundations.

After a period of some disorder in the last quarter of the eleventh century, the administration of the provinces went back to being organized into large districts in which a duke supervised all the provincial departments, including the tax administration. In order to prevent an official's putting down roots, the emperor did not leave the same governor in place for too long, although sometimes a civil servant held the same position twice over the course of his career. The seals of governors seldom mention where they held their charge. Instead they refer to the family ties that linked them to the emperor. From this point on, these links determined the hierarchy. The personal tie with the sovereign was reinforced, as the expression "emperor's man" attests, which became official in documents and on seals beginning in the eleventh century.

An expanding hierarchy of titles, many of them honorific, also indicates this change. Under the Komnenoi, the title of *sebastos* was reserved for family members and those closely connected to the emperor. The brothers of the sovereign, for example, were *sebastokratores*, and so on. The *roga* was progressively, though not entirely, replaced by the *pronoia*, a temporary grant of a stream of income that could be revoked by the emperor. The beneficiary of a *pronoia* received the right to take a certain amount of taxes or public revenue, determined in advance by the document awarding this *pronoia*. Holders of *pronoia* sent their own agents to collect the revenues, who replaced imperial tax collectors. The emperor saw advantages in this, since this institution reduced the number of levies and fiscal civil servants required. The family of the emperor received immense *pronoiai*, whereas simple officers received only those in keeping with their status. The danger that the holder of the *pronoia* might end up acting as its permanent owner was limited, since the *pronoia* was an annuity, or offered as compensation for a specific function, and was returned as soon as it was completed. In principle,

17 Nikolaos Antōniu Oikonomidès, "L'évolution de l'organisation administrative de l'empire byzantin au xie siècle (1025–1118)," *Travaux et Mémoires* 6 (1976): 125–52.

strict control and recourse to the courts prevented the holder of the *pronoia* from taking more than his due.

This very centralized administration narrowed the possibilities for opposition, although this did not prevent several dukes placed at the head of frontier provinces from plotting with the adversaries of the Empire against the sovereign. For example, Andronikos Komnenos when he was duke revolted against Emperor Manuel I (1143–80). But this "legacy" system ensured interior peace, and in fact, from 1081 to 1180, no large military revolts took place as had happened in the preceding centuries.

The place of the Empire in the concert of nations also changed after the Macedonian dynasty ended in 1056 and especially after the Komnenoi came to power. Basil II had agreed to give his sister, Anna Porphyrogenita, in marriage to Prince Vladimir of Kiev because, faced with the revolts of Asia Minor, he was in a critical military situation. He also demanded Vladimir's conversion. Beginning with the dynasty of the Doukas, the emperors, while continuing to claim superiority over other sovereigns in principle, agreed to negotiate as equals with other Christian sovereigns, notably with the German emperors. Their matrimonial policy reflects this change. Traditionally the emperors had married within the Byzantine aristocracy, except in rare moments of crisis. However, beginning with Michael VII Doukas, and except for usurpers who were already betrothed or married, the Byzantine emperors married foreign princesses in order to reinforce ties with other sovereigns. Even Manuel I Komnenos, whose official panegyrics made him out to have restored Roman universal grandeur, adopted a very pragmatic attitude. Concerned with the Empire's defense and the restoration of secure borders, he married the sister-in-law of the German emperor Conrad III and then the daughter of the French ruler of one of the Western states.

Power relationships changed because of the strength of economic and demographic growth of the Latin West. The Venetians promised military support to Alexis Komnenos in exchange for important trade benefits, sanctioned by the chrysobull, or imperial decree with a golden seal, of 1082. This trade and defensive agreement was at first beneficial to the large Byzantine landowners who exported grains, oil, cheese, but it also placed the merchants of Constantinople at a disadvantage. Italian trading cities, among them principally Venice, became ever more powerful. Their fleets became the masters of the Mediterranean, even if Manuel I was still capable of constructing Byzantium's last great war fleet. Foreign princes also had the means to form large armies. The Crusaders, whose arrival benefited the

Empire with regard to the Turks, demonstrated the capacity of the Latins to send powerful expeditionary forces very far from their borders.

This ambiguous relationship with the Latins, who were at times allies and at times adversaries, was made more difficult by religious quarrels. These became poisonous after the crisis of 1054, when the popes, shaped by the Gregorian reforms, claimed hegemony over all Christians.

Continuing problems and final collapse

At the beginning of the thirteenth century, the classic schema of Byzantine weakening happened again. The instability of imperial succession after the death of Manuel I Komnenos in 1180, the victorious revolt of the Bulgars, the exacerbation of "nationalist" sentiment in the population of Constantinople – wary of those who were not Greeks – and the arrival of the knights of the Fourth Crusade, resulted in the unexpected installation of a Latin emperor in April 1204. This left the Byzantines with an unprecedented situation: the emperor who was established on the throne was a foreigner. Certain Greeks might have rallied to a sovereign capable of restoring imperial grandeur, but the Latin forces were defeated at Adrianople by the Bulgars in 1205, which eliminated that possibility.[18]

The people from the provinces stopped looking toward Constantinople for leadership and instead endeavored to reconstruct a Greek state without the city. Two attempts were somewhat successful: that of Theodore Lascaris in the East and that of Theodore Doukas in Epirus on the Ionian Sea, both of whom re-established the title of emperor. The Lascarids rapidly became the more powerful. In 1211, at the battle of Antioch-on-the-Meander, Theodore Lascaris saved his small nation from conquest by the Seljuk Turks thanks to the sacrifice of the Latin mercenary cavalry. His grandson, Theodore II Lascaris (1254–8), proposed the recruitment of a national army, which was supposed to cost less than Latin mercenaries and to remain loyal to the emperor, but he reigned for too short a time to put his project into place. Such proposals worried the Latin mercenaries, however, and they supported the seizure of power by their leader, the commander Michael Palaiologos (r. 1259–82). In Asia Minor, which was the Lascaris' power base, Michael VIII

---

18 On the Greeks of Latin Constantinople, cf. David Jacoby, "The Greeks of Constantinople under Latin Rule 1204–1261," in Thomas F. Madden (ed.), *The Fourth Crusade: Event, Aftermath, and Perceptions: Papers from the Sixth Conference of the Society for the Study of the Crusades and the Latin East, Istanbul, Turkey, 25–29 August 2004* (Aldershot: Ashgate, 2008): 53–73.

had deposed and blinded the young John IV, the Lascaris claimant to the throne, in his rise to power. He continued to clash with supporters of the Lascaris dynasty, which alienated the Palaiologoi from a large part of the population on a long-term basis.

Despite his victory over Guillaume of Villehardouin, the Latin prince of Achaea, in 1259 at Pelagonia, Michael VIII was unable to convince the Greeks of Epirus to accept his legitimacy. Instead they remained independent, although the price of this was an alliance with the Latins.[19] Other Greeks, who half a century earlier had founded the small state of Trebizond on the Black Sea coast of Asia Minor, also preserved their complete independence, and were preoccupied with surviving amidst potentially hostile emirates.

In 1261 Michael VIII Palaiologos took Constantinople back from the Latin emperor and his Venetian allies. This return to the capital did not cancel out the events of 1204, however, because when Michael Palaiologos returned to the city, the Greeks did not all rally around him. Provincial people had gotten into the habit of governing themselves without the existence of a central power.

Michael VIII had the ambition of reconstructing the empire of the Komnenoi and the institutions had changed little. The armies were thus still composed of mercenaries, which was the most economical solution for recruiting soldiers, of whom the most effective were the Latins.[20]

Michael VIII was able to create the illusion of the Empire's power by pushing back the challenges of Charles of Anjou, king of Naples and Sicily, but this was at the price of the Asian provinces. The defense of Constantinople cost dearly, because it was necessary to maintain and reinforce the walls. This effort could not be continued under his son, Andronikos II, during whose long reign (1282–1328) the collapse in Asia took place. The responsibility was not only the emperor's, however, because the pressure of the Mongols, who took control in Asia Minor, pushed the Turkish tribes toward the Byzantine provinces. The necessity of finding further financial resources had pushed Michael VIII to eliminate the tax advantages given to soldiers who guarded the border on the Turkish side, and some deserted. In less than three decades, the rich provinces of Asia were lost to the emirates, the most dynamic of which, the Ottomans, was established in Bithynia, directly across

---

19 On the Palaiologoi, see Donald MacGillivray Nicol, *The Last Centuries of Byzantium: 1261–1453* (Cambridge University Press, 1993).

20 Mark C. Bartusis, *The Late Byzantine Army: Arms and Society, 1204–1453* (Philadelphia: University of Pennsylvania Press, 1992).

the Bosphorus from Constantinople. In a last-ditch effort, the emperor Andronikos II recruited Western troops comprised of Catalans. But the state had no more resources to pay them, and therefore, despite their superiority over Turkish forces, they turned toward the European part of the Empire, which they laid waste. It was no longer possible to maintain a local army of sufficient size.

Andronikos III (1328–41) failed in Asia Minor, but assisted by an active general, his relative John Kantakouzenos, he succeeded in reconstituting a homogenous state in Europe that stretched, with the recovery of Dyrrachion, from the Bosphorus to the Adriatic. The Frankish barons of the Peloponnese and Attica were just about to rally around him, but Andronikos III died suddenly, which provoked a terrible civil war between the young John V Palaiologos, son of Andronikos III (r. 1341–76 and 1379–91), and John VI Kantakouzenos (r. 1347–54, as co-emperor with John V Palaiologos), who temporarily won the day in 1347. John Kantakouzenos introduced Serbian and Turkish foreigners into the Byzantine provinces on a massive scale, thus laying the ground for the ultimate dismemberment of the Empire. The return of the plague added to the general pessimism and provoked a demographic disaster. The civil war also revealed sharp new tensions at the heart of society, as violence included the murder of landed aristocrats by the mercantile classes of the cities. In Thessalonica, an anti-aristocratic group called the Zealots took over the city for seven years. Constantinople's resistance to Kantakouzenos was also led by merchants and craftsmen.

These developments led to the final transformations of Byzantine society. The resistance to taxes increased. Certain people felt that the emperor should live on his own revenues, and the monasteries refused to see their lands broadly confiscated. Beneficiaries of *pronoiai* succeeded in making them more or less hereditary, depriving the emperor of money and room to maneuver. The emperor gave cities such as Ioannina and the great port city of Monemvasia important tax concessions in exchange for their loyalty. The territory of the Empire ceased to be maintained. The emperors relied upon privileges conferred to family members.

In the second half of the fourteenth century, the aristocrats lost the greater part of their lands during the rapid advance of the Ottomans in the Balkans. Those who did not succeed in changing to careers in commerce and banking were ruined. The governors of Morea, a province that included most of the Peloponnese, were temporarily an exception to this, as they managed to extend their territory as the Ottomans advanced and were not conquered by the Ottomans until 1460.

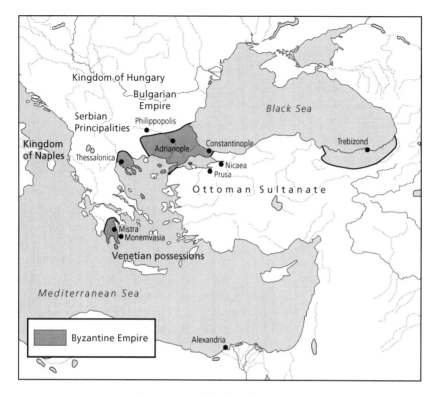

Map 21.3. Byzantine Empire in 1350 CE

The emperors, notably John VI Kantakouzenos, tried in vain to break free of the hold that the Italian merchants had on the economy, but the Italians continued to dominate trade. John VI even failed at ousting the Genoese, who were settled at Galata on the Golden Horn across from the port of Constantinople. However, some Greeks succeeded in making a fortune in trade, most often in association with such Italian merchant families as the Notaras or the Goudelai. They cautiously placed their fortunes in Genoese or Venetian banks, and often combined a great confidence in Italian banks with a hostility toward the papacy.

The Empire temporarily recovered a few territories after Timur defeated the Ottomans at Ankara in 1402, but Constantinople was reduced to a city-state of around 50,000 inhabitants. It still represented a major stakeholder, for it prevented the Ottomans from having a completely unified state, and allowed Latin merchants access to the foreign trading posts of the Black

Sea. Despite the wealth of its elites, however, the state was devoid of the means of self-defense. It could only count on Western assistance: in 1430 Thessalonica was besieged by the Ottomans, and the defense was entrusted to the Venetians. The price consisted of concessions regarding the Union of the Western and Eastern churches. Motivated by the inability of the Empire to defend itself, John VIII Palaiologos (r. 1425–58) even agreed to such a union, under papal leadership. The Union was approved by representatives of both churches at the Council of Florence-Ferrara in 1439. This provoked strong tensions in the Byzantine church and within the population. George Scholarios, the first patriarch of the Ottoman period, opposed the Union, and it was never accepted by the Eastern Church.[21]

The Latins present in Constantinople participated heroically, often at the cost of their lives, in the siege of 1453, and the city's Greek residents fought vigorously as well. They were not successful, and Ottoman forces took the city, in a battle in which Emperor Constantine XI Palaiologos (r. 1449–53) himself was killed. The entry of Mehmed II into Constantinople on 29 May 1453 led inevitably to the surrender of other parts of the Empire, including Trebizond and Morea.

Conclusion

Contrary to the image of stability emanating from official discourse, the structures of the Byzantine Empire were constantly being transformed. Byzantium's greatest weakness came from the system of selecting the emperor, which several times provoked civil wars and, combined with invasions, ended up bringing about its downfall. The evolution of the Empire is to be located in a European context. It benefited from the common demographic growth that continued from the eighth century to the beginning of the thirteenth, and suffered from the same catastrophic epidemics as did the rest of Europe. Social transformations were not as radical as in western Europe. However, under the Palaiologoi, the importance of Byzantine cities and their populations of merchants and craftsmen can hardly be differentiated from those of contemporary Italian cities, nor can their hostile reactions to the landed aristocracy or their challenging of taxes. On the other hand, the great Western monarchies, France and England, progressively

---

21 Marie-Hélène Blanchet, *Georges-Gennadios Scholarios (vers 1400–vers 1472): un intellectuel orthodoxe face à la disparition de l'Empire byzantin* (Paris: Institut Français d'Études Byzantines, 2008).

formed state structures around a sovereign, whereas the Empire followed an opposite path, which led from a quasi-absolute monarchy to disintegration into more or less autonomous entities around an impotent sovereign, Constantine XI, who was unable, at a crowning moment in 1453, to mobilize the fortunes of the last opulent Greeks for the defense of the city.

Translated by
Michelle Bolduc

FURTHER READING

Angold, Michael, ed. *The Byzantine Aristocracy, ix to xiii Centuries*. Oxford: BAR, 1984.

Ahrweiler, Hélène. *Byzance et la mer. La marine de guerre, la politique et les institutions maritimes de Byzance aux viie–xve siècles*. Paris: Presses universitaires de France, 1966.

Bartousis, Mark C. *The Late Byzantine Army: Arms and Society, 1204–1453*. Philadelphia, PA: University of Pennsylvania Press, 1992.

Blanchet, Marie-Hélène. *Georges-Gennadios Scholarios (vers 1400–vers 1472): un intellectuel orthodoxe face à la disparition de l'Empire byzantin*. Paris: Institut Français d'Études Byzantines, 2008.

Brandes, Wolfram. *Finanzverwaltung in Krisenzeiten: Untersuchungen zur byzantinischen Verwaltungsgeschichte*. Frankfurt am Main: Löwenklau, 2002.

Cheynet, Jean-Claude. *The Byzantine Aristocracy and its Military Function*. Aldershot: Ashgate, 2006.

Pouvoir et contestations à Byzance (963–1210). Paris: Publications de la Sorbonne, 1990.

Cheynet, Jean-Claude, Angeliki Laiou, and Cécile Morrisson, eds. *Monde byzantin*, 3 vols. Paris: Presses universitaires de France, 2004–11.

Foss, Clive. *Cities, Fortresses and Villages of Byzantine Asia Minor*. Aldershot: Variorum, 1996.

Dagron, Gilbert. "Byzance et le modèle islamique au xe siècle: à propos des *Constitutions tactiques* de l'empereur Léon VI," *Comptes rendus de l'Académie des Inscriptions et Belles-Lettres* 2 (1983): 219–43.

Haldon, John F. *Byzantine Praetorians: An Administrative, Institutional, and Social Survey of the Opsikion and Tagmata, c. 580–900*. Bonn: Habelt, 1984.

State, Army and Society in Byzantium. Aldershot: Variorum, 1995.

Warfare, State and Society in the Byzantine World 565–1204. London: UCLA Press, 1999.

Jacoby, David, ed. *Latins, Greeks and Muslims: Encounters in the Eastern Mediterranean, 10th–15th centuries*. Farnham: Ashgate, 2009.

Janin, Raymond. *Constantinople byzantine: Développement urbain et répertoire topographique*. Paris: Institut Français d'Études Byzantines, 1964.

Jeffreys, Elizabeth M. and John H. Pryor. *The Age of the Dromon: The Byzantine Navy ca 500–1204*. Boston: Brill, 2006.

Jeffreys, Elizabeth M., John Haldon and Robin Cormack, eds. *The Oxford Handbook of Byzantine Studies*. Oxford University Press, 2008.

Lemerle, Paul. *Le monde de Byzance: Histoire et institutions*. Aldershot: Variorum, 1978.

Madden, Thomas F., ed. *The Fourth Crusade: Event, Aftermath, and Perceptions: Papers from the Sixth Conference of the Society for the Study of the Crusades and the Latin East, Istanbul, Turkey, 25–29 August 2004.* Aldershot: Ashgate, 2008.

Magdalino, Paul. *Constantinople médiévale: Études sur l'évolution des structures urbaines.* Paris: De Boccard, 1996.

Mango, Cyril. *Le développement urbain de Constantinople (ive–viie siècles).* Paris: De Boccard, 1990.

Nicol, Donald MacGillivray. *The Last Centuries of Byzantium: 1261–1453.* Cambridge University Press, 1993.

Oikonomidès, Nikolaos Antōniu. *Fiscalité et exemption fiscale à Byzance (ixe–xie s.).* Athens: Institut de Recherches Byzantines, 1996.

——— "L'évolution de l'organisation administrative de l'empire byzantin au xie siècle (1025–1118)," *Travaux et Mémoires* 6 (1976): 125–52.

——— *Les listes de préséance byzantines des ixe et xe siècles.* Paris: Éditions du Centre national de la recherche scientifique, 1972.

Treadgold, Warren T. *A History of the Byzantine State and Society.* Stanford University Press, 1997.

Zuckerman, Constantin. "Learning from the Enemy and More: Studies in 'Dark Centuries' Byzantium," *Millennium: Jahrbuch zur Kultur und Geschichte des ersten Jahrtausends n. Chr.* 2 (2005): 79–135.

22

Early polities of the Western Sudan

DAVID C. CONRAD

From the late eighth century to 1500, a series of major polities emerged in the Sudanic zone between the Niger River and the Atlantic. All drew significant resources from long-distance and trans-Saharan trade in gold, salt and slaves, according to contemporary chroniclers writing in Arabic. Ghana (or Wagadu, as the Soninke remember their ancient state) and Gao (Songhay "Gaawe," Tamasaq "Gawgaw") are both mentioned between the late eighth–tenth centuries, with considerable detail – especially for Ghana – provided by the Muslim geographer al-Bakri in the eleventh century. Al-Bakri also makes the earliest mention of Takrur, located on the Senegal River. In the thirteenth century, all these areas were consolidated within the hegemony of the Empire of Mali, known to us from Ibn Battuta's eyewitness account in the mid-fourteenth century, among others, and from versions of the epic tradition of Sunjata (described below).

The history of Western Sudanic states during our chronological period centers on three main polities. The earliest was the Soninke kingdom of Wagadu/Ghana (not to be confused with the modern coastal state of that name) that emerged during the period 500–700, and was in decline by the second half of the eleventh century. Following a period of political turmoil of unknown duration, most likely in the first half of the thirteenth century, Manding chiefdoms in the region of the Upper Niger and its tributaries unified into what would become the Mali Empire that attained its apogee in the fourteenth century and was in decline by the mid-fifteenth century. By c. 750–950, the kingdom of Gao farther east on the Middle Niger Bend had become sufficiently prosperous as a terminus for trans-Saharan trade that it expanded into the Songhay Empire by the 1490s. Songhay replaced Mali as the dominant power in the Western Sudan until 1591, when it was conquered by an invading Moroccan army. This chapter will examine these three states

This chapter is dedicated to the memory of Nehemia Levtzion.

in more detail, but will first discuss the role of oral traditions and recent interpretations of archaeological findings in West African history.

The importance of oral tradition for West African history

West African oral tradition rarely reveals facts about the past that can be accepted according to strict European historiographical standards, because the existence of people and events that are described in the narratives usually cannot be confirmed by independent evidence such as written documentation involving contemporary eyewitnesses. Nevertheless, oral tradition does convey useful information, both literally and metaphorically, about African perceptions of the past and how those perceptions affect present-day cultural values. In many rural West African communities, traditional social values and customs have not been submerged by foreign influence, as has been the case in capital cities and other urban centers. In agricultural villages and market towns of the countryside, notions of what happened in the distant past are still expressed through oral traditions that provide part of the framework for the way people live from day to day. The deeds of ancestral heroines and heroes are described in narratives that are passed down from one generation to the next in chains of oral communication that can be measured in spans of time ranging from several generations to many centuries. In some cases, the discourse rises to the level of epic that is filled with rich and colorful imagery in both narrative and song, reflecting the values of the cultures that produced them. Epic narratives vary in length, content and complexity depending on the desires and composition of the audience, and on the knowledge, purpose, and momentary whim of the performer. They tell the stories of village communities, kingdoms and empires that were peopled by charismatic leaders both male and female, who founded family lineages and accomplished momentous deeds during periods that are recalled as defining moments of the past.

Populations descended from the medieval West African states boast unsurpassed levels of oral art and consciousness. In the epic narrative of the Manding and some culturally related societies, the ancestors remain as they have apparently been for many centuries, the means of identification for every stranger entering a town or village, and for every householder receiving the strangers. The ancestors are evoked during any serious greeting, they are regularly praised in songs by the ubiquitous bards, their spirits are present at every council meeting, and sacrificial offerings are made to them before any serious project is undertaken. It is no exaggeration to say that the ancestors described in *kuma koro* or "ancient speech" define the identity of each and every member of Mande society, regardless of gender. Therefore, if the ancestors were to be forgotten, the fundamental essence of indigenous values – as perceived by the people themselves – would disappear. For foreign scholars to maintain that it is not possible for, say, the hero Sunjata and his companions to be known after so many centuries and that they and their deeds are entirely mythical (that theirs is "imaginary history" as one writer has phrased it), is to deny a fundamental fact of an extraordinarily vibrant culture: genuine reverence for the ancestors has kept certain aspects of the past more alive than could have been accomplished with the written word.

Cities and trade as a basis of state power

In the late 1970s, some important strides forward in the acquisition of archaeological data in West Africa were made when an archaeological team first visited the site of Jenne-jeno in the Middle Niger Delta of the republic of Mali. They were impressed by the vastness of an ancient settlement littered with ruins of clay-brick houses, exposed and still occupied burial urns, evidence of extensive iron works, and many tons of broken pottery among other surface artifacts. However, in what appeared to be an ancient urban landscape (later dated to *c.* 400–1000 CE with earliest settlement in the third century BCE), they saw nothing erected on the surface to indicate its import-ance as a heavily populated wealthy city and center of pre-Islamic trade. At one time, archaeological wisdom expected that an ancient city grounded in pre-industrial economies would exhibit something indicating the seat of power of a coercive kingdom or state. Colonial-era historians and archaeolo-gists had been aware of the Jenne-jeno site, but they failed to recognize it as an ancient urban center because of the absence of permanent, monumental architecture reflective of an exalted titleholder ruling a powerful state.

Nowadays it is evident that monumental manifestations of state power are absent in ancient settlements of the Middle Niger because they evolved without the kinds of power hierarchies and accompanying symbols charac-teristic of urban centers of the ancient Middle East and elsewhere. One developing argument is that the more familiar kinds of despotic, state-driven societies lack sustainability, being fragile and prone to eventual collapse because of their rigid hierarchical infrastructure. In the Middle Niger Delta, archaeologists found a different species of ancient urbanism, with non-despotic communities of diverse corporate groups in no need of a king or other indications of a state-based city. Influenced by the unpredictable and potentially hazardous sub-Saharan Middle Niger environment, these communities spontaneously evolved into what Roderick McIntosh calls a "self-organizing landscape." Passing through multiple stages of development, the process culminated by the middle of the first millennium CE in a kind of "multi-satellite, multi-corporate urban complex" that was innovative and flexible enough to achieve the type of long-term sustainability that the McIntosh expeditions found at Jenne-jeno and other partly explored locations in the Middle Niger Delta.[1]

Research of the last several decades indicates that sociopolitical development during the first millennium CE was influenced by a wide range of economies involving various degrees of mobility. At some point near the end of a long period of drought from *c.* 300 BCE to *c.* 300 CE camel-herders appeared and began transforming the desert economy. This and other responses to the great period of increased dryness had social, political, and economic consequences which then shaped responses to a climate upturn that occurred after 300 CE. Noting the importance of horses during the first millennium, some scholars have speculated about what their impact might have been on the political economies of the time and place in question. For example, horses might have increased people's ability to trade with neighboring groups, or to raid and exact tribute from them. These and related issues involving mobile, sedentary, and combinations of both types of economies, form an important part of the long-tem chronological framework within which the development of early Western Sudanic polities is now considered.

The antiquity of both trans-Saharan trade and the trade-based polities of the Western Sudan has been the subject of considerable discussion. Some scholars argue for a trade route from North Africa to the Niger Bend in the mid-first millennium BCE. Recoveries of Roman coins are limited to only three sites in southern Mauritania, but Kevin MacDonald has presented evidence on behalf of "a pre-existing network of down-the-line exchange" in semi-precious stones.[2] Susan McIntosh has outlined a significant amount of evidence for a variety of regional exchange systems throughout the southern Sahara and Sahel. According to her archaeological findings at Jenne-jeno, the

---

1 Roderick J. McIntosh, *Ancient Middle Niger: Urbanism and the Self-Organizing Landscape* (Cambridge University Press, 2005): 32–3, 43.

2 Kevin C. MacDonald, "A View from the South: Sub-Saharan Evidence for Contacts between North Africa, Mauritania and the Niger, 1000 BC – AD 700," in Amelia Dowler and Elizabeth R. Galvin (eds.), *Money, Trade and Trade Routes in Pre-Islamic North Africa* (London: The British Museum Press, 2011): 72–80.

earliest unambiguous evidence discovered to date for the re-establishment of links between desert and savannah is the presence of copper by the fifth century CE, which also indicates the likelihood of a desert salt trade.[3] Discussion of trade routes has of course included the question of when gold began to be transported along the Saharan networks to reach North Africa. Evidence from North African mints suggests that the reactivation in 296 of the mint at Carthage, which continued to strike imperial gold coins until it closed in 695, might have been made possible by a West African source reaching North Africa during that period . However, alternative views must also be considered, pending results of research that could reveal evidence for a trans-Saharan gold trade prior to 750–800.

Imports of copper and glass in sites just south of the Sahara increased during the period 400–800. The latter half of this period coincides with the initial Arab advance into North Africa, and the establishment of trading centers at Tahert and Sijilmasa in the Maghreb. Large-scale transport of heavy commodities such as salt and metals was made possible by the spread of the camel as a desert pack animal in the first millennium CE. With the spread of Islam and literacy, more expansive trade networks carrying far more goods were in place by 1000. In the eleventh century, a desert confederation of the desert-dwelling Berbers known as Sanhaja established the powerful Almoravid Empire, which provided a unified political field for trade from the Senegal River Valley to the Maghrib (i.e. northwestern Africa), southern Spain, and Egypt.

Wagadu / Ghana

The first major West African state in this era was the kingdom of Wagadu / Ghana, which emerged in the Sahel – the semi-arid region between desert and savannah – from villages established during the period 500 to 700 CE. The principal people of Wagadu / Ghana were the Soninke, who were the northernmost of the Mande peoples, a large family of culturally related groups that would subsequently populate the Mali Empire. Some ancestors of the Soninke were probably among the Neolithic farmers who began cultivating sorghum and millet in the Sahelian grasslands during the period 3000 to 1000 BCE. By about 1000 BCE the Soninke ancestors began establishing small settled communities, and around 600 BCE these grew into large villages

---

3 Susan Keech McIntosh, *Excavations at Jenné-jeno, Hambarketolo, and Kaniana: The 1981 Season* (Berkeley: University of California Press, 2005).

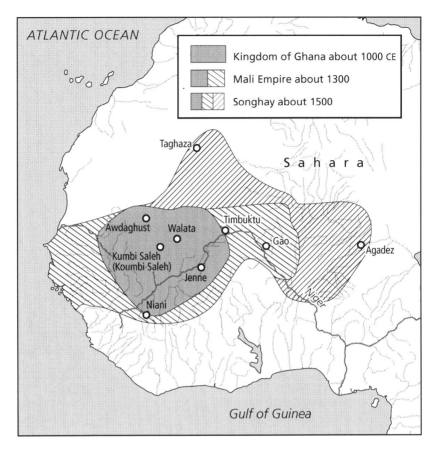

Map 22.1. Ghana / Mali / Songhay

administered by chieftaincies. The early farmers were among the first to take advantage of the iron technology that developed in West Africa by about 500 to 400 BCE. As the most northern of the Mande peoples, the Soninke were also in contact with the nomads of the Sahara, from whom they acquired small horses brought from North Africa. The early Soninke's superior iron weaponry and horses made it possible for them to develop some level of a nascent polity. They gradually expanded their territories and dominated neighboring rulers until, by the tenth century, they had established a state (see Map 22.1).

Was Wagadu/Ghana a kingdom, an empire, or something else? Some have questioned the use of the term "empire" to describe ancient Ghana because it tends to obscure what scarce information is available in the sources. When applied to African polities like Wagadu/Ghana, questions of what is actually meant by such terms as "state," "kingdom," and "empire" have generated a steady flow of theories by anthropologists, historians and geographers about African political systems in colonial times, through early post-colonial colloquiums on topics like the origin and development of state systems and into the present era of discussion about urbanization and state formation. West African scholars with the insider's perspective[4] have contributed valuable alternative theories to outsider's notions of "pristine states" versus "secondary states" or the ownership and application of technological developments. The amount of theoretical literature on these complex topics vis-à-vis West Africa is indeed extensive, even without taking into account evidence from the archaeology of pre-colonial cities and states. Considerable archaeological progress has been made in recent decades, but even so, Susan McIntosh concludes that given the present condition of the evidence, "any discussion of the development and political organization of early Sudanic polities must be both theoretical and speculative."[5] An example of current informed archaeological theorizing in this regard, would be the model of Wagadu/Ghana suggested by Roderick McIntosh, to the effect that it was not so much a despotic conquest state, as it was a "slowly consolidated confederation of many 'chiefdoms' in various relations to the core (from nominal, tribute-paying parity to fully administered)." McIntosh explains that his reconstruction is in line with recent views regarding "origins of states out of an earlier landscape of small-scale polities." Regarding the later Mali and Songhay empires, he observes that "during times of dynastic struggles or other sources of political turmoil at the core, the elements of the periphery slipped easily into states of greater or lesser political autonomy." Moreover, says McIntosh, during the rise of Wagadu/Ghana, "parts of the Middle Niger, such as the Jenne region, probably maintained their status as fully self-administering, independent, and friendly polities."[6]

The Soninke people's own ideas about their history are expressed in the "Legend of Wagadu," an oral tradition told by many generations of *gesere*,

---

4 Raymond N. Asombang, "Sacred Centers and Urbanization in West Central Africa," in Susan Keech McIntosh (ed.), *Beyond Chiefdoms: Pathways to Complexity in Africa* (Cambridge University Press, 1999): 80–7.
5 Susan Keech McIntosh, "Reconceptualizing Early Ghana," *Canadian Journal of African Studies* 42 (2008): 366.
6 Roderick J. McIntosh, *The Peoples of the Middle Niger* (Oxford: Blackwell Publishers, 1998): 256.

professional oral historians and musicians of the Soninke. Details vary from one version to the next, but it generally describes the origins and early deeds of different Soninke clans. The story often begins by describing how the ancestor Dinga came from somewhere in the Middle East and settled in successive locations in what is today's Mali. In the Middle Niger Delta region he was at Jenne for a time, then at Dia, where he produced offspring who became Soninke ancestors elsewhere in the Sahel. Dinga is said to have eventually arrived at a place southwest of Nioro that was dominated by spirits of the bush, which in the story are called "genies." Various versions describe a kind of magician's duel between Dinga and the genies with Dinga emerging victorious and marrying the three daughters of the chief genie. The sons from these wives became the ancestors of many Soninke clans, one of which was that of the Cissé. It was the Cissé clan that became the ruling lineage of Wagadu.

The next episode in the legend is reminiscent of the story of Jacob and Esau in the Bible. Dinga has grown old and blind, and before he dies he wants to pass his chiefly power on to his elder son Khiné. But a younger son named Diabe disguises himself as the eldest brother and deceives his father into bequeathing him the chiefly powers. After Dinga dies, Diabe flees the wrath of his enraged elder brother and takes refuge in the wilderness where a mysterious drum falls out of a tree and lands at his feet. At the sound of the drum, four troops of cavalry come out from the four corners of the wilderness. The four commanders recognize Diabe as their superior and become his lieutenants. Later, after the Wagadu kingdom is established, they become chiefs or governors of the four provinces.

Diabe sets out to find a location where he can settle, arriving at a place called Kumbi, which was located in the southern part of what is now Mauritania, just north of the border presently shared with Mali. Arriving at the site where the town of Kumbi is to be established, Diabe finds it guarded by a giant snake called Bida. Significantly, the great snake is usually described as a python, implying the presence of water at the new settlement's location. A pact is made allowing Diabe to settle there with Bida as guardian, on the condition that every year a young virgin girl would be sacrificed to the great serpent. In return, Bida guarantees abundant rain for Wagadu and a plentiful supply of gold.

With its capital at Kumbi, Wagadu prospers under the rule of Diabe Cissé and his descendants known by the title *Maghan*. The descendants of Diabe and the four *Fado* or commanders of the provinces are still recognized as aristocratic Soninke clans called *Wago*. That term is probably related to "Wagadu" which is a contraction of *wagadugu*, a word that can be translated as "land of the Wago."

According to the legend, representatives of the four provinces of Wagadu would assemble at Kumbi each year to participate in the virgin sacrifice to Bida, the guardian serpent. This ceremony was the annual renewal of the pact between Diabe Cissé and Bida, to ensure the continued supply of gold and abundant rainfall. According to some versions, each year a different province was required to supply the virgin for the sacrifice. If this was the actual practice, it was a custom that probably helped maintain unity in the kingdom.

After an unspecified number of generations have passed, a year arrives when the virgin to be sacrificed happens to be the fiancée of a young man of noble birth. As the sacrifice is about to be made, the young man decapitates the snake with his sword, thus triggering the destruction of Wagadu. As Bida's severed head bounds into the sky it pronounces a dreadful curse that henceforth no rain would fall on Wagadu and no more gold would be found there. Deprived of rain and gold, Wagadu declines into ruin, its Soninke people are dispersed, and the countryside becomes a desert.

The Wagadu legend's mythical elements are obvious, but parts of it reflect both social and environmental realities that could have actually been involved in Soninke history. The kind of competition seen between the younger brother Diabe Cissé and his elder brother Khiné, is a common form of stepbrother rivalry called *fadenya* in Manding society of which the Soninke are a part. At the state level of the early Western Sudanic kingdoms, there are many stories of brothers being involved in bloody rivalries for succession to the throne (especially in the Songhay Empire).

With regard to environmental elements in the legend, it is a fact that pythons are equally at home in the water and on land. Their presence was a sure sign of a climate with adequate wet phases to support a settlement, as suggested by the bargain struck between Bida and Diabe Cissé. In early times before the arrival of Islam and Christianity, the great pythons were sacred religious symbols throughout sub-Saharan West Africa from the Sahel to the Atlantic coast. In recent times, zoologists have found that during the heat of the day in the dry season, pythons usually seek water in which to submerge themselves. Thus, it is not difficult to see how the idea of the great snake as a highly spiritual water oracle could develop.

For the early Arab geographers who wrote about "Ghana," it was a tantalizing land of mystery and fabled wealth. They had some inaccurate and even fantastic notions of what was there, but they also provide important information. In 738 a governor of the Maghrib sent a commercial expedition to "the land of the blacks," and the merchants returned laden with slaves and gold. The trade seems to have originated with the peoples of the desert, the most powerful of whom were the Sanhaja who carried on trade with the Soninke to the south of them. The Soninke's early involvement with the traders of the Sahara is one reason that Wagadu/Ghana emerged as a great power ahead of other chiefdoms of the medieval Sahel. The other main reason is that Wagadu controlled the sources of both salt and gold. As Ibn Hawqal, writing in 988, described it, "the ruler of Ghana is the wealthiest king on the face of the earth because of his treasures and stocks of gold extracted in olden times for his predecessors and himself."[7]

Efficient food production, early control of iron technology for superior weaponry and the acquisition of horses, helped the Soninke achieve early superiority over their neighbors. The Muslim writer al-Ya'qubi (d. 897) described Ghana as one of the two most powerful kingdoms of the Western Sudan, with a ruler who had other kings under his authority. What eventually raised the Soninke kingdom to the imperial level was its control of both regional and trans-Saharan trade. The inter-regional trade involved the exchange of salt, copper and dates from the Sahara. Savannah products included slaves, livestock, iron tools, weapons and utensils, animal hides, leather goods such as sandals, cushions and bags, locally woven and dyed cloth, clay pottery, woven grass products like baskets and sleeping mats, medicinal herbs, and foodstuffs like dried fish, rice, various grains and condiments, spices, honey, and fruit. From farther south nearer the forest came gold and kola nuts.

On a broader scale, Wagadu/Ghana was well positioned to dominate the international caravan trade across the western Sahara. One of the most important reasons for that commercial development had been the introduction of the camel into North Africa by the Romans during the first century CE. The one-humped camel was originally domesticated in southern Arabia around 5000 BCE, and introduced into northeastern Africa around 3000 BCE. From northeastern Africa the camel arrived in the Sahara Desert sometime during the first centuries CE. It was from that time on, thanks to the camel, that regular and extensive trade across the Sahara became possible.

In the second and third centuries CE the use of camels expanded among North African Berber peoples. The Sanhaja Berbers acquired significant numbers of camels by the fourth and fifth centuries, and began to develop and control increasingly busy desert trade routes. The trans-Saharan caravans

7 Nehemia Levtzion and J. F. P Hopkins (eds.), *Corpus of Early Arabic Sources for West African History* (Cambridge University Press, 1981): 49.

could consist of as few as a half-dozen camels, or as many as two thousand. They usually left North Africa in April or May, led by professional Berber guides who could find the wells and waterholes. The dangerous journey lasted from two and a half to three months, depending on the size of the caravan and conditions of the route. Unusually dry years could leave the wells with insufficient water, and if a severe sandstorm came up the entire caravan could perish.

In pre-Islamic times, the Maghrib and southern Sahara were already linked by Berber-speaking nomads who interacted with Sahelian sedentary populations of the Bilad al-Sudan ("land of the blacks"). Sometime during the eighth century the Zanata and other Berber peoples of the Atlas region became Muslims, but it was not until the first half of the eleventh century that the Sanhaja Berbers of the southern Sahara became committed to Islam when they were coerced into joining the Almoravid movement. Extensive conversion of the Berber peoples brought with it wider commercial connections, increased the scale and complexity of their trade, and generally enhanced their prosperity. This was evident in sub-Saharan commercial centers including the much-contested city of Awdaghust, which originally gained commercial prominence under Berber authority. During the early decades of the eleventh century, the Soninke of Wagadu/Ghana seized control of Awdaghust, but Almoravid Sanhaja retook it in 1055–6.

By the eleventh century, black sub-Saharan rulers of Wagadu/Ghana in the western Sahel and Gao on the Niger Bend were accepting the presence of North African Muslim traders in designated quarters of their cities while most of the local population continued with their traditional spiritual practices. For merchants, participation in the vast Sahelian commercial network became dependent on at least nominal conversion to Islam, even for black sub-Saharan traders that included Fula, Wolof and Manding. It was the latter who linked the savannah goldfields of Bambuk and Buré with the sub-Saharan entrepôts of Walata, Jenne, and Timbuktu.

Wagadu/Ghana's advantageous location in the Sahel enabled the Soninke to function as middlemen controlling commerce from the savannah and forest zones in the south, and the Sahara and Maghrib in the north. From tributary states in the Senegal Valley the Tegdaoust/Awdaghust entrepôt received salt, gold, ivory, dried/salted fish, produce, and craft products. From the broader savannah region and the forest it received gold, elephant and hippopotamus ivory, ebony, slaves, ostrich feathers, wild and domestic animal hides, gum arabic, produce such as dates and kola nuts, pottery, leatherwork, and other craft goods. The geographer Yaqut (1179–1229), a freed slave of Greek origin who became a Muslim, described the country's commercial position: "Merchants meet in Ghana and from there one enters the arid wastes towards the land of Gold. Were it not for Ghana, this journey would be impossible, because the land of Gold is in a place isolated from the west in the land of the Sudan. From Ghana the merchants take provisions on the way to the land of Gold."[8]

The north–south trade employed a network of routes connecting Wagadu's Tegdaoust / Awdaghust entrepôt with its counterpart trading city of Sijilmasa in the Maghrib, as well as with al-Andalus, Tripoli and Egypt. From those sources came manufactured objects and luxury goods from the Mediterranean world, Europe, and North Africa. They included iron products like knives, scissors, needles, and razors; brass and copperware; textiles including silk, velvet, and brocade; ornaments and jewelry, including glass and porcelain beads; and other luxury goods, including silver, glassware, mirrors, carpets, perfumes, paper, tea, coffee, and sugar. Horses from North Africa were one of the most important items moving south, as were cowrie shells, which were used as currency in West African markets.

As the twelfth century unfolded, the dominance of Wagadu/Ghana gradually faded away. Desert encroachment on formerly productive land as well as generations of struggle with powerful desert nomads prompted many Soninke to abandon their ancestral lands and move to a less difficult and capricious environment. The decline of Soninke power left a vacuum that was filled for a time by some smaller savannah kingdoms to the south in areas closer to rivers and lakes, and with more reliable rainfall. In the first half of the thirteenth century some Mande chiefdoms (*jamanaw*) of the Upper Niger began to unify into a new state that would eventually develop into the Mali Empire.

The Mali Empire

All of the above-mentioned goods that were traded in the markets of Wagadu / Ghana from the tenth to twelfth centuries continued to generate revenue in the markets of Mali from the thirteenth to fifteenth centuries, but gold was the most important commodity. There were three principal goldfields below the Sahara. One of the main ones, which had also been a source for Wagadu / Ghana, was at Bambuk, between the Senegal and Faleme rivers.

8 Levtzion and Hopkins, *Corpus of Early Arabic Sources*, 172.

Another, also formerly controlled by Wagadu/Ghana, was at Buré above the Upper Niger in what is now northeast Guinea. The third was in Akan territory near the forest in the modern republics of Côte d'Ivoire and Ghana. Mali drew on all three goldfields for the trans-Saharan trade in precious metal for which merchants from North Africa, the Middle East, and Europe competed. The exact routes or frequency of shipment from the individual goldfields are not entirely known, but much of the gold from Buré was moved along the Niger River to Jenne, where camel caravans headed overland across the Sahara, with some continuing to Timbuktu before turning north.

The Mande people's oral tradition, "Mande Maana," which presents their own perceptions of the origins of the Mali Empire, is usually referred to outside the culture as the "Sunjata Epic." In recent decades the corpus of indigenous oral sources has grown enormously, and many previously unknown variants of the Sunjata epic, among other important narratives, have come to light. The additional oral sources have been accompanied by increasingly sophisticated methodologies for determining reasonable degrees of probability for elusive elements of historical evidence.

The Sunjata epic is named for Sunjata Keita, who, along with several other charismatic ancestors of both genders, is credited with a major role in establishing the foundations of the Mali Empire. The story begins sometime around the beginning of the thirteenth century in Farakoro, a Mande chiefdom. The identification of Farakoro and other places as important locations in Mali's political history is relatively recent. From the early 1960s when D. T. Niane introduced the Sunjata Epic to the world outside West Africa, the town of Niani on the Guinean side of the Sankaran River was said to be the home of Sunjata's father and the "capital" of the Mali Empire. More recently, a significant amount of evidence has been found to indicate that Konfara was the chiefdom of Sunjata's father and his village was Farakoro. This was near the goldfields of Buré, which had been one of the main sources of gold for Ghana in earlier centuries and proved to be similarly important for the Mali Empire. One of Sunjata's most important towns was Dakajalan, said to be the place where he spent his early years, to which he returned from exile, and which served as his headquarters during the war with Soso.

Like all powerful men of Mande culture, Sunjata's father, Maghan Konfara, had diviners who would forecast the future. They told him that he would be the father of a great hero, but that the woman who would be the hero's mother had not yet been found. After a long search the woman is finally located in the kingdom of Do ni Kiri. She is Sogolon Condé, a sister of the *mansa* (king) of Do ni Kiri. Sogolon is an ugly, hunchbacked woman with formidable powers as a sorceress and is recognized as the woman who is destined to give birth to Sunjata. She is brought to Farakoro and married to Maghan Konfara, who already has many other wives. Jealous of the diviners' prediction favoring Sogolon, the co-wives do everything they can to stop her from giving birth to the hero. After several years of trouble the predicted birth takes place, but the child is born crippled. He is called "Sogolon's Jara" (*jara* = lion). It takes years for Sogolon's Jara (Sunjata) to learn to walk, but when he finally does he becomes a great hunter. One of Maghan Konfara's other wives has a son who was born before Sunjata. Despite the diviners' forecast of greatness for Sunjata, she is determined that her son will be the next chief. After a failed attempt to kill Sunjata, Sogolon moves him and her other children into exile, eventually settling in the old Soninke kingdom of Mema in the Middle Niger Delta.

While Sogolon and her children are in exile, the Mande chiefdoms are conquered by the army of Soso led by its powerful king Sumaworo Kanté. After long suffering under his tyrannical rule, the Mande people recall the diviners' prediction that Maghan Konfara's wife Sogolon would give birth to a great leader. A search party locates Sunjata in Mema and returns him to Manden where he organizes the Mande chiefdoms into a powerful army against Soso tyranny. Sunjata's army eventually vanquishes the army of Soso, and the unified Mande chiefdoms form the basis of a powerful kingdom that expands into neighboring territories and becomes the Mali Empire. The Mande oral traditions do not give dates for the events they describe, but according to the Arabic sources, Mande's defeat of Soso happened sometime during the 1230s. The most detailed information about Mali is provided by three Arab geographers and historians: Al-'Umari (1301–1349), Ibn Battuta (1304–1368/9 or 1377) and Ibn Khaldun (1332–1406). Of these, only Ibn Battuta actually visited the court of Mali.

Ibn Khaldun heard that Mali became the greatest power in the Western Sudan. He reported that the greatest king of Mali, who overcame the Soso and conquered their country was named Mari Jata (a.k.a. Sunjata), who ruled for twenty-five years. Sunjata was succeeded by his son Mansa Wali (*mansa* = "king" or "emperor") who survived in memory because he made a pilgrimage to Mecca during the reign of the Mamluk Sultan Baybars, who ruled Egypt and Syria (1260–77). The relatively sparse information available about rulers other than a famous few indicates that Mali had major leadership problems at various times, evidently suffering the fatal flaw of never establishing an effective standard of royal succession. In the decades between

Sunjata's reign and those of Mansa Musa and Mansa Sulayman in the fourteenth century, the country endured repeated periods of dynastic instability, a pattern that would be repeated after the latter's death. Failed rulers ranged from the merely undistinguished to the insanely homicidal. They included a vicious tyrant, an assassin, a brazen plunderer of state wealth, some well-intended but ineffective weaklings, and usurpers who stepped in at times with mixed results. The Arabic name of Mansa Abu Bakr reflects the continuing influence of Islam among the ruling elite, and the reign of a formerly servile military commander named Sakura (1298–1308) underlines the periodic failures of some descendants of Sogolon Condé's offspring, Sunjata and Manden Bori. Upon Sakura's death the kingship reverted to two forgettable descendants of Sunjata before power passed to descendants of Manden Bori. This finally resulted in the reign of one of Mali's great rulers, Mansa Musa (r. 1312–37).

By this time the desert city of Walata had overtaken Tegdaoust/Awdaghust as the main western terminus of trans-Saharan trade. However, Jenne was linked to Timbuktu by the Niger River, and it subsequently became the key distribution center for salt moving southward from the central Sahara via Timbuktu and, among other products, gold transported north to the Maghrib. At the regional level, the main difference between Wagadu/Ghana and Mali had been that at the height of Mali's power it controlled far more territory than Ghana ever did, so it had more resources to exploit. By the beginning of the fourteenth century, Mali's expansion into the Inland Delta, Gao, and what would eventually become eastern provinces of Songhay, had added enormously to the farming, grazing, hunting and fishing resources of the empire. The new territories also provided additional sources of slaves for trade, military service and farm production. Tribute from newly subordinated kings and chiefs, and tariffs from newly controlled trade routes enriched the government treasury.

Thus, Mansa Musa's twenty-five-year reign is thought of as the "golden age" of Mali. Among sub-Saharan West African rulers who made the pilgrimage to Mecca, Mansa Musa was the most famous. His caravan is said to have included eighty loads of gold dust, and his 1324 arrival in Egypt created a sensation because Mansa Musa distributed so much gold as gifts, and the Malians spent such large amounts in the market, that it took several years for the value of gold to recover (see Figure 22.1). Publicity resulting from the sensational visit brought increased awareness of Mali to North Africa, the Middle East, and Europe. An impression spread throughout the Mediterranean world of vast wealth to be had south of the Sahara. Trade with the

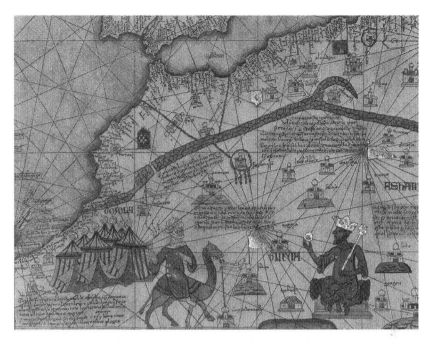

Figure 22.1 Illustration of Mansa Musa in detail from the Catalan Atlas, 1375 (vellum), Cresques Abraham (1325–87) (Bibliothèque Nationale, Paris, France / Bridgeman Images)

Maghrib was especially boosted by Mansa Musa's exchange of diplomatic embassies with the sultan of Morocco. Increasing numbers of traders from throughout North Africa embarked on commercial ventures across the Sahara. By the mid-fourteenth century these included Egyptian traders making regular visits to Mali. Citizens in commercial centers like Walata were dressing in clothes and buying other imported goods from Mediterranean shores.

Another especially significant result of Mansa Musa's pilgrimage was the arrival in Mali of a Muslim architect recruited from Spain named Abu Ishaq al-Sahili. The architect built Mansa Musa a rectangular domed house covered with plaster that was decorated with colorful designs, thus introducing an architectural style that can still be seen in many towns and cities of the Western Sudan. One of Mansa Musa's residences was in Timbuktu, location of the still-famous Sankoré Mosque which is believed to have been designed by al-Sahili.

When Mansa Musa died in 1337, his son Mansa Magha succeeded him, but was replaced after a few years by Musa's brother, Mansa Sulayman

(r. 1341–60). Although not popular with his subjects, Sulayman was a powerful and effective ruler of the empire. In 1352–3 his court was visited by the North African geographer Ibn Battuta who later wrote an eyewitness account indicating that the royal court of Mali was as rich and splendid as any in the Muslim world. The palace throne room is described as a "lofty pavilion" with curtained, gilded arches and silken accessories. An upholstered outdoor throne was shaded by a large silken parasol topped by a golden falcon. Royal audiences featured elaborate pageantry and ceremony, with marching drummers and trumpeters with elephant tusk horns, and hundreds of armed guards formed in ranks. Ibn Battuta describes the pomp and circumstance of the *mansa*'s ceremonial approach to the throne wearing a golden headdress and red robe, carrying a bow and quiver of arrows, and preceded by singers and musicians "with gold and silver stringed instruments."[9] Nevertheless, grand as Ibn Battuta found the royal court to be, the pious traveler was deeply offended by the casual social relationships he saw between men and women. In the royal compound, he witnessed the public nudity of scores of female slaves and servants, which Jerry Bentley points to as clearly indicating that "pagan traditions" survived there, with Islamic law being established in only limited and selective fashion.[10]

The reigns of Musa and Sulayman spanned the years 1312–60 and marked the apogee of the Mali Empire. When Mansa Sulayman died in 1360, his sons and the sons of Mansa Musa fought over the succession. Civil war ensued, opening the way to generations of power struggles and leadership gone awry. By the end of the fourteenth century, generations of power struggles and weak leadership had undermined Mali's power to the point where it became impossible to retain control of the empire's distant frontiers; indeed Mali lost control of Timbuktu sometime around 1433. Beyond the Niger Bend, the more distant eastern provinces, including Gao, had probably been lost even earlier.

The kingdom of Gao

Among the early people of the Niger Bend region were the camel-riding Sanhaja of the Sahara Desert. Locally known as Tuareg, they rode out of the great desert to establish trading camps near the Niger River. Other early

---

9 Levtzion and Hopkins, *Corpus of Early Arabic Sources,* 290–1.
10 Jerry H. Bentley, *Old World Encounters: Cross-Cultural Contacts and Exchange in Pre-Modern Times* (New York: Oxford University Press, 1993): 131.

settlers were a riverine people known as Sorko, who moved northward into the region from an area known as Dendi, which was downstream from Gao. Sorko origins are obscure, but they were early speakers of proto-Songhay, either bringing it with them or adopting it later under the rule of Songhay horsemen who followed them upriver from Dendi and established control over them. Between 750 and 950, while Ancient Ghana was prospering as "the land of gold" far to the west, the trading center at Gao became an increasingly important southern terminus for trade across the Sahara Desert. By the tenth century the rulers of Gao had established it as a small kingdom, taking control of the peoples that lived along the trade routes. By around 1300, Gao had become so prosperous that it attracted the attention of Mali's rulers and, as we saw earlier, was conquered by them. Until recently, modern scholarship on the history of the Songhay polity relied largely on chronicles written in Timbuktu during the second half of the seventeenth century. According to these chronicles, the Songhay state was ruled by a series of three dynasties. They began with rulers who carried the title Zuwa, the first fourteen of which ruled before the arrival of Islam. The second dynasty was that of the Sii or Sonyi (c. 1430–1492), and they were followed by the Askias who held power from 1493 until the Moroccan invasion of 1591.

Linguistic and other evidence suggests a fair likelihood that the rulers known as Sii or Sonyi, originated as a Mande warrior group that moved in from Mali. According to the now familiar narrative presented in the Timbuktu chronicles and supplemented by oral tradition, the Sii dynasty was highlighted by the reign of Sii Ali Beeri ("The Great"), who transformed the kingdom of Gao into the empire of Songhay, which would replace Mali as the great power of the Western Sudan. Sii Ali commanded a large, well-disciplined army and a fleet of riverboats with which he expanded Gao's territory throughout the Middle Niger Delta. Ali's control of the Niger Bend brought with it the rich gold and salt trade that passed through Timbuktu and Jenne, which became the second and third most important cities of the Songhay state.

According to the Timbuktu chronicles, the Sii dynasty was followed by one that adopted the title Askia, which has long been said to date from the 1480s,[11] although epigraphic evidence uncovered by Paulo Moraes Farias reveals that the title was in use in Gao by 1234, two and a half centuries earlier. Under the first Askia, who became known as Askia Muhammad the

---

11 Ibn al-Mukhtar, *Ta'rikh al-fattash*, ed. and trans. Octave Houdas and Maurice Delafosse (Paris: Adrien-Maisonneuve, 1964): 88.

Great (1493–1529), Songhay would flourish into the early decades of the sixteenth century. Imperial control eventually expanded northward to the saltpans of Taghaza in the Sahara Desert, westward to former territories of the Mali Empire, and eastward to the Tuareg sultanate of Agadez. The empire became so large that its army was divided into two, one for the western provinces based in Timbuktu, and one for the eastern provinces based in Gao. The sons of Askia Muhammad were mostly half-brothers, and in 1529 Askia Muhammad was deposed by one of them. Similar to the case of Mali, failure to establish an effective process of succession would eventually lead to Songhay's downfall. Askia Muhammad's son Musa (1529–31) had no compunctions about killing rival brothers to stay in power. This set the tone for the triumphs and vicissitudes of the seven succeeding Askias up to the time of the Moroccan conquest of Songhay in 1591.

With the publication of *Arabic Medieval Inscriptions from the Republic of Mali* in 2003, Paulo Moraes Farias has introduced epigraphic evidence revealing that the Timbuktu chronicles were not the product of detailed historical records extending back over several centuries as had been previously thought, but were constructed on ideological grounds. He describes their production on one level as being "an exercise in catastrophe management," catering to emotional and intellectual needs that resulted from the destruction of the Songhay Empire by the Moroccan invasion of 1591. Moraes Farias reasons that through artful reconstruction of the past the chroniclers were coming to terms with the disastrous events that reduced the Askias to puppet roles and caused personal suffering for the literate urban elite and downgraded their political and social status. He argues, moreover, that on another level the Timbuktu chroniclers were endorsing acceptance of the post-invasion Arma (Arabic: *al-rumāh* – "musketeers") regime while at the same time formulating grounds for its reform. Thus, the chroniclers' political agenda required consolidation of the Songhay and Timbuktu past into a seamless narrative with chronological depth and political continuity. Moraes Farias argues that the chroniclers, in pursuit of their aim to represent the Songhay state as an unbroken narrative spanning three successive dynasties, manipulated their lengthy king lists, obfuscating periods of dynastic change and interval. The epigraphic evidence has convinced Moraes Farias that the Timbuktu chronicles artificially shorten Mali's period of domination of the eastern arc of the Niger Bend, and that they also prolong the length of the Zuwā (or Za) dynasty into the past and possibly forward in time.

In the epigraphic evidence there are four identifiable series of royal titleholders, with two of the series of rulers known as Malik (pl. Mulūk).

The earlier Mulūk (kings) held power from an undetermined date up to 1083–4,[12] and the later series of Mulūk reigned from *c.* 1084 to *c.* 1203. Names of ancestors appear in the later Mulūk series of inscriptions, but without explicit reference to royal titles, which leads Moraes Farias to the tentative conclusion that the series of rulers known as Mulūk was based on a system of circulating kingship, which was apparently more important to them than claims to royal ancestry.

The third series of rulers featured women known by the title Malikāt (queen) which Moraes Farias believes existed parallel to, but relatively autonomous from, the Mulūk series. The last-known inscription date for the later Mulūk series is 1203 and the earliest date for the officeholders called Zuwā is 1127, so there is a chronological overlap of the two. Moraes Farias qualifies as "provisional" his description of the Zu'a/Zuwā series as a succession of kings, because it is not possible to be sure of the exact nature of their politico-ritual role, especially in regard to the earliest of them. Moreover, the title Malik is explicitly attached to only two of the inscriptions. Among possible explanations, Moraes Farias hypothesizes that during the twelfth century, political power over Gao and neighboring areas might not have been unified, with some communities governed by different rulers who coexisted peacefully. Another possibility is that twelfth-century Zuwā served under the Mulūk in offices that did not challenge their authority, and then replaced the Mulūk with overall power after 1203.

The last inscription date found for the Zuwā officeholders can be read as either 1280 or 1299, and this appears to mark the end of independence for Gao and the beginning of Mali's rule over the Middle Niger.[13]

Other states

Although Wagadu/Ghana, Mali, and the Gao/Songhay state tend to receive the most attention in the historical literature, they were by no means the only significant polities in medieval West Africa. In the ninth to the eleventh centuries, the Kingdom of Takrur was the dominant power in the Senegal River Valley, competing for trade with Wagadu/Ghana as a zealously Islamic

12 Moraes Farias reminds us that al-Bakri's description of them suggests they were a riverine people rather than Berbers from the Sahara: P. F. de Moraes Farias, *Arabic Medieval Inscriptions from the Republic of Mali: Epigraphy, Chronicles and Songhay-Tuāreg History* (Oxford University Press for The British Academy, 2003)

13 Moraes Farias, *Arabic Medieval Inscriptions* clix, clxii, cvi–cvii, clxv–clxvi, clxvii, and 29–30.

ally of the rising Almoravid movement of the western Sahara. The Almoravid movement commenced in the second half of the tenth century when 'Abdallah ibn Yasin (d. 1059), a Berber of the desert-dwelling Sanhaja people, began to establish what would become a formidable Islamic empire which, as we saw earlier, rose to power during the decline of Wagadu/Ghana. The Almoravids took control of the Soninke territories on the way to achieving political hegemony for the next two centuries throughout the western Sahara and the Maghrib, where they founded the city of Marrakesh in 1062. At its apogee, the Almoravid Empire included present-day Mauritania, western Sahara, Morocco, western Algeria, and southern Spain.

Some relatively ephemeral kingdoms of the period were, for a time, client states or provinces of Wagadu/Ghana. These chiefdoms or smaller states were generally much slower to adopt Islam, in most cases incorporating Muslim elements into traditional belief systems that constituted the indispensable underpinnings of power and authority for local rulers. Such was the case with Kaniaga and Diafunu, each of which briefly occupied a Sahelian power vacuum left by the decline of Wagadu/Ghana, as well as Kingui and Mema, which were located west of Gao in the Middle Niger Delta and later absorbed by the Mali Empire. But the most powerful state in the interim between the decline of Wagadu/Ghana and the rise of Mali was the Kingdom of Soso, whose imperial ambitions ended in the first half of the thirteenth century with the alliance of rival Mande chiefdoms that conquered Soso and established the foundations of the Mali Empire.

Conclusion

In the period between 500 and 1500 CE, West African settlements between the southern edge of the Sahara Desert and major riverine environments, including Senegal and Niger, experienced varying degrees of success in taking advantage of their geographical locations and control of natural resources to establish and sustain urban centers and satellite communities that eventually emerged as polities of the Western Sudan. Key values held in common were elaborate kinship systems, customs and rituals addressing issues of inter-ethnic relations, and spiritually based constructions of power and authority. These archetypal core values of Mande society made it possible for ancient urban centers to emerge by themselves and endure for more than a millennium and a half. In place of despotic rule as found in later-developing hierarchical state systems like Wagadu, Mali, and Songhay, urban centers passed through multiple stages of development in a process that culminated by the beginning of the Middle Millennium in an urban complex that was innovative and flexible enough to achieve long-term sustainability. In the earliest instances, prior to the emergence of ruling hierarchies, these were governed through heterarchy, i.e. a network of groups of competing, overlapping interests including farmers, herders, fishermen, hunters, artisans, and merchants.

Among the Western Sudanic polities that subsequently developed under hierarchical authority, Wagadu/Ghana was one of the earliest to experience the benefits of the trans-Saharan trade and expand into neighboring territories. Well placed to function in a middleman capacity, Wagadu/Ghana gained control of sources of artisanal, agricultural, and mineral goods, commanding the gold-producing center of Bambuk and, by the eleventh century imposing control over the important Berber trading center of Awdaghust in the south-western Sahara. The eleventh-century rise of the Almoravids and the decline of Wagadu/Ghana from the late twelfth century resulted in the use of trade routes farther east in what became the heartland of the Mali Empire. By the fourteenth century, as Mali became the dominant Western Sudanic power, the Buré goldfields, near tributaries of the Upper Niger in present-day Guinea, came into play, with Jenne and Timbuktu emerging as important trading centers, all under Malian control. Meanwhile, farther east and sometime before the tenth century, the arc of the Niger Bend had been settled by hunters, fishermen, boatmen, farmers, herders, and artisans. They were subsequently joined by horse-riding Songhay speakers who brought both their language and political dominance to the region. During the first half of the fifteenth century, the kingdom of Gao emerged, prospered, and began filling a power vacuum left as the Mali Empire slid into decline. Gao subsequently expanded into the third of the great empires of medieval West Africa, with both people and state known as Songhay. Established in 1493, the last ruling dynasty (the Askias) of the Songhay Empire prevailed until the Moroccan invasion of 1591 brought to a close the era of the great medieval states of the Western Sudan.

FURTHER READING

Brooks, George. *Landlords and Strangers: Ecology, Society, and Trade in Western Africa, 1000–1630*. Boulder, CO: Westview Press, 1993.

Cisse, Youssouf Tata and Wa Kamissoko. *La grande geste du Mali des origines à la fondation de l'Empire*. Paris: Karthala-Arsan, 1988.

Soundjata, la gloire du Mali. Paris: Karthala-Arsan, 1991.

Connah, Graham. *African Civilizations: Precolonial Cities and States in Tropical Africa: An Archaeological Perspective*. Cambridge University Press, 1987.

Conrad, David C. "From the *Banan* Tree of Kouroussa: Mapping the Landscape in Mande Traditional History," *Canadian Journal of African Studies* 42 (2008): 384–408.

"Mooning Armies and Mothering Heroes: Female Power in Mande Epic Tradition," in Ralph Austen (ed.), *In Search of Sunjata: The Mande Epic as History, Literature and Performance*. Bloomington, IN: Indiana University Press, 1999: 189–229.

"Oral Tradition and Perceptions of History from the Manding Peoples of West Africa," in Emmanuel Kwaku Akeampong (ed.), *Themes in West Africa's History*. Athens, OH: Ohio University Press, 2006: 73–96.

"A Town Called Dakajalan: The Sunjata Tradition and the Question of Ancient Mali's Capital," *Journal of African History* 35 (1994): 355–77.

Conrad, David C. and H. J. Fisher. "The Conquest that Never Was: Ghana and the Almoravids, 1076," *History in Africa* 10 (1983): 53–7.

Garrard, Timothy. "Myth and Metrology: The Early Trans-Saharan Gold Trade," *Journal of African History* 23 (1982): 443–61.

Hunwick, John, trans. and ed. *Timbuktu & the Songhay Empire: Al-Sa'di's Ta'rikh al-sudan down to 1613 and Other Contemporary Documents*. Leiden: Brill, 1999.

Kea, Ray A. "Expansions and Contractions: World-Historical Change and the Western Sudan World-System (1200/1000 B.C. – 1200/1250 A.D.)," *Journal of World-Systems Research* 10 (2004): 723–816.

Law, Robin. *The Horse in West African History*. Oxford University Press, 1980.

Levtzion, Nehemia. *Ancient Ghana and Mali*. London: Methuen, 1973.

"The Western Maghrib and Sudan," in *The Cambridge History of Africa*, vol. III. Cambridge University Press, 1977: 331–462.

Levtzion, Nehemia and Randall L. Pouwels, eds. *The History of Islam in Africa*. Athens, OH: Ohio University Press, 2000.

McDougall, E. Ann. "The Sahara Reconsidered: Pastoralism, Politics, and Salt from the Ninth through the Twelfth Centuries," *African Economic History*, 12 (1983): 263–86.

"The View from Awdaghust: War, Trade and Social Change in the Southwestern Sahara, from the Eighth to the Fifteenth Century," *Journal of African History* 26 (1985): 1–31.

McIntosh, Roderick J., Joseph A. Tainter, and Susan Keech McIntosh, eds. *The Way the Wind Blows: Climate, History, and Human Action*. New York, NY: Columbia University Press, 2000.

McIntosh, Susan Keech. "Floodplains and the Development of Complex Society: Comparative Perspectives from the West-African Semi-Arid Tropics," in Elizabeth A. Bacus and Lisa J. Lucero (eds.), *Archaeological Papers of the American Anthropological Association* 9 (1999): 151–65.

"A Reconsideration of Wangara/Palolus, Island of Gold," *Journal of African History* 22 (1981): 145–58.

Mitchell, Peter. *African Connections: Archaeological Perspectives on Africa and the Wider World*. Walnut Creek, CA: Altamira Press, 2005.

Moraes Farias, P. F. de. "Intellectual Innovation and Reinvention of the Sahel: the Seventeenth-Century Timbuktu Chronicles," in Shamil Jeppie and Souleymane Bachir Diagne (eds.), *The Meanings of Timbuktu*. Cape Town: HSRC Press, 2008: 95–107.

Munson, P. J. "Archaeology and the Prehistoric Origins of the Ghana Empire," *Journal of African History* 21(1980): 457–66.

Niane, Djibril Tamsir. *Sundiata: An Epic of Old Mali.* Trans. G. D. Pickett, London: Longman, 1965.

Nicholson, Sharon. "Saharan Climates in Historic Times," in M. A. J. Williams and Hugues Faure (eds.), *The Sahara and the Nile: Quaternary Environments and Prehistoric Occupation in Northern Africa.* Rotterdam: A. A. Balkema, 1980: 173–200.

as-Sa'di, 'Abd ar-Rahman b. 'Abdullah. *Ta'rikh as-Sudan*, trans. and ed. Octave Houdas and Maurice Delafosse. Paris: Librarie d'Amérique et d'Orient Adrien-Maisonneuve, 1964.

Sutton, John E. G. "West African Metals and the Ancient Mediterranean," *Oxford Journal of Archaeology* 2 (1983): 181–8.

Webb, James. *Desert Frontier: Ecological and Economic Change Along the Western Sahel 1600–1850.* Madison, WI: University of Wisconsin Press, 1995.

Willis, John Ralph. "Ancient Ghana and Mali," *International Journal of African Historical Studies* 8 (1975): 175–81.

23

Mesoamerican state formation
in the Postclassic period

MICHAEL E. SMITH

During the period under consideration in this volume, Mesoamerican societies underwent two major episodes of fundamental transformation
and restructuring. The year 500 CE saw the height of development of the
so-called "Classic" period societies, including the well-known Maya of
the southern lowlands, Teotihuacan, and Zapotec society of Oaxaca. The
following centuries saw the breakdown or collapse of these and other
societies for poorly understood (and much debated) reasons. After an interval
of ruralization and stagnation in most areas, processes of demographic and
economic growth, political expansion, and cultural florescence generated a
dynamic and highly interconnected world system. The diverse cultures and
society of Mesoamerica became more closely connected than they had ever
been previously. In 1519, at the point of greatest expansion, Hernan Cortés
arrived to bring the Aztec Empire and other Mesoamerican societies to a
crashing halt.

The stories of the Classic-period societies are told in other volumes of this
series. In this chapter I begin with the Classic period in order to establish the
background for the changes that followed. I focus on the Mesoamerican
Postclassic period, c. 700–1519. The levels of technology in Mesoamerica and
other New World societies were considerably lower than in contemporary
Europe and Asia in many domains, from transport to weaponry to industry
to writing and literacy. But Postclassic Mesoamerica saw the operation of the
same kinds of processes operating in other parts of the world at this time.
Peoples migrated, demographic levels fluctuated, commerce expanded,
empires and city-states rose and fell, and ideas and styles traveled widely.

The region known as Mesoamerica was initially defined by anthropologists and archaeologists following the "culture area" approach popular in
mid-twentieth century North American anthropology. Although there were
few cultural traits shared by all of the peoples and cultures of ancient
Mesoamerica, a number of cultural and social traits were shared by many

Mesoamerican groups, who were in active communication with one another in most periods.[1] Mesoamerica is characterized by considerable environmental diversity. Most lowland areas are hot and humid with poor soils, but intensive cultivation methods can produce sufficient agricultural surplus to support urban civilizations such as the Classic Maya. A chain of volcanic mountains runs the length of Mesoamerica, and highland zones range from well-watered mountainous forests to semi-arid plains and deserts.

The volcanically derived soils in highland areas are quite fertile, and the topography is no major barrier to human occupation. Large highland valleys – such as the Basin of Mexico and the Valley of Oaxaca – were centers of population and society over the several millennia of the agricultural epoch. The environmental diversity within Mesoamerica acted as a stimulus for commerce, and archaeologists have documented extensive long-distance exchange in all periods.

Scholarly approaches

Scholarship on ancient Mesoamerica has traditionally been dominated by the anthropological archaeology approach, in which cultural evolution has long been a major research theme. Mesoamerica is one of the areas of the world where important crops were domesticated and where state-level societies developed from earlier non-state societies independently. Because of their emphasis on cultural evolution and the very earliest, or pristine, states, archaeologists have emphasized early farming societies and the initial states in the Classic period, with a relative neglect of the Postclassic period. This bias is compensated by the far greater abundance of written documents for the final pre-Spanish period in comparison with earlier eras. The study of Mesoamerican texts is usually referred to as ethnohistory, although research by art historians and linguists is also important. Ethnohistory is closely allied intellectually with anthropology, and many university-based ethnohistorians are affiliated with anthropology departments rather than departments of history.

The anthropological basis of Mesoamerican studies has a number of implications for comparative and world-historical analysis. First, many or most research topics within Mesoamerica have developed out of the

---

[1] Robert M. Carmack, Janine Gasco and Gary H. Gossen (eds.), *The Legacy of Mesoamerica: History and Culture of a Native American Civilization*, 2nd edn. (Englewood Cliffs, NJ: Prentice-Hall, 2007) and Susan T. Evans, *Ancient Mexico and Central America*, 2nd edn. (New York: Thames and Hudson, 2008).

traditional emphasis of cultural anthropology on non-western, non-state societies. One consequence is that Mesoamericanists have been slow to recognize some of the more sophisticated economic and political institutions (such as price-setting markets, forms of fiscal organization, and empires) that developed in the Postclassic period. Second, this anthropological emphasis has channeled comparative considerations more in the direction of recent tribal societies or ancient states in the Near East and less in the direction of societies in Europe or Asia that were contemporaneous with Postclassic Mesoamerica. Third, the disciplinary separation between anthropology and history has contributed to a lack of knowledge about Mesoamerica among historians, and hence its poor representation in comparative research by historians. Another contributing factor is the lower levels of empirical data from Mesoamerica compared to other world areas during the target period.

Data and methods

Archaeological data for Postclassic Mesoamerica is particularly strong for economic phenomena such as agricultural systems, craft production, and long-distance exchange.[2] Nevertheless, the small number of fieldwork projects to focus on the Postclassic period limits the resolution of the available data. For example, archaeologists working on the early farming villages of the Formative period in the Valley of Oaxaca count on time periods on the order of a century, while the Postclassic period in the same region has yet to be reliably subdivided chronologically. Needless to say, it is virtually impossible to generate reliable interpretations of economic or political phenomena when the relevant chronological resolution is on the order of five centuries.

A variety of kinds of written texts are informative of Postclassic Mesoamerican dynamics. Several indigenous writing systems were in operation at this time, including the Aztec script of central Mexico and the Mixtec script of Oaxaca. These writing systems were more limited in their ability to encode spoken language than was the earlier Classic-period Maya script, and the range of phenomena described is somewhat limited. Nevertheless, we do have some Aztec cadastral maps and tax records, as well as dynastic histories and ritual texts.[3] The writings of the Spanish conquerors are crucial for

2 Michael E. Smith and Frances F. Berdan (eds.), *The Postclassic Mesoamerican World* (Salt Lake City: University of Utah Press, 2003).

3 Elizabeth H. Boone, *Stories in Red and Black: Pictorial Histories of the Aztecs and Mixtecs* (Austin: University of Texas Press, 2000).

providing an outside perspective on native society at the time of conquest, and during the century after conquest a number of Spanish friars and others made systematic attempts to gather information about history, society, and religion in ancient times.

The native rulers of Mesoamerican states maintained historical accounts of dynasties, ethnic groups, and a limited range of other phenomena. The purpose of these accounts was to legitimize and glorify dynasties and ethnic groups. The keeping of history combined oral and written accounts, and the level of detail in written histories varied among regions. For the Classic Maya no oral accounts have survived, but the written histories contain detailed descriptions of rulers and dynasties, framed by an accurate calendar. By contrast, indigenous historical documents for the Postclassic period were mostly mnemonic devices whose calendrical dates and schematic outlines of events were meant to aid professional historians in recounting oral accounts. After the Spanish conquest, Spanish chroniclers recorded many histories – predominantly from the Aztec capital Tenochtitlan – by interviewing nobles and sometimes consulting the painted documents themselves.

This body of indigenous historical scholarship is often referred to as the native historical tradition. The historical accuracy of these accounts is similar to oral political history in other parts of the world, as analyzed by David Henige and others.[4] That is, many events that had occurred shortly before the accounts were first written down were accurately recorded, and as one moves back in time accuracy declines and history blends into myth. Aztec native histories often begin with creation by the gods, then they recount migrations of ancestor groups, and they end up with quotidian political history of kings and battles. Most of the primary historical sources on Postclassic Mesoamerica are published and there are substantial bodies of historiographic analysis. Early colonial administrative documents also provide rich details about many pre-Spanish phenomena, and these include both Spanish language documents as well as those recorded in various indigenous languages.[5]

4 David P. Henige, *Oral Historiography* (New York: Longman, 1982); Michael E. Smith, "Tula and Chichén Itzá: Are We Asking the Right Questions?," in Jeff Karl Kowalski and Cynthia Kristan-Graham (eds.), *Twin Tollans: Chichén Itzá, Tula, and the Epiclassic to Early Postclassic Mesoamerican World* (Washington, DC: Dumbarton Oaks, 2007): 579–617.
5 Charles Gibson, *The Aztecs Under Spanish Rule: A History of the Indians of the Valley of Mexico, 1519–1810* (Stanford University Press, 1964); James Lockhart, *The Nahuas After the Conquest: A Social and Cultural History of the Indians of Central Mexico, Sixteenth Through*

Mesoamerica in the Classic period

Most regions of Mesoamerica experienced two major demographic peaks prior to the Spanish conquest. The first came late in the Classic period, immediately prior to the various regional collapses of states and cities, and the second occurred shortly before the Spanish conquest. The best-documented of Classic-period societies was the Classic Maya society in the southern lowlands of present-day Guatemala, Mexico and Belize (see Map 23.1). Sprawling settlement surrounded towering stone pyramids and palaces in a lush jungle setting. Urban population densities were quite low, leading many to categorize these settlements as "non-urban" in character. Nevertheless, they were the location of administrative and religious activities that integrated whole regions, and thus the Maya centers can be called urban from a functional perspective. The entire landscape filled up, and urban food supply became a problem as the Classic period proceeded. Written inscriptions describe hereditary kings who competed with one another through warfare and theatrical ritual productions. Economic phenomena are not well documented; they are largely absent from the written record, and archaeological research has only begun to address patterns of production and exchange.

During the ninth century, the major cities in the southern lowlands were abandoned and the fates of millions of people are unknown. Elite culture, including writing, the calendar, and courtly life, came to an end. Paleoclimatic data indicate a series of droughts across the Maya lowlands, although their timing and severity are not yet well understood. The end of Classic Maya civilization is one of the "textbook cases" for societal collapse, and it fits four out of five of Jared Diamond's features of collapse: (1) overpopulation in relation to the environment; (2) increasing warfare; (3) droughts at key times; and (4) rulers who do not respond well to these problems and crises. Recent environmental data suggest that Diamond's fifth feature – deforestation and soil erosion – may not have been a significant factor in the collapse.[6] The

Eighteenth Centuries (Stanford University Press, 1992); Matthew Restall and John F. Chuchiak, IV, "A Re-evaluation of the Authenticity of Fray Diego de Landa's *Relación de las Cosas de Yucatán*," *Ethnohistory* 49 (2002): 651–70; Michel R. Oudijk, *Historiography of the Bènizàa: The Postclassic and Early Colonial Periods (1000–1600 A.D.)* (Leiden: Research School of Asian, African, and Amerindian Studies, Universiteit Leiden, 2000), vol. 84.

6 Jared Diamond, *Collapse: How Societies Choose to Fail or Succeed* (New York: Viking, 2004); Cameron L. McNeil, David A. Burney and Lida Pigott Burney, "Evidence Disputing Deforestation as the Cause for the Collapse of the Ancient Maya Polity of Copan, Honduras," *Proceedings of the National Academy of Sciences* 107 (2010): 1017–22; David Webster, *The Fall of the Ancient Maya: Solving the Mystery of the Maya Collapse* (New York: Thames and Hudson, 2002).

Map 23.1. Maya sites

Classic Maya collapse did not affect all of the Maya-speaking regions of Mesoamerica. The Puuc Maya culture was a distinctive variant that flourished in Yucatan, north of the southern lowlands. Its cities developed somewhat later than their southern neighbors, and they were unaffected by the collapse in the latter area.

Another Classic-period society was that of Teotihuacan, a city whose ruins lie close to Mexico City in the Valley of Mexico. Teotihuacan stood out as a unique settlement in Mesoamerica for its large size (c. 100,000 residents) and strict orthogonal planning. Its rulers forged a small empire in central Mexico through conquest, and they traded with cities as far away as the Maya lowlands. After a growth surge around the first century of the Common

Era, Teotihuacan maintained its size and influence for many centuries until brought down by invasion or rebellion in the seventh century. Many public buildings show signs of burning, but the city was never completely abandoned and continued as a smaller urban center into the Postclassic period. Large urban centers (although not as large as Teotihuacan) were also the norm in other parts of Classic-period Mesoamerica. Monte Alban, a powerful hilltop capital in the Valley of Oaxaca, is one of the best known of these. Although never completely abandoned, like Teotihuacan, its political power declined and the settlement shrunk significantly at the end of the Classic period.

Postclassic society: regional trajectories

By the year 900 all of the major Classic-period capital cities had collapsed or declined in size and power, and only a few major urban centers were flourishing. Although the basic processes such as urbanization and the growth of commercial exchange occurred throughout Mesoamerica, each region exhibited its own distinctive trajectory of change. In this section I review briefly the nature of Postclassic society and its change in seven key regions of Mesoamerica. I begin with the central Mexican highlands, the best-documented region of Postclassic Mesoamerica. There has been more archaeological fieldwork in this area, and more native and Spanish documents describing Postclassic societies have survived from central Mexico.

Figure 23.1 shows the basic archaeological periods for Postclassic Mesoamerica. In some areas one or more of these periods have been further subdivided chronologically, whereas in others the chronological resolution is much coarser.

Central Mexico

Central Mexico consists of the Basin of Mexico and surrounding highland valleys. The Basin of Mexico is the largest of the highland valleys/basins of Mesoamerica, and it has good rainfall and rich soils. At around the first century of the Common Era, the Basin became the center for a large urban society (Teotihuacan), and it has remained the dominant urban and political core of Mesoamerica and then Mexico through the present day. Because of the abundance of archaeological sites and the presence of Mexico City, the Basin of Mexico has seen more archaeological fieldwork than most other parts of Mesoamerica. Excavations in the early twentieth century at Teotihuacan, Tula, and other sites established a basic archaeological

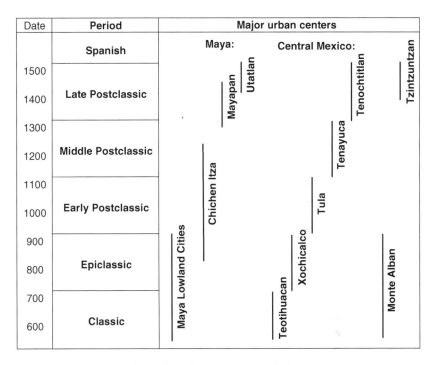

Figure 23.1 Chronological outline for Postclassic Mesoamerica

chronology, and then in the 1960s and 1970s William T. Sanders and colleagues directed the innovative Basin of Mexico Archaeological Survey Project. This was the first time in Mesoamerica that archaeologists had walked over a large continuous portion of the landscape, recording thousands of archaeological sites. Although fieldwork in Oaxaca has now surpassed the Basin of Mexico in the extent of surveyed area and quality of data-collection, the central Mexican research transformed archaeological knowledge of central Mexico.[7]

The two major Mesoamerican demographic peaks mentioned above (in the Late Classic and in the Late Postclassic periods) were first identified by the Basin of Mexico Archaeological Survey Project. The hyper-urbanization of Teotihuacan in the Classic period resulted from simultaneous processes of population growth throughout the Basin of Mexico and rural depopulation in

7 William T. Sanders, Jeffrey R. Parsons and Robert S. Santley, *The Basin of Mexico: Ecological Processes in the Evolution of a Civilization* (New York: Academic Press, 1979).

many areas as people moved into the city. The decline of Teotihuacan led to both ruralization and demographic decline at the regional level. After several centuries of a cyclical rise and fall of urban centers, population rebounded in the Middle and Late Postclassic periods, reaching its peak at the time of the Spanish conquest. This pattern of twin population peaks has been identified in subsequent survey and excavation projects in most parts of Mesoamerica, although the specific contours of change in each region varied.

Much of Teotihuacan's civic architecture was burned and destroyed in the sixth century, and this episode is often referred to as the "collapse" of the city. Nevertheless, a significant population – perhaps 30–40,000 people – continued to reside in the city in the following Epiclassic period (700–900), and Teotihuacan remained the largest city in central Mexico. Unfortunately we know very little about the post-collapse city or its residents, although it is almost certain that it had ceased to be an influential polity at this time.

The Epiclassic period saw the rapid growth of a series of large, fortified, hilltop cities throughout central Mexico. The regions of these new cities had all previously been part of the large zone of influence of Teotihuacan, whether part of that city's empire or not. Xochicalco, located near Cuernavaca in the state of Morelos, is the most extensively studied Epiclassic fortified city.[8] The city was founded with a small population during the Classic period, but reached its largest extent in Epiclassic times. Monumental civic architecture was concentrated on top of a small mountain, whose slopes were terraced for residential occupation. A series of walls and ditches helped protect much of the city. Archaeologists have located an abundance of public-relief sculpture that adorned temples and other civic buildings. These images stress dynastic and military themes, with several elements of Classic Maya style and content (the Epiclassic period in central Mexico coincided with the final flourishing of the Classic Maya cities).

The basic parameters of Xochicalco's setting and external connections were duplicated at other Epiclassic central Mexican cities such as Cacaxtla and Teotenango. Cacaxtla is best known for an elaborate series of mural paintings showing battles and rituals, executed in Maya style. These were found in excavations at a palace compound located on a hilltop, surrounded by a large fortification ditch. Archaeological research at these and other sites suggest that Epiclassic central Mexico was a period of political decentralization and warfare. Long-distance social interaction with the Maya cities,

---

8 Kenneth G. Hirth (ed.), *Archaeological Research at Xochicalco*. 2 vols. (Salt Lake City: University of Utah Press, 2000).

involving imagery and art styles, increased dramatically from Teotihuacan's day, although the social processes responsible have yet to be determined. The Epiclassic cities also traded with one another and shared a series of artistic and intellectual traits.

The Epiclassic cities collapsed after two centuries, leaving their hinterlands in a highly decentralized state with ruralized populations. At Xochicalco, the collapse involved the burning and destruction of much of the city, including defacement of much of the public art. Only a few small pockets of the city continued to be occupied by small communities. The multiple Epiclassic capitals were replaced in the Early Postclassic period by a single large urban center, Tula. Away from the Tula region, most parts of central Mexico had small, dispersed populations in Early Postclassic times.

Tula was the home and capital of the historically documented Toltec peoples.[9] This is the earliest city and people to receive unequivocal treatment in the Aztec native historical sources, but scholars cannot agree on the level of accuracy or relevance of those sources with respect to Toltec society. The Aztec kings traced their origin and legitimacy to their descent from the Toltec kings, and the descriptions of Tula and the Toltecs contain many obviously mythological elements (e.g. buildings constructed of gold, or fantastic god-kings who lived hundreds of years). Earlier credulous interpretations of the Toltecs have given way recently to more skeptical accounts, and many scholars now doubt that Aztec native history contains any reliable historical information about the Early Postclassic period.[10]

If the later native historical accounts are not useful for historical analysis, archaeology does provide considerable information about political and economic phenomena in the Early Postclassic period. With a population of 50,000, Tula was the largest city since Classic-period Teotihuacan. The urban plan of Teotihuacan had been highly aberrant in Mesoamerica, including numerous unusual traits such as strict orthogonal planning, the lack of a large central civic plaza, and Axial layout around a central avenue. These planning traits were abandoned by the Epiclassic cities, and then the designers of Tula returned to ancient Mesoamerican planning canons in an extreme form. Tula is the most formally planned urban center in all of Mesoamerica, with a highly symmetrical and monumental layout of buildings around a formal plaza.

---

9 Alba Guadalupe Mastache, Robert H. Cobean and Dan M. Healan, *Ancient Tollan: Tula and the Toltec Heartland* (Boulder: University Press of Colorado, 2002).
10 Smith, "Tula and Chichén Itzá: Are We Asking the Right Questions?"

Although some scholars argue that Tula was the capital of an empire, this judgment owes more to a loose interpretation of Aztec native history than to empirical evidence. Nevertheless, Tula did engage in some kind of intensive interaction with the distant Maya city of Chichen Itza in Yucatan. One portion of the Maya city is laid out in a similar fashion to the civic center at Tula, and the two cities share a number of architectural forms and styles that are otherwise rare in Mesoamerica (such as buildings employing numerous stone columns). The nature of this relationship has been debated actively for over a century, and although there is now a consensus view backed by archaeological evidence, many details remain obscure. The architectural and urban commonalities between Tula and Chichen Itza developed at approximately the same time, and it is impossible to assign temporal priority to either city. The current model stresses dual processes of commercial exchange and movements of elites, who generated the stylistic similarities between the cities.

The collapse and abandonment of Tula around 1100 are not well understood. At approximately this time, a series of migrating central Mexico from the north. The native histories from many of the Aztec city-states assert that their ancestors came from Aztlan, a perhaps mythological homeland to the north.[11] Linguists have reconstructed a northern homeland for Nahuatl (the Aztec language) and an arrival date in central Mexico sometime between 200 and 1200. Because the timing of their arrival is not well established, it is not known whether the Nahuatl peoples played a role in the collapse of Tula. Archaeologically, however, it is clear that new cities were founded throughout central Mexico in the twelfth century, with new types of artifacts and architecture. These new cities, of the Middle Postclassic period, developed into the Aztec cities that flourished at the time of the Spanish conquest. The simplest explanation is that the Nahuatl migrants arrived in central Mexico in the eleventh or twelfth century to found cities and states, whether or not they contributed to the end of Tula and the Toltecs.

The Middle Postclassic period was a time of population growth and the expansion of cities and settlement across the landscape of central Mexico. Numerous city-states (*altepetl* in Nahuatl) were founded. These consisted of small urban centers with modest monumental architecture (a royal palace and one or more temple-pyramids, arranged around a central plaza), small resident populations, and surrounding farmland settled with villages and

---

11 Michael E. Smith, "The Aztlan Migrations of the Nahuatl Chronicles: Myth or History?" *Ethnohistory* 31 (1984): 153–86.

towns. Kings and nobles pursued marriage alliances across city-state lines, and soon an interlocking nobility covered all of central Mexico. City-states also traded with one another, and a dynamic system of periodic marketplaces soon developed. Alongside these friendly relations, city-states also engaged in antagonistic activities. Kings waged wars with their neighbors to extract tribute, and some managed to create conquest-states or small empires. Tenayuca was one of the largest and most powerful Middle Postclassic cities in the Basin of Mexico, and it may have been the capital of a small empire. The entire political situation in central Mexico was highly dynamic, however, and no polity lasted very long.

As populations grew and settlement expanded, a variety of intensive agricultural methods were employed.[12] Rivers were dammed and canals built, leading to large and productive irrigation systems in some areas. Hillsides were terraced, and the swampy lakes in the Basin of Mexico were converted to highly productive raised fields. Population growth and agricultural intensification continued into the Late Postclassic period, and by 1500 irrigation and terracing covered much of the central Mexican landscape. Nevertheless, droughts brought crop failures and famines to the Basin of Mexico with increasing frequency, although other areas seem to have fared better.

For the Late Postclassic period, scholars can rely on an abundance of written documentation assembled in the early decades of Spanish rule.[13] This material permits a detailed reconstruction of social, political, economic, and cultural patterns in central Mexico, although the sources are heavily biased toward Tenochtitlan and the Basin of Mexico. Society was divided into two legally defined classes, nobles and commoners. Nobles monopolized the positions of power in city-state government, and they owned most of the land. Although this was not "private property" in the modern sense, much of the land could be sold (only to other nobles). Commoners gained access to farmland through a variety of arrangements, including rental and sharecropping. Many commoners belonged to a corporate group called the *calpolli,* which consisted of a group of households residing in the same community, subject to the same noble overlord, and usually sharing economic occupations or activities. *Calpolli* councils allocated land to individual households,

---

12 Sanders, Parsons and Santley, *The Basin of Mexico*; Thomas M. Whitmore and B. L. Turner II, *Cultivated Landscapes of Middle America on the Eve of Conquest* (New York: Oxford University Press, 2001).

13 Lockhart, *The Nahuas After the Conquests*; Gibson, *The Aztecs Under Spanish Rule*; Michael E. Smith, *The Aztecs*, 3rd edn (Oxford: Blackwell Publishers, 2012).

and organized collective activities. Commoners who did not belong to a *calpolli* had to work directly for a lord or king, and they were less well-off economically and had less control over their own destiny.

In the first part of the Late Postclassic period two small empires formed in the Basin of Mexico, based in the cities of Azcapotzalco and Texcoco. By this time the native historical accounts provide relatively good information on political dynamics. Then in 1428, war broke out leading to a major political realignment. Azcatpotzalco, the more powerful capital, was defeated and three cities – Tenochtitlan, Texcoco and Tlacopan – formed an alliance to conquer other city-states and generate taxes. This "triple alliance" soon became a powerful empire of conquest. Although the alliance remained intact officially until the Spanish conquest, Tenochtitlan grew in power and wealth at the expense of its allies until it could be regarded at the sole capital of the empire. This polity was organized around several practices of indirect rule, and most of the rulers and governments of the conquered city-states were left in power.

Yucatan

After the collapse of the southern lowland Maya cities, the focus of Maya urban society shifted to the northern part of the Yucatan peninsula. A group of cities with a distinctive style of public architecture known as "Puuc" had been founded prior to the lowland collapse, and these cities grew and flourished after it. Although some populations fleeing the southern area probably moved into the Puuc cities, the demographic growth was insufficient to account for more than a small part of the southern population loss. The Puuc cities exhibited only a small portion of the set of elite cultural traits that had characterized the southern lowland cities. The long-count calendar, whose dates were so prominently displayed on public stone monuments in the south, was not used in the Puuc area; other Maya calendars, however, continued in use. A more limited version of the Maya script was used at these sites.[14]

The overall configuration of urban form at the Puuc cities resembled the earlier southern cities. Monumental stone pyramids and palaces, often arranged around large formal plazas, dominated the city centers, and housing surrounded the centers in a low-density pattern. Chemical analyses of soils at some of these cities have established that the areas between the houses were

14 Nicholas P. Dunning, *Lords of the Hills: Ancient Maya Settlement in the Puuc Region, Yucatan, Mexico* (Madison, WI: Prehistory Press, 1992).

farmed with a high degree of intensity. As these cities grew, one of them – Chichen Itza – outpaced the others and began a program of political expansion. Although the nature and extent of this city's political domination is not clear, this was the largest Puuc city and it exhibits the most extensive record by far of interactions with distant areas (including Tula), as measured in both art styles and imported goods.[15]

As noted above, in spite of an extensive record of research and publication on Tula and Chichen Itza – the largest urban centers in Mesoamerica at the time – scholars have still not determined the nature of their relationship. One of the few firm conclusions now agreed on is that an older model positing the Toltec conquest of Chichen Itza and Yucatan is not correct. In the twelfth century Chichen Itza started to decline, and by around 1200 the city had been largely abandoned. Soon after, the nearby city of Mayapan expanded rapidly as an imperial capital, its armies conquering much of Yucatan. The final centuries before the arrival of Cortés in 1519 saw much warfare in the Maya region. Mayapan was one of the few large walled cities of ancient Mesoamerica. The rulers of Mayapan emulated some of the architectural forms of Chichen Itza, but on a much smaller scale. Mid-twentieth-century archaeologists thought the simpler, smaller buildings of Mayapan were pale reflections of those at Chichen Itza and earlier Maya cities, and labeled Mayapan's period as one of cultural "decadence." This concept of the decadence of Postclassic Maya culture is parallel to older views of the decadence of post-Roman Mediterranean society ("late antiquity" in current parlance). During the fifteenth century Mayapan too came to an end, and when the Spaniards arrived, Yucatan was the setting for a large number of warring petty states or chiefdoms.

Other regions

Much less is known about regions other than the Valley of Mexico or the Yucatan. Scholars generally identify five of these: the southern Maya lowlands, the Maya highlands, the Gulf of Mexico Coast, the Valley of Oaxaca, and west Mexico.

After the Maya collapse, the southern Maya lowland environment (Guatemala and Belize) was converted from a densely settled landscape with numerous bustling urban centers, to a quiet isolated jungle setting with only a few scattered villages. The area would never return to its former condition

---

15 Kowalski and Kristan-Graham (eds.), *Twin Tollans: Chichén Itzá.*

of high population, urbanization, and intensive agriculture. New villages were founded, most likely by refugees fleeing the warfare and chaos of the collapsing central cities; many of these sites were located on the eastern edge of the region, in what is now Belize. This area witnessed a gradual growth of population and its residents traded and interacted with other parts of Mesoamerica, but it would never again be the setting for large states or cities. In the Late Postclassic period, a series of migrating groups moved into, and through, the southern lowlands. Many of these were fleeing south to avoid the troubled situations after the falls of the cities of Chichen Itza and Mayapan. Some of these groups set up fortified towns deep in the lowland region.[16]

The Maya highlands, consisting of a chain of mountainous regions that parallels the Pacific coast from Mexico through Guatemala and into Honduras, had been the home to speakers of Maya languages for millennia. With the exception of the city of Copan in Honduras, this area was largely isolated from the processes of urbanization and cultural fluorescence that characterized lowland Classic Maya society. During the Middle and Late Postclassic periods, populations grew and numerous small city-states emerged. Their capitals were typically placed on the tops of mountains or ridges and fortified with walls and ditches. Many of these polities corresponded to language groups. The largest and most powerful of these groups was the Quiché (or Kich'e) Maya, whose capital city, Utatlan, was a large and complex settlement with a series of individually fortified hilltop zones or neighborhoods. The Kakchiqel group, centered at Iximché, was another large powerful polity.[17]

The art and material culture of the highland Maya polities included a large number of exotic elements, including both individual motifs and styles that also appear in the art of central Mexico. The traditional interpretation views these traits as spread by migration or conquest from central Mexico in a process called "Mexicanization." The world systems model (see below), on the other hand, interprets these traits as components of what has been called the "Postclassic International Style," a widespread phenomenon whose place of origin is difficult or impossible to identify.

---

16 Prudence M. Rice and Don S. Rice (eds.), *The Kowoj: Identity, Migration, and Geopolitics in the Late Postclassic Petén, Guatemala* (Boulder: University Press of Colorado, 2009).

17 Robert M. Carmack, *The Quiché Mayas of Utatlan: The Evolution of a Highland Guatemala Kingdom* (Norman: University of Oklahoma Press, 1981), and Linda Schele and Peter Mathews, *The Code of Kings: The Language of Seven Sacred Maya Temples and Tombs* (New York: Simon and Schuster, 1998).

Along the Gulf of Mexico, the Postclassic epoch was a time of smaller cities, capitals of small polities or city-states, after a Classic period of high populations and large, highly planned urban centers. The people of this area were a complex mix of different linguistic and ethnic groups, some of which had distinctive styles of architecture and material culture. Many of the elements of the Postclassic International Style were incorporated into the artistic repertoire of Gulf Coast peoples in mural paintings and painted ceramic vessels. The southern portion of the Gulf Coast presents a major enigma of interpretation: early Spanish explorers described large, dense populations, but archaeologists cannot identify sites from the Late Postclassic period.

The Valley of Oaxaca, south of the Basin of Mexico and the second largest highland valley in Mesoamerica, was home to speakers of the Zapotec language. The Classic-period capital city, Monte Alban, declined in power during the ninth century, setting in a process of decentralization. Smaller cities were founded throughout the valley, and in the fifteenth century the area was conquered by the expanding Aztec Empire. Postclassic processes of change will remain impossible to reconstruct, however, until archaeologists succeed in establishing and applying a more refined chronological scheme. Presently, the entire interval from the fall of Monte Alban (*c.* 900) until the Spanish conquest consists of a single archaeological period. To judge from native historical sources of the Zapotec and Mixtec peoples, the ruined city of Monte Alban retained a symbolic importance for the rulers of the many Postclassic city-states in and around the Valley of Oaxaca. Although the city was largely abandoned, important individuals were still buried there in tombs with rich offerings. Some of these contain objects from the Mixtec culture, another Oaxacan group based outside of the central valley.[18]

West Mexico is a vast region whose ancient cultures remain very poorly understood, largely because much of the area is difficult to access today and has seen far less archaeological research than other regions. Two major developments of the Postclassic period can be emphasized. First, the technology for smelting bronze was introduced into west Mexico from South America early in Postclassic times. Merchants or other voyagers brought the knowledge by sea along the Pacific coast. Within a century or two, west Mexican metalsmiths were developing a distinctive tradition of both utilitarian items (sewing needles and punches) and ritual objects (bells and

18 Jeffrey P. Blomster (ed.), *After Monte Albán: Transformation and Negotiation in Oaxaca, Mexico* (Boulder: University Press of Colorado, 2008).

tweezers); bronze in Mesoamerica was not used for agricultural tools or weapons. A second development was the formation and expansion of the powerful Tarascan Empire in the final century prior to Spanish arrival. From a base in the Lake Patzcuaro Basin, the Tarascan kings expanded their control quickly at the same time as the Aztec Empire, culminating in a major defeat of the Aztec armies in the 1480s. Outside of Tarascan hegemony, most regions of west Mexico were organized into small polities at the time of Spanish conquest.[19]

Processes and connections

The Postclassic period in Mesoamerica was a time of major change and growth in many dimensions, from demography to political organization to economics. Although archaeological coverage is uneven and native historical accounts do not contribute useful information until well into the Late Postclassic period, it is possible to summarize the major processes and changes on a large scale.

Demographic and agricultural growth

As a broad pattern, almost every region of Mesoamerica experienced its two greatest demographic peaks at the end of the Classic period and during the Late Postclassic period. The best-documented regions, however – the southern Maya lowlands and central Mexico – exhibit contrasting demographic trajectories. In the Maya region, Classic-period population growth was exponential in form, starting slowly and accelerating into a major surge just prior to the collapse of the ninth century. Although there was a slow recovery from the demographic disaster of the collapse, leading to higher populations in 1500 than in 1000, the region never fully recovered its population after the Classic period. In central Mexico, Teotihuacan's Classic-period demographic profile was radically different from its Maya contemporaries: rapid early growth, followed by several centuries of stability. Other parts of central Mexico witnessed more population growth within the Classic period, leading to a region-wide peak in the seventh century. Populations then dropped rapidly in most areas in Epiclassic times, only to begin an exponential growth surge in the Late Postclassic period.[20]

---

19 Helen Perlstein Pollard, *Tariacuri's Legacy: The Prehispanic Tarascan State* (Norman: University of Oklahoma Press, 1993), and Christopher S. Beekman, "Recent Research in Western Mexican Archaeology," *Journal of Archaeological Research* 18 (2010): 41–109.
20 Sanders, Parsons, and Santley, *The Basin of Mexico*.

Paleoclimatologists working in central Mexico have used lake sediments to identify a period of lower rainfall between approximately 600 and 1200, and recent research on tree rings suggests a series of shorter droughts.[21] Although we do not yet have sufficient evidence to link these data firmly to the changes identified by archaeologists, climate changes must have impacted the demography and historical trajectories of the region. Without proposing causal models, I will simply point out that the start of the period of lower rainfall coincides with the fall of Teotihuacan, and its end coincides with a major demographic surge.

Migrations

The topic of Postclassic migrations is a difficult one, for both empirical and historiographic reasons. Empirically, it can be difficult to identify migrations through archaeological data. When extensive excavations of many kinds of contexts have been carried out, coupled with scientific analyses of skeletal remains, migrations are amenable to archaeological study. Unfortunately this level of coverage is only available for a few sites and regions of Postclassic Mesoamerica, and the evidence for migrations is equivocal and controversial.

The nature of Mesoamerican native historical accounts introduces another obstacle for the study of migrations. For Late Postclassic peoples, ancestral migrations were important parts of group identity. Many ethnic groups claimed to have migrated to their Late Postclassic locations from elsewhere, and native histories are full of migration stories. A still significant Mesoamerican historiographic tradition tends to accept native historical accounts at face value, and thus many scholars interpret what appear to be mythological charters as empirical events.[22]

From a critical perspective, two sets of Postclassic migrations can be accepted as valid, based on both native historical traditions and archaeological fieldwork: the Aztlan migrations that brought Nahuatl speakers to central Mexico from the north, and a series of southward movements from Yucatan into the southern lowlands and beyond in the final century of the

---

21 David W. Stahle et al., "Major Mesoamerican Droughts of the Past Millennium," *Geophysical Research Letters* 38 (2011): 1–4; Sarah L. O'Hara, Sarah E. Metcalfe and F. Alayne Street-Perrott, "On the Arid Margin: The Relationship Between Climate, Humans and the Environment: A Review of Evidence from the Highlands of Central Mexico," *Chemosphere* 29 (1994): 965–81.

22 Smith, "Tula and Chichén Itzá: Are We Asking the Right Questions?"

Postclassic period. Both of these migrations had significant effects on their destination areas. There were probably other migratory movements in Mesoamerica during Postclassic times, but they cannot be regarded as historical events until additional historical and archaeological evidence becomes available.

Polity growth and decline

With numerous examples of the rise and fall of states, the expansion and contraction of empires, and wars, Postclassic Mesoamerica was very dynamic politically. Within this complex region of multiple historical trajectories several long-term political trends can be identified. Three of these trends are illustrated schematically in Figure 23.2: changes in the duration, size, and despotism of polities.

First, in terms of duration: The major cities included in the chronology chart (Figure 23.1) illustrate a trend that started with the long-lasting states of the Classic period and ended with the much shorter-lived polities of the Late Postclassic period. The table in Figure 23.1 does not include the entire Classic period (which began in the first century CE), which would have accentuated the contrast to a greater degree. The reduction of duration of Maya polities is particularly striking in Figure 23.1. After the fall of Teotihuacan, central Mexico witnessed a somewhat regular rise and fall of states, each of which lasted about two centuries. In contrast, Teotihuacan had flourished for five or six centuries. The downward arrow in Figure 23.2 for polity duration levels off at the end of the sequence. Although some of the Middle Postclassic Aztec cities (such as Tenayuca) did not survive into the Late Postclassic period, most did continue, giving them a lifespan of three or four centuries before being cut short by Hernan Cortés.

Second, in terms of size: With the exception of the (Late Postclassic) Aztec Empire, the Mesoamerican states with the largest areal extents flourished during the Classic period. The Epiclassic and Early Postclassic states that followed were smaller polities; the Epiclassic polities and Tula in central Mexico, and the Puuc cities of Yucatan are the best documented of these. Finally, the city-state form spread throughout all of Mesoamerica in the Middle and Late Postclassic periods. In the latter period, the expansionist Aztec and Tarascan empires created a counter-trend of increasing size (Figure 23.2). Even with the expansion of the Aztec Empire, the city-state remained the predominant form of polity in both central Mexico and the outer imperial provinces. The growth of systems of city-states, what Mogens

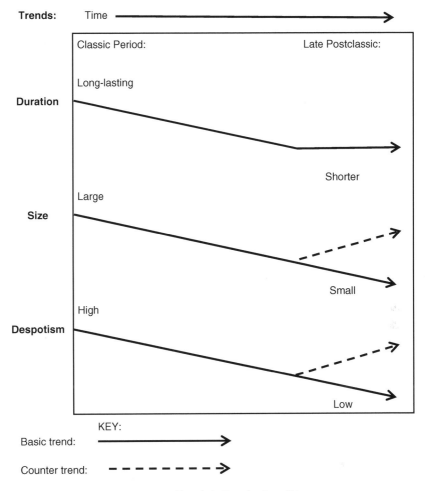

Figure 23.2 Trends in Postclassic polities

Hansen calls "city-state cultures," is one of the most striking Postclassic trends in Mesoamerica.[23]

Third, in terms of despotism: Although the documentation of patterns of political dynamics such as despotic versus participatory rule is difficult for

---

23 Mogens Herman Hansen (ed.), *A Comparative Study of Six City-State Cultures* (Copenhagen: The Royal Danish Academy of Sciences and Letters, 2002); Smith and Berdan (eds.), *The Postclassic Mesoamerican World*.

archaeologists, new methods and data reveal some general trends during the Postclassic period.[24] As revealed by spatial patterns of civic architecture, the content of public art, and other measures, the decline in polity size was accompanied by a reduction in what Michael Mann calls "despotic power," or the ability of rulers to carry out their will without consultation with other groups.[25] This trend is best documented in central Mexico, but in most regions the conquest-era city-states were less despotic than their Classic-period antecedents. Again, the two late empires (Aztec and Tarascan) developed in contradistinction to this trend. As documented by historical records, the Aztec emperors of Tenochtitlan were engaged in a systematic effort to exclude from power not only their allied kings but the nobles and other civic groups within Tenochtitlan. The decline of despotic power was in many cases accompanied by increases in Mann's "infrastructural power," referring to the ability of the state to penetrate civil society to implement its actions throughout its territory. Although this is difficult to monitor with archaeological data, historical documents reveal elaborate systems of taxation and state monitoring in the conquest-period city-states.[26]

Cities and urbanization

Nearly all Mesoamerican cities were capitals of polities, and city size was correlated with the territorial extent and power of states. The two largest Mesoamerican cities – Teotihuacan and Tenochtitlan – were capitals of empires. The Epiclassic and Early Postclassic cities were smaller than Teoti-huacan and ruled smaller domains, while the city-states of Late Postclassic Mesoamerica were ruled by small cities. The median size of Late Postclassic cities was 11,000 residents in an area of 2.5 square km.[27] Most Mesoamerican cities had relatively low population densities, leaving considerable open space

24 Richard E. Blanton and Lane F. Fargher, *Collective Action in the Formation of Pre-Modern States* (New York: Springer, 2008); Gary M. Feinman, "Variability in States: Comparative Frameworks," *Social Evolution and History: Studies in the Evolution of Human Societies* 7 (2008): 54–66; Lane F. Fargher, Verenice Y. Heredia Expinoza, and Richard E. Blanton, "Alternative Pathways to Power in Late Postclassic Highland Mesoamerica," *Journal of Anthropological Archaeology* 30 (2011): 304–26.
25 Michael Mann, "The Autonomous Power of the State: Its Origins, Mechanisms and Results," *European Journal of Sociology / Archives européennes de sociologie* 25 (1984): 185–213; Mann, "Infrastructural Power Revisited," *Studies in Comparative International Development* 43 (2008): 355–65.
26 Michael E. Smith, "Aztec Taxation at the City-State and Imperial Levels," in Andrew Monson and Walter Scheidel (eds.), *Fiscal Regimes and the Political Economy of Premodern States*, forthcoming.
27 Michael E. Smith, "City Size in Late Postclassic Mesoamerica," *Journal of Urban History* 31 (2005): 403–34.

available for urban agricultural production. Although farming within Post-classic cities has been established conclusively for only a few cases, it is likely that the practice was quite common.

Just as Mesoamerican cities were generally small in size, the urbanization levels (the percentage of population living in cities) were small in most Mesoamerican societies. As is the case in many other realms, Classic-period Teotihuacan stands out as different from other Mesoamerican cities as the most urbanized society in ancient Mesoamerica. The Classic-period city's rapid growth was fed by rural to urban migration, probably through coercion, leaving the countryside largely empty. Fully 80 per cent of the population in the Basin of Mexico resided in the city at its height. After the collapse of Teotihuacan, conditions in central Mexico quickly returned to the Mesoamerican baseline of low urbanization. Of the population of the Basin of Mexico, 30 per cent lived in cities in Epiclassic times, none in the Early Postclassic period, and 35 per cent in the Late Postclassic. Of the Late Postclassic urban population, 70 per cent lived in the capital Tenochtitlan and 30 per cent in city-state capitals.[28]

The two best-known Mesoamerican cities – Teotihuacan and Tenochtitlan – were not only the largest urban centers, but also the most aberrant in terms of their planning and layout. These imperial capitals showed strict orthogonal planning of the entire city, including residential neighborhoods. In contrast, most Mesoamerican cities (Postclassic and earlier) had carefully planned civic centers surrounded by unplanned residential zones. Mesoamerican urban planning followed a set of principles that differed from cities in other parts of the world. The formal civic plaza was the nucleus of urban design. Plazas were usually framed by the royal palace, temple-pyramids, and other monumental civic buildings. These central buildings were often aligned orthogonally and linked together with platforms and subsidiary plazas. Many of the Aztec city-state capitals explicitly copied the ancient urban plan of Tula, which included a large square plaza with the largest temple-pyramid on the east side, opposite a ballcourt. The conjunction of archaeological and historical data show how the kings of Aztec city-states employed urban planning to legitimize and extend their rule.[29]

As capitals of polities, all Postclassic cities showed the stamp of rulership, including royal palaces, large temple-pyramids of the state religion, and

28 Sanders, Parsons, and Santley, *The Basin of Mexico*.
29 Michael E. Smith, *Aztec City-State Capitals* (Gainesville: University Press of Florida, 2008), 124–50.

planning models that were expressions of ideological precepts. Much more variable, however, was the influence of economic factors on urban processes and layouts. The extent of urban-based craft production varied greatly. Just within the small sample of well-studied Aztec city-state capitals, archaeologists have identified one example with numerous major craft industries (Otumba), one city with no craft production beyond the ubiquitous Aztec household textile industry (Huexotla), and several cities (Yautepec, Xaltocan) with varying levels of production between these extremes.[30] In contrast to this variation in craft activities, Postclassic cities show more uniformity in the prevalence of markets and commercial exchange practices.

Growth of commercial networks

The expansion of commerce was one of the most significant social trends in Postclassic Mesoamerica. Historical sources describe a flourishing commercial economy in all parts of Mesoamerica at the time of Spanish conquest. The very first group of Mesoamerican people encountered by Christopher Columbus were Maya merchants traveling along the coast in 1502 in a large canoe (with twenty-five people) full of trade goods and money, and when Cortés entered Tenochtitlan eighteen years later the central marketplace was the feature that most impressed the conqueror and his soldiers.

Documentation of commercial institutions is strongest for Aztec central Mexico.[31] Cortés wrote that 60,000 people attended the central marketplace of Tenochtitlan every day, and there are several lengthy first-hand descriptions of this facility. Hundreds of goods were offered for sale, by both petty vendors and professional merchants. Stalls were arranged in an orderly fashion, and a panel of judges heard complaints. Most or all cities in central Mexico had marketplaces that met once a week (the Aztec week was five days in length). Several types of merchants traveled among marketplaces buying and selling. A number of forms of money were used, of which the most common were cacao beans (for small purchases) and cotton textiles of a standard length. The Aztec economy was a commercial economy but it was not a capitalist one. Wage labor was extremely rare, as were sales of land. Commercial practices such as account books, partnerships, and loans existed in only rudimentary fashion.

Although historical documentation is much sparser in other regions, existing accounts do indicate the presence of similar commercial practices

---

30 Smith, *Aztec City-State*, 180–3.   31 Smith, *The Aztecs*, 108–26.

and institutions in all parts of Mesoamerica at the time of Spanish conquest. Furthermore, archaeologists have identified increasing exchange during the course of the Postclassic period.[32] Although it is difficult to determine the full extent of commercial institutions during the Classic Period, recent methodological innovations now aid the identification of markets and commercial exchange using archaeological data.[33] These methods suggest that commercial exchange was far less widespread in the Classic Period. The timing and contours of the expansion of commerce between 700 and 1300 have yet to be established, however.

Writing systems and literacy

Changes in the nature of writing and literacy accompanied the political and economic trends of Postclassic Mesoamerica. The Classic Maya had developed the only complete phonetic writing system in ancient Mesoamerica; anything that could be expressed in spoken Mayan could be recorded with hieroglyphs. After the Maya collapse, only a more restricted form of writing was used by the Maya peoples. Several Mesoamerican societies, including Teotihuacan and Xochicalco, had limited scripts whose nature is debated by linguists. At the time of Spanish conquest, the Aztec and Mixtec peoples were using distinctive limited-purpose written scripts. Mixtec writing primarily recorded royal genealogies, while Aztec writing was used for mnemonic dynastic histories, tax and land records, and esoteric religious lore.[34]

The most significant development in writing during the Postclassic period was the creation of a distinctive art style and a set of common symbols that were used all over Mesoamerica. This style and symbol set are often called "international" because they spanned many diverse polities, cultures and languages. The scripts of the Mixtecs and Aztecs are components of the Postclassic International Style and the Postclassic Symbol Set, as are painted murals, polychrome ceramics, and painted manuscripts from many regions. These media were not restricted to a particular language or group of languages, and thus they did not comprise a complete phonetic writing system. Their independence from a particular language, however, facilitated communication between speakers of different languages, and contributed to

32 Smith and Berdan (eds.), *The Postclassic Mesoamerican World*.
33 Christopher P. Garraty and Barbara L. Stark (eds.), *Archaeological Approaches to Market Exchange in Ancient Societies* (Boulder: University Press of Colorado, 2010).
34 Boone, *Stories in Red and Black*.

long-distance communication. In the Late Postclassic Period, Mesoamerica reached its highest level ever of aesthetic and religious interaction and similarity.[35]

Postclassic Mesoamerica and world history

When Cortés landed on the Gulf Coast of Mexico in 1519, Mesoamerica had reached its highest level ever of social and cultural integration, and the accompanying similarities of social and cultural phenomena. Through much of the twentieth century scholars posited migrations, conquests, or vague processes such as "Mexicanization" as the mechanisms for creating the Late Postclassic similarities across Mesoamerica. Starting in the 1980s, such explanations were recognized as inadequate, however. Mesoamerica was never united linguistically or politically. The region was always the home to many diverse language groups and numerous independent polities.

At an international conference in 1999, a group of scholars developed a new model for the dynamics of Postclassic Mesoamerica. They identified six major processes of change and innovation: population growth; proliferation of small polities; greater diversity of trade goods; commercialization of the economy; new forms of writing and iconography; and new patterns of stylistic interaction. To understand these changes across the area of Mesoamerica, these scholars adopted a modified version of the world systems theory first articulated by Immanuel Wallerstein, based loosely on research by Janet Abu-Lughod, Christopher Chase-Dunn and Thomas Hall.[36] Their model differed from other world-systems models in its incorporation of religious and intellectual dynamics alongside political and economic processes. This modified world-systems model integrates a diverse range of processes and developments, helps scholars understand the nature of Mesoamerica as it was observed by Columbus and Cortés, and allows for comparisons with other contemporaneous regions.

If "world history" is about connections among geographically separated societies, then Postclassic Mesoamerica is irrelevant to mainstream world history in the Old World prior to the adventures of Hernan Cortés between

---

35 Boone, *Stories in Red and Black*; Smith and Berdan (eds.), *The Postclassic Mesoamerican World*.

36 Janet L. Abu-Lughod, *Before European Hegemony: The World System, A.D. 1250–1350* (New York: Oxford University Press, 1989); Christopher Chase-Dunn and Thomas D. Hall, *Rise and Demise: Comparing World-Systems* (Boulder: Westview Press, 1997); Smith and Berdan (eds.), *The Postclassic Mesoamerican World*.

1519 and 1521. But if world history is about a broadly comparative approach to history, then the "expanding webs of exchange and conquest" in Postclassic Mesoamerica provide a unique case study that can help illuminate general processes of societal change. Many of the economic, political, and social processes that characterized the Old World between 500 and 1500 have parallels in Postclassic Mesoamerica. The levels of technological proficiency, economic development, and societal scale were lower in the New World, but such differences can be illuminating in broad comparative studies.[37]

FURTHER READING

Abu-Lughod, Janet L. *Before European Hegemony: The World System, A.D. 1250–1350*. New York, NY: Oxford University Press, 1989.

Beekman, Christopher S. "Recent Research in Western Mexican Archaeology," *Journal of Archaeological Research* 18 (2010): 41–109.

Blanton, Richard E. and Lane F. Fargher. *Collective Action in the Formation of Pre-Modern States*. New York, NY: Springer, 2008.

Blomster, Jeffrey P., ed. *After Monte Albán: Transformation and Negotiation in Oaxaca, Mexico*. Boulder, CO: University Press of Colorado, 2008.

Boone, Elizabeth H. *Stories in Red and Black: Pictorial Histories of the Aztecs and Mixtecs*. Austin, TX: University of Texas Press, 2000.

Carmack, Robert M. *The Quiché Mayas of Utatlan: The Evolution of a Highland Guatemala Kingdom*. Norman, OK: University of Oklahoma Press, 1981.

Carmack, Robert M., Janine Gasco and Gary H. Gossen, eds. *The Legacy of Mesoamerica: History and Culture of a Native American Civilization*, 2nd edn. Englewood Cliffs, NJ: Prentice-Hall, 2007.

Chase-Dunn, Christopher and Thomas D. Hall. *Rise and Demise: Comparing World-Systems*. Boulder, CO: Westview Press, 1997.

Diamond, Jared. *Collapse: How Societies Choose to Fail or Succeed*. New York, NY: Viking, 2004.

Diamond, Jared and James A. Robinson, eds. *Natural Experiments of History*. Cambridge, MA: Harvard University Press, 2010.

Dunning, Nicholas P. *Lords of the Hills: Ancient Maya Settlement in the Puuc Region, Yucatan, Mexico*. Madison, WI: Prehistory Press, 1992.

Evans, Susan T. *Ancient Mexico and Central America*, 2nd edn. New York, NY: Thames and Hudson, 2008.

37 Charles Tilly, *Big Structures, Large Processes, and Huge Comparisons* (New York: Russell Sage Foundation, 1984); Michael E. Smith (ed.), *The Comparative Archaeology of Complex Societies* (New York: Cambridge University Press, 2012); Jared Diamond and James A. Robinson (eds.), *Natural Experiments of History* (Cambridge, MA: Harvard University Press, 2010).

Fargher, Lane F., Verenice Y. Heredia Expinoza and Richard E. Blanton. "Alternative Pathways to Power in Late Postclassic Highland Mesoamerica," *Journal of Anthropological Archaeology* 30 (2011): 306–26.

Feinman, Gary M. "Variability in States: Comparative Frameworks," *Social Evolution and History: Studies in the Evolution of Human Societies* 7 (2008): 54–66.

Garraty, Christopher P. and Barbara L. Stark, eds. *Archaeological Approaches to Market Exchange in Ancient Societies*. Boulder, CO: University Press of Colorado, 2010.

Gibson, Charles. *The Aztecs Under Spanish Rule: A History of the Indians of the Valley of Mexico, 1519–1810*. Stanford University Press, 1964.

Hansen, Mogens Herman, ed. *A Comparative Study of Six City-State Cultures*. Copenhagen: The Royal Danish Academy of Sciences and Letters, 2002.

Henige, David P. *Oral Historiography*. New York, NY: Longman, 1982.

Hirth, Kenneth G., ed. *Archaeological Research at Xochicalco*. Salt Lake City, UT: University of Utah Press, 2000.

Kowalski, Jeff Karl and Cynthia Kristan-Graham, eds. *Twin Tollans: Chichén Itzá, Tula, and the Epiclassic to Early Postclassic Mesoamerican World*. Washington, DC: Dumbarton Oaks, 2008.

Lockhart, James. *The Nahuas after the Conquest: A Social and Cultural History of the Indians of Central Mexico, Sixteenth through Eighteenth Centuries*. Stanford University Press, 1992.

Mann, Michael. "The Autonomous Power of the State: Its Origins, Mechanisms and Results," *European Journal of Sociology / Archives européennes de sociologie* 25 (1984): 185–213.

Mastache, Alba Guadalupe, Robert H. Cobean and Dan M. Healan. *Ancient Tollan: Tula and the Toltec Heartland*. Boulder, CO: University Press of Colorado, 2002.

McNeil, Cameron L., David A. Burney and Lida Pigott Burney. "Evidence Disputing Deforestation as the Cause for the Collapse of the Ancient Maya Polity of Copan, Honduras," *Proceedings of the National Academy of Sciences* 107 (2010): 1017–22.

O'Hara, Sarah L., Sarah E. Metcalfe and F. Alayne Street-Perrott. "On the Arid Margin: The Relationship between Climate, Humans and the Environment: A Review of Evidence from the Highlands of Central Mexico," *Chemosphere* 29 (1994): 965–81.

Oudijk, Michel R. *Historiography of the Bènizàa: The Postclassic and Early Colonial Periods (1000–1600 A.D.)*. Leiden: Research School of Asian, African, and Amerindian Studies, Universiteit Leiden, 2000.

Pollard, Helen Perlstein. *Tariacuri's Legacy: The Prehispanic Tarascan State*. Norman, OK: University of Oklahoma Press, 1993.

Restall, Matthew and John F. Chuchiak IV. "A Re-evaluation of the Authenticity of Fray Diego De Landa's *Relación de las Cosas de Yucatán*," *Ethnohistory* 49 (2002): 651–70.

Rice, Prudence M. and Don S. Rice, eds. *The Kowoj: Identity, Migration, and Geopolitics in the Late Postclassic Petén, Guatemala*. Boulder, CO: University Press of Colorado, 2009.

Sanders, William T., Jeffrey R. Parsons and Robert S. Santley. *The Basin of Mexico: Ecological Processes in the Evolution of a Civilization*. New York, NY: Academic Press, 1979.

Schele, Linda, and Peter Mathews. *The Code of Kings: The Language of Seven Sacred Maya Temples and Tombs*. New York, NY: Simon and Schuster, 1998.

Smith, Michael E. *Aztec City-State Capitals*. Gainesville, FL: University Press of Florida, 2008.

"Aztec Taxation at the City-State and Imperial Levels," in Andrew Monson and Walter Scheidel (eds.), *Fiscal Regimes and the Political Economy of Premodern States*, forthcoming.

The Aztecs. 3rd edn. Oxford: Blackwell Publishers, 2012.

"The Aztlan Migrations of the Nahuatl Chronicles: Myth or History?", *Ethnohistory* 31 (1984): 153–86.

"City Size in Late Postclassic Mesoamerica," *Journal of Urban History* 31 (2005): 403–34.

ed. *The Comparative Archaeology of Complex Societies*. New York, NY: Cambridge University Press, 2012.

"Tula and Chichén Itzá: Are We Asking the Right Questions?", in Kowalski and Kristan-Graham (eds.), *Twin Tollans: Chichén Itzá, Tula, and the Epiclassic to Early Postclassic Mesoamerican World*, 579–617.

Smith, Michael E. and Frances F. Berdan, eds. *The Postclassic Mesoamerican World*, Salt Lake City, UT: University of Utah Press, 2003.

Stahle, David W., José Villanueva-Díaz, Dorian J. Burnette, Julián Cerano Paredes, Richard Heim Jr, Falko K. Fye, Rodolfo A. Soto, et al. "Major Mesoamerican Droughts of the Past Millennium," *Geophysical Research Letters* 38 (2011): 1–4.

Tilly, Charles. *Big Structures, Large Processes, and Huge Comparisons*. New York, NY: Russell Sage Foundation, 1984.

Webster, David. *The Fall of the Ancient Maya: Solving the Mystery of the Maya Collapse*. New York: Thames and Hudson, 2005.

Whitmore, Thomas M. and B. L. Turner II. *Cultivated Landscapes of Middle America on the Eve of Conquest*. New York, NY: Oxford University Press, 2001.

24

State and religion in the Inca Empire

SABINE MACCORMACK

The Incas built the largest imperial state of pre-Columbian America, which at its height extended over 4,000 kilometres along South America's Pacific coast, and across the cordillera of the Andes from what is now southwestern Colombia to Ecuador, Peru and Bolivia into Chile and Argentina. The earliest traces of a distinct Inca presence in Cuzco, the city that became the imperial capital, go back to *c.* 1000 CE. The Spanish invaders who ended up destroying the empire began arriving in 1532 and in the following year killed the Inca emperor Atahuallpa. After years of warfare, a Spanish viceroyalty was established in 1549, but a small Inca state in exile endured in the Andean highlands until 1571. The Inca presence, however, was felt until the century's end and beyond. Indeed, in the modern republics where Inca power had prevailed, most especially Peru, this presence is still discernible today. But the name of Peru is a Spanish neologism, and Inca concepts of geographical and cultural space differed from those obtaining today. The Incas called their empire Tahuantinsuyu, 'Realm of the Four Parts'. Seen from Cuzco in the South Central Andean sierra, the four parts, *suyos*, related to each other in an ordered sequence, each *suyo* characterized by its peoples and resources, its deities and the diverse religious observances, customs and dress codes of its peoples: Chinchaysuyo towards the north, Antisuyo towards the Amazonian lowlands, Collasuyo towards Lake Titicaca and beyond, and Cuntisuyo towards the south and the Pacific coast. Within the empire, the *suyos* related to each other not simply as a sequence, but as interdependent pairs, so that people in Chinchaysuyo saw themselves as paired with Collasuyo and vice versa. Also, the *suyos* were not primarily a set of four measurable territories delimited by frontiers, but a world order. They expressed how the Incas conceptualized their empire, which was not just as a state with certain boundaries beyond which other polities prevailed. Rather, the Inca state in itself constituted the world. Beyond, there were inchoate human groups awaiting the ordering presence of the Incas, children of the Sun. On the edges of Antisuyo accordingly, the distinction between human and animal life remained as yet unclear, and Antisuyo itself bordered on the land of the *yskays singas*, people with 'two noses'. Or, possibly, beyond Tahuantinsuyu, there was 'nothing at all'.[1]

Sources of Andean history

News of Tahuantinsuyu, the empire that was 'destroyed before it became known',[2] caused a sensation in Spain and Europe. Reports by some of the invaders were soon printed in Seville, and before long several of them circulated across Europe. So did historical works based on more detailed information that were published during subsequent decades. Examples are the *Chronicle of Peru* by the soldier Pedro Cieza de León and the *Royal Commentaries of the Incas* by Garcilaso de la Vega, the son of an Inca lady and a conquistador. Numerous other historical works, however, remained in manuscript until the nineteenth or twentieth century, most notably the *Narrative of the Incas* by Juan de Betanzos, a conquistador who lived in Cuzco and married a relative of Atahuallpa, the *Historia Indica* of Pedro Sarmiento de Gamboa, and the *First New Chronicle and Good Government* by the Andean nobleman Guaman Poma de Ayala. Collectively, these texts are known as *crónicas*, 'chronicles'. Documents produced by Spanish officials containing demographic, administrative and economic information supplement these accounts, especially regarding the provinces of the Inca Empire. There is also the important, and partially autobiographical, *History of How the Spaniards arrived in Peru* by Titu Cusi Yupanqui, a grandson of Guayna Capac (r. 1493–1527), the last Inca emperor to rule before the arrival of the Spanish.[3] Even so, what for the most part is missing is information produced by the

1 Two noses: John H. Rowe, 'Probanza de los Incas nietos de conquistadores', in Rowe, *Los Incas del Cuzco. Siglos XVI – XVII – XVIII* (Cuzco: Instituto Nacional de Cultura, 2003): 93; 'Runa Yndio ñiscap Machoncuna ñaupa pacha ... (c. 1608)', in Frank Salomon and J. Urioste (eds.), *The Huarochiri Manuscript: A Testament of Ancient and Colonial Andean Religion* (Austin: University of Texas Press, 1991): 22 and 278.

2 Garcilaso Inca de la Vega, *Primera parte de los Comentarios Reales de los Incas* (1609), ed. Carmelo Sáenz de Santa María in *Biblioteca de Autores Españoles* (Madrid, 1960–65), vols. 133–5, 1 and 19.

3 Raúl Porras Barrenechea, *Los cronistas del Perú (1528–1650) y otros ensayos*, ed. Franklin Pease, 2 vols. (Lima: Banco de Crédito del Perú, 1986); Francisco Esteve Barba, *Historiografía Indiana* (Madrid: Gredos, 1992); Franklin Pease, *Las Crónicas y los Andes* (Mexico City: Fondo de Cultura Económica, 1995); Joanne Pillsbury (ed.), *Guide to Documentary Sources for Andean Studies 1530–1900*, 3 vols. (Norman: University of Oklahoma Press, 2008).

Incas themselves. Some Spanish administrative documents contain transcripts or summaries of *khipus*, the knot records on which the Incas and their subjects recorded numerical and narrative information.[4] But no European we know of learned how to make and read a *khipu*, although recent progress in the study of the small fraction of *khipus* that survived from among the many thousands that had existed constitutes a notable advance in knowledge, with promise of more.[5]

The Inca Empire was not the first imperial polity in the Andes. Pedro Cieza de León noted the distinct architectural and sculptural style of Tiahuanaco on Lake Titicaca, where – so he was told – Titu Cusi Yupanqui's father Manco Inca was born. But all that Cieza was able to learn about the site, some of it abandoned and ruined, was that it had been built by 'people of understanding' who 'will have perished in the wars', and that 'the first Incas spoke of setting up and making their court and its seat in this Tiahuanaco'. Another impressive abandoned site that Cieza noticed, with buildings 'that are not of the same design as those the Incas built or ordered to be built, because this building is square and those of the Incas are elongated and narrow', was a place he called Vinaque, now known as Huari, on the edge of the Ayacucho Valley. And at Mohina, now Pikillacta, some 30 kilometres east of Cuzco, Cieza noticed ruined 'grand buildings' where the Spanish had looted 'much gold and silver and even more precious clothing'.[6]

But these sites remained enigmatic and silent until, from the late nineteenth century, they and many others attracted the attention of archaeologists, historians and linguists. The ruins of Tiahuanaco, Vinaque and Mohina that interested Cieza pertain to the two contemporaneous imperial cultures of Tiahuanaco and Huari that flourished between *c*. 500 and *c*. 1000 CE. Tiahuanaco and Inca pottery sequences point to the stylistic and ideological influence that the Tiahuanaco culture exercised on the Incas.[7] It was an influence that the Incas themselves acknowledged. The vast archaeological site of Vinaque or Huari was an imperial centre that held sway in the central

---

4 Gary Urton, 'From Knots to Narratives: Reconstructing the Art of Historical Record Keeping in the Andes from Spanish Transcriptions of Inka Khipus', *Ethnohistory* 45 (1998): 409–38; Frank Salomon, *The Cord Keepers: Khipus and Cultural Life in a Peruvian Village* (Durham, NC: Duke University Press, 2004).

5 Jeffrey Quilter and Gary Urton (eds.), *Narrative Threads: Accounting and Recounting in Andean Khipu* (Austin: University of Texas Press, 2002).

6 Pedro Cieza de León, *Crónica del Perú* (Seville, 1553), ed. Franklin Pease and Miguel Maticorena (Lima: Pontifica Universidad Católica del Perú, 1986), chapter 87, 97, and 105.

7 Alan L. Kolata, *The Tiwanaka: Portrait of an Andean Civilization* (Cambridge: Blackwell, 1993).

Peruvian sierra and along the Pacific coast from Lambayeque nearly as far as Chile.[8] Among the numerous Huari colonies founded in the valley of Cuzco in the course of the seventh century, the principal one was Pikillacta. Extending over nearly two square kilometres it was designed as the administrative centre for the entire region. Although never completed, parts of this enormous site, consisting of residential and ceremonial structures and an entire section probably intended for storage, were occupied until sometime after 900.[9] Pikillacta thus speaks not only of Huari success but also of its decline or failure. Success in that Pikillacta, designed as the residence of Huari officials for the administration of the region, is testimony to major mobilizations of local labour and resources over an extended period. Beyond that, the spread of Huari ceramic styles in the valley of Cuzco documents Huari cultural influence and the cooptation of regional elites into the imperial project. But ultimately the Huari withdrew. Pikillacta was systematically evacuated, and the same appears to have happened in other Huari settlements.[10] In short, the Huari were unable to integrate the region into an imperial structure in any enduring sense – precisely what, in time, the Incas did succeed in accomplishing.

During the period of Huari hegemony in the Cuzco valley, Cuzco itself was a chiefdom producing an agricultural surplus that was probably sent to Pikillacta, along with individuals performing labour service there. Huari cultural influence in the close vicinity of Cuzco is revealed both by imported Huari ceramics and by locally produced ceramics that display Huari influence. But the absence of Huari architecture in the archaeological record of that vicinity seems to point to a merely indirect Huari presence in this region, rather than to the direct control so clearly manifest at Pikillacta. In the Cuzco valley as a whole, the demise of the Huari state, contemporaneous with that of Tiahuanaco, gave rise to more dispersed settlement patterns during a period of demographic growth. Concurrently, new agricultural terraces and irrigation canals for cultivating maize were constructed in the valley, and Cuzco grew far beyond the size of any of the villages of the region, indicating that Cuzco elites were able to bring smaller neighbouring settlements,

---

8 William Isbell and Gordon McEwen (eds.), *Huari Administrative Structure: Prehistoric Monumental Architecture and State Government* (Washington, DC: Dumbarton Oaks, 1991).

9 Gordon F. McEwan (ed.), *Pikillacta: The Wari Empire in Cuzco* (Iowa City: University of Iowa Press, 2005).

10 Brian S. Bauer, *Ancient Cuzco: Heartland of the Inca* (Austin: University of Texas Press, 2004).

polities and resources into their orbit. The emergence of the Killke ceramic style (so named after a small settlement near Cuzco), with possible Huari antecedents, gave rise to the development of a clearly identifiable Inca style.[11] During this same period, Killke- and Cuzco-style ceramics, along with architectural styles and techniques showing Inca influence, extended northwards into the Vilcanota River Valley, also known as the Sacred Valley.[12] These archaeological indicators – the development of distinct Inca styles in architecture, ceramics, textiles and metallurgy, and a hierarchy of settlements of different sizes among which Cuzco, surrounded by smaller satellite towns was the most extensive – point to a considerable degree of centralization and the existence of an Inca elite in the process of creating an Inca homeland; in short, to the presence of an Inca state by 1300 or before.

Inca origins in documentary sources

Documentary sources provide a very different perspective on Inca origins. Versions of the Inca myth of origin that were included in the *crónicas* during the sixteenth and seventeenth centuries were all collected in Cuzco. They begin with an account of Creation in the Andes, followed by the emergence of the first Incas, a group of four brothers and their four sister consorts from 'windows' in a rock located in a perhaps mythic place called Pacaritambo or 'inn of the dawn'. Mythic or historical, Pacaritambo is an Andean *pacarina*, 'place of the dawn', a rock, lake, spring or other feature of the landscape, from which Andean peoples – not just the Incas – traced their origins.[13] During their migration to Cuzco, two of the Inca brothers were metamorphosed into stone: that is, they became *huacas*, sacred markers in the landscape and recipients of cult. The fourth brother, Manco Capac, with two sister consorts, made his abode in Indicancha, 'enclosure of the Sun', in lower Cuzco alongside the Alcaviças, an ethnic group already resident there, who occupied upper Cuzco. The foundation legend, therefore, attributes to the advent of the Inca ancestors in Cuzco the establishment of the pan-Andean numerical, spatial and social order whereby upper and lower, left and right,

---

[11] Gary Urton, *The History of a Myth: Pacariqutambo and the Origin of the Incas* (Austin: University of Texas Press, 1990).

[12] R. Alan Covey, *How the Incas Built their Heartland: State Formation and the Innovation of Imperial Strategies in the Sacred Valley, Peru* (Ann Arbor: University of Michigan Press, 2006).

[13] Juan de Betanzos, *Suma y narración de los Incas (1551)*, ed. Maria del Carmen Martín Rubío (Madrid: Atlas, 1987): 1, 1–4.

male and female are paired in a complementary and reciprocal order, each indispensable to the other, an order also expressed in the paired hierarchy of the four *suyos* of Tahuantinsuyu.[14]

Having brought the Inca ancestors to Cuzco, these accounts of Creation and first settlement shift into a different narrative mode by recounting the doings of some eleven or twelve Inca rulers (who were known by the title of 'the Inca'), generation by generation, down to Guayna Capac and Atahuallpa. Forging marriage alliances with neighbouring lords, engaging in conflicts and conciliations over irrigation rights and territory in the Cuzco Valley and the Sacred Valley, and waging wars to gather plunder with which to meet ever-growing demands of gift exchange and reciprocity, the early Inca rulers as portrayed in the *crónicas* gradually enhanced their power and status. Where thus archaeology sees process and behaviours conditioned by economic, environmental and cultural conditions, the narrative traditions recorded in the sixteenth and seventeenth centuries foregrounded specific events and named individuals, Inca rulers, their consorts, allies and enemies. In these narrative traditions the interests and commitments of the individuals – mostly Spaniards – who did the recording inevitably played as large a role as did the material they collected.

The Huari Empire is nowhere mentioned in these narratives because, even if some form of recollection about it might have endured in the Cuzco Valley and elsewhere, the Incas deliberately portrayed themselves as the founders and originators of civilization in the Andes. In the words of Pedro Cieza de León: 'From the accounts that the Incas of Cuzco give us, there was in ancient times great disorder in all the provinces of this kingdom that we call Peru', the ancient times being the times before the advent of the first Inca ruler.[15] Here, the narratives that Cieza and others picked up in Cuzco reflect an Andean pattern. It is probably no accident that not one of the Andean Creation myths recorded during the century or so after contact with the Spaniards describes a universal origin that was valid once and for all. Instead, these myths open with a prior Creation that failed because of dysfunctional relations between the creating deity and the beings he made, and because the creating deity omitted establishing an order of worship and a social order. The operative, present Creation thus represented a correction and improvement of a preceding one.

[14] Gary Urton, *The Social Life of Numbers: A Quechua Ontology of Numbers and Philosophy of Arithmetic* (Austin: University of Texas Press, 1997): 54–65.
[15] Cieza, *Crónica del Perú*, 38.

Take the Creation myth told at the great oracular pilgrimage shrine of Pachacamac, the 'Maker of the World', near Lima. The original world order brought into existence by Pachacamac contained people, but no food. The resulting cosmic turmoil was remedied by a child of the Sun, to whom the Sun gave three eggs, one of gold, another of silver and the third of copper. From these eggs proceeded the lords and rulers of society, their womenfolk and the common people respectively. In short, the revised Creation entailed a social order and, along with it, an order of nature and cult, whereby Pachacamac and the remnants of the prior world that remained alive as integral parts of this present world, would receive the reverence and offerings due to them. This idea, that what matters above all is an ordered society in which functions of governance and religion are fittingly distributed, also speaks in Inca self-perceptions as rendered in our sixteenth-century Spanish accounts. The origin of the Incas as seen by themselves was not tantamount to the origin of life or human life. Rather, it was tantamount to the origin and nature of ordered human life, of life in society.

The *crónicas* all describe the gradual expansion of Inca power and influence in the vicinity of Cuzco during the reigns of the first eight rulers, which led to rapid conquests and the extension of a system of roads with their way stations (*tambos*), and of imperial administration into the four *suyos*. The contrast between these historical narratives, centred as they are on persons and events, and the results of archaeology which describe gradual transformations of settlement patterns, the refinement of agricultural techniques, territorial consolidation and the accumulation of resources that together facilitated the formation of the Inca state, is striking. But this does not mean that historical narratives have nothing to tell us. As remembered by the Inca informants whose statements are reflected in the *crónicas*, the shift from small-scale warfare by the early Inca rulers to Andean-wide campaigns occurred in the course of conflicts with the neighbouring Chancas, a loose confederation of fortified agro-pastoralist settlements centered around Andahuaylas.[16] A grand assault launched on Cuzco by two Chanca lords representing the upper and lower moieties of the confederation caused the Inca Viracocha and his designated son and successor Inca Urco to take flight. With the Chancas in possession of Cuzco, Viracocha's younger son Pachacuti (r. 1438–71) received in a vision the Creator's promise of assistance, which

---

[16] Brian S. Bauer, Lucas C. Kellett, and Miriam Aráoz Silva, *The Chanka: Archaeological Research in Andahuaylas (Apurimac), Peru* (Los Angeles: Cotsen Institute of Archaeology Press, 2010).

became manifest when stones, henceforth known as *pururaucas*, rose up, turned into soldiers and helped to defeat the enemy. The mythic quality pervading these narratives conveys the importance with which the Incas endowed the Chanca war. The very name of Inca Pachacuti, 'Turning of the Time', designates cataclysm and recovery.

The Inca and the Sun

The Chanca war differed from earlier wars not only because of its scale, resulting in the incorporation of Chanca territory under Inca administration, but because it generated a theoretical and religious reconceptualization of the Inca ruler's power and position in relation to other lords. Betanzos, who collected this information from his Inca wife's kinsfolk, described Inca rulers collectively as Capac Cuna or Ingas Capac Cuna, and explained the title Capac as meaning 'very much more than king'.[17] The title was used widely throughout the Andes to differentiate paramount lords and kings from chieftains, *sinchi*. But times were changing, and after his Chanca victory Pachacuti was ready 'to subject those other towns and provinces to the city of Cuzco and to remove the title of Capac that each little lord of those towns and provinces was holding, because there would only be one single Capac and that was he himself'.[18]

According to Cieza, the very first Incas claimed to be 'sons of the Sun'. Like *Capac*, however, this title also was claimed by other lords in the Andean world. For Inca rulers, the title became more concrete when they brought the Titicaca region and Tiahuanaco under their control. For it was at Tiahuanaco that, according to local sacred histories, the Creator had made 'the sun and the day, the stars and the moon', and it was on the Island of the Sun in the lake that the sun had first risen from a rock.[19] These histories provided a basis for incorporating the Inca myth of origin from Pacaritambo with the grander story of the origin of the Sun: according to the resulting expanded origin myth, the Sun had sent the first Inca ancestors from Lake Titicaca via Pacaritambo to Cuzco.[20] The Sacred Rock on the Island of the Sun from which the sun had risen was already a local *huaca* (sacred marker) before 400 CE and was then incorporated into a sacred precinct, the goal of a

---

[17] Betanzos, *Suma*, I, 27; Catherine Julien, *Reading Inca History* (Iowa City: Iowa University Press, 2000): 23–48.

[18] Betanzos, *Suma*, I, 18.   [19] Creator: Betanzos, *Suma*, I, 1.

[20] Garcilaso de la Vega, *Comentarios Reales*, I, 1,15.

pilgrimage, by the Tiahuanaco state. With the demise of this state, the rock receded once more into local obscurity, until Pachacuti visited the island and initiated the development of the site into a major sanctuary, empire-wide pilgrimage centre and oracle, where sacred history enshrined in ritual imparted legitimacy on the Inca conquest of Collasuyo, and of the empire at large. The project was brought to completion by Pachacuti's son and successor Tupa Yupanqui (r. 1471–93), and was designed to inculcate Inca might and majesty. The access of pilgrims to the Sacred Rock was guided and controlled even while they were still on the mainland, and more carefully once they crossed to the island, their progress being punctuated by repeated confession of sins in the presence of religious specialists. Finally, having walked the length of the island, they reached a sequence of three gateways, the last of which opened towards an offering area with the Sacred Rock, which was draped in precious textiles and adorned with plaques of gold and silver at one end. In front of it stood a golden brazier for offerings.[21]

In Cuzco also, the cult of the Inca Sun became more prominent in the time of Pachacuti, who according to Betanzos built the Sun's temple of Coricancha, the 'golden enclosure', perhaps on the site of Manco Capac's house Indicancha. Echoing the building's name, its external walls were later adorned with a band of plates of gold affixed on all sides beneath the thatch roof.[22] After solemnly consecrating Coricancha, Pachacuti ordered the image of the Sun, represented as a one-year-old boy, to be cast of solid gold. The image was dressed in the finest Inca cloth, its head adorned with the Inca royal headband and a golden solar paten. Having been solemnly placed on a royal seat, the image received daily offerings that were burnt in a brazier for the Sun's sustenance 'as if the Sun were a person who ate and drank'. At his inauguration, the Inca ruler, as 'son of the Sun', received the royal headband from the hand of the Sun's image, and a priest with the title *vilaoma*, 'diviner who speaks', was specially appointed to attend the image and to deliver oracular pronouncements on its behalf. In Coricancha, as on the Island of the Sun, access to the holy of holies was strictly regulated. Only the Inca and the *vilaoma* were permitted to appear in the image's presence; Inca nobles came as far as the patio leading to the Sun's chamber, and the people at large worshipped from outside and in Cuzco's main square.

---

[21] Brian S. Bauer and Charles Stanish, *Ritual and Pilgrimage in the Ancient Andes: The Islands of the Sun and the Moon* (Austin: University of Texas Press, 2001).

[22] Betanzos, *Suma*, I, 28.

Offerings similar to those given the Sun were made to deceased Inca rulers. When his father Viracocha died, Pachacuti, in accord with Andean and Inca custom, instituted the cult of his mummified body. Viracocha's mummy was clothed in royal textiles, and was honoured 'exactly as if he were alive'.[23] Before the mummy, 'llamas, clothing, maize and coca were burned, maize wine was poured out, and Pachacuti declared that the mummy ate, was a son of the Sun and was with him in the sky'. Concurrently, Pachacuti reorganized the ceremonial, social and political life of all earlier Incas. Their mummies, ensconced on ceremonial benches, received offerings for their daily sustenance and were attended by members of their kinship group, *panaca*, who also had the task of reciting ballads detailing the deeds and accomplishments of each Inca, 'beginning with the song, story and praise of the first Inca Manco Capac, and then these retainers would sing about each lord as they had succeeded one another up to that time. This was the order that was followed from then on, and in this way they preserved the memory of them and their antiquities.'[24] Commemoration of the past went hand-in-hand with organizing the present and the future, for the Inca ancestors were not merely treated 'as if they were alive', they actually were alive in the sense that their attendants, speaking in their voices, pronounced oracular statements about current and future policies, and most especially about the Inca succession.

The transformation of Cuzco from village to town to city predated Pachacuti, but the informants of Betanzos attributed to this Inca the construction and organization of Cuzco as an imperial capital. This entailed canalizing the city's springs and the twin rivers that ran through it, improving nearby agricultural land, building storage for foodstuffs, clothing and other products, and above all, reorganizing the population, which amounted to expelling the original inhabitants and demolishing their houses before building new ones resting on solid stone foundations. Cuzco is built on an incline sloping from below the majestic structures of Sacsayhuaman (often misdescribed as a fortress) that were built in the time of Pachacuti and Tupa Yupanqui, down into the Cuzco valley. Upper Cuzco, extending uphill from Coricancha towards Sacsayhuaman, was set aside for the dwellings of Pachacuti and his *panaca* (kinship group) and for the *panacas* of former Inca rulers;

---

[23] Betanzos, *Suma*, I, 17, 85b. William Harris Isbell, *Mummies and Mortuary Monuments: A Postprocessual Prehistory of Central Andean Social Organization* (Austin: University of Texas Press, 1997).

[24] Betanzos, *Suma*, I, 17, 86a.

Pachacuti's successors and their *panacas* also resided there. Lower Cuzco on the incline into the valley southwest of Coricancha became the home of other Incas.[25] Coricancha itself was the religious centre of both Cuzco and the empire. From here, forty-one sight lines or *ceques*, subdivided into four groups, each *ceque* being punctuated with shrines both great and small, radiated towards and beyond the horizon in the direction of the four *suyos*.[26] Within each group, the *ceques* were ordered in a threefold hierarchy where one may remember the three eggs of gold, silver and copper which, according to the myth of Pachacamac gave origin to the three-ranked orders of human society. Accordingly, the ranked *ceque* shrines were looked after by the families and kinship groups of Cuzco who were also ranked.

While Coricancha represented Inca myth and cult on an imperial scale, the *ceque* shrines expressed more intimate concerns closer to home. Many shrines were very small indeed, such as a simple stone or stones. Others were features in the landscape, fountains, springs, boulders, or a piece of ground where an earthquake had been felt. There were also the places that became shrines because an Inca ruler had slept or dreamt a dream there. Other shrines marked episodes in Inca history, most especially Guanacauri on the road to Collasuyo, the most venerable of all the *ceque* shrines, where, when the Inca ancestors were travelling to Cuzco, one of them was turned into stone. There also were the *pururaucas* who, after having helped Pachacuti Inca win his victory, became stones again, and there was Çapi, the root of a quinoa tree, said to be 'the root from which Cuzco originated'.[27] Collectively, the shrines speak of the nature of Inca religion, which drew no dividing line, or only a rather tenuous one, between human beings and a natural environment that was imbued with an energy on which humans could draw and which they revered. On a different level, the *ceques* anchored the city of Cuzco in its historical past, aspects of which were re-enacted every time representatives of each of the kinship groups walked along their *ceque* to make the appropriate offerings to its shrines. In this way, the sacred and the secular, the Inca and the Inca's ancestors along with traces of his supernatural helpers and protectors were intertwined with ongoing manifestations of the Inca's power and were inscribed on the landscape surrounding Cuzco and in the city itself. Systems of *ceque* shrines existed elsewhere in the Andes, which

[25] John H. Rowe, 'What Kind of Settlement was Inca Cuzco?' *Ñawpa Pacha* 5 (1967): 59–77.
[26] Tom Zuidema, *The Ceque System of Cuzco: The Social Organization of the Capital of the Inca* (Leiden: Brill, 1964).
[27] Susan A. Niles, *Callachaca: Style and Status in an Inca Community* (Iowa City: University of Iowa Press, 1987).

meant that Inca ideas about the relation between human beings and the supernatural fitted into a larger Andean order of belief and practice.[28]

In one sense, the city of Cuzco was the outcome of its past going back to the time of Manco Capac and indeed beyond. The *crónicas* described what archaeology has amply confirmed, how during centuries Cuzco grew from a settlement of adobe huts into a city the beauty of which astonished even the hardbitten Spanish invaders. In another sense, however, the city that the Spanish admired was the outcome of Pachacuti's energies. This, at any rate, was the opinion of the informants consulted by Betanzos, at least some of whom appear to have belonged to Pachacuti's kinship group, whose task it was to remember his deeds and recite his praises. When planning the new Cuzco, Pachacuti arranged for the fields near the city to be painted and measured for distribution to their future owners, and surveying the contours of the land to be built on, 'he imagined within himself the order' to be followed.[29] The houses and lots of upper and lower Cuzco were modelled in clay before construction began, and the clay model was later used to distribute the dwellings among the new residents. Similarly, the Inca painted and drew bridges and roads near Cuzco and elsewhere, generating puzzlement among his followers who found these activities to be 'beyond their understanding'.[30] However, these particulars permit a glimpse into the significance and intent of Inca architecture and urban planning, where the aim was not so much simply to build, but to complement and refine what had been provided by climate and environment, and in doing so to shape society.[31] Put differently, the work of the Inca paralleled the work of the Creator. For when, at Tiahuanaco, after making the sun and the day, and the moon and the stars the Creator populated the land, he 'made certain people of stone as a model of the people he would produce later. He made them in this way, that he made of stone a certain number of people and a lord who would govern and rule over them, and many pregnant women and

---

[28] Tom Zuidema, *El calendario Inca. Tiempo y espacio en la organización ritual del Cuzco. La idea del pasado* (Lima: Fondo editorial del Congreso del Perú, 2010); Sabine MacCormack, 'History, Historical Record and Ceremonial Action: Incas and Spaniards in Cuzco', *Comparative Studies in Society and History* 43 (2001): 329–63; Brian S. Bauer, *The Sacred Landscape of the Inca: The Cusco Ceque System* (Austin: University of Texas Press, 1998).

[29] Pachacuti measured fields, Betanzos, *Suma*, I, 12, and imagined within himself. Betanzos, *Suma*, I, 13.

[30] Betanzos, *Suma*, I, 17; I, 37.

[31] Jean-Pierre Protzen, *Inca Architecture and Construction at Ollantaytambo* (New York: Oxford University Press, 1993); Susan A. Niles, *The Shape of Inca History: Narrative and Architecture in an Andean Empire* (University of Iowa Press, 1999).

others who had given birth and had their babies in cradles, according to their custom', proceeding in the same way for all the provinces of Peru. The Creator's companions then placed these stone models into their *pacarinas* ('places of the dawn') – springs and rivers, caves and crags – and from there called them to come forth into life.[32] When thus the Inca painted and made clay models of the distribution of fields and houses, roads and bridges, thereby giving order to society, he continued in a human, historical context what the Creator had done at the beginning. In a sense, as the Inca Atahuallpa said of himself, an Inca ruler, in imitation of the Creator, had to begin 'a new world'.[33]

Conquest and diplomacy in Inca expansion

Pachacuti's victory over the Chancas and the incorporation of the Chanca settlements under Inca rule that followed led to further campaigns that, combined with diplomatic overtures, brought increasingly distant polities into the framework of Tahuantinsuyu. The combination of diplomacy and warfare, which is a regular theme in the *crónicas* that narrate the conquests of Pachacuti and his successors Tupa Yupanqui and Guayna Capac, is adumbrated in two distinct strands in the Inca myth of origin. In some versions of this myth, the first Inca Manco Capac's consort was a ferocious warrior and untiring enemy of any and all opponents whom the first Incas encountered, a most effective partner of her not quite so ferocious husband. Other versions, in which Manco Capac is portrayed as a cultural hero and religious founder, make of his consort the teacher of the art of spinning and weaving that in the Andes was seen as both the most useful and the most prized of arts. As for the Incas' long-distance conquests, the *crónicas* are not always compatible with each other because they all reproduced narratives derived from the Inca kinship groups, each of which exalted the deeds of its own ancestor. Even so, it is clear that a different scale of campaigning began with the expeditions by Viracocha and then Pachacuti into Collasuyo. Pachacuti also initiated expeditions into Chinchaysuyo, which Tupa Yupanqui extended as far as Quito and beyond. But Tupa Yupanqui's most extensive conquests were in Collasuyo as far as Chile and Argentina, and in Antisuyo. He also finalized the integration of the chiefdoms of the central coast near Lima and visited the great shrine of

---

[32] Betanzos, *Suma*, I, 1–2.
[33] Supno Collapiña, *Relación de la descendencia, gobierno y conquista de los Incas (1542)*, ed. Juan José Vega (Lima: Biblioteca Universitaria, 1974): 20.

Pachacamac on the Pacific coast. Guayna Capac, the last Inca to rule before the Spanish invaded, undertook further campaigns in Chinchaysuyo, extending the Incas' reach north of Quito.[34] The incorporation of this region into the empire was a long process, having been envisioned even in the time of Pachacuti. The project was brought to completion by Guayna Capac, who built a northern capital at Tomebamba, which he named after his kinship group and deliberately planned to be 'another Cuzco', a northern capital (see Map 24.1). Apart from dwellings for the use of the Inca, agricultural terraces and storehouses to supply the needs of the court, there was a temple of the Sun and other sacred buildings, one of which housed the gold statue of Guayna Capac's mother Mama Ocllo, which enshrined the remains of her womb. 'This famous residence of Tomebamba', Cieza wrote, 'was one of the most magnificent and sumptuous in all of Peru, with the grandest and most beautiful buildings. Whatever the Indians say of this residence is dwarfed by the remains that are still left of it.'[35]

Prolonged warfare strained relations among the Inca nobles. The *crónicas* mention periodic friction and rivalry between the Inca ruler and those who served in or conducted his wars. On the one hand, the Inca ruler counted on the success of his delegates, but on the other, too much success posed a threat to his pre-eminence. Fearing an usurpation, Pachacuti thus arranged for his brother Capac Yupanqui to be killed, rather than allowing him to celebrate his victory over the lord of Cajamarca. The emergence of a delicate, appropriately maintained equilibrium is exemplified by Guayna Capac's long and hard-fought campaign south and north of Quito. While withdrawing from a difficult engagement, Guayna Capac's entourage of Inca nobles fled and he fell from his litter. He therefore humiliated those nobles by excluding them from the customary distribution of clothing and rations. But he had not calculated the possible consequence, for the disenchanted lords decided to leave the Inca to his war and to return home to Cuzco. By way of saving face and of averting a military disaster, Guayna Capac sent after them the image of his mother Mama Ocllo along with its priestess, whose task was to deliver oracular statements in the voice of Mama Ocllo. Speaking with Mama Ocllo's

---

34 Martti Pärssinen, *Tawantinsuyu: The Inca State and its Political Organization* (Helsinki: Societas Historica Finlandiae, 1992): 85–140; Supno Collapiña, *Relación de la descendencia*, 76; Sabine MacCormack, *On the Wings of Time: Rome, the Incas, Spain and Peru* (Princeton University Press, 2007): 207–8.

35 Cieza, *Crónica del Perú*, 44.

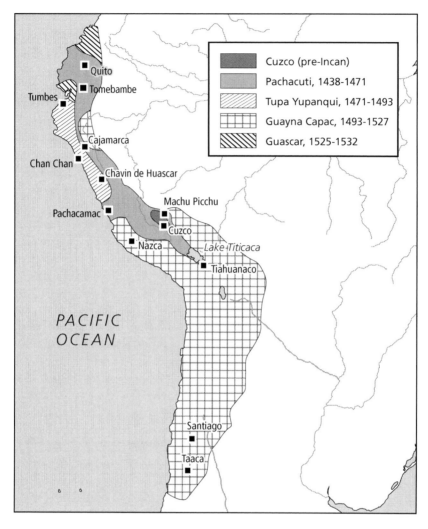

Map 24.1. Inca expansion

authority, this lady pleaded with the nobles to relent, and when they did so, exceptional honours and gifts were their reward.[36]

Sweeping as the Inca conquests were, warfare was also a matter of negotiation and conciliation between the Incas and the peoples they planned

36 Sabine MacCormack, *Religion in the Andes: Vision and Imagination in Early Colonial Peru* (Princeton University Press, 1991): 134–5.

to conquer or annex, and between the Incas and those already conquered or annexed. Although Pachacuti took grim vengeance upon his defeat of the Chancas, he then sent two of their lords with their followers on an expedition of conquest to Lake Titicaca, 'and they subjected all under the dominion of the Inca'. Yet old enmity was not so easily forgotten: during a subsequent expedition, one of the two lords with some of his men escaped beyond Inca reach to the Amazonian lowlands, while the other, seeing no alternative, reaffirmed his submission to Pachacuti. In return he was rewarded with 'a stool of honour decorated with gold, and with other distinctions', which acknowledged his status while also serving as tokens of Inca overlordship.[37] Later, when an Inca army attacked the lord of Cajamarca in the northern sierra, the ruler of the coastal kingdom of Chimor – the only state even remotely comparable to the Incas in power and resources – came to his help, but in vain. In a subsequent campaign Chimor was conquered and its ruler, like other Andean potentates before him, was taken to Cuzco as hostage. The kingdom's very considerable treasure of gold, having been displayed in 'the most splendid and proud triumph' that the city of Cuzco had ever seen, was used to adorn Coricancha. Even so, in the towns and valleys of the former kingdom of Chimor, descendants of its ruler governed as hereditary lords under Inca and later Spanish oversight, and so did numerous other lords of ancient elite families. But unlike other defeated polities whose troops were incorporated into Inca armies, Chimor appears never to have contributed soldiers to fight in Inca wars.[38]

Expansion by military conquest was frequent but not universal. The powerful and populous lordship of Chincha on the central coast was annexed by generally peaceful means. In the time of Pachacuti, an Inca lord passed through, and later Tupa Yupanqui annexed Chincha by means of gift giving and conciliation, without prior warfare. The Inca built an administrative and religious compound in Chincha's capital city, juxtaposing it with the local palace, and the pyramid of the oracular deity Chinchaycamac was reoriented in relation to the Inca compound. Chincha ceramics display a high degree of Inca influence that endured even after the Spanish invasion – a suggestion that the Incas may not have been entirely unwelcome. Most notably, the lord

---

37 Betanzos, *Suma*, 1, 10; Cieza, *Crónica del Peru*, 48 and 50; Miguel Cabello Valboa, *Miscelánea Antártica (1586)* (Lima: Universidad Nacional Mayor de San Marcos, Instituto de Etnología, 1951): 3 and 16.
38 John V. Murra, 'The Expansion of the Inca State: Armies, War and Rebellions', in Murra, Nathan Wachtel, and Jacques Revel (eds.), *Anthropological History of Andean Polities* (Cambridge University Press, 1986): 49–58.

of Chincha enjoyed the privilege of having his litter carried side-by-side with that of the Inca, which 'seemed a remarkable thing, because no person, however distinguished, was allowed to appear before the Inca without a load on his shoulders and with bare feet'.[39]

These episodes, detailing different methods of expansion, also highlight the diversity of the peoples and polities that the Incas brought under their control and of the different geographical environments in which they lived, from sea level to the high altitudes of the Andes, from the Inca homeland around Cuzco to recently incorporated regions.[40] Even long before the Incas, Andean polities had taken account of the enormous range of the ecological environments of the Andes and the resources they offered by creating networks of exchange, including maritime exchange, both within Tahuantinsuyu and also extending to peoples living far beyond its boundaries. Establishing colonies in diverse ecological niches yielded direct access to crops and resources not available locally. The Tiahuanaco state maintained colonies at lower altitudes not only near Cochabamba and Larecaja, but also near Moquegua on the Pacific coast and near Arequipa, where in due course the Incas followed.[41] Colonies in outlying ecological niches and ranging in size from a handful of households to village communities were also planted, independently of any state, by ethnic polities desirous of securing access to crops and resources not available in their homes. As emerges from governmental inspections conducted by the Spanish, such colonists were not counted by the Inca state in the places to which they migrated, but as members of their original polities and kinship groups. Finally, there were persons described as *yanacona*, retainers of individual Incas, dead or still living. The people who were resettled in the Sacred Valley to work on the estates of Inca rulers there were *yanacona*, individuals no longer subject to the *curacas* (regional lords) in their places of origin. Other *yanacona* were detailed for the service Tahuantinsuyu's many temples and sanctuaries, and also for work on Inca estates other than those in the Sacred Valley. Yet other *yanacona* had been 'given' by their communities to serve their *curacas*, and in this sense were no longer incorporated in those communities. The status

---

39 Pedro Pizarro, *Relación del descubrimiento y conquista de los reinos del Peru (1572)*, ed. Guillermo Lohmann Villena (Lima: Pontifica Universidad Católica del Perú, 1978): 37.

40 Terence N. D'Altroy, *Provincial Power in the Inka Empire* (Washington, DC: Smithsonian Institution Press, 1992).

41 Charles Stanish, *Ancient Titicaca: The Evolution of Complex Society in Southern Peru and Northern Bolivia* (Berkeley: University of California Press, 2003): 6–11; 169–72; 191–3; R. Alan Covey, 'Inka Administration of the Far South Coast of Peru', *Latin American Antiquity* 11 (2000): 119–38.

of *acclacona*, women chosen for the service of the Sun – whom the Spanish liked to compare to nuns, even though the Inca might give them in marriage to followers and servants – resembled that of *yanacona*, because they also were separated from their communities of origin. Possibly therefore these individuals were more intimately bonded with the Inca state than the many others who identified primarily with their own ethnic communities. The existence of *yanacona* and *acclacona* would then lead to the conclusion that the Incas were in the process of building a state transcending ethnic identity.

Regions and households

The Incas endeavoured to impose a certain uniformity on these different regions and peoples – at least in principle. The Spanish were often under the impression that the Incas imposed their language on their subjects, or at any rate on *curacas*. But in effect, Tahuantinsuyu was a linguistic mosaic, even if Quechua, the language of the Inca, was widely understood.[42] As for Inca administration, viewing it as an ideal scheme, populations were organized into age groups and decimal units of households, sometimes with intermediate subdivisions, from ten to ten thousand, the units being adjusted periodically in accord with demographic fluctuations. Two or three units of ten thousand made a province, with an Inca official – *tokoyrikoq*, 'who sees everything' – at its head. He had under him the chiefs of the smaller units, many of them *curacas*, lords from local elite families who continued in power under the Inca. All this information, sorted into the moieties of upper and lower that were ubiquitous in the Andes, was recorded on *khipus* of which duplicates were kept locally and in Cuzco. Garcilaso explained the functioning of such demographic *khipus*:

> they recorded first the inhabitants of each village, and then those of each province. On the first thread they would enumerate the old people of sixty or more, on the second men in their maturity of fifty upwards, the third stood for those of forty, and so on in groups of ten years, down to babes and sucklings. Women were counted similarly by age groups.

42 Rodolfo Cerrón-Palomino, *Lingüistica Quechua* (Cuzco: Centro de estudios rurales andinos 'Bartolomé de las Casas,' 1987); Bruce Mannheim, *The Language of the Inka since the European Invasion* (Austin: University of Texas Press, 1991); Alfredo Torero, *Idiomas de los Andes. Lingüistica e Historia* (Lima: Editorial Horizonte, 2005).

Some strings had finer ones attached to take account of exceptions:

> for instance the finer thread on the string referring to men or women of a
> certain age, who were assumed to be married, would mean the number of
> widows or widowers of that age in a given year, for all their records were
> annual.[43]

When a region was incorporated into the Inca Empire, after boundary stones
had been placed and a painting or map of the province had been made, all the
land was seen as belonging to the Inca, who assigned portions of it for the
purposes of religion, for the use of the Inca, and for the people at large.

The demographic counts recorded on *khipus* were the basis for assessing
tribute, which in the absence of currency in the Andes was taken in labour
(not in kind), household by household. In the most basic sense, labour was
agricultural, the crops cultivated in the fields of the deities being used for
their cult, and the crops from the fields of the Inca for his use, and finally the
crops from the fields of each household for the sustenance of its members.
Households of artisans – miners, weavers, metalworkers, potters,
stonemasons, specialists who made sandals, military equipment, cloth of
feather work and much more – likewise were assessed in terms of labour.
There were also the postal runners who carried messages from one end of
Tahuantinsuyo to the other, and the specialists who carried the Inca in his
litter, and with this occupation and work they paid their tribute. To them as
to all others working for the Inca state, the state – seen as the person of the
Inca ruler – supplied sustenance and materials, and in order to do so,
redistributed the products that the state gathered from one group of workers
and one region to another. People thus worked for the Inca, but did not give
the Inca anything they counted as theirs. The supreme giver of gifts was the
Inca, and redistribution was a primary task of the Inca state, without which it
could not have functioned. Moreover, in an ideal framework, and even in the
framework of every day, labour performed for the Inca took place in a
context of feasting and gift giving, of reciprocal benefits. The huge *kallankas* –
long halls that are so distinct a feature of Inca provincial capitals – were
designed for accommodating crowds during feasts and festivals. When thus,
according to Betanzos, Inca Pachacuti was planning to rebuild Cuzco on a
grander scale, the regional lords came with gifts which were placed into
nearby storehouses. The next five days were taken up with fiestas and

---

43 Garcilaso de la Vega, *Comentarios Reales*, I, 6,8; Catherine Julien, 'How Inca Decimal
   Organization Worked', *Ethnohistory* 35 (1988): 257–79.

celebrations, and only then did the Inca inform the lords of the work to be accomplished next. Once this work was completed, further tasks followed, interspersed with fiestas. Labour for the Inca state was performed in a celebratory framework of reciprocity and of the Inca's generosity; from very different vantage points, Garcilaso and Guaman Poma de Ayala chose to remember it in this way some eighty years after the Inca was gone.[44]

But we must not underestimate the economic, and hence military and political power that, thanks to this system of reciprocity and redistribution, the Inca state came to possess. The products resulting from all the work performed by the Inca's subjects, accounted for by *khipu*, were kept in state storehouses. For example, at the provincial capital of Huanuco Pampa, several hundred well-ventilated and insulated storehouses contained agricultural products, cloth, sandals and weaponry. In some places, the stores that had been accumulated by the Inca for times of need and for the uses of the state lasted, despite Spanish depredation, until the early seventeenth century.[45] Military service was another form of labour performed for the state, often at great cost of life and limb. Equally, if not more, intrusive on the lives of groups and individuals was the resettlement of entire populations for the purpose of working for the Inca. The colonies that ethnic polities within Tahuantinsuyu maintained at distances from their homelands were replicated by the Incas on a much larger scale and also, frequently, for different reasons. When Tupa Yupanqui organized the cult of the Sacred Rock on the Island of the Sun in Lake Titicaca, he removed the entire population of the island and replaced them with colonists, *mitimas*, who were to look after the shrine and were selected from forty-two different nations, the intention perhaps being to represent all of Tahuantinsuyu on the island.[46] Most resettlements, however, were undertaken for political or economic reasons. For example, after a series of difficult campaigns against the Chachapoyas and the Cañari, large numbers of colonists from both these polities were resettled to work on the estates of Inca rulers in the Sacred Valley so as to diminish the likelihood of rebellions in their homelands. With good reason, because when the Spanish invaded, the Chachapoya and

44 Betanzos, *Suma*, 1, 13; Garcilaso de la Vega, *Comentarios Reales*, 1, 5, 2; Felipe Guaman Poma de Ayala, *Nueva Crónica y buen gobierno (1615)*, ed. John V. Murra, Rolena Adorno and J. Urioste (Madrid: Historia 16, 1987): 251; John V. Murra, *The Economic Organization of the Inca State* (Greenwich, CT: JAI Press, 1980); Brian S. Bauer, 'Legitimization of the Inca State in Myth and Ritual', *American Anthropologist* N.S. 98 (1996): 327–37.
45 Craig Morris and Donald E. Thompson, *Huánuco Pampa: An Inca City and its Hinterland* (London: Thames and Hudson, 1985).
46 Sabine MacCormack, 'From the "Sun of the Incas" to the Virgin of Copacabana', *Representations* 8 (1984): 30–60.

Cañari became their willing allies. They were not alone: as an old man from Hatuncana said in an administrative enquiry in 1571, his father had been resettled by Tupa Yupanqui because he 'was a valiant man' and the Inca moved him from his home 'lest he rebel against him'.[47]

On a far larger scale was the resettlement program involving some 14,000 colonists from many different parts of Tahuantinsuyu that Guayna Capac undertook in the Cochabamba valley. Here, the rationale was economic. Most of the local people were moved elsewhere, and the colonists, who came with their lords for life and for the lives of their descendants, were therefore no longer enumerated on the *khipu* of their group of origin; they were employed in growing maize for the Inca state. Supremely disruptive as such resettlement was for all involved, the Incas for the most part governed through local lords, who were left in place after a region's incorporation into Tahuantinsuyu and, inter alia, were in charge of organizing work for the Inca, such as raising crops, weaving textiles and transporting whatever had been produced to Inca store-houses. Other work was taken in turns, *mita,* and involved travel: for example a number of Lupaqa men from Chucuito on Lake Titicaca worked in turn as *mitayoc* (one who works in turn) to make walls and houses for the Inca in Cuzco.

Such being the contours of the ideal scheme of Inca governance, different aspects of which obtained primarily in the core regions of Tahuantinsuyu, more recently integrated regions displayed much variety. Decimal administration does not appear to have been imposed in either the northern or the southern reaches of the empire, where the elegant Inca stone carving of Cuzco and the Inca heartland is rarely found. The southernmost part of Collasuyo, reaching from the heights of the Andes to the desert along the Pacific coast of Chile and somewhat beyond contemporary Santiago, was much more sparsely populated than the southern sierra of Peru. Like other regions conquered by the Incas, some parts of the southlands saw intensified agriculture, herding and mining. The roads built by the Inca, with *tambos,* way stations at intervals, reached beyond Santiago, and the region was protected by a line of forts in the foothills of the Andes that were designed to protect settlements, control movement and discourage raids, but were not designed to maintain a fixed or closed border (see Figure 24.1).[48] The absence

47 Roberto Levillier, *Don Francisco de Toledo, supremo organizador del Perú. Su vida, su obra (1515–1582)* (Buenos Aires: Biblioteca del Congreso Argentino, 1940), vol. II: 108.
48 Terence N. D'Altroy, Verónica I. Williams and Ana Maria Lorandi, 'The Inkas in the Southlands', in Richard L. Burger, Craig Morris and Ramiro Matos Mendieta (eds.), *Variations in the Expression of Inka Power* (Washington, DC: Dumbarton Oaks, 2007): 85–133.

Figure 24.1 Sacsayhuaman: Inca Ruins (Aivar Mikko / Alamy)

of such a border is also evident from the archaeological record of eastern lowland Bolivia. Here the splendid site Samaipata with its huge *kallanka* (long hall), remembered by the descendants of Tupa Yupanqui who conducted a long campaign there, proclaimed the Inca presence in what appears to have been a ceremonial and religious much more than a military sense. As for the northern end of Tahuantinsuyu, which, if the descendants of Tupa Yupanqui were to be believed, was conquered by their forebear, it was in effect only integrated into the empire after long wars by Guayna Capac.

Religion in the Inca Empire

When in the 1570s the Spanish conducted enquiries as to how the Incas had governed, many Andean respondents claimed that force had been a major factor – which was the answer that the Spanish were expecting and wanting to hear.[49] But this was far from being the whole story. Polities like Chincha that had been incorporated into Tahuantinsuyu by negotiation and gift giving are regularly mentioned in the *crónicas*, war being chosen as a last resort, or if

49 Levillier, *Don Francisco de Toledo*; Catherine Julien, 'Francisco de Toledo and his Campaign Against the Incas', *Colonial Latin American Review* 16 (2007): 243–72.

a polity already under Inca control rebelled. In whichever way incorporation into Tahuantinsuyu was achieved, it entailed participation in Inca religion, and the Inca ruler's participation in the religion of his subjects. This two-way incorporation took place at many levels, beginning with the allotment of land and work for the cults of the Inca Sun, of deceased Inca rulers and of further supernaturals, whether Inca or other.[50] Aside from such economic arrangements, diverse existing cults were reorganized within the Inca religious framework. Some were effectively transformed into Inca cults, most especially that of the Sacred Rock on the island in Lake Titicaca. At the coastal sanctuary of the oracular deity Pachacamac, incorporation took the form of juxtaposition. Pachacamac was a religious centre possibly as early as c. 500 CE, and the influence of Huari and Tiahuanaco styles in the ceramics of the site indicate its importance beyond its immediate environment. The crónicas attribute the first Inca visit to the sanctuary of Pachacamac to Pachacuti or Tupa Yupanqui. The latter was said to have spoken of Pachacamac while still in his mother's womb, and later to have visited the sanctuary because he had dreamt that the 'Creator of all' was to be found there. Pachacamac, revered as world maker and world destroyer, gave oracles which were sought out by pilgrims from far and wide, who were allowed to approach the shrine only after undergoing extended rites of purification and confession. Given the power of the oracle, the Incas did not redesign the existing temple, but built another one, a huge pyramid dedicated to the Sun and the Day next to it.[51] Where Tupa Yupanqui associated himself with Pachacamac, his successor Guayna Capac sought out the oracle Catequil near Huamachuco, whose influence reached far into the northern Andean highlands. Catequil, manifest in a rocky crag, was a founding ancestor of the people of Huamachuco, and also a deity of thunder and lightning who was revered along with two other supernaturals – crags flanking the central one of Catequil himself – called Mamacatequil and Piguerao. Like Pachacamac, Catequil had numerous offspring whose oracular statements were sought out at shrines often located at considerable distances from the central sanctuary. One such manifestation of Catequil accompanied Guayna Capac on his northern campaigns.

The Incas sought to introduce some kind of conformity among the multiplicity of divine oracular voices that resonated all over the Andes by

---

50 Justin Jennings, 'Inca Imperialism, Ritual Change and Cosmological Continuity in the Cotahuasi Valley of Peru', *Journal of Anthropological Research* 59 (2003): 433–62.

51 María Rostworowski, *Pachacamac y el Señor de los Milagros. Una trayectoria milenaria. Señoríos indígenas de Lima y Canta* (Lima: Instituto de Estudios Peruanos, 2002).

sending offerings to their shrines to obtain good harvests, avert disasters and pray for the Inca, especially at his inauguration. These offerings, carried in procession from Cuzco to their various destinations were known as *capacocha*, 'supreme sacrifice', and for especially solemn occasions included human victims, especially children. This movement of offerings that radiated from Cuzco throughout Tahuantinsuyu was balanced by a movement in the opposite direction by the principal oracles of all the provinces who visited Cuzco annually to deliver their prognostications for the coming year. The oracles were questioned one by one, and each individually, wrote Cieza, 'answered by the mouth of the priests who were in charge of their cult'. In the following year, the oracles that had predicted correctly were rewarded with a *capacocha*, while those who had not received 'no offering but rather, lost reputation'.[52]

Put differently, by listening to the oracles, the Incas were able to collect news and assess climates of opinion in the different parts of Tahuantinsuyu, or, as Cieza put it, they would learn 'whether the year would be fertile or there would be drought, if the Inca would live a long time or might perhaps die that year, if enemies were to come from somewhere, or if some peaceful subjects would rebel'.[53] In effect, however, things were more complicated. Not only did subjects rebel regardless of these efforts, but also, the oracles and local deities did not always comply with the Inca's wishes. Over a century after the event, the people of Huarochirí still remembered how Tupa Yupanqui, when contending with a series of rebellions, had summoned all the local deities and oracles to Cuzco for a consultation. Even Pachacamac went, but Pariacaca the principal deity of Huarochirí refused and only sent his son Maca Uisa. After a long and awkward silence, with the local deities refusing to converse with the Inca, Maca Uisa spoke up and then washed the Inca's enemies away in a mudslide, only to reject the Inca's offerings and require that the Inca come in person and dance for him at his annual festival, thereby challenging the order of dignity in which the Inca stood at the top. Guaman Poma also remembered the incident, but thought that Maca Uisa had said that 'there was no more time for talking and governing' because soon the Spanish would arrive.[54] Later, in the Chillón valley, a regional lord, displeased with Inca interference, ordered his people to 'speak to their local deity so that the Inca Guayna Capac should die, because his predecessor Tupa Yupanqui had already died for the very reason that they had requested

---

52 Cieza, *Crónica del Perú*, 29.   53 Cieza, *Crónica del Perú*, 29.
54 *Runa Yndio ñiscap Machoncuna ñaupa pacha'*, 261–2.

it, and the local deity would do the same thing again if they requested that Guayna Capac should die'.[55] In due course, Guayna Capac's son Atahuallpa fell out not only with Pachacamac but also with Catequil, who criticized the Inca for causing the death of many people. Whereupon Atahuallpa ordered Catequil's shrine to be destroyed, but in vain, because the oracle revived and multiplied in the guise of its many descendants.

It was not only the oracles that frequently spoke with discordant voices. The Inca ancestors, to whose instructions their *panacas* (kinship groups) attributed their own opinions and interests, did the same. As a result, Inca successions were usually complicated by conflicting claims, all the more so because among the Incas, as in the Andes at large, successors were chosen for their ability, not by primogeniture. In addition, a successor of a regional lord or of the Inca might be his son, but could also be his brother or the son of his sister. Hence, in order to reduce the number of possible candidates for the succession, Inca Pachacuti ordained that the Inca, however many other consorts he might have, should in his capacity of Inca also marry a sister, making a son of this union the preferred successor. Even so, Pachacuti chose Tupa Yupanqui as his successor because he considered him to be his ablest son. Tupa Yupanqui's son Guayna Capac died unexpectedly of one of the infectious diseases that preceded the Spanish invaders, and so, shortly thereafter, did his designated successor. This left, in Tumebamba, Guayna Capac's son Atahuallpa whose mother belonged to the *panaca* of Pachacuti, and in Cuzco, Guayna Capac's son Guascar, whose mother belonged to the *panaca* of Tupa Yupanqui. It was in the aftermath of the resulting civil war between Atahuallpa and Guascar, from which Atahuallpa emerged the victor, that the Spanish invaders arrived.[56]

The destruction of Tahuantinsuyu can thus be seen, in one sense, as the consequence of civil war, and in another as the consequence of discordant divinatory voices, both those of the diverse Andean oracles, and those of the Inca ancestors who were looked after by their *panacas*. It was only after 1565,

55 María Rostworowski, *Conflicts over Coca Fields in Sixteenth Century Peru* (Ann Arbor: University of Michigan Press, 1988), vol. IV, fol. 212v.
56 María Rostworowski, *History of the Inca Realm*, trans. Harry B. Iceland (Cambridge University Press, 1999): 97–134; Sabine MacCormack, 'Inca o español? Las identidades de Paullu Topa Inca', in P. Kaulicke, G. Urton and I. Farrington (eds.), *Identidad y transformación en el Tawantinsuyu y en los Andes Coloniales. Perspectivas arqueológicas y etnohistóricas. Tercera Parte* (Lima: Pontificia Universidad Católica del Perú, Fondo Editorial, 2004): 99–109; Sabine MacCormack, 'The Scope of Comparison: The Roman, Spanish and Inca Empires', in Benjamin Z. Kedar (ed.), *Explorations in Comparative History* (Jerusalem: Magnes Press, 2009): 53–74.

over thirty years after the onset of the Spanish invasion, that the Andean oracles were thought to speak in one voice in the movement known as *Taqui Onqoy*, 'Song of Disease', the disease to be expelled being the Spanish. The *pacarina* ('place of the dawn') of the Incas, Titicaca, Tiahuanaco, the volcano Chimborazo near Quito, Pachacamac and some sixty or seventy other local deities and oracles were asking for the traditional Andean offerings that the Incas had been so careful to provide, so as to fight the Christian god, whose turn, *mita*, must surely be coming to an end. But by that time, when the Spanish hold on Tahuantinsuyu was tightening and the realm of the Incas was on its way to becoming the viceroyalty of Peru, it was too late.[57]

FURTHER READING

Bauer, Brian S. *Ancient Cuzco. Heartland of the Inca*. Austin, TX: University of Texas Press, 2004.
    The Sacred Landscape of the Inca: The Cusco Ceque System. Austin, TX: University of Texas Press, 1998.
Bauer, Brian S. and Charles Stanish. *Ritual and Pilgrimage in the Ancient Andes: The Islands of the Sun and the Moon*. Austin, TX: University of Texas Press, 2001.
Benson, Elizabeth P. and Anita G. Cook, eds. *Ritual Sacrifice in Ancient Peru*. Austin, TX: University of Texas Press, 2001.
Boone, Elizabeth Hill and Gary Urton, eds. *Their Way of Writing: Scripts, Signs, and Pictographies in Pre-Columbian America*. Washington DC: Dumbarton Oaks, 2011.
Burger, Richard L., Craig Morris and Ramiro Matos Mendieta, eds. *Variations in the Expression of Inka Power*. Washington, DC: Dumbarton Oaks, 2007.
Covey, R. Alan. *How the Incas Built their Heartland: State Formation and the Innovation of Imperial Strategies in the Sacred Valley, Peru*. Ann Arbor, MI: University of Michigan Press, 2006.
Curatola Petrocchi, Marco and Mariusz S. Ziolkowski, eds. *Adivinación y oráculos en el mundo andino antiguo*. Lima: Pontífica Universidad Católica del Perú, 2008.
D'Altroy, Terence N. *The Incas*. Oxford: Blackwell, 2002.
Hyslop, John. *The Inka Road System*. New York, NY: Academic Press, 1984.
Julien, Catherine. *Reading Inca History*. Iowa University Press, 2000.
Kolata, Alan L., ed. *Tiwanaku and its Hinterland: Archaeology and Paleoecology of an Andean Civilization*. I. *Agroecology*. II. *Urban and Rural Archaeology*. Washington, DC: Smithsonian Institution, 1996–2003.
Lamana, Gonzalo. *Domination without Dominance: Inca-Spanish Encounters in Early Colonial Peru*. Durham, NC: Duke University Press, 2008.
MacCormack, Sabine. *On the Wings of Time: Rome, the Incas, Spain and Peru*. Princeton University Press, 2007.

---

57 Gonzalo Lamana, *Domination without Dominance: Inca-Spanish Encounters in Early Colonial Peru* (Durham, NC: Duke University Press, 2008).

'Processions for the Inca: Andean and Christian Ideas of Human Sacrifice, Communion and Embodiment in Early Colonial Peru', *Archiv für Religionsgeschichte* 2,1 (2000): 1–31.

'The Scope of Comparison: The Roman, Spanish and Inca Empires', in Benjamin Z. Kedar (ed.), *Explorations in Comparative History* (Jerusalem: Magnes Press, 2009): 53–74.

McEwan, Gordon F., ed. *Pikillacta: The Wari Empire in Cuzco.* University of Iowa Press, 2005.

Murra, John V. *The Economic Organization of the Inca State.* Greenwich, CT: JAI Press, 1980.

Murra, John V., Nathan Wachtel and Jacques Revel, eds. *Anthropological History of Andean Polities.* Cambridge University Press, 1986.

Niles, Susan A. *The Shape of Inca History: Narrative and Architecture in an Andean Empire.* University of Iowa Press, 1999.

Pärssinen, Martti. *Tawantinsuyu: The Inca State and its Political Organization.* Helsinki: Societas Historica Finlandiae, 1992.

Pillsbury, Joanne, ed. *Guide to Documentary Sources for Andean Studies 1530–1900.* 3 vols. Norman, OK: University of Oklahoma Press, 2008.

Quilter, Jeffrey and Gary Urton, eds. *Narrative Threads: Accounting and Recounting in Andean Khipu.* Austin, TX: University of Texas Press, 2002.

Rostworowski, María, *History of the Inca Realm,* trans. Harry B. Iceland. Cambridge University Press, 1999.

Salomon, Frank. *The Cord Keepers: Khipus and Cultural Life in a Peruvian Village.* Durham, NC: Duke University Press, 2004.

Native Lords of Quito in the Age of the Incas: The Political Economy of North Andean Chiefdoms. Cambridge University Press, 1986.

Stanish, Charles. *Ancient Titicaca: The Evolution of Complex Society in Southern Peru and Northern Bolivia.* Berkeley, CA: University of California Press, 2003.

Urton, Gary. 'From Knots to Narratives: Reconstructing the Art of Historical Record Keeping in the Andes from Spanish Transcriptions of Inka Khipus', *Ethnohistory* 45,3 (1998): 409–38.

'Sin, Confession and the Arts of Book- and Cord-keeping: An Intercontinental and Transcultural Exploration of Accounting and Governmentality', *Comparative Studies in Society and History* 51,4 (2009): 801–31.

Zuidema, Tom. *El calendario Inca. Tiempo y espacio en la organización ritual del Cuzco. La idea del pasado.* Lima: Fondo editorial del Congreso del Perú, 2010.

25

"Proto-globalization" and "Proto-glocalizations" in the Middle Millennium

DIEGO OLSTEIN

As the editors were planning this volume, they hoped that the widely celebrated Israeli sociologist Shmuel N. Eisenstadt (1923–2010) would be able to write the final chapter, because his ideas about the interplay among cultural, political, and social processes of change throughout world history have been so influential. With more than fifty books authored or edited, Eisenstadt's prolific work covers wide chronological, spatial, and thematic scopes running from ancient to contemporary societies worldwide. However, he never encompassed this entire chronology or synthesized the full range of his central ideas in a single book.

A possible outline for such an undertaking might portray the core of his historical vision as two major transformations and a long-lasting continuity. In such a schematic view of Eisenstadt's work, the "Axial Age" and "modernization" are the two crucial breakthroughs of world history. Conversely, the "system of empire" that consolidated in the wake of the Axial Age, is the political feature that provided institutional continuity along most of human history until its replacement by the autonomic state – that is, one that is independent from the ruler's patrimony – as modernization unfolded.

The Axial Age comprehends a period running from the eighth to the fifth centuries BCE, the nearly simultaneous foundational moment of many major intellectual traditions. In China, many philosophical schools emerged during this period, of which Legalism, Daoism, and predominantly Confucianism were the most important. In India, Buddhism and Jainism emerged, fostering also the reformulation of Hinduism. In southwest Asia, Zoroastrianism appeared in Iran as a dualist religion, while Judaism as a monotheist religion entered its prophetic phase. In time, Judaism gave rise to Christianity and Islam. In the Mediterranean, Greece witnessed the emergence of rationalistic philosophy. These traditions all led to the creation of distinctive regional civilizations.

According to Eisenstadt, all Axial Age traditions institutionalized the division between the mundane and the transcendental orders. This institutionalization was represented by the emergence of a new type of social elite, a spiritual leadership that challenged and restrained the already established political elite. Using moral considerations, this new spiritual elite restrained the old political one and demanded accountability from it. This reordering of the world of knowledge, ideas, ideals, and morality also led to the reordering of the political and social spheres, which crystallized in the form of a new political institution, the empire. In Eisenstadt's view, the system of empire emerged as a political framework capable of achieving territorial centralization for long periods of time precisely because the goals of the rulers and those of the autonomous social, political, and economic elites were properly balanced. The better balanced these interests were, the longer the empires lived, although the system of empire also required sufficiently complex and productive societies in order to emerge and flourish.

A second dramatic increase in complexity and productivity brought about by modernization displaced both the system of empire and the civilizations of the Axial Age, and resulted in the second major transformation in world history. Industrialization, urbanization, social differentiation, political revolution in thought and praxis, democratization, the emergence of autonomic states, the expansion of the public sphere, and the growing prominence of the civil society are the leading factors that Eisenstadt pointed to as the shapers of a new worldwide modern civilization. For all of the homogenizing force of this new encompassing civilization, however, each of the contributing factors emerged entangled with the singular traditions of the different regional civilizations, resulting in "multiple modernities."

In his later works, Eisenstadt entwined the unfolding of modernization and the emergence of multiple modernities with the process of "globalization." For one, he inquired about the interplay between globalization and modernization by assessing their reciprocal influences. While globalization as a homogenizing force influences the multiplicities of modernization, these multiplicities still find expression amidst globalization, which makes this phenomenon also plural. The same dichotomy between homogeneity and heterogeneity already observed in the tension between modernization and multiple modernities re-emerges in his discussion of globalization. Monolithic and pluralistic trends leading towards both integration and resistance are at the core of globalization.

Within this overall framework the Middle Millennium seems to fall within a long-lasting parenthesis opened by the Axial Age and closed by modernization, multiple modernities, and globalization. In fact, the Middle Millennium is widely represented in the system of empire by the Chinese, Mongol, Muslim, Byzantine, Carolingian, and Inca Empires. And yet, as Eisenstadt prepared the outline for the present chapter, he advanced the notion of "proto-globalization" and sketched some of its features, thus proposing the Middle Millennium as a prelude to the radical transformations of the second breakthrough of world history. Cultural changes in the Middle Millennium itself may have also brought about a second Axial Age of sorts.

In short, the Middle Millennium appears through the lenses of Eisenstadt's later thinking as one in which the civilizations of the Axial Age enjoyed a new lease on life, the system of empire thrived as never before, and the foundations for globalization and modernization were laid. In this spirit, and inspired by Eisenstadt's outline, the following synoptic chapter aims to encapsulate some of the major developments and trends presented in this volume through the lens of Eisentadt's notion of "proto-globalization."

Although this concept remained undefined in his drafted outline, Eisenstadt presented proto-globalization as the action of three pervading forces promoting regional integration: religion, commerce, and conquest. In addition, he listed four types of movements as capable of furthering interaction between the world's main regions: those of people, animals and plants, goods, and ideas. These forces of regional integration and movements of interaction led to the articulation of three levels of proto-globalization. The first level comprehends commercial, political, military, and cultural relations between the realms of Islam, China, India and Europe. The second level entails relationships that gave rise to hybridization of traits derived from two of these four realms. The third level consists of the success of some states in constructing hegemonies within the realms of Islam, China, India and Europe, and the reactions to these.

As the geographical scope of these three levels concerns only Afro-Eurasia, one way of understanding proto-globalization is as globalization falling short of encompassing the globe. Indeed, rather than a globalized world, the world of the Middle Millennium was one of "worlds together" for Eurasia and the northern half of Africa and "worlds apart" for the rest of the world's societies. In addition to this limitation, and despite all the importance of regional integrations and trans-regional movements, local conditions of social life were fundamental not only for the worlds apart of the western and southern hemispheres but also for the relatively connected societies of Afro-Eurasia.

In other words, a complementary way of understanding proto-globalization is as globalization falling short of making global trends prevail upon local ones. These local conditions, therefore, also need to be addressed in a discussion of proto-globalization. Attention to both proto-global and local conditions brings us close to the notion of "proto-glocalization." Glocalization, a term invented in the 1980s by Japanese economists and popularized in the 1990s by sociologists to describe adaptation of a global product to local conditions and standards, has more recently been used widely to describe processes that blend globalization and localization. Glocalization stresses the tensions between the local and global origins of – and inputs into – structures and processes in any given society, as well as tensions in the outcomes of such processes.

One way to assess proto-globalization during the Middle Millennium is to follow the changing balance between local structures and processes and regional and trans-regional ones as time passed by. Thus the point of departure for this chapter is a summary of the prevailing local conditions at the beginning of the period, around 500 CE. Then, it focuses on the forces and movements of proto-globalization throughout the period (c. 500–1500 CE). Finally, the chapter assesses the impact of proto-globalization by looking at Middle Millennium societies around the end of the period (c. 1500 CE). In doing that, this chapter relies on the vantage points provided by the twenty-four chapters of this volume.

The local

As the Middle Millennium opened up c. 500 CE, the world was made of an immense variety of little worlds, usually unrelated. Each of these worlds consisted of societies differentiated by their family structure, education, religion, law, and government. Deeply embedded patterns of marriage, child-raising, living arrangements (patrilocality, matrilocality or neolocality), kinship, and kinship-like ties distinguished societies from one another. Idiosyncrasy also predominated in education as these singular family and household arrangements also functioned as primary educational institutions: mothers taught daughters the skills that women were expected to possess, and fathers taught sons. Also formal education, provided by institutions that resulted from particular local combinations of religious and intellectual traditions, as well as by social, political, and economic structures, was essentially local. Local customary patterns of instruction prevailed, transmitted in both written and oral forms, as well as through practice.

Beyond close-kin relations, most people probably felt most solidarity with their local communities. Solidarities evolved within the relatively small polities of nomadic societies, among neighbors in settled agricultural societies, and within towns. It is upon the strength of these local relations that larger polities emerged and consolidated, reaching political unity, based upon the acceptance of local hierarchies and solidarities. However, solidarity at the level of whole polities was probably felt only by their leading members, in control of the rest of the population, rather than by local communities. As war leaders and their followers acquired resources, they turned from mere tribute-taking to more systematic collection of taxes, rents, and tolls, and spent more on their courts, rituals, and patronage. Throughout the course of the Middle Millennium, courts were created around central authorities. In time, local authorities also established their own courts modeled to a greater or lesser extent on the central ones. This duplication reflects the fact that government came in layers, with either the central government delegating authority through a formal hierarchy of offices over different regions and smaller areas, or with local people of high status who ruled their own domains being recognized by the central authority. Whichever direction authority was transferred, local power centers, whether religious, administrative, or private landowners, remained important.

The prominence of the local is certainly true for the rule of law. The legal departing point for most societies was some kind of unwritten customary law. Because it was unwritten it tended to vary, even within one polity, from place to place and from time to time. For example, rules about such matters as inheritance and the use of land varied among societies and among classes of people within them, and were variably enforced. Similarly local were religious customs, as societies probably started out with their own belief systems and practices. These local belief systems and practices were later influenced by the religions of those societies with which they came into contact, or were even partially displaced by the religion of central polities. Still, such displacements resulted in syncretistic beliefs and practices that blended impositions from the outside and local elements.

Despite these local differences, some crucial social features were similar in all societies during the Middle Millennium. Those for which there are records all seem to have been more or less unequal. The least unequal, with the fewest layers of government, were the smallest and poorest: pastoral nomads or hunter-gatherers, with little or no agriculture. Societies based on agriculture had larger populations, greater wealth, greater inequality and power, greater complexity of government, and therefore more cause for conflict both within societies and between them. In this type of society land remained the chief source of wealth, status, and power, so that the largest landowners remained the top elite. Out of this landowning class came the rulers of localities, regions, and polities. Some kind of monarchy was the norm.

Moreover, not only similar underlying features bring these varied local worlds together, but also actual contacts between them. Increased production promoted markets, towns, and trade, both local and long-distance, and with this came more development of more crafts, more movement and mixing of people, both in space and status, as well as movement of goods, both everyday and luxury items. Long-distance trade, though, was just one of the main ways through which wider contacts impacted the local worlds. Together trade, the diffusion of religions, and conquests represented the forces of 'proto-globalization.'

The "proto-global" forces

The Middle Millennium opened with a series of shifts in relative wealth and power within Afro-Eurasia. First, pastoralist nomadic societies conquered and extracted wealth from agricultural ones. Second, among the latter, India and West Asia prospered while Europe and China declined. There is a connection between these two shifts. The military might of the Sasanian Empire (226–651 CE) was able to restrain the expansion of raiders from the pastoral societies of the steppes of Asia, thus enabling political stability and continuity in West Asia while at the same time the Roman and Han empires collapsed. Third, these imperial collapses brought about political fragmentation and trade decay. Fourth, the power vacuum created by political fragmentation was filled in by the spread of universal religions, as the political power vacuum allowed religions to spread more widely, and as religious institutions substituted for secular political ones as the means by which power was organized. Christianity continued to expand, and from India Buddhism spread to Southeast and Central Asia, China, Korea, and Japan. A century and a half later, with the advent of Islam a new universal religion as well as a new civilization came to the fore, ultimately reaching the Atlantic shores westward and the Pacific Ocean eastward. Indeed, the spread of agriculture, city dwelling, and state formation to vast new areas of Afro-Eurasia is the fifth outstanding development highlighting this period. On the western end of Eurasia forest and swamp were transformed into arable land. In East and South Asia floodplains were transformed into rice paddy fields that provided the material base for the consolidation of a unified Korea under the Silla dynasty (618–935), the Yamoto state in Japan (538–710), and the emergence of new states in the main river valleys of Southeast Asia.

These five developments set the stage for the "proto-global" dimension of the Middle Millennium, the irruption of outside forces that transformed the local worlds in Afro-Eurasia. There were three major such forces: empire building, the expansion of trade networks, and religious conversion. Although these political, economic, and ideological developments operated independently, they also appeared sometimes in pairs or as an entangled triad. Sometimes empire building fostered commercial integration and religious conversion, but the establishment of trade networks and the spread of religions also unfolded outside imperial contexts, sometimes entangled with one another. Along with these three, other factors also shaped local worlds, including migration, and the diffusion of languages, knowledge, and technology.

The expansion of Islam exemplifies the intertwining of empire construction, the establishment of trade networks, and religious conversion. The Muslim conquests of the seventh and eighth centuries initially resulted in a huge empire. This fragmented in the tenth century, but even after its fragmentation the political units of the Islamic world were larger than those in place before Islamic expansion. These political transformations were associated with processes of Islamization and Arabization, as Islam and, to a lesser extent, the Arabic language were disseminated in the conquered lands. Manifold local worlds were absorbed within the realm of Islam, as local traditions became displaced or entangled with the external forces brought by Islam. Moreover, the geographic expansion of Islam from Iberia to India and from Morocco to Southeast Asia resulted in the establishment of a corridor directly connecting the Asian far east and the European far west. Islam also spread through the Indian Ocean long-distance trade routes, and had an impact throughout this ocean basin from the shores of East Africa to the ports of southern China. This combination of large political units and maritime networks facilitated the articulation of contacts between faraway societies via trade interactions through which technologies and ideas also flowed. The challenge to local traditions extended beyond the lands that were politically part of the Islamic world or in which Islam was the dominant religion. Islam was, instead, truly a Afro-Eurasian proto-global phenomenon.

The diffusion of Buddhism was also initially associated with empire building, but this was before the Middle Millennium, during the Maurgan Empire of the second century BCE and the Kushan Empire of the first century

CE. During the Kushan period, Mahayana Buddhists began to develop their unique philosophical tradition, texts, and images, which later spread to Central Asia, China, Japan, and Korea. The Theravada variety of Buddhism became dominant in Sri Lanka and most of Southeast Asia. During the Middle Millennium, these consolidated centers of Buddhism exchanged teachings, texts, and images. Religious exchanges were frequently intertwined with commercial activity, as trade routes were their vehicle and itinerant traders and merchants were their agents. Networks of Buddhism and trade overlapped and were interdependent, and they flowed in all directions. Buddhist monks from India, for example, went to China not only to transmit the doctrine, but also to pay homage to Buddhist divinities purportedly living in Chinese mountains. Similarly, ideas formulated in Japan seem to have influenced Buddhist schools in China, although these Chinese schools are also considered to be the main source of Buddhism in Japan. The spread of Buddhism included a process through which Buddhist ideas were transmitted back to places recognized as the central realms of Buddhism.

Linked to these Buddhist networks were many other types of cross-cultural exchanges, including diplomatic relations between various courts and kingdoms, the transmission of scientific and technological knowledge, and borrowings in art, literature, and music. Thus, the spread of Buddhism must be understood as a multifaceted and dynamic process of cross-cultural interactions and influences. Bonds were tighter within areas that practiced similar varieties of Buddhism: Mahayana Buddhists had their own sphere of influence radiating from China into East Asia while Theravada Buddhists in southern Asia maintained close relationships with Tibet. Despite the divergence between the Mahayana and Theravada forms of Buddhism, however, Buddhist interactions between China and southern Asia continued throughout the Middle Millennium. The exchange of monks, the translation of Indian Buddhist texts into Chinese, and the import of Buddhist artifacts from southern Asia reached unprecedented levels under the Song dynasty (960–1279). Buddhist interactions between China and southern Asia continued during the Mongol Yuan dynasty, albeit with less intensity.

The Mongol expansion in the thirteenth century was also an instance of empire building entwined with the thickening of trade relations, although without the dissemination of the conquerors' religion. Instead, their expansion resulted in their own conversion to either Islam or Buddhism. The emergence of the Mongol Empire, the largest continental empire the world has ever seen, was the culmination of a proto-globalizing phenomenon that recurred throughout the Middle Millennium: pastoralist nomadic migrations and conquests. In fact, because at the beginning of this period there were already no unutilized and unclaimed pastures anywhere in Eurasia, the Middle Millennium stands out as a period of large-scale pastoralist nomadic migrations and conquests. This pattern unfolded for the first time between the second half of the sixth century and the middle of the eighth century. In this period, Turkic peoples subjugated many oasis states in Central Asia and established Turkic khaqanates. These conquests resulted in the spreading of Turkic languages from East Siberia to the Middle Volga region and to the Balkans, a Turkification that was the counterpart to the Arabization produced by the Islamic conquests. During the Qarakhanid period in the eleventh and twelfth centuries, nomads migrated into and settled in the agricultural areas of Central Asia in considerably larger numbers than they had previously. These waves of nomadic migrations and conquests shaped manifold local worlds because trade, migrations, information flows, and cross-cultural contacts accompanied them. Even when they did not result in the formation of new empires, nomadic conquests were a major challenge for existing empires. In the western end of their reach, the extension, nature, and fate of the Byzantine Empire fluctuated according to the threats posed by nomadic societies. In the eastern end, nomadic challenges made major imprints on the political history of China.

The Mongol conquest in the thirteenth century was part of the recurrent waves of pastoral nomadic migration and conquest. It represented not only the final and largest wave, however, but also a transition from mediated to direct rule. In contrast to earlier steppe empires that were usually administered indirectly through local elites, Mongol rule was generally direct. It relied on mobile secretariats appointed by a central government and depending upon a mounted postal courier system. Under Mongol auspices various commodities, technologies, and knowledge, as well as human, animal, and plant populations were disseminated across Eurasia. For instance, the Mongols promoted the transfer of those branches of knowledge in which they were interested, such as medicine (i.e. healing), astronomy and divination (reading of heaven), geography and cartography (reading of earth). Similarly, numerous skilled professionals and specialists were transferred across the empire to provide for its needs.

Because the nomadic empires brought political stability and transportation facilities to Central Asia, overland trade flourished along the Silk Roads during the Middle Millennium. Moreover, nomadic states stimulated trade though increased demand for luxury commodities and prestige goods, and they were the main suppliers of slaves to their sedentary counterparts.

Conversely, the collapse of nomadic empires resulted in the decline of Eurasian trade.

Once again, the Mongol Empire is the best example of this overall trend. As Mongol expansion paved the way to political consolidation and as taxation replaced booty, trade was privileged; its pace accelerated and its scope enlarged. Most of Afro-Eurasia was virtually connected by means of overland and maritime routes, as well as the intertwining of these: from the ports of South China to Southeast Asia and India, and from there to the Persian Gulf or the Red Sea; by land route to West Asia and Europe; or from Aden to the shores of East Africa. Merchants from Southeast Asia, India, the Muslim world, and Europe were all part of this global trade network, with the key non-Mongol players the Indian kingdoms and the Italian city-states.

Along with the spread of religions and empire building, trade was the third trans-regional process penetrating the fabrics of local societies. In this regard as well, the Afro-Eurasian world was a very different place in 1500 CE than it had been in 500 CE. A more professional merchant class moved larger cargoes of more varied commodities over longer distances to more destinations serving a wider consumer base than could have been imagined at the close of the fifth century. Although most trade took place on the local and regional levels, trans-regional linkages had become stronger as the Afro-Eurasian world slowly drew together. Towards the second part of the middle millennium, China focused more and more on maritime outlets leading into the Indian Ocean. India's trade routes pointed in many directions. Going eastward, they led from the Coromandel Coast to Southeast Asia and from there to China. Going westward, they led from the Malabar Coast to the realm of Islam. The realm of Islam was itself the great Afro-Eurasian trade nexus by both sea and land, reaching as far as West Africa through camel caravans. The Silk and Steppe Roads systems provided more overland routes, connecting trade from the north to the Indian complex, and providing a direct link from China to Persia through the Black Sea and from there to the Russian river system and the Mediterranean Sea.

Trade provided many benefits, but also created problems. Along with goods and ideas, disease traveled along trade routes. One dramatic example of this was the plague pandemic of the fourteenth century, which apparently traveled on the trade routes of the Mongol Empire across Asia to Europe and Africa. Combined with economic and political problems, plague led to a decline in overland trade, so that by the early fifteenth century the Steppe Road was permanently defunct, the Silk Roads resumed their long decline, and the Trans-Sahara caravan trail lost most of its inter-regional importance.

Thus, by the end of this period, maritime routes were becoming even more important than they had been earlier. Technological innovations allowed larger ships to travel more safely in shorter times than ever before, which made maritime travel more cost-effective. Until the twelfth century, advances in navigation and maritime technology are primarily attributed to the Arabs, Indians, and Malays. After that, the Chinese took the lead; they introduced the magnetic compass, watertight bulkheads, fore-and-aft rigging, and ships employing five or more mainmasts, steered by rudders up to fifty feet in length, and they greatly enhanced the seaworthiness of their ships by using iron nails instead of coir. The growth of maritime traffic was a favorable trend for Europe, perched at the far end of Eurasia with a coastline far out of proportion to its interior, and the Italians took the lead in the Mediterranean and Black Sea from the twelfth century on.

Empire building, religious conversion, and trade networks were the three forces of inter-regional integration during the Middle Millennium. None of these forces was new. The unification of China by a short-lived dynasty (Sui, 589–618), successfully succeeded by a long lasting one (Tang, 618–907), is reminiscent of the original unification (Qin, 221–206 BCE / Han, 206 BCE–220 CE). And nomadic empires had emerged in the steppes of Inner or Central Asia before 500. But certain aspects of these political developments were very different to earlier examples. The reach of the short-lived Mongol Empire was unprecedented, and the emergence, expansion, and consolidation of the Muslim Empire was an even more dramatic change. Not only was the Islamic world large, but it shared borders with all other regions of Afro-Eurasia.

Along with being a new type of empire, Islam was also a new religion in the Middle Millennium. Buddhism had emerged about a thousand years earlier, and its spread into Central, East and Southeast Asia had begun long before the Middle Millennium. What was new in this period was the reinvigoration of its diffusion to a re-unified China and from there to the new polities in Korea and Japan. The situation of Christianity is rather similar to that of Buddhism: it began before the Middle Millennium and was already widely disseminated by 500. A major distinction, though, is that during the Middle Millennium Christianity doubled its geographical scope. Christianity became the hegemonic religion in Europe, in a successful missionary effort that was tightly connected with empire and state-building. In lands far afield from Christian states, such as southern India, Malaya, Central Asia, and China, missions were associated with trade activity. Although in terms of numbers of converts their degree of success was very modest, the range of

Christian expansion in the Middle Millennium represents a major innovation in terms of religious diffusion. Nevertheless, the ultimate religious innovation of the age, as was the case for empire building, is the rise of Islam.

As for the third driving force of trans-regional integration, trade networks, none of the major webs – the Silk and Steppe Roads, the North African caravans, or the Indian Ocean and Mediterranean Sea routes – were new. They had entered a phase of decline at the beginning of the Middle Millennium, however, then recovered and became more tightly connected until the outbreak of the Black Death.

"Proto-glocal": Afro-Eurasian integration forces on the local scene

At the beginning of the Middle Millennium the political situation of most of Afro-Eurasia was one of fragmentation. The large empires of the previous era had disappeared, devolving political power to numerous smaller entities. Together with these empires trans-regional trade networks had also declined. Under these conditions, in both Afro-Eurasia and the rest of the world, local norms and patterns mattered the most in defining life arrangements and conditions. This continued in the Middle Millennium, but the new wave of empire building, interrelated with commercial revival and religious conversion sketched above, also made major imprints in local conditions in such areas as family structure, education, law, and government.

Islamic conquests introduced the Quran and shari'a law, and the process of Islamization resulted in their dissemination. These developments transformed the structures of family life. For example, on the one hand Islam contributed to the protection of women by specifying a marriage gift to a wife (*mahr*). By the end of the Middle Millennium in East African societies, where conversion was often achieved through trade rather than conquest, shari'a introduced a dower paid to a wife by contract and in Muslim Spain a marriage contract included a similar dower. These practices persisted throughout Islam and women were understood to embody the honor of the family. On the other hand, Islam favored the subordination of women as expressed by veiling and seclusion, and it allowed polygyny, although it did limit the number of wives a man could have to four, and specified that he was to treat them equitably. Islam failed to eliminate all regional differences in its wide reach, however. In many places, especially among rural residents, women and girls worked outside of the home as a matter of course and *'urf*, or exigent custom, structured family life along with religious law throughout Islam. Family life in the lands of Islam was, then, a result of "proto-glocal" tension.

The Mongol expansion also brought proto-glocal tensions as Mongol social norms penetrated their subjects' lives. For instance, levirate marriages (in which a widow married her husband's brother) were condemned by both Islamic law and Confucian ethics, but were not rare in Ilkhanid Iran and Yuan China. Similarly, following in the footsteps of their Mongol counterparts, Persian and Korean princesses attained an elevated status and became intimately involved in politics.

Other proto-global tensions transformed family lives all across Afro-Eurasia as exogenous factors made their varied impact upon local arrangements. War, conflict, and invasions constituted threats that often led to subordinating women through a more pronounced emphasis on gender difference; the spread of Confucianism and other hierarchical ideologies did so as well. In general, gender systems moved from somewhat diverse and flexible to more rigid in this era. Patriarchal institutions dominated, and in some places by the end of the era became more hierarchical among men – favoring wealth and advanced age – as well as between men and women. Around the world marriage had become more monogamous, which meant that married couples were more responsible themselves for providing care for elderly parents and investment in their offspring's welfare, which might include marriage gifts for daughters and some type of inheritance for all sons at the death of a father.

All across Afro-Eurasia the shape of education was transformed by the spread of Confucianism, Buddhism, Islam, and Christianity. Confucian ideas began to spread to Korea before the Middle Millennium with the Han occupation of the northern part of the Korean peninsula (c. 100 BCE–400 CE). This intensified when the Silla dynasty unified the peninsula in 668 and modeled their state structure on that of Tang China (618–907). In 682, they also established a Confucian Academy in the capital, Kyongju, for the education of officials. Later on, the cultural exchange between China and Korea facilitated by the Mongol conquest even resulted in an increasing number of Korean students passing the Chinese civil service examinations in Beijing. In 1314 Ch'ungson abdicated the throne in favor of his son and retired to Beijing, where he founded a large library that became a meeting place for Korean and Chinese scholars to discuss Neo-Confucianism. Buddhism, well established in Tang China, was another dominant cultural and ideological influence flowing from China to Korea, one of the many examples of the spread of Buddhist teachings and educational institutions throughout South, East, and Southeast Asia.

The flourishing institutions of Buddhist education throughout South, East, and Southeast Asia represented a unifying force coming from the outside and bringing both religious and secular education. For a polity and culture that was already unified, such as China, this meant an additional layer of unity. Conversely, for a region like Southeast Asia, with its large variety of cultures, peoples, and states, Buddhist education brought some unity to a varied local landscape. Central to this process of educational diffusion were some centers of Buddhist learning with trans-regional projections, the most famous of which was founded at Nālandā (Bihar, India) probably in the mid-fifth century. Another major center in Vikramaśīla (also in Bihar) housed 160 scholars and 5,000 ordained monks maintained by royal patronage beginning in the eighth century. These centers that set in motion the trans-regional spread of Buddhism were displaced by another trans-regional development in the early thirteenth century, however, when they were razed with the Muslim conquest of Bihar.

Muslim conquests were followed by the establishment of educational institutions for the transmission of religious knowledge: the *maktab* or *kuttab* (a "place of writing" that arose in the seventh century CE to provide elementary education), the mosque, and the madrasa (place of study). The emergence of these institutions coming from the outside contended with local educational practices. For example, the exclusivity that the *griot* (West African bard) had for the transmission of learning, understood as the knowledge a society had of itself and its past, ended with the establishment of Muslim educational institutions. And yet, as elsewhere, local traditions clearly prevailed in the domestic sphere with the acquisition of skills necessary for the sustenance and survival of the community transmitted through family lines as done before for generations.

These proto-global tensions are also observed in Europe. To the fragmentation of educational practices following the collapse of the Roman Empire, the spread of Christianity subsequently provided the unifying context for the development of educational institutions. Singular to Europe, though, is the development of universities as corporations with well-defined rights and duties.

The restructuring of family relations and education because of trans-regional influences contributed to the reshaping of some aspects of social life. Moreover, for all the local idiosyncrasy of social life some features were apparently shared globally. The assumption of political and social inequalities was pervasive in all societies. Most people seem to have taken their inequality for granted and regarded it as just, as long as those above them treated them according to their society's ideas of justice. Moreover, inequality was not at all incompatible with consultation and hierarchy seems to have imposed duties, however often unfulfilled, on the people at the top. Hierarchies came in different shapes and layers, while as a rule smaller and poorer societies were less unequal. The richer and more complex societies of this period were liable to have more conflicts of interest between economic (and political) classes.

The creation of courts across Eurasia also entailed "glocal" tensions. On the one hand, everywhere courts developed, based upon local traditions. Courts in China relied upon Chinese Han court traditions. Roman imperial courts set the model for the Byzantine court and the papal court. On the other hand, these local models reached new areas, as in the adoption of the Chinese Han model by the Japanese from *c.* 500, or the embracing of the Roman model by the Germanic kingdoms. Moreover, in the case of Islamic courts we observe a truly inter-regional synthesis as both Roman and Sasanian traditions were at its base. Finally, as local courts developed around local power centers emulating the central courts, regional and inter-regional diffusion further penetrated the local scene.

Also economic life was mostly locally based by the beginning of the period in terms of production, consumption, and even in terms of trade. However, as the Middle Millennium progressed, commodities found their way increasingly from one end of Afro-Eurasia to the other. European cotton textiles, Chinese porcelain, Southeast Asian pepper and spices, Arabian perfume, Mediterranean glassware, Persian and Central Asian horses, and in many regions slaves, were among the most traded commodities. Certainly, this trans-regional trade was mostly one for luxuries, but this did not mean it had only a marginal impact on local economies. The shape of local economies was determined to a large extent by local elites willing to consume these luxuries brought through trans-regional trade as symbols of power and status. Some non-luxury items, such as food and cloth as well as medicine and entertainment, also found their way into trans-regional trade. Diffusion of these items by trade was amplified when their production was imitated locally, thus enhancing their consumption. That was the case, for example, with "Tatar dress," rugs and tapestries, and pasta. Trans-regional trade also resulted in the adoption of silver across most of Eurasia as the standard unit for pricing transactions, even when they were paid by other means. In fact, the period spanning the 1280s and 1360s witnessed a sharp rise in the use of silver from England to Bengal and North Africa.

The Mongols were also decisive in bringing about a global cartographic turn. Aiming to consolidate their rule of their huge domains and looking even beyond, the Mongols relied on Islamic maps and Muslim scholars, who launched vast cartographic projects. These projects paved the way to the drawing of a world map in Korea in 1402, which cartographers see as part of a transition from ethnocentric to global cartography. This transition was also evident in the drawing of world maps in Byzantium and western Europe around 1300 as the Pax Mongolica enabled Western travelers to report on their Eurasian voyages. Marco Polo's accounts enabled the preparation of the Catalan Atlas. Other accounts by travelers, such as those of Benjamin of Tudela, Ibn Jubayr, Ibn Battuta, and Wang Dayuan, as well as of pilgrims, returning prisoners of war, and merchants provided descriptions of far-away countries. Despite the growing amount of information on other societies, however, the Middle Millennium witnessed just one attempt at proto-global historiography, the *Compendium of Chronicles* by Rashīd al-Dīn. Otherwise, writing on the past was locally framed or, at the most, encompassed within the writer's own civilizational framework.

Other forms of scientific and technological knowledge were transmitted by practitioners, diplomatic exchanges, translations, and artifacts. There are well-documented processes of scientific transmission along certain tracks within the Afro-Eurasian realm, such as the transmission of astronomical knowledge from Sindh and Hind to Baghdad or that of pharmacological knowledge traveling from Constantinople to Cordova. More ambitious processes of transmission covering a huge chunk of Afro-Eurasia are hypothesized, such as the scholastic method presumably formulated among Buddhists in Central Asia being carried into Islamic madrasas, and finally spreading to western Europe. Regardless of means and scale, all transmissions of scientific knowledge entailed tensions between the local and the proto-global as translation, interpretation, and framing added local components to external formulations. Occasionally proto-glocalization also took another form when local and foreign bodies of knowledge coexisted. Medicine in South Asia represents a case in point. There Ayurvedic medicine, associated with local Buddhist and Hindu traditions, existed side-by-side with ancient Greek (*Unani*) medicine, transmitted by Muslim intermediaries.

Technologies for civil and military purposes, daily life, and the production of luxuries were also transferred across Afro-Eurasia. Hydraulic technologies, irrigation systems, and gunpowder artillery exemplify this trend. The processes by which new technologies were adopted and adapted were predominantly local, however. New developments often lingered for a while before they took root and became widespread in an area, or they were even invented several times. Whether it was adopted, adapted, or rejected, innovation from the outside was always in tension with the local conditions in which peopled lived.

Processes of transmission were facilitated by go-between populations that emerged as proto-global interactions unfolded. A case in point is that of the local Christian populations that fell under Muslim rule. From Persia to Iberia, Muslim conquests brought Christians under Muslim rule as protected people (*dhimmi*). Since Christian communities retained many of the cultural attributes of their pre-Islamic life, they offered traditions, local knowledge, and administrative experience to the Muslim rulers. Simultaneously, their own Arabization positioned them as cultural bridges between the realm of Islam and their original civilizational sphere.

The transmission of manifold branches of knowledge unfolded during the Middle Millennium amidst "Ecumenical Renaissances," a reassertion by Eurasian societies in the tenth to the thirteenth centuries of their cultural legacies. This reassertion was associated with the strengthening of the clerical elites, although the growth of their degree of autonomy also represented a challenge to the political elites, whose exclusivity in the political arena was brought into question. Moreover, with this challenge posed by clerical elites underway, additional social groups also attempted a degree of power-sharing. This dynamic is reminiscent of that of the Axial Age as defined by Eisenstadt. The late Eisenstadt, for his part, identified the Middle Millennium as the age of proto-globalization.

Conclusions

The pre-modern world was also a pre-global one, for globalization requires the encompassing of the globe and its articulation in a way that local societies are significantly transformed by developments radiating from that articulation. This is neither the geographical scope nor the degree of interdependence reached during the Middle Millennium. Geographically speaking, the world of the Middle Millennium was one of worlds together in northern Africa and Eurasia but worlds apart in the western and southern hemispheres. In terms of intensity, interdependence was not structured on a permanent basis but was rather an intermittent situation.

The worlds apart westward across the Atlantic Ocean underwent important transformations during the Middle Millennium. In Mesoamerica, Maya civilization was at its height in what archaeologists term the Classic period (*c.* 250–900 CE), as were other societies, including those centered on the cities of Teotihuacan and Monte Alban. During the eighth and ninth centuries, many Maya cities were abandoned, building stopped, and inscriptions ended in what has been called the Classic Maya collapse. Many cities throughout Mesoamerica that had been important in the Classic period shrank in size and power. In the succeeding Postclassic period (*c.* 900–1520), a series of processes transformed the region. They include: the proliferation of small polities, new forms of writing and iconography, new patterns of stylistic interaction, commercialization of the economy, and greater diversity of trade goods. Population grew again, so that it was higher in 1500 than it had been in 1000. The expansion of commerce was one of the most significant trends, allowing the diverse cultures and societies of Mesoamerica to become more closely connected than they had ever been. Moreover, merchants or other voyagers brought Meso- and South America into contact along the Pacific coast. This linkage enabled the transmission of the technology for smelting bronze into west Mexico from South America, and may have involved other trade goods or technologies as well. In South America, conquest was the major driving force leading towards regional integration. The Inca Empire established the largest imperial state of pre-Columbian America.

Trade and conquest, then, were driving forces of integration in the New as in the Old World. Religion was as well. All Postclassic Mesoamerican cities included large temple-pyramids of the state religion as well as royal palaces and markets. In the Inca Empire, the cult of the Inca Sun became increasingly prominent as conquests generated theoretical and religious reconceptualization of the Inca ruler's power and position in relation to other lords. Diverse existing cults were reorganized within the Inca religious framework and empire-wide pilgrimage centers were established, where sacred history enshrined in ritual imparted legitimacy on the Inca conquest. Whether incorporation into the Inca realm was achieved by conquest or diplomacy, it entailed participation in Inca religion, and the Inca ruler's participation in the religion of his subjects.

To the comparability of these integrative forces, that of periodization and sequencing could be added. In both Mesoamerica and Afro-Eurasia the early part of the Middle Millennium saw the collapse of the largest political entities, political fragmentation, and decline in trade. Subsequently, these trends were reversed in both hemispheres with population growth, the emergence of new polities, and commercialization at the core of these transformations. However, and most crucially, for all their potential comparability, the hemispheres remained worlds apart.

Even while looking at the worlds together of northern Africa and Eurasia this world was composed by manifold little idiosyncratic worlds, which were not articulated into an interdependent whole. Nevertheless, very many of them became entangled throughout the Middle Millennium through a series of large-scale transformations whose epicentres could have originated thousands of miles apart. These transformations were the emergence and expansion of Islam, the diffusion of Buddhism and Christianity, the Mongol conquests, and the tightening of commercial webs. Most aspects of local life were touched to different degrees by these forces. Family life was impacted throughout Afro-Eurasia by the introduction of the shari'a law, the diffusion of Buddhism and Christianity, and the practice of Mongol social norms. Religious institutions also radically transformed the field of education. Economies were impacted by the arrival of new plants, new technologies, and commodities. In the political field, besides fluctuations in power distribution, the courts – central and local – adopted styles and habits from counterparts abroad. Exposure to other societies and cultures and acquaintance with their scholarly achievements increased noticeably.

It is in view of this combination of limiting conditions for a globalized world and the presence of such powerful forces that permeated so many local lives that Eisenstadt's quest for a proto-global Middle Millennium makes full sense. Eisenstadt's outline of a proto-global world was partially matched by a growth of proto-global consciousness in the Middle Millennium itself, reflected in cartographical innovation and interest in travelers' accounts. Eisenstadt has also not been alone among recent scholars in highlighting the growing connectedness of this era. His idea of a proto-global Middle Millennium echoes Marshall Hodgson's description of Afro-Eurasia as an *Oikoumene* linked by the corridor established by Islam, Janet Abu-Lughod's emphasis on eight commercial circuits between the Atlantic and the Pacific under the Pax Mongolica, and Jerry Bentley's highlighting of distinctive patterns of cross-cultural encounters that transformed Asia and Europe during this period.

Other scholars do not agree. For A. G. Hopkins, proto-globalization was the two-century-long threshold that began with the process of encompassing the globe and its articulation into a single unit starting in the sixteenth century. It involved the simultaneous growth of pre-industrial manufacturing, financing, services, and markets combined with the strengthening of political entities, taxation and sovereignty that resulted in the enhancements of circuits of exchange on a planetary scale. This is the proto-globalization that paved the way for the "modern globalization" of the nineteenth century characterized by industrialization, nation-state formation, a global integration of producers of raw materials and manufacturing centers, faster and cheaper communication and transportation, and price convergence. For many other authors, however, the combination of the "Columbian" and "Magellan" exchanges in the sixteenth century, epitomized by the launching of Manila as a trans-oceanic entrepôt, already represents full-fledged globalization. And if so, then the Middle Millennium's proto-globalization represents its threshold.

Whatever the preferred periodization and conceptualizations are, the questions remain: How does the proto-globalization of the Middle Millennium inform the history of globalization? Are there developments coming from the Middle Millennium's proto-globalization that opened early path dependence or other developments that conditioned later globalization, whether of the nineteenth century or today? These are open-ended questions to be answered in subsequent volumes of this series, indispensable for establishing links and contrasts between the periods, and possibly warranting a further quest for continuities and changes.

Index

Aachen, 126, 180
'Abbasid Baghdad, 186, 346
'Abbasids, 48, 100, 166, 187, 194, 200, 252, 398,
    411, 505–6
  Caliphate, 24, 168, 199, 211, 213, 238, 252,
    346, 402, 406
  Court, 180, 195, 199
'Abd al-Malik, 505
Abd al-Rahman III, 346, 349
Abelard, Peter, 129
absolutism, 99, 113
Abu Ishaq al-Sahilil, 601
Abu-Lughod, Janet, 634, 683
Abū Mufarrij, Shaykh, 299–300, 302
Acciaiuoli, 259, 266
Achaea, 580
adab, 191–2
adaptation, 22, 34–5, 328, 415, 476, 500, 559,
    668
Aden, 4, 279, 301–4, 552, 674
administration, 123, 134, 180, 432–3, 532, 534,
    539–42, 576–7
  centralized, 24, 332, 506, 578
  imperial, 33, 555, 644
  indirect, 539–40
  tax, 561, 570, 575, 577
administrative expertise, 518, 521
administrative models, 32, 381
admirals, 259, 271
Adrianople, 575, 579
adultery, 87
advisers, 73, 184, 515
Aegean Sea, 274, 564
aesthetics, 191, 436
Afghanistan, 26, 165, 373, 375, 396, 406
Africa, 2, 5, 9, 12, 109–10, 340, 342, 415, 562–4
  East, *see* East Africa.
  hierarchies and solidarity, 109–12
  Horn of, 170, 394, 486

Islam and educational institutions, 135–7
North, *see* North Africa.
northern, 681–2
sub-Saharan, *see* sub-Saharan Africa.
West, *see* West Africa.
western coast of, 8, 254
Afro–Eurasia, 31, 33, 142, 667, 670–1, 674–7,
    680, 682–3
  trade and commerce, 233–54
afterlife, 200, 546
agrarian reformers, 52–3
agricultural growth, 216, 626
agricultural production, 220–1, 246, 318,
    336, 531
agricultural societies, 95, 105, 669
agriculture, 20, 45, 53, 97–8, 100, 107, 148,
    334–6, 376–7, 669
  permanent, 49, 54
  rainfed, *see* rainfed agriculture.
  wet-rice, 518, 525
agro-literate societies, 212, 217, 225
agro-urban civilizations, 29, 145, 149–50
Akroinon, 157, 564
Albertus Magnus, 45
alchemy, 125, 340
Aleppo, 72, 134, 354, 391, 432, 571
Alexander the Great, 343–4
Alexandria, 155, 263–4, 269–70, 273–4, 276,
    279, 292, 345, 418
Algeria, 402, 606
alliances, 80, 155, 253, 389, 495, 518, 562, 580,
    606, 622
  marriage, 35, 147, 621, 643
  political, 185, 190, 545
Almagest, 347, 349
Almohads, 12, 162
Almoravids, 372, 394, 596, 606–7
Alps, 277, 322
alum, 259, 268, 275, 282, 524

Amalfi, 274, 567
Amarāvatī, 451, 457
Amaury, king of Jerusalem, 12
ambassadors, 201, 347, 349, 540
Americas, 8, 18–19, 33–4, 71, 83, 117, 141–2, 174, 328–9
    educational institutions, 137–40
    hierarchies and solidarity, 109–12
Amoghavajra, 462, 464–5
Anagarika Dharmapala, 477
anal intercourse, 86–7
Anastasius, Emperor, 560, 562
Anatolia, 155, 158, 373, 377, 400, 535, 540, 564, 566, 569
ancestors, 403, 587, 590, 593, 605, 620, 650
    Inca, 642, 645, 647–8, 662
    Soninke, 590, 593
Ancona, 269, 276
Andahuaylas, 644
al-Andalus, 71, 237, 276, 279, 326, 349, 431, 433, 597
Andalusia, 277, 281, 329
Andes, 638, 642–5, 648, 650, 654–6, 658, 660, 662
Andronikos II, 580–1
angels, 416, 438
Angkor, 16, 60–1
Angkorean Cambodia, 16, 24
animal husbandry, 46
    combined with rainfed agriculture, 52–5
Ankara, 582
anthropological approach, 55
anthropologists, 46, 109, 111–12, 310, 592, 610–12
Antioch, 154–5, 160, 274, 418, 420, 569, 571, 575
Antisuyo, 638, 650
Antwerp, 273, 277
apostasy, 430
apostles, 7, 418–19, 422
Apulia, 272, 281, 572
Aquinas, St. Thomas, 129
Arab, tribes, 394, 400, 402, 405
Arab conquests, 11, 15, 21, 25, 395, 399, 401–2, 411, 430, 433
Arabia, 2, 20, 236, 239, 373, 399–400, 403–4, 411, 559–60
    western, 389, 404
Arabian Sea, 290
Arabic, 12–13, 131–2, 297, 299, 345–7, 349–50, 378, 401–2, 409
    inscriptions, 297, 436
    script, 299, 391, 396, 400
Arabic erotic literature, 88

Arabic science, 341, 353, 356
Arabization, 671, 673, 681
arable land, 334, 371, 472, 670
Arabs, 12–13, 271, 343, 353–4, 368, 399–403, 411–12, 564, 566
    warfare, 155–8
Aragon, 276–7, 281, 497
Aramaic, 292, 399, 401, 411
archaeological research, 311, 614, 618, 625
archaeologists, 112, 588, 610–12, 617–18, 625, 627, 629, 633
archaeology, 16, 23, 109, 394, 592, 619, 643–4, 649
archbishops, 12, 428–9, 441
archery skills, 163, 168
architectural forms, 550, 620, 623
architectural styles, 601, 642
architecture, 72, 138, 182, 195, 311, 315, 321–2, 620, 625
    civic, 618, 630
    monumental, 588, 620
Arghun, Ilkhan, 443, 549
arid regions, 44, 47, 51, 403–4
aristocracy, 118, 120, 160, 164, 189–90, 258, 520–1, 531
    Guanzhong, 515–16, 520
    military, 370, 575
aristocratic clans, 220, 514–16, 521
aristocratic patronage, 183, 195
Aristotle, 45, 126, 129, 339, 345, 351, 356
arithmetic, 129, 132, 350
Armenia, 154, 267, 420, 427, 540, 543, 546, 560, 568
Armenians, 22, 424, 432, 546, 564, 569, 571, 575
armies, 102, 153–4, 156–7, 162–5, 371–2, 565, 567–70, 575–6
    large, 149–50, 362, 578
    Mongol, 530, 547
    Roman, 154, 158
    standing, 83, 514, 520, 523, 526, 531
    thematic, 571–2
armor, 149, 152, 170, 173
Arras, 260, 262
arrows, 146, 156, 161, 173, 447, 602
arsenals, 270–1, 331
art, 15, 316, 320, 322, 326, 329, 335, 545, 624, 650
art forms, 32, 468, 474, 476–7
art styles, 34, 633
Arthaśāstra, 99, 287, 292
artisanal expertise, 318, 320
artisanal processes, 316, 335
artisans, 302, 320–4, 326, 329, 331, 457, 542–4, 607

Ascalon, 15
asceticism, 80, 200, 420, 422, 434
Ashikaga period, 121, 125
Asia, 317–18, 340, 415, 443–4, 447–8, 454,
    460–2, 466–7, 476–7, 580
  Central, *see* Central Asia.
  East, *see* East Asia.
  Inner, 365–7, 370, 375, 537
  northeast, 542
  South, *see* South Asia.
  Southeast, *see* Southeast Asia.
  southern, 46, 58, 452–3, 672
  southwest, 18, 665
  West, 11, 166, 424, 436, 443, 492, 670
  western, 340, 385, 442, 537
Asia Minor, 226, 277, 374, 416, 559, 564–6, 576,
    578, 580–1
Askia Muhammad, 348, 603
Askias, 603–4, 607
Aśoka, King, 304, 447, 450–2, 460
assemblies, 99, 102, 105, 127, 228
associations, 30, 85, 90, 95, 127, 223, 238, 257,
    261, 264–5
  merchant, 30, 261, 305–6
Asti, 259
astrolabe, 330, 350, 352
astrology, 125, 138, 194, 343, 345, 348, 355
astronomy, 129, 132, 343, 348–9, 352, 354–5,
    410, 432, 543–4
  Western, 349, 355
Atahuallpa, 639, 662
Athens, 343
Atīśa, 467–9
Atlantic Ocean, 70, 257, 681
Augsburg, 261, 283–4, 368
Augustine, St., 57, 417, 419
Australia, 18, 310, 328, 427
authority, 70, 73–4, 97, 99, 342–3, 418–24, 504,
    571–2, 606
  central, 179, 370, 571, 669
  centralized, 244, 538
  ecclesiastical, 127, 347, 441
  personal, 134, 141
  political, 190, 296, 455, 471, 474, 532
  religious, 138, 156, 504, 506
  supreme, 515, 518
autocratic rule, 494, 499, 515
automata, 321, 330
autonomic states, 665–6
autonomy, 106, 220, 226, 252, 495, 559, 564,
    681
Avars, 366, 437, 486, 513, 564
Averroes, 356

Avignon, 180, 266
Awdaghust, 596, 607
Axial Age, 206–7, 209, 212–13, 216, 218–19,
    225–6, 665–7, 681
  legacies, 207–12
  religions, 208, 211
'Aydhāb, 279, 299, 301
'Ayn Jalut, 162, 165
ayurveda, 85
Ayyavole, 305
Ayyubids, 238, 279
Azerbaijan, 377, 535, 554
Aztecs, 3, 25, 137, 140, 610, 613, 619–20, 626,
    628–33
Aztlan migrations, 627

bāb mandū, 14
baccalaureus, 129
Bactria, 345, 375, 514
Baghdad, 130, 133, 246, 248, 263, 276–7, 346–8,
    565
  'Abbasid, 186, 346
  court, 190, 263
  Jews, 237
  Mongol occupation, 227, 318
al-Bakri, 135, 586
balance of power, 491, 509, 531, 570
Bali, 47, 306
Balkans, 154–5, 171, 224, 267, 392, 564, 569–70,
    576, 581
Balkh, 246, 345
Baltic Sea, 30, 160, 243, 261, 269, 276–7, 279
Bambuk, 596–7, 607
Banākatī, Muhammad, 14
banking, 78, 90, 244–5, 249, 259–60, 263, 266,
    271, 371, 581
banquets, 185, 193, 196, 198
Banu Hud, 352
Banyeres of Barcelona, 260
Bar-sur-Aube, 272
barbarians, 147, 151–2, 180, 220, 320, 559
barbers, 296
Barcelona, 260–1, 266, 269, 276–7, 281, 283
Bardi, 259, 266
Barlaam, 22
barter, 53, 111, 264, 551
Barygaza, 292, 304
basic education, 126, 132, 140
Basil II, 568, 570, 575–6, 578
Basin of Mexico, 611, 616–17, 621–2, 625, 631
Basmils, 367
Basra, 72, 266
Bateson, Gregory, 47

battering engines, 150
battles, 146, 149, 153–6, 159, 162, 165–6, 170–1, 576
   see also names of *individual battles.*
   cavalry, 165
Bay of Bengal, 290, 451, 455
Beckwith, C., 346
Bedouins, 361, 372–3, 376, 378
bees, 44
Beijing, 4, 168, 180, 441, 467, 554, 677
Beirut, 270, 274, 276, 279
belief systems, 476, 606, 669
beliefs, 410, 417–18, 427–8, 434, 440–1, 464,
   469–71
Belize, 614, 623
Ben Yijū, Abraham, 301–4
Benedict, St., 126
benefices, 128, 198
Bengal, 73, 215, 238, 290, 312, 552, 679
   Bay of, 290, 451, 455
   Bihar-Bengal region, 464, 467–8
   West, 458
Benjamin of Tudela, 15, 680
Bentley, Jerry, 602, 683
Berber nomads, 394, 596
Berbers, 342, 372, 402, 595–6, 606
   Sanhaja, 595–6
Berg-op-Zoom, 273
Bergen, 274, 277, 279
Bernard of Clairvaux, 44
Bertrand, Georges, 52
Betanzos, Juan de, 639, 645–7, 649, 656
Bhadresvara, 297
Bharuch, 288, 304
Bible, 14, 110, 347, 416–17, 593
Bida, 593–4
Bihar, 331, 450, 454, 464, 467–8, 678
biodiversity, 61, 67
Biraben, Jean-Noël, 18
Biran, Michal, 33, 534
birch-bark documents, 16
biremes, 268, 270
bishops, 12, 352, 417–19, 422, 429, 434, 436, 438,
   441, 443
Bisson, Thomas, 211, 217–18
Bithynia, 267, 565, 580
Black Death, 18, 62, 67, 248–9, 253, 315, 676
Black Sea, 244, 246–8, 269–70, 274, 279–81,
   283, 437, 580, 582
black stone, 289, 468
Bloch, Marc, 53–4, 81
boats, 149, 268–70, 296, 320
   flat-bottomed, 277
   sewn, 291–2

bodhisattvas, 22, 452, 465
bodyguards, imperial, 181, 184
Bohemia, 160, 282
Bologna, 128
Bonnassie, Pierre, 260
Bonsignori, 259
Book of the Eparch, 262
booty, 147, 152, 492, 538, 542, 552
Bordeaux, 260, 272, 277
   wines, 281
borders, 25, 149, 491, 525–6, 559, 562, 565–6,
   578–9
Borobudur, 465
Borromeos, 260
Boserup, Esther, 55
Bosphorus, 561, 581
Boucher, Guillaume, 20–1
Bourgneuf, salt, 277, 281
bows, 146, 158, 324, 602
   composite, 154, 171
boys, 70, 87, 126, 132, 146, 184
brahmanas, 296, 304
Brahmanism, 464, 468
Brahmins, 73, 185, 199, 502
brass factories, 300, 302
bribery, 148
brides, 72–3, 77, 83, 85–6
brocade, 242, 597
'Brog-mi, 469
brokers, 78, 82, 263, 299, 527
bronze, 23, 174, 458, 626
   coins, 522, 524
   prestige items, 243
   smelting, 625, 682
   statues, 331, 524
brothers, 74, 90, 147, 189–90, 419, 516, 577, 593,
   642
Bruges, 261–2, 266, 272–4, 277, 279
bubonic plague, *see* plague.
Buddha, 447–8, 450–1, 453, 455, 458, 471, 473,
   475, 477
   images, 14, 126, 455
Buddhism, 121–2, 124–6, 448, 450–62, 468–77,
   549–50, 672
   across Asia, 454–61
   Chan, 466, 473–4
   diffusion, 447, 451, 671, 683
   doctrines, 447–50, 452, 455, 457–8, 461,
     465–6, 471
   East Asian Buddhist world, 469–74
   and educational institutions, 122–6
   India-Tibet Buddhist world, 468–9
   Mahāyāna, 122, 125, 452, 672

persecution, 467, 469, 548
Pure Land, 470, 473
sangha, 124
schools, 469, 474–5
spread, 447–77
  between 5th and 10th centuries, 454
  early, 450–4
Sri Lanka–Southeast Asia Buddhist world,
  474–6
Tantric, 465, 468
Theravada, 125, 475, 504
Tibetan, 469, 473, 546, 549–50
transmission, 447, 457, 460
Buddhist artifacts, 455, 471, 672
Buddhist communities, 447, 460, 471–2
Buddhist ideas, 447–8, 453, 462, 466, 470,
  476–7, 672
Buddhist institutions, 451, 470, 474
Buddhist interactions, 448, 454, 460, 475, 672
Buddhist law, 549
Buddhist learning, 452, 454, 457
Buddhist literature, 450, 454
Buddhist monastic institutions, 104, 118,
  121–3, 125–6, 140, 152, 466, 470–2
Buddhist monks, 447, 453–4, 457, 467, 469,
  471, 474, 672
Buddhist monuments, 471, 515
Buddhist networks and exchanges, 448, 454,
  462–7, 470, 473, 672
Buddhist paraphernalia, 457, 462, 471
Buddhist relics, 455, 475
Buddhist rituals, 472–3
Buddhist teachings, 32, 124–5, 448, 452, 476, 677
Buddhist temples, 121, 124, 181, 306, 455, 460
Buddhist texts, 124, 453, 457, 461–2, 471–2
Buddhist universities, 122
Bulgars, 560–1, 566, 569–70, 574, 579
Bulghars, 243, 367, 389–91, 395
  rulers, 389–90, 392
bureaucracy, 28, 100, 346, 419, 424, 539, 542
  civil, 33, 182, 531
  Iranian, 369, 374
  sclerotic, 167
  Weberian, 111
bureaucratic entrepreneurship, 527
Burgundio of Pisa, 347
Burma, 305, 452, 534
Burmese, 125, 503
butchers, 376, 574
Byzantium, 262, 270–1, 273–4, 400–1, 415–16,
  419–21, 427–8, 559–84
  11th century developments, 572–6
  army, 154, 435, 570, 576

Church, 560, 583
continuing problems and final collapse,
  579–83
court, 179, 181, 184–5, 679
emperors, 11, 100, 154–5, 179, 181, 190, 197,
  562–3
see also names of individual emperors.
Komnenoi, 572, 575–80
merchants, 572, 574
reorganization and recovery
  750-1000, 566–70
state formation and empire building,
  508–9
tagmata, 164, 569
warfare, 153–5

Cacaxtla, 618
Caesarea, 155, 200, 274
  Frankish, 17
Caffa, 248, 274, 276, 552
Cahorsins, 262
Cairo, 72, 78, 131, 133–4, 238, 272
  Geniza, 271, 276, 292, 299–300
Cajamarca, lord of, 651–3
Calais, Wool Staple of, 262, 275, 277
calendars, 138, 183, 407, 613–14
Calicut, 254, 279
caliphate, 11, 160, 162, 237, 389–90, 406, 408,
  504, 506–7, 571
caliphs, 11–13, 163–4, 186, 190, 200, 389–90,
  405–6, 408
Cambay, 288, 297
  Gulf of, 288, 294
Cambodia, 15, 331, 458
Cambrai, 262, 281
camel caravans, 236, 245, 277, 598, 674
camels, 242, 245, 296, 336, 363, 590, 595
camphor, 237, 444
canals, 47–8, 235, 621
  irrigation, 641
Cañari, 657
Canary Islands, 283, 395
cannibalism, 50
canon law, 77, 128
Capac, 645
capacocha, 661
capital, 264–5
capital cities, 180, 399–400, 411, 587, 616, 624
  imperial, 416, 561, 623, 631, 638, 647
captives, 149, 170, 174
caravans, 552, 595, 600
  camel, 236, 245, 277, 598, 674
caravanserais, 246, 248, 300

caravels, 329, 381
careers, 78, 119, 131, 134, 183, 192, 198, 575, 577, 581
cargo(es), 30, 233, 250, 282–3, 290, 551, 674
Carlowitz, Hanns Carl von, 62
Carolingian Renaissance, 126, 496
Carolingians, 45, 100, 166, 188, 200, 214, 283, 496–7, 566, 667
carpets, 242, 597
cartography, 1–10, 195, 543, 673, 680
  Sino-centric, 2
cash, 157, 265, 300, 566, 568
caskets, 22
Caspian Sea, 241, 243
castes, 73, 99, 107, 185, 197, 252, 408, 525
Castile, 162, 259, 267, 282, 497
castles, 159, 162, 166, 168
Catalan Atlas, 8, 680
Catalans, 275, 279, 581
Catalonia, 12, 260, 271, 282
Catequil, 660, 662
Cathay, 13, 348 *see also* northern China
cathedral schools, 126, 128–9, 131, 141, 350
Catherine of Siena, 79
Catholic Church, 158, 493
cattle, 109, 334, 518
Caucasus, 399, 421, 535, 567, 574–5
  North, 368
cavalry, 149–50, 152, 154, 156, 158, 161, 170–2, 569, 593
  heavy, 159, 161, 514, 517
  light, 154, 161
  mamluk, 165, 170
  tribal, 153
cavalry battles, 165
caves, 290, 426, 650
celibacy, 87–8, 419
censuses, 540, 542
Central Asia, 241–2, 364–7, 369–70, 376–7, 424, 437, 451–2, 488–9, 553–4
central control, 164, 506, 530
Central Europe, 52, 63, 65, 244, 249, 254
central Germany, 281
central governments, 100, 515, 520–1, 524, 527–9, 531, 539, 541, 669, 673
central India, 215, 375, 455
central Java, 241, 465
central power, 98, 179, 370, 374, 502, 566, 571, 580, 669
centralization, 239, 541, 642, 666
centralized administration, 24, 332, 506, 578
centralized empires, 24, 381
centralized government, 244, 402, 531, 538

centralized states, 33, 120, 518, 553
ceque shrines, 648
ceramics, 296, 312, 320, 642, 660
  styles, 641–2
ceremonies, 111, 185, 196–8, 465–6, 473, 594, 602
  imperial, 185, 561
  religious, 137, 185, 198, 457
Ceylon, 3, 393, 450
Chach, 242–3
Chachapoyas, 657
Chaghadaids, 535, 547–8
Chalcedon, Council of, 427, 560
Chaldeans, 343, 417
chamberlains, 184, 186–8
Champagne, fairs of, 259, 262, 266, 272–3, 277
Chan Buddhism, 466, 473–4
Chancas, 644, 650, 653
chancellors, 129
chanceries, 182, 186, 188, 515
Chang'an, 180–1, 345, 438, 514–16, 520, 524
chants, 197–8, 426, 464
Chapar b. Qaidu, 552
Chapaṭa, 475
chapels, 181, 188
charisma, 189, 419–22, 440, 537
  dynastic, 492, 507
charity, 72, 156
Charlemagne, 24, 65, 126, 157, 159–60, 180, 195, 198, 572
Charles Martel, 158–9, 368
Charles the Simple, 12
charter of Visnusena, 295–6
charters, 188, 295–6
cheeses, 272, 281, 578
chelandia, 270–1
Chiang Mai, 125
Chichen Itza, 620, 623–4
chiefdoms, 110, 240, 592, 595, 598, 606, 623, 641, 650
  Mande, 597–9, 606
chiefs, 99, 110–11, 121, 184, 246, 287, 295, 593, 599–600
  provincial, 138–40
Chieri, 259
child-raising, 70, 668
childhood, 189, 424
children, 83, 89, 113, 116, 137–8, 146, 164, 181, 187, 599
Chile, 638, 641, 650, 658
Chimor, 653
Chin, 370, 380, 675

China, 4–7, 24–7, 74–6, 166–7, 233–7, 452–7,
      469–74, 516–20, 543–5
Confucianism and educational
      institutions, 118–19
court, 181, 183, 201, 306, 443, 453, 455
eastern, 393, 410
economy, 235, 237, 470, 532
emperors, 189, 196, 455, 514
      see also names of individual emperors.
Five Dynasties Interregnum, 523–4
Grand Canal, 167, 331, 516, 524
Great Wall, 514, 525
Han, *see* Han.
institutions, 121, 498, 503
internal challenges and decline of Tang
      power, 519–21
Liang, 460
localist turn under Southern Song, 528–30
long-term trends in state-society relations,
      530–2
Ming, *see* Ming.
Mongols, 2, 11, 166–8, 378, 393, 440, 548
new policies of Wang Anshi, 527–8
North, 166–8, 370–1, 437–8, 455, 488–9, 491,
      522–3
post-An Lushan transformation of
      government and society, 521–2
post-Han, 448
prosperity and crisis under Song, 524–6
reunification, 33, 533
Song, *see* Song.
South, 217, 220, 246–7, 393, 514, 522–3, 539,
      551
state formation
      Sui through Song, 513–32
Sui, *see* Sui.
Sui–Tang, *see* Sui–Tang.
Tang, *see* Tang.
warfare, 152–3
Yuan, *see* Yuan.
Chincha, 25, 653, 659
Chinchaysuyo, 638, 650–1
Chinese culture, 121, 214, 320, 401
Chinese diasporic communities, 27, 476
Chinese maps, 2–4
Chinese models, 33, 180–1, 184, 499, 501, 516,
      518
Chinese monks, 454, 462–4, 472
Chinese scholars, 319, 344, 346, 677
Chinese ships, 251, 293
Chinese silk, 239, 378
Chinggis Khan, 24, 246, 440–1, 491–2, 534,
      537–9, 546, 550

Chinggisids, 534–5, 541–3, 545, 547–51,
      553–4
Chioniades, Gregory, 349, 352
Chios, 259, 274, 279, 281
Chola kingdom, 168, 236, 299, 300, 494
Chonai, 273
Chosŏn, 119, 307
Christ, *see* Jesus,
Christendom, 7, 27, 32, 155, 211
      Christian life in Sassanid and Muslim
            polities, 427–36
      Christian life outside Abrahamic sphere,
            437–41
      Eastern, 225, 442
      life in Christian polities, 420–7
      regional systems, 415–45
      Western, 26, 214–15, 219, 223–4, 494–8,
            501–2, 507, 510
Christian communities, 416, 421, 429, 432,
      434, 437, 444, 681
Christian ethics, 420
Christian faith, 130, 260, 422
Christian institutions, 32, 141, 416–20, 442
Christian life, 32, 415–19, 422, 426, 433, 437–8,
      440, 443
      outside Abrahamic sphere, 437–41
      in Sassanid and Muslim polities, 427–36
Christian monasteries, 77, 126, 140
Christian polities, 100, 416, 419–20, 422,
      426–7, 437, 440, 442
      life in, 420–7
Christian regions, 32, 416, 422, 424, 429, 442,
      444–5
Christian rulers, 32, 130, 135, 347, 416, 421, 495
Christian worship, 428, 432
Christianity, 56, 103–4, 156, 427, 430–1, 438,
      441–2, 560, 675, 683
      and European universities, 126–9
      Mesopotamia, 418
      Nestorian, 194, 208, 225, 227, 426–8, 437–8,
            441, 444
      Orthodox, 427, 534, 544
      Protestant, 124
Christians, 87, 345–6, 415, 424–38, 440, 442,
      444
      Eastern, 434, 436
      European, 415, 418, 442
chrysobulls, 274, 578
church courts, 418, 421
Church of Holy Wisdom, *see* Hagia Sophia.
Cieza de León, Pedro, 639–40, 643, 645, 651,
      661
circular maps, 5, 8

cities, 260–1, 343, 561, 564–5, 581, 614–16, 618–20, 622–3, 630–2, 648–9
  major, 261, 407, 515, 614, 628
citizens, 140, 197, 261, 270, 601
city-states, 34, 101, 104, 107, 495, 554, 621–2, 625, 628–30
  conquest-era, 630
  Italian, 322, 552, 674
  Mayan, 137
civil bureaucracy, 33, 182, 531
civil service, 84, 101, 119, 122, 126, 138, 183, 354, 515, 570
  examinations, 117–21, 124, 140–2, 183, 515, 525, 527, 529
civil society, 630, 666
civil wars, 152–3, 155, 157, 159–60, 163–4, 581, 583, 662
civilian elites, 101, 151, 319
class conflict, 108–9
classes, 104, 109, 113, 129, 194, 224, 235, 542, 669, 679
  commercial, 236, 252, 581
  military, 149, 158, 199
  upper, 108, 437, 450
  warrior, 221
Classic Maya, 611, 613–14, 618, 624, 633, 682
clay models, 649–50
clergy / clerics, 32, 124, 128, 200, 418, 420–1, 440, 515–16, 519
clerical elites, 217, 220, 224, 226, 681
climate, 15, 57–8, 241, 249, 373, 564, 594, 649, 661
  change, 57–8, 61
  Medieval Climate Optimum, 58, 61, 334, 336
climatological approach, 55, 57
cloth, 75, 242, 261, 277, 282, 296, 304, 514, 656–7
  precious, 258–9
  woolen, 259, 262, 266, 272–3, 282–3
cloth of gold, 75
Clovis, 12
coal, 335
coastal navigation, 268, 270, 277
coercive power, 63, 211, 217, 229, 361, 631
Coeur, Jacques, 261
coins, 90, 95, 238, 244, 396, 405–7, 523–4
  bronze, 522, 524
  gold, 267, 553, 561, 590
  iron, 524
  silver, 243, 290, 296
coir, 250, 291, 675
coitus, 85–6, 89

Collasuyo, 638, 646, 648, 650, 658
collective identities, 224
collective worship, 32, 424
Cologne, 261
colonialism, 318, 328
colonies, 274, 654, 657
  trade, 242, 415, 437
colonists, 654, 657–8
colonization, 54, 83, 313, 477
Columbus, Christopher, 174, 632, 634
command, 128, 211, 250, 567
commanders, 75, 165, 187, 538, 547, 575, 577, 593, 600
commentaries, 45, 131, 349, 356, 529
commerce, 233, 238–9, 245–7, 251–2, 259–60, 287–8, 290–2, 443, 595–6, 673–4
  activities, 258–60, 262, 267, 675
  Afro-Eurasian, 233–54
  colonies, 242, 415, 437
  expansion of, 244, 471, 551, 632–3, 682
  foreign, 235, 251, 275, 526–7
  gold, 250, 590
  goods, 632, 682
    diversity, 634, 682
  international, 34, 262, 264, 271, 276–7, 535, 550
  long distance, 30, 159, 233, 239, 242–3, 245–6, 249–50, 252–3
  maritime, 270, 287–8, 290, 295, 548
  networks, 276–9
  objects, 279–84
  overland, 247, 378, 381, 673–4
  private, 235–6
  retail, 272
  routes, *see* routes.
  salt, 266, 590, 603
  slaves, 170, 258, 283, 303, 552
  state and papal intervention, 274–6
  trans-Saharan, 34, 109, 586, 589, 595, 598, 600, 602, 607
  transit, 236, 239, 244, 390
  tribute, 235, 250
commercial centers, 237, 245, 259, 266, 596, 601–2
commercial classes, 236, 252, 581
commercial diasporas, 27, 396
commercial economy, 77, 141, 239, 243, 246, 249, 252, 257–8, 632
commercial exchanges, 470–1, 476, 616, 620, 633
commercial growth, 225, 228, 239, 520
commercial markets, 264–5, 267
commercial networks, 34, 257, 471, 596

Mesoamerica, 632–3
commercial revolution, 90, 244, 471
commercial taxes, 522, 525, 540
commercial techniques, 30, 264
commercialization, 634, 682
commodities, 233, 238, 241, 243–4, 250–1, 287,
    290–1, 296–7
    luxury, 251, 281, 287, 550–1, 597, 602, 670,
        673, 679–80
commoners, 83, 90, 119, 137, 362, 374, 404,
    456–7, 531, 621–2
commons, tragedy of the, 63
communities, 105–6, 113, 122, 124, 290–1, 297,
    416, 424–6, 504, 654
    agricultural, 105
    Buddhist, 447, 460, 471–2
    Christian, 416, 421, 429, 432, 434, 437, 444,
        681
    Jewish, 78, 130, 237, 301, 304, 417, 428, 430
    local, 102, 105, 215, 297, 505, 669
    maritime, 30, 287
    merchant, 438, 450, 476
    monastic, 122, 450, 452, 455, 475, 504
    sailing, 30, 291
    seafaring, 30, 291, 306
    settled, 428, 590
    trading, 287, 290, 295–6, 451
    village, 531, 587, 654
compasses, 313, 317
    magnetic, 250, 675
Compendium of Chronicles, 12, 14, 543,
    549, 680
competition, 29, 189–91, 194, 201, 262, 283,
    523, 594
complexity, 98, 196, 201, 238, 312, 587, 596,
    666
    economic, 28, 109
    of government, 97, 669
composite bows, 154, 171
concubines, 74, 81–2, 87–8, 107, 183, 191, 245,
    304
confiscations, 252, 575
Confucian ethics, 76, 87, 531
Confucian schools, 121–2, 140
Confucian statecraft, 516, 530
Confucianism, 28, 75, 140, 142, 156, 191, 225,
    339, 521, 677
    and educational institutions, 117–21
    Japan, 120–1
    Korea, 119–20
    Neo-Confucianism, 120–1, 214, 220, 486,
        500, 522, 530–2
    texts, 118–20, 122, 124, 140, 183, 354

Vietnam, 121
conquered countries, 32, 365, 371–2, 377, 379,
    381, 671
conquerors, 146, 151, 156, 227, 370, 380, 403,
    411–12, 489, 491
    Spanish, 16, 487, 612
conquest dynasties, 153, 158, 163–4, 488,
    500–1, 504
conquest-era city-states, 630
conquests, 359–60, 363–5, 371, 375–7, 380–1,
    491, 538–9, 650, 673, 682
    Inca, 650–5, 682
    Islamic, 71, 89, 101, 122, 158, 671, 673, 676,
        678, 681
    Mongol, 9, 24, 30, 96, 227, 391, 393, 673,
        677, 683
    nomadic, 31, 52, 376, 379, 381, 673 *see also*
        pastoral nomadism, migrations
        and conquests.
    Ottoman, 262, 283, 392, 396
    Seljuk, 373, 377
    Spanish, 613–14, 618, 620, 622, 625–6,
        632–3
consolidation, 147, 215, 296, 531, 671, 675
    internal, 160, 172
    political, 513, 674
    religious, 295
    territorial, 644
Constantine the Great, 561–2
Constantine V, 157, 565, 569
Constantinople, 155, 258, 276–9, 347, 560–8,
    572–5, 579–80, 582–3
    see also Byzantium.
    Great Palace, 560–1, 574
    merchants of, 262, 578
consumers, 30, 196, 233, 525, 550, 674
contact zones, 310, 328–9
continuity, 180, 214, 221, 440, 490, 492, 495,
    508, 513, 665
    and change, 313–18
contracts, 15, 71, 77, 82, 90, 259, 265, 676
    oral, 198
    written, 82
control, 34, 117–18, 152, 164–5, 169, 188, 503,
    595, 602–3, 606–7
    central, 164, 506, 530
    direct, 138, 486, 641
    effective, 100, 502
conversion, 71, 73–4, 390–2, 416, 430, 437, 507,
    547–8, 671, 676
    forced, 104, 448
    royal, 547–9
convoys, 264, 268–9, 302

copper, 23, 34, 282, 295, 302, 524, 590, 595, 644, 648
Coptic, 343, 401, 424, 432, 435–6
Coptic martyrs, 431
Copts, 427, 432
Cordova, 12, 346, 349, 680
Coricancha, 646–8, 653
Cornwall, 277, 282
Coron, 274, 279
corruption, 471, 528
Cortés, Hernan, 610, 623, 628, 632, 634
cosmology, 137, 206, 209, 213, 223
Cossacks, 426
cotton, 238–9, 253, 282, 284, 295, 305, 317, 632, 679
Council of Chalcedon, 427, 560
Council of Florence-Ferrara, 583
councils, 102, 112
    ecclesiastical, 421, 428
    royal, 99, 102, 112
    ruling, 98, 102, 107
court astrologers, 185, 198
court ceremonial, 196–9
court culture, *see* courtly cultures.
court life, 29, 190, 196, 201
court poets, 193–4
court rituals, 197, 395, 421
court traditions, 35, 179–80
courtiers, 181–2, 184, 186, 189, 191–3, 195, 197, 330
    male, 184, 189
courtliness, 189, 191–2, 196
courtly cultures, 120, 179–201, 324
    competition and courtliness, 189–92
    court and critics, 199–201
    court ceremonial, 196–9
    cultural production in courts, 192–6
    membership and function, 182–9
    power and place, 179–82
courtly love, 196
courts *see also* courtly cultures.
    'Abbasid, 180, 195, 199
    Byzantine, 179, 181, 184–5, 679
    church, 418, 421
    and critics, 199–201
    India, 179, 181, 197
    Islamic, 179, 194, 201, 679
    Japan, 180, 183, 193, 519
    papal, 179–80, 679
    royal, 182, 186, 188, 191, 195–6, 200, 551, 602
    Western, 188, 190, 195, 200
cowrie shells, 245, 597

crafts, 77, 98, 109, 116, 316, 321–2, 324, 335, 360, 670
craftsmanship, 8, 147, 542
craftsmen/people, 95, 107, 252, 290, 305, 320, 456, 572, 581, 583
creation myths, 35, 643–4
credit, 249, 266, 273, 527, 537
Cresques Abraham, 8
Crete, 83, 274, 279, 281
crime, 86–7, 105–6
Crimea, 243, 274, 366, 391, 543
critical reflexivity, 206
crop failures, 55, 249, 621
crops, 26, 111, 216, 336, 654, 656
cross-cultural exchanges, 32, 462, 672
    Mongol empire, 541–5
cross-cultural interactions, 297, 378, 672–3
cross-gender behavior, 87
cross-regional interactions, 462, 469
crossbows, 152, 160, 172–4, 315
Crusader States, 162, 347, 578
crusaders, 17, 329, 426, 578
crusades, 12, 78, 274, 329, 424, 436, 442, 444
    First, 7, 12, 17, 130, 161
    Fourth, 24, 274, 579
crystallizations, cultural, 29, 206, 209, 212, 216, 229
cuicacalli, 137–8
cultivation, 44, 48, 75–7, 117, 192, 259, 281, 360, 410
cults, 418, 472, 642, 644, 646–8, 656–7, 660–1, 682
    relic, 450, 475
cultural crystallizations, 29, 206, 209, 212, 216, 229
    and trans-regional reorientations, 208–12
cultural dominance, 206, 320
cultural ecumenes, 29, 212–13, 216, 225, 227
cultural exchanges, 312, 347, 378, 677
cultural frameworks, 310, 490, 493
cultural heritage, 138, 212, 346
cultural legacies, 24, 29, 225, 499, 537, 681
cultural practices, 211, 215–16, 321
cultural production, 192, 194–5, 201, 436
cultural supremacy, 33, 333
cultures, 29, 31, 44, 60–1, 195–6, 219, 309–10, 316, 335, 543
    elite, 317, 402, 411, 614
    irrigation, 50, 67
    material, 329–30, 545, 624
    political, 380, 507, 550
    religious, 33, 483, 496, 503
    sedentary, 50–1

currency, III, 245, 266–7, 522, 524, 527, 597,
      656
   exchange, 244, 266, 273, 552
   gold, *see* gold, coins.
   metal, 30, 264
curricula, educational, 132, 141, 322, 350, 527
custom duties, 259, 275
customary law, 295, 380, 407
   unwritten, 104, 669
customary practices, 116, 295–6
customs, 89, 102, 130, 192, 211, 303, 514, 587,
      606, 638
   religious, 103, 669
Cuzco, 25, 138, 638–49, 651–3, 655–6, 658,
      661–2
   Lower, 642, 648–9
   Upper, 642, 647
   Valley, 641, 643, 647
Cyprus, 270, 273, 279, 281, 396, 564

da Gama, Vasco, 254, 415
Dahbattan, 302
Dai Viet, 121
Dakajalan, 598
Dalmatia, 569, 572
Damascus, 4, 133–4, 155, 180, 411, 432, 564, 599
dance, 81, 138, 661
Dao Learning, 529, 531
Daoism, 121, 156, 225, 546, 665
Datini, Francesco di Marco, 260, 265, 267
Datong, 456, 460
daughters, 74–5, 90, 128, 131, 138, 185, 224, 304,
      430, 578
de la Vega, Garcilaso, 639, 655
Deccan, 451
decimal units, 537–8, 542, 655
defenders, 150, 380, 530
defense, 151, 162, 167, 172, 261, 274, 519, 578,
      580, 583
deforestation, 59–60, 335, 614
deities, 197–8, 546, 638, 643, 660
   local, 661–3
Delhi, 248, 297, 375
   sultanate, 82, 164, 169, 215, 238, 548
Demetrius, St., 273, 574
democracy, 106–7, 113, 210
demographic decline, 562, 572, 618
demographic growth, 159, 216, 572, 578, 583,
      622, 641
deserts, 47, 51, 57, 241, 360–1, 363, 590, 594–5
despotic power, 101, 628–30
Despotism, Oriental, 96, 99, 105
deviance, 86–8

dharma, 85, 549
Dharmapāla, Pāla ruler, 468
dhimmi, 275, 429, 432, 681
Dhu'n-Nun, 44
Diabe Cissé, 593
Diafunu, 606
dialectical reasoning, 129, 350
Diamond, Jared, 55, 61, 614
diasporas, commercial, 27, 396
diet, 371, 545
dikes, 47, 65, 325, 329
Dinga, 593
Diogenes, Romanos, 576
Dioscorides, 349–51
diplomacy, 35, 419, 443, 650, 682
diplomatic missions, 467, 553
diplomatic relations, 389, 466, 502, 517, 672
direct taxes, 522, 531
disciples, 124, 321, 417, 450
discovery, voyages of, 313, 317, 341
disease, 59, 248, 315, 471, 663, 674
   infectious, 66, 662
ditches, 150, 618, 624
divergences, 224, 233, 311, 336, 497, 501, 672
diversification, 266, 314, 316–17, 326
diversity, 34, 43, 53, 73, 76, 267, 410, 415–16,
      441–2, 444
   of trade goods, 634, 682
divination, 197, 322, 438, 543, 673
diviners, 598
division of labor, 148, 159
divorce, 71–2, 76, 78, 434
doctors, 12, 78, 128, 194, 345, 352, 354–5
domestic skills, 116, 140
domestic slavery, 28, 80, 83
dominance, 56, 85, 152, 262, 502, 518, 529, 582,
      597
   cultural, 206, 320
   political, 34, 377, 387, 607
domination, 95, 214, 228, 604
   political, 363, 623
   world, 494, 510
Dominican order, 129, 442
donations, 289, 295, 451–2, 472, 475, 477
donkeys, 245
donors, 73, 91, 123
Dore, Elizabeth, 50
Dorestad, 258, 276
dower, 71, 676
dowries, 73–4, 77–8, 90
drainage, 47–8, III
dreams, 354, 453, 648
dried fish, 595–6

dromedaries, 245, 363, 373
dromons, 270–1
droughts, 43, 46, 58, 589, 614, 621, 627, 661
drums, 194, 593
Du Huan, 15
duchies, 102, 274, 567, 569
dukes, 160, 569, 577–8
Dunhuang, 438, 457, 467
durability, 26, 33
Dust Bowl, 45, 54
duties, 13, 85, 100, 113, 181, 185, 191, 296, 305,
    678
  parish, 444
  religious, 132, 156
dykes, *see* dikes
dynastic change, 189, 485, 498, 604
dynastic charisma, 492, 507
dynastic instability, 366, 600
Dyrrachion (Durrazzo), 273, 564, 569, 581

Early Middle Ages, 53, 258–9, 276, 281, 283
Early Postclassic period, 619, 631
East Africa, 71–2, 108–9, 169, 251, 291, 294,
    393–4, 396
East Asia, 122–3, 447, 463–5, 470–2, 485,
    498–501, 503, 519, 531
  Buddhism and educational institutions,
    124–5
  genesis, 519–33
East Europe, 365, 367–9, 372
East Siberia, 377, 673
Eastern Christendom, 225, 442
eastern Europe, 166, 215, 224, 243, 548
eastern hemisphere, 1–2, 5, 20, 24–6, 83, 341
eastern Mediterranean, 21, 24, 30, 58, 133, 160,
    257, 273, 349, 385
ecclesiastical authorities, 127, 347, 441
ecclesiastical laws, 90, 420
ecological instability, 48
ecology, 15, 47, 52, 57, 60
economy, 90–1, 244–6, 249, 525, 527, 589, 682
  Chinese, 235, 237, 470, 532
  commercial, 77, 141, 239, 243, 246, 249, 252,
    257–8, 632
  development, 222, 245, 252, 501, 635
  economic activities, 213, 222, 296, 303, 360,
    476–7
  economic foundations of societies in
    Eurasia, 96–8
  economic phenomena, 612, 614, 619
  growth, 30, 90, 121, 159, 218, 284, 523, 530,
    610
  market, 530–1

pastoral nomadic, 359–60
  political, 287, 589
  private, 528, 531
  resources, 148, 151, 386, 522, 544
  sustainable agricultural, 48–9
  transformations, 220, 223
ecumenes, 26, 29, 214, 219, 229
  cultural, 29, 212–13, 216, 225, 227
  religious, 24, 26, 207
Edessa, 155, 428, 575
education, 116–19, 121–6, 130–41, 668, 676
  basic, 126, 132, 140
educational institutions, 28, 35, 116–42, 677–8
  Americas, 137–40
  and Buddhism, 122–6
  China, 118–19
  and Christianity, 126–9
  and Confucianism, 117–21
  development, 126, 678
  formal, 117, 132, 140–2
  and Islam, 131–5
    Africa, 135–7
    Japan, 120–1
  and Judaism, 130–1
    Korea, 119–20
    primary, 116, 668
    Vietnam, 121
educational resources, 122, 124, 126
Egyptian traders, 601–2
Egyptians, 258, 343
Eisenstadt, Shmuel N., 206, 226, 665–7, 681,
    683
elderly parents, 90, 677
elite culture, 317, 402, 411, 614
elite families, 224, 655
elites
  civilian, 101, 151, 319
  clerical, 217, 220, 224, 226, 681
  educated, 124, 220
  landed, 224, 379
  literati, 119, 220
  local, 34, 106, 499, 505, 559, 562, 567, 673,
    679
  military, 151, 221, 331, 379, 506
  political, 151, 221, 226, 303, 361, 379, 389, 521,
    666, 681
  regional, 164, 641
  religious, 207, 217, 221
  ruling, 378, 520, 545
  traditional, 221, 226
  urban, 133, 160, 222, 226, 604
Ellenblum, Ronnie, 58
Elvin, Mark, 49

emancipation, 107, 304
embassies, 236, 389, 455, 518, 553, 601–2
emirates, 571, 580
emirs, 567, 571
empire, system of, 665–7
empire building, 33, 35, 156, 171, 488, 671–2,
    674–6
  Mongols, 537, 541
  and state formation, 483–510
employment, 185, 235, 311, 314
empresses, 183, 198, 576
endowments, 118, 122, 128–9, 133, 297–8
enemies, external, 80, 157
energy, 43, 157, 316, 334–5, 464, 648
  kinetic, 161, 173, 314
engineers, 154, 167, 170, 354, 539
engines, 30, 233, 244, 252, 528
  battering, 150
  stone-throwing, 150
English merchants, 275, 277
English peasants, 108, 333
enlightenment, 79, 125, 450, 466
enslavement, 82–3, 149, 171
entertainers, 31, 306
entertainment, 181, 197, 542–3, 679
entrepreneurs, 195, 250, 333, 527, 552
environment, 27, 94, 309, 316, 323, 334–6, 400,
    410, 434
  and humans, 43–68
  natural, 361, 648
  physical, 309, 334
environmental change, 335, 489
environmental damage, 28, 62
environmental historians, 46, 59, 62, 334
environmental history, 45, 51, 54, 56, 59, 61,
    64–5, 67
environmentalism, 47, 57
envoys, 27, 453, 455, 461, 475
epic narratives, 587
Epiclassic period, 618, 626, 628, 630–1
epidemics, 66–7, 565–6, 583
Epirus, 569, 579–80
Equal Field system, 514, 522, 530–1
espionage, 262, 520
estates, 74, 158–9, 163, 223, 552, 575
  small, 167, 568
Esterlins, 261
ethics, 130, 191, 220, 350
  Christian, 420
  Confucian, 76, 87, 531
Ethiopia, 24, 109–10, 135, 415–16, 437, 440, 442,
    444, 487
ethnic groups, 102, 613, 625, 627, 642

ethnic identities, 292–3, 495, 497, 535, 655
Euclid, 126
eunuchs, 84, 183, 185, 187, 189, 197, 245
Eurasia, 29, 96–7, 111, 219–20, 340–2, 535–8,
    541–5, 673, 679
  class conflict, 108–9
  Eastern, 490, 516
  economic foundations of societies, 96–8
  hierarchy and government, 98–101
  Inner, 484, 486–92, 499, 501, 507, 510, 514
  law, 104–6
  local society, 106–7
  religions, 103–4
  solidarities within polities, 101–3
  western, 179, 494
Eurasian steppes, 31, 145, 360, 362–3, 365–7,
    371–4, 380, 389
Europe, 5–9, 95–6, 106–8, 223, 228, 252–4, 340,
    422–4, 443–4, 674–5
  Central, 52, 63, 65, 244, 249, 254
  East, 365, 367–9, 372
  Medieval, 45, 58, 76–7, 94, 96, 99, 109,
    125–6, 314–15
  military revolutions, 171–4
  northern, 17, 53, 95, 128, 215, 257, 261, 279,
    284, 310
  southeastern, 387, 392, 484
  southern, 211, 329
  western, 26, 160–1, 179–80, 182, 214–15, 220,
    222, 226
European Christians, 415, 418, 442
European scholars, 126, 142, 320, 322, 436
European trade networks, 257–84
European universities, 117, 126–9, 135, 141,
    223, 350
Euthymius the Georgian, 22
examinations, civil service, 117–21, 124, 140–2,
    183, 515, 525, 527, 529
exchanges
  commercial, 470–1, 476, 616, 620, 633
  cross-cultural, 32, 462, 541, 544–5, 672
  cultural, 312, 347, 378, 677
  diplomatic, 349, 462, 680
  technological, 328–9
exile, 199, 264, 420, 506, 521, 598–9, 638
expertise, 136, 166, 320, 324, 328, 419
  administrative, 518, 521
  technical, 318, 323, 329, 333
experts, 31, 185, 329, 337, 539, 542, 546, 548–9
exports, 242, 253, 262, 264, 275, 282,
    524, 574
expulsions, 78, 104, 121
extortion, 252, 275

fairs, 257, 259, 271, 471
of Champagne, 259, 262, 266, 272–3, 277
faith, *see* religions.
Fakhr al-Din, 553
families, 28, 81–3, 85, 87–9, 116, 197–9, 424–6
Central and East Asia, 73–6
elite, 224, 655
Europe, 76–9
imperial, 181, 183–4, 193, 197, 473, 567
Islamic world and South Asia, 71–3
family life, 16, 80, 434, 676–7, 683
structured, 71, 676
family members, 81, 134, 492, 567, 575, 577, 581
famines, 98, 154, 252, 305, 435, 621
Farakoro, 598–9
farmers, 48, 163, 314, 527, 542, 607
farming, 52, 55, 97, 322, 361, 600, 631
see also agriculture.
families, 514, 522, 525
pasture, 48, 51
terrace, 47, 49–50
wet rice, 49–50, 518
fathers, 72, 90, 131, 138, 189, 191, 298, 303, 570, 576
paternal rights, 82–3, 89
Fatimids, 238, 264, 271, 576
Faulkner, Edward H., 54
female slaves, 81–3, 304–5, 602
Fertile Crescent, 32, 279, 404, 411–12
fertility, 48
fertilizers, 48–9, 53
festivals, 103, 196, 656
feudalism, 95, 105, 210
Indian, 238
Fez, 26, 134
financial incentives, 329–30
fines, 86, 407
fiscal policy, 527, 552
fish, 259, 270, 273, 277, 281
dried, 595–6
fishermen, 607
fishing, 30, 291
Five Dynasties period, 523–4
Flanders, 259, 261–2, 269–70, 272–3, 281
Flannery, Timothy F., 55
flat-bottomed boats, 277
fleets, 167, 169, 240, 250, 264, 578, 603
Hanseatic, 268
Italian, 160, 268–9
Mongol, 167
Flemish, 261, 273, 275, 279
Florence, 260–1, 266, 269

Florentines, 259, 275
flutes, 193
food, 49, 72, 74, 111–12, 316, 320, 332, 335, 538, 543
food, production, 34, 241, 336
food supplies, 54, 162, 281, 614
footmen, 149, 161
forced conversion, 104, 448
foreign merchants, 237, 262, 272, 275, 303, 306
foreign trade, 235, 251, 275, 526–7
foreigners, 113, 150, 275, 301, 352, 471, 542, 574–5, 579
forestry, sustainable, 62–3
forests, 52–5, 57, 60–3, 65–6, 97, 595–6, 598
fortifications, 17, 150, 154, 166–7, 182
fortresses, 110, 153, 569, 647
trace italienne, 174
Fourth Lateran Council, 81–2
fragmentation, 128, 252, 496, 499, 671, 676, 678
political, 11, 101, 238, 495, 513, 524, 537, 670, 682
France, 90, 96, 165, 260–1, 273, 275, 277, 419, 424, 497
northern, 130
southern, 77, 157, 262, 442
Franciscans, 129, 421
Frankfurt, 273
Franks, 12–14, 17, 22, 27, 84, 102, 153, 158–60, 366, 368
see also Carolingians.
warfare, 158–62
freed slaves, 304, 597
freedom, 191, 304, 440, 521, 546, 550, 564
Frescobaldi family, 259
Friday prayers, 389–90, 405, 407–8
Frisian merchants, 258, 272, 276
Frisians, 243, 261, 279
fubing militias, 152–3, 168, 514, 516, 520–1, 530
Funan, 455, 458
funduq, 272
furs, 237, 243, 263, 273, 277, 282, 320, 390, 551
Fustat (Old Cairo), 263, 293, 301, 353, 431
fustians, 282–3

Galata, 574, 582
Galen, 85, 126, 355, 410
galley ships, 268–70, 282
galleys, 25, 268
gantowisas, 80
Gao, 34, 136, 348, 586, 596, 600, 602–5, 607
Gaon, 130, 141
Gaozong, Chinese emperor, 520

gardens, 7, 52, 105, 181–2, 198
Gaul, 22, 158, 416, 484
gender, 15, 28, 70–1, 79, 85, 89, 140, 588, 598
    assumptions, 70, 76, 89
    difference, 71, 677
    expectations, 70, 89
    and slavery, 80–4
    systems, 28, 71, 677
    third, 87
gendered space, 187
genealogies, 107, 109–10, 194, 342, 412, 538, 633
generals, 169, 520, 525, 576
    slave-eunuch, 164
generosity, 72, 110, 192, 568, 657
Geniza, 263, 267, 299–300, 302–3
Genoa, 160, 248, 259–60, 269, 274, 276,
    279–83, 574
Genoese, 274, 282–3, 574, 582
genres, 10, 58, 131, 200, 353, 409, 454
gentry, 96, 500
geographers, 5, 7, 544, 592
geographical knowledge, 32, 476
geography, 5, 112, 145, 245, 292, 401, 543, 673
geometry, 129, 350
Georgia, 267, 427, 540, 567
Georgian, 22, 432, 434–5
Germans, 158, 276, 279
Germany, 102, 130
    central, 281
    northern, 54
    southern, 277, 282–3
Ghana, 135–6, 395, 487, 586, 590–1, 594–5,
    597–8, 600, 603
Ghazan, Ilkhan, 74, 547, 553
Ghaznavids, 373, 392, 402
Gibraltar, 259, 402
gifts, 164, 198, 200, 287, 290, 450, 550, 652–3,
    656
    exchange of, 186, 643
    marriage, 71, 90, 676–7
Giovanni de' Marignolli, 11
girls, 70–2, 138, 287, 676
Glacken, Clarence J., 56
glass, 238, 283, 320, 590, 597
glassware, 243, 597, 679
globalization, 30, 35, 284, 535, 666–8, 681, 684
    proto-globalization, 35, 665, 667–8, 670,
    681, 683–4
globalized world, 35, 555, 667, 683
glocalization, 35, 665, 668, 680
God, 44, 192, 405, 407, 409–10, 416–17, 427–8,
    434–5
    grace of, 207, 420

goddesses, 80, 354
godhead, 438, 464
gods, 99, 103, 197, 207, 502, 613
gold, 195, 239, 245, 267, 593–8, 600–2, 646, 653
gold, coins, 267, 553, 561, 590
gold trade, 250, 590
golden ages, 193, 239, 600
Golden Horde, 74, 365, 369, 371, 391, 426, 545,
    547, 552–3
Golden Horn, 272, 574, 582
goldfields, 596, 598, 607
Goryeo, *see* Koryŏ
Goths, 153, 437
Gottfried, Robert S., 62
government, 101–2, 107–10, 112, 118, 211, 217,
    252, 668–9
    central, 100, 515, 520–1, 524, 527–9, 531, 539,
    541, 669, 673
    centralized, 244, 402, 531, 538
    complexity of, 97, 669
    Eurasia, 98–101
    layers of, 97, 669
    officials, *see* civil service.
    units of, 94–5, 101
governors, 187, 405, 570–1, 577, 581, 593–4
grace of God, 207, 420
grain, 147, 163, 197, 238, 242, 259–60, 275, 281,
    295
    tithe, 262, 281
    trade, 258, 260, 281
grammar, 122, 129, 132, 194
Granada, 134, 162, 279
Grand Canal, 167, 331, 516, 524
grandsons, 7, 346, 579, 639
Great Palace, 560–1, 574
Great Silk Road, 366, 378
great snake, 593–4
Great Wall, 514, 525
Great Zimbabwe, 60, 109
Greece, 207, 218, 409, 665
Greeks, 22, 271, 273, 342–3, 345–7, 349, 427,
    434–5, 579–80
Gregorian reforms, 579
griots, 135, 678
Grove, A. T., 63
growth, 53, 55, 68, 106–7, 216, 223–4, 471–2
    agricultural, 216, 626
    commercial, 225, 228, 239, 520
    economic, *see* economy, growth.
    population, *see* population growth.
    unsustainable, 49
    urban, 281, 450, 499, 522
Guaman Poma de Ayala, 639, 657, 661

Guangzhou, 235, 237, 526
Guanzhong aristocracy, 515–16, 520
Guascar, 662
Guatemala, 614, 623–4
Guayna Capac, 639, 650–1, 658–62
guilds, 95, 262, 287, 323, 334
  merchant, 216, 306, 451
Guillaume of Villehardouin, 580
Gujarat, 104, 238, 290, 294, 296–7, 299, 301, 303
  coast, 288, 294, 297, 548
Gulf of Cambay, 288, 294
Gulf of Mexico, 623, 625, 634
gunpowder, 171, 313, 545
  weapons, 29, 166, 171, 173–4, 381, 554
guns, *see* gunpowder, weapons.
Guptas, 49, 238–9, 484, 502

hadith, 86, 132, 134, 194, 430
Hagia Sophia, 181, 185, 197, 444
hagiography, 420, 568
Haithabu, 258, 276
Hamburg, 261, 267
Hamdān al-Athāribī, 12
Han, 179–80, 448, 452–3, 455, 498, 515,
  517, 521, 679
Han, Southern, 524
Han Suyin, 60
handguns, 171–3
Hangzhou, 235, 331, 528, 530, 554
Hanse, 261, 268, 274, 277, 279, 284
Hardin, Garrett, 63–4
harems, 79, 81, 84, 86
Harold Godwinson, 161
Harris, Marvin, 50, 55
Harun al-Rashid, 11, 346
harvest, 197, 271, 540
Harz mountains, 267, 282
Hasan b. Bundār, 301, 303
healing, 543, 547, 673
heaven, 80, 87, 155–6, 189, 196–7, 207, 227,
  490, 520, 537
heavy cavalry, 159, 161, 514, 517
heavy ploughs, 53–4, 313, 315
heavy soils, 53, 55, 336
Hebrew, 22, 131, 300, 304, 344, 347
Heian Japan, 120, 164, 180, 221, 330,
  448, 473
heirs, 11–12, 72, 82, 138, 160, 164, 513, 516,
  534, 539
Hellas, 569
Henan Province, 456
Heraclius, Byzantine emperor, 21, 155–7,
  563–4

Herat, 246, 248
herds, 111, 150, 359, 371, 489, 538
heresy, 87, 420–1
heretics, 81, 104
Hermann of Carinthia, 354, 356
Hermes, 342–3
hermits, 103, 426
Herodotus, 247
hierarchies, 100–2, 190, 228, 489, 577, 642,
  648, 669, 679
  and government
    Eurasia, 98–101
  local, 98, 107, 669
  political, 100, 108
  religious, 34, 103, 562
  social, 28, 75, 98, 103, 109, 420, 531, 553
  and solidarity, 94–113
hieroglyphs, 341, 633
High Middle Ages, 53, 57, 210, 257, 281, 315,
  334
high officials, 133, 187, 194, 200, 527, 538
Hijaz, 300, 404
Himalayas, 122
Hindu traditions, 215, 680
Hinduism, 30, 85, 104, 125, 288, 293, 306, 355,
  402, 665
Hippo, 417–18
hippodromes, 181, 185
historical records, 142, 145, 330, 458, 501, 604,
  630
historiography, 12, 67, 95–6, 320, 330, 680
Hocquet, Jean-Claude, 281
Holy Land, 435, 444
Holy Roman Empire, 222, 419, 497–8, 510
homosexuality, 86–7
Honduras, 624
honey, 44, 243, 277, 595
Honnecourt, Villard de, 326
honor, 71, 74, 84, 153, 185, 460, 676
Horden, Peregrine, 59, 257, 276
Hormuz, 279, 297
Horn of Africa, 170, 394, 486
horsemanship, 147, 163
horsemen, 149–50, 154, 161, 163, 170
horses, 170, 174, 239, 242, 333–4, 363, 589, 591,
  595, 597
  war, 245, 524
hostages, 543, 653
hostels, 129, 132
household work, 305
households, 28, 72, 74–5, 77, 81–2, 116, 188,
  621, 654–6
  imperial, 181–2

houses, 74–5, 80, 133, 137–8, 299, 647, 649–51, 657–8
Hsiung-nu, 365–6
Huamachuco, 660
Huang Chao, 11, 523, 166
Huanuco Pampa, 657
Huari (Wari), 640–1, 643, 660
Huarochirí, 661
Hugo of Santalla, 352–3
Huichang Persecution, 470
Huizinga, Johan, 43, 47, 63, 68
human nature, 46, 56, 117
Hungarians, 166, 368–9
Hungary, 20, 162, 166, 171, 282, 368, 390, 392–3, 534–5
hunger, 58, 147, 162
Huns, 66, 375
hunters, 187, 607
husbands, 71–5, 77, 80, 87–9, 91
hydraulic societies, 47
hydraulic works, 323, 329
Hyech'o, 464

Iberian peninsula, 2, 81, 126, 269, 276, 395, 506, 569, 671, 681
Ibiza, 260, 281
Ibn 'Abdun, 351–2
Ibn Battūta, 43, 50, 293, 543, 586, 599, 602, 680
Ibn Fadlan, 389–91, 395
Ibn Jubayr, 15, 293, 680
Ibn Khaldun, 110, 134, 361, 377, 379, 599
Ibn Khurdadhbih, 263
Iceland, 22, 243, 277, 340
iconography, 196, 441, 634, 682
idealization, 192, 196
ideals, 100, 125, 666
ideologies, 51, 235–6, 318, 500–1, 537
  political, 525, 531, 553
Ifriqiya, 263, 276–7
Ilkhanate, 535, 540, 547–8, 553
Ilkhanid Iran, 539, 545, 677
Ilterish, 146, 152
imitation, 208, 261, 320, 326, 518, 650
immigrants, 102–3, 121, 332, 518, 522, 548
imperial administration, 33, 555, 644
imperial bodyguards, 181, 184
imperial capitals, 416, 561, 623, 631, 638, 647
imperial ceremonies, 185, 561
imperial courts, 75, 182–3, 217, 221, 226, 235, 306, 531
imperial expansion, 157, 488, 491, 496, 504
imperial families, 181, 183–4, 193, 197, 473, 567
imperial households, 181–2

imperial ideology, 490, 560
imperial power, 180–1, 222, 487, 494, 508, 576
imperial rule, 214, 220, 227, 491, 494
imperial sovereignty, 33, 508, 530
imports, 23, 239, 294, 304, 601, 623, 672
Inca, 3, 50, 137, 140, 638–40, 642–63, 682
  ancestors, 642, 645, 647–8, 662
  capital, 25, 138
  conquests and diplomacy, 650–5, 682
  empire, 16, 35, 639–40, 656, 667, 682
    state and religion, 638–63
  homeland, 642, 654
  myth of origin, 642, 645, 650
  origins in documentary sources, 642–5
  regions and households, 655–63
  religion, 648, 659–63, 682
  rulers, 35, 111, 643, 645–6, 648, 650–1, 656
  sources of Andean history, 639–42
  state, 111, 638, 642, 644, 654, 656–8
  and Sun, 645–50, 660, 682
Inca Pachacuti, 645, 648, 656, 662
India, 11–13, 89–90, 98–9, 103–4, 218–19, 224–5, 241–2, 263–4, 301–5
  central, 215, 375, 455
  courts, 179, 181, 197
  eastern, 451, 462
  northern, 72–3, 165, 169, 238–9, 447, 451, 462, 468–9, 543, 545
  northwest, 82
  and pastoral nomads, 375–6
  peninsular, 238–9
  southern, 108, 169–70, 240, 250, 305, 429, 451, 474, 548, 675
  state formation and empire building, 501–4
  trade, 288, 300–1, 674
  west coast, 290–2, 299–300, 304
Indian Ocean, 5, 235–6, 239, 250–2, 287–8, 290–3, 393–5
  interconnectedness, 305–6
  Islamic civilization, 393–4
  western, 287–8, 290, 292, 294, 299, 302
Indian slaves, 82, 303
Indian subcontinent, 19, 215–16, 219, 224, 287, 299, 303, 305, 316
Indicancha, 642, 646
indigo, 296
indirect taxes, 522, 524–5, 531
Indonesia, 241, 276, 503
industrial revolution, 68, 213, 220, 254, 314
industrialization, 666, 684
inequality, 94, 97, 102–3, 110, 113, 669, 678
infantry, 149–50, 154, 161, 167

infectious diseases, 66, 662
infidels, 547, 571
information, 2, 4, 7–8, 11, 13, 15–16, 94, 362,
    639
infrastructures, 31, 158, 235, 243, 316, 336, 381,
    509, 551
inheritance, 28, 72, 89–90, 98, 104, 112, 164,
    197, 220, 223–4
Inner Asia, 365–7, 370, 375, 537
Inner China, 500
Inner Eurasia, 484, 486, 488–92, 499, 501, 507,
    510, 514
    interactions with adjacent civilizations,
        487–93
Inner Mongolia, 370
Innocent III, 82, 421
innovation, 31, 68, 214, 250, 266–7, 309–10, 353,
    489, 514, 539
    and technologies, 309–37
inscriptions
    Somanath-Veraval, 297–8
    Tamil, 73, 305
instability, 34, 52, 562, 576, 579
    dynastic, 366, 600
    ecological, 48
institutions, 32–3, 116–17, 122–4, 133–4, 142,
    209, 419–20, 505–6
    Christian, 32, 141, 416, 442
    educational, *see* educational institutions.
    Islamic civilization, 405–8
    monastic, 450, 452, 464, 467–70, 473, 475–6
    political, 151, 207, 215, 516, 519, 612
    religious, 103, 299, 329, 519, 532, 670, 683
insurance, 260, 266–7
integration, 33, 120, 225, 303, 311, 554, 650, 666,
    682
    large-area, 20, 24
    political, 1, 361
    regional, 35, 667, 682
intellectual life, 213, 435, 529
intensive cultivation, 488, 522, 611
interactions
    cross-cultural, 297, 672
    cross-regional, 462, 469
    social, 94, 217
    stylistic, 634, 682
interconnectedness, 233, 290, 305
interdependence, 117, 419, 506, 681
internal consolidation, 160, 172
international markets, 252, 551, 602
international trade, 34, 262, 264, 271, 276–7,
    535, 550–1
Inuit, 61

invaders, 154, 172, 213, 489, 502, 639
    Spanish, 111, 638, 649, 662
invasions, 71, 73, 76, 165–7, 373, 375, 572, 575
    Mongol, 18, 166, 180, 221, 335, 376, 528
    Muslim, 72, 81–2
    nomadic, 365, 368, 377
inventions, 53, 62, 87, 267, 310, 317–19, 322,
    341, 471
investment, 90, 122, 160, 253, 282, 315, 323–4,
    336, 476, 527
investors, 265, 301, 550
Ioannina, 273, 581
Iodasaph, 22
Ionian Sea, 274, 579
Iran, 371, 373–4, 378–80, 391–2, 399–401, 491,
    493, 543–4
    see also Persia.
    bureaucracy, 369, 374
    Mongol, 380, 443, 543
    religions, 208, 225
Iranians, 271, 344, 402, 411, 488, 544
Iraq, 246, 248, 263–4, 393, 396–401, 411, 426–7,
    534–5
Ireland, 95, 349, 416, 424
iron, 109, 111, 154, 162, 275, 282, 314, 518, 524–5
    coins, 524
    nails, 250, 675
    technology, 591, 595
    tools, 34, 595
irrigation, 47–8, 97, 111, 315, 621
    canals, 641
    cultures, 50, 67
    networks, 65, 376
    systems, 46–51, 58, 60, 680
Islam, 71–2, 134–6, 140–1, 389–95, 401–6, 430–1,
    436–8, 545–7, 670–1
    central Islamic lands, 298, 346, 403
    and educational institutions, 131–5
        Africa, 135–7
    expansion, 215, 218, 385, 484–7, 504, 508–9,
        671
    madrasas, 131–4, 136, 141, 217, 350, 408, 678,
        680
    Sunni, 133, 374, 405
Islamic civilization, 32, 83, 133–4, 215, 217, 227,
    484, 506–7, 671
    African interior, 394–5
    Atlantic, 395–6
    centrality, 385–412
    components, 405–12
    culture, 408–11
    far north, 389–93
    Indian Ocean, 393–4

institutions, 405–8
origins, 411–12
regions around 1500
    Arabian homeland, 403–4
    former Byzantine provinces,
        400–1
    former Persian Empire, 398–400
    old lands, 396
    second wave of conquests, 401–3
    state formation and empire building, 504–8
    Turks, 391–3
Islamic conquests, 71, 89, 101, 122, 158, 671,
    673, 676, 678, 681
Islamic courts, 179, 194, 201, 679
Islamic heartland, 30, 236–8, 241, 246, 252–3,
    372, 507
Islamic law, 106, 132, 298, 405, 407, 430, 554,
    602; *see also* shari‘a law
Islamic world, *see* Islamic civilization.
Islamization, 27, 133, 391, 393, 547–9, 671, 676
Italian cities, 244, 332, 574, 578, 583
Italian city-states, 322, 552, 674
Italian fleets, 160, 268–9
Italians, 262, 266, 271–3, 275–6, 279, 284, 396,
    497
Italy, 7, 77, 126–8, 258–9, 273, 277–9, 545,
    562–4, 568, 572
    northern, 159, 223, 497
    southern, 160, 347, 567, 572
itinerant traders, 476, 672
ivory, 109, 195, 245, 348, 416, 572, 596

Jacobite Church, *see* Syriac Orthodox
    Church.
Jacques Coeur, 261
al-Jahiz, 147
Jains, 73, 288
Jam, 540–1
Jamāl al-Dīn, 4
James of Venice, 347
Japan, 2–3, 29, 63, 100, 179, 454–5, 458–61, 473,
    516–19, 672
    Confucianism and educational
        institutions, 120–1
    court, 180, 183, 193, 519
    Heian, 120, 164, 180, 221, 330, 448, 473
    Kamakura period, 121, 125, 221, 473
    Kyoto, 180, 189, 221, 473, 519
    Tokugawa regime, 222, 485
Jaroslav, Prince of Rus', 261
Java, 167, 240–1, 306, 393–4, 410, 465, 468, 476
    see also Indonesia.
    central, 241, 465

eastern, 241
west, 305
al-Jazari, 326
jealousy, 84, 88, 102, 599
Jenne, 109, 136, 588–9, 593, 596, 598, 600,
    602–3, 607
Jerusalem, 7, 130, 155, 160, 162, 391, 418, 421,
    432, 442–3
    Kingdom of, 12, 17, 162, 442
Jesuits, 344, 355
Jesus, 356, 417, 419–20, 422–4, 427–8, 436, 560,
    618, 620
    sutras, 438
jewelry, 22, 85, 186, 597
Jewish communities, 78, 130, 237, 301, 304,
    417, 428, 430
Jewish law, 130, 304
Jewish merchants, 27, 237, 263, 276, 301
Jewish scholars, 27, 347
Jewish women, 78, 89, 131
Jews, 13–14, 87, 130–1, 141, 263–4, 344, 346,
    351–2, 429–30, 433–4
    Baghdad, 237
    Radhanite, 237, 263, 276
jihad, 571
Jiménez de Rada, Rodrigo, 12
Jin, 331, 528
Joan-Joan, 366
Joannes of Dalyatha, 434–5
Joannes of Phanijoit, 431
John IV Lascaris, 580
John V Palaiologos, 581
John VI Kantakouzenos, 581–2
joint family ownership, 90
Josaphat, 22
Joseph, husband of Mary, 424
Joseph b. David Lebdi, 301
Joseph Ibn ‘Awkal, 263
Judaism, 28, 141, 243, 369, 389, 404, 433, 437,
    491, 665
    and educational institutions, 130–1
Junagarh, 297
Jurchen, 65, 166–7, 324, 370–1, 380
Jurchen Jin, 317, 324, 528
jurisprudence, 132, 430, 535
justice, 28, 94, 99, 108–9, 156, 186, 191, 407,
    493, 679
Justinian, Byzantine emperor, 82, 126,
    154, 200, 345, 427, 484, 513,
    560

Kaifeng, 166, 181, 324, 331, 524, 528, 554
kallanka, 656, 659

Kalyan, 288
Kamakura period, 121, 125, 221, 473
Kamalaśīla, 466
Kamalaśrī, 13
Kanheri, 290
Kaniaga, 606
kapikulu, 171
Karimis, 238, 264
Kashmir, 13, 348, 549
   women, 73
Kedah, 458
keshig, 538–9, 541
khagans, 146, 152, 569–70
khanates, 243, 270, 426, 534, 540–3, 547, 551,
      554
   Chaghadaid, 535, 548
   Mongol, 267, 547–8, 551
khanqah, 133–4
khans, 74, 277, 365, 538–40, 550
khaqanates, 516, 537
   Khazar, 365, 368–9, 399
   Turkic, 365–6
   Uighur, 367
khatīb, 299
Khazar khaqanate/state, 365, 368–9, 399
Khazars, 12, 243, 263, 365, 367–9, 389, 399, 437,
      486, 491
khipus, 16, 140, 640, 655–8
Khitan Liao, 166, 317, 532
Khitans, 166, 367, 370–1, 380, 471, 523, 542, 554
Khosro I Anushirwan, of Persia, 154–5, 344–5
Khotan, 452, 457
Khubilai Khan, *see* Qubilai.
Khurasan, 132, 277, 373, 375
Khwarazm, 369, 376, 378
Kiev, 508, 554, 578
Killke, 642
Kimeks, 369
kinetic energy, 161, 173, 314
King of Kings, 399, 408
Kingui, 606
kinship, 70, 97, 112, 334, 668
   groups, 137, 647–8, 650–1, 654, 662
   rules of, 97, 112
   ties, 70, 183, 437
knights, 161, 224, 363, 579
knowledge, 15, 116–18, 129–30, 135, 141–2,
      319–21, 324–8, 351–4, 356, 680–1
   astronomical, 438, 680
   cultures, 328, 336
   flows, 311, 378
   geographical, 32, 476
   religious, 28, 117, 134, 140–1, 678

scientific, 31, 342, 344, 351, 432, 680
technological, 312, 315, 337, 672, 680
transmission of, 26, 28, 117, 134, 329, 354
Kocho, 457
Koguryŏ, 459–60, 517–18
kola nuts, 595–6
kommerkion, 262, 274
Komnenoi, 509, 572, 575–80
Koran, *see* Quran.
Korea, 2, 120, 455, 459–60, 470, 472, 516–18,
      531–2, 677
   Confucianism and educational
      institutions, 119–20
Korean monks, 464, 472, 518
Korean Peninsula, 118–19, 467, 516–18, 677
Koryŏ, 120, 313, 472, 524
Kucha, 452, 457
Kumbi, 593
Kuṣāṇas, 451–2
Kutch, 288, 294, 297
Kwŏn Kūn, 2, 5
Kyoto, 180, 189, 221, 473, 519
Kyrgyzstan, 548, 554

labor, 66, 71, 77, 80, 265, 268–9, 313, 316, 332,
      656–7
   division of, 148, 159
   services, 108, 111–12, 514, 522, 531–2, 641
   ladies-in-waiting, 183–4, 193
Lagny, 272
Lake Pátzcuaro, 50
Lake Titicaca, 638, 640, 645, 653, 657–8, 660
land grants, 106, 157, 180, 303
land revenues, 262, 519
land routes, 25, 277, 463, 574, 674
landed elites, 224, 379
landlords, 105–6, 108
landowners, 101, 105, 271, 568, 670
   private, 121, 521, 568, 669
languages, 10, 345–7, 399, 401, 409, 411–12, 441,
      633, 655
   vernacular, *see* vernaculars.
Languedoc, 281–2
Lascaris dynasty, 580
La Tana, 273, 276–7, 281
Late Middle Ages, 61, 67, 78, 322–3
Late Postclassic period, 617–18, 621–2,
      624–6, 628
lateen sails, 268, 270–1
Latin Christendom, 26, 162, 214–15
Latin merchants, 273, 574, 582
Latins, 8, 11–12, 22, 126–8, 344, 347, 351–2, 424,
      441, 579–80

law, 77, 81, 128–30, 132, 136, 138, 264–5, 407–9, 419
  Buddhist, 549
  canon, 77, 128
  codes, 28, 83, 519
  Eurasia, 104–6
  Islamic, 106, 132, 298, 405, 407, 430, 554, 602
  Jewish, 130, 304
  natural, 46, 322
  religious, 71, 86, 88, 130, 676
  Roman, 82–3, 158, 493
  shari'a, 71, 89–90, 676, 683
leaders, 108, 152, 298, 301, 545–6, 567, 570, 575–6
  military, 138, 516, 525
  religious, 156, 331
  spiritual, 546
leadership, 266, 373, 435, 530, 547, 566, 579, 602
  political, 504, 530
learning, transmission of, 116, 135, 141–2, 678
Lebdi, Joseph, 301
Lebdi family, 301, 303
Lechfeld, 368
legacies, cultural, 24, 29, 225, 499, 537, 681
legal partnerships, 90
legends, 10, 22, 342, 344, 422–4, 440, 465, 593–4
legitimacy, 151, 228, 492, 495, 507, 519, 535, 537, 547, 580
legitimation, 102
Leipzig, 273
Lekhapaddhati, 303, 305
lenders, 259, 265
lenses, 85, 667
Leo III, Byzantine emperor, 157, 159, 569
Leo VI, Byzantine emperor, 262
lesbians, 88
levirate marriages, 74, 545, 677
Li Yuan, 516
Liang China, 460
Liao, 166, 331, 370, 380, 440, 471, 491, 523–4
libraries, 136, 343, 347
  monastic, 125–6
  private, 136
Libya, 2, 136
licenses, 129, 141, 276, 421
life-estates, 154
lifestyles, 149, 252, 385, 424
light cavalry, 154, 161
Lille, 262, 272
Lima, 644, 650
linen, 238, 282
linguistic practices, 215, 224

linguists, 310, 611, 620, 633, 640
literacy, 72, 75, 77–8, 91, 98, 100, 116, 121, 131, 633
  basic, 124, 126
literary traditions, 32, 199, 411, 519
literati, 213, 220, 227, 312
  elite, 119, 220
literature, 59, 86, 132, 195–6, 393, 399–400, 543, 672
  Arabic erotic, 88
  Buddhist, 450, 454
  classical, 45, 194
litters, 651, 654, 656
Little Ice Age, 58, 61, 249
liturgy, 124, 418–19, 427–9
Liu Ji, 75, 322
livestock, 146, 160, 272, 282, 360, 595
loans, 249, 259, 264, 471, 528, 632
local authorities, 254, 500, 669
local communities, 102, 105, 215, 297, 505, 669
local conditions, 35, 545, 667–8, 676, 681
local deities, 661–3
local elites, 34, 106, 499, 505, 559, 562, 567, 673, 679
local hierarchies, 98, 107, 669
local lords, 25, 98, 105, 226, 658
local rulers, 169–70, 303, 475, 502, 606
local societies, 531, 674, 681
  Eurasia, 106–7
local trading communities, 287, 290–9, 451
local traditions, 410, 430, 444, 671, 678–9
localization, 454, 668
logistics, 29, 145, 166, 528, 530
Lombards, 153, 158, 259, 281
Lombardy, 282
London, 261–2, 266, 274, 277, 279
long-distance trade, 233, 239, 242–3, 245–6, 249–50, 252–3, 670–1
long-term sustainability, 589, 607
longbows, 173–4, 315
longevity, 34, 546
looting, 169, 361, 370
lords, 185, 191–2, 198, 644–5, 647, 653, 655, 657–8
  local, 25, 98, 105, 226, 658
  regional, 654, 656, 661–2
  territorial, 66
Lorenzo the Magnificent, 260
Louis IV d'Outremer, 12
love, 44–5, 88, 190, 192–3, 198, 422, 434
lower Cuzco, 642, 648–9
loyalty, 163–4, 185, 538, 543, 566, 581

Lübeck, 261, 267, 277, 284
Lucca, 260, 282
Luhmann, Niklas, 57
Luoyang, 453, 456, 514–16, 524
Lupaqa, 658
An Lushan Rebellion, 166, 520–2, 525
lust, 89, 431
luxury commodities/goods, 251, 281, 287,
    550–1, 597, 602, 670, 673, 679–80
Lyon, 273, 282, 418

Maca Uisa, 661
Macedonian dynasty, 213, 270, 576, 578
Machin, 13, 348
machines, 31, 311, 314, 319, 322, 326
McNeill, John R., 67
McNeill, John R. and William H., 46
Madhyamikā, 466
Madmun b. Hasan b. Bundār, 301, 303
madrasas, 131–6, 141, 217, 350, 408, 678, 680
Maghreb, 263, 267, 276–9, 590, 594, 596–7,
    600, 602, 606
Magyars, 159, 224, 368
Mahāyāna Buddhism, 122, 125, 452, 672
Mahdiya, 160, 263, 276, 301
Maitrakas, 295–6
maize, 46, 641, 647
maize wine, 647
Malabar Coast, 238–9, 254, 279, 293, 302, 418,
    429, 437, 674
malaria, 49–50
Malay Peninsula, 240, 305, 393, 458, 486
Malaya, 335, 429, 675
Malays, 250, 526, 675
male courtiers, 184, 189
male prostitutes, 87
male relatives, 24, 190
male slaves, 81
Mali, 109–10, 135–6, 395, 586, 588, 592–3,
    597–607
    Empire, 34, 586, 590, 597–602, 604, 606–7
Malindi, 4, 135
Mallorca, 260, 269, 276
Malukus, 241
Mama Ocllo, 651
Mamacatequil, 660
Mamluks, 133, 135, 169, 171, 225, 249, 268, 363,
    545
    warfare, 162–6
Manchuria, 367, 378, 488, 514, 517, 523, 528,
    535, 540, 551
Manco Capac, 642, 646–7, 649–50
Mande, 588, 590, 598–9, 606

chiefdoms, 597–9, 606
Manding, 586–7, 596
Mangalore, 301–4
manhood, 88, 165
Manichaeism, 208, 219, 225, 392, 401, 491, 546
Manigramam, 305
Mañjuśrī cult, 465, 472
manpower, 29, 145, 157, 237, 538
Mansa Musa, 110, 136, 600–2, 604
    Mansa Sulayman, 600–2
al-Mansur, Caliph, 348, 433
Manuel I Komnenos, 347, 574, 578
manufactured goods, 242, 253
manumission, 81, 83, 304
Manzikert, 374, 435, 576
mapmakers, 5–8, 10
mappa mundi, 14
maps, 2–10, 14, 387, 447, 543–4, 612, 656
    Chinese, 2–4
    circular, 5, 8
    imported, 2, 10
    world, 1–2, 5–10, 14, 680
Marco Polo, 8, 15, 84, 97, 443, 543, 548, 552,
    555
maritime communities, 30, 287–306
maritime networks, 297, 299, 460, 474, 476,
    671
maritime routes, 30, 247, 250, 274, 277, 452,
    455, 551–2, 674–5
maritime technology, 250, 675
maritime trade, 59, 270, 287–8, 290, 295, 548
markers, sacred, 642, 645
market economy, 530–1
market inspectors, 300, 303
marketplaces, 271, 283, 290, 298, 395, 621, 632
markets, 82, 264, 266, 271–4, 471, 597, 632–3,
    682–3
    commercial, 264–5, 267
    expanding, 244, 525
    international, 252, 551, 602
    rural, 271–2
    urban, 271–2
Marks, Robert B., 67
marriage, 72–4, 76–7, 87, 89, 91, 196–7, 304,
    436
    alliances, 35, 147, 621, 643
    contracts, 71, 676
    deeply embedded patterns of, 70, 668
    levirate, 74, 545, 677
    same sex, 87
Marriage at Cana, 436
marriage gifts, 71, 90, 676–7
Marseille, 2, 7, 261, 269, 276–7

Martin of Troppau, 13
martyrs, 418, 422, 431, 571
 Coptic, 431
Mary, Virgin, 416, 422–4, 435–6, 444
masts, 251, 268, 271
al-Mas'ūdī, 11, 292
material culture, 329–30, 545, 624
material resources, 362, 542
mathematics, 16, 128, 132, 138, 322, 346
matrilocality, 70, 668
mats, 330, 595
Mauritania, 402, 404, 411, 589, 593, 606
Maveraunnahr, 369
Maximus the Confessor, 420, 435
Maya, 16, 50, 60, 85, 137, 174, 610, 622–4, 633
 cities, 137, 618, 682
 Classic, 611, 613–14, 618, 624, 633, 682
 collapse, 60
 culture, 16, 60
 highlands, 623–4
 lowlands, 614–15, 622–3, 626
Mayapan, 623–4
Mecca, 134, 136, 156, 273, 298, 300, 404, 406,
 599–600
mediation, 328, 424, 432, 436–7
 trade, 361
medicine, 122, 125, 128–9, 132, 342, 355, 543,
 679–80
Medicis, 260, 266
Medieval Climate Optimum, 58, 61, 334, 336
Medieval Europe, 45, 58, 76–7, 94, 96, 99, 109,
 125–6, 314–15
Medina, 156, 298, 404, 408, 432, 564
Mediterranean, 5–7, 59, 247, 257, 269–70, 276,
 279–84, 427, 552, 572
 eastern, 21, 24, 30, 58, 133, 160, 257, 273, 349,
 385
 western, 259, 269
Mediterranean trade networks, 257–84
Melitene, 571, 575
Meloria, 259
Mema, 599, 606
memorization, 132, 134, 324, 395
memory, 102, 214, 399–400, 402, 453, 599,
 647
merchandise, 252, 254, 263–5, 268, 270, 275,
 277, 300, 328
 heavy, 268, 271
merchant associations, 30, 261, 305–6
merchant class, 238, 245, 252–3, 259
 professional, 30, 233, 674
merchant communities, 438, 450, 476
merchant guilds, 216, 306, 451

merchants, 30–1, 237–8, 243–4, 258, 260–5,
 290, 295–6, 299–301, 551
 Byzantine, 572, 574
 Egyptian, 601–2
 English, 275, 277
 foreign, 237, 262, 272, 275, 303, 306
 Frisian, 258, 272, 276
 German, 261
 itinerant, 476, 672
 Jewish, 27, 237, 263, 276, 301
 Latin, 273, 574, 582
 Muslim, 109, 135, 237, 262, 266–7, 297, 393,
 550
 Saxon, 258, 276
 and their associations, 258–64
 wealthy, 276, 431
Merchants Venturers, 262, 283
Merinids, 259
Mesoamerica, 23, 25, 34, 137, 331, 487, 681–2
 ancient, 610–11, 623, 631, 633
 Classic, 614–16
 Postclassic, 25, 34, 682
 regional trajectories, 616–22
 state formation, 610–35
 cities and urbanization, 630–2
 data and methods, 612
 demographic and agricultural
 growth, 626–7
 growth of commercial networks, 632
 migrations, 627
 polity growth and decline, 628
 processes and connections, 626
 scholarly approaches, 611–12
 writing systems and literacy, 633–4
 and world history, 634–5
 Yucatan, 622–3
Mesopotamia, 48, 154, 218, 281, 372, 398, 432,
 564–5
 Christianity, 418
Messines, 272
metal, currency, 30, 264
metallurgy, 23, 518, 642
metals, 244, 261, 268, 275, 283, 287, 320, 405,
 468, 590
 precious, 239, 249, 267, 550, 598
metaphysics, 339, 350
Mexicanization, 624, 634
Mexico, 23, 50, 614–16, 623–4
 Basin of, 611, 616–17, 621–2, 625, 631
 central, 612, 615–18, 620–1, 624, 626–32
 City, 615–16
 Gulf of, 623, 625, 634
 west, 23, 25, 623, 625–6, 682

Michael VII Doukas, 576, 578
Michael VIII Palaiologos, 259, 580
Middle Ages, 43–4, 52–3, 56, 58, 66–8, 95,
    279–81, 310–11
  Early, 53, 258–9, 276, 281, 283
  High, 53, 57, 210, 257, 281, 315, 334
  Late, 61, 67, 78, 322–3
Middle East, 98, 363, 369, 372, 386, 407, 411,
    598, 600, 602
Middle Millennium, 31–4, 55–9, 209–10,
    309–10, 667–9, 671–6, 681–4
  political landmarks defining, 483–7
  for today's historians, 15–17
Middle Niger, 136, 588, 592, 605
  Bend, 586
  Delta, 588–9, 593, 599, 603, 606
Middle Persian, 191, 409
Middle Volga, 243, 367, 377, 673
middlemen, 236, 239, 244, 596
migrations, 359–60, 362, 364–5, 371, 373, 377–9,
    624, 627–8, 671
  Aztlan, 627
  nomadic, 31, 152, 359–60, 362, 364–5, 372,
    375–6, 381, 672–3
  Postclassic Mesoamerica, 627–8
Milan, 261, 266, 282, 418
military aristocracy, 370, 575
military classes, 149, 158, 199
military commanders, *see* commanders.
military elites, 151, 221, 331, 379, 506
military leaders, 138, 516, 525
military service, 74, 153, 159, 164, 185, 366, 370,
    374, 438, 569
military skills, 363, 426
military training, 138, 149, 362
milk, 73, 146
mills, 133, 313–14
  oil, 296
  paper, 26
mines, 150, 244–5, 267, 331
Ming, 119, 121, 168, 220, 235–6, 249–50, 315,
    317, 499, 532
  Emperor, 453
mining, 62, 65, 68, 150, 318, 525, 658
  regions, 269, 315, 322
mints, 249, 303, 396, 590
missionaries, 429, 437, 440, 477, 547, 560
mita, 658, 663
mitayoc, 658
Mixtecs, 625, 633
mobile secretariats, 539, 541, 673
mobility, 51, 154, 156, 348, 589
  social, 101, 107, 118

mobilization, 33, 493, 497–8, 542–3, 554
modernity, 53, 222, 485
  industrialized, 336
modernization, 665–7
Modon, 274, 279
Mogadishu, 4, 135
Moheyan, 466
Mohina, 640
Mon, 125, 457
monasteries, 7, 103, 124–6, 138, 140, 434, 454,
    456, 468–9, 515
  Buddhist, 140, 453, 466, 471
  Christian, 77, 126, 140
  Vikramaśīla, 467–9
monastic communities, 122, 450, 452, 455, 475,
    504
monastic institutions, 450, 452, 464, 467–70,
    473, 475–6
  Buddhist, 104, 118, 121–3, 125–6, 140, 152,
    306, 470, 472
monastic libraries, 125–6
monastic life, 124, 421
monastic orders, 129, 215, 223–4
monastic schools, 117, 122–3, 126, 131
Monemvasia, 262, 581
monetary policies, 523–4, 554
monetization, 33, 245, 518, 527
money, 23, 43, 83, 239, 244, 249, 567, 569, 571,
    632
moneychangers, 266, 574
Möngke, 20, 441, 539, 541
Mongol China, 2, 11, 378, 393, 440, 548
Mongol conquests, 9, 24, 30, 96, 227, 391, 393,
    673, 677, 683
Mongol empire, 11, 13, 225, 246–7, 491–2, 548,
    672, 674
  building of, 537–41
  cross-cultural exchange, 541–5
  economic exchange, 550–3
  and inter-civilizational exchange, 534–55
  legacy of Mongol statecraft, 553–4
  religious exchange, 546–50
Mongol fleets, 167
Mongol invasions, 18, 166, 180, 221, 335, 376,
    528
Mongol Iran, 380, 443, 543
Mongol khanates, 267, 547–8, 551
Mongol princes, 167, 548, 551
Mongol statecraft, 553
Mongol Yuan, *see* Yuan.
Mongolia, 367, 372, 375, 378, 469, 534, 537, 551
  Inner, 370
  Outer, 370

Mongolian silk, 274, 277
Mongols, 13–14, 20–1, 165–7, 246–7, 371–2,
    491–2, 535–51, 553–5*see also* Mongol
    empire.
  armies, 530, 547
  China, 2, 11, 166–8, 378, 393, 440, 548
  empire building, 537–41
  warfare, 162–6
  with China, 166–70
monks, 124–5, 200, 424–6, 447, 460, 463–6,
    470, 472–4
  Buddhist, 447, 453–4, 457, 467, 469, 471,
    474, 672
  Chinese, 454, 462–4, 472
  Korean, 464, 472, 518
Monophysites, 560, 563
monopolies, 238, 252, 261–2, 275, 281, 527, 572
monotheism, 404, 411
Monte Alban, 616, 625, 682
Montpellier, 261, 276
monumental architecture, 588, 620
monuments, 111, 456, 622
  Buddhist, 471, 515
  Islamic, 297
Moore, R. I., 216
Moraes Farias, Paulo, 603–5
morality, 328, 666
  Confucian, 76
Morea, 581, 583
Morocco, 5, 26, 348, 389, 395, 402, 601–2, 606
  Sultan of, 601–2
mosaics, 195, 416, 444, 572
Moscow, 426, 554
  princes, 365
Moses, 130
Moses of Bergamo, 347
mosques, 133, 135–6, 294, 299, 408, 432, 601
  local, 299
Mosul, 160, 346
mothers, 72, 84, 189, 422–4, 428, 662, 668
  see also parents
mounted postal courier system, 540, 673
Mozarabs, 347
mudae, 269–70, 279
Mughals, 215, 229, 484–5
Muhammad ibn al-Muzallik, 264
Muhammad (Prophet), 11, 13, 81–2, 404–6,
    409–10, 429–30, 433, 548–9
multilingual dictionaries, 543
multiple modernities, 666–7
Mulūk, 604–5
mural paintings, 618, 625
Murasaki Shikibu, 75

Muscovy, 535, 553
music, 81, 129, 138, 182, 193–4, 196, 340, 545,
    672
musicians, 197, 290, 345, 593, 602
Muslim conquests, *see* Islamic conquests.
Muslim faith, *see* Islam.
Muslim invasions, 72, 81–2
Muslim merchants, 135, 262, 266–7, 297, 393,
    550
Muslim rule, 392, 396, 424, 681
Muslim rulers, 32, 136, 331, 392, 406, 408, 432,
    563, 681
Muslim scholars, 4, 134, 377
Muslim societies, 72, 406–10
Muslim Spain, 26, 263, 346, 394, 396, 403, 676
Muslim states, 171, 395–6, 404, 561
Muslim traders, 109, 237
Muslim world, 136–7, 262–3, 265, 282–3, 404,
    406, 543–5, 551–4
Muslims, 78–9, 141, 275, 292–3, 390–5, 409–10,
    431–2, 440–1, 548
Myanmar, 452, 457, 468, 474–6
mystics, 44, 79, 409
  women, 79
myth of origin, Inca, 642, 645, 650

Nagapattinam, 306
Nāgārjunakoṇḍa, 451, 457
Nahray b. Nissim, 263
Nahrwāra, 301
Nahuatl, 620
Naiman, 424, 437
Nalanda, 122, 125, 331, 454, 457, 462–4, 467,
    678
Naples, 276, 283, 567, 580
Nara, 180, 519
Narasimhavarman II, 306
Narbonne, 261
narrative traditions, 35, 643
narratives, 309, 417, 424, 587, 643, 645
  epic, 587
  historical, 644
  religious, 424
Nasir al-Din, 348
Native Americans, 174
natural environment, 361, 648
natural laws, 46, 322
natural pastures, 359, 363
natural resources, 56, 62–4, 237, 252, 360, 606
natural science, 128, 339, 344–5, 350, 353
Nava Vihara, 345
navigable waterways, 245, 522
navigation, 250, 268–71, 279, 675

navigation, (cont.)
  coastal, 268, 270, 277
Nawbahar, 345
Needham, Joseph, 340
needles, 319, 597, 625
negotiation, 35, 150, 652, 659
Negroponte, 274, 279
neighbors, 101, 106, 159, 161, 166, 169–70, 336,
  519, 554
Neo-Confucianism, 120–1, 214, 220, 486, 500,
  522, 530–2
neolocality, 70, 77, 668
Nestorian Christianity, 194, 208, 225, 227,
  426–8, 437–8, 441, 444
Netherlands, 47, 273, 281, 494, 497
networks, 236–7, 291, 293, 448, 451, 454, 476–7,
  560–1
  Buddhist, 462, 473, 672
  commercial, 34, 257, 471, 596, 632
  of exchange, 465, 654
  global, 341, 552
  irrigation, 65, 376
  maritime, 297, 299, 460, 474, 476, 671
  trade, *see* trade networks.
New Deal, 45, 51
Niane, D.T., 598
Niger, 135, 245, 586, 598, 600, 602, 606
  Bend, 589, 596, 602–4, 607
  Middle, *see* Middle Niger.
  Upper, 586, 597–8, 607
Nile, 48, 403, 564
  Valley, 394, 401
Nineveh, 155, 346, 434
nobility/nobles, 101, 112, 137–8, 196, 201, 211,
  218, 621, 651–2
noble savage, 55
nomadic conquests, 31, 52, 376, 379, 381, 673
  see also pastoral nomadism,
  migrations and conquests
nomadic invasions, 365, 368, 377
nomadic migrations, 31, 152, 359–60, 362,
  364–5, 372, 375–6, 381, 672–3
nomadic realms, 46, 50–2
nomadic rulers, 31, 377, 380–1, 544
nomadic societies, 29–30, 145, 362–3, 489,
  669–70, 673
nomadic statehood, 364, 366
nomadic states, 361, 366, 369, 375, 378, 470,
  489, 673
nomadic tribes, 366, 437, 471, 476
nomadic warriors, 363, 564
nomadism, 50–2, 57, 373, 375, 488–9
  pastoral, *see* pastoral nomadism.

nomads, 50–2, 146, 148–9, 360–7, 369–81,
  437–8, 488
  Berber, 394, 596
  Oghuz, 369, 373
  steppe, 146, 161, 437, 516–17, 530
  Turkic, 367–9, 371, 373–4, 377
non-Deistic religions, 208, 339
non-state societies, 611–12
Nordic route, 277–9
Norfolk, 281
Normandy, 161, 283
North Africa, 19, 51, 160, 245, 377–8,
  402–3, 416–17, 589–90, 597–8,
  600–2
North Caucasus, 368
North China, 166–8, 370–1, 437–8, 455, 488–9,
  491, 522–3
North Sea, 243, 257, 261, 276
Northampton, 272
northern Europe, 17, 53, 95, 128, 215, 257, 261,
  279, 284, 310
northern India, 72–3, 165, 169, 238–9, 447, 451,
  462, 468–9, 543, 545
Northern Song, 65
Northern Wei, 152, 455, 513–16, 521, 530
  political legacy, 513–14
Northern Zhou, 524
Northwest India, 82
Notaras, 262, 582
notaries, 188, 265
Novara, 259
Novgorod, 16, 261, 274, 277, 279, 416
  Peterhof, 261, 274
Nubia, 135, 267, 394, 427
nuns, 73, 76–7, 79, 122, 124–5, 128, 447, 470
Nuremberg, 261, 284

oars, 268, 270
oases, 244, 403–4, 477, 488
oasis states, 365, 451, 457, 673
oaths, 103, 199
Oaxaca, 610–11, 616, 623, 625
Odantapurī, 468
offerings, 197, 644, 646–8, 661
officials, 101, 104, 106, 118–19, 290, 527, 531,
  540, 577
  high, 133, 187, 194, 200, 527, 538
  literati, 380, 520
Oghuz, 369, 373, 391–2, 399
Ögödei, 379, 440, 539–40
oil, 268, 281, 298, 330, 404, 578
  mills, 296
Öljeitü, Īl-Khān, 14

Oman, 294, 404
openness, 227, 322, 389
oracles, 646, 660–3
oral contracts, 198
oral traditions, 34, 137, 592, 598–9, 603
  importance for West African history,
    587–8
oral transmission, 31, 306
Oriental Despotism, 96, 99, 105
Orthodox Christianity, 427, 534, 544
ortoqs, 551–2
Ostrogoths, 427, 484
Ostrom, E., 47, 64
Otto I, 368, 441
Ottomans, 49, 171–2, 229, 271, 318, 484, 506–8,
    561, 580–3
  conquests, 262, 283, 392, 396
Outer Eurasia, 491
  state
    empire and religion, 493–4
Outer Mongolia, 370
overgrazing, 51
overland routes, 135, 235, 237, 247, 250, 452,
    525, 551–2, 674
overland trade, 247, 378, 381, 673–4
overlordships, 366, 510
owners, 83, 290, 293, 299, 541, 649
ownership, 77, 83, 160, 223, 269, 302, 568, 592
  joint family, 90
Oxford, 128–9

pacarinas, 650, 663
Pacaritambo, 642, 645
Pachacamac, 644, 648, 650, 660–3
Pachacuti, 644–53, 656, 660, 662
Pacific, 70, 237, 545, 670, 683
  coast, 25, 624–5, 638, 641, 651, 654, 682
pacification, 6, 224
pack animals, 245, 248
Paekche, 459–60, 517–18
Pagan, 125, 305, 474
pagan populations, 390–1
pageantry, 198, 602
painting, 194–5, 321, 330, 467, 545, 656
  wall, 196, 444
Pāla period, 468–9
Pāla Tantric art, 468
palaces, 180–1, 183, 186–8, 190, 197–9, 331, 618,
    620, 622, 631
Palaiologoi, 262, 561, 574, 580, 583
Palermo, 347, 349
Palestine, 51, 157, 415–16, 420, 432, 436, 563
pamphyloi, 268, 270

pan-Asianism, 477
panacas, 647, 662
Pannonia, 365–7
Paolino Veneto, 7
papacy, 224, 484, 495–6, 501, 510, 582
papal court, 179–80, 679
paper mills, 26
Parākramabāhu I, 474–5
paraphernalia, 454–5, 462, 474
  religious, 326, 447, 456, 465
parents, 80, 83, 86, 88 *see also* fathers;
    mothers.
  elderly, 90, 677
Pariacaca, 661
Paris, 7, 107, 128, 181, 266, 271–2
parish duties, 444
partners, 86, 88, 244, 263, 265, 301, 551
  trading, *see* trading partners.
partnerships, 30, 245, 297, 301, 303, 632
  legal, 90
passageways, 30, 233, 239, 250
pastoral nomadism, 241, 359–60, 364, 375
  migrations and conquests, 359–81
    causes, 360–3
    effects, 376–81
    Eurasian steppes
      semi-deserts and deserts, 363–72
    India, 375–6
    Near and Middle East and North Africa,
      372–5
    regional developments, 363–76
pastoralism, 52, 241, 362, 375, 378, 488
pasture farming, 48, 51
pastures, 52–4, 105, 360
  natural, 359, 363
  unutilized and unclaimed, 360, 673
paternal rights, 82–3, 89
patriarchate, 181, 197, 418, 560–1
patrilocality, 70, 668
patronage, 100, 102, 183, 329, 447, 451, 468,
    474, 567, 570
  aristocratic, 183, 195
patrons, 12, 72, 133, 138, 163, 192, 194, 353–4
pattana, 292
Pátzcuaro, Lake, 50
Pax Chazarica, 368
Pax Mongolica, 8, 247, 329, 348, 680, 683
peace, 88, 149–50, 152, 155, 247, 315, 551
Pearl River, 49
peasants, 49, 53, 62–3, 65–6, 100, 105, 108,
    565–6, 568, 575
  English, 108, 333
Pechenegs, 368–9

Pegolotti, Francesco Balducci, 267
Pelagonia, 580
Peloponnese, 273, 564, 569, 581
pepper, 239, 251, 262, 264, 301
perfumes, 574, 597
periodizations, 483, 485, 682, 684
peripheries, 157, 243, 310, 328, 387, 497, 501, 567, 592
Periplus Maris Erythraei, 291–2, 304
Perpignan, 260
persecution, 27, 78, 104, 130, 420, 427–8, 431, 470
Persia, 153–4, 157, 164, 166, 236, 246–7, 432, 560, 564 *see also* Iran.
   Empire, 396–400, 429, 437
   northern, 420
   Sasanian, 154, 484, 487
   warfare, 153–5
Persian Gulf, 24, 238, 250–1, 279, 293, 297, 428, 474, 551, 553
Persian statecraft, 505, 507
Persians, 12–13, 154, 292, 343, 346, 349, 352, 399–401, 438
Peru, 16, 638–9, 643, 650–1, 658, 663
Peruzzi, 259, 266
Peter, St., 418
Peterhof, 261, 274
petitions, 16, 188
Petrus Alfonsi, 342, 350
Philoponus, John, 345
philosophy, 120, 122, 208, 211, 339, 344–6, 348, 351–3, 409
   political, 117, 515
Phocaea, 259, 274
physical environment, 309, 334
physical stability, 29, 201
physicians, *see* doctors.
Piacenzans, 259
Picardy, 281–2
piepowders, 258
piety, 72, 134, 422
Piguerao, 660
Pikillacta, 640–1
pilgrimage sites, 288, 462, 464, 467, 472–3
pilgrimages, 134, 136, 288, 294, 435–6, 442, 462–4, 599–600, 602
pilgrims, 14, 17, 27, 31, 44, 126, 300, 306, 420, 426
pillaging, 149, 571
piracy, 169, 251, 268–9, 291, 331, 564
Pisa, 160, 260, 266, 269, 271, 274, 276, 283, 574
Pisans, 259, 274

plague, 62, 66, 91, 98, 248, 334, 379, 562, 565–6, 674
Planhol, Xavier de, 57
plants, 44, 316, 335–6, 667
   new, 316, 683
Plato, 126, 351, 353
ploughs, 45, 54, 109, 111, 311
   heavy, 53–4, 313, 315
plundering, 35, 51, 152, 159, 240, 243, 249, 550, 643
pluralism, 214, 222–3, 227, 497
   religious, 225, 499, 542
poetry, 15, 75, 87, 118, 193–5, 199, 215, 409, 412
poets, 77, 194–5, 351
   court, 193–4
Poitiers, 158, 418
Poland, 5, 162, 419
political alliances, 185, 190, 545
political authority, 190, 296, 455, 471, 474, 532
political elites, 151, 221, 226, 303, 361, 379, 389, 521, 666, 681
political fragmentation, 11, 101, 238, 495, 513, 524, 537, 670, 682
political hierarchies, 100, 108
political ideology, 525, 531, 553
political institutions, 151, 207, 215, 516, 519, 612
political leadership, 504, 530
political orders, 33, 142, 207–8, 217, 219–22, 224–8, 406, 516, 519
political organization, 60, 365, 592, 626
political philosophy, 117, 515
political power, 116, 118, 201, 222, 226, 235, 392, 403, 458, 466
   real, 182, 228
   vacuum, 670
political practices, 207–8, 220
political stability, 332, 670, 673
political unity, 101, 237, 442, 669
politics, 51, 104, 113, 119, 165, 200, 252, 260, 496, 504
poll taxes, 429, 432
Pollock, Sheldon, 218–19, 224, 435
Polo, Marco, 8, 15, 84, 97, 443, 543, 548, 552, 555
polygamy, 73, 88, 190
polygyny, 71, 76, 84, 676
Poma de Ayala, Guaman, 639, 657, 661
popes, 13, 56, 103, 129, 141, 189, 442–3, 560, 566 *see also* names of individual popes.
   rival, 180
popularity, 466, 471, 473, 475

population
  estimates, 19, 98, 181, 244, 248–9, 253,
    618–19, 626, 631
  growth, 53–4, 91, 522, 525, 617, 620–1, 624,
    626, 682
  and history, 18–20
  pressures, 66, 336
porcelain, 239, 251, 294, 312, 335, 522, 679
ports, 82, 259, 269, 276–7, 294, 452, 574
Portugal, 22, 174, 281, 498
Portuguese, 170, 254, 284, 328
post-Han China, 448
postal courier system, mounted, 540, 673
Postan, Michael M., 53
Postclassic International Style, 624, 633
Postclassic Mesoamerica, *see* Mesoamerica,
    Postclassic.
potters, 296, 305, 312, 656
pottery, 16, 293, 595–6; *see also* ceramics;
    porcelain
power, 151, 157–8, 179–80, 189–90, 199–201,
    490–1, 509–10, 575–8, 605–6,
    669–70
  balance of, 491, 509, 531, 570
  caliphal, 505–6
  central, 98, 179, 370, 374, 502, 566, 571, 580,
    669
  centres, 29, 98, 179, 218, 328, 404, 497, 503,
    669, 679
  coercive, 63, 211, 217, 229, 361, 631
  distribution of, 190, 683
  imperial, 180–1, 222, 487, 494, 508, 576
  of life, 80, 85
  military, 164, 516, 531
  political, *see* political power.
  social, 151, 314, 328, 496, 500
  state, 122, 247, 332, 509, 522, 546, 588, 630
  structures, 496, 506–7
Prato, 260, 265
prayers, 44, 132, 197, 199, 434–5, 440, 458
  Friday, 389–90, 405, 407–8
pre-Columbian America, 3, 35, 137, 638, 682
preachers, 200, 298, 426, 457, 547
precious metals, 239, 249, 267, 550, 598;
    see also gold; silver
prefectures, 95, 562, 565
Prester John, 440
prestige, 73, 132, 157, 250, 484, 519, 541, 551,
    561–2
prices, 81, 83, 170, 252, 264, 276, 564, 566, 580,
    583
priests, 31, 79, 88–9, 103, 124, 137–40, 418, 424,
    437–8, 441

primogeniture, 90, 189–90, 197, 224, 662
princes, 182–4, 186, 190, 192, 197, 199–200, 550,
    552
  Mongol, 167, 548, 551
princesses, 183–4, 545, 578, 677
printing, 75, 124, 313, 317
  woodblock, 14, 26, 124, 314
prisoner's dilemma, 63
prisoners of war, returning, 14, 680
private landowners, 121, 521, 568, 669
private libraries, 136
private trade, 235–6
privileges, 102, 127, 129, 153, 261, 322, 329,
    352–3, 542, 546
productivity, 217, 268, 316, 360, 525, 666
professional merchant class, 30, 233, 674
professional soldiers, 153, 569
professionals, 106, 182, 375, 542, 673
profits, 157, 168, 170–1, 174, 236, 246, 264, 290,
    551
pronoiai, 171, 577, 581
property, 74, 77, 84, 105, 112, 129, 146, 164,
    220, 298
  intellectual, 545
  landed, 90, 500
  personal, 72, 247
  private, 575, 621
  rights, 105, 112
prophecies, 417, 429, 505, 507
prophets, 54, 190, 237, 342–3, 389, 405, 434,
    504, 549
  see also Muhammad
prose, 16, 193–4
prostitutes, 87, 199
  male, 87
Protestant Christianity, 124
proto-global forces, 670–6
proto-globalization, 35, 665–84
proto-glocal forces, 676–81
proto-glocal tensions, 677–8
proto-glocalization, 35, 665, 668, 680
Provence, 281
Provins, 260, 272
Pseudo-Ptolemy, 353
Ptolemy, 5, 126, 343
  Almagest, 347, 349
  Geography, 5, 8
public spaces, 217, 221, 228, 406
public worship, 131, 133
publicity, 600, 602
punishments, 182, 184, 407, 433
Purcell, Nicholas, 59, 257, 276
Pure Land Buddhism, 470, 473

pururaucas, 645, 648
Puuc cities, 622, 628
pyramids, 653, 660
Pyrenees, 158–9
pythons, 593–4

qaghans, *see* khagans.
Qanun, 407–8
Qara Qorum, 537, 539, 551
Qarakhanids, 369–70, 377, 380, 673
Qarluks, 367
Qayrawan, 263
Qing, 221, 485, 510
Qipchaqs, 369, 554
Qu Geping, 66
quadrivium, 129, 339
Quanzhou, 235, 237, 305, 441, 526, 551
Qubilai, 13, 74, 84, 329, 372, 473, 475, 530, 532, 549–50
Quechua, 138, 655
queens, 187–8, 190, 197–8, 605
quipus, *see* khipus.
Quito, 650–1, 663
Quran, 71, 79, 132, 191, 298, 395, 400, 402, 430, 436
Quraysh, 405–6
Qus, 279, 299
Quseir al-Qadim, 299–300, 302

Rabban Sauma, 443–4
rabbis, 89, 130–1, 141
Rackham, Oliver, 63
Radhanite Jews, 237, 263, 276
rafts, 25, 291
Ragusa, 67, 269, 276
Ragusans, 270, 275
raiding, 147–9, 152, 163, 166, 245, 361–2, 369–70, 374, 564, 571
rainfall, 403–4, 594, 627
rainfed agriculture, 46, 48
   combined with animal husbandry, 52–5
rakkad, 263
ranks, 29, 73, 94, 97, 165, 183–4, 186, 299, 569, 572
Rapondi, Dino, 260
Rashid al-Din, 12–15, 22, 27, 348, 543, 680
Ravenna, 180, 418, 566
Ravensburg, 261, 266, 283
raw materials, 30, 245, 268, 282, 524, 684
rebellions, 11, 151, 157, 366, 521, 575–6, 578, 657, 661
rebels, 108, 154, 159, 167, 199, 237, 661

reconquests, 562, 569, 571, 575
recruitment, 29, 121, 145, 316, 335, 354, 362, 525, 542, 579
rectangular sails, 268, 271
Red Sea, 238, 251, 263, 271, 275, 279, 299–300, 302, 551, 574
reformers, 124, 432, 527
   agrarian, 52–3
   statist, 499
reforms, 31, 191, 220, 337, 473, 497, 527, 541, 565, 604
   Gregorian, 579
   social, 109, 531
refugees, 489, 542
regents, 72, 184
regional elites, 164, 641
regional integration, 35, 667, 682
regional lords, 654, 656, 661–2
regional specialization, 236, 523
regional states, 70, 406, 502, 524
   centralized, 33
regional trade networks, 24
relatives, 71, 259, 430, 527, 540
   male, 24, 190
relic cult, 450, 475
relics, 198, 442, 450, 456, 460, 471, 473–5, 560
   Buddhist, 455, 475
religions, 138–42, 355–6, 401–2, 421–2, 429–32, 504, 546, 549, 669–71
   Axial Age, 208, 211
   Buddhist, *see* Buddhism.
   Christian, *see* Christianity.
   Eurasia, 103–4
   Inca, 648, 660, 682
   Iranian, 208, 225
   Islam, *see* Islam.
   Judaism, *see* Judaism.
   Muslim, *see* Islam.
   new, 113, 132, 394, 400, 402, 433, 675
   non-deistic, 208, 339
   and science, 356
   state, 141, 416, 631, 682
   universal, 79, 501, 670
   and women, 79–80
   world, 32, 117, 140, 142, 207, 209–10, 386, 390–1, 546–7
religious affiliations, 30, 293, 303
religious authority, 138, 156, 504, 506
religious ceremonies, 137, 185, 198, 457
religious conversion, *see* conversion.
religious cultures, 33, 483, 496, 503
religious customs, 103, 669

religious duties, 132, 156
religious ecumenes, 24, 26, 207
religious elites, 207, 217, 221
religious exchange, Mongol Empire, 546–50
religious hierarchies, 34, 103, 562
religious institutions, 103, 299, 329, 519, 532,
  670, 683
religious knowledge, 28, 117, 134, 140–1, 678
religious law, 71, 86, 88, 130, 676
religious leaders, 156, 331
religious life, 130, 200, 421
religious narratives, 424
religious paraphernalia, 326, 447, 456, 465
religious–philosophical approach, 55–6
religious pluralism, 225, 499, 542
religious rituals, 47, 103, 422, 472–3
religious scholars, 395, 404, 548
religious specialists, 124, 646
religious traditions, 399, 407, 409, 547
religious unity, 560
rents, 33, 95, 98, 100, 105, 108, 129, 669
resettlements, 657–8
residential colleges, 122, 129
resilience, 46, 59, 61, 89, 500
resistance, 108, 156–7, 328, 370, 399–400, 402,
  566, 570, 581
resource extraction, 490, 550
resources, 159, 161, 163, 387, 490–1, 539, 550–1,
  641–2, 654
  educational, 122, 124, 126
  financial, 329, 563, 575, 580
  fiscal, 398, 565
  material, 362, 542
  natural, 56, 62–4, 237, 252, 360, 606
restorations, 6, 119, 500, 520, 524, 532, 539, 570,
  578
retail trade, 272
retainers, 182, 542, 647, 654
retinues, 287, 551
returning prisoners of war, 14, 680
revenues, 290, 295, 522, 524, 526, 528, 530,
  551–2, 577
  land, 262, 519
  tax, 47, 122, 157, 167, 570
revolts, *see* rebellions.
rhetoric, 63, 129, 320, 322, 332
Rhineland, 196, 258
Rhodes, 276, 279
rice, 46, 197, 241, 314, 329, 595
Richards, John F., 59
rihla, 134, 141
rites, 182, 196–7, 546

ritual items, 23, 32, 476
rituals, 100, 103, 196–8, 201, 319, 321, 422, 515,
  519
  Buddhist, 472–3
  court, 197, 395, 421
  religious, 47, 103, 422, 472–3
rival popes, 180
rivalry, 88, 104, 270, 468, 497, 501–2, 524, 594,
  651
roads, 27, 35, 235, 290, 443, 538, 540, 644,
  648–50
Roger II of Sicily, 5, 195
Roman armies, 154, 158
Roman Empire, 126, 242, 416, 418, 433, 483,
  487, 559–62
  see also Byzantium.
  Western, 152, 416
Roman law, 82–3, 158, 493
Roman traditions, 34, 180, 195, 562
Rome, 11, 15, 98, 153, 158, 180, 418–19, 560–3,
  572
Rouen, 277
round ships, 268, 270–1
routes, 237–8, 269, 271–3, 276–9, 451, 589–90,
  674
  maritime, 30, 247, 250, 274, 277, 452, 455,
    551–2, 674–5
  Nordic, 277–9
  overland, 135, 235, 237, 247, 250, 452, 525,
    551–2, 674
  spice, 274, 277, 279
royal clans, 182–3, 366
royal conversions, 547–9
royal courts, 182, 186, 188, 191, 195–6, 200, 551,
  602
rudders, 250, 271, 675
rugs, 545, 679
rulers, local, 169–70, 303, 475, 502, 606
ruling classes, 95, 221, 253, 370, 374, 379, 547
ruling elites, 378, 520, 545
ruling powers and technological
  innovations, 330–4
rural markets, 271–2
ruralization, 34, 561, 610, 618
Rus', 12, 224, 243, 369, 416, 419, 426, 440, 508
Russia, 22, 263, 276, 381, 469, 508, 554, 560
  river system, 236, 247, 674
Russian principalities, 281–2, 365, 371, 535

sacraments, 418–19, 422, 435
sacred landscapes, 33, 477
sacred markers, 642, 645

Sacred Rock, 645–6, 657, 660
Sacred Valley, 642–3, 654, 657
sacrifices, 111, 579, 594
Sacsayhuaman, 647
Safavids, 171, 229, 484
Sahara, 20, 135–6, 394–5, 590–1, 595–8, 600,
    602–4, 606
  southern, 244, 589, 596
  southwestern, 136, 607
  trans-Saharan trade, 34, 245, 250, 586,
    589–90, 595, 598, 600, 602, 607
  western, 136, 394, 595, 606
Sahel, 170, 394–5, 589–90, 593–4, 596
sailors, 31, 169, 269, 271, 292
sails, 268, 270
  lateen, 268, 270–1
  rectangular, 268, 271
St Augustine, 57, 417, 419
St Benedict, 126
St Demetrius, 273, 574
Saint-Ives, 272
St Peter, 418
St Thomas Aquinas, 129
St Thomas the Apostle, 418
St Vitale, 418
saints, 32, 77, 79, 197–8, 422
Saladin, 17, 133, 162, 275
salaries, 132, 408, 562, 570
salinization, soil, 48
salt, 268, 270, 273, 277, 281, 287, 291, 524–5, 595
salt, Bourgneuf, 277, 281
salt trade, 266, 590, 603
salvation, 44, 155, 420, 433, 571
Samaipata, 659
Samanids, 370
Samarkand, 14, 26, 52, 242–3, 246,
    248, 437
same sex relations, 87–8
Samguk sagi, 458
sandals, 595, 656–7
sangha, 124
Sanhaja, 590, 595–6, 602
Sanskrit, 125, 194, 215, 290, 292, 297–8, 345–6,
    452, 458, 465
Sanskrit-based cultural world, 218, 228
Sasanians, 154–5, 163, 207, 213, 416, 419, 427–8,
    484, 487
Saurashtra, 294–5
Saxon merchants, 258, 276
Sayf al-Dawla, 354, 571
scale models, 320, 323
Scandinavia, 89, 243, 276–7, 282
Scandinavians, 222, 243, 261, 276, 279

Scania, 277, 279, 281
Scarsella, 267
scholars, 126–7, 136, 194, 321–2, 347–9, 406–9,
    457–8, 619–20, 623
  Chinese, *see* literati.
  European, 126, 142, 320, 322, 436
  Jewish, 27, 347
  Muslim, 4, 134, 377
  religious, 395, 404, 548
scholasticism, 129, 350, 680
schools, 91, 116–17, 119–21, 132–3, 136–8, 225,
    428, 448
  cathedral, 126, 128–9, 131, 141, 350
  Confucian, 121–2, 140
  monastic, 117, 122–3, 126, 131
science, 195, 339, 341–3, 346, 348, 351, 353, 400,
    409, 419
  Arabic, 341, 353, 356
  diffusion from one source or independent
    discoveries, 339–42
  legends about diffusion, 342–4
  methods of transmitting, 348–51
  modern, 62, 340
  natural, 128, 339, 344–5, 350, 353
  politics of communicating, 351–3
  and religion, 356
  social, 210, 217, 228
  transformation of, 356
  transmission of, 31, 344, 355–6
  with whom should it be shared, 353–5
scientific knowledge, 31, 342, 351, 432, 680
  hubs, 344–8
scientists, 194, 343, 354, 544, 548
Scotland, 416
Scott, James C., 61
Scotto, Alberto, 259
scriptural exegesis, 124, 292
scriptures, 122, 124, 402, 409, 418, 438
sculptures, 109, 194, 323, 456, 458
sea routes, *see* maritime routes.
sea trade, *see* maritime trade.
seafaring communities, 30, 291, 306
seasons, 44, 193, 196, 269, 407, 552
seaworthiness, 250–1, 675
secretariats, 182, 515, 520, 522, 539
  mobile, 539, 541, 673
security, 246, 272, 275, 277, 378, 424, 435, 550
sedentary countries, 360, 362–3, 369, 371, 376,
    380
sedentary cultures, 50–1
sedentary populations, 363–4, 366, 369–70,
    375, 379, 538, 596
sedentary societies, 33, 361, 364, 376, 380, 490

sedentary world, 360–1, 376, 491, 551
self-cultivation, 119
self-government, 222, 495
self-images, 29, 212
Seljuks, 164, 371, 373–5, 440
    conquests, 373, 377
semen, 85
semi-deserts, 31, 360, 363
Semirechie, 367
Senegal River Valley, 590, 605
serfs, 95, 107
sermons, 299, 303
servants, 81–2, 94, 97, 110, 113, 188, 191, 303–4
settled communities, 428, 590
Seville, 276–7, 342, 351, 639
sewn boats, 291–2
sexual excess, 88
sexual pleasure, 85
sexual practices, 84–6, 89
sexuality, 28, 70, 80, 84–9, 422
Shari'a law, 71, 89–90, 676, 683
Shingon, 465, 473
ship-owners, 238, 262, 264, 290, 292, 297, 301
shipbuilding, 65, 291, 329, 522
shippers, 299, 301, 304
ships, 248, 250–1, 254, 257, 268–71, 297, 300, 302, 675
    Chinese, 251, 293
    crews, 160, 174, 251, 268
    galley, 268–70, 282
    round, 268, 270–1
    treasure, 174, 251
shipyards, 251, 259, 328
shoemakers, 81, 296
shoes, 75, 78, 311
shops, 133, 272, 288, 298, 572
Shōtoku, Prince, 461, 518
shrines, 181, 297, 420, 426, 476, 515, 648, 657, 660–1
Siberia, 510, 535, 540, 551
    East, 377, 673
Sichuan, 241, 521, 525
Sicily, 5, 263, 271, 276, 281–3, 347, 349, 563, 566–7
sieges, 159, 161, 166, 172–3, 565, 583–4
Siena, 79, 426
Sii, 603
Sijilmasa, 590, 597
silk, 82, 147, 186, 251, 262, 281, 301, 329–30, 568, 572
    Chinese, 239, 378
    Mongolian, 274, 277
    Spanish, 263

Silk Roads, 97–8, 235–6, 247–8, 250, 345, 348, 437–8, 673–4
    Great, 366, 378
Silla, 119, 459, 464, 472, 517–18, 671, 677
silver, 239, 243–4, 267, 524–5, 552, 646, 648, 679
    coins, 243, 290, 296
    uncoined, 524, 552
Sindh, 288, 348, 389, 392, 396, 402–3, 485, 680
Sino-centric cartography, 2
sins, 85, 87, 223, 433, 515, 646
Siraf, 293
sisters, 74, 578, 598, 642, 662
skills, 136–8, 140, 189, 191, 193, 224, 316, 323, 329, 538–9
skins, 73, 236, 245, 263
slave-eunuch generals, 164
slave-markets, 163
slave-raiding, 29, 170
slave-soldiers, 164, 171
slave trade, 170, 258, 283, 303, 552
slavery, 21, 107, 283, 329
    domestic, 28, 80, 83
    and gender, 80–4
slaves, 81–3, 109–10, 174, 237, 243, 245, 303–4, 393, 594
    domestic, 81–2, 84, 443
    female, 81–3, 304–5, 602
    freed, 304, 597
    Indian, 82, 303
    male, 81
    manumission, 81, 83, 304
Slavs, 12, 82, 243, 273, 347, 513, 564, 570
small polities, 101, 625–6, 634, 669, 682
smallpox, 66
soap, 273, 283
social hierarchies, 28, 75, 98, 103, 109, 420, 531, 553
social interactions, 94, 217
social life, 488, 499, 530, 667, 678
social mobility, 101, 107, 118
social norms, 103, 545, 677, 683
social order, 88, 217, 223–4, 381, 406, 642–3
social power, 151, 314, 328, 496, 500
social reforms, 109, 531
social science, 210, 217, 228
social status, 116, 118, 120, 138, 326, 330, 604
social stratification, 15, 361, 404, 489
sociology, 210, 340, 668
sodomy, 86
Sogdians, 242, 366, 452, 520
Sogolon Condé, 598, 600
soil erosion, 45, 50, 58, 60, 614

soils, 45, 47–8, 53–4, 260, 336, 376, 622
  barren, 54
  heavy, 53, 55, 336
  salinization, 48
soldiers, 149–50, 152–3, 157–8, 163–5, 167, 538, 547, 570–1
  professional, 153, 569
  slave-soldiers, 164, 171
solidarity, 28, 88, 568, 669
  and hierarchies, 94–113
  within polities in Eurasia, 101–3
Somnath, 288–9, 294, 297–8
Song, 118, 166–7, 213–14, 235–6, 312–14, 324–6, 354, 470–2, 499–500, 524–6, 530–1
  court, 471, 528–9
  new policies of Wang Anshi, 527–8
  Northern, 65
  prosperity and crisis under, 524–6
  Southern, *see* Southern Song.
  Yingzao fashi, 324–6
Songdetsen
  Tri, 466–7
Songhay, 34, 348, 487, 586, 592, 594, 600, 603–4, 606–7
Soninke, 586, 590, 592–7, 599
  ancestors, 590, 593
sons, 90, 138, 189–90, 299–300, 304, 538, 576, 580–1, 599, 662
Sonyi, *see* Sii.
Sopara, 288, 294
Sorbonne, 129
Soso, 598–9, 606
soul, 85, 200, 353, 549
South Asia, 80, 122–3, 215, 447–8, 451, 454, 458, 460–5, 468
  Buddhism and educational institutions, 122–3
South China, 217, 220, 246–7, 393, 514, 522–3, 539, 551
South China Sea, 241, 251, 474
southeastern Europe, 387, 392, 484
Southeast Asia, 125–6, 239–40, 250–1, 454–8, 462, 474–6, 501–3, 674, 677–8
  Buddhism and educational institutions, 125–6
  maritime, 454–5, 457–8, 474, 476
  state formation and empire building, 501–4
Southern Han, 524
southern India, 108, 169–70, 240, 250, 305, 429, 451, 474, 548, 675
Southern Song, 119, 220, 235, 528, 530
  localist turn, 528–30

Souyri, Pierre François, 211
sovereigns, 200, 262, 502, 519, 560–1, 567, 572, 577–9, 584
  universal, 250–1, 570
  western, 568, 572, 578
sovereignty, 426, 495, 499, 683
  imperial, 33, 508, 530
Spain, 77, 154, 157–8, 192, 283, 347, 396, 402–3, 406
  Muslim, 26, 263, 346, 394, 396, 403, 676
  southern, 590, 606
Spaniards, 347, 623, 639, 643
Spanish conquerors, 16, 487, 612
Spanish conquest, 613–14, 618, 620, 622, 625–6, 632–3
Spanish invaders, 111, 638, 649, 662
Spanish silk, 263
spears, 146, 156, 158, 162, 319
specialists, 132, 426, 545, 656, 673
  religious, 124, 646
specialization, regional, 236, 523
spice routes, 274, 277, 279
spices, 239–41, 258, 262–4, 273, 281–4, 312, 378
spiritual leaders, 546
Sri Lanka, 5, 125, 239, 251, 450, 452, 464–5, 474–6, 672
Śrīvijaya, 240–1, 306, 463, 503
stability, 239, 525, 532, 561–2, 626
  physical, 29, 201
  political, 332, 670, 673
stagnation, 34, 68, 233, 610
Stamford, 272
standing armies, 83, 514, 520, 523, 526, 531
stars, 21, 353, 356, 645, 649
state formation, 33, 471, 486, 488–90, 493–5, 497–8, 501, 503–4
  in China
    Sui through Song, 513–32
  and empire building, 483–510
  Mesoamerica in Postclassic Period, 610–35
  processes, 483, 494
state power, 122, 247, 332, 509, 522, 546, 588, 630
state religions, 141, 416, 631, 682
statecraft, 317, 477, 516–18, 531, 553
  Confucian, 516, 530
  Mongol, 553
  Persian, 505, 507
statehood, 33, 369–70, 497, 502, 506, 509
  nomadic, 364, 366
statist reformers, 499
status, 28, 30, 72, 74, 98–100, 117, 185–6, 670
  high, 99, 101, 130, 545, 669, 677

social, 116, 118, 120, 138, 326, 330, 604
steppe-based states, 523–4, 526, 532
steppe nomads, 146, 161, 437, 516–17, 530
Steppe Road, 247–8, 250, 674, 676
steppes, 51–2, 145, 147, 364–5, 369, 371, 437,
        537–8, 550–1, 553–5
    eastern, 159, 513, 516
    Eurasian, 31, 145, 360, 362–3, 365–7, 371–4,
        380, 389
    western, 390, 493, 537
Steps to an Ecology of the Mind, 47
stereotypes, 96, 112
stirrups, 159, 161, 514
stone, 16–17, 174, 194, 297, 320, 642, 645, 648–9
    black, 289, 468
stone-throwing engines, 150
storehouses, 10, 656, 658
strategoi, 566–7, 569
strategy, 29, 145, 154, 162, 172, 191, 441, 488,
        491, 493
stratification, social, 15, 361, 404, 489
stringed instruments, 193, 602
students, 118–19, 121–3, 127–9, 132–6, 138, 141,
        353–4
styles
    architectural, 601, 620, 642
    art, 34, 416, 458, 619, 623–4, 633
Su Song, 324, 333
sub-Saharan Africa, 5, 25, 70–1, 109, 117, 142,
        174, 267, 387
submission, 156, 159, 169, 361, 429, 516, 653
subordination of women, 71, 80, 676–7
subsidies, 361, 366, 370, 404
successions, 34, 189–90, 417, 498, 504, 562,
        566, 602, 604–5
successor states, 365, 486, 490, 492, 541
successors, 133, 166, 180, 213, 218, 371–2, 379,
        514, 516, 662
    designated, 190, 662
Sudan, 378, 597
    northern, 394
    western, *see* western Sudan.
Sufism, 72, 132–3, 409, 432, 547
sugar, 238, 522, 597
Sui, 24, 33, 152, 208, 366, 513–14, 516, 518, 523
    court, 461, 516, 518
Sui–Tang, 513–14, 516, 519, 530–1
    reunification, 514–16
Sumatra, 32, 240–1, 251, 305, 448, 458, 467–8,
        548
Sumerians, 48
Sun, 80, 140, 355, 638, 651, 655, 660
    and Inca, 645–50, 660, 682

Sunjata, 586, 588, 598–600
Sunni Islam, 133, 374, 405
supplies, 81, 150, 157, 159, 233, 254, 274–5,
        300, 594
    food, 54, 162, 281, 614
suq, 272
surpluses, 258, 271, 298, 570–1, 611, 641
Susruta, 86, 346
sustainability, 28, 59, 62–4, 588
    long-term, 589, 607
sustainable agricultural economy, 48–9
sustainable forestry, 62–3
sutras, 122, 124, 453
    Jesus, 438
suyos, 638, 643–4, 648
suzerainty, 169, 506, 517
Sweden, 273, 282
Switzerland, 424, 497
swords, 86, 154, 156, 434, 594
symbiosis, 63–4, 489
symbols, 10, 45, 239, 339, 432, 460, 679
    common, 34, 633
syntheses, 45, 52, 119, 129, 223, 492, 510
Syri, 258
Syria, 154, 156–7, 165, 248, 253, 267, 269,
        415–16, 562–3
    armies, 162, 564
    northern, 428, 377, 436, 567, 575
Syria–Palestine, 274, 281
Syriac, 346, 417–18, 424, 427, 429, 432, 435,
        438, 571
Syriac Orthodox Church, 427, 560
Syrians, 262, 343, 347, 436
system of empire, 665–7

Tabriz, 14, 348, 352, 552, 554
tactics, 29, 145, 156, 160–1, 165, 172, 319
Taghbač, 514–15
tagmata, 164, 569
Tahuantinsuyu, 639, 643, 650, 654–5, 657–9,
        661–3
Tai, 125, 503
Taizong, 516, 520
Takrur, 586, 605
Talas River, 153, 371
Tale of Genji, 75, 193
Talmud, 130
tambos, 644, 658
Tamerlane, *see* Timur.
Tamil, inscriptions, 73, 305
Tana, 281, 302, 552
Tang, 119–20, 152–3, 157–8, 462–4, 499, 516,
        518, 520–3, 677

Tang, (cont.)
  court, 438, 462, 467, 520–1
  decline, 519–21
  early, 152, 521
  late, 312, 523, 525
  rulers, 118, 153, 465, 516, 518
Tangier, 543, 599
Tanguts, 371, 471, 554
Tantric Buddhism, 438, 464–5, 468–9
Tantric practices, 86, 464
Taoism, 339, 438
tapestries, 545, 679
Taqui Onqoy, 663
Tarascan Empire, 34, 628
Tarsus, 564, 571
Tashkent, 153, 242
tastes, 31, 192, 197, 312, 333, 444, 545, 549
Tatar dress, 545, 679
Tatars, 391, 544, 554
tax revenues, 47, 122, 157, 167, 570
taxes, 98, 100, 275, 290, 296, 540, 550–2, 563–4,
    568–9
  administration, 561, 570, 575, 577
  commercial, 522, 525, 540
  direct, 522, 531
  indirect, 522, 524–5, 531
  poll, 429, 432
Taxila, 451–2
tea, 522, 524–5, 597
teachers, 122, 127, 130–2, 134–6, 141, 408, 419,
    462, 650
technical expertise, 318, 323, 329, 333
technical instruction, 320, 322, 326
technical knowledge, 31, 317, 320, 337
technological change, 312, 328, 332, 335–6
technological developments, 311–13, 318, 320,
    337, 592
technological exchange, 328–9
technological innovations, and ruling
    powers, 330–4
technological knowledge, 312, 315, 337, 672,
    680
technologies, 30–2, 35, 171, 174, 671, 673, 680,
    682
  building, 313, 328
  discourses of technology, 318–20
  and environmental factors, 334–6
  and innovation, 309–37
  maritime, 250, 675
  new, 112, 253, 680, 683
  scholarship on, 310–13
telpochcalli, 138
temple-pyramids, 620, 631, 682

temples, 97, 99, 103–4, 123, 138, 140, 288–90,
    294–5, 651, 654
  Buddhist, 121, 124, 181, 306, 455, 460
temporality, 206, 209
temptations, 79, 113, 185
Tenayuca, 621, 628
Tendai school, 473
Tengri, 537, 546–7
tennō, 518–19
Tenochtitlan, 138, 613, 621–2, 630–2
Teotenango, 618
Teotihuacan, 610, 615–19, 626–8, 630–1, 633,
    682
terrace farming, 47, 49–50
terracing, 110–11, 621
Texcoco, 622
textiles, 75, 78, 241, 245, 259, 282, 301, 311, 524,
    597
Thailand, 452, 457, 474–5
  Gulf of, 251
thematic armies, 571–2
Theodore I Lascaris, 579
Theodore II Lascaris, 579
theology, 104, 128–9, 132, 194, 345, 428, 543
Theophanes the Confessor, 11
Theophilus of Edessa, 432
Theotokos, 416, 418, 428, 444
Theravada Buddhism, 125, 475, 486, 504, 672
Thessalonica, 273, 574, 581–3
Thirsk, Joan, 53
Thomas the Apostle, St., 418
Thourout, 272
Thrace, 281, 421, 565
three-field system, 45, 52
three-realms model, 46
Tiahuanaco, 487, 640–1, 645, 649, 654, 663
Tibet, 5, 13, 100, 122, 348, 355, 465–9, 531, 534,
    540
Tibetan Buddhism, 469, 473, 546, 549–50
Tibetan Empire, 98, 467, 488, 499
Tigris, 346, 403, 428
Tikal, 60
timber, 55, 63, 524
Timbuktu, 136–7, 348, 596, 598, 600–4, 607
  chronicles, 603–4
  'ulama, 137
Timur, 24, 52, 247, 372, 493, 535, 582
tin, 275, 277, 282, 302
Titicaca, Lake, 638, 640, 645, 653, 657–8, 660
titles, 184–6, 405, 408, 562, 567, 570, 577, 579,
    645
Toghrul, 374
Tokharistan, 345

Tokugawa regime, 222, 485
Toledo, 12, 343, 347, 352, 418
toleration, 225, 430, 440
tolls, 98, 100, 669
Toltecs, 619–20
Tomebamba, 651
tones, 193, 432, 604
tools, 31, 302, 311, 321, 336, 543, 626
    iron, 34, 595
Torah, 130–1, 346
Totman, Conrad, 63
Tours, 158, 282, 368, 418
Toynbee, Arnold, 60
trace italienne fortresses, 174
trade, *see* commerce.
trade mediation, 361
trade networks, 24–5, 283, 288, 290, 294,
    451–2, 671, 675–6
    European and Mediterranean,
        257–84
    expansion, 35, 671
    regional, 24
    trans-regional, 207, 676
traders, *see* merchants.
trading centers, 34, 258, 299, 590, 603
    on Red Sea, 299–305
trading communities, 287, 451
    local, 287, 290–9, 451
trading partners, 273
    across Indian Ocean, 287–306
traditions, 117, 189–92, 214, 333–4, 355, 399,
        408, 469
    Byzantine, 195, 271
    court, 35, 179–80
    Hindu, 215, 680
    literary, 32, 199, 411, 519
    local, 410, 430, 444, 671, 678–9
    oral, 34, 137, 587, 592, 598–9, 603
    religious, 399, 407, 409, 547
    Roman, 34, 180, 195, 562
training, 122, 126, 130–1, 137, 140–1, 217, 224,
        362–3
    military, 138, 149, 362
trans-regional reorientations, 206–29
    age of, 225–9
    Axial legacies, 207–8
    conditions and causes, 216–18
    and contexts of change, 213–16
    and cultural crystallizations, 208–12
    diverging patterns and pathways of
        transformation, 218–25
trans-Saharan trade, 34, 245, 250, 586, 589–90,
    595, 598, 600, 602, 607

Transcaucasia, 243, 371, 374
transit trade, 236, 239, 244, 390
translations, 26–7, 96, 343, 345, 347, 349–51,
    356, 453, 680
translators, 21, 356, 472
transmission
    of knowledge, 26, 28, 117, 134, 329, 354
    of learning, 116, 135, 141–2, 678
    oral, 31, 306
    processes, 310, 328–30, 681
    of science and philosophy, 339–56
Transoxania, 157, 164, 247, 389, 396, 401, 403,
    440
transport, 242, 244–5, 268, 270, 291, 293, 313,
    318, 324
trans-shipment, 240, 279
travelers, 8, 14, 84, 137, 440, 680, 683
travelogues, 442–3
treasure, 155, 160, 277, 595, 653
treasure fleets, 169, 250
treasure ships, 174, 251
treasuries, 152, 184, 188, 354, 561
treaties, 274–5, 303, 429, 525, 574
treatises, 99, 104, 106, 321, 409, 569
Trebizond, 74, 273, 276–7, 565, 580, 583
trees, 22, 44, 50, 60, 444, 593
Tri Songdetsen, 466–7
tribal cavalry, 153
tribal groupings, 489–90, 507
tribes, 110, 145, 332, 366, 402, 404, 406, 489–90,
    538
    Arab, 394, 400, 402, 405
    nomadic, 366, 437, 471, 476
tributary states, 162, 596
tribute, 101, 110–11, 166, 169, 236, 365–6, 368,
    370, 656
tribute trade, 235, 250
Tripoli, 2, 271, 274, 301, 597
Troyes, 260, 272
Tuareg, 136, 602
Tula, 616, 619–20, 623, 628, 631
Tunis, 271, 421, 599
Tunisia, 263, 301, 396, 401
    west of, 402–3
Tupa Yupanqui, 646–7, 650, 653, 657, 659–62
Turco-Mongols, 375, 469
Turkestan, 3, 539–40, 542
    eastern, 367, 371
    western, 489
Turkic Empire, 486, 490
Turkic khaqanates, 365–6
Turkic languages, 31, 368, 377–8, 673
Turkic nomads, 367–9, 371, 373–4, 377

Turkic origins, 366, 499, 507
Turks, 242, 365, 367, 375, 391, 400, 537, 559, 576
    Islamic civilization, 391–3
Tuscany, 266, 347
tutors, 128, 346
Tyre, 84, 130
Tzetzes, 574

Uighurs, 13, 242, 367, 489, 491, 537, 542, 550–1,
    554
ulama, 132, 141, 380
    Timbuktu, 137
Umayyads, 100, 157–8, 162, 166, 200, 402, 411,
    430, 565
Unani medicine, 355, 680
unbelievers, 156, 406, 507
unity, 101, 168, 237, 354, 385, 406, 594, 678
    political, 101, 237, 442, 669
    religious, 560
universal religions, 79, 501, 670
universities, 79, 116, 126–9, 142, 223,
    350
    Buddhist, 122
    and Christianity, 126–9
    European, 117, 126–9, 135, 141, 223, 350
unwritten customary law, 104, 669
upper Cuzco, 642, 647
Upper Niger, 586, 597–8, 607
urban centers, 451–2, 468, 587–8, 606, 618–19,
    623, 625 *see also* cities
urban civilizations, 361, 611
urban elites, 133, 160, 222, 226, 604
urban growth, 281, 450, 499, 522
urban life, 216, 377, 450
urban markets, 271–2
urban planning, 318, 631, 649
urban population, 259, 361, 614, 631
urban societies, 103, 361, 489, 616, 622
urbanization, 253, 316, 334–5, 452, 592, 616,
    624, 630, 666
usurpation, 190, 515, 520, 651
usurpers, 500, 578, 600
Uyghurs, *see* Uighurs.

Vadrapalli, 295
Vajrabodhi, 462, 464–6
Valabhi, 288, 294–5
Valarapattanam, 302
Valencia, 81, 260, 269, 276, 281, 283
Vandals, 153, 427
vaniggrāma, 295
vassalage, 95, 369
    ceremony, 198

vassals, 95, 146, 186, 191, 198, 365, 367, 371
Veckinchusen brothers, 261
Vedas, 122
Venetians, 258, 274, 282, 443, 578, 583
Venice, 268–9, 271, 273–4, 276, 279–83, 347,
    574, 578
vernaculars, 22, 196, 215, 224, 378, 400, 422,
    519
Vienna, 171, 261
Vietnam, 3, 117–18, 167, 251, 470, 476, 501, 503,
    517, 531
    Confucianism and educational
        institutions, 121
viharas, 350
Vijayabāhu I, 474
Vijayangaran empire, 169
Vikramaśīla Monastery, 467–9
village communities, 531, 587, 654
villages, 95, 100, 105–6, 424, 431, 434, 587, 590,
    641, 647
Vinaque, 640
violence, 190, 200, 224, 431, 493, 520, 539, 581
Viracocha, 644, 647, 650
virginity, 85–7
virgins, 87, 140, 356, 438, 594
Visby, 261, 274
Visnusena, charter of, 295–6
visual representations, 319–20, 549
Vitale, St., 418
Vivas de Provençals, 260
viziers, 12–13, 133, 187, 348
Volga, 277, 385, 389–91, 548
Volga, Middle, 243, 368, 377, 673
Volga Bulgaria, 365, 371
voyages of discovery, 313, 317, 341

Wagadu/Ghana, 34, 586, 590–7, 600, 605–7
Walata, 136, 596, 600–2
wall painting, 196, 444
walled cities, 162, 166, 623
Wang Anshi, 527–9, 531
Wang Dayuan, 15, 680
waqf, 133, 137, 298
warhorses, 245, 524
warehouses, 262, 300
warfare, 80–1, 138, 145–74, 269–70, 315, 651–2
    Africa
        Atlantic and slave trade, 170–1
    Arab explosion, 155–8
    China, 152–3
    Europe's military revolutions, 171–4
    Franks, 158–62
    horsemen, footmen, and empires, 149–71

Mamluks and Mongols, 162–6
Persia and Byzantium, 153–5
steppes and agro urban empires,
145–9
Wari *see* Huari (Wari)
warriors, 52, 120, 137, 140, 158–9, 163–4, 167,
303, 362
mounted, 65, 363
nomadic, 363, 564
women, 89
water, 44, 48, 61, 66, 311, 316, 333, 335, 593–4
management, 47, 318
mills, 67, 315
shortages, 335–6
water-lifting devices, 314, 321
waterways, 271, 303, 331
navigable, 245, 522
Watson, Andrew M., 48
wax, 243, 277
way stations, 35, 644, 658
wealth, 77, 83, 89–91, 97, 151, 164–5, 174, 295,
531
weapons, 34, 149, 167, 170, 172, 174, 243, 259,
270, 282; *see also individual weapon
types*
weavers, 275, 296, 305, 656
weaving, 140, 314–15, 317, 321, 650
Weber, Max, 44, 53, 100, 210
Weberian bureaucracy, 111
Wei, Northern, *see* Northern Wei.
West Africa, 135–6, 244–5, 394–5, 487, 587–8,
590–2, 597–8
West Asia, 11, 166, 424, 435, 443, 492, 670
West Bengal, 458
Western astronomy, 349, 355
Western Christendom, 26, 214–15, 219, 223–4,
494–8, 501–2, 507, 510
state formation and empire building,
494–8
Western courts, 188, 190, 195, 200
western Europe, 26, 160–1, 179–80, 182,
214–15, 220, 222, 226
Western Sudan, 34, 586, 589, 595, 599, 601,
603, 606–7
cities and trade as a basis of state power,
588–90
early polities, 586–607
Gao, 34, 136, 348, 586, 596, 600, 602–5, 607
importance of oral tradition for West
African history, 587–8
Mali Empire, 34, 586, 590, 597–602, 604,
606–7
Wagadu/Ghana, 34, 586, 590–7, 600, 605–7

wet-rice agriculture, 49–50, 518, 525
wheat, 46, 48, 66, 253, 262, 272–4
wheel-turning king, 530, 532
White, Lynn, Jr., 54, 56–7
White Horse Monastery, 453
widows, 75, 77–8, 656, 677
Wilhelmy, Herbert, 60
William of Rubruck, 21, 73, 424, 441, 444
William of Tyre, 12
William I of Sicily, 349
Winchester, 78, 272
wine, 242–3, 260, 268, 273–4, 277, 281, 296, 436
Bordeaux, 281
maize, 647
Wink, André, 288
wisdom, 339, 343–4, 354, 356
Wittfogel, Karl August, 47
wives, 71–2, 74, 84, 87, 192, 676
women, 70–80, 83–6, 88–9, 131, 134, 183–4,
188–9, 676–7
Central and East Asia, 73–6
Europe, 76–9
Islamic world and South Asia, 71–3
Jewish, 78, 89, 131
Kashmir, 73
mystics, 79
and religion, 79–80
sequestration, 71, 79, 89
single, 73, 77
subordination, 71, 80, 676–7
women warriors, 89
wood, 17, 60, 65, 162, 174, 237, 262, 275,
277, 282
woodblock printing, 14, 26, 124, 314
wool, 260, 262, 266, 268, 272, 275, 277, 282
Wool Staple of Calais, 262, 275, 277
woolen cloth, 259, 262, 266, 272–3, 282–3
world domination, 494, 510
world maps, 1–2, 5–10, 14, 680
world religions, 32, 117, 140, 142, 207, 209–10,
386, 390–1, 546–7
worship, 132, 419, 432, 440, 442, 546, 643
Christian, 428, 432
collective, 32, 424
public, 131, 133
writing, 111, 132, 136–7, 320–1, 326, 349, 519,
538–9, 612, 633–4
written histories, 10–15, 613
Wu, Emperor, 153, 455, 460
Wu Zetian, Empress, 153, 520
Wu Zhao, 519
Wutai, Mount, 465–7
Wuzong, Emperor, 470

Xenophon, 59
Xia, 524–6
Xiaowen, 514–15
xingsheng, *see* mobile secretariats.
Xixia, 471, 523
Xochicalco, 618–19, 633
Xuanzang, 14, 462, 468
Xuanzong, 520–1

Yamato, 517–18
yanacona, 654
Yang Jian, 513–16
Yangdi, Emperor, 516, 518
Yangzi, 514, 522
    Delta, 516, 522, 528, 530
Yānshū, 11
al-Yaʿqubi, 595
Yaqut, 596
yasa, 408, 492, 538
Yehlu Ch'uts'ai, 379
Yellow River, 65
Yemen, 135, 264, 300–2, 304, 404,
    427, 543
yeshivas, 130–1, 141
Yi Xing, 352–3

Yijing, 462–4
Yingzao fashi, 324–6
Ypres, 262, 272
Yuan, 74–5, 119, 213–14, 249–50, 534–5, 539–40,
    542–5, 551–4
    rulers, 75, 119
Yucatan, 60, 615, 620, 622–3, 627
Yunnan, 241, 312, 468, 548

Zaccaria, Benedetto, 259
Zanj, 12, 108, 303
Zhang Zhongyan, 324
Zhao Kuangyin, 524–5
Zheng He, 4, 169–70, 250, 475
Zhong Gongfu, 49
Zhou, 319, 520
Zhou, Northern, 524
Zhou Daguan, 16
Zhu Xi, 119, 529
Zhu Yuanzhang, 168, 323
Zimbabwe, 60, 110, 548
    Great, 60, 109
Zoroastrianism, 208, 219, 225, 293, 345, 401,
    416, 546, 665
Zuwā, 604–5

Made in the USA
Coppell, TX
17 February 2021